THE
ROMAN REPUBLIC

IN THREE VOLUMES
VOLUME THREE

THE
ROMAN REPUBLIC

BY

W. E. HEITLAND, M.A.

FELLOW OF ST JOHN'S COLLEGE

VOLUME THREE

GREENWOOD PRESS, PUBLISHERS
NEW YORK

First published in 1909 by the Cambridge University Press
Reprinted by permission of the Cambridge University Press

First Greenwood Reprinting 1969

Library of Congress Catalogue Card Number 69-13930

SBN 8371-2079-9

PRINTED IN UNITED STATES OF AMERICA

TABLE OF CONTENTS
VOLUME THREE

Book VII.

Revolution. Sulla to Caesar.

Book VIII.

The last struggles and transition to the Empire.

ADDITIONAL NOTES AND CORRECTIONS, 1922

VOLUME THREE

§ 941. In a paper in the University of California publications in Classical Philology 1918 Professor M E Deutsch discusses the accounts of the death of Lepidus and concludes that it was probably due to violence.

§ 942. The date of Caesar's birth is disputed. The year 102 BC is assumed here, after Mommsen and W W Fowler. But Prof M E Deutsch in Trans[ns] of Amer[n] Phil Assoc[n] 1914 reverts to the old date 100 BC. See M[r] Rice Holmes in Journ Rom Stud 1917.

§ 969. Asia under Lucullus. See Waddington, *Fastes des provinces Asiatiques* (1872), N° 20.

§ 976. Communications. That this point is important may be inferred from the precautions found necessary by Corbulo AD 58 when campaigning in these countries. See Tacitus *ann* XIII 39.

§§ 991. The *edictum*, not intended for a special case but for the whole course of the praetor's year of office, was a 'standing notice' [*perpetuum*]. To a great extent taken from his predecessors, it was so far traditional [*translaticium*]. Roby, *Introd to Digest* p clxiv. But (when cited as an authority) it was regarded not as a body of rules. 'It was an utterance on a single point, however general that point might be.' So I interpret these words of Greenidge *l c*. The drafting of the *edictum perpetuum* in a permanent form with statutory force was the work of Salvius Iulianus under Hadrian. See Bryce, *Studies* II 274 foll. Buckland, *Text-book of Roman Law* pp 9 foll.

§ 1000. Euphrates frontier. Note that Pompey, by claiming to decide the possession of Gordyene and Sophene, had asserted authority beyond the Euphrates.

§ 1002. For Caesar's later relations with the Jews see §§ 1239, 1241.

§ 1005. Note that the arrangements of Pompey in the East were followed by Augustus.

§ 1006. The meeting with Cato. The chronology here needs further clearing. If the story given in § 1044 is true, the meeting at Ephesus must surely have taken place in 63, and early in the year, to allow time for Cato's return to Rome and election as tribune for 62.

§ 1009. It is not here implied that Caesar was actually a party to this conspiracy of 65 BC. But that he was concerned in the intrigues of the time is hardly doubtful.

§§ 1020—3. Some of the detailed expressions used here of the bill of Rullus are invalidated by the criticism of D[r] E G Hardy (Journ Phil N° 64). He agrees that the measure was really a move of Caesar. But he makes havoc of Cicero's representation of its scope and contents in a way not easy to answer. With a great part of his article I fully agree, but I am not yet convinced that the relation of this affair to the events of the year 63 needs revision. The article is a masterly treatment of the details, and I wish I were free to recast §§ 1020—2 in connexion with it. But this would require more time than I have at disposal, and I am not quite certain that the evidence of Cicero is to be so completely rejected.

§ 1024. The part of this section dealing with the trial of Rabirius has been rewritten in view of the masterly article by Dᵣ E G Hardy (Journ Phil Nᵒ 67), the only convincing treatment of this much-debated affair that has come to my notice.

§ 1031. 'In a crafty reply.' In his *Orator* § 129 Cicero claims to have silenced Catiline (*obmutuit*). The truth seems to be that the latter's attempt at reply was howled down.

§ 1036. This threat to kill Caesar (Sall *Cat* 49 § 4) may possibly be another version of that which Suetonius *Iul* 14 puts on 5 December. Or it may have been repeated.

§ 1055. Defeat of Aedui. Mommsen places their submission to their rivals about 61 BC.

§§ 1059—61. 1068—71. For the land-legislation of Caesar's first (59 BC) Consulship see M Cary in Journ Phil Nᵒ 70.

§§ 1067, 1187, 1188. Dᵣ Hardy (Journ Phil Nᵒ 65) argues with great force that Comum became a Latin colony in 89 BC under the *lex Pompeia Strabonis* (see above, § 853), and that Caesar made it into a Roman colony, acting under the *lex Vatinia* in 59 BC. The brutal act of M Marcellus in 51 BC appears thus as part of a move to declare this Vatinian law invalid, and thus to deprive the *Comenses* of citizen rights, and treat Comum as a Latin Colony once more. This version is directly contrary to the views of Prof Reid, and I cannot in haste offer an opinion on the dispute. Dᵣ Hardy gives a full discussion (Journ Rom Stud 1916) of the Transpadane Question, and I believe his general conclusions are right. If, as he holds, the *lex Pompeia* of 89 was really the *lex provinciae* of Cisalpine Gaul, we must no longer attribute that step to Sulla [§ 921]. Mᵣ G H Stevenson (in JRS 1919) seems to accept Dᵣ Hardy's view, and discusses the interesting inscription recording the enfranchisement of *equites Hispani* by Strabo, probably in 89 BC after the fall of Asculum.

§ 1126. Mediterranean seamen. See Lucretius v 35—36. For the Mediterranean galleys see Smollett's *Travels*, letter xiv. The remarks of Macaulay *Hist Eng* on Tourville's galleys in 1690, and of the writer of 'the shipwrights of Rome' in the *Yachting Monthly* of Dec 1911 must be received with considerable reserve. See on § 245 above.

§ 1138. The literary relations of Caesar and Cicero at this time attracted the notice of later writers. See Apoll Sidonius *epist* VIII 6 § 1.

§ 1165. In *Syria as a Roman Province* p 26 Mᵣ Bouchier gives a more favourable view of Gabinius.

§ 1181. From Cic *ad Att* VII 1 § 4 it seems that Pompey also put pressure on Cicero to influence Caelius.

§ 1185. For the slovenly record and custody of laws in this age see Cic *de legibus* III § 46.

§ 1187. Dᵣ E G Hardy (Journ Phil Nᵒ 65) holds that Caesar made Comum a Roman colony. See on § 1067.

§§ 1194—5. Pompey owned great landed estates. Plin NH XVIII 35 notes his practice of scattering these, never buying *agrum conterminum*.

§ 1210. In Journ Phil N° 66 M^r J D Duff shews reasons for believing that Cicero never actually resigned his official charge, but in effect allowed it to lapse after Pompey abandoned Italy.

§ 1226. Caesar in the open boat. Compare the case of William III in Jan 1691, off the Dutch coast.

§ 1263. The statement in Tac *ann* XIV 27 § 4 seems to contradict this. But the words *ut olim* are too loose to justify us in rejecting the evidence of Dion Cass XLII 54, Suet *Iul* 38, cited by Marquardt *Stvw* I 115.

§ 1264 note 6. This matter of *recensus* is the subject of a controversy between Prof Elmore and Dr Hardy. See Class Quarterly 1918 and 1919.

§ 1265. The controversy on the so-called *lex Iulia municipalis* between Prof J S Reid and Dr Hardy, in Journ Rom Stud 1914—15 and Journ Phil 1919, is a matter much too intricate for me to offer an opinion on it in the short time now at my disposal. So I have left the old view to stand in the text.

§ 1281. For Caesar's colonizing projects see Mommsen in *Hermes* XVII.

§ 1301. According to Appian *Civ* III 2, 7, 12, 24, Caesar had designed Macedonia for Brutus and Syria for Cassius as provinces after their praetorship. Antony upset this arrangement by a vote of the Assembly, and thus bought the support of Dolabella by giving him Syria with the prospect of command in a Parthian war. See Lange RA III² pp 490, 498. The statement in the text is based on the conclusions of Schwartz in the articles there cited.

§ 1350. See Mr Storr-Best's translation of Varro (1912). For the luxurious country seats cf Cic *de legibus* III §§ 30—1.

§ 1351. For *calles* see Pelham, essays N° XIV. For weapons of *pastores* cf Livy IX 36 § 6.

§ 1354. Labour. I have dealt with this subject more fully in *Agricola* (1921).

§ 1370. Nepos. Jacob Bernays' *Phokion* note 5 p 104 contains a good treatment of this writer's allusions to matters of his own time as shewing his Republican point of view.

§ 1372. Speeches in Sallust. Fronto p 123 Naber says that Ventidius borrowed one of these orations for the celebration of his victory over the Parthians in 38 BC.

§ 1375. *sacra*. See Cic *de legibus* II §§ 46—53.

§ 1378. That the oratorical profession was still in full vogue in the 4th century AD is evident from the passage in which Ammianus Marcellinus [xxx 4] digresses to speak of it and its abuses.

§ 1384. Weakness of *insulae*. See Mayor and Friedländer on Juvenal III 193—6, and Seneca *de beneficiis* VI 15 § 7, *de ira* III 35 § 5. In the Digest XIX 2 § 57 we hear of a wall damaged by damp from the heaping of earth against it. See above on § 5.

§ 1399. The emperors and the mob. See the remarks of Fronto pp 21, 210, Naber.

CHAPTER XLVIII

936. THE death of Sulla ushers in the final period of revolution, the period in which the Roman Republic, deprived of its master, proved that it could not do without one. That contemporaries should recognize this necessity, and tamely acquiesce in it, was of course impossible: the Roman nobles, proud of the glorious past and profiting by the imperial conditions of the present, were not the men to submit without a struggle. Nearly another half century elapsed before exhaustion and an emperor brought peace to the Roman world. At this point we may well pause for a moment and briefly review the situation with which the Roman government had to deal at home and abroad.

To begin with Italy. Bit by bit the Roman franchise had been extended over all the country south of the Po, and the communities of Latins and other Italian Allies were settling down in their new capacity of *municipia*, towns of Roman citizens, whose members enjoyed the Roman city franchise and also a local one. Each municipality[2] had its local senate and magistrates, who carried on the government in local affairs and exercised jurisdiction in all cases save those reserved for the higher courts in the capital. Rome was now not only the centre of empire but the capital of Italy, and with the spread of Roman law and the Latin tongue the Romanizing of the more distant parts of the peninsula went on apace. Sulla had not seen his way to annul the various extensions of the franchise, and the whole of Italy should by rights have been ere now incorporated in Rome. There were however some notable exceptions, such as the Etruscan cities and Samnite cantons which he punished for their

---

[1] The general authorities for this chapter are Livy epit. 90—98, and Plutarch's lives of Sertorius, Lucullus, Crassus, Pompey, Caesar, Cato minor, Cicero. The Verrine orations of Cicero are very important, and Orelli's *Onomasticon* and *Index Legum* are indispensable. The lost History of Sallust dealt with this period, and supplied the Marian party view of events. The fragments edited (1893) by Maurenbrecher in a connected form, and his Prolegomena (1891), are of the highest importance and interest. Later writers drew largely from this work of Sallust; who and what and how much, it is Maurenbrecher's endeavour to determine, with marked success in many cases.

[2] See Greenidge, *Legal Procedure*, pp. 99—104.

stubborn resistance. And it is highly probable that of the Italians admitted by law to the citizenship of Rome a large number had not as yet been able to take formal possession of their rights. How many of them had found places in the registers of the Tribes, we do not know. In the more elaborate organization of the Centuries, which under the Sullan system had regained much of its old importance, very few can have been included. After the census of 86 no other was held till 70, and we do not hear of consuls discharging this part of the censorial functions. Altogether the confusion in the body politic must have been extreme, and discontent rife in Italy. Matters would not be improved by the presence of Sulla's military colonists; and the chief result of the changes of ownership, the revival of great estates and increase of the slave-population, was from every point of view a serious evil.

937. Of the numbers dispossessed by the acts of Sulla, those who remained in their native districts were a disaffected element, ready for revolutionary movements. Those who flocked to Rome would certainly strengthen the more turbulent elements of the Roman mob. They could not be prevented from voting, at least in the Tribe-Assembly. The immense majority of them would be hostile to the rule of the nobles under the Sullan system. One of their objects would certainly be the reestablishment of the cheap corn-supply. Nor could they be blind to the truth that the first step toward attainment of their wishes must be the restoration of the tribunate to its former power. In short, there were at work, both in Italy and in Rome, forces tending to produce a counter-reaction, overthrowing the constitution of Sulla. The 'popular' or Marian party had been struck down but not crushed, and any demagogue had ready to his hand the prospect of powerful support from the capitalist Knights, eager to recover the control of the public courts. The senators placed by Sulla in the seat of power had among their various difficulties none more persistent than the dilemma facing them as jurors in the court of extortion. If by severity they encouraged good governors in punishing bad ones, they inflamed the wrath of the financial syndicates thirsting for provincial plunder: if by laxity they left the guilty unpunished, they gave great occasion for scandal. The demagogue might denounce them, and the financier, ever willing to take their place, would applaud the attack. Yet all these embarrassments might be successfully encountered so long as the military leaders commanding the allegiance of armies remained at the Senate's disposal. Once the relations between the two powers became strained, once the military men found that their ambitions could be more easily promoted by a 'popular' policy, the rule of Sulla's

restored Senate would be at an end. And that this situation would arise was only too likely from the nature of the Senate itself. An aristocratic body must so far as possible maintain equality within its own ranks, and this tendency most readily expresses itself in a jealousy of successful rivals.

938. It may not be sheer waste of time to explain the objections to the use of the term 'oligarchy' in referring to the dominant power of the senatorial nobility. Truth is, this technical term has a quite definite connotation in the political vocabulary of the old Greek republics. However much the use of the term wavered, both in common speech and the writings of political thinkers, one point at least is always clear. Of the freemen belonging to a state, and enjoying civil rights therein, only a part (in practice a minority) enjoy political rights. These are the Few (ὀλίγοι), who alone have votes in elections and other state-issues : those excluded from this class have no votes at all. In practice the line was normally drawn by means of a property-qualification. That all freemen belonging to the state should be entitled to vote, but that they should be grouped and organized in such a way that their votes were frequently of little or no effect, was assuredly a plan that would have seemed monstrous to a Greek. If all citizens in a Greek state had votes, government of the people by the people (δημοκρατία) was the sure and logical result. But in Rome, with her wide empire and her widely-scattered citizens, things had shaped themselves differently. The issues of public policy were ever widening, and the Assembly was wholly incompetent to deal with them. Nor was it an Assembly of the whole people, for the majority of the citizens were non-resident and seldom or never appeared to vote. But under the constitution the Assembly was in the last resort supreme. The Senate, the one competent body, had to manage the Assembly somehow, and the pressure of influence and corruption was the readiest way, perhaps the only possible one. Such a situation differed fundamentally from Greek oligarchy. It was a system of make-believe and compromise. Sulla had tried to give it a more logical character, by making the Senate practically supreme. But he could not impart to the senatorial nobles the virtues (perhaps superhuman) necessary for successful conduct of government in the circumstances of the time. The Assembly, though weakened, still existed as the traditional sovran power: the Senate after all was a mere aristocratic Ring, with internal jealousies undermining its apparent strength.

939. By whatever name we call the government of Rome as left by Sulla, that government had many difficulties to deal with. In the provinces the condition of Spain was most alarming. A great part of

the peninsula was in rebellion, with Sertorius at the head of it. Macedonia was never really at rest from the inroads of its barbarian neighbours. In Asia Minor the presence of Mithradates was a source of anxiety, and there was danger of complications from Rome becoming involved in the affairs of Egypt. Meanwhile the pirates were more than ever the terror of the seas, and it was imperatively necessary to check them. Under the strain of discontents and agitations within and the pressure of these difficulties from without, it is not wonderful that the ten years from the retirement of Sulla (79—70) brought his political fabric to the ground. We will briefly trace the steps by which this result was brought about.

940. It has been already pointed out that the consuls of the year 78 began by quarrelling over the funeral of Sulla. All through the year they were at loggerheads, and Catulus with much ado held his vain ambitious colleague[1] in check. Lepidus, relying on the general discontent, came forward with proposals to upset a number of the acts of Sulla. There was already a serious movement on foot to revive the powers of the tribunate. This he successfully opposed, most likely foreseeing that it would not suit with his own designs. But he proposed to recall the Marian exiles, to undo Sulla's land-settlement by restoring the dispossessed Italians to their confiscated lands, and to renew the supply of cheap corn to the city populace. This last measure he seems to have carried. An outbreak at Faesulae in Etruria, in which a party of Sulla's military settlers were overpowered with loss, and the lands reoccupied by their former owners, gives us a glimpse of the state of things existing in some parts of Italy. But the Sullan settlers, and others interested in keeping things as they were, were still too strong to allow any wholesale reversal of the dictator's policy. Lepidus was preparing to overthrow the Sullan system by force of arms. But he delayed, having prospects of a better opportunity in the following year. The Senate, alarmed at the quarrel of the consuls, had required them both to swear that they would not engage in civil war. But Lepidus held that this oath only bound him as consul. In the allotment of provinces for 77 he had drawn Transalpine (Narbonese) Gaul, and he would as proconsul have a good pretext for raising an army. The disturbances in Rome prevented the holding of the consular elections, and at the beginning of 77 the gaps had to be filled by resort to an *interregnum*, while Lepidus, having a free hand, set to work with his revolutionary pro-

---

[1] Affair of Lepidus. Livy ep. 90, Appian *civ.* I 107, Plutarch *Pomp.* 16, Suetonius *Jul.* 3, Florus II 11, Orosius V 22, Zonaras X 2. In particular Sallust *hist.* fragm. Also Licinianus pp. 43, 45, Bonn, Valer. Max. VI 2 § 8, Macrobius I 13 § 17. Maurenbrecher vol. I pp. 14—20, II 20—37, 59—67.

ject.   There was at first nobody to stop him, for until he committed
some overt act of hostility nobody had power to interfere.   No doubt
some preparations were being made, and the Senate went so far as to
summon the proconsul to Rome to give an account of his proceedings.
Lepidus had now two forces under arms.   His lieutenant M. Junius
Brutus remained in Cisalpine Gaul to secure the North, while he
himself with the main army in Etruria marched upon Rome.   Such
was his answer to the Senate, little more than a year after the death
of Sulla.

941.   The accounts of this affair of Lepidus are in many respects
conflicting and obscure.   Whether his proposals eventually included
the restoration of the tribunician power, whether civil war began
while he was still technically consul, whether he marched on Rome
once or twice, are points[1] on which opinions may well differ, and
which matter little.   The Senate met him with a force nominally
under the command of Catulus, of which Sullan veterans doubtless
formed the backbone.   But Catulus was a man of civilian pursuits,
so Sulla's lieutenant Pompey was called in[2] to supply military skill.
The occasion is notable.   Pompey, Sulla being now dead, appears as
the indispensable man, through whom the Senate gives effect to its
will; a position which he was never afterwards content to abandon.
The attempt of the Senate to use him without becoming subject to
him, in fact to dispense with him, is one of the most significant
episodes in the history of the Roman revolution.   Lepidus was
defeated in a battle[3] fought on the northern side of Rome, and driven
back into Etruria.   He seems to have had transports ready to convey
his army to Transalpine Gaul.   Once convinced that his present
undertaking had failed, he put to sea and landed in Sardinia, with
what design is uncertain.   He was not able to get control of the
island, and in a short time fell ill and died.   His army partly dispersed, but the best part of it was taken by his lieutenant Perperna to
join Sertorius in Spain.   Meanwhile Pompey had crushed the rising
in Cisalpine Gaul and put Brutus to death, treacherously and cruelly,
as was said by some: perhaps with truth, for his treatment of Carbo
in 82 had been base and cruel enough.   The son of this victim,
M. Brutus, and his nephew D. Brutus, were in 44 notorious among
the murderers of Caesar.

942.   The senatorial government was not to be upset by force of

---

[1] See Maurenbrecher cited above.

[2] We must not forget that Pompey had supported the candidature of Lepidus for the
consulship against the warnings of Sulla.   Plutarch *Pomp.* 15.

[3] Whether Pompey took part in this part of the operations has been doubted, and his
chief work was certainly in Cisalpine Gaul.   See Livy epit. 90, Plut. *Pomp.* 16, Florus II 11.

arms, at least not for the present. But the political reaction against it remained, and the corruption of the nobles at times offered chances of attack.   The opposition or Marian party were wanting leaders of courage and eloquence, able to take advantage of opportunities. Cicero, since his defence of Roscius, had found it convenient to seek change and self-improvement in the centres of Greek culture. Young Caesar too, after his escape from the wrath of Sulla, had been away in the East, where he had served with distinction at the siege of Mitylene.   In 79 the consul P. Servilius was appointed to the province Cilicia with charge of the war against the pirates, who were infesting the eastern seas.   When he took command Caesar joined him, but on the news of Sulla's death returned to Rome.   The young man (he was about 23) had already chosen his side in politics : indeed as nephew of Marius' wife and son-in-law of Cinna he was naturally marked out as an opposition leader.   But it was as yet too soon to carry measures of reform, and with foolish ventures likely to end in fruitless bloodshed he would have nothing to do.   So he bore no part in the silly enterprise of Lepidus. He knew the man, and did not trust him.   But there was work to do in exposing the iniquities[1] of the ruling nobles, and the court of extortion was already a field in which rising young orators turned their talents to account.   Cn. Cornelius Dolabella (consul in 81) had been proconsul in Macedonia, the governor of which province had a general supervisory authority over the nominally free communities of Greece.   The provincials charged him with oppressive extortion, and Caesar took up their cause and brought him to trial.   That he was acquitted by the senatorial jury was no proof of his innocence.   But the impeachment had served Caesar's turn, for to discredit senatorial juries was politically not less important than to convict and punish Dolabella.   A number of Greeks had given evidence for the prosecution, no doubt at considerable trouble and expense.   To encourage these useful supporters Caesar went on to another case.   During the Mithradatic war one C. Antonius had been employed by Sulla in Greece, where he had used his power to squeeze bribes out of the wretched people.   Caesar brought him to trial.   His guilt was clear, but again the prosecution failed.   In short, for the provincials there was no redress, but the senators had added to the record of scandals that might serve as a convenient weapon in the hands of their adversaries.   Such was the practical working of the Roman Republic as an imperial power.

943.   The suppression of the rising of Lepidus was in itself a relief to the Senate, but the sequel clearly exposed the real weakness

---

[1] See Sueton. *Jul.* 4, Plutarch *Caes.* 4, Q. Cicero *de petit. cons.* § 8, Valer. Max. VIII 9 § 3, and index to Cicero.

of that body. To the news of the victories of Sertorius in Spain was now added the knowledge that Perperna had carried off a considerable force to strengthen still further the rebellion in that troublesome province, and so to give a more Italian character to the war. To put down this rising before it became irresistible, and perhaps involved Italy, was necessary. But who was there to do this? The Senate was at a loss, and Pompey took advantage of their perplexity. After he had stamped out the revolt in Italy, he contrived to keep together the army which it was his duty to disband. Meanwhile he intrigued through his friends to obtain the command in the Spanish war. His position was a strong one. The House was loth to confess that it had to rely on a young man, still only a Roman Knight who had served in no magistracy, to get it out of a serious difficulty. But the thing had to be done, and Pompey was duly invested with the *imperium pro consule* and made equal with Metellus already in Spain. That the consuls of the year were neither of them fit for the charge was generally admitted; and the sarcastic Philippus is credited with the acid remark that he proposed to send out Pompey not in place of one consul (*pro consule*) but of both (*pro consulibus*). How Pompey prospered in his new command we shall see below. For the present the important point is that pressure had been put upon the Senate by their young military champion, and the Senate had seen no way of avoiding compliance with his wishes. Many must have felt that they were rather obeying a master than employing an agent. To them the future may well have been clouded by misgivings; the weary Sulla had resigned his despotic power in their favour, but Pompey, trained in Sulla's school, was only at the beginning of his career, and already famous for successful defiance of precedent.

944. The removal of Pompey left the field clear for movements of the Marian party in Rome. In the next year (76) we find a tribune named Sicinius[1] openly agitating for restoration of the tribunician power. The consuls of the year opposed him, but he persisted, and was only silenced by some arbitrary procedure, perhaps by a fine imposed on him for a technical breach of the *lex Cornelia*. But the fact of a tribune venturing to attack Sulla's limitation of the tribunate was in itself highly significant of the public temper, and the year 75 saw the agitation continued. Times were bad for the Roman government. The wars in Spain and Thrace were costly, and the necessity of taking over new provinces in the East was now pressing: a fresh Mithradatic war was clearly inevitable: altogether the strain on the finances of the state was extreme. Corn was scarce[2] and dear, and

---

[1] Sallust *hist.* II 23—27, III 48 § 8, Maur.
[2] Cicero II *in Verr.* III § 215, *pro Plancio* § 64, Plutarch *Cic.* 6.

the Roman populace irritable, for there was no spare money in the treasury, and no prospect of exceptional measures of relief. Cicero, who was then quaestor in Western Sicily, took great credit to himself for his exertions in forwarding corn to Rome. But public discontent was so great that the consuls were attacked by the mob and for a time unable to shew themselves in the streets. The tribune Q. Opimius was keeping up the agitation begun by Sicinius in the previous year, and one of the consuls, C. Aurelius Cotta, saw that some concession was inevitable. A former ally of Drusus, banished by the Varian commission in 90, restored by Sulla, he had much experience, and he was now one of the first orators of the day. He proposed and carried a law[1] repealing that clause of the *lex Cornelia* which disqualified ex-tribunes for holding any further office. The Senate grumbled but could not venture to block the measure, as it might have done. Better men would now be got to hold the tribunate. That was all; but it was something, and more would follow. The resentment of the governing nobles found expression in the next year (74), when Opimius the ex-tribune was prosecuted for an alleged violation of the *lex Cornelia*. The court, presided over by the praetor C. Verres, found him guilty, and a heavy fine harshly exacted was the ruin of him. So at least said Cicero[2], who referred to this affair as one of the iniquities of Verres.

945. In the year 74 the external embarrassments of the government were even greater. What with the desperate state of affairs in Spain, the ceaseless warfare on the Macedonian frontiers, the revival[3] of activity on the part of the pirates after what had been fondly deemed their effectual suppression by Servilius, and the alarming preparations of Mithradates, there was trouble on every side. Meanwhile it was decided to take over[4] the Cyrenaica and Bithynia as provinces, and this was a challenge to both Mithradates and the pirates. Both were interested in opposing further extensions of the Roman dominion, and we shall see that a connexion was formed between the Pontic king and Sertorius through the help of the pirate cruisers. These matters will be dealt with in the next chapter. It was evident that the greatest exertions would be needed to assert the power of the imperial republic East and West by land and by sea. That Rome did not succumb to the strain of all these dangers is a proof of her real strength, even after the awful losses of the Italian and civil wars. Still more is it a proof of the weakness of her

---

[1] Asconius pp. 66, 78.   [2] Cic. II *in Verr.* I §§ 155—7.
[3] See §§ 964—6.
[4] Cyrene bequeathed to Rome in 96, Bithynia in 75, made provinces in 74. See §§ 805, 968.

enemies. The ruling nobles, to do them justice, competed for the posts of danger and glory: in all their luxury and corruption they were still a soldier-aristocracy. The two Luculli[1], Lucius the former lieutenant of Sulla, and his brother Marcus, were typical men of the time, but above the average in virtue. The ex-Marian renegade Cethegus, a clever but dissolute fellow, was just now a very influential person. The complications and intrigues then rife are illustrated by the arrangement come to for the Sertorian and Mithradatic wars. L. Lucullus, one of the consuls of the year, wanted to command against Mithradates. He had been regarded by Sulla with marked favour, and between him and Pompey, who posed as Sulla's military heir, there was keen jealousy. The present policy of Lucullus was to keep Pompey busy in Spain while he secured for himself the command in the East. He therefore supported the proposal to send reinforcements and money for the Spanish war, and it was carried. But in the allotment of provinces he had the bad luck to draw Cisalpine Gaul. While he was casting about for a way to avoid being thus shelved, news came that the governor of Cilicia, L. Octavius (consul in 75), was dead. Lucullus set himself to secure this vacancy, which would probably carry with it the command in the eastern war. To this end it was all-important to win the favour of Cethegus, but this debauchee and the respectable Lucullus were open enemies. Lucullus stooped to conquer. He made interest with the notorious courtesan Praecia, and through her help won the favour of Cethegus and the Cilician province. Of the Mithradatic war we shall speak below. The manœuvres of Lucullus concern us here as illustrating the state of things in the upper circles of political and social life.

946. If the merits of Lucullus might excuse the jobbery of his appointment, the same could not be said in the case of his colleague M. Aurelius Cotta, who received Bithynia and with it the charge of the naval department of the Pontic war. He was a failure. Worse still was the appointment of the praetor M. Antonius to the command against the pirates. His father, the famous orator, one of the victims of. Marius, had gained some credit by his operations on the Cilician coast in 102, the first attempt on the part of Rome to check eastern piracy. He might urge a quasi-hereditary claim, but it seems to have been the influence of Cotta and Cethegus that brought about his preferment, worthless though he was known to be. To disregard aristocratic equality[2] in favour of such a man as Antonius was a

---

[1] On what authority Ferrero I 133 asserts that the family was poor, I know not. Nicolaus Damasc. fragm. 83 (*FHG* III 416—7) only refers to the σωφροσύνη of L. Lucullus. I agree with Drumann (not Drümann) IV 165 'er war begütert, ehe er als consul nach Asien gieng.' It is true that he returned from Asia a *millionaire*.

[2] See § 966.

blunder that brought its own punishment. It is no wonder that there
was trouble in home politics, when the ruling nobles were thus given
over to jobbery in the face of gathering perils. A tribune of mean
origin, one L. Quinctius[1], carried on the agitation against the senatorial government. He was in some way connected with the restless
and unprincipled Cethegus, but was, if we may believe Plutarch, a
good deal calmed and restrained by the influence of Lucullus. But
in the course of the year a grave judicial scandal[2] encouraged him to
come forward again and attack the present constitution of the public
courts. A citizen from a municipal town was charged by his stepson
with attempting to remove him by poison. He was found guilty by
a jury in the murder court at Rome. There were suspicious circumstances attending the verdict, and the opinion gradually spread that
bribery had been used to procure the condemnation of a man innocent
at least of this particular crime. Quinctius took up the matter,
harangued popular meetings on the subject of judicial iniquities,
himself brought to trial the president of the court that had corruptly
condemned an innocent man, and got him fined and his prospects in
public life ruined. The man had been to blame for some technical
irregularities, but what was fatal to him was the terrorism of popular
enthusiasm at the back of Quinctius. The affair served to inflame
the general hatred of the senatorial juries, and to draw the capitalist
Knights into closer sympathy with the popular agitators. That there
was good reason for discontent with the courts as conducted by venal
senators we need not doubt. The city praetor of this year 74 was no
other than the notorious Verres.

947. The year 73 brought no lessening of anxieties abroad. If
things were a little better in Spain, they were worse in the East.
L. Lucullus was not doing badly, but M. Cotta had been utterly
defeated. As for Antonius, he was a burden to Rome's maritime
subjects, and ineffective against the pirates. Frontier war in Macedonia dragged on as before. One of the consuls of the year,
M. Lucullus, drew that province, and commanded there with more
success in the two following years. To these troubles was now added
a terrible danger[3] in Italy itself. We have often noticed the perilous
state of the country under the system of rural slavery, and referred to
the training of slave-swordsmen for public entertainments. These

---

[1] Cicero *pro Cluentio* §§ 77—9, 84—5, 89—94, 108—113, with Plutarch *Luc.* 5, Sallust
hist. index Maur. This is the man referred to by Cicero in his speech *pro Tullio*, as counsel
for the other side.

[2] The case of Oppianicus.

[3] Spartacus. Appian *civ.* I 116—20, Plutarch *Crass.* 8—11, Florus II 8, Eutrop. VI 7,
Orosius V 24, Velleius II 30 § 5, Pliny *NH* XXXIII 49, Horace *odes* III 14, *epod.* XVI 5.
Maurenbrecher vol. I pp. 40—46, II pp. 146—55, 165—72.

two abominations now bore their natural fruit. A school of gladiators at Capua broke out and overpowered their warders. Their leaders were two Gauls, Crixus and Oenomaus, and above all the Thracian Spartacus. Thracian and Gallo-German slaves were in request for a profession requiring strength and courage. Spartacus is said to have once served in the Roman army, to have been taken prisoner, and so to have reached his present position by way of the slave-market. He and his band, some 70 in number, took post in the crater of Vesuvius, where they were joined by runaway slaves and ruined freemen. They were soon the terror of the country side, and the breaking-open of barracoons and liberation of chained slaves quickly raised their numbers. Two Roman forces were hastily levied and sent to quell the rising, but were routed one after the other, and their defeat equipped the slaves with proper weapons. The rebels now ranged freely over southern Italy, plundering and gaining recruits. By the end of the year they were 70,000 strong, all hardy and desperate men. There was no police-force in Italy, and raw emergency-levies were of no use: it was clear that nothing but an organized army could effect anything, and an insurrection of slaves must be treated as a serious war. The war indeed lasted two years and more, and it was doubtless a great check on projects of reform. But for the present the popular agitation was carried on by a man of considerable ability, the tribune C. Licinius Macer. This man was the author[1] of a Roman History, afterwards used by Livy and others, for the purpose of which he consulted old records, genuine in his eyes, though suspected by some modern critics. His bent was rhetorical, and he was an orator of some merit. He was a bitter partisan of the 'popular' party, and eager to overthrow the system of Sulla. A trace of his activity survives in the fact that he prosecuted[2] a senator for the murder of Saturninus 27 years before. The man had boasted of the deed, but was of course acquitted by his peers. A short quotation[3] from a speech in which he denounced the cruel eviction of the Etruscan landowners also exists.

948. There was no lack of oratorical talent in Rome at this time. But Hortensius, the leader of the Roman bar, was of the government party. C. Cotta, the aristocratic reformer, was dead. Cicero was now back from Sicily, disappointed to find that his services were ignored by the people at home, and bent on rising to eminence. But he was a 'new man' with his way to make, and for the present unwilling to risk his chances by openly facing the storms of politics. A

---

[1] See H. Peter, *Histor. Rom. fragmenta.*
[2] Cicero *pro Rabir. perd.* § 7.
[3] In the grammarian Priscian X 42.

Roman Knight, and at heart a Marian, he could not yet lend a hand to overthrow the constitution of Sulla. Julius Caesar stood on a different footing. He had returned from a tour in the East, rich in varied experiences. He had studied rhetoric in Rhodes. He had been captured by pirates[1] on the high seas, and held to ransom. While waiting for the money, he amused these ruffians by the threat that he would presently come back and hang them ; but he meant to keep his word, and did. When the Mithradatic war broke out, he raised some troops and did some volunteer service in preventing some of the Asiatic cities from joining the enemy. But when Lucullus came, and all commands were in the hands of Sullan partisans, he seems to have felt that his place was in Rome. Early in 73 he was back again, and at once threw himself into public affairs. In him Macer found a formidable ally. He had kept in touch with the popular leaders, to whom the cooperation of the young Patrician was most welcome. Family influence may probably be traced in the fact of his being coopted[2] into the pontifical college while still in the East. His social charm made him a favourite with all classes, while his boldness and decision marked him out as a leader of men. He was at once chosen as one of the elective military tribunes. His political position was asserted by a speech[3] on behalf of a Samnite who had been doomed in the Sullan proscriptions, but had escaped, and was now needing support in some way. Macer and he aimed at the full revival of the tribunician power and general reversal of Sulla's policy, but for this the time was not yet come. A bill for the restoration of men in exile[4] through complicity with the rising of Lepidus was carried. But the chief concession wrung from the government was in connexion with that old story, the supply of cheap corn. The consuls of the year, M. Terentius Varro Lucullus (by birth brother of L. Lucullus) and C. Cassius Varus, carried[5] a *lex Terentia Cassia*, which provided for the yearly purchase of a quantity of corn in Sicily (and perhaps elsewhere), to be retailed to the urban populace at a cheap rate. Such a measure might stop the clamour of the hungry for the moment, but it had grave objections. It tended to draw more of the idle poor to swell the overgrown mob of Rome, and it furnished such governors as Verres with further openings for illicit gains. That the treasury in any case stood to lose on the transaction was no longer in these days a serious consideration. The general discontent was

---

[1] The adventure variously told, Suetonius *Jul.* 4, 74, Valer. Max. VI 9 § 15, Plutarch *Caes.* 1—2, Velleius II 42, Polyaenus VIII 23 § 1. Date (76) settled by Pliny *NH* II 100.

[2] Velleius II 43 § 1.

[3] Cicero *pro Cluent.* § 161, Tacitus *dial.* 21.

[4] Suetonius *Jul.* 5, Gellius XIII 3 § 5.

[5] Cic. II *in Verr.* III § 163, V § 52. Marquardt *Stvw.* II 116.

not effectively appeased by such concessions, and the foundations of the Sullan system were imperceptibly undermined. Before we leave this year 73 we may note two significant details of the time. A Vestal[1] was accused of having broken her vow. That the man involved in the charge was the notorious Catiline gave rise to the presumption of guilt. But the case was dismissed, hushed up by influence, said the gossips. And it was in this year that Verres began his governorship of Sicily, in which the Senate left him to work his wicked will for three years.

949. The year 72 brought some relief abroad. The two Luculli were doing well in Macedonia and Asia Minor, though Antonius was making no way against the pirates. In Spain the murder of Sertorius led to the speedy suppression of the revolt, though Pompey had several months more work in restoring order, and did not come home till the following year. In Italy the servile war reached its height. Three Roman armies took the field against the rebels. Of four battles, three were confessedly Roman defeats. Yet the signs of failure were beginning to appear on the insurgent side. The Gallo-German and Thracian elements formed two separate armies and did not act in effective combination. Spartacus knew that they could not for any long time withstand the power of Rome; so after victories in northern Italy he wanted to pass the Alps and give his men a reasonable chance of regaining their native homes. But the slaves, flushed with victories, would not obey him. Their numbers were now greater than ever. They marched back southwards, revelling[2] in the plunder of Italy, and never after had a chance of escape. The Senate saw that the ordinary nobles-in-office could not deal with this Hannibalic slave-war, in which all Italy was going to rack and ruin, and the consuls for 71 were men of no more efficient type than their predecessors. They pitched upon Crassus, who was a praetor in that year. Since the battle of the Colline gate[3] Crassus had turned to civil life. By his ready services as advocate he had won wide popularity, and by speculating in forfeited estates he had become the richest man in Rome. He accepted the command, and we cannot doubt that he stipulated for a free hand in respect of martial law. Nothing was to be done with the demoralized troops till discipline was restored. This Crassus did with a severity long fallen into disuse. After destroying other detachments of the enemy, he penned up the main body under Spartacus in the Bruttian peninsula. A pirate fleet was cruising in those waters, capturing merchant-vessels

---

[1] Orosius VI 3 § 1.   [2] See Horace *odes* III 14.
[3] To him the victory of Sulla had been chiefly due, so far as that battle was concerned.

and taking toll of misgoverned Sicily. Spartacus bargained with them to transport him with a strong force over to that island. But the rascals insisted on prepayment and then left him in the lurch. He turned back and broke away towards Apulia with Crassus at his heels. His men still fought well, but he could not keep them together, and they were beaten in detail. Spartacus fell fighting, and the rising was at an end: but the work of suppression had not been all done by Crassus. M. Lucullus, returning victorious from Macedonia, had saved Brundisium at a critical moment, and so driven Spartacus back upon Crassus' army. And at the very last a body of slaves in flight to the North were met and cut to pieces by Pompey on his way back from Spain. Still Crassus had done well, and he was now in the front rank of Roman leaders. The waste of looted homesteads and devastated lands, the corpses of captured slaves rotting on crosses by the road-side, were for a time the visible signs of the Italian slave-war, when order had been restored and the blood had ceased to flow.

950. Things had so fallen out that a sort of general concentration at Rome took place in this year 71, and it was soon clear that a great crisis was at hand. No less than four commanders appeared in the course of the year, each with more or less claim to triumphal honours, for beside Pompey Crassus and M. Lucullus there was Q. Metellus Pius, at length released from his long service in Spain. The hard work of L. Lucullus in the East, and the failure of Antonius, would seem of little moment compared with the strife of powerful interests at the centre of the Roman world. By far the most important point at issue was the relation of Pompey to the two great parties. Would he conform to the wishes of the Sullan Senate, and become one of the normal aristocracy? Would he follow the example of Sulla, and become despot by force of arms? Or would he find a readier means of gratifying his ambitions by an alliance with the popular leaders? Those who feared that he would choose the second of these alternatives did not understand the man. To take the responsibility of boldly assuming despotic power would have been foreign to his character. To his dainty political appetite it was a main object to avoid a surfeit, and the abdication of his master Sulla had probably had some influence upon his mind. He did not want to seize a throne once for all, and to be certainly hated, if possibly obeyed. His aim was rather to attain such a position in the state that, while a mere citizen, he should be recognized as the first of citizens; that, while rivalling the most commonplace in heavy respectability, he should be the leader and guide to whom all looked to deal with the problems and emergencies of peace and war; that, while setting little store by the ordinary magistracies, the goal of ordinary ambition, he should solemnly hold a dissembled royalty with perpetual refusal of the crown.

951. It would seem that the Senate had a fair chance of keeping Pompey loyal to the existing system by themselves cheerfully making the concessions required by his vanity. But they were not willing to pay the price. He wanted a triumph, though he had never been consul or praetor : he wanted to stand at once for the consulship, though he had held none of the lower posts as required by the law. As for the first claim, he had already had a triumph, but this was in a time of confusion, and by the leave of Sulla. The second demand was surely not the act of a man who meant to uphold the constitution as Sulla had left it. The only reason for granting these concessions was that there was no effective means of preventing them. It is hard to blame the nobles for their unwillingness to sanction so direct a violation of the constitution on which their own power rested. Beside the jealousy of some and the pedantry of others, there must have been many clearsighted enough to foresee that these concessions would not be final. The Roman nobility were not prepared to submit to a master ; still less would they set up a master by their own act. The Senate was in an awkward position, for Pompey had played his cards well. In his references to the recent war he had been careful to represent it as a Spanish rebellion, and on the trophies erected to record his victories he had omitted all mention of Sertorius and the Marians. Thus he could not be charged with a wish to triumph over fellow-citizens. Again, it was rumoured that Perperna, when beaten and captured, had offered him a number of autograph letters from Romans of quality expressing their sympathy with Sertorius. Pompey had burnt the letters and put Perperna to death, and many a discontented man in Rome breathed more freely at the news. When the first soldier of the state had given evidence of so much discretion, who could be better qualified for the consulship? The ordinary citizen cared little for rules about the tenure of offices that he had himself no prospect of holding, and to him the constitutional scruples of senators might seem the outcome of self-interested pedantry. The leaders of the opposition party naturally wished to gain the support of Pompey, and he, seeing the sulky humour of the Senate, came to terms with these new allies. The Senate was now powerless. Armies lay before Rome, kept together on the pretext of taking part in triumphs, and it was not possible to play off Crassus against Pompey as Pompey had been used against Lepidus. Crassus was profoundly jealous of Pompey, but he was ruled by his own interest. He did not feel a match for his younger rival if it came to a fight, and he had no mind to share the growing unpopularity of the Senate. So

he made overtures to Pompey, and was graciously received. It was agreed that they should combine forces and stand for the consulship together, and their election was practically certain.

952. As the principle of senatorial government was that of a normal equality among its noble members, so it was inevitable that those who in fact stood out above their peers should resent the jealousy of the less eminent, and should look outside for support. The misgovernment of provinces, now the chief hope of financial salvation to embarrassed nobles, was not enough to glut the ambition of the really eminent men: they began to see that they could get more important appointments from the Assembly. Nor would such men be content to stay in Rome and improve their financial position by the precarious and disreputable gains of judicial corruption. Pompey, though he had come to the front as a partisan of Sulla, seems to have made no difficulty about accepting the democratic programme. The present leader of popular agitation was M. Lollius[1] Palicanus, a native of Picenum, a district in which Pompey had a following. He had been active in calling public attention[2] to the misdeeds of Verres, and in denouncing the scandalous proceedings of the courts of justice. These were indeed notorious enough. Even the Senate had been constrained to authorize the introduction of a new and severer law for punishment of judicial corruption; but three years[3] had passed, and the law was not yet carried. In truth nothing could be looked for in the way of democratic reform until the powers of the tribunate were fully restored.

953. The coalition of Pompey and Crassus was far too strong for the Senate to resist. To begin with, each had an army at hand. The democratic opposition leaders were with them, for they pledged themselves to the restoration of the tribunate. The Knights were won by the promise of a reform of the jury-courts. We may probably infer also that the claims of the new citizens to proper registration were not overlooked, and that some assurance was given that a census should be held in the coming year. And so all formal hindrances were swept aside. Votes of the Assembly were procured, granting Pompey the right to triumph, and also to stand for the consulship. Crassus, who was praetor in 71 and so not yet legally eligible, was probably dispensed from the statutory limitation at the same time. It is hardly necessary to add that the pair were elected consuls. Thus, so far from the Senate being able to do without Pompey, Pompey, by means of the army and the mob, had been able to defy

---

[1] Valer. Max. III 8 § 3, Sallust *hist.* IV 43 Maur.
[2] Cicero II *in Verr.* I § 122, II § 100.
[3] Cicero *pro Cluent.* §§ 136—7.

the Senate. It was an object-lesson to all observers, and we cannot doubt that young Caesar laid these phenomena to heart. The various triumphs were a feature of the latter part of the year. To Crassus only the *ovatio* or minor triumph was allowed for his victories in the slave-war. The importance attached to these distinctions at Rome is illustrated by the fancy[1] of Crassus. The wreath of the victor in an ovation was the *corona myrtea*. Crassus knew that he had saved the state from a great danger, and claimed the *corona laurea* used in regular triumphs. The Senate, perhaps not unwilling to do honour to some one other than Pompey, granted his request. Metellus had a triumph for the Spanish war, and M. Lucullus (in this year or the next) for his victories over the Dardani. Pompey contrived to put off his triumph till the last day of the year. Thus he enjoyed the dramatic situation of triumphing for the second time in defiance of precedent, and continuing the process by entering on his consulship next morning in defiance of constitutional law.

954. The consulship of Pompey and Crassus in B.C. 70 includes several measures of great importance, the outcome of the struggles and agitations of recent years. The two consuls distrusted each other, and at first neither was willing to disband his army according to promise. But the popular leaders had no mind to see all their schemes of reform wrecked by such personal dissensions, and their pressure led to a formal[2] reconciliation. Sincere and hearty cooperation was out of the question, but the Senate was at least well beaten, and the programme could be carried out. A bill for restoring the former powers of the tribunate was proposed by the consuls and passed. The Senate could not venture to refuse their consent. The next great step was the reform of the jury-courts. This was not so simple a matter: it was easy to decry the corruption of senatorial juries, but not easy to suggest a certain means of improvement. The Knights claimed to be reinstated in their position of privilege. But Sulla had not taken away that privilege without good reason. The case of Rutilius is enough to remind us that equestrian juries had grossly abused their power. The mere proposal to substitute equestrian for senatorial juries did not command unanimous support, and the Senate was resolved to fight on this question and concede as little as possible. The consuls themselves did not bring forward a bill to deal with the matter; and indeed the promises of Pompey seem to have been given in guarded language[3] from the first. What was done was to provide for the election of censors. This revival of that

---

[1] Cicero *in Pison.* § 58, Pliny *NH* xv 125, Gellius v 6 § 23.

[2] Appian *civ.* I 121.

[3] See Cicero I *in Verr.* §§ 44—5.

disused office was a popular move, if we may believe Cicero. The censors L. Gellius Poplicola and Cn. Cornelius Lentulus Clodianus (consuls in the year 72) were especially concerned to purge the Senate. A number of disreputable fellows had of late years found their way into the House through having taken part with Sulla. Among this class were many, perhaps most, of the venal jurors who made the public courts a public scandal. There was perhaps some hope that the sacrifice of the worst of these scoundrels might save the senatorial juries. The censors struck 64 members off the roll. Of the proceedings in the registration of citizens we hear nothing, but we learn incidentally that a great number of visitors flocked to Rome in the course of this summer, attracted, says Cicero[1], by the elections the public shows and the census. It would seem that on this occasion the registration was thoroughly carried out. The traditional numbers[2] are perhaps not to be trusted, but in marking an enormous increase as compared with the census of 86 they may very well be right. The number of persons who had since the great Italian war acquired the Roman franchise as a right, and yet had never been placed on the register, may have been (and probably was) very large. And at this time, what with the armies returned from abroad, and the feelings aroused by the prospect of a final settlement of long admitted claims, it is likely that the attendance of citizens, old or new, would be more than usually complete.

955. If the progress of the census served to keep open for a time the question of the juries, public interest was kept alive by the most famous of Roman trials. Verres had governed Sicily for three years (73—71). The embarrassments of Rome, in particular the war of Spartacus, had given his influential friends an excuse for not recalling him in the regular course. The obvious successor was somehow always wanted elsewhere. The enormities of Verres were not unknown; we have seen that he had been already denounced in public. Leading Sicilians, with the approval of Romans settled in the island, were bent upon bringing their tormentor to justice, and looking round for a Roman to undertake the prosecution. They wanted not only an eloquent advocate, but one who would throw himself heart and soul into the case, and fight it to the end. Personal grudge and self-advertisement, the vulgar motives of many Roman impeachments, could not be relied on here: both were liable to be stifled by the ill-gotten money of Verres. They bethought them of the kindly and upright man who had been quaestor at Lilybaeum five years before, and a deputation was sent to Rome to engage the services of Cicero. The orator had

---

[1] Cic. I *in Verr.* § 54.

[2] In 86 B.C. 463,000, in 70 B.C. 910,000. See Beloch, *Bevölkerung* pp. 348, 352.

hitherto confined his activity to pleadings for the defence: as a 'new man' his policy was rather to gain support in his public career by laying men under obligations than to achieve notoriety as a dangerous accuser. But at the present juncture, with jury-reform in the air, it was possible to convince even senatorial jurors of the risks incurred by a corrupt acquittal. To wring from them the condemnation of so notorious a criminal would be a signal triumph won before the eyes of the whole civilized world. Moreover Cicero had a genuine sympathy for the oppressed provincials, a sound conception of imperial duty, rare among the statesmen of republican Rome. And, though he was now a senator himself, his real attachment was to the Equestrian Order to which he belonged by birth. In putting pressure on a jury of senators he could speak with all the unstudied force of sincerity. If the tardy repentance of the senators should miss its aim, and the Knights nevertheless regain judicial power, from his point of view so much the better. He was now 36 years of age, and a grand opportunity was not to be missed. He gladly undertook the case, and the Marian reform-party followed his proceedings with interest. Whether the Sicilians did or did not gain redress, the Roman opposition at least saw in the prosecution a stick with which to beat their enemies.

956. From first to last Verres lost no chance of hindering the course of justice. In giving formal notice to the praetor Cicero found himself faced by a competitor, Q. Caecilius, who had served under Verres as quaestor and pretended a better right to prosecute. This necessitated a preliminary trial (the so-called *divinatio*) in which Cicero vindicated his own claim and exposed the ill faith of this sham-accuser, who was of course acting in collusion with Verres. But time had been wasted. A further means of delay was sought by getting up a case against another provincial governor, so planned as to come on earlier than the case of Verres and engage for some time the attention of the court. This device was foiled by the diligence of Cicero. All depended on the speed with which he could gather the necessary evidence in Sicily. Out of 110 days allowed him for this purpose he only used 50. The eager zeal of the provincials can be faintly imagined. The other case was a sham, and fell through, not having even served its turn. The elections for 69 now came on, and the nobility interested in protecting Verres gained some important successes. Hortensius, who was leader for the defence, was returned as consul with Q. Metellus, who was of the same party leanings. Among the praetors was a M. Metellus, and the lot assigned him for the next year the charge of the court of extortion. Against this was to be set the election of Cicero as curule aedile, which was not much, save as a victory over influence and bribery. It was clear that, if the

trial could be protracted into the next year, Verres would enjoy
official support to such a degree that his escape would be almost
certain.   And there were circumstances peculiarly favourable to
delay.   The case was to be opened on the 5th of August.   Between
the middle of August and the middle of November no less than four
sets of games were due.   These would take up about 50 days in all.
By spinning out the defence it was hoped that the available court-days
might be wasted and the case finished under more favourable conditions
in the coming year.   But this calculation assumed that Cicero would
open the case for the prosecution in the usual way with a long elaborate
speech.   To him however it was just now more important to win his
cause than to air his eloquence.   He opened quite briefly, but he
found room in his short speech to utter a plain threat, that anyone
concerned in taking or giving bribes in connexion with this case would
be brought to justice by himself when aedile.   He then made a bare
statement of the specific charges, and proved them by crushing
evidence.   Nine days sufficed for the whole of the prosecution.   Hortensius was in a sad fix.   In default of evidence he had doubtless
relied on picking to pieces the prosecutor's speech; but now his
famous memory had no detailed defences to recall, and, having no
great highly-coloured oration to criticize, his rhetorical skill had
nothing to adorn.   He made some effort to reply, but he could make
no head against the facts and threats of Cicero.   Bribery had been
tried, and for once had failed, and Hortensius saw that the game was
up.   He threw up the case.   Verres fled into exile.   Cicero became
the head of the Roman bar.   He had indeed done magnificently.
But the political agitation of the time, pressing severely on the
senators and menacing their privileges, was by far the most efficient
cause of his success.

957.   If Cicero had been already taking a leading part in politics,
and had been about to stand for one of the higher offices of state, his
services to the opposition party would doubtless have met with immediate reward.   But he was already aedile-elect for 69, and could not
be praetor till 66.   He saw an opportunity of turning the recent trial
to account as a literary theme.   He would thus call further attention
to the greatness of his achievement, and produce at leisure a lasting
monument of his powers.   The outcome of this was the great written[1]
speech, supposed to be delivered on the second hearing of the case,
which had in fact not got beyond a first hearing.   It was a political
pamphlet in the form of a fictitious oration.   Under five heads he
gave a full exposure of the infamous career of Verres, from his base
treachery in the time of the Italian war, his misdeeds in the East, and

---

[1] The so-called *actio secunda in Verrem.*

his shameless conduct as city praetor, to the crowning abominations of his government of Sicily. He reviewed in detail with scathing comments the total disregard of the charters and customs of the province guaranteed by Rome ; the boundless ingenuity of extortions, particularly in connexion with the corn-supply ; the robbery of works of art belonging to cities temples and private owners, the cherished heirlooms of the Greek past ; reserving to the last and most effective place the acts by which Rome and Romans were directly injured. When he told how Verres combined heartless cruelty to provincials with corrupt lenity to pirates, he exposed the perils created for the republic by the conduct of its own officers. When he told of the crucifixion of a Roman citizen, he was sure of a sympathetic hearing from Roman ears in all parts of the Roman world. When he made it clear all through that greed of gain was the inspiring motive of all these hideous enormities, that a Verres desired vast wealth in order to buy impunity by bribes, to satisfy the demands of his disreputable companions of both sexes, and to live in wanton luxury among his brother senators, he was striking a blow that reached further than the criminal of the hour. All men knew that there were plenty of others of the same type as Verres, though perhaps less thorough in their doings. All knew that Verres had had bad luck in being tried at a moment when bribery of jurors was hardly possible, and that such a moment might not occur again. All those to whom the present abuses appeared shocking, those who had no prospect of enjoying similar license, those who thought that Verres had been too greedy and so had consumed at once what should have been enough for a long series of predatory governors, philanthropic jealous and cynical alike, would be roused to interest by the invective of Cicero. The circulation of this splendid work was no doubt very wide, wherever there were men to whom Roman literature appealed. For the present it assuredly told in favour of reformers. But the admiration of posterity for this masterpiece must not blind us to the probability that the picture is somewhat overdrawn. Cicero worked himself up into a fury, mostly genuine at the time. But how differently he could depict extortion we may see from the professional levity with which he defended Flaccus eleven years after.

958. While Cicero was busy with the composition of his great Verrines, the agitation against senatorial juries went on with renewed vigour, headed by the praetor L. Aurelius Cotta. It gradually became clear that the proposal simply to substitute Knights for senators would be stubbornly opposed and not easy to carry. It would seem that there was a counter-proposal (of course in the senatorial interest) to form each jury of two sections, one of senators, the other of Knights. This would not have served the purpose of the reformers : the least they could accept was that the senators should be in a minority. A compromise had to be found, and before the end of the year the *lex Aurelia*[1] was passed, to the following effect. Every jury was to consist of three sections, one of senators, one of *equites*, one of *tribuni aerarii*. Who these last were, is one of the many obscure points in Roman antiquities. That they were in some way not easily distinguishable from *equites* may be inferred from the loose language of several passages in which the latter term is used to cover both. It is probable that they were either men whose property was up to the equestrian standard, but who were not actually included in the 18 centuries of Knights, or men of somewhat smaller property, in short a class of lesser capitalists. The name was doubtless an ancient survival, but what were the precise functions of the class to whom it originally applied is a doubtful matter of minor importance. In voting on a verdict each of these three sections (*decuriae*) voted by ticket in a separate box or jar (*urna*), so that the verdict of each section was known; but, if the meaning of a passage of Cicero[2] be rightly interpreted, it would seem that the verdict was decided by the votes of the jury counted as a whole. All the efforts of the senators had thus only succeeded in keeping one third of the voting-power in their own hands. Experience was to prove that this change by no means secured purity of verdicts: it might be a check on class-prejudice, for senators could no longer by their own votes protect evil-doers of their own Order, but against bribery it was no safeguard whatever. Politically the effect of the *lex Aurelia* was great. Taken in connexion with the restoration of the tribunate, it meant that the rule of the Senate was at an end. It had never been a true oligarchy, for the *populus Romanus* (such as it was) had never ceased to be the ultimate depositary of sovran power. The cords with which Sulla had bound the Assembly were now snapped. But the result was not a true democracy. Not only did Roman group-voting place a check on the power of a numerical majority. There was far too much friction, caused by religious hindrances and collision of equal official authorities, to allow the Assembly to become a Greek Demos, even had that been otherwise possible. And things had now gone so far that neither Senate nor Assembly could in the last resort decide anything of vital importance. It was not for these venerable names, the worn-out institutions of the City-Republic, that the professional soldier of those days would march and fight. The result was virtual anarchy, which opportunists like Cicero might vainly strive to ignore, but which went from bad to worse, and could neither be mended nor ended by purely political means.

---

[1] See Greenidge, *Legal Procedure* pp. 442 foll., Mommsen, *Staatsrecht* III 189—91, 482—8, 532—3, Lange *RA* III 196—8.   [2] *ad Quintum fratrem* II 4 § 6.

CHAPTER XLIX.

959. FROM the retirement of Sulla to the consulship of Pompey and Crassus we have traced the failure of the constitution as re-modelled by the great Dictator. A clearly-marked stage in the Roman revolution has been reached. We must now turn to the wars and general external policy of this period. In themselves the wars are not of great interest, and the record, save in the case of the Mithradatic war, is scanty. In the case of the Spanish war superficial narratives are mixed up with sensational legends of which Sertorius is the hero.

We have seen that Sertorius[1] withdrew to Spain in 83, foreseeing the failure of the Marian cause in Italy. For two years or more he went through a series of adventures. Unable to hold his ground in Spain against the Roman governors, who were on the side of Sulla, he fled to Mauretania. Repulsed by barbarians, he joined some pirates then cruising in the West, and tried to wrest the island Pityussa (Iviza) from the Roman garrison. Here also he failed, and it is said that he would now gladly have sought a peaceful retreat in the 'islands of the blest' of which he heard enthusiastic accounts from seafaring men. Whether Madeira or the Canaries are meant, it matters not. He could get no following, and we next hear of him serving as a soldier of fortune in a dynastic war between Mauretanian chiefs. It seems to have been in the year 80 that he was invited by the Lusitanians to return to Spain and take the lead in a rising against Rome. He accepted the offer, and went. The handful of Marians with him supplied him with Roman officers, and he soon organized the native rebels on the model of a Roman army. From the first he regarded himself as fighting not against Rome, but against the usurping faction of Sulla. He defeated both the governors of the Spanish provinces. The governor of Narbonese Gaul came to their aid, and was badly beaten. Sertorius was now in a fair way to

---

[1] General authorities. Livy ep. 90—96, Plutarch's *Sertorius and Pompey*, Appian *civ.* I 108—115, Florus II 10, Eutropius VI 1, Orosius V 23, etc. Sallust was used by most later writers, in particular by Plutarch. See Maurenbrecher I pp. 20—40 for a discussion of the relations of our authorities.

become master of Spain, and fugitive Marians rallied to the one leader in whom there was still some hope for their cause. Sulla thought the matter so serious that he sent out Metellus Pius (son of old Numidicus), one of his best generals, to take command in the war. This was in 79. But, by the time Metellus was ready to fight Sertorius, the latter had made further progress. He shewed remarkable versatility in the management of his various followers. To his Roman supporters he was not a desperate rebel, but a true Roman leader. He formed a Senate of his chief partisans from Italy, and employed others in the army and the administration of civil government. To him and them Spain was part of the Roman empire, in fact a province of which he was still the rightful governor. At last the Marian cause had found a leader, and Marians proscribed in Italy could be loyal citizens in Spain. But, while asserting Roman supremacy, he had the power of winning the respect and allegiance of the natives, from whom he drew the great mass of his army. His influence with the chiefs was so great that a number of them were induced to send their sons to a school in which he provided them with a Roman education. The boys were at the same time informal hostages for the loyalty of their fathers. His Spanish soldiers were devoted to him, and he shewed full confidence in them. But in appealing to their generous instincts he did not forget that they were superstitious. The story of the white fawn of Sertorius, which he tamed and kept as a pet, and from which he pretended to receive advice as from a familiar spirit, illustrates his skill in dealing with these simple warriors. Roman governors had been generally remarkable for their oppressions and their blundering. Sertorius was able to maintain military discipline and civil order by justice and tact.

960. Metellus did his best, but the task was too great for him. The nimble and hardy troops of Sertorius could move without heavy baggage and live on scanty food. Their commander was a master of the strategy of surprises, and, what with the mobility of his forces and superior means of information, he was able to defy the ponderous efficiency of the Roman army. And in 77 he received a reinforcement from Italy, the better part of the troops raised by Lepidus and now brought to Spain by Perperna. The Italian element was thus strengthened, and the war took more the character of a civil war. How far the chances of Sertorius were really improved by this accession we do not know. It is said that Perperna at first wanted to act against Metellus on his own account, but was forced to join Sertorius by the clamours of his men. Their number is put at 53 cohorts, perhaps about 25,000 men, a very doubtful story. And it is clear that the situation was complicated by the presence of Perperna. He

was deeply committed to the Marian faction, so he remained with Sertorius, jealous and disloyal himself and stirring up discontent in others. Pompey was now sent out to Spain with another army, to cooperate with Metellus. He came by land, opening a new route[1] through the western Alps. But the two proconsuls fared little better than the one. In the campaign of 76 Sertorius had the upper hand. In 75 the operations of the Roman army were more effectively combined, and Metellus defeated one of Sertorius' lieutenants. But in other battles the results were indecisive ; Pompey in particular was beaten by Sertorius himself, whose power and renown were now at their height. Mithradates, now on the eve of war, sent an embassy[2] and made a treaty with him. This was easier than it might seem, for communication was by sea, and both parties were on friendly terms with the pirates. It is said that Sertorius would abate nothing of the rights of Rome: when the king claimed the province of Asia, he would not hear of the proposal. Another version of the story makes him agree to the cession of Asia. In any case a treaty was made, and Rome had to face war in the East as well as the West. Pompey passed the winter[3] of 75—74 in southern Gaul, and wrote[4] to the Senate, calling for more men and money, and pointing out the danger of the war being transferred from Spain to Italy. He was accordingly reinforced, and the war went on in Spain.

961. The tide now began to turn. In the campaigns of 74 and 73 the fortune of war varied, and with the strain of occasional failure the real weakness of Sertorius began to appear. Spanish enthusiasm was perhaps slackening. His Roman supporters were more and more an embarrassment to him. Officials did things offensive to the natives, and the blame recoiled upon the governor whose orders they professed to obey. The resident 'Senate' must have been a nuisance. What useful function it performed, other than that of appeasing vanity, we do not know. Men impatient of being ignored would probably resent the concentration of power in the hand of Sertorius, though on this concentration depended the success of their cause. And Perperna and his clique were a constant source of mischief. It was not the arms of Pompey, but the canker of disaffection, that wrecked the Spanish rising. We begin to hear of desertions and mutual distrust. Sertorius was compelled to deal severely with some offenders, and lost much of his popularity. That

---

[1] Probably by the pass of Mont Genèvre and along by the river Druentia (Durance) into the Rhone country. Mr Strachan-Davidson discusses the matter in an appendix to Appian *civ.* I.

[2] Appian *Mithr.* 68. [3] See Cicero *pro Fonteio* §§ 13—16.

[4] A version of this letter is given in Sallust *hist.* II 98 (Maur., III 1 Kritz).

he became suspicious, and occasionally harsh, as troubles gathered round him, is doubtless true. He killed or sold into slavery a number of the school-boys under his care, to punish the defection of their fathers. It was the act of a madman. But the hostile tradition, which represents him as having become lazy and debauched, is probably a slander due to admirers of Pompey or at least to writers of the anti-Marian party. A plot was formed against his life, and in the year 72 he was treacherously murdered at a banquet. Perperna, who was at the bottom of the business, succeeded to the command, but was soon after defeated and taken prisoner by Pompey, who put him to death. Order was now speedily restored in Spain. A few sieges were still necessary, but the natives for the most part had had enough of war. It was desirable to reward those Spaniards who had served Rome well. With this view the consuls of 72 by direction of the Senate carried a *lex Gellia Cornelia* by which Pompey was authorized to confer the Roman franchise on deserving individuals. Pompey acted on this law, probably passed at his suggestion. It happens that a case of enfranchisement thus granted[1] is traceable in the later history. A native of Gades, who was rewarded by Pompey, took the name L. Cornelius Balbus, and migrated to Rome. He became a person of great importance, and was connected with all the leading men of the time. Pompey returned to Rome in 71, shortly before his colleague Metellus. The latter had done good work in Spain, but was thought slow and averse[2] to roughing it. So at least said the admirers of Pompey, who managed to get most of the credit of success.

962.   The province of Macedonia was one of the most troublesome parts of the Roman dominions. We have seen how the Senate tried to evade direct annexation after the overthrow of Perseus, and how they were at last forced to take over the government. We have noted a case of a governor[3] left in charge there for a number of years; an exception so remarkable, that we can only account for it by assuming that this *provincia* was shirked by all that respected their own comfort and desired wealth or glory. It was indeed far too much for a single governor. The two kingdoms of Perseus and Gentius formed the main part of it, the province proper; but the governor had a sort of supervisory authority over the nominally free states of Greece. We might call him Commissioner for the Greek states. In this capacity he might find congenial occupation, settling disputes and receiving flattery and gifts. But it would seem that most governors of Mace-

---

[1] See Reid's Introduction to Cicero *pro Balbo*, essay on this Balbus in Tyrrell and Purser's *Correspondence of Cicero* vol. IV.

[2] See Valer. Max. IX 1 § 5.   [3] C. Sentius. See above §§ 803, 879.

donia had enough to do in the province itself. The Macedonian kingdom, created by conquest, had never been able to exist safely without a strong army. The barbarous tribes on the North and East were only restrained from invasion by fear. Since the formation of the Roman province things had changed for the worse. The provincials were disarmed, all save a few borderers, and Rome, now responsible for their defence, did not take the one effective step of maintaining a strong standing army of occupation. And so the history of Macedonia was largely made up of frontier wars. Inroads made in times of Roman weakness or neglect were followed by punitive expeditions beyond the Roman border, and the advance had on occasion even reached the Danube. But these fitful campaigns led to no lasting conquest. When the Romans retired, the barbarians closed in again and took the first opportunity of renewing their raids. Nothing short of conquest followed by annexation to the North and East could give peace to Macedonia, and of this there was at present no prospect. Already the great migratory peoples beyond the Danube, urged on by others[1] pressing on their rear, were beginning to cross the stream, and the pressure was destined to continue. And, beside these general causes of unrest, the Thracian tribes had in recent years been more than usually troublesome, stirred up by emissaries of Mithradates.

963. We know of four governors[2] of Macedonia in this period. They seem to have held office for two years each. Cn. Cornelius Dolabella (79—7) had been consul in 81, Appius Claudius Pulcher (77—5) consul in 79, C. Scribonius Curio (75—3) consul in 76, and M. Terentius Varro Lucullus (73—1) consul in 73. All four are credited with victorious campaigns; Dolabella and Claudius against the Thracians. About the same time we hear of one C. Cosconius[3] waging a successful war in Dalmatia, which shews that there was trouble on that side also. Curio made a great expedition to the North, defeated the Dardani and pushed on to the Danube. M. Lucullus took command at a critical moment. The war with Mithradates was in full course, and with it the Macedonian war was closely connected. While L. Lucullus pressed the king hard in Asia Minor, his brother dealt with the king's allies in Europe. The campaigns of Marcus led him far afield. After beating the Thracian tribes, he took a number of cities, in particular some Greek or half-Greek towns on the coast of the Euxine. Mithradates, who claimed to be the head and champion of the Greeks, especially of these outposts of Hellenism in northern lands, could not help them. Nor could they and their

---

[1] See Jordanes, *Getica* 11.

[2] See in general Livy ep. 91—97, Florus I 39 § 6, Eutrop. VI 2—10, Orosius V 23, VI 3.

[3] See Eutropius VI 4, Orosius V 23 § 23, and Cicero *pro Cluentio* § 97.

barbarian neighbours help him. So Rome gained ground in both
parts, thanks to a rational scheme of war. For a time quiet was
restored in the Balkan countries, but there was nothing like a real
conquest of Thrace.

964. Among the difficulties of Macedonian governors was doubtless one of which we do not directly hear, that of communication with
Italy. It is true that the Adriatic passage was short, and that from
Apollonia and Dyrrachium a Roman road (*via Egnatia*) had been
made through the mountains to the Macedonian lowlands and the
Aegean seaboard. But we do hear that even the Adriatic was
infested by pirate squadrons, and Cicero (exaggerating no doubt)
declares[1] that the transport of troops from Brundusium was never
attempted but in the heart of winter. If we believe this statement to
contain any truth at all, it is plain that serious interruption might
ensue from the fear of exposing a convoy of helpless transports to
attack. In any case the march through the mountains was no easy
matter in the winter, which in those parts is notoriously severe. This
consideration leads us to the great development of piracy[2] and its
causes. On a small scale it was a very ancient evil. Athens and Rhodes,
each in its day of maritime greatness, had maintained some sort of
police of the seas, and earlier powers had probably done the same
before them. But Athens was nautically dead, and Rhodes withered.
It rested with Rome to take the initiative in such matters now. Not
only did Rome shirk this duty ; her policy directly tended to promote
the growth of the evil. We have seen that the enormous demand for
slaves encouraged the kidnapping of men in time of peace by sea and
land. The slave-dealer was not likely to ask awkward questions ; he
took his men and paid for them. The slave-supply inevitably fell
more and more into the hands of the pirates. Their numbers grew
fast as every war set adrift ruined and desperate men, and the civil
wars in Italy[3] were no exception. Adventurers from Crete and elsewhere, deserters, and rough spirits generally, flocked to them. Every
slave-war in Sicily or Italy created a fresh demand for slaves. The
pirate leaders were evidently men of intelligence. Their enterprises
were carried on in all parts of the Mediterranean, by bands which
acted independently of each other. A central sovranty was impossible,
but the various bodies recognized a common[4] interest, helped each
other at a pinch, and took care not to spoil each other's game. They

---

[1] Cic. *de imper. Cn. Pomp.* § 32.

[2] The pirates. Florus I 41—2, Eutrop. VI 3, Orosius V 23, Dion Cass. XXXVI 20—23,
Strabo XII 6 § 2, Appian *civ.* I 111.

[3] We must remember that the Sullan proscriptions and confiscations were not reversed.
Men feared to reopen dangerous questions, which might cause another civil war.

[4] See Dion Cass. XXXVI 20—22.

well understood that their real enemy was Rome, and for the most part kept on good terms with other powers, especially with any power at war with Rome. They were of service to Sertorius and Mithradates. If they swindled Spartacus, we must not forget that he was already a thorn in the side of Rome, and that his destruction would mean a demand for more slaves.

965. When Sulla patched up a peace with Mithradates, in haste to return to Italy, he had no time to attend to the pirates. But they had been very troublesome, and he had not forgotten them. One of the consuls of 79, P. Servilius Vatia, was appointed to the Cilician province, and commissioned to suppress piracy. The province was supposed to include Pamphylia and a considerable Hinterland, but it would seem that the power of Rome had been very ineffectively asserted in most of it. All along the southern coast of Asia Minor from Lycia to Cilicia the pirates now had settlements. They held the harbours, and their cities were populous and wealthy, thriving on the slave-trade and the plunder of commerce. Servilius, who was an able and upright man, got to work boldly. He defeated the corsair fleets, for their swift barks, designed to catch the slow and escape from the strong, were no match[1] for his ships in battle. He took a number of towns on the coast, and made a campaign inland among the mountains of Isauria. He annexed at least a part of the mountainous western Cilicia. All these successful operations occupied him for about three years. But the chief fruits of his exertions were the captives and the rich booty, of which it was pointedly remarked[2] that he rendered full account on his return to Rome. The pirates were dispersed, and a few of them killed or taken captive. But the mass of them easily found shelter in Crete and other haunts till the proconsul's back was turned. While he was triumphing as *Isauricus* in 75, they were reoccupying their old headquarters, and piracy was going on[3] merrily as ever; indeed it had never ceased.

966. In the year 74 the Roman government had three serious wars on its hands. But so pressing were the dangers created by piracy, threatening the corn-supply of the Roman populace and the communication with the armies abroad, that another effort was made to put it down. The plan of assailing the pirates in their headquarters had failed; it was now proposed to hunt them down wherever they could be found, and for this purpose to confer on a single commander very wide powers. M. Antonius[4], a son of the orator, was invested

---

[1] See Cic. II *in Verr.* v § 89 for a comparison of a quadrireme with piratical light vessels.

[2] Cic. II *in Verr.* I §§ 56, 57.

[3] It was in 76 that Caesar fell into the hands of pirates near Miletus.

[4] Antonius. Velleius II 31, Livy ep. 97, Cicero *div. in Caecil.* § 55.

with a general proconsular *imperium* over the sea and sea-coasts. This power he was to exercise in the various provinces also, as the needs of his mission might require, concurrently with that of the local governors. Such powers were necessary for the object aimed at, but in the hands of an incompetent and worthless man they were worse than useless. So long as Antonius confined himself to making requisitions[1] on Rome's provincial subjects, he merely added to burdens already too grievous. But, when he began to make war, his failure was disastrous, and a material addition to the dangers of Rome. Crete, the nursery of mercenaries and centre of disturbances from time immemorial, was now a congenial resort of the pirates. Its independence was inconsistent with the peace of its neighbours : it was clear that it must be conquered. So far well, but Antonius, who attacked the island with boastful confidence, seems to have been defeated and compelled to make a treaty with the Cretan leaders. This had to be referred to Rome, and the Cretans, anxious to end the war, sent envoys[2] to plead with the Senate for ratification of the pur- posely moderate terms granted to the beaten Antonius. But the Senate insisted on terms such as might have followed a Roman victory. So apparently nothing came of the treaty, but the Cretans henceforth could be under no delusion as to the intentions of Rome. Antonius, whom the Roman wits nicknamed *Creticus* in derision, died in Crete. How the Romans dealt with Crete and with the pirates in general we shall see below. For the present we may well take note of the extreme naval weakness of Rome. Since the destruction of Carthage she had been under no necessity of keeping up a fleet save for purposes of maritime police, and a succession of wars on land had taxed her resources to the utmost. Her old policy had been to occupy or control all islands within reach, and this policy, in default of an efficient navy, had sufficed to make her virtually mistress of the seas. She now stood in danger of losing her island empire, and with it her communication by sea with her transmarine provinces. How much might depend on a speedy restoration of the peace of the waters, no man could tell.

967. I must endeavour in a few words to give a slight sketch of the state of things in the East, so far as it concerns Roman history. In Egypt the degenerate Ptolemies were entering upon the last stage of their downward career. Murders depositions restorations, such were the chief events in the Lagid house. In 81 the throne was vacant[3], and Sulla placed a refugee Lagid prince (Ptolemy XII or

---

[1] Cic. II *in Verr.* III § 213.
[2] Diodorus XL 1, Dion Cass. fragm. 111.
[3] Appian *civ.* I 111.

Alexander II) upon it. He murdered his queen, and was himself murdered by the mob of Alexandria. It was said that he left a will[1] bequeathing Egypt to the Roman people. But this is a very doubtful story. Rome did not take possession, and revolutions and anarchy went on for some years yet. The outlying province of Cyrene and its neighbouring cities had been left to Rome in 96, but was, as we saw, not occupied as a province. In 74 it was at last taken over[2] and for the present placed under a quaestor with the powers of a praetorian governor. This step was probably connected with the resolution to put down piracy, for it closed what was then[3] a harbour to the pirates and provided a convenient naval base facing the south coast of Crete. Syria had for some time past been the scene of frequent revolutions and wars. It was tending to fall under the power of the Parthian kings; but a Scythian invasion weakened Parthia for a time, and in 83 Tigranes king of Armenia annexed some Parthian provinces, and with them Syria, to his dominions. A Seleucid prince still survived, and eventually sat upon the Syrian throne afterwards for a few years, but the great house of Seleucus had practically come to an end. Tigranes was now a powerful monarch. Rome was not at present inclined to meddle with him. It remained to be seen what sacrifices he would be willing to make for his father-in-law and ally. He was a Great King of the type common in the East since the days of the great Alexander. One of the appliances of royalty was a splendid capital city, and Tigranes resolved to create one. He, like Mithradates, was impressed by the talent of the Greeks, and admired Greek cities. So he laid out a great city, and planted there a number of people drawn[4] from the semi-hellenized cities of Cappadocia and eastern Cilicia. He named it Tigranocerta, and did all he could to encourage Greek civilization and literature. But the whole spirit of the Armenian Great King was oriental. He and Mithradates were essentially a pair of Sultans. For the present they had a common interest, the opposition to Roman dominion in the East: but, if Rome had been beaten back, one of the two would assuredly have devoured the other. From the death of Sulla till the renewal of the Pontic war in 74 the Roman government had not effectively asserted itself in Asiatic affairs. Tigranes annexed Syria and even Cappadocia, and Rome looked on.

968. The actual breach with Mithradates came about in connexion with Bithynia. In 75 the worthless Nicomedes III died, and

---

[1] Cicero *de lege agr.* II §§ 41—4.
[2] Sallust *hist.* fragm. II 43 (Maur., II 47 Kritz).
[3] Since destroyed by the subsidence of that coast.
[4] See in particular Appian *Mithr.* 67.

bequeathed[1] his kingdom to the Roman people. The bequest was accepted, as was indeed necessary, if it was not to fall into the hands of the king of Pontus. Moreover, the prospect of a new province to plunder whetted the imperial appetite of the Roman capitalists. But Mithradates meant to have Bithynia, and no better chance than the present was likely to occur. He had a large army ready, recruited mainly from the hardy peoples of the steppes beyond the Euxine and the Thracians of the Balkan. His fleet, raised among his maritime allies and subjects, was organized and commanded by Greeks, and was efficient according to the standards of those days. A large part of his army was trained on the Roman model, for the civil wars and proscriptions had provided the king with Roman officers; two of his chief advisers were Marians who had escaped from the legions of Fimbria when they went over to Sulla. Experience had taught him that Roman armies, if well led, were not to be overwhelmed by mere numbers, and his first care now was to improve the quality of his troops. He knew that most of the peoples of Asia Minor wished him well, and the Pisidians and Isaurians had lately been irritated by the expedition of Servilius. Any success against Roman generals would cause a widespread rising in his favour. At his back was his ally Tigranes of Armenia. It is true that he could not rely on the Galatians. These Celtic tribes did not readily accommodate themselves to the system of an oriental despotism, and some of them at least preferred a connexion with Rome. But his good friends the pirates enabled him to extend his views. By the advice of his Marian refugees he opened negotiations with Sertorius in Spain, and a treaty was concluded in the year 75, by which the king was bound to support the Spanish rising with money and ships, while the Marian leader on behalf of Rome agreed to let all the parts of Asia Minor not as yet in Roman possession be incorporated in the Pontic empire. He also sent him a Roman general. Mithradates now set to work. He put up a son of Nicomedes as claimant of the Bithynian kingdom. This was in effect a declaration of war against Rome, and he prepared to support his claim by force of arms.

969. We have already remarked that the consuls[2] of 74, L. Lucullus and M. Cotta, were appointed to Cilicia and Bithynia. The former was meant to take charge of the chief operations by land, the latter

---

[1] Authorities criticized by Maurenbrecher I 58—60, who prefers the other version, of intestacy followed by Roman occupation. See § 946.

[2] Mithradatic war, general authorities. Plutarch *Lucull.* 6—36, Appian *Mithr.* 67—90, Livy ep. 93—98, Florus I 40 §§ 13—21, Eutrop. VI 6—9, Orosius VI 2, 3, Dion Cass. XXXVI 3—19, Memnon (*FHG* III 545—58), Phlegon 12 (*FHG* III 606). Much of interest in Cicero *de imper. Cn. Pomp.*

was primarily to conduct the naval war, though he had some land-force as well. It would appear that some arrangement was made by which the province of Asia was also placed under[1] Lucullus (not at first as governor, for we have traces of other governors), for it is clear that he did not start his campaign from the distant South. We hear of him later striving to check abuses in Asia, and it is highly probable that he advanced by one of the roads from Pergamum to Cyzicus. The war opened as usual with a Roman disaster. Mithradates found Cotta posted at Chalcedon, and defeated him both by sea and by land. He pushed on to the West and received the submission of the coast districts of Mysia, which was a part of the province Asia. Among the Greek towns of the Propontis was the flourishing city of Cyzicus, one of the republics whose autonomy was respected by Rome. The Cyzicenes, 'our very loyal allies,' as Cicero calls them, refused to admit the king, who thereupon laid siege to the place with an immense army and a strong fleet. Cyzicus lay on an island joined to the mainland by a small causeway or neck of land perhaps improved by art. The ground on which it stood[2] was low, and Mithradates occupied a height on the mainland opposite the isthmus and another on the island at the back of the town, thus commanding all the space outside the walls. But the walls were strong, and the defence stubborn. All the skill of his Greek engineers was foiled, and the king himself came near to being captured in a mine. His own forces were in danger from their very numbers, for food ran short in his camp. Lucullus marched to relieve the besieged, and cut off the besiegers' supplies by land. Winter was coming on, and the supply by sea became difficult. Mithradates still pressed on the siege, but famine and pestilence carried off many of his trained troops, and he had to give way. He sent home his fleet, and fled with the remains of his army to Lampsacus on the Hellespont, whence he transported them home by sea. Lucullus did not neglect to pursue him. If there had been an effective fleet cooperating with the Roman army, the war would probably have ended there and then. But the fleet of Mithradates (perhaps a second squadron) had the upper hand in the Aegean, and kept him in touch with the pirates and with Crete. He had also other armies operating in the interior of Asia Minor, mostly with success: only Deiotarus, a Galatian chief, made a vigorous stand on the side of Rome.

970. Lucullus wintered at Cyzicus (74—3), preparing for a

---

[1] See Cicero *pro Flacco* §§ 45, 85. Lucullus was there *consulari imperio*, for war purposes, till 72 or 71.

[2] Cyzicus. Strabo XII 8 § 11, Pompon. Mela I 98, Pliny *NH* v 142, and the Admiralty charts.

vigorous campaign in the spring. His first care was to destroy the Pontic fleet, which threatened his line of communications with Italy, and might even attempt something against Italy itself. His lieutenants had been busy collecting naval contingents from Rome's maritime allies. The new fleet beat the enemy in two battles and cleared the Aegean. Lucullus had now secured most of Bithynia, and he advanced against Mithradates by land, while Cotta with a fleet entered the Euxine. Things had gone ill with the king on his homeward voyage. Storms and wrecks had cost him many ships and men. But he held most of the coast-cities, and he had thrown a garrison into Heraclea. The town[1] was a strong fortress. As a Greek republic of more than average vitality, the Heracleots would gladly have stood neutral ; but Mithradates got the town by treachery, and left the wretched citizens to bear the penalty of opposing Rome. While Lucullus pushed on into the Pontic kingdom, and C. Triarius held the sea with the fleet, Cotta undertook the siege of Heraclea. For about two years the place kept him at bay, but supplies began to fail, and it was at length betrayed by the king's own officers. The Heracleots, after being bullied and starved by the garrison, were now handed over to be murdered or enslaved by the Roman troops, who barbarously sacked the town. Works of art were shipped for Rome and mostly lost at sea. The brutality and rapacity of Cotta seem to have been notorious. After his return to Rome his enemies charged him with misconduct and peculation. The Senate could not screen him, and bills were passed for setting free the prisoners and making all possible restitution to the injured Heracleots. But when it came to hunting up the survivors in order to restore the city, only a poor remnant could be found. So the restitution did not come to much, nor does this Cotta seem to have received any adequate punishment. It is well to take note of this affair, for it throws light on the imperial methods of the Roman Republic.

971. We must return to Lucullus. He had nothing to do with this shameful business of Heraclea. His aim was to catch Mithradates and bring him to battle, but he could not do this until the sea had been cleared and the coast districts of Pontus secured in his rear. Sieges of the Pontic strongholds thus engaged most of his time and forces in a good part of the years 73 and 72. But he marched up the country as far as Cabeira on the Lycus, and gained a decided success over the king, whose army was no longer so good in quality as it had been. Mithradates was for the moment beaten. He sent orders that his wives and female relatives should be put to death,

---

[1] The extracts from Memnon (*FHG* III 545—58), himself a native of this city, are interesting and important as giving a non-Roman version of events.

as he could not withdraw them from the place where he had lodged them. He fled to Armenia, and took refuge with Tigranes. But Tigranes had as yet no open quarrel with Rome. He had enough on hand, what with his provinces taken from the Parthians and his other annexations such as Syria. So he received Mithradates as a refugee, but did not employ his immense army to support his cause. For many months he did not even admit his father-in-law to an audience. Meanwhile the chief Pontic cities, Sinope Amisus and others, fell into the hands of the lieutenants of Lucullus, only after a stubborn resistance in many cases. No doubt the garrisons contained many desperate men, who could expect little mercy from a Roman conqueror. There were some excesses when these places were taken, but nothing like the ruin of Heraclea. The policy of Lucullus was very different to that of Cotta. By about the middle of the year 70 it seems that the ancestral kingdom of Mithradates had been brought under the dominion of Rome. But during a great part of this war of sieges the proconsul was busy with administrative duties further to the West.

972. The state of the province of Asia was truly deplorable. The exactions of Sulla had compelled the cities to raise large sums of money on loan at exorbitant interest, and the Roman financiers, backed by corrupt and rapacious governors, held the wretched provincials in their grip. Good care was taken that the debts should not be paid off but go on mounting. The amount of the public debts is said to have been 20,000 talents (say £4,750,000) at first, and after some 12 years to have now reached 120,000 talents (over £28,000,000). These amounts are only worth mentioning as a record of Roman usury which Plutarch found in his authority (probably Sallust) and does not seem to have felt any difficulty in believing. Of the private indebtedness we have no estimate, but it was enormous. As the cities were constrained to sell their public property, so men with families had to part with marketable sons and daughters. Slaves they had to be, somewhere or other ; and, once they belonged to a Roman owner, they had at least a maintenance and protection. There may be some exaggeration in these stories, but they are nowise incredible : Verres had, according to Cicero, done things as bad or worse. This was one of the ways in which the Roman brokers got hold of the works of art and attractive slaves for which Roman society could always supply rich purchasers.

973. Lucullus was not the man to tolerate a system of such infamous oppression. If Mithradates was to be put down effectually, Asiatics must be taught to look upon Roman sovranty as better, or at least not worse, than the absolute monarchy of a Great King. We

must remember that the constitution of Rome provided no standing army to overawe the province in time of peace. He probably saw that continual wars would consume more than the revenues of the province could supply. Asia was meant to be a mainstay of the Roman treasury. But complete exhaustion was manifestly near, and the province would be a burden if the process were allowed to go on. Romans in the name of Rome were for their own private gain ruining one of Rome's most valuable assets. He set to work with drastic measures of relief. The rate of interest[1] was reduced to 1%. The accumulated burdens of usury were cancelled. An arrangement was made by which the creditor received yearly a fixed share (25%) of the debtor's income towards payment of the reduced debt. The public debt was to be discharged in double (40,000 talents for 20,000) instead of sixfold (120,000) as claimed by the Roman capitalists. It was a desperate remedy for a desperate evil. We are told that in less than four years the province was cleared of debt by this bold policy. But if there was joy in Asia[2] there was a bitter cry in Rome. It may be that Lucullus hardly understood the trend of Roman politics during the three or four years of his absence. The senatorial government was greatly weakened, in fact falling fast. The rage of disappointed greed only drove the capitalist Knights into closer alliance with the 'popular' party, and there began a series of attacks upon the absent proconsul which only ended with his recall. It mattered not that the money-lenders had richly deserved his interference; that he had acted in the true interest of Rome, whose power he was representing; that the grateful provincials founded festivals in his honour. He was now held up to the Roman mob as a typical noble, full of pride and ambition, overbearing to fellow-citizens, and accused of protracting the eastern war for his own glory. It was not yet possible to get him superseded in command, so the capitalists had to wait: but they neither forgot nor forgave.

974. Lucullus had made enemies at home by his uprightness. With his army he had trouble on the score of discipline. He seems never to have had a large force at disposal. Five legions formed the core of it, and two of these were the legions of Fimbria, left behind by Sulla when he returned to Italy. The bulk of the men in them were the original levies, seasoned veterans of splendid fighting qualities, but apt to be unruly, and corrupted by living at free quarters among the submissive people of Asia. The first great task of Lucullus had been to restore discipline in the legions, particularly among the

---

[1] That is, 1% per month, I imagine. See Plutarch *Lucullus* 20.

[2] In Cicero *pro Flacco* § 85 we read of bequests to Lucullus, apparently from grateful provincials, but the passage is somewhat obscure.

Fighting Fimbrians. And in the earlier years of the war he seems to have been on the whole successful in this respect. But as time went by a deterioration set in. Men wearied of campaigns, and wintering in Armenia was not the same thing as wintering in the province Asia. No doubt those who had filled their purses wanted to be where pleasures could be bought, while the unlucky or unthrifty were sick of the whole business. Nor was the latter part of the war under Lucullus an unbroken series of victories. His lieutenants were more than once defeated. The proconsul himself still led his troops to victory, but then he was too strict, and too much concerned to protect the goods of conquered enemies. In short the Roman soldiery of that age were spoilt children, and to command their best services for any length of time was only possible to a man at once genial and attractive. With all his merits, Lucullus had not the necessary sympathy and magnetism to carry his army with him by sheer personal attachment and so to complete his task. And in the last stage of his career in the East, when the loyalty of his officers was being sapped by the news from Rome, and rumour foreshadowed his recall, he had so far lost control of his men that he could effect nothing. Thus the splendid achievements of Lucullus did not bring him the glory he desired. He had sown, but his rival Pompey was to reap.

975. It appears to have been in the year 70 that Lucullus, having now got a firm hold of Pontus and done his work of reform in Asia, sent an ambassador to Tigranes with a demand for the extradition[1] of Mithradates. Tigranes was away in Syria, busy with the organization of his new provinces, and generally playing the Great King. The envoy, Lucullus' brother-in-law Appius Claudius, turned his long journey to good account by treating secretly with some of the chiefs of principalities and head men of cities now become dependent on the king. He encouraged them in hopes of deliverance by Roman help, but warned them to wait quietly for the present. As for Tigranes, he flatly refused to give up Mithradates, and Appius answered by a declaration of war. Mithradates was now openly taken into favour, and Tigranes prepared to back him up with a great army. It was the old story of Antiochus and Philip over again : he first let Mithradates be overthrown, and then faced Rome single-handed. Lucullus saw his opportunity. He was at Sinope, which he had recently taken,

---

[1] No doubt this was a bold step, and may be viewed as beyond the instructions from Rome. But Lucullus had been sent to put down Mithradates. No army of occupation would be maintained in conquered Pontus. To capture or kill the king was the only possible security for peace. Ferrero's (I 199) comparison of Lucullus to Napoleon seems to me a misleading analogy.

and he was free to move. His brother's campaigns had pacified the Thracians for the time, and Machares, a son of Mithradates, who was governing the Bosporan (Crimean) kingdom, had sought the friendship of Rome. He now left a detachment behind in Pontus, and hastened up the country with a very small but efficient force, to strike Tigranes and forestall an invasion. His men were already grumbling and loth to march. But he pushed on, crossed the Euphrates, and entered the districts to the north of Mesopotamia, making for Tigranocerta. Tigranes, like a true Sultan, put to death the first man who reported the approach of the Romans. At last the truth had to come out, but even then the king had no notion of his danger. Before he was well aware of it, Lucullus had routed and cut up a force sent to meet him, and was besieging Tigranocerta. The king had left his new capital in a hurry, to get together his main army : indeed he had left behind his concubines, who were only recovered by a special party of cavalry making a dash through the Roman lines. Against the advice of Mithradates and others he soon advanced to relieve the city at the head of a motley host reckoned at about 250,000 men. Lucullus did not abandon the siege, but marched to meet the enemy with his main force. The odds were about one to twenty, but that mattered not. Generalship and skill turned the day. Rolled into a helpless mass, the oriental foot was butchered, and the horse ran away, but were mostly cut down. Mithradates had not been present. He now came to the front again and was left to command the new army which the two kings began to raise. Lucullus soon took Tigranocerta, and allowed his men to enjoy the plunder of private goods. Games and shows were held to celebrate the victory. It is said that, among the Greeks brought there by Tigranes to give a Hellenistic tone to the place, there were some actors, who were now employed to entertain the victorious Romans. Lucullus had some[1] Galatian and Thracian auxiliaries in his army, and the gathering must have been a strange one. The mongrel population of the city were soon scattered to their former homes, and the new capital of Tigranes was deserted.

976. Such were the chief results of the campaign of 69 B.C. A number of principalities and cities made submission to the conqueror, who wintered with his army in the land of Gordyene by the upper Tigris. Tigranes was cut off from Syria. A prince of the house of Seleucus[2] still remained, and he now became king for a little while. The winter of 69—8 was an anxious time. Lucullus knew, it seems, of the agitation against him in Rome. It is said that he had made

---

[1] Plutarch *Lucull.* 28—9, Memnon 56 (*FHG* III 556).
[2] Appian *Syr.* 70.

arrangements[1] for quieting some of the agitators by bribes. This may remind us of a difficulty not mentioned in our authorities. He was some 500 miles or more distant from the force left behind in Pontus and from the seaports of that region. Until he summoned that force to join him, his line of communications can only have been held by a few weak posts, for he had no men to spare. Yet he seems to have been able to communicate with his lieutenants in the rear without hindrance, and this through a wild mountainous country. I will not attempt to solve this difficulty by guesses, but merely state it, to shew the unsatisfactory nature of our record. The scene of interest now shifts for a time to the Parthian court. Both Mithradates and Lucullus were wishing to get help from that quarter. But the Parthian king played a double game, and would help neither. Lucullus resolved to coerce him, and ordered up the rest of his troops from Pontus in preparation for a Parthian war. But they were mutinous and would not come. News of their refusal encouraged the discontent of his own army, so he gave up the plan, and marched northwards instead. He hoped to reach Artaxata, the Armenian capital, and effect the conquest of Armenia. He met the new army under Mithradates, and won another victory. But when he continued his advance his men openly refused to go on. The campaign of 68 had been begun late, owing to delays and change of plan, and the cold and wet of the Armenian mountains were more than they would endure. There was nothing for it but to march south again. Lucullus therefore returned to the districts he had lately left, and besieged and took the strong town of Nisibis. After this he wintered again in Gordyene, his men more mutinous[2] than ever, and clamouring for their discharge. In the case of the Fimbrian veterans this was not wonderful. They had been raised by the Marian leaders in 86, and by the winter of 68—7 they had served quite 18 years in the East.

977. Things now got rapidly worse for Lucullus. In Armenia Tigranes recovered his lost ground. Soon news came that Mithradates had entered Pontus, won back a number of towns, beaten one of the proconsul's lieutenants and shut him up in Cabeira. Old age and a wound could not check him, and the natives preferred his rule to that of the Romans. Triarius moved up and relieved Cabeira, and even gained some success against the king. But Mithradates was still dangerous, and Lucullus had to hurry back to meet him. Before

---

[1] See Maurenbrecher on Sall. *hist.* fragm. IV 71.

[2] Among the officers who promoted this mutiny was P. Clodius (see § 977), whose relations with Lucullus are described in Plutarch *Luc.* 34. He worked in the interest of Pompey, no doubt intriguing in Rome, and may have been an agent, as Ferrero thinks. See § 984. He was brother of the Claudius named in § 975.

he arrived, another disaster had occurred. Mithradates had threatened a small depot of the Romans, the relief of which the clamours of his men, now quite out of hand, forced Triarius to attempt. This brought on a battle, in which the Roman force was utterly defeated, and only escaped annihilation by a strange device of a brave man. The king had from the first had with him a number of Roman exiles. It seems that some of these were still left, for a Roman centurion made his way unsuspected to his side and wounded him. Another version makes the centurion actually one of those in the service of Mithradates. The fall of the king threw his army into confusion, and so the Romans had time to rally. Whether true or not, this story gives us a very credible picture of the character of the two armies at this time. Mithradates soon recovered. When Lucullus came up, he could do nothing. The king held a strong position, and waited. The Roman camp was a scene of mutinous disobedience. An Armenian army was advancing into Cappadocia, cutting off scattered Romans on the way. An appeal for help (how sent[1] we do not hear) to the governor of Cilicia met with no response. Lucullus heard that Tigranes was approaching with his main army, and set out to meet him ; but he had not gone far when his men finally refused to follow him any longer. Weary no doubt they were of hard campaigning under a stern and scrupulous commander. Ambition was for him, not for them. But the movement of politics in Rome was the chief cause of the collapse of Lucullus. It was known that he was about to be recalled, and even his officers no longer heeded him. A certain P. Claudius had begun to make mischief while at Nisibis. Afterwards he found it better to withdraw from the proconsul's service, and Marcius the governor of Cilicia received him on his staff. This was the same Clodius afterwards notorious as a violent mob-leader.

978. Early in the year 67 the enemies of Lucullus had at last carried their point. Already the province of Cilicia had been assigned to Q. Marcius Rex, consul in 68. And now a *lex Gabinia*[2] gave Bithynia and Pontus to M' Acilius Glabrio, consul in 67. Lucullus having reported the conquest of Pontus, ten commissioners[3] were also appointed to make the usual regulations for the new province. But, when the new governor and his colleagues reached Bithynia, they found that there was nothing to be done in Pontus. The mere news of their appointment had sufficed to take from

---

[1] Dion Cass. XXXVI 17 seems to make Lucullus apply to Marcius on his way to Cilicia, perhaps drawing from Sallust (v 14 Maur.) who says *per Lycaoniam*. The matter is a mystery to me.

[2] Maurenbrecher on Sall. *hist.* frag. V 13.

[3] See Cicero *ad Att.* XIII 6 § 4. It seems that some at least of the ten were friends of Lucullus.

Lucullus all that was left of authority. He could do nothing but look on while Mithradates was recovering his lost kingdom and Tigranes overrunning Cappadocia. The Fimbrian troops had heard of their discharge, and wanted to start for Italy ; but at the entreaty of their comrades they agreed to wait for the end of summer, so as not to expose the rest of the army to destruction. The disgrace of Lucullus was complete. The people in power at Rome had indirectly dropped the war without making peace. Glabrio remained in Bithynia, for the prospect of taking over Pontus under present conditions was not an attractive one. Both he and Lucullus must at least have suspected that at the back of this weak renunciation of the fruits of victory there was an intention of reserving the power and glory of command for another man. Such was the connexion between war and politics in this age of the Republic. The treatment of Lucullus established a principle for the guidance of leaders. Already it had been proved that the army was the dominant force in politics, and that the road to preeminence lay through military glory. But as yet no leader was prepared to use the sword as a means of gaining and keeping a despotic power. The connexion between politics and war had to continue for a while yet. The means of working this system had been roughly outlined by Marius at the time of the Cimbric war. It consisted in the alliance of a general in command with a tribune at home. Sulla's muzzling of the tribunate had checked its development. Pompey had in the restored power of the tribunate an instrument ready to his hand, and it was he that first regularly turned it to account. The tribunate had long been the tool of the Senate. Now for a few momentous years it became the tool of the great proconsuls. The example of Pompey was boldly followed by Caesar, who was thus enabled to use a democratic appliance for the overthrow of the worn-out Republic.

The interest of the story of Lucullus in the East is great, for it throws much light on the conditions of Roman public life at this time. But in telling it, though briefly, with omission of a mass of doubtful or irrelevant detail, we have got down to the year 67. It is time to turn back and consider the events which were contemporary with the failure of Lucullus and which were in part connected with his recall.

CHAPTER L

INTERNAL AFFAIRS 69—66 B.C.[1] POMPEY'S PREEMINENCE 67—62 B.C.

979. THE restoration of the powers of the tribunate in the consulship of Pompey and Crassus was a measure that soon made itself felt in the public life of Rome. The armies were disbanded, political parties faced each other, and the ambitions of individuals were left to seek their fulfilment in the sphere of politics. For the only war on foot was that in the East, and as yet Lucullus was apparently well able to finish his task. In the year 69 the restoration of the Capitoline temple, begun by Sulla, was so far complete that the dedication was performed by Catulus[2] (consul 78), whom the censors of 70—69 had chosen as *princeps senatus*. He was a bold and determined aristocrat, and till his death nine years later was the head of the Sullan party. As an orator he was not in the first rank, but the eloquence of Hortensius was employed on the same side. Hortensius was consul in this year with Q. Metellus. In the allotment of the provinces, the charge of the Cretan war (for the failure of Antonius had to be repaired) fell to Hortensius. He did not wish to leave Rome, where all his interests were centred, and resigned the province to his colleague. Metellus conquered Crete, but it took him three years (68—6) of rough work, as we shall see below. The new juries were now sitting, and we find Cicero[3] engaged in the defence of a M. (or M') Fonteius, who had been governor of Transalpine Gaul at the time when Pompey was sent to Spain. The services rendered by him in sending supplies, and in providing winter quarters for the army beaten by Sertorius, were the strong part of Cicero's case. The necessities of advocacy compelled him to disparage the worth of provincial evidence, on which he had almost entirely relied in the prosecution of Verres. That he laid stress on the great extent to

---

[1] General authorities. Dion Cass. fragm. 111, XXXVI 23—XXXVII 23, Velleius II 31—40, Suetonius *Jul.* 6—8, Appian *Mithr.* 91—119, Cicero *de imper. Cn. Pomp.*, Livy ep. 99—103, Florus I 40—42, Eutropius VI 11—16, Orosius VI 4—6, Plutarch's *Pompey, Lucullus, Caesar.* Also Maurenbrecher's Sallust II 195—9.

[2] See inscription in Wilmanns 700. The story of the offering intercepted by Verres is interesting, Cicero II *in Verr.* IV §§ 60—71.

[3] Cic. *pro Fonteio*, especially §§ 11—17.

which Roman capital was employed in the province, and the great number of Roman financial agents doing business there, was probably a move to interest the Equestrian part of the jury on the side of his client.

980. For the present the position of Cicero was that of a leading counsel, whose services in court all parties were anxious to secure. But he had entered on an official career, and it was certain that he would soon have to come forward as a political speaker. The state of the public courts was not materially improved by the introduction of the composite juries. The attempt to check provincial extortion by playing off senators and Knights against one another was doomed to failure. A governor could no longer restrain the malpractices of Roman usurers and tithe-farmers, for his fellow-senators could no longer protect him. But, if he left the capitalists a free hand, or helped them, he might freely enrich himself. If brought to trial, his conviction was most unlikely, and would almost certainly depend on the influence of his personal enemies. And the revival of interest in politics, which followed the restoration of the tribunate, did not tend to lessen the demand for money. The tribunate was now again worth competing for. A tribune could make himself felt as the leader of the 'Roman people,' that is the sovran mob, or, failing this, he could sell himself to the nobles as an organ of obstruction. And there were ten tribunes to be elected every year. Moreover, it was noticed that the recent removal of 64 senators from the roll had increased the number of candidates for offices. Many of these men were seeking to regain as magistrates a place in the House. With more competition there was more bribery, and more extravagance in public games and entertainments. In 68 we hear that C. Piso won his election as consul by bribery. Accusers appeared to threaten a prosecution, but he bought them off, and was actually consul in 67. After this he was governor of Transalpine Gaul. For his conduct there he was prosecuted by Caesar on a charge of extortion, and successfully defended by Cicero. He belonged to the party of senatorial nobles led by Catulus, and seems to have been a notable specimen of his class. The truth was simply that money ruled most things in the later Republic. Speaking generally, a man had to be corrupt himself in order to have the means of corrupting others. Few could win promotion by the sword, like Pompey, or by laying clients under obligation, like Cicero. But the power of a full purse was any man's weapon, and the purse emptied had to be refilled.

981. These details will suffice to give us some slight notion of the political atmosphere of Rome in the time following the changes of the year 70. The two really important men, Pompey and Crassus, were

for a while nursing their ambitions in private life, watching opportunities and each other. Crassus was the elder, and he had spent
enormous sums in winning popular favour by bounties and entertainments. But in military reputation he was inferior to his rival, so he
set himself to gain ground in other ways. He was not a great orator,
but a very painstaking counsel, and ever ready to serve those who
needed his help. His wealth enabled him to attach to his interest a
number of useful persons by judicious loans, and his affable and
popular bearing disposed people generally in his favour. And yet
there was something in Crassus that prevented him from ever enjoying the affection and full confidence of his fellow-citizens. Self-
interest was in him too transparent a motive. Those who found in
him an enemy knew that he might at any moment become their friend,
but his friends were also conscious that he had in him the making of
an enemy. He was thought by some a dangerous man to meddle
with, and the sinister rumours of his doings in the time of the proscriptions can hardly have died away. In the eyes of the now
reviving Marians Pompey might appear to have been a hard conqueror, but Crassus had made his millions out of the ruin of families.
Pompey no doubt lost surface-popularity by his adherence to the role
of Indispensable Military Man in time of peace. He stood aloof from
the minor affairs of public life as far as possible, and shewed none of
the accommodating assiduity of Crassus in the relations of private
life. Neither sought an ordinary provincial governorship: Crassus
was doing well for his own interests in Rome, while Pompey waited
for some exceptional call to draw him from his proud seclusion. At
the time of the census he had betrayed his self-satisfaction in having
shewn that the rules made for ordinary men did not apply to him.
In passing the inspection as an *eques*, he was asked 'Have you served
all the campaigns required by law?' His answer was 'Yes, and all
under my own command.' This spirit he had carried into his retirement, and it was inevitable that he should soon become restless, with
Crassus flourishing at home, and Lucullus winning victories abroad.
We shall see that he had not long to wait for the coveted opportunities of coming dramatically to the front.

982. These two pupils of Sulla, mutually jealous, had for a
moment combined to gratify common ambitions by overthrowing
their master's system. The Senate naturally distrusted them, while
to the reviving Marians a genuine representative of the 'popular'
party was more congenial. The heir of their tradition was in every
way a striking contrast to these two rival personalities. They were
men of ability, Pompey indeed really great as a soldier, but Caesar
was a genius. The Roman people had produced one at last: the

Julian house was of the bluest blood of the Roman patriciate, and in Caesar the steely nerve of the true-born Roman of the olden time was equipped with Greek clearness of vision and tempered by a wide and various experience. Pompey and Crassus were narrow, Caesar was broad. They had both an evil record of conduct towards fellow-citizens, while Caesar was clear. They had so managed things that their political position was already ambiguous, while about Caesar's adhesion to the 'popular' cause there was no doubt whatever. That the championship of that cause must lead him to ruin or to monarchy was probably as yet hidden even from himself. Men, and still more women, succumbed to his social charm. Money he spent so lavishly that to superficial observers he seemed to be sacrificing all future prospects for the pleasure of the hour ; but it was afterwards remarked that he had got good value for his outlay. Before he began his official career he was, it is said, already deep in debt. Of course his creditors were now interested in his welfare, and this bold mortgaging of his future was in truth a proof that he had confidence in himself. Nor was his intimacy with the Roman ladies a mere diversion or a vulgar fruition of the lax morality of the age. He seems to have taken a genuine pleasure in female society, and to a man walking in dark slippery paths the chances of gaining secret information were no doubt invaluable. That he was found loveable by good judges, and that in after life he found faithful adherents, is no great wonder ; he was neither a man of greed like Crassus, nor a man of blood like Pompey. Of course the Roman aristocrats were not to be mitigated by generosity and mercy. Caesar was their open and consistent adversary, and from the vital antipathy between the two opposing forces there was destined to proceed one of the saddest tragedies of the world.

983.   In 69 Caesar began the regular 'course of honours' by being elected quaestor, an office which he served in the next year under the governor of the Further Spain. But before he left he had to bear a chief part in two funerals. His aunt Julia, widow of old Marius, had of course none of her husband's family left to do her honour. Suetonius preserves the words of the funeral speech in which he called attention to the illustrious origin of his aunt, and thereby of himself. Her mother's stock were Marcii who claimed descent from king Ancus, while the Julii were the offspring (through Aeneas) of a goddess, Venus, mother of the legendary founder of Rome. This was no idle manifesto. He was proud of his birth. That he was disqualified from holding the tribunate, the office of plebeian brawlers, was probably to him a relief. Now that a Patrician had as such enjoyed no political privilege for hundreds of years, there was nothing against a popular leader in the fact of his being a son of the ancient

nobility.   A keen student of human nature, as Caesar was, must have been aware that his traditional rank was all in his favour with the common people.   His wife Cornelia was also lately dead, and he went out of his way to speak over her also, though it was only customary to deliver these panegyrics over ladies who died in a ripe old age.   But the public exposure of grief was thoroughly Roman: the joy and sorrow of great houses was in fact a part of the life of Rome.   The display of the face-mask (*imago*) of Marius at the funeral of Julia was quite in order.   The point was that Caesar dared to shew it.   Times had changed, and the conqueror of the Cimbri was no longer a public enemy.   Of Caesar's service as quaestor in Spain we only know that he went to hold the assizes for the governor in the South-West, in fact that he went through the usual administrative and judicial duties of his post.   It has been well remarked[1] that he must have taken a great interest in the achievements of Sertorius.   But news of movements on foot in Rome soon drew his active spirit to the centre of things.   He returned in 67 as soon as he could get leave to go. He seems to have journeyed by land, perhaps for fear of the sea-rovers, and so passed by Pompey's new route through Cisalpine Gaul. There he found excitement prevailing in the towns north of the Po. In contrast to the communities south of the river, which received the Roman franchise, they had been left by Sulla in the position of Latin colonies.   Looking at the history of the last twenty years, it was natural to regard this as a preliminary to full enfranchisement, and the Transpadanes, now fast becoming Romanized, were conferring and agitating.   It was, they thought, high time that this transitional stage should come to an end.   Both his own opinions and the traditions of his party inclined Caesar to sympathize with a movement tending to add many thousands of good citizens to the strength of Rome.   It was said that he encouraged their claims so strongly that a demonstration in arms seemed imminent.   But the Senate was opposed to the concession, and indeed so remained.   For the present a show of force induced the Transpadanes to wait.   But Caesar had made up his mind, and he did not forget his clients.

984.   Things had been moving fast in Rome during his absence. The failure of Antonius in Crete had only served to encourage piracy. Metellus was now hard at work there, conquering the island thoroughly, but provoking resistance by his severities.   The pirates, reinforced of late by refugees from the beaten fleets of Mithradates, were as strong as ever, and Metellus, locked up in Crete, was no check upon their movements.   They infested the western seas, landed in Sicily, and finally made several descents on the coast of Campania and Latium.

[1] By Mr W. W. Fowler in his *Life of Caesar*.

So long as only the provinces suffered by the sack of towns and inter-ruption of trade, no effective measures had been taken to put an end to the evil. But now even the Appian way was not safe. Persons of quality were carried off as they journeyed on their pleasure or duty, among them two praetors. The port of Ostia itself was surprised, ships burnt, cargoes seized or destroyed, and other damage done. All this with impunity: and the Senate, well aware doubtless that only an individual entrusted with immense powers could be of any use, still preferred to let the scandal and losses go on, sooner than place such powers in the hand of the inevitable Pompey. But the pirates cut off the corn-ships that brought the food of Rome, and the price of corn rose. Stocks were wasting, and the prospect of famine soon brought matters to a crisis. It is evident that the general discontent of the poor had led to the election of 'popular' tribunes for the year 67, and that a vigorous attack on the Senate and its policy was in con-templation. The two most active tribunes were A. Gabinius and C. Cornelius, the latter of whom is spoken of as a respectable man. That they worked in connexion with Pompey is certain. It is also highly probable that from the first there was a design of transferring to Pompey the command in the East, where Lucullus was now known to be in difficulties. Once more the Senate was opposed to the elevation of Pompey: once more Pompey leagued himself with popular leaders to overcome their opposition. And at this juncture the nobles could do nothing with the hungry mob by influence. Even bribery was useless, for it could not be so continuous as to compensate the daily pressure of the rise in corn.

985. Whatever may have been the order in which the measures of this year (67) were brought forward, it is best to speak first of the famous Gabinian law for the better suppression of piracy. It was a simple proposal to appoint a single commander to do the work. He was to be an ex-consul, and was to be appointed for a term of three years. He was to be supreme in the whole Mediterranean, and his power was to extend inland fifty miles from the coast, equal to that of the local governors in their respective spheres. He was to have a number of lieutenants of senatorial rank, a strong fleet with troops and oarsmen as required, and authority to draw money not only from the treasury but from the[1] revenue-farmers. The number of lieutenants and the strength of the fleet seem to have grown as the agitation pro-ceeded. Pompey, who had practically dictated the bill, did not shrink from raising his demands when it had passed. Yet he was not named

---

[1] That is, I take it, in the provinces, by way of an advance on the credit of the state. Remittance of money by sea was risky just now. See the picture drawn in Cicero *de imp. Pomp.* §§ 31—3.

in the bill. But it was known to all who was meant, and, if we may trust our authorities, the debates on the question were carried on with direct reference to Pompey. One of the consuls of the year, M' Acilius Glabrio, had been appointed to go out and take over Bithynia and Pontus from Lucullus. As this had been done by a *lex Gabinia*, it is a reasonable inference[1] that it was a part of the general scheme, intended to get rid of Lucullus in advance, before appointing Pompey as his real successor. Glabrio had either gone or was preparing to go. The other consul, C. Calpurnius Piso, was one of the most stubborn nobles, and ran some risk of violence for his opposition to the bill. The chief speakers against it before the people were Catulus and Hortensius. Caesar supported Gabinius. Constitutional arguments, against the concentration of such enormous powers in the hand of one man, would have little weight with Caesar, and indeed they were out of date. The populace were quite resolved to vote for their daily bread, and the opponents of the bill offered no practical alternative. Talking was useless, but two tribunes had been induced to undertake to defeat it. Of these, L. Trebellius openly vetoed the bill when put to the vote, whereupon Gabinius took a vote on the question of his deposition, as Gracchus had dealt with Octavius years before. Trebellius gave way when the first 17 Tribe-votes announced were all against him. L. Roscius Otho, another tool of the nobles, then tried to persuade the people to appoint two[2] commanders instead of one, but was howled down. So the bill became law. The election of Pompey followed, and so great was the confidence inspired by the belief that the time of obstruction and half-measures was past, that the holders of stocks at once began to sell, and the price of corn went down.

986. We shall see presently how Pompey discharged his trust. Meanwhile let us review the legislation[3] of the year, which consists of a resolute attempt to check the various practices by which directly or indirectly the nobles contrived to retain a great deal of their former power. Part of this activity belongs to the first half of the tribunes' year, the rest to the second, and the elections in the summer come in between. One of the inveterate scandals of Roman public life was connected with the visits of foreign ambassadors and provincial deputations. Their object was to get an early hearing from the Senate, to receive a favourable answer, and to go home. The process

---

[1] Lange *RA* III 207.

[2] Such is the story in Dion Cass. xxxvi 30. But I doubt it. Amendment should have come at an earlier stage, before the voting *comitia*. Plutarch puts the attempt of Roscius at a *contio*, and ignores Trebellius altogether.

[3] Chief authorities are the fragments of Cicero *pro Cornelio*, with the introduction and notes of Asconius, and Dion Cass. xxxvi 38—41.

was not so simple as it might seem.   The proper person to introduce envoys to the House was a consul, and the traditional time for their reception was the beginning of the year.   It was no new discovery that promptitude was a marketable commodity, and it was now customary to make the envoys pay for official complaisance.   In promoting the success of their application no means was found so effective as the bribery of senators.   The art of organizing corruption behind the scenes with careful decency was carried to great perfection in the upper circles of Rome, and it was easy to ascertain what a favourable decision would cost.   The next thing was to get the ready money.   This presented no difficulty, for a banker or bankers were at once found willing to make the necessary advances.   The rate of interest was no doubt high, and the people at home would grumble at the burden laid on them by their representatives.   But by this time it was too late to draw back and defer the whole matter.   The hopes of senators and money-lenders had been raised by the prospect of a lucrative transaction, and to play fast-and-loose with greedy Romans was a dangerous game.   The business had to go through, cost what it might.   The wished-for decree of the Senate was procured, subject of course to be rescinded or superseded by a later one, or to be evaded with impunity by Roman officials abroad.   A new burden had been laid on the community which had thus procured the granting of its request.   The debt would be collected strictly enough, and repudiation was impossible when the creditors could in the last resort bring to bear the irresistible might of Rome.   To escape some of this extortion by bringing cash to Rome, and paying bribes without a Roman banker's kind help, was probably not practicable, for two reasons. First, the discovery of the arrival of a large sum of money would assuredly have sent up prices all round, and secret gossip would exaggerate the amount to be shared.   Secondly, the meaner sort of senators (and some of the more eminent) were often sleeping partners in financial syndicates, and in any case invested much of their moneys through their bankers.   The whole fabric of corruption and capitalism hung together, and to keep the normal process of investment going was the interest of all well-to-do Romans.   Any means employed to keep foreign or provincial communities out of the clutch of Roman usury would be resented, and would have to be paid for in some form or other.   So the infamous conspiracy went on, and the recipient of a bribe need only pay the amount in to his own credit with his banker to set it going perhaps in another transaction of the same kind.

987. Of course it was unofficially known that this sort of thing went on.   The Senate as a body was not likely to make any serious

effort to check a practice deplored by its more nonourable members. Yet it was not to the interest of Rome that her provinces and client-kings should sink into insolvency. The ordinary citizen could not but know that the immunities and perquisites of the citizenship were only possible through the revenue drawn from the provinces, and he had popular tribunes to remind him of the fact. Even the ignorant and apathetic rabble was shocked at the roguery of their betters, the profits of which were not shared by the poor. Gabinius and Cornelius were giving voice to a popular feeling when they came forward with bills directed against these scandals. Gabinius proposed to forbid the lending of money to provincials in Rome; to this end all governors of provinces[1] were to treat bonds for securing such debts as invalid and not to grant actions for recovery of the money. Cornelius followed with a similar proposal to forbid loans to ambassadors of foreign powers. But this seems never to have got beyond the stage of a debate in the Senate. An order of the Senate in this sense had been passed relative to some Cretan envoys 27 years before, and quite recently repeated. It was solemnly pretended that this declaration had done all that was necessary, and hypocrisy prevailed. But the bill of Gabinius passed into law. He carried also a law that the Senate should be obliged to grant audience to envoys from abroad on all days in the month[2] of February. The arrangement of introductions was no longer to be a profitable traffic for greedy consuls. But the Senate could still find pretexts for adjournment and delay. No legislation could suppress the craving of itching palms. Cornelius now proposed a bill imposing severer penalties for corrupt practices (*ambitus*) at elections, and rendering even the subordinate agents (*divisores*) who distributed bribes liable to punishment. We are told[3] that a remarkable criticism was directed against this proposal in the Senate. When penalties, it was urged, go beyond a certain degree of severity, then either prosecutors hang back or juries refuse to convict. It was agreed that the bill required amending from this point of view, and the consuls were instructed to modify the tribune's draft and carry it through the Assembly as a law of their own. The 'consuls' really meant Piso, for Glabrio was gone or just going out to Bithynia. Now Piso, as we have seen, had bought his own consulship by bribery, and immunity from prosecution by blackmail.

988. It is most difficult to give an intelligible account of the complicated series of events at Rome in the middle part of this year. The obstinate Piso, bent on asserting his power to the utmost in the

---

[1] See below § 1194.

[2] Already a conventional season for this business, to judge from Cic. II *in Verr.* I § 90.

[3] Dion Cass. XXXVI 38.

interest of the Senate, and on thwarting Pompey where possible, is
for the time the central figure. We must bear in mind that Pompey's
organization of his forces was going on all the time, and that his
successful operations in the western Mediterranean were completed in
the first half of the year. Piso, like his colleague, had a province
placed under him while still consul, but he could not quit Rome. The
province, Narbonese or Transalpine Gaul, must have been ruled for
the present by his lieutenants. Here as elsewhere it was necessary
for Pompey to control the coast and raise troops for his great undertaking. Piso not only hindered the preparations in Rome, but by his
disloyal orders obstructed those in Gaul. When Pompey, having in
40 days quieted the western seas, paid a flying visit to Rome, he was
welcomed with enthusiasm. Sicily, Sardinia, Africa, were now able
to send the Roman populace their cheap food, and Gabinius seized
the opportunity to give notice of a bill for depriving the unpopular
Piso of his office. Pompey however knew better than to fall in with
this proposal. The best part of his work still remained to be done,
and to embitter the strife of factions in Rome was not the surest
means of keeping up his own influence while absent, and so of
smoothing the way for his further designs. He urged moderation,
and Piso escaped the danger. Piso was now in charge of two
important pieces of business, the corrupt-practices bill and the
consular elections. The Senate was anxious to get the bill passed
into law in time for the election. There was every prospect of trouble.
M. Lollius Palicanus, the tribune-agitator of 71, had announced his
candidature for the consulship, and riotous gangs were parading the
streets, bent on mischief. To carry the law before the time fixed for
the election was impossible, for a legislative Assembly was always
liable to be broken up by the announcement of unfavourable signs, as
provided by the Aelian-Fufian laws. This *obnuntiatio* was not allowed
in elective Assemblies, but it was also provided that an Assembly
summoned for election could not be employed to legislate. Thus
laws, formerly passed to enable the ruling nobility to check un-
desirable legislation, now stood in the way of their successors. In
order to carry out their present purpose the Senate resorted to an
exercise oi authority which rested on no statute, but which the House
had gradually assumed in its palmy days. An order was passed
dispensing the presiding consul from the provisions of the inconvenient laws. Piso could now bring his bill before an Assembly
summoned for elections, and could proceed unhindered by omens:
the one thing still necessary was to secure the attendance of voters
well affected to the cause of the 'Best Men.' He was equal to the

occasion. He issued a proclamation[1] calling on all citizens concerned for the safety of the commonwealth to attend and vote for the bill. No doubt, even before this appeal was put forth, messages from nobles to their friends in country towns had whipped up a large body of supporters. And here we must reflect for a moment on the features of Roman practical politics that might enable such an effort, even at a time when the resident voters were chiefly hostile, to be crowned with success. First, to overcome the laziness of non-residents a considerable stimulus was needed, and this was in a great degree supplied by a double object; for to be able in one short visit to vote both on a law and in an election was a rare occurrence. Secondly, the citizens who could afford to come from a distance would be men of property. Such men would be sure to bring with them slaves, probably stout fellows able to guard their masters from insult, and at a pinch to commend their opinions with sticks. Lastly, there was the working of the group-system. I have pointed out the inequality of the Tribes in respect of number of voters. A large proportion of the non-residents would belong to rustic Tribes of small numerical strength, and their votes would tell with great effect. To carry 18 Tribes meant the passing of the law, no matter how small the majority in each, and the remaining 17, however numerous and solid, must take their defeat as best they might. The election of consuls and praetors took place in the Assembly by Centuries. But a Century was now only a subdivision of a Tribe, and in this grouping special advantage was given to wealth and age. The effective influence of the nobles on this occasion may not improbably be traced in the election of two consuls of the type dear to the Roman aristocracy, men unlikely to offend the Senate by venturing to think and act for themselves.

989. But the Assemblies[2] at this juncture were scenes of violence and even bloodshed. As for the consular election, Piso flatly refused to accept Lollius as a candidate. He would not treat as valid votes given for a bad and seditious citizen, and there was no means of compelling him to do so. The election of praetors was so disturbed that it could only be completed after the Assembly had been more than once dismissed and proceedings resumed on another day. Cicero was a candidate, and he tells us with pride that he was thrice over returned first, that is, he made up his majority of Centuries before any

---

[1] *edixerat* Asconius p. 75, who puts this step after the failure of a first attempt to carry the law.

[2] The matter of this section is drawn from Valer. Max. III 8 § 3, Cicero *ad Att.* I 11 § 2, *de imper. Pomp.* § 2, Dion Cass. XXXVI 38—9, Asconius pp. 74, 75. In some points the combination of fragmentary notices is very difficult.

of his competitors. The voting on the law was interrupted by a riot[1] got up by the election-agents (*divisores*) who resented the clauses rendering them liable to punishment. The consul was mobbed, but he provided himself with a more efficient guard and carried the law in a second Assembly. It remains to inquire why the 'popular' leaders objected to this law, as it seems certain they did. The original draft of Cornelius had included the agents of corruption as well as their principals. But its chief aim was to punish principals more severely, probably[2] by outlawry, driving them into exile. The *lex Calpurnia* of Piso[3] was a move of the Senate with a very different aim. It retained (but perhaps reduced) the penalties for *divisores*, while it made[4] the punishment of principals less severe than the tribune had intended, though more severe than those of the existing statutes. Cornelius was in short 'dished,' and the employment of Piso to carry out the manœuvre was particularly irritating. It is not wonderful that he now dealt a blow directly at the Senate, and he had no difficulty in finding a vulnerable spot.

990. I have already remarked that the power of granting dispensations[5] from the laws did not strictly speaking belong to the Senate at all. The initiative fell naturally to that body, because it was always ready to act in emergencies. But the ancient procedure was that the order passed by the House contained a clause requiring the matter to be laid before the Assembly. In the days of their virtual supremacy the Senate had gradually dropped this recognition of popular sovranty. But that sovranty still existed, though dormant, and with the revival of activity in 'the Assembly it was easy to make it real. There was all the more temptation to do so, because cases had occurred in which the suspensory order had been passed when the attendance of members was small, and that a thin House should venture to assume such a power was an encroachment not easy to justify. Cornelius brought forward a bill to forbid the granting of such dispensations save by the people, that is by vote of the Assembly. To this the Senate, the leading nobles in particular, offered a stout resistance, and procured a tribune to block it. On the day of voting[6] the two tribunes fell out, and Cornelius was preparing to disregard

---

[1] Whether the riot spoken of by Asconius took place at the voting or at a *contio* is not clear. There may well have been riots at both.

[2] As Lange supposes, *RA* III 213.

[3] See Greenidge, *Legal Procedure*, index (*lex*). Reid's Introduction to Cicero *pro Sulla* §§ 9, 13.

[4] See Orelli's onomasticon, *lex Calpurnia de ambitu*.

[5] Asconius pp. 57—8, Dion Cass. XXXVI 39.

[6] In a *concilium plebis* with the tribune presiding. But this had long been the legislative equal of *comitia tributa*. See index, *Assemblies*.

the 'intercession' of his colleague, when the consul Piso loudly protested against his conduct.   A riot arose, Piso was assaulted, and Cornelius broke up the meeting.   The matter was now discussed in the Senate, and Cornelius as the result of the debate recast his proposal in a much milder form.   No dispensation was to be granted by the Senate in a House of less[1] than 200 members.   But, if the matter was subsequently brought before the people, no tribune was to be allowed to intervene to prevent a vote of the Assembly being taken. This modified bill passed.   The compromise did away with the worst part of the abuse, and legalized what might prove a convenient power; at the same time popular sovranty was reserved, and could at need be appealed to without interruption.   It is to be noted that we hear of no reference to the 'last decree' or declaration of a state of siege, employed by the Senate against C. Gracchus and Saturninus.   That too was soon to be called in question: for the present it seems to have been let pass as constitutional.   On the whole the Senate evidently made the best bargain it could in the circumstances.   But the nobles knew that their power was not strengthened by the questioning and definition of rights.   Indefiniteness and creation of precedent were in their favour.   So they submitted to the new compromise, but they did not like it.

991.   The same effort to bind the governing class by strict rules is apparent in another law[2] carried by Cornelius, enacting that the praetors should in the exercise of their jurisdiction follow the principles laid down in their own edicts.   The edict of the *praetor urbanus* was the most important of these yearly[3] announcements.   Each holder of the office issued one on succeeding to the post, and with its publication that of his predecessor became void.   There was thus always an edict in force at any given moment, from which it was possible to learn what principles the praetor in office proposed to follow in granting legal remedies, that is, what interpretation he proposed to put upon ancient statute and custom in applying them to the civil disputes of his own day.   The series of these edicts was continuous, and hence the edict of the juridical praetor was spoken of as *edictum perpetuum*. But there was as yet no statute binding the praetor not to deviate from his published principles, and cases had occurred[4] in which praetors had abandoned rules laid down by themselves in order to suit the convenience of favoured litigants.   In the glaring instance of

---

[1] Thin Houses seem to have been common in this period.   For the slackness of senators see Fowler, *Social Life* pp. 124—5.

[2] Asconius p. 58, Dion Cass. XXXVI 40.

[3] See Cic. II *in Verr.* I § 109, Greenidge, *Legal Procedure* p. 87.

[4] See Cic. II *in Verr.* I § 119, *pro Cornelio* fragm. 18 b.

Verres the suspicion of corruption was probably quite justified, perhaps in others. Cornelius in short had a very strong case in legislating to put down these arbitrary inconsistencies, but that many (senators, no doubt,) took his interference ill was no great wonder. We hear that he proposed a number of other bills, but could not carry them. Some were blocked by other tribunes, and in any case, as we have already observed, the latter part of the year was a time not favourable to legislation. The tribunes of the current year were inevitably somewhat overshadowed and weakened by the presence of the tribunes-designate already elected for the next.

992. The year 67 was one of great political unrest, and it is clear that the popular tribunes could rely on the discontent of the city populace for support in measures aimed at weakening the power of the Senate. Yet the Senate had on the whole held its ground remarkably well, though it no longer held the position of vantage assigned it by Sulla. To account for this we must remember that the two active popular leaders were both connected with Pompey, and that Pompey did not wish to see party-violence pushed too far. Even more important was the effect of the new system of composite juries in the public courts. Senators and Knights began to be conscious of a common interest, and to draw together. Thus was developed the *concordia ordinum* to maintain which was one of the principal objects of Cicero in his public life. The harmony of the wealthy Orders tended to accentuate the unhappy contrast of Rich and Poor, and did not really tend to promote good government. But it certainly strengthened the governing class. It was at present only beginning: the memories of Sulla were not dead yet. But, at a time when Rome was not under the direct pressure of an army, the alliance with the financial and commercial class was already enough to enable the Senate to make a fair stand against mob-rule. It is significant that in this very year a tribune whom we have seen acting as a partisan of the opposition to the *lex Gabinia*, one L. Roscius Otho, brought forward a bill to gratify the Equestrian Order. We are told that he assigned to them reserved seats[1] in the theatre, namely 14 rows behind those reserved for senators. Some accounts represent this as a restoration to the Knights of an old privilege which had been taken away, presumably by Sulla. Such honorary privileges were highly valued at Rome, and sitting 'in the 14 rows' became a regular expression connoting Equestrian rank. Roscius carried his law. We need not believe that the populace were eager for it and would take

---

[1] *lex Roscia*, perhaps carried early in the year, before the chief conflicts. Livy ep. 99, Asconius pp. 78—9, Cic. *pro Murena* § 40, Velleius II 32 § 3. More in Orelli's onomasticon.

no refusal, as Cicero[1] found it convenient to suggest. If the men of money had the support of the dependants of senators as well as their own, and the question did not touch the people's bread: we need look no further to explain the result.

993. While in Rome the tide of political strife swayed to and fro, Pompey had been making the most of his grand opportunity. His task was first to catch the nimble sea-rovers, then to crush all open resistance, and lastly to effect a settlement that would finally secure the peace of the waters. He divided the whole Mediterranean into naval departments, for each of which one of his lieutenants was responsible, with a squadron sufficient for that particular duty. All the best naval stations were thus closed to the pirates, and became bases for the Roman fleets. The pirate vessels, built specially to chase or run, were ill suited to give battle, and the simultaneous pressure of the Roman squadrons soon forced them to withdraw from the seas west of Italy. Sicily was no longer open to them, as in the time of Verres. The Adriatic was closed and the coasts of Greece and northern Africa watched. The Hellespont and the northern Aegean were strongly held. The islands were not safe: Delos[2] they had themselves laid waste. Crete was in the grasp of Metellus, Cyprus was watched by a squadron cruising off the coasts from Lycia to Phoenicia. Thus there was nothing to be done but to fall back on their old haunts in Pamphylia and the Rough Cilicia, and here, driven into a corner, they at last turned to bay. Pompey drew together a powerful fleet and utterly defeated them in a battle off Coracesium. The capture of their strongholds might well have been a long business, if he had followed the usual practice of Roman commanders, and left the vanquished no hope of life or freedom. But he did not thus bungle matters. When it was found that he accepted surrender on honourable terms, and treated his captives with humanity, all resistance to his overwhelming force quickly ceased; there was more hope in surrender than in a protraction of a life-and-death struggle, and these motley bands of refugees from all countries had no national traditions to sustain a fury of despair. Forty days had swept the pirate rovers out of the West: forty-nine effected the submission of their combined forces in the East. Pompey destroyed all their arms and a vast stock of materials in their dockyards: he set free the captives in their prisons, and turned most of the pirates into peaceful colonists. He settled them in various spots, for good reasons. Many helped to re-people failing towns both inland and on the seaboard. Soli in Cilicia was a noted case. It was one of the cities out of which Tigranes had

[1] Cic. *pro Cornel.* I fragm. 28.
[2] Phlegon fragm. 12 (*FHG* III 606).

transplanted citizens to fill his mushroom capital, and it had never recovered the loss. It was now repeopled with reformed pirates, and named Pompeiopolis in honour of its new founder. Far and wide the colonies were scattered. One was at Dyme in Peloponnesus, an old Achaean city now shrunken or deserted. Another is traced to the Calabrian heel of Italy by Vergil's reference[1] to the old man of Corycus (in Cilicia) whom he found contentedly tilling an unkind soil near Tarentum. So great was the impression made by the mild treatment of the conquered enemy, that embarrassment was thereby caused to Metellus in Crete. Some besieged Cretans sent a message asking Pompey to accept their surrender and protect them from Metellus, who was destroying enslaving and executing in the old style. Pompey, eager to appropriate the credit of this war also, accepted the offer, and even sent an officer to represent him. What with the interference of this man, and an exchange of angry letters between the two generals, a very sharp quarrel arose out of this collision of authorities. But Metellus stood firm, and finished the conquest of Crete. He presided over the organization of the island as a Roman province, and afterwards had a triumph and the title *Creticus*. The Senate did not desert their man, and the ambition of another Roman noble was fulfilled.

994. Pompey was too busy with his settlements of pirates to follow up this bickering seriously, and the prospect of new opportunities of renown began to engage his chief attention. Even his friends regretted his jealousy of Metellus; but, setting this aside, we must grant that he had now fairly earned the name of Great. None of his later achievements, great though they were, will stand comparison with the prompt and thorough suppression of piracy as an exhibition of statesmanlike tact and strategic skill. We may faintly imagine the effect of the news in Rome: the exultation of the politicians who had striven for his appointment, the claims of trimmers to a share of the credit, the relief of the populace at the new security for cheap corn, and not least the keen unostentatious delight in mercantile and financial circles. To the nobility this exposure of the needless futility of their previous half-measures would be less welcome. The inefficiency of the average noble had been clumsily attacked by Marius; it was now quietly demonstrated by Pompey in a way that none could ignore. Even Lucullus, though a thoroughly competent soldier, had not the gift of understanding the psychology of an army, and his political opponents had only set their seal upon a failure which his own stiffness had prepared. A man was wanted to assert Roman supremacy in the East, to secure old provinces and it might be to

---

[1] Servius on Verg. *georg.* IV 127, referring to Suetonius.

annex new. If what was at present a wasteful war could be given a more business-like turn, and if an advantageous peace should open up further fields for Roman enterprise, might not the patient capitalist hope to reap a golden harvest? Mithradates could hardly be left in triumphant possession of his kingdom lately recovered, for to allow this would jeopardize all Rome's Asiatic dominions. Yet Lucullus was paralysed, and Glabrio was no match for the king of Pontus. So men's minds were prepared for a proposal to transfer the command to Pompey, and give him a free hand for restoring peace and revising the relations of the East according to the interest of Rome.

995. On the 10th December 67 the tribunes for the year 66 came into office. The tradition of the tribunate pointed to early action, before a tribune's official prestige grew stale; and C. Manilius, one of the 'popular' party, began work at once with a bill for allowing freedmen to vote in the same Tribes as their respective *patroni*. This would open all Tribes, even the most select, to a large and growing class of men whose influence, as being unrepresentative of Roman traditions and prejudices, the nobility wished to restrict. It is said that he carried this bill into law[1] on the last day of the month (29 Dec.), and the festival *Compitalia* fell on that day, which gave the Senate an excuse for annulling the law on the day following (1 Jan.) as void on religious grounds. Thus the revival of a law carried by Sulpicius in 88 and annulled on his fall, undertaken by Manilius at the instigation of Cornelius, miscarried. Manilius now sought to strengthen himself by becoming the agent of some bigger man. We are told that he approached Crassus and others, but people fought shy of him. So he took up the question of the East, and brought forward a bill[2] for appointing Pompey to the command. The powers already conferred on him by the Gabinian law were not to cease, but he was to be entrusted with the conduct of the war on land, and empowered to conclude alliances, to make peace, in fact to settle oriental questions as he thought best. Cilicia and Bithynia were placed under him, probably Asia[3] also. On no Roman had such powers, or anything like them, been conferred by the free act of the sovran people. It was indeed sheer monarchy. The patronage at Pompey's disposal would be enormous. Manilius had marked the rise of Gabinius, and hoped to raise himself too by Pompey's favour:

---

[1] Clearly the time of *promulgatio* (*trinum nundinum*, see § 819) had not been duly observed. Cicero refers to this *celeritas actionis*.

[2] For the *lex Manilia* see in particular Cicero *de imper. Cn. Pomp.* (*pro lege Manilia*), Plutarch *Pomp.* 30, Dion Cass. XXXVI 42—3, Appian *Mithr.* 97, Velleius II 33 § 1.

[3] It seems that there were propraetors as local governors of Asia during Pompey's command, but that he, like Lucullus, had a superior power there as proconsul. See Cicero *pro Flacco* § 76 where two propraetors are named.

he seems to have taken no notice whatever of the Senate. In him we clearly see the up-to-date tribune of the failing Republic, the tool and dependant of a military chief. The bill went through without effective opposition. Speeches against it were delivered by Catulus and Hortensius. Even the senatorial majority was divided on the question; some of them even spoke in favour of the measure. But the two most notable supporters were Cicero and Caesar. The latter had to keep himself to the front as a popular leader by supporting what was in any case certain to pass, and he probably felt no repugnance to a precedent that might some day serve the turn of another than Pompey. Cicero had already declared himself on the side of the popular favourite, and on this occasion made his first public speech on a matter of state. He understood the situation well, and knew the weakness of the opposition. By lending his eloquence to the popular side the praetor pleased the voters who had elected him, and also the capitalists to whom it offered hopes of profit. Many a senator too would secretly approve his arguments, whether as a private shareholder in financial syndicates, or as a possible governor of some province when the number of such posts was increased.

996. Pompey lost no time in putting his new powers to use, upsetting arrangements[1] made by Lucullus for the punishment or reward of persons whose deserts he knew and Pompey did not. We need not doubt that he meanly lowered his predecessor in the eyes of all, and mortified him in every way. Jealousy of rivals, and an eagerness to reap where others had sown, were marked features of his character. The two proconsuls met in Galatia, but their conference ended in unprofitable bickering. To Pompey we shall return below. Of the experiences of Lucullus we will speak briefly. On his return to Rome he was made an object of attack by the popular faction. He was accused of peculation in the matter of war-booty, and every effort made to deny him a triumph. But the nobles succeeded in preventing this ungracious treatment of a soldier who, with all his faults, had bravely borne a heavy burden. He disappointed the better men of his party, who had hoped to find in him a stout defender of the aristocracy. But he had no longer a stomach for such political life as he found in full swing. He was now very rich and fond of ease, and to fight for the failing cause of the *optimates* was a duty that it was a downright luxury to neglect. He lived an elegant and refined life, noted for the splendour of his household and entertainments. We hear of him as the typical dilettante noble of the revolutionary age, surrounded with works of art, and rich appointments

---

[1] He continued this spiteful conduct even after his return to Rome. Strabo XII 3 § 33. Retaliation of Lucullus, Plut. *Luc.* 42.

of which he kept no account; the builder of villas, and layer-out of gardens and fishponds; the collector of a library and associate of literary men. Lucullus appeared as a character in some of Cicero's dialogues, and was an author himself. On the occasions when he took part in politics after his retirement, he did not intervene with much good result. The lack of insight into the feelings of others, which we have seen marring the effectiveness of his great military talents, is probably to be detected in another relation. Though he tried marriage twice, he either chose or managed badly, for he was compelled to divorce both wives.

997. Pompey spent about four more years in the East. He kept more or less in touch with Rome, and the news of his successive conquests coming in from time to time served to encourage his agents and partisans, and to remind all that the real decision of questions at home must in the last resort depend on the will of the master of the ever-victorious army. Till his return none could tell what line he would take in public affairs, and the generation then living could remember the homecoming of Sulla. Meanwhile he went about his imperial work. A negotiation with Mithradates failed, for the king was not prepared to surrender at discretion. But his forces were small compared with the huge armaments of his earlier days, and in quality they had never been a match for Roman troops. Lucullus had broken him, and Pompey could now defeat him with ease. The winter of 66—5 found him a fugitive resting on the eastern coast of the Euxine, Tigranes having refused to give him further shelter and support. He was never really dangerous again, but he still shewed a bold front to his enemies, and the last stages of his career were highly instructive illustrations of his true character. The oriental despot, before whom the common run of mankind had no rights, who could insult and torture to death a Roman proconsul, now appeared as the indomitable hero in adversity, abating none of his royal pretensions and capable of gigantic schemes. In 65 he made his way with the relics of his force to his Bosporan (Crimean) kingdom, where his son Machares was governor. Him he deposed and drove to suicide, and then set to collecting a new army with a design, it is said, of marching through the Danube countries, crossing the Alps, and making havoc in Italy as a second Hannibal. He was still an object of awe to the Scythian chiefs of the Steppes, and the Greek towns still owned his rule. But from that outlying northern kingdom he was never destined to emerge as a conqueror. The accounts of his furious energy read like the tale of a wild beast at bay. Revolts are caused by the misdeeds of his eunuchs, in whom he now seems to find his most trusty ministers. His wives or concubines (for he had

several left) take a part either as faithful companions or as making terms with Pompey. His daughters, destined to wed Scythian princes, were carried off by their escort and handed over to Pompey, but he still had two left with him. One son he murdered to punish the treachery of the boy's mother. Pharnaces, his favourite son, finally rebelled against his father. For the army was now disaffected and sick of his enterprises. He had detected the conspiracy of Pharnaces, but spared him. Pharnaces thereupon secured himself by winning over the army, and Mithradates had now no course open but to die. Poison, according to the famous story, took no effect on him, for with true oriental suspicion he had habitually fortified his system with antidotes. A Gaulish officer in his service killed him at his request. This took place in the year 63, so that he was scheming and raging in his Bosporan kingdom for about two years.

998. So died the great Mithradates Eupator, somewhat less than 70 years of age. We are concerned with him only so far as his career[1] affected Roman history. It is to be noted that in spite of his wonderful gifts, though aided by Greek generals and Roman exiles, though he greatly impressed the princes and peoples of the Orient, and posed as a champion of East against West, though he recruited his armies from warlike peoples, he never gained any marked success against Roman troops competently led. His strategic capacity was probably overrated, and the phenomena of his wars with Rome shew many traces of the weakness as well as the strength of the autocrat. The wonderful way in which he recovered from great disasters, and appeared formidable as ever, illustrates the advantage of power concentrated in one vigorous hand. Such a gross miscalculation as that of bringing to besiege Cyzicus a vast army which he could not feed shews us a Great King, a belated Xerxes, who has never, among his courtiers and eunuchs, learnt to adapt himself to practical necessities, and to recognize that the nature of things imposes limitations on his sovran will. It is hard to imagine that such a potentate could, if successful, have been a sincere and large-minded protector of eastern Hellenism. That he was in himself incomparably superior to Tigranes, is not to be doubted. But, if he had driven the Romans out of Asia, we may well doubt whether the Greek cities would have fared better under him than at the hands of the founder of Tigranocerta. He, like Jugurtha, registers for us the weakness and inefficiency of the Roman government as conducted by the Senate in its degenerate days. Once a serious effort was made, there was no standing against

---

[1] He has been the subject of a great monograph, *Mithridate Eupator*, by Theodore Reinach (Paris 1890), the appendix of which gives a full collection of the epigraphic and numismatic evidence. The writer's estimate of the king's achievements and character is on p. 299.

the power of Rome.   But to get such efforts made when called for—
there was the difficulty.   It was necessary to overcome the inertness
of the Senate by the pressure of the Assembly.   This weakened the
Senate, but did not set up an alternative government in its place.
The Senate remained, for the ordinary business of the state had to be
done, and the Assembly could not do it.   An inevitable consequence
was the growth of the power of individuals and the fall of the Republic.
The rise of Marius and the predominance of Pompey mark stages in
the process.   Both were essentially due to causes within, set in motion
by occasions without, and must ever be associated with the names of
Jugurtha and Mithradates.

999.   The years following the final defeat of Mithradates were
spent by Pompey in a victorious progress through the countries and
peoples of the East.   He had ample forces at his disposal.   With his
fleets he commanded all the seas, including the Euxine.   His forces
on land included his own army, the troops of the governors of Cilicia
and Bithynia, who had to make way before their proper time, and the
remains of the army of Lucullus.   Even the Fimbrian legions, who
had got the discharge for which they clamoured, took service again
under a general who understood how to manage them and in whose
good luck they trusted.   We find him able to maintain and protect
his convoys of supplies, and to employ lieutenants with sufficient
detachments in operations subsidiary to the main advance.   No doubt
the necessary numbers were procured by the use of auxiliary corps
(Galatian Thracian etc.), and we read of deserters from the Pontic
army in its later days of disheartenment.   And the condition of
things in the East was highly favourable.   Phraates, who had lately
succeeded to the Parthian throne, made some kind of compact with
him, and took the opportunity of reconquering some provinces that
had been annexed by Tigranes.   There was no great combination of
oriental powers to resist the Roman general, and the only man able to
direct such a combination was a fugitive.   Pompey could move on
boldly, without much fear of disaster.   It is characteristic of the man
and the age that he took with him a Greek writer to hand down to
after times the story of his wars and other achievements.   This author,
Theophanes of Mitylene, seems to have given satisfaction[1] to his
employer, in whose favour he afterwards stood very high.   But the
honest truth was not to be expected from such a court-historiographer,
and Theophanes was suspected of carrying the glorification of his
patron so far as malignantly to calumniate persons against whom his
patron had a grudge.

---

[1] Strabo XIII 2 § 3, who several times cites him on points of geography and natural
history.   See also Plutarch *Pomp.* 37, and Orelli's onomasticon.

1000.   The first fruit of the overthrow of Mithradates was the submission of Tigranes.   Threatened by the Parthians, and troubled by the rebellion of a son, the Armenian saw his best hope in the mercy of Pompey, and promptly drank the cup of humiliation to save his kingdom.   Pompey left him his throne, but we shall see that he had to give up his conquests.   The assertion of Roman supremacy was so far complete, and the young Tigranes, who shewed anger at his father's being forgiven, was seized and imprisoned to grace Pompey's triumph. In 65 Pompey, giving up the notion of pursuing Mithradates, made a campaign among the Albanians and Iberians, independent peoples dwelling south of the Caucasus.   These were well beaten.   On the Colchian coast he met his fleet, and in a fort, delivered up to him by a concubine of Mithradates commanding there, he found a collection of the king's private writings, letters and memoranda many of which are said not to have been to their owner's credit.   From this region he returned to the southward, having much work awaiting him, and not feeling able to pass the barrier of the Caucasus.   Meanwhile his lieutenants in southern Armenia and the adjoining districts had come into collision with the Parthians, who were asserting claims to Gordyene.   Pompey firmly refused to concede the point, but sent commissioners to arbitrate in the dispute, and avoided an inconvenient war.   The chief result was that Mesopotamia was recognized as Parthian, and the normal frontier of Roman and Parthian territory became the line of the Euphrates.   But it seems that a certain soreness remained in the mind of Phraates, to whom Pompey refused the title of King of Kings; for to the eastern potentate the omission of a diplomatic courtesy would appear significant of unfriendly designs on the part of Rome.

1001.   In the year 64 Pompey was engaged in restoring order in the kingdom of Pontus and arranging for the future government.   A number of minor kings and chiefs attended to make terms, and a distribution of rewards to deserving allies took place.   He had resolved to annex Syria and to effect a general settlement of the principalities in that part of the world.   So he moved southwards, crossed the Taurus, and wintered in Antioch.   In Syria all was anarchy.   A descendant of Seleucus, Antiochus XIII, had nominally been king since Lucullus had put an end to the rule of Tigranes.   But he was little more than a powerless claimant of a broken throne.   The neighbouring princelets, formerly vassals of the Seleucids, were now independent, and some of them, as the prince of the Nabataean Arabs, were extending their influence unchecked.   The Jewish kingdom had grown owing to its favourable position between the decaying kingdoms of Syria and Egypt.   A disputed succession rendered it at present a special source of disturbance.   The Greek or Greek-modelled cities suffered from the continual troubles and desired the restoration of order.   The main principle adopted by Pompey was to refuse to recognize Antiochus as king, to treat Syria as a country vacant by the withdrawal of Tigranes, and thus fallen to Rome by right of conquest. He meant to organize it as a Roman province.   But the undertaking was far from easy.   Several clearly-marked nationalities, Jewish Arab Phoenician, occupied parts of the country, while the mass of Syrians proper were the population of the larger district in the north extending roughly from the Taurus to the Lebanon and from the Euphrates westward to the sea.   And planted here and there were the numerous Greek cities, long possessed of important privileges and now most of them practically independent.   To make such a country into a province of the ordinary type was not a promising venture.   It was probably present to the mind of Pompey that the cities were in general accus- tomed to govern themselves, and the people of the minor principalities to be ruled by despots of their own, while the tradition of a great imperial power, dominating all alike, was not extinct.   Indeed, if Rome did not step in and claim the sovranty, it was highly probable that some one else would.   Even Tigranes had at first been welcome in that land of general anarchy.   Some umpire was necessary, to arbitrate in disputes and keep jarring interests at peace.   At all events his scheme for the new province was such as these con- siderations might dictate.   The province Syria was a collection of cities and principalities enjoying local self-government under the guarantee of Rome and the presidency of a Roman governor.   Of course they were tributary, and their independence meant that they were free to do what they were told by the Roman government and by nobody else.   But interference was in theory reduced to a minimum: it amounted in fact to the substitution of Rome for the kings of the house of Seleucus.

1002.   While Pompey was in these parts[1] his most serious opera- tion of war was the siege of the temple of Jerusalem.   Two brothers, Hyrcanus and Aristobulus, were disputing the Maccabaean throne. Pompey had decided in favour of the former, but was compelled to advance upon Jerusalem to enforce his decision.   The city was sur- rendered by partisans of Hyrcanus, but the temple, a fortress in itself, was stoutly held for Aristobulus, and was only captured through the Romans taking advantage of the religious scruples of the fanatical defenders.   They pushed on their siege-works on sabbaths, and delivered the final assault on a day of fasting and sacrifice, when the priests stood to be cut down rather than cease officiating.   Pompey

---

[1] Pompey in Judaea.   Josephus *Ant.* XIV §§ 1—79, Dion Cass. XXXVII 15—19.

installed Hyrcanus in power as High Priest at the head of the local government, and included Judaea in the province, but detached from Jewish government a number of conquered Hellenistic cities, to which he granted 'freedom' of the usual kind. Jewish feelings were deeply outraged by his insisting on violating the sanctity of the Holy of Holies. He did not carry off the sacred treasure found there, and his act was probably a deliberate piece of policy, to teach the turbulent Jews what their folly must bring upon them. Nor would a Roman polytheist easily understand the horror with which the worshippers of one unseen god regarded such a profanation. It was enough to shew that those who wished their prejudices respected had better keep on good terms with Rome. Aristobulus was added to the collection of notables destined for the triumph.

1003. On his march to Jerusalem Pompey received the news of the death of Mithradates. In the army there were great rejoicings, and the general himself was doubtless much relieved to be rid of so troublesome an enemy without further exertion. The storm-centre of the East had disappeared. He finished off his business in Judaea, contented himself with a formal submission of the Arab king, and returned to Pontus, leaving his lieutenant M. Aemilius Scaurus to carry the new province through the early stages of the settlement. He was now anxious to clear up matters generally and take back his veterans to Italy. The corpse of Mithradates, received from Pharnaces, he ordered to be honourably buried at Sinope in the sepulchre of the Pontic kings. The winter of 63—2 was occupied in determining the future boundaries of territorial units, and their various relations to the sovran power. The arrangements made were generally marked by moderation and good sense. Two points in particular deserve attention. First, there was the practical recognition of the value of Greek influences as tending to promote order and good government. Hellenism naturally expressed itself in city life. Pure Greek populations were not to be had, but the 'hellenistic' civilization based on community of culture was a living fact, capable of being made more widely operative than it had ever been in the past. Pompey not only encouraged city life in the East by granting privileges to existing cities, but restored or repopulated others, ruined or dwindling through misfortunes or disturbance of trade, and added new foundations to extend the system and record his fame. This policy had lasting results and was afterwards imitated by emperors. It was the foundation on a great scale of the later or Roman Hellenism which flourished so vigorously in the East as a continuation of the foundations of the Macedonian kings. Secondly, we may remark the general recognition of monarchy as suited to certain peoples, in other words, to a certain stage of civilization. The old notion, that 'liberty' was somehow conferred by the deposition of a king, as in the case of Macedonia after the fall of Perseus, or by letting the kingship lapse, as in Cappadocia before the election of Ariobarzanes in 95, has simply disappeared. The proconsul sits at his headquarters and serves out thrones wholesale to kings and chiefs on suitable terms. These principalities are not buffer-states. They are a convenient and cheap form of asserting Roman supremacy, rather analogous to the aristocratic or plutocratic governments set up by Rome long ago in communities whose loyal allegiance it was desired to secure. They are in the language[1] of Tacitus 'appliances of empire,' an extension on a large scale of a practice that had been growing up for some time. Among them are to be reckoned some of those strange communities[2] the centre of which was a temple and the ruler the High Priest. The general principle of this great settlement was in short to interfere with existing arrangements as little as possible, only to take care that power was not left in the hands of governments hostile to Rome.

1004. I can only give details of the settlement in a very condensed form, under general heads.

A. PROVINCES. *Syria* was wholly new. *Cilicia* was enlarged by the addition of the eastern or level Cilicia, and of the districts to the North-West, so far as they had not yet been effectively annexed. *Bithynia* was enlarged to the East by adding to it the coast districts of Paphlagonia and western Pontus.

B. CLIENT KINGDOMS. In the inland parts of *Paphlagonia* the native dynasty was recognized. In *Cappadocia* Ariobarzanes was confirmed on the throne with addition of some districts to the East. *Galatia* was left with its constitution[3] of three cantons each with its four tetrarchs, but the real head was Deiotarus, who had been loyal and useful to Rome. Eastern Pontus was attached to Galatia in reward of his services, and it seems that the other chieftainships were soon extinguished, and he became ruler of the whole. A minor principality was also established in the district of *Commagene* to the north of *Syria*. In *Colchis* Pompey is said to have appointed a prince, but this distant land was hardly brought under the direct influence of Rome.

C. ALLIED KINGS. Tigranes of *Armenia*, and Pharnaces in the *Bosporan kingdom.* The former was weakened by the payment of an

---

[1] Tac. *Agr.* 14, *instrumenta servitutis.*

[2] See Strabo XII 3 § 34 for an appointment made to one of these (Pontic Comana) by Pompey. Also Marquardt *Stvw.* I 385 (Olbe in Cilicia). Good general account in Mahafïy, *Silver age of the Greek World* pp. 263—5.

[3] Strabo XII 5 §§ 1, 2, Appian *Mithr.* 114, Orelli's *onomasticon.*

immense war-indemnity and by cession of much territory. The latter retained the small remnant of the kingdom of Mithradates as a reward for having brought about his father's death.

The omissions in the above enumeration should be referred to. The province *Asia* remained as Sulla had organized it. Lucullus had merely tried to improve the working of the administration by putting down abuses. *Lycia*, which had been a loyal ally of Rome, retained its freedom as recognized by Sulla. This interesting federal league was 'free' for more than another 100 years. More notable was the fact that Pompey did not intervene in the affairs of Egypt. True, Egypt was not included in the spirit of his commission, but he is said to have been invited by the king to come and put down a rebellion, and pretexts would not have been wanting, if he had wished to interfere. But the Egyptian question was a thorny one, and the record of invasions of the country by no means one of successes. Pompey acted wisely in letting it alone. Cyprus also was not disturbed.

1005. The relations between the principalities included within provincial boundaries and the sovran power represented by the provincial governor, a delicate matter liable to lead to friction, were no doubt considered to some extent by Pompey. These relations were not exactly the same in all cases. In Syria, where there were many local dynasties, the Arab princes of Damascus were only compelled to accept the overlordship of Rome after Pompey's departure. If Palmyra, the famous caravan-station in the eastern desert, was really reckoned in the province, its subordination can hardly have been more than nominal. Lying between the Roman and Parthian empires, each side was interested to see that it was not made a base of attack by the other. In course of time there were many changes in the relations of the principalities to Rome, but complete absorption was the end. The free cities on the other hand were a more permanent institution, in fact the basis of Roman-hellenistic civilization and government. Each had a territory of its own, in some cases considerable, managed its internal affairs under an aristocratic constitution, and collected its own share of the dues payable to Rome. Pompey was evidently convinced of their importance, and of the fundamental distinction between them and the purely oriental natives, to whom monarchic rule was a law of nature. He relieved some cities from tyrants who in troubled times had seized a despotic power. Speaking generally we may say that his settlement of the East was a reasonable and practical one, judged from the point of view of his own time. That abuses might arise out of it through the misdeeds of those to whom its working was entrusted, was no fault of his. In no part of the

Roman dominions, at home or abroad, did theory and practice exactly correspond. But it is notable that, while he so greatly extended the empire and authority of Rome, and added largely to the public revenues, he left behind him a good reputation in the East. He had enjoyed enormous power, and on the whole he had used it well. That is, he had shewn the qualities that the East looked for in its rulers. And when, in a few years, the great civil war engaged all the forces of the imperial Republic, we find the solid goodwill and resources of the East supporting Pompey and sharing his defeat.

1006. The homeward journey of the great commander was slow and ceremonious. This was probably intentional, for he loved to do things in a dignified and rather pompous way, and he had not as yet had a chance of displaying himself to the Greek cities of the Aegean. We find him at Mitylene, a place recently disgraced and punished for its obstinate adherence to Mithradates. Here he made a dramatic appearance as public benefactor and patron of Theophanes, at whose request he conferred 'freedom' on the city. He honoured a competition of poets with his presence. The theme of the composers was his own exploits. At Ephesus he is said to have met Cato, already noted for his precise and refractory virtues, and to have been glad to see him start for Rome. We may believe that the plain-spoken Roman was not congenial to Pompey, engaged in advertising his own exploits and gorged with adulation and applause. Before turning westwards he visited Rhodes, where the sophists and rhetoricians performed before him. Lastly he came to Athens. Athens, like Mitylene, had suffered for Mithradates. Here too he patronized the professors, and gave fifty talents (nearly £12,000) towards the needful restoration of the city. Thus by systematic complaisance and bounties he had made the chief centres of Greek culture his trumpeters. He had also contrived to please his army. Out of war-indemnities fines and plunder even private soldiers had received substantial dividends. The rumour of these things of course preceded him to Rome, where his slow movements raised expectation to a very high pitch. When he reached the city early in 61 it was not wonderful that his possible plans were a subject of intense interest to all and alarm to some. But it is time to turn back and see what had been happening in Rome during his absence in the East.

CHAPTER LI.

CICERO AND CATILINE. 66—63 B.C.

1007. The years 67 and 66 had seen the seas cleared by Pompey, navigation freely resumed, and immediate anxieties removed; they had left Pompey entrusted with immense general powers, and committed to a task which was certain to engage his energies for a considerable time. In the absence of the first man of the hour a confused struggle took place in Rome, a jarring conflict of interests ambitions grudges intrigues. With worthless factions using the cry of public good as a cloak for party ends, with a constitution utterly unworkable, with morals very generally corrupt, and scruples non-existent, it is little wonder that the problems of the age were insoluble. The few honest statesmen in whom the love of their country outweighed sectional or private objects could do nothing effective to save the Republic, and the stream of revolution, ever gathering force and volume, swept them helplessly along. The biographical tendency in the history of the revolutionary age becomes more and more marked, and for good reason. As a movement from monarchy to a Republic is an assertion of principles against the man, so a movement from a Republic to monarchy is a putting of the man in the place of principles. At Rome the years 65 to 60, confused and complicated though their story is, have a certain unity given them through the peculiar position of Pompey and his relation to the various forces striving for mastery in the state. At first he is far away, and others use his absence as an opportunity for pushing their own designs unchecked. But his return at the head of a great and victorious army—the only considerable force then on foot—is ever in prospect, and all farsighted men are reckoning on it and anxious to stand well with one who can be a new Sulla if he will. Then he does return, and does not seize the monarchy that awaits its monarch. Confusion then becomes worse confounded, and no sure direction of affairs is possible until the genius of Caesar brings about a coalition, under the domination of which the Republic ceases to be a reality.

1008. In these years the evils of which we have spoken above are going on and becoming worse. The growth of legislation continues, but no good comes of it. The Assembly is more than ever a futile mob. Corruption is rampant, but is beginning to take the form of paying gangs of ruffians, that is of organizing disorder, rather than mere bribery of voters. There are no true parties with definite policies, but factions directed by individuals. No ties bind public men: the apparent interest of the moment forms combinations and oppositions on personal grounds, and the widespread embarrassment arising from debt is a silent cause of mischief that is always at work. To find our way in the complexity of phenomena is difficult indeed, and it is not rendered less by the abundance of detail preserved. Our authorities are copious, but for the most part their evidence is given with a purpose, to justify the action of this or that side. Accordingly the judgments of modern writers on the events of this time have differed widely, and will no doubt continue to differ. To discuss conflicting views is impossible here. It must suffice to make a few remarks on the character and action of Cicero, who, though not the most powerful person, is by chance the central figure of this troubled time. Cicero was a 'new man,' and his first political connexion had been with the 'popular' movement against the Sullan constitution, by heading which Pompey had risen to be the first man in the state. But Cicero was from first to last a loyal republican. As it gradually became clear that the Republic was menaced, and that the danger was coming primarily and directly from the 'popular' party, factiously raising leaders to positions of unconstitutional power, it was only natural that he should feel drawn to the party of the nobles and their adherents, the so-called *optimates* or 'best men.' They (that is, the Senate, their organ,) had misused the powers given them by Sulla; their mismanagement had been a real danger to the state. But after all they were the only body that had any qualifications for government. Once let the Senate lose its remaining power, and nothing could prevent monarchy; nothing was left but a contest for the throne. That the adhesion of Cicero to the Optimate party, and his endeavours to strengthen it by alliance with the Equestrian Order, did not save the Republic, cannot be fairly held to prove him a blunderer or a trimmer. The time for saving the Republic had gone by, but it was not for a patriot republican at that moment to recognize this truth or give up the struggle in despair. No doubt he suffered from indecision, but this was due partly to his power of seeing both sides of a question, partly to the fact that his aim was the good of the Roman Republic and not his own elevation to despotic power. It was not always clear by which of two or more courses the good of the Republic was most likely to be reached, and an honest patriot may temporize and concede much in the hope of gaining more. Cicero is sometimes compared, not to his advantage, with his contemporary

M. Porcius Cato, the great-grandson of the famous censor. In Cato, a hard positive temperament was developed by Stoic principles to such a degree that doubt and hesitation had no part in his life. As the consistent fighting man of the republican cause, he earned and engrossed the admiration of Roman Stoics of the next age. But our business is not with the opinions of the malcontents and martyrs of the early Empire. The fact is that as a statesman Cato was a failure. The patriotic opportunist did more for their common cause than the patriotic prig. Each did his best, each made mistakes. To weigh the man who would sacrifice his principles to save his country against the man who saw his country's salvation only in the assertion of his principles is to compare incommensurables. Yet even Cato, who scorned corruption himself, could stoop to condone corruption in the interest of his own party.

1009. The year 66 was full of conflicts after the extension of Pompey's commission by the Manilian law. The courts were busy with cases which, under cover of various charges, were really political moves. The 'popular' leaders sought to make those who had profited by the bounty of Sulla disgorge some of their gains, or to rake up old charges against aristocratic opponents. Another object, if we may believe Cicero[1], was to extend the penalties for judicial misconduct to the non-senatorial members of juries. Sulla's law only took account of senatorial jurors; the others claimed to evade liability by pressing the letter of the law. The point was raised in the trial of Cluentius, but his acquittal left things as they were. Two thirds of each jury could still act corruptly with impunity. Cicero, who defended Cluentius, presided himself as praetor in the court of extortion, and had before him cases promoted by the other party. C. Licinius Macer[2] (the reformer and historian) killed himself, seeing his condemnation certain. On quitting office, Manilius himself was prosecuted: Cicero fixed the hearing on the last day of the year available, and the trial was broken up by a riot. The ex-tribune Cornelius was also put on his trial for *maiestas* because of his treatment of his colleague Servilius in the preceding year. But the intentional absence of the praetor of that court, followed by a riot, brought this prosecution also to nought for the present. The consular elections this summer were also the occasion of grave scandal. The elected consuls P. Autronius Paetus and P. Cornelius Sulla were at once prosecuted for *ambitus* and unseated, and others elected in their stead. A further interest attaches to this election in that the

---

[1] Cic. *pro Cluent.* § 152.
[2] Valer. Max. IX 12 § 7, Plutarch *Cic.* 9, Cic. *ad Att.* I 4 § 2, Dion Cass. XXXVI 44.

notorious Catiline intended to be a candidate. He had been praetor
in 68 and governor of the province Africa in 67, where he had
followed the example of his friend Verres. Returning in 66 to stand
for the consulship, he was threatened with a prosecution for extortion
by P. Clodius, a young aristocrat then seeking notoriety. He found
that the presiding consul would not receive[1] votes for him, and so did
not formally enter his name as candidate. The trial of Catiline did
not come on till the next (65) year, and much had happened in the
meantime. A conspiracy was formed to murder the two new consuls
on the first of January and to recover the consulships for the two unseated men by force. The design became known and failed. It has
long been supposed on the authority of Sallust that Catiline was the
prime mover in this plot. But the best evidence, carefully weighed,
does not[2] bear this out, nor is it probable. He was no doubt concerned in it, but in a subordinate capacity. So too was the turbulent
and reckless Cn. Calpurnius Piso. We may call Autronius the
nominal leader; that his colleague Sulla knew of the plot is most
likely, though he appears to have kept out of the way and taken no
active part. But none of these men were strong enough to undertake
so daring a revolutionary design. The truth undoubtedly is that it
was part of a much larger[3] plan, at the back of which stood Crassus
and Caesar. Their main object was to build up a power with which
they could hold their own against Pompey whenever that conqueror
should return, and neither was scrupulous as to the means. So their
secret favour emboldened Autronius and the rest to conspire. A
second murderous attempt was planned for early in February, but
this also was foiled by precautions and exposed by the consul
Torquatus. And now the forces at work in Roman politics shewed
their real tendencies. No resolution could be formally passed in the
Senate for dealing with the now notorious conspiracy. This was
blocked by a tribune, no doubt instructed by the 'popular' leaders.
So far all was as usual, but the sequel was strange even for those
days. The matter was hushed up, and no proceedings taken. Later
in the year, when Catiline was on his trial for extortion, Torquatus
appeared in full state as consul to support in court the man who had
meant to murder him. The case of Piso was equally significant.
It had been part of the main plan to send him out to Spain with a
commission to raise forces there and establish a military base for the

[1] Asconius 89, 90.
[2] See the note at the end of this chapter.
[3] See Sueton. *Jul.* 9, Asconius p. 83. But the alleged plan of making Crassus dictator
and Caesar his master of horse is probably mere crazy gossip.

party interested in the opposition to Pompey. The Senate was now actually induced to make a special appointment[1] for Piso as governor of the Hither Spain.

1010. There can be no doubt that we have before us the outcome of a secret negotiation between Caesar and Crassus on the one hand and the chief senatorial nobles on the other. Underlying all intrigues at this time was the desire felt in several quarters to set up some power able to hold Pompey in check. His elevation was not welcome to the Senate, and Crassus was bitterly jealous of him. Hence the plan of sending Cn. Piso to Spain was officially taken up. But this scheme miscarried. The young man soon irritated the proud Spaniards and was murdered. Roman gossip said that adherents of Pompey did the deed, for that he had been selected as an enemy of Pompey was no secret. That the aristocrats were strengthened by the great man's absence in the East is indicated in the election of censors. The chosen were Catulus the chief of the Senate and the shifty but powerful Crassus. Both were opposed to the aggrandisement of Pompey, Catulus as a republican, Crassus as a rival. But Crassus was secretly under the influence of Caesar, and Caesar's promptings soon set the colleagues quarrelling. Crassus was for enrolling the 'Latins' of Transpadane Gaul as citizens, but Catulus would not hear of it. Crassus was for declaring Egypt a province, and deposing the worthless Ptolemy Auletes. It was true that this creature was not a legitimate member of the Lagid house and that Rome had not recognized him. But the alleged bequest of the kingdom to Rome by the last king was a doubtful[2] matter, and the Senate had at any rate not accepted the legacy. The real object in view was to keep Egypt out of Pompey's hands and to occupy it as a post of vantage from which the master of the East might be watched and held in check. But Catulus set his face against this also, and a bill already prepared for sending out Caesar to take over the new province had to be allowed to drop. The 'best men' were willing no doubt to check Pompey, but they did not mean to play into the hands of Crassus, still less of Caesar. So the censors[3] were fairly at loggerheads, and ended by resigning without performing any of the duties of their office. This result was a sort of victory for the aristocrats led by Catulus, and was followed up by a law[4] for the

---

[1] As *quaestor pro praetore.* See Asconius pp. 93—4, Sall. *Cat.* 18, 19, inscription in Wilmanns 1105.

[2] Cic. *de lege agr.* II §§ 41—2.

[3] Plutarch *Crass.* 13, Suet. *Jul.* 11, Dion Cass. XXXVII 9. Hence a contract was let by the consuls, the censors having abdicated. Cic. *in Catil.* III § 20.

[4] *lex Papia.* Dion Cass. XXXVII 9, Cic. *ad Att.* IV 18 § 4 (=16 § 12), Reid's Introd. to *pro Archia* p. 12.

expulsion of aliens from Rome. No doubt this old-fashioned measure was aimed primarily at the Transpadanes.

1011.   The war of prosecutions continued fiercely. The case of Catiline now came on. That he had plundered Africa cruelly was notorious, and he had no political party at his back to support him. But he had influential friends, mostly on the 'popular' side, and even Cicero[1] was within a little of undertaking his defence, though convinced of his guilt. But he bought his way out, bribing his accuser Clodius to let him secure a jury of suitable men, and then bribing them. Thus his ill-gotten money was spent, and he was left bankrupt in purse and character. The trial was protracted long enough to prevent him from standing for the next (64) year's consulship, and a point was thus gained by his enemies. Another trial of political importance was the case of Cornelius, now resumed and pressed by the leading Optimates. Cicero[2] defended him, and the praetor presiding in the court of *maiestas* did what he could to favour him : even his former colleague Globulus, whom he was said to have treated unconstitutionally, appeared on his behalf. The influence of Pompey's connexion also helped him, for he had once been quaestor under the great man. In short, whether Cornelius had or had not technically 'lessened the majesty' of the Roman people was not the real issue. The forces of the popular party were not going to let one of its leaders be sacrificed to gratify the aristocrats, and the result was a triumphant acquittal.

1012.   The doings of two notable magistrates, Caesar and Cato, were very characteristic, and throw light on the state of public affairs. Caesar was this year curule aedile[3] with M. Calpurnius Bibulus, one of the aristocratic party. The practice of using this office as a means of winning popular favour was followed by Caesar with unprecedented thoroughness. Such shows had never yet been seen, such splendid booths and stalls, such plenty and cheapness to gratify the idle mob. That the Senate interfered to limit the number of gladiators in th interest of public safety would not lessen the popularity of the lavish aedile. Expense was no consideration. He borrowed immense sums, no doubt chiefly from Crassus. Caesar was now a man of 37, and well aware that a great struggle of some sort lay before him. He was not the man to let slip the opportunity of marking himself out as the coming popular leader. He did not fear his debts, and he dexterously managed cooperation with his colleague so that he monopolized the credit of their joint expenditure. A

---

[1] See Cic. *ad Att.* 1 1 § 1, 2 § 1, Tyrrell's Introduction pp. 8, 9.

[2] See fragments of Cic. *pro Cornel.*, and the valuable notes and introduction of Asconius.

[3] See Suetonius *Jul.* 10, Plutarch *Caes.* 5, 6, Dion Cass. XXXVII 8.

dramatic stroke further concentrated attention upon himself. One morning people were all talking of a surprise that had been prepared for them during the night. The trophies of the Jugurthine and Cimbric wars, removed by decree of the Senate when Marius was declared a public enemy, were found to have been put back in their places on the Capitoline hill, all bright and clean. It was no secret who had thus revived the memory of one peculiarly honoured by the Roman Commons. That the Senate's leave had not been asked only made the act more popular. Catulus protested, and charged Caesar with designs against the Republic; the plausible aedile offered some ingenious explanations, with which the House thought it wiser to seem content. If Caesar with cool foresight thus made ready the path for his own ambition, on the other hand Cato rigidly upheld the public interest, disregarding all personal considerations. He was one of the city quaestors[1], and as such had charge of the state treasury, in which, besides coin and bullion, a number of public documents were deposited. The charge was a highly responsible one, and it seems that average quaestors were slack in attending to their duties. The real work of the office was done by the permanent underlings, who alone knew the ins and outs of the business, and thus could often exercise a power which did not belong to them. To be a mere ornamental head, the puppet of his subordinates, was a position intolerable to a man of Cato's temper. So he set himself to master the details of the department, and to reform the abuses which his diligence soon discovered. A sharp lesson or two quelled the insubordination of saucy clerks, and he was able to make good progress with getting rid of arrears. Overdue debts to the state were called in, payments due from the state were no longer delayed. Documents were no longer received into state custody without proper evidence of their genuineness. The interruption of many malpractices gained him much respect, but his example was not enough to establish a precedent for continuous imitation. In the present state of things, to expect average quaestors to give up the easy-going ways of republican officials was too much. Still Cato probably did some good. He attended regularly in the Senate, and firmly opposed remissions and grants, such as the House was only too ready to vote—jobs, in short,—under the pressure of influential members. In the course of his inquiries he came upon the record of sums paid out by order of Sulla as rewards to informers and murderers at the time of the proscriptions. These sums Cato addressed himself to recover, and a number of trials[2], and some convictions, followed in

[1] Plutarch *Cato min.* 16—18.
[2] Dion Cass. XXXVII 10, Sueton. *Jul.* 11, Asconius 92, Plutarch *Cato min.* 17. The

the next year. Thus the well-meant efforts of Cato on behalf of the treasury set in motion a campaign of the Marian popular leaders against the surviving bloodhounds of Sulla. This was conducted warmly, for instance by Caesar, who in 64 presided over one of the divisions[1] of the murder-court. These Sullan agents had been exempted from future prosecution by special clauses of the dictator's laws. The democrats now found a grand opportunity for calling this exemption in question. Cato, who was all for the Senate, had so far played into their hands. It was a characteristic feature of the political game that the opportunity furnished by Cato was turned to account by Caesar.

1013. We must bear in mind that all this while news of the continued success of Pompey in the East was reaching Rome and having a powerful influence on the various designs and relations of public men. The more genuine democrats could not wish to see Pompey follow the example of his old master Sulla. Caesar, whose views were widening, could not desire to see him in a position to thwart the ambitions of others. Crassus, who thought he had bought Caesar by becoming his obliging creditor, could not welcome the prospect of being thrust back into a secondary position by the return of the eminent conqueror with his tiresome airs of superiority. But Caesar and Crassus had not yet gained enough power to enable them to hold their ground against Pompey. The plot of which they would have reaped the fruits had failed. They were still in league with Catiline and others, but Catiline was not the man to be permanently kept in the background. He wanted the consulship, and in view of Pompey's return there was no time to be lost. His trial for extortion had prevented him from standing in 65 for the consulship of 64, but there was nothing to stop his candidature in 64 for that of 63. This then was his plan, and his prospects seemed good. Caesar and Crassus were ready to back him, of course for their own purposes, and it was by no means clear that the conservative nobles could or would offer any effective opposition. They were just now at cross purposes among themselves. The 'new man' Cicero, and the business-men with whom he was so much in sympathy, were staunch adherents of the absent general, and could point with pride to the success of their policy. But to the senatorial leaders, such as Catulus, the Luculli, Servilius Isauricus, Metellus Creticus, the preeminence of one man was hateful, and the majority of the House undoubtedly feared Pompey's return and looked with a friendly eye on any movement

mention of *scribae* tried for *peculatus* in Cic. *pro Mur.* § 42 may refer to cases of pilfering treasury-clerks.

[1] As *iudex quaestionis* (§ 928). See Greenidge, *Legal Procedure* 356, 432.

likely to avert a monarchy. In general Pompey passed for a much more dangerous person than he really was. None had gauged his limitations. That he did not clearly understand the impossibility of maintaining the Republic is almost as certain as that he did not attempt to overthrow it. But for the present he was credited with far-reaching designs for which he had neither the insight nor the nerve. Men of very different party-leanings agreed in favouring policies and persons of anti-Pompeian tendency. Hence the design on Egypt, the despatch of Piso to Spain: hence also the astounding apathy and even connivance that encouraged the enterprises of Catiline. In the year 64, if his acquittal in the murder-court was partly due to the friendly offices of Caesar, it is remarkable that a number of ex-consuls were among the witnesses[1] to character (*lauda-tores*) who came to plead for the accused. It was not that parties were inclined to draw together for the public good. Censors were appointed this year, the failure of Crassus and Catulus having left all the business undone. They were of course nobles, ex-consuls. But they were soon involved in a quarrel with some of the tribunes, and they too resigned without carrying out the duties of the office. After this failure no more attempts were made seriously to carry out a census, though censors were appointed on four other occasions (61, 55, 50, 42) before the final establishment of the Empire. The census of 70 was the last effectively completed under the Republic.

1014. The year 64 brings us to the middle stage of this series of intrigues. Crassus and Caesar are still pursuing the same ends, but no longer by such crude methods as the abortive conspiracy of Autronius. Their immediate aim was to capture the chief magistracy by procuring the election of Catiline as consul for 63 with a suitable colleague. A great attack on the conservative position was contemplated, and was indeed delivered in the following year. There was as yet no conspiracy with Catiline at its head. All depended on the blindness or apathy of the leading nobles. If fear of Pompey held them back, and the 'popular' leaders filled the consulships with their creatures, Caesar and Crassus would be the real masters of Rome by constitutional means, and the 'best men' would either have to submit to them or to place themselves under the protection of Pompey. They had of course no mind for either alternative, as the sequel was to shew. The election was to come on in the summer (64), but intending candidates had been known long before. We need only mention three. Of Cicero it is to be noted that as a rising 'new man' he could not, however respectable himself, afford to appear stuck-up and squeamish beyond his fellows. Therefore in 65, when

---

[1] Cicero *pro Sulla* § 81.

Catiline was prosecuted for extortion, the orator was for a time inclined[1] to undertake the defence of a man whose guilt was as clear as the noonday. The accuser (Clodius) had played into the hands of the accused so that an acquittal was almost certain, and the acquitted criminal would be a convenient ally in their common candidature. Yet Cicero very well knew the character of the man. A ruined Patrician, of a house once illustrious but now long obscure, his connexion with the enormities of the Sullan proscriptions was notorious. Other crimes and abominations were attributed to him on more or less credible evidence. But Roman society was no longer shocked at these things, and Catiline was able to suit himself to various company. Eight years after this Cicero[2] declared that he had almost been imposed upon by Catiline, and it is at least certain that he did not at this time avoid him. The truth seems to be that Cicero in the early stages of his candidature had little hope of support from the great nobles, and was driven to look for it elsewhere. Why then did his notion of defending Catiline come to nothing? That it did, is practically certain. We are left to infer that he found things not quite as he had expected. If Catiline had already made sure of the venal jury, Cicero's eloquence would be a mere luxury. Still more, if Catiline had already agreed to a joint candidature with another man, he could not offer a bargain that it would be worth Cicero's while to accept. And both these suppositions are highly probable. Caesar and Crassus were behind the scenes, and it is most unlikely that their designs had been left to chance and risked by delay. It was already known that C. Antonius, a son of the famous orator and brother of the man who had failed so disgracefully against the pirates, was going to stand. We find him making common cause with Catiline at the election, and their joint candidature had probably been arranged by Caesar long before. Antonius was a dissolute fellow, deeply in debt, and ready, as the sequel shewed, to do anything for his own profit and relief. For him the only question was whether the path of duty or the path of treason would lead him most surely to the desired end. Such a man was well suited to follow the lead of Catiline and promote the interests of the popular leaders. In himself he was of no great importance, and he does not seem to have had any personal following. Catiline on the contrary was a leading spirit among the corrupt and criminal circles of Roman society. The plausible debauchee, whose iron constitution was still not seriously impaired by riotous living, was attractive to numbers of ruined men and women. To them it mattered not that the sway of passions had weakened his judgment. Many young Romans of the upper classes

---

[1] See on § 1011.   [2] Cic. *pro Caelio* §§ 10—14 (56 B.C.).

were drawn to him as a specialist in sport or advanced vice. Thus to rouse the nobility as a body to oppose his candidature was no easy matter, for there were all the while plenty of powerful persons to whom any influences likely to tell against the supremacy of Pompey seemed worthy of countenance. Backed by Crassus and Caesar, and with the senatorial nobles lukewarm or divided, he seemed to have a good chance of success and of carrying in Antonius along with him.

1015. The position of Cicero was one of great difficulty. He was the only candidate who belonged by birth to the Equestrian Order, and among these capitalists he had doubtless a good percentage of supporters, all the more as the misdeeds of Catiline in Africa appear to have affected the financiers there and caused them to testify against him. Many men were also bound[1] to support Cicero on the ground of his services as counsel to themselves or their friends. Others might be glad to establish a claim to help from the first pleader in Rome, in case they should come to need it. A few non-residents from municipal towns might look kindly on a man who never belied his municipal origin. And, whatever adroit canvassing[2] could do, had assuredly been done by Cicero. But tradition was very powerful with the Roman electorate, and 'new men' had very seldom got beyond the praetorship. The consulship was still in practice reserved for men whose families were already noble. So it would have been on the present occasion, for all Cicero could do. He never forgot the elevation of Marius, his fellow-townsman : but his services were those of the tongue, while Marius had risen by the sword. The nobility affected to regard his pretensions as absurd, when the course of events suddenly changed their tone. Catiline was making himself conspicuous by his activity in raising a body of gladiators on behalf of a friend. Antonius was boasting that, encumbered though his estates were, he had still enough slave-herdsmen to seek redress by force if defeated at the poll. Their behaviour was an open menace, and care was no doubt taken to call attention to it. The noble senators saw at once that them-selves stood in grave danger if these two were elected consuls. There was no time for dallying, with the election close at hand, and it was no longer merely the Roman Republic that was in jeopardy. The most flagrant bribery was going on, with the purse of Crassus to back it. A motion in the Senate for a severer law to be introduced against *ambitus* was blocked by a tribune, and members had to find a policy in a hurry. Leaving aside candidates who were commonplace or

---

[1] Asconius pp. 86—7, citing Cicero.
[2] See his remarks in the *pro Murena*, and the *de petitione consulatus* addressed to him by his brother Quintus.

certain of defeat, they threw their influence on the side of the only man who had some qualifications for the post of danger and had also some following of his own. The Centuries voted, and Cicero was triumphantly returned first. The second place fell to Antonius, but he only beat Catiline by a few votes.

1016. The situation just before the election is known to us chiefly through the fortunate preservation of the notes of Asconius on Cicero's speech 'in the white gown' (the dress of the Roman office-seeker), containing many quotations from the speech itself. It was delivered in the Senate, after the motion for a new bribery-law had been blocked, and shortly before the election. The majority of the House were indignant and alarmed. It was plain that the action of the blocking tribune was not a mere matter of impulse, but part of a concerted scheme, a move arranged by those who meant to make Catiline consul at all costs. Who these were, everybody knew. Clearly they meant to stick at nothing, and even those who saw in the expected Pompey the chief menace to the Republic must now have seen that the daring enterprise of Crassus and Caesar was a far more immediate peril. At this critical moment, when the shock of a sudden awakening was on the minds of the great nobles, Cicero struck in with a speech which gave them a lead. He assailed Antonius and Catiline with fierce invective. But to expose the infamies and crimes of this precious pair was easy, and the facts were for the most part notorious. So far the orator was aiming at convincing his hearers that he was a stalwart opponent of the coalition, in particular that he had broken off all relations with Catiline for ever. Far more important than this display of abusive rhetoric were the passages in which he called attention to the fact that the two persons publicly put to the front were not the real heads of the movement causing so much uneasiness. The vital forces of this movement were to be found elsewhere, and Cicero artfully pointed this out, not mentioning Crassus and Caesar by name, but using descriptive language the reference of which was unmistakeable. He connected the joint candidature of Catiline and Antonius with the plot of 66—5 and the mission of Cn. Piso to Spain. The House knew very well to whom those schemes had been due. It was only necessary now to indicate that the present design was a substitute for the former one, and to inform members that the headquarters of the flagrant bribery now going on were in the mansion of a Roman noble[1] a notorious adept in transactions of the kind. He was also at pains to shew that the aims of Catiline, judged by his past, could not be compatible with the interests of either the nobles or the Equestrian capitalists ; while the common people, long ago disgusted with his bar-

[1] Certainly either Crassus or Caesar, it matters not which.

barities as a satellite of Sulla, could hardly regard him with favour now. Catiline and Antonius retorted by reviling the orator as an upstart, but the outcome of the debate was that Cicero had captured the warm support of the noble and moneyed interests. The effect of this stroke upon the election we have seen above.

1017. After the election the position may be summed up thus. Cicero had broken with the ' popular' party and gone over to the ' best men,' the aristocrats among whom it was the ambition of the ' new man' to find a place. They on their part were committed to the support of Cicero—for the present. They depended on his watchful energy to see them safely through the coming year : that year once past, the orator would of course deserve their gratitude. Whether this would dispose them to make any sacrifice on his behalf in case he should need protection, was for the future to shew. Meanwhile the immediate designs of the ' popular' leaders had received a check, and they were left to find other means of promoting them. That this result had been achieved was surely due in the first instance to the support of the financiers. It is true that the Equestrian Order had been on the side of Marius and Cinna, and had suffered severely under Sulla. But there was enough in the present composition of parties to make them reconsider their allegiance. If Caesar posed as the successor of Marius, Crassus was one of Sulla's men, and at this time he was to all appearance the more important personage of the two. And Catiline was one of the Sullan butchers, whose deeds were fresh in the memory of all moneyed men. On the other hand Cicero, a loyal son of their own class, whose connexions were Marian, was a man after their own heart. The Knights had recovered most of the privileges of which Sulla had deprived them, and had little sympathy with democratic movements. Moreover the news from the East suggested a prospect of new countries to exploit, and in the financiers' calculation this prospect would count for more than the jealousy of Pompey. Therefore it cost the Knights nothing to follow Cicero, even when the senatorial nobles took up his cause. And Roman politics had not yet reached the stage at which the two wealthy Orders could cooperate and yet be unable to control the Assembly of Centuries. For the moment the two combined formed a dominant party of order; that is, the interests of the rich had prevailed, and it was more than ever clear that the true line of division in the state was that between Rich and Poor. That Catiline saw this we shall presently find. The immediate necessity for Cicero was to neutralize the opposition of a hostile colleague during their year of office. This was done by a bargain. Of the two provinces assigned to be held by the consuls of 63, Cicero drew Macedonia, Antonius Cisalpine Gaul. The latter was dissatisfied. In Macedonia (which included the protectorate of Greece and many districts not strictly Macedonian) there was money to be made, as Dolabella had recently shewn. A triumph too might seem attainable there on easy terms[1] since the successful campaigns of M. Lucullus. The Cisalpine offered no such opportunities of enrichment and cheap glory. Cicero promised to make over Macedonia to Antonius on condition of his abstaining from factious opposition while consul. The bait was eagerly swallowed. Thus the 'popular' leaders lost the help of their official confederate, while the 'best men' were relieved of much uneasiness; for a man so deeply in debt as Antonius was thought capable of anything. And Cicero sacrificed nothing. Rome was his field of action, now more so than ever, and the plunder of provincials was never to his taste. He did not even accept Cisalpine Gaul in exchange. He had gained what for a 'new man' had not been easy, a strong position in the Senate. Henceforth he was one of the *optimates*, and the 'best men,' if not willing to risk much for his sake, were willing to have their own doubtful merits commended by the accession of so much eloquence and virtue.

1018. We must not omit to notice the war of prosecutions that took place in this year (64) before and after the consular elections. Cato had as quaestor in 65 been active in recovering moneys from the agents of Sulla, as we saw above. Caesar was now presiding in the murder-court, and used his position[2] as ground of vantage against these Sullan murderers, thus assailing the Sullan aristocrats interested in the validity of the dictator's acts. Treating the exemption-clauses of Sulla's laws as invalid, he accepted accusations brought against such persons, and some of them at least were condemned. This was before the election. In order to put a stop to these proceedings, and to turn the tables on Caesar, the 'best men' caused L. Lucceius to bring a charge of the same kind against Catiline, perhaps the guiltiest of all. The trial did not come on till the autumn, but the plain reference of Cicero shews that it was in preparation months before. It has been acutely conjectured[3] that on some pretext Caesar had managed to prevent the proceedings from reaching the stage at which the jury would have been chosen, and the day of hearing fixed, before the election. This would explain why Catiline was able to appear as a candidate, and in default of direct evidence it may be accepted as the most probable suggestion. Another scandalous acquittal was the result of the trial: even now ex-consuls were found to appear on

[1] See Cic. *in Pisonem* §§ 38, 44, 55, 56.
[2] See Asconius pp. 91—2, Suet. *Jul.* 11.
[3] By John, *Jhb. für class. phil.* 1876 pp. 735—6, and accepted by von Stern p. 53. See note at end of this chapter.

behalf of the accused, and Caesar favoured him. Indeed he was useful for party purposes. But the prosecution had partly served its turn, for the Sullan agents had after this to be left in peace. It was most likely in the latter part of 64 that P. Sittius[1] (of whom we shall hear again) was sent out to Spain to see whether he could do anything for the 'popular' cause as a private adventurer, Piso's death having upset that part of their plans. But we need not dwell on this matter here.

1019. The beginning of the tribunician year (10 Dec.) before the consular (1 Jan.) was important now, as always in stirring times. It enabled active tribunes to get the start of the consuls by giving notice of proposed measures, and addressing meetings in support of them, before the new consuls entered on office. Cicero found himself face to face with a number of proposals put forward by tribunes, doubtless under the influence of Crassus and Caesar, to which he was bound to offer opposition. It was not in his favour that a number of prodigies were being reported, and the ceremony[2] known as the 'augury of Safety,' performed at the beginning of the year in times of peace, was attended by omens at which the augurs shook their heads. We hear of bills for restoring the children of those proscribed by Sulla to the full rights of citizens, for remission or reduction of debts, for a grand scheme of land-allotment and colonization, and for relief of the consuls unseated for *ambitus* in the year 66. Under the Calpurnian law of 67 these men were for ever disqualified from holding office. It was now proposed to limit their disqualification to ten years, in fact to return[3] to the previous law. The two culprits were P. Autronius Paetus and P. Cornelius Sulla, a nephew of the dictator. This proposal, with the consent of Sulla, was withdrawn on the first of January, under circumstances far from clear. As for attempts to relieve debtors at the expense of creditors, we only know that Cicero contrived somehow to foil them, though they were persistently made, and that he was proud of having borne a leading part[4] in the maintenance of credit. In connexion with the latter proposal it should be remarked that some of the most striking instances of indebtedness were of a peculiar kind arising out of the land-system of Italy. Many men owned immense landed estates part at least of which had once been *ager publicus* held in 'possession.' The failure of the policy of the Gracchi had converted

---

[1] See below §§ 1253, 1257.

[2] Dion Cass. XXXVII 24—5, Cic. *de divinatione* I § 105. See Preller's *Röm. Mythol.*, index under *augurium Salutis*. The war in the East must have been regarded as practically ended.

[3] See Cic. *pro Sulla* §§ 62—66, with Reid's notes and Introd. § 13 on this *rogatio Caecilia*.

[4] See Cic. *Catil.* II § 18, *de officiis* II § 84.

most of these lands into private property, but the old name of
possessiones still remained.   A certain importance inevitably clung to
the great landlord.   He generally lived in Rome and managed his
estates through slave-bailiffs.   His income therefrom, consisting in the
return from sales of stock or other produce, was probably far less than
could have been got out of the land under a better economy.   Money
soon melted in Rome, and he got into debt.   Soon the interest on the
loans became larger than his income from his estates, though the land
was worth in the market enough to have paid off the capital of his
debt.   We are assured by Cicero that there were not a few of these
embarrassed landlords who would not part with their land to clear off
their encumbrances, and by such mad finance as this were sinking
into utter bankruptcy.   Such men cherished a muddle-headed hope
that a revolution might cancel their debts and yet leave them their
lands.   Cicero, ridiculing their delusion, had afterwards to admit that
they formed a contingent in the motley following of Catiline.

1020.   Of all the schemes now put forth none was more subtly
conceived than the so-called agrarian bill of the tribune P. Servilius
Rullus, backed by several of his colleagues, but beyond doubt really
the handiwork of Caesar.   It appeared as a popular move of the
Marian party, but interests likely to be adverse were carefully conciliated.   Its promoters hoped to carry it with a rush and begin actual
business before the end of January.   The bill was ready drawn, but
seems not to have been published till just before the beginning of the
new year.   It was the subject of much talk beforehand, but Cicero
complains that he could get no official version of its provisions.
Indeed the tribunes had good reasons for not gratifying the new
consul's curiosity.   It will be best to sketch as briefly as may be the
scope of this ingenious measure before discussing the real design
cleverly hidden under apparently beneficent proposals.   It professed
to provide for a great scheme of colonization, by which the poor
citizens were to be settled on lands in Italy, each with a sufficient
allotment.   These allotments were to pass from father to son, but the
holders were to have no power of sale.   Thus the pauper mob of
Rome was to be drained away from the crowded capital to people and
till the depopulated country side of Italy.   The scheme might sound
well, but the state could only distribute *ager publicus* (agrarian laws
did not deal with *ager privatus*), and of this there was in Italy only a
very small quantity left.   Sulla had confiscated the territory of some
few communities, and some at least of this remained state property.
Beside this there was only the land in Campania, which had been
forfeited to Rome in the second Punic war, and was one of the surest
resources of the treasury, being let to tenants who paid a rack-rent, and

apparently a few stray properties (woodlands etc.) also in the hands of lessees.   These remnants were what the earlier land-reformers had spared; they were already occupied by Roman citizens, and on terms remunerative to the state.   No material gain could be expected from turning out present occupiers to make room for new ones.   There was of course a great deal of land held under the Sullan assignations, which the Marian party would not have been loth to resume.   But the opposition of the 'Sullan possessors' would have been fatal to the bill. To keep them quiet, clauses were inserted expressly guaranteeing these (and perhaps other) questionable titles, provided they were later than a certain date; the date (year 82) being fixed so as to include and confirm all the grants of Sulla.   There was in short only one way to get Italian land available for distribution, namely by purchase, and for purchase on a large scale a vast sum of money must be found.   It is in the methods of raising this necessary capital that we come upon the essential portions of the bill.

1021.   If we may trust the statements of Cicero, quoting professedly from the text, the clauses giving powers of sale were astoundingly wide.   It was not merely that they referred in express terms to such an immense area of public property in so many countries.   Loose general expressions were also there, capable of a still wider application.   If Cicero[1] spoke of a 'sale of the Roman people's effects,'—as in a case of bankruptcy, is the obvious insinuation,—he was at least able to give good reasons for using strong language.   The sale was to include all remaining state property in Italy, and all state property abroad (with one or two trifling exceptions); in particular, all the acquisitions made in the first consulship (88) of Sulla or since.   The extent of the power of sale under this head may be gauged by the single case of Bithynia, which was all acquired within the period named, and by observing that the recent annexations of Pompey were included also.   More remarkable still was the fact that, though Egypt was not expressly mentioned, the empowering clauses were so drawn as to leave it an open question whether that country could or could not be dealt with under the provisions of the bill.   Bearing in mind that an attempt had lately been made to occupy Egypt in force as a check to the all-powerful Pompey, and that the last legitimate Ptolemy was alleged to have bequeathed his kingdom to Rome, the suspicion that Rullus (or rather Caesar) had designs upon the Nile would seem to be just.   It was of course clear that all the vast territories potentially affected by the bill could not in practice be actually sold.   To meet this difficulty power was given to lay a rent or tax on whatever was not disposed of by

[1] Cic. *de lege agr.* I § 4, II § 48.

sale. The money and other booty recently acquired in the East was further to be appropriated to the purposes of the bill. Thus in one way or another an enormous fund was to be created, which was to be invested in Italian land for distribution to the Roman poor. To complete the scheme large judicial and administrative powers were necessary. For the executive officials, to carry out its provisions, would have (*a*) to determine what was state property and what not (*b*) to be armed with an authority sufficient to enforce compliance with their orders (*c*) to decide on purchases, what land to buy for distribution and what not. Words are weak to give an idea of the extent of these powers. For they carried with them the further necessity of long continuance. If the work was to be done at all, a reasonable time must be allowed for it. The great powers conferred on Pompey had their justification in the military needs of the moment. The bill of Rullus, whatever its merits, was dealing a deadly blow at the republican system of short magistracies in a time of peace.

1022.   These powers were to be entrusted to a commission of ten, elected[1] by the majority of 17 Tribes chosen by lot. These commissioners were to have the *imperium* of propraetors, and to hold office for five years. By a clause requiring candidates to appear in person, the exclusion of Pompey was decently secured. If the bill had become law, Caesar would doubtless have been on the commission, and of course would have been the real master. Cicero was bound to come forward in opposition to the scheme, both as representing the views of the Senate and as a leader among the supporters of Pompey. Besides, he no doubt had a genuine objection to it himself as a loyal republican and an opponent of corruption and extravagance. He delivered four speeches against it, of which three survive. The first, in the Senate on the first of January, is not complete. The second is the address to the people in which he gained the greatest oratorical triumph of his life, by setting the common people against a bill professedly brought forward in their interest. Of this the third is a short sequel. Misrepresentations and exaggerations occur in them, as in nearly all political oratory: but some of the arguments throw so much light on the state of popular feeling that they call for brief mention here. In exposing the insidious attack on the position of Pompey, the orator created the impression that the real aim of the promoters was different from that professed. In pointing out the boundless opportunities for favouritism and corruption he appealed to a widespread and well-grounded belief in the dishonesty of public men, and no effective personal reply was possible, as the names of commissioners were not proposed in the bill. Nor could it

[1] See § 1025.

be denied that the project was one offering endless openings for black-mailing those whom, for good or for evil, the decisions of the commission would affect. The mere handling of the immense sums that might be realized by the sales would expose the commissioners to great temptation, a point not likely to be viewed charitably by needy citizens, who would themselves have no access to the fund. As for the land in Italy, there was no guarantee that what was bought would be such as the poor citizens would find it worth while to accept in allotments. There was room for infinite jobbery. Numbers of men had estates where the soil was barren or cultivation impossible through drought or malaria : others had acquired lands in discreditable circumstances, the spoils of the proscribed. All these would be on the alert to relieve themselves by making a good bargain with the state. Rullus himself was known to be connected with a landowner anxious to part with some ineligible property. Was it wise to sell state property in a glutted market for what it might fetch, to sacrifice healthy sources of revenue, in order to put it in the power of ten politicians to buy useless lands from their friends at fancy prices ? In these lines of argument the art of the great advocate appears. The lounging mob of the Forum had no real stomach for the patient toil required of those who would earn a living on the land. The passages in which Cicero delicately suggested to them what the scheme meant, no shows, no corn-doles, no city gossip, no chance of using votes that had a market-value, no prospect of being feasted and courted as the sovran people, were surely the most effective in defeating the bill. As a practical means of relieving poverty and ridding Rome of a surplus population, the bill was a sham. Caesar of course knew this, but he wanted a ' cry ' to serve his real purposes. Cicero exposed the trick with consummate boldness and skill.

1023. A tribune was held in readiness[1] to block the bill when it came on for voting, but this disagreeable necessity, and the riot likely to arise from it, were happily avoided. Popular enthusiasm was not to be evoked, and the measure was withdrawn. Caesar was for the moment foiled. But we may reflect that, if it had become law, and Caesar had gone to the East with such extensive powers, it would hardly have suited his purpose to have Catiline upsetting everything behind his back by murder and robbery. Now that the bill was dropped, and he remained in Rome watching events, it was always possible for him in case of disturbance to take advantage of some false step on the part of the government. That there was as yet no Catilinarian conspiracy is practically certain, but Catiline was still to the fore, and eager to avenge his defeat. To let him embarrass the Senate and the

---

[1] Cic. *pro Sulla* § 65.

consul might be convenient.   Accordingly Caesar and Crassus still
supported him[1] as a candidate for the next year's consulship.   It is
hardly possible to believe that they would have continued to encourage
so dangerous a person, had it not been for the failure of the
agrarian law.

1024.   There were other events in which the discontents and
intrigues[2] of the time are to be traced.   An outcry was raised against
the reservation of seats for the Knights in the theatre, and the
eloquent consul had to talk the rabble into good humour.   The affair
had perhaps not occurred without some wire-pulling.   The next move
was the trial of C. Rabirius, an aged senator.   It was said that he had
been the actual slayer of Saturninus 37 years ago.   It was another
of Caesar's attacks upon the Senate.   The facts of the case have
come down to us in a confused form.   Recent criticism has however
shewn that the charge was one of high treason [*perduellio*].   Begun
with revival of an obsolete and barbarous procedure, a tradition of
the regal period, it ended in a trial on appeal to the Assembly of
Centuries.   The Assembly was broken up by a trick[3] equally obsolete, doubtless arranged by Cicero.   The prosecution was not an attack
on the legality of the 'last decree' of the Senate, but a warning against
the misuse of martial law, such as was alleged in the case of the
death of Saturninus.   The matter seems not to have been dropped
at once, but further proceedings were of too little interest to be clearly
recorded for us.   The consul made a speech on behalf of the old man,
but, as he himself said afterwards, it was the right of the Senate to
issue such a decree that he was really defending.   Nobody cared
about Rabirius, and nothing seems to have happened to him.   So the
performance ended.   It had served to worry the consul and his noble
friends, but the position of the Senate as a body was if anything
strengthened by the attack.   The proposal to repeal the disqualification[4] for public office, inflicted by a law of Sulla on the children of
his victims, was also troublesome.   Cicero had supported previous
attempts to upset Sulla's arrangements, and now in opposing the
present one had to appear at a disadvantage.   But the restoration of
these unfortunate youths would just now have led to further agitation,
which it was most important to avoid.   It was better[5] that a few should

---

[1] See below § 1026.

[2] See Cic. *ad Att.* II 1 § 3, *in Pisonem* §§ 4, 5.

[3] The pulling down of the red flag on the Janiculum.   This signified that the guard
posted to watch against a sudden raid of Etruscans was no longer on duty, and the *exercitus*
or *comitia centuriata* could not lawfully continue in session.

[4] Dion Cass. XLIV 47 speaks of Caesar's relief of these persons as an instance of his
consistency.   So he was probably at the back of the present proposal.

[5] See argument given in Quintilian XI 1 § 85.

suffer unjustly than that the state should be upset by admitting them to office. The orator again pleaded with success. We must remember that the pauper mob would probably be indifferent, while the wealthier classes were satisfied with the existing order of things. How well Cicero understood the temper of the populace was shewn in the matter[1] of the so-called 'free delegations.' This abuse had existed for some time. A Senator would want to go abroad on private business, to take up an inheritance or look after his investments in the provinces, and he used his influence in the House to get himself made a titular *legatus*. This enabled him to travel in style as a servant of the state at the public cost, though he had no public mission to discharge. The expense of these trips fell almost wholly upon the provincials, and was a most vexatious addition to burdens already heavy enough. To attack this scandalous privilege, assumed for the profit of a few rich men, was a popular move, and Cicero, who sincerely sympathized with the subject peoples, saw that there was now a chance of getting something done. The poorer citizens grudged these perquisites of the rich, and the consul cleverly introduced several references to this particular topic into his speeches on the agrarian law. He now drew up a bill to prohibit the practice altogether, but a tribune was found to block this. He had to be content with proposing to limit such 'deputations' to a duration of one year. In this form the bill became law, but of course it did little or nothing to check the abuse.

1025. All through the movements of the year 63 we can feel the opposition of policies represented by Cicero and Caesar. But in a matter where personal popularity was the one important point Caesar could have his own way. In the winter of 64—3 Q. Metellus Pius the chief pontiff died, and it was certain that there would be severe competition for this post, politically important and held for life. Caesar meant to fill it himself, for it was exactly what he wanted, and the absence of Pompey was in his favour. He began operations by putting forward the tribune T. Atius Labienus (who had also done duty as prosecutor of Rabirius) to propose a bill for restoring the method of appointment in use before the legislation of Sulla. This was in short a selection[2] of one of the existing pontiffs by a majority (9) of a minority (17) of the 35 Tribes, the 17 being chosen by lot. The proposal was carried into law, and the close system of selection by the college itself was thus abolished. Caesar had now to compete with two men of the first rank and of ripe age, Catulus the chief of the

[1] *legationes liberae.* See Cic. *de legibus* III § 18.
[2] See Dion Cass. XXXVII 37, Cic. *de lege agr.* II §§ 16—19, Velleius II 43, Plutarch *Caes.* 7, Sueton. *Jul.* 13.

Senate and Servilius Isauricus.   Catulus knew of Caesar's debts, and
it is said that he offered Caesar a good round sum to retire.   But he
misjudged his man.   Caesar went into the contest determined to win[1]
at all costs, and he did.   Thus the religious headship of the state,
including the trusteeship of sacred property, the jurisdiction in religious
questions and determination of religious scruples, the charge of the
calendar, and other powers capable of being used to advantage in
politics, passed into his possession either as chairman of the pontifical
college or as part and parcel of his primacy.   The choice of the spirit
in which the ancient superstitions, still powerful with the ignorant
masses, should be manipulated in a freethinking age was henceforth
to be guided by the most far-sighted man and one of the most
advanced freethinkers in Rome.

1026.   Thus the earlier part of the year 63 had been a time of
ceaseless disturbance.   The aristocracy in possession of the government were exposed to a series of attacks only foiled with difficulty.
What would have happened had Catiline and not Cicero been consul
we can only guess: at all events it was in the 'new man' that the
nobility had hitherto found their effective champion.   And now the
time for the elections was at hand, and a sharp contest for the consulship of the next year (62) was in prospect.   There were four candidates.
D. Junius Silanus had already sustained defeat, but he was popular on
account of the splendid shows he had given when aedile.   L. Licinius
Murena, lately propraetor in Transalpine Gaul, had served with his
father under Lucullus in the East.   The triumph of Lucullus, delayed
by factious opposition for about three years, only took place shortly
before this election.   Some of his old soldiers came to attend this
function, and these, together with a great throng of followers assembled
by influence treating and bribery, were for Murena.   Servius Sulpicius
was an orator of note, and the first jurist of the day.   These three
were all on the side of the government.   The fourth was Catiline.
He was still supported[2] by Crassus and Caesar, and enjoyed the open
or secret sympathy of the embarrassed and desperate.   His chances
of success had probably not improved with time.   Another year's
extravagance had surely not left him richer; another year of intrigues
and gossip had surely put the propertied classes more on their guard.
Nor was his election so important to Caesar and Crassus as it had been
when Antonius was to have been his colleague.   From what we hear
of Catiline's conduct at this time it would seem that he was fully
conscious of the change in his position, and beginning more and more

---

[1] He is said to have bribed heavily.   Probably the others did too.
[2] I think this is to be assumed.   Their support was no doubt half-hearted, and von Stern
may be right in denying it altogether.

to take a line of his own. He had been the tool of those who were using the forces of a political faction (the *populares*) for their own ends. But neither he nor his more intimate associates really cared for party divisions and party cries. Unless Crassus and Caesar were prepared for a cancelling of debts and a general attack on property, ruined men and women would gain little or nothing by their victory over Catulus Lucullus Servilius and the rest of the party of order. It might be well to try for the consulship once more, and see what could be done through official powers. But we can hardly doubt that the bankrupt gang were already beginning to desire some practical result from their efforts, and considering what they were to do in the event of their leader's defeat. It cannot have escaped their notice that Crassus was the prince of capitalists. If they still fancied that Caesar would favour a general repudiation of debts (which we know was not his policy), at all events they knew that he was financed by Crassus. In these two there was therefore no hope from the point of view of the more desperate companions of Catiline. Nothing could really serve their turn but an anarchist revolution, but for the present they had not got beyond growling and talking big over their wine.

1027. The canvass went on, each party using to the utmost the resources at its disposal. It was natural that the Catilinarian circle should look for support to the discontented outside Rome. In particular there were numbers of men restless and impoverished in northern Etruria, chiefly old soldiers of Sulla who had failed as farmers, but also the former occupiers, dispossessed Marians. On the common ground of wishing for change these heterogeneous elements could combine and attract other desperate fellows, of whom there was no lack in Italy after the troubles of recent years. A certain C. Manlius, a former centurion under Sulla, gathered together a number of these men, and fixed his headquarters at Faesulae. He was in league with Catiline, and money enough was sent to enable him to conduct a large body to Rome (about 200 miles by the *via Cassia*) in order to bear a hand in the election. Meanwhile Sulpicius had been acting after his kind. Corrupt practices of all sorts were notoriously going on flagrantly, perhaps beyond all precedent. But the upright man of law, dealing with a corrupt and disorderly electorate, looked to the laws to secure purity of election, for which the populace cared nothing. He addressed the Senate on the matter, and induced the House to take two decided steps. First, an order was passed declaring certain practices, such as the hiring of escort-gangs and various forms of treating, to be breaches of the existing (Calpurnian) law. Secondly, the consuls were instructed to prepare a new law of *ambitus* with severer penalties. The laws about signs from heaven were suspended in order to prevent delay, and this *lex Tullia* was hurried through in time for the election in July. It is a striking fact that no tribune blocked these proceedings, when we remember what had happened in the previous year. If Crassus and Caesar had still been deeply interested in Catiline's behalf and had seriously objected to the new law, surely the efforts of Sulpicius would have been foiled at some stage. Probably they and Catiline were drawing apart, and anyhow laws were nowadays made to be broken. Another sign of Catiline's detachment from the political programme of the 'popular' leaders is to be detected in the rumour of a speech[1] delivered by him at this time to a meeting of his supporters in his own house. He was credited with having declared that only a man himself ruined could be trusted to act loyally and boldly as the champion of ruined men ; to war with wealth and heal their own financial wounds they must have a leader who would stick at nothing. Whether he spoke thus or not, we may believe Cicero that he was so reported. Shortly before this he had had an altercation with Cato in the Senate, in the course of which he uttered words capable of being represented as a threat of violent revolution in case he were thwarted in his present designs. Cicero now induced the House to put off the election due the next day, and demanded an explanation from Catiline. He drew from him no apology for the utterances reported, but a defiant reply that he meant to be the leader of the poor but unorganized Many, if they would only back him up, against the rich but rotten minority and their shaky head, that is Cicero. Soon after—in July[2], not in October, as some have thought—the adjourned election was held, Cicero presiding. He had now for some time been at open enmity with Catiline, and may have had good reason to fear violence. At all events he gave out that there was danger, and a number of the party of order armed themselves and escorted him to the Field of Mars in the interests of public safety. As a dramatic reminder addressed to popular sentiment, he let it be seen that he was wearing a cuirass under his robe. There appears to have been no fighting, and there is no proof that an attack had been intended. The voting took place, and Silanus and Murena were elected. The latter seems to have owed his success partly to the support of some who, seeing that Sulpicius had spoilt his own chance, threw over the lawyer at the last moment, and voted for Murena to keep out Catiline. Sulpicius was furious, and at once prepared to prosecute Murena under the Tullian law. Cato, indignant at the corrupt means used, readily agreed to appear in support of the charge.

---

[1] Cic. *pro Murena* § 50.
[2] This crucial point is established by John. See note at end of this chapter.

1028. On the occasion of Catiline's defiant reply to Cicero, the Senate, though angered by his audacity, had avoided committing itself to any strong resolution. The caution of the House[1] was a disappointment to the consul. No doubt members were afraid that the chief magistrate, in the view of many men an upstart of theatrical bent, might lead them into a position from which they could not recede. But events moved in favour of Cicero. Catiline had no longer any hope of reaching his ends by what passed for constitutional means. He had gathered round him the ruined men of all classes in Rome, and brought in from outside numbers of desperate characters. To his company any change from their present indigence was alluring. They looked to their leader for relief, and he, whatever his faults, did not lack courage. At this point the designs of Catiline took their final shape, and we come to the genuine Catilinarian conspiracy. The would-be revolutionary magistrate passes into the secret plotting anarchist. The details of the enterprise are not of first-rate importance, but its relation to the life of the Roman state deserves careful consideration. The political social and moral atmosphere of the time favoured wild revolutionary designs. The Senate, the only permanent organ of government, was by no means powerless, but its authority had suffered from collision with the Assembly under the restored tribunate. It was also internally weakened by containing many timid members, and not a few embarrassed untrustworthy and disloyal. The city was full of gossip, scandal, suspicion. Prodigies of the old sort had been abundant two years before (65), when even the famous group of the she-wolf and the twins was struck by lightning. A new series now began. Educated Romans might refer such phenomena to natural causes, but with their enlightenment too often went a selfishness that left them indisposed to effort and self-sacrifice. Superstition had still a strong hold on the rabble, and by this time a large percentage of the Roman mob must have been of alien extraction, lacking patriotic tradition, but not less superstitious than those of Italian blood. Italy swarmed in many parts with discontented men, and no regular police-force for the maintenance of order existed. Who or what was there to resist a bold revolutionary stroke? Certainly not the cooperation of free patriotic burghers in Rome, or the automatic rally of a contented Italy. The government had no troops ready to hand. Thus an anarchist conspiracy was a serious peril, though the resources at its disposal were absurdly small. In Rome itself[2] men

---

[1] Cic. *pro Mur.* § 51.

[2] Disorder in Rome was greatly promoted by the *collegia*, which served to give an organization to the mob. These associations, generally formed under cover of a religious worship of some kind, were put down by a decree of the Senate in the year 64. Only a

could be found to undertake the work of arson pillage and massacre. But to carry out such a business with effect, so as to supersede the magistrates and the Senate, was a matter for organization, and sure to need time.   We have no ground for supposing that the inner circle of conspirators had any plans of political reform, or that mere massacre and pillage would have answered their purpose.   To murder rich men was useless unless the plunder fell into the right hands, that is, their own.   Catiline was virtually pledged to place them once more in a position to lead wanton and extravagant lives.   It was no easy task, and the time needed for preparations could only be gained by secrecy. Manlius and his band returned to Faesulae and continued to raise men and arms, in readiness for an insurrection in Etruria whenever orders came from Rome.   But here also there were difficulties caused by the peculiar aims of the conspiracy.   By arming rural slaves from the great plantations a force might surely have been raised with which the government would have been quite unable to cope.   But the rural slaves, rough hardy sullen animals, were no fit allies for men who aspired to become themselves the proprietors of confiscated estates.   To let the slave-gangs loose upon the land would be to find themselves, after overthrowing the government, face to face with a ruinous slave-war, perhaps at the mercy[1] of a luckier Spartacus. This was no prospect for men whose ambition was to enjoy the spoils of wealthy victims and to live in luxurious ease.   It is therefore quite credible that Catiline, while willing to allow the employment of domestic slaves when the time came for the rising in the city, would not have rural slaves enlisted in Etruria.   According to Sallust, he stood by this refusal[2] to the last, in spite of the pressure of his confederates.

   1029.   Months went by without any open move on the part of Catiline.   That secret conclaves met from time to time to discuss plans and report progress, we hardly needed to be told : that horrid oaths, sealed with cannibal solemnities, were taken by the chief plotters, even if true, matters not.   The important fact is that the conspirators were watched.   The nervous consul, left by the Senate with the whole responsibility for the Home government and un-provided with troops, took his own measures, and played the game of secrecy more skilfully than Catiline.   He was well served by spies, but espionage could not do much.   At this juncture a lucky chance

few old and useful ones, such as that of the *fabri*, were licensed.   See Asconius pp. 8, 75. We shall hear of them again.

   [1] See Cic. *Cat.* II § 19 end.

   [2] Sallust *Cat.* 44 § 6, 56 § 5, Cic. *Cat.* III §§ 8, 12.   The words of Dion Cass. XXXVII 33 § 2 and Cic. *Cat.* I § 27 cannot be set against these passages.   That he enlisted *latrones*, escaped slaves, is very likely.

opened up to him a new source of information. A light-headed
conspirator, one of the men turned out of the Senate by the censors
of the year 70, was the lover of a lady of quality named Fulvia.
This man, one Q. Curius, in order to satisfy his mercenary mistress,
boasted to her of a good time coming when his purse would be full.
She soon got at his secret, but could not keep it.   Cicero heard of it,
and took the lady into pay as a spy.   Thus the progress of the plot,
so far at least as Curius was in the confidence of the chief movers,
was regularly reported through Fulvia to the consul.   It may be well
to mention some of the anarchist leaders.   The first man, or rather
figure-head, for the city part of the enterprise was P. Cornelius
Lentulus Sura, formerly praetor, consul in 71, turned out of the
Senate in 70, but now again praetor and once more in the House.
He was dreamy and lethargic, no fit ringleader in a dangerous
business.   A dubious prophecy, that three Cornelii were destined to
win supreme power in Rome, is said to have encouraged him to look
for the succession of Cinna and Sulla.   Of other senators the most
notable were L. Cassius Longinus, a corpulent wily rogue who had
stood against Cicero for the consulship, and C. Cornelius Cethegus,
hot-headed and hasty.   There were a few Knights.   The municipal
element was represented by such men as T. Volturcius of Croton,
M. Caeparius of Terracina, and P. Furius a Sullan colonist from
Faesulae. Freedmen too were admitted, in particular one P. Umbrenus,
who had done financial business in Gaul beyond the Alps, probably
as an agent.   We can see from these specimens what a motley band
the company of Catiline were.   Desire of money to gratify their
passions was their one bond of union.   They had also in common the
fact of being failures in the past, and of being now betrayed by the
traitor Curius.

   1030.   The position of Cicero was now this.   He had plenty of
private information, and knew that the outbreak of the conspiracy
was arranged for a day late[1] in October.   From his colleague Antonius
he had no fear of hindrance.   To make sure of the man he had
publicly[2] clinched the bargain about Macedonia before the elections
in the summer.   But he had not as yet induced the Senate to grant
him full powers by passing the 'last decree,' nor was there much
prospect of their doing so until they were convinced of their own
immediate danger.   How was he to alarm them?   At this point
we must refer to a story recorded[3] by Plutarch and Dion Cassius,

---

[1] Perhaps the 25th or 27th. See discussion by von Stern pp. 87—9.

[2] In the *oratio cum provinciam in contione deposui*, as he says *ad Att.* II 1 § 3. It is lost.
The transaction was unusual, and no doubt he thought it well to address a meeting on the
subject.

[3] Plut. *Cic.* 15, Dion Cass. XXXVII 31.

probably drawn from Cicero's own memoirs.   The consul was called
up at night by a visit of Crassus and two other nobles.   Crassus
produced a packet of letters addressed to various leading men, left at
his house by a mysterious messenger.   One, which bore no address,
he had opened, and found it to contain a warning that Catiline was
preparing a massacre, and advice to withdraw from Rome.   We may
observe that Crassus had been placed in a dilemma.   If he suppressed
the letters, he would seem to be an accomplice in the plot, in case
anything more should come out and the story be true.   He chose
rather to clear himself, and so played into the hands of the consul.
It has been suggested[1] that the letters had been prepared under the
direction of Cicero himself, and that the farce was got up deliberately
to put pressure on Crassus and ultimately on the Senate.   The
consul took the letters, summoned the House early next morning,
handed the letters unopened to the members addressed, and bade
them read out the contents.   All were found to contain the same
warning.   A senator also announced that he had news of military
preparations made by Manlius in Etruria.   The Senate was now
really alarmed, and Cicero followed up the impression created in a
speech.   He shewed that he was well informed of the conspirators'
plans, and asserted that a day close at hand was fixed for a concerted
outbreak in Etruria and Rome.   The House believed him now, and
at this memorable sitting the 'last decree' was passed.   This was on
the 21st of October.   Members separated to look after their own
safety, and the 'new man' of Arpinum had the city under martial
law at last.   Days went by, the dreaded date passed by without an
insurrection in Rome, and men began to doubt the necessity of the
measures that were being taken, and to fancy that the fussy and over-
nervous consul had made much out of little.   But about the last day
of October news arrived that Manlius had actually raised the standard
of revolt.   That it was a preconcerted affair was clear.   The rising
in the city had been stopped just in time, while the leader had not
had time enough to countermand the rising of Manlius.

   1031.   The position of Catiline was now wellnigh desperate.
There was a general rally of all who had anything to lose : the consul
must be supported at all costs.   He had already sent Q. Metellus
Celer to Picenum, to raise troops and provide for the security of the
North.   Other officers were despatched to various points.   Rome
itself was carefully patrolled by guards, and men enrolled for the
service of the government.   An accuser came forward to prosecute
Catiline for public violence (*vis*).   This gave the arch-conspirator the

---

[1] By von Stern pp. 85—6.   I would remark that we hear nothing of Caesar in connexion
with this matter.   Did Cicero think him less likely than Crassus to fall into a trap?

opportunity of posing as an injured innocent, only too glad of the
chance of clearing himself.   He offered himself to be kept in custody
by leading nobles.   One after another declined the proposal, but a
person was at length found to receive him.   Of course his real aim
was to gain time, to find his way out of the web spun round him by
the consul.   Some modification of his plans was necessary, so he
acted the part of innocence, and waited.   But he was not idle.   By
way of securing a military post near at hand, he organized a party to
seize the citadel of Praeneste on the first of November, but it was
found already held[1] by a government force.   He turned now to
wilder schemes of bloodshed and anarchy, which were indeed the
logical consequence of his recent designs.   But above all things it
was an object to get rid of the consul whose watchful care had thus
far foiled all his efforts.   On the night of the 6th November a secret
meeting of the chief conspirators was held at which the working
arrangements were made for firing the city in a number of places at
once and for a massacre of the wealthy in the general confusion.   The
parts in this tragedy were assigned to definite persons, each to
operate in a particular district.   The consul was to be murdered at
once under pretext of a morning call, a service for which two of the
company volunteered.   This done, Catiline would be free to set out
to join Manlius, while the other leaders worked their will on the
helpless city.   But Cicero was promptly informed of their plans, and
the callers on the morning of the 7th found his house guarded and
were refused admission.   So the departure of Catiline for northern
Etruria was delayed by this miscarriage.   On the 8th the Senate
met, and Cicero delivered the famous speech[2] in which he set forth
the facts of the conspiracy and exposed fully the designs of Catiline,
bidding him quit Rome and take his proper place as an enemy at the
head of his army.   Catiline was even now present in the House, and
in a crafty reply deprecated a harsh judgment of his conduct: was
it likely that a Patrician of ancient race would attempt the destruction of Rome, that a latter-day lodger[3] might pose as its saviour?
But the members had now had enough of him, and he strode out,
defiant to the last.   After conferring with some of his chief associates,
he left the city by night.   A small armed force already awaited him
on the Aurelian road: these he now joined, assumed the dress and
style of a consul, and marched on to join Manlius.   It was given out
that he had gone into voluntary exile at Massalia, but Cicero knew
better.   Next day the consul addressed[4] a public meeting, told the

[1] Cic. *Cat.* 1 § 8.   [2] The first of the existing collection.
[3] *inquilinus*, that is the 'new man' from Arpinum.   See Juvenal VIII 231—44.
[4] Second Catilinarian speech.

people what had occurred, and reassured them as to the sequel.   The
forces of the insurrection were far inferior to the forces of order, and
the conspirators still remaining in the city had better beware how
they exposed themselves to certain detection and punishment.   But
the tell-tale part of the speech[1] is that in which he admits that he
has not dared to seize and punish Catiline in Rome, because of the
calumnies and accusations that would surely follow such a step.   He
thought it better to 'give him rope' and let him prove his guilt to
the satisfaction of all.   Thus, he urged, it would be possible to act
boldly against his confederates in the city.   That all this caution
should have been necessary, after the Senate had passed its 'last
decree,' is a highly significant fact.   Not only was the consul resolved
to make assurance doubly sure, but the senators who stood behind
him were evidently afraid of a reaction in which they themselves
might suffer.   It was no easy task to rouse the multitude to indignation against the conspirators, whose designs seemed to offer a chance
of promiscuous pillage.   What made Cicero's task all the harder was
that he had to walk warily, in order not to compromise his noble
supporters.

1032.   After the departure of Catiline came a time when both
sides were preparing for the inevitable conflict.   On his way north
Catiline raised and armed more men, and joined Manlius at Faesulae.
The Senate[2] declared them both public enemies, and fixed a date
before which their followers might disperse and escape punishment.
But neither this nor the offer of rewards had any effect in causing
desertion in the field or betrayal in Rome.   Troops had meanwhile
been raised for the government, and the consul Antonius was
instructed to take command in Etruria, while Cicero was on duty in
the city.   The nervous strain on the latter must have been terrible,
but he rose to the occasion as he usually did.   At this juncture he
had to meet another call upon his powers.   Murena's trial for corrupt
practices came on, and in the interest of the government it was most
necessary to secure his acquittal.   A conviction would mean a fresh
election with all its risks.   If, as was not unlikely, hindrances
occurred, the state might have to face the beginning of the new year
with only one consul in office.   The new tribunes would be in office on
the 10th December, and one of them (Q. Metellus Nepos) was already
beginning to give trouble by seditious harangues.   But Sulpicius the
man of legality, enraged at his defeat, and Cato, determined to act
on principle in season or out of season, cared for none of these things.

---

[1] In truth he had hoped that the other leaders would depart with Catiline. Theiɪ
presence in Rome was a great anxiety.

[2] Sallust *Cat.* 36 § 2.

The defence was conducted by Hortensius Crassus and Cicero. Crassus, it is said, had warned Cicero of the armed rising in Etruria, and his interest[1] in the case of Murena is an additional reason for believing that he was not a party to the conspiracy of Catiline.   The speech of Cicero was a masterpiece.   He made merciless fun of the pretensions of the bookworm man of Law, and the paradoxical dogmas of the Stoic man of principle.   He discussed the practices of Roman electioneering with apologetic ingenuity, which came strangely from the lips of the author of the last new law against *ambitus*. Even Cato remarked that the consul was a master of ridicule.   But the real gist of the speech was the argument that in this hour of peril the jury, as patriots, ought not to be too extreme in vindicating purity of election.   A reminder that the conspiracy was still a menacing reality clinched the matter.   Murena was acquitted.   Indeed to condemn a man at a highly inopportune time, merely because he was guilty, would have been an outrage on Roman commonsense.   The criminal courts had inherited something of the spirit of the old trials before the popular Assembly, where the real issue was—Do you mean to punish him, or do you not?

1033.   By this success the continuity of government policy was assured.   As for the new tribunes, Cato was one, and his tough loyalty was a tower of strength.   Murena bore him[2] no grudge; Cato's little ways were well known.   But Cicero's anxieties were great.   The conspirators in Rome were enlisting all sorts of men in their cause, so as to be ready to cooperate with Catiline whenever he should appear.   Moreover it was known that risings might at any moment occur in various parts of Italy to which he had sent emissaries.   In particular Capua, where the gladiatorial barracks were more than usually full (owing to the removal thither of some companies from Rome), was a danger-spot.   But the energy of the quaestor P. Sestius was successful in preventing any serious outbreak.   Meanwhile the campaign of slander against Cicero was not abandoned, for even now it seemed possible to detach from him some of his noble supporters, who had no mind to incur odium for his sake.   It was said that he had driven Catiline into banishment without a fair trial; and the outlaw wrote to a number of the nobles in the same tone, asserting his innocence and explaining his flight by the patriotic wish not to provoke civil strife.   But in a letter to Q. Catulus he told a very different[3] story, admitting that since his

[1] Evidence about Crassus and Caesar neatly summarized by Summers on Sallust *Cat.* 48.

[2] Plutarch *Cato min.* 21.

[3] Sall. *Cat.* 35. I believe with von Stern that this letter is in substance genuine. Sallust is much more correct in the latter part of his story. Compare 44 §§ 4—6 with Cic. *Cat.* III § 12.

defeat for the consulship he had become the champion of ruined men (*miseri*). This was nothing less than a declaration of war on the propertied classes. He added a reference to the elevation of unworthy persons, meaning Cicero. This letter Catulus read out to the Senate, and the members saw that after all Cicero was their man. This episode seems to belong to the latter part of November. The position of the conspirators in Rome was now an embarrassing one. To wait for Catiline's appearance was hopeless, he being held in check by gathering forces. Still the slow Lentulus dallied. The hot hasty Cethegus urged action, for their enterprise was not one suited for a waiting strategy. At last he moved Lentulus, and the festival of the Saturnalia (19 Dec.) was fixed for carrying out their urban programme[1] of fire and blood. So long a further delay was of course a blunder. To give time to Catiline was to give time to Cicero. But as yet no evidence had come to hand sufficient to make it safe for the upstart consul to arrest Roman nobles. There must be no sort of mistake, or the 'new man' would pay dearly for his haste.

1034. An accident relieved him of his difficulty in a highly dramatic manner. The Allobroges, a tribe on the Rhone, now included in the Transalpine province, had got into the hands of the Roman usurers who swarmed in Gaul. Growing restive under their burdens, they sent a deputation to Rome to seek redress from the Senate, and these deputies happened to arrive just at this juncture. It occurred to Lentulus that here was a very useful alliance ready to hand, for the Gauls were discontented and brave, and well able to furnish cavalry, of which the rebel army was in great need. The envoys, approached by Umbrenus, were quite ready to listen to proposals. They were introduced to the leading conspirators, who foolishly told them of the plot. But the Gauls, fickle by nature and indifferent to Roman quarrels, soon reflected that it would pay them better to betray the conspiracy and earn (so they hoped) the gratitude of the government. Through their Roman patron[2] they were introduced to the consul, who told them to go on approving the plot and making offers of help until they had secured damning evidence against the chief conspirators. This could hardly be other than their own autographs, for Roman citizens would never have been convicted of treason on the sole evidence of barbarians. The dissolute and stupid plotters, weary no doubt of long delays, walked into the trap.

---

[1] Plut. *Cic.* 18 has preserved a characteristic story that in the massacre the children of Pompey were to be spared and held as hostages till terms could be made with the conqueror of the East.

[2] Q. Fabius Sanga, probably a relative of the Q. Fabius (Allobrogicus) who conquered the tribe in 121 B.C.

They gave the envoys solemn pledges, written and sealed, and addressed to the Allobrogian authorities. Volturcius was to accompany them home by way of Faesulae, with a letter to Catiline, urging him to enlist slaves, and they were to make a treaty with the chief conspirator. Cicero then sent two praetors with soldiers to arrest the party as they left for the North. They were neatly ambushed and seized on the Mulvian bridge, which crossed the Tiber a little way above Rome, on the night of the second of December.

1035. The consul had now his witnesses and documentary evidence. He did not open[1] the letters, for fear of being accused of tampering with them. He sent out to fetch Lentulus and the other leaders, and to summon the Senate. Meanwhile the house of Cethegus was searched, and a large store of arms and combustibles discovered. At the meeting of the Senate the evidence of Volturcius[2] and the Gauls was taken, the seals and handwriting of the letters verified, and the contents read. Some feeble attempts to explain away the facts were made, but soon collapsed; the guilt of the culprits was too plain, and the House was in no mood to stand shuffling. An order was passed requiring Lentulus to resign his praetorship, after which he and the rest, being now all private citizens, were to be put under the charge of certain named senators, of whom[3] Crassus and Caesar were two. In the absence of a proper gaol, this was the only way, to make men of position responsible for the safe-keeping of state-prisoners. Lentulus resigned his office, doubtless trusting that this storm, like many others, would blow over. Cicero, still alive to the danger of a reaction in public opinion, had taken care[4] to have the examination of the witnesses and the evidence of the plot fully reported by skilled senators. All this information he at once had copied out by a staff of clerks, and sent out copies broad-cast over Italy. The debate on the fate of the conspirators was adjourned. But before dispersing the House passed a vote of thanks to the watchful consul, and ordered a public thanksgiving[5] (*supplicatio*) to the gods for having enabled him to save the state. It was now urgently necessary to calm the agitation in the city and to bring the multitude, which contained so many disorderly and disloyal elements, into sympathy with the government. Accordingly that very afternoon (3rd Dec.) Cicero addressed the people in a speech[6] of great

[1] Disregarding the advice of some noble advisers, who still doubted the guilt of the accused. Cic. *Cat.* III § 7.

[2] He was allowed to turn state-evidence under promise of pardon. Cic. *Catil.* III § 8.

[3] Presumably selected purposely in order to place them in a difficulty.

[4] Cic. *pro Sulla* §§ 40—44. It appears that Sulla's prosecutor accused Cicero afterwards (in 62) of having garbled the report.

[5] Hitherto only voted for signal victories in war.   [6] Third Catilinarian speech.

skill. The telling points are easily detected. The completeness of the proof is an answer to possible expressions of doubt. The references to intended arson are meant to bring home to the poor the fact that the conspirators would have burnt their roofs over their heads. Shelter was the one thing that all, even the poorest, had to lose, and Sallust points out that nothing turned the masses against the conspirators so much as the belief that they were going to have burnt down Rome. The design of employing Gauls in Italy enabled the speaker to appeal to old prejudices and fears. A passage recounting recent signs from heaven, inferring the interest of the gods[1] in the well-being of the state, and attributing to them the present escape from imminent destruction, is especially notable. It is not only an appeal to the forces of superstition, but also an indirect way of investing the acts of the consul and the Senate with divine sanction. Cicero knew his audience : it is only in addressing the masses that he gives so much credit to the immortal gods as compared with himself. In this speech he even went so far as to forestall future attacks of his enemies. He artfully compares his victory at home with those of Pompey abroad. But, he adds, I cannot go away and leave my foes dead or prostrate behind me, I must live among those whom I have defeated ; it is for you to protect the man who has protected you. This foreboding was no groundless nervousness, as the sequel was to shew. For the present the consul was popular with the crowd.

1036. The 4th December was not an idle day. An informer gave evidence implicating Crassus in the plot, but the Senate voted the man a liar. Some suggested that it was a trick got up to shield the guilty by interesting the millionaire in their safety. Others thought it a move of Cicero to muzzle one who was a confirmed popularity-hunter and might give trouble. Nobody really trusted Crassus, and nobody but Caesar understood how to manage him. More strange still is Sallust's other story, that Catulus and C. Piso, the stubborn consul of 67, put great pressure on Cicero to arrange for information to be laid against Caesar, whose notorious indebtedness gave colour to suspicion. Cicero refused to be concerned in such an iniquity, so these rancorous nobles circulated lying reports on their own account, with such effect that some Roman Knights, standing on guard before the temple where the Senate was sitting, threatened to kill Caesar as he came out of the House. Sallust was a Caesarian,

---

[1] He also called attention to the fact that the new statue of Jupiter, ordered two years before but only now completed, had just been set up overlooking the Forum. Halm on § 20 of the speech well remarks that this strange coincidence was probably due to the management of Cicero himself.

and this version is supposed to be a partial[1] one, designed to clear his great chief from an awkward stain on the record of his earlier days. It may be so. Our evidence does not admit[2] a final condemnation or acquittal of Caesar. At the worst it may serve to illustrate the fine discretion of Cicero, who had enough on his hands already. At the best it is one more testimony to the consul's sense of honour. The voting of rewards to the informers was another business transacted on this day. In the background of public events another sort of persons were astir. Freedmen and clients of Lentulus and Cethegus got together slaves and ruffians, and prepared to rescue their patrons by force. But the consul's guards were found already posted, and the attempt had to be abandoned. On the following day he summoned the Senate, and laid before them the question what was to be done with the men in custody. It is above all things necessary to bear in mind that the Senate was not a court of justice, and had no power to condemn a man to death or banishment. Death could be inflicted by a general in the field in virtue of the *imperium* (*militiae*) in its fullest degree. From a sentence of the magistrate within the city precincts, resting on the *imperium* (*domi*) in its lesser degree, the citizen at least had the right of appealing to the people. The responsibility for executing a sentence of death lay on the magistrate, not on the Senate. The question underlying that raised by the consul was, How far could the Senate relieve him of that responsibility? Did the proclamation of martial law by the 'last decree' and the declaration that the culprits were public enemies justify the consul in dealing with them as on the battlefield? The challenge to the Senate in the recent case of Rabirius had been a failure. But Saturninus was at any rate killed in a riot. Was it not a step further to put prisoners to death in cold blood?

1037. The famous debate[3] of the 5th December has reached us in a more copious tradition than any similar event of antiquity. We know too that special pains were taken by Cicero to secure a full and accurate report of the speeches. Yet we have various versions, not only of proposals made but even of the sequence of debate. We are only concerned with the issues raised on this memorable occasion, and

---

[1] But it is to be observed that in comparing Cato with Caesar (*Cat.* 54) he certainly shews no preference for the latter.

[2] The posthumous imputation contained in Cicero's memoirs cannot go for much. Plut. *Crass.* 13.

[3] Authorities. Sallust *Cat.* 50—53, Cic. *Catil.* IV and *ad Att.* XII 21 § 1, Suetonius *Jul.* 14, Plutarch *Cic.* 20—22, *Cato min.* 22—24, *Caes.* 7, 8, Velleius II 35, Appian *civ.* II 5, 6, Dion Cass. XXXVII 35, 36. An admirably fair account is given in Mr Strachan-Davidson's Life of Cicero.

the forces that came into play, throwing as they do much light on the condition of the Republic in this stormy period. The following account is based on the versions of Sallust and Cicero. Silanus consul elect moved that the prisoners, and four others if and when caught, should suffer the extreme[1] punishment. All the rest of the consular members followed suit. Of the praetorians, Caesar, praetor elect, first offered opposition. By taking part in the debate[2] he waived any objection to the procedure by which the House was virtually acting as a court of justice. His objections were largely legal, but this particular line of argument might well seem to him inopportune, more likely in the present state of feeling to rouse suspicion against himself than to save the lives of the prisoners. Nor again did he attempt to minimize their guilt. But he urged that to give free course to the wrath of the moment was both un-Roman and unwise, and hinted at the reaction that would surely follow. Not that death, the end of sufferings, was the worst of penalties; but it could not be recalled. He no doubt meant his hearers to reflect that reaction would assail the living, being unable to revive the dead. Moreover, what about the law of the matter? If the criminals were not to be scourged because of the Porcian laws, why should they be put to death in disregard of the facilities for voluntary exile now normally granted by the statutes even to men found guilty by regular courts? Was not this to swallow the greater scruple while straining at the less? Did not history shew that the sequel of evil precedents could not be controlled, and who knew but they might recoil on their creators? Would it not be well to imitate the wise moderation of their fathers? He wound up by moving that their property be confiscated, that they be put in chains and handed over for custody to the strongest *municipia* of Italy, that these towns be held severally answerable, under heavy penalties, each for the safe detention of the prisoner assigned to it, and that any proposal to Senate or Assembly for their release should be forbidden: any attempt of the kind was to be declared a treasonable attack on the public safety. On which we may remark (1) unless we are grossly misinformed, the conspirators were for the most part bankrupt or nearly so, (2) the Senate had no more right to put citizens in chains and imprison them than to put them to death, (3) to impose such a burden on corporate towns of Roman[3] citizens was unfair, perhaps unprecedented, as a command,

---

[1] In Plutarch ἐσχάτην δίκην, no doubt a translation of *ultimum supplicium*. See Summers on Sall. *Cat.* 50 § 4.

[2] Of course the speech given by Sallust is in form the writer's own work. But the points are certainly in the main authentic.

[3] The confinement of Perseus and of the suspected Achaeans took place before the Latin colonies had received the Roman *civitas*. See Cic. *Catil.* IV §§ 7, 8, and above §§ 845, 847.

while if put as a request it was not likely to be granted, (4) nobody knew better than Caesar that to prohibit proposals for reléase was idle talk, for even a statute to that effect could itself be repealed, and the demagogues of that time would pay little regard to a mere decree of the Senate. In short, if the House had accepted this impudent motion, it would still have assumed powers not belonging to it. It would have caused great irritation in Italy, and it would have effected nothing. Caesar had asserted the prisoners' guilt in the strongest terms, but his proposal offered a ready means of setting them at large. Some tribune of his own circle would probably soon have done so, and earned the gratitude of several *municipia* to boot.

1038. But Caesar knew his men. The average senator was above all things anxious to save his own skin, and some of them, playing to the 'popular' faction, had stayed away. The suggestion of legal scruples, and the hints of reaction to follow, had shaken the nerve of many a noble member. Silanus himself tried to explain away the force of his motion. Cicero's own friends[1] leant to Caesar's proposal, as exposing the consul to less danger. But the next set speech was that of Cicero[2] himself. We have it as edited, perhaps rather freely, for publication. The points on which he insists most effectively are these. The House is not to consider his personal risk, but to vote for what it deems best in the interest of the whole state. It must make up its mind speedily, for the conspiracy is widespread, and a faltering policy will only encourage risings outside. No penalty can be too severe. As for the Sempronian law, reserving the extreme penalty for the vote of the Assembly, it applies to citizens only, and these criminals are public enemies and cannot benefit thereby. Gracchus himself was put to death without a vote[3] of the people. Senators must not be daunted by talk of opposition. Their decision can and shall be carried out, whatever it be. And in this crisis all sorts and conditions of men are displaying unanimity to a degree hitherto unknown. There is no doubt a certain half-heartedness about the speech, as of a man neither convinced nor convincing. The fact of his taking Caesar's proposal seriously shews how great the effect of its suggestions had been. The point about citizens and enemies was on the face of it a quibble, but it must be admitted that if we assume the prisoners to be *cives* it is not easy to justify the motion of Caesar. It was only as *hostes* that the Senate could claim to judge them at all, and even then only in the form of giving its sanction and approval to a course of action for which the consul, not the Senate, might

[1] His brother Quintus, then praetor elect, is said to have been one of these.
[2] Fourth Catilinarian speech.
[3] (But not in cold blood.)

afterwards be called to account. Cicero did not demand a sentence of death, but he shewed that he preferred it. In arguing that Caesar's proposal was the more severe, he can hardly have convinced his hearers.

1039. What really decided the issue of the debate was the speech of Cato. Hearty and unwavering, he lashed the nerveless hesitation of the nobles, engrossed in the pursuit of ease and luxury. He ascribed the lenient proposal of Caesar to sympathy, if not direct connexion, with the conspirators. He declared that the crisis was vital, and would brook no delay. The sentence on the prisoners would decide the fate of the insurgents in Etruria. Heaven helped those who helped themselves. Assuming that the House meant to save the state, he ended with a motion declaring the proved guilt of the accused, and requiring their execution as criminals taken[1] in the act. This was a logical deduction from the Senate's 'last decree.' If that decree was valid, what we call a 'state of siege' existed, and Rome was under martial law. To draw back now meant no less than to abdicate for ever the power of dealing with emergencies, and for the present to increase indefinitely the prestige of Catiline. The Senate took heart, and the motion of Cato was carried[2] by a great majority. A feeble attempt was made at the last to defer a final decision on the pretext of giving time for further inquiries and preparations, but this proposal, made by Tiberius Claudius Nero[3], a man probably already connected with Caesar, was never actually put to the vote. The position was now this. In using the extreme powers of the *imperium* under stress of dire necessity, to prevent the spread of the insurrection becoming a danger to the public safety, the consul had the moral support of the Senate. The sequel fully justified the forecast of Cato. The execution of Lentulus and the rest utterly ruined the enterprise of Catiline.

1040. Every moment was precious, and Cicero did not court further danger by delay. The five traitors[4] were promptly taken to the dungeon (*carcer*), beneath which was a noisome chamber, the ancient *tullianum* or 'well-house,' originally a cistern hewn in the tufa rock. Into this dark and filthy hole, where Jugurtha and many another Enemy of the Roman People had met a cruel fate on the day of their victor's triumph, they were lowered one by one, and strangled. The

---

[1] Sallust *Cat.* 52 § 36 *de manifestis rerum capitalium* is really no more than an assertion of the power of the consul under the *senatusconsultum ultimum*. See Greenidge, *Legal Procedure* pp. 569—571.

[2] The assertion of Clodius (58 B.C.), that Cicero garbled the decree of the Senate, was a mere lie. See Cic. *de domo* § 50.

[3] Grandfather of the future emperor Tiberius.

[4] Lentulus, Cethegus, Statilius, Gabinius, Caeparius, were the five actually caught.

consul, true to the conventional avoidance of words of ill omen, announced that their lives were over.   As he made his way home, he was escorted by a cheering crowd, and the joy of many houses was testified by the flare of torches and lamps lighting up the darkness of the night.   It may be true that even with the mob Cicero was for the moment a hero.   The execution of members of the upper classes was a small concern to them.   But they would soon forget their escape from the perils of conflagration.   Caesar on the other hand was under a cloud.   His persistent opposition to the vote for death had caused his life to be threatened in the Senate, and until the new year, and with it his praetorship, began he thought it well to stay away from the sittings of the House.

1041.   While the detection and punishment of the chief confederates left behind by Catiline was engaging the attention of Rome, several minor outbreaks had occurred elsewhere.   Those in Apulia and Bruttium seem to have been quite trivial.   In the North, where the neighbourhood of Catiline's main army made the movements more dangerous, full precautions had been taken.   Q. Metellus Celer, to whom Cicero had passed on Cisalpine Gaul, promptly arrested suspected persons, and C. Murena, whom his brother had left in charge, did the same beyond the Alps.   The force under Catiline himself is said to have reached the number of 20,000 men, but only part were properly armed, and the news from Rome at once led to wholesale desertions.   He knew not where to turn.   Metellus barred the way northwards, the army of Antonius was advancing from the South.   It was commanded by the consul's lieutenant M. Petreius, a veteran officer, for Antonius, unwilling to fight against his former associate, was opportunely disabled by gout.   The battle took place[1] near Pistoria.   The government forces lost heavily, and of the insurgents, now reduced to about 3000 desperate men, not a single free Roman survived.   Their leader sold his life dearly.   His head was sent to Rome, but after this proof of his death he seems to have been allowed burial.   We may believe that he was a fine man wasted, if we lay stress on the attachment of his friends and blame the age for his crimes.   There were those who regretted his fall, and, when the base Antonius a few years after was condemned in a criminal trial, we hear that some wild fellows celebrated the occasion[2] by a feast and offerings of flowers at the grave of Catiline.

---

[1] 5 Jan. 62 B.C.
[2] Cicero *pro Flacco* § 95 (59 B.C.).

1042. Note on the history of the conspiracies comprised in the above chapter.

I had long been convinced that the old view, in which Catiline appears as the head of two conspiracies, or one spread over several years, was highly improbable, if not incredible. It rests on the authority of Sallust, who wrote as a Caesarian advocate and with a fine disregard of chronology. Thorough examination and comparison of the other authorities has I think completely destroyed the credit of his narrative where it conflicts with them. I would mention the following treatises as having in my opinion settled all the important points, and enabled me to give what I hope is a fair and consistent version of the events in question. The learned authors refer to many other works (for the subject has a large literature of its own) and their criticisms correct the errors of standard writers such as Drumann and Mommsen.

(i) *Catilina's und Cicero's Bewerbung um den Consulat für das Jahr* 63. By H. Wirz. (Zürich, 1864.)

(ii) *Sallustius über Catilinas Candidatur im Jahr* 688. By C. John. (Rheinisches Museum, 1876.)

(iii) *Die Entstehungsgeschichte der Catilinarischen Verschwörung.* By C. John. (Jahrbücher für classische Philologie, achter Supplementband, 1876.)

(iv) *Catilina und die Parteikämpfe in Rom der Jahre* 66—63. By E. von Stern. (Dorpat, 1883.)

(v) *Die Berichte ueber die Catilinarische Verschwoerung.* By E. Schwartz. (Hermes, 1897.)

Of these, the third is a massive article, a classic of its kind; the fourth the best general account I have seen; the last is mainly concerned with divining the genesis of Sallust's perversions, how far convincingly, I will not venture to say.

Note added in 1922. I have refrained from rewriting parts of this chapter to suit with the conclusions of Dr Hardy's great article in *Journ. Rom. Stud.* 1917. That the analysis of Caesar's policy during the year 63, the relations of Crassus and Caesar to Catiline, their probable reversion to an understanding with Pompey through Metellus Nepos in the latter half of the year, are presented with singular fairness and force, can hardly be denied. The psychological treatment is most acute, and generally convincing. But the restoration of history is so thoroughgoing that I am at present not quite able to keep pace with it. Therefore, as the article in several important points confirms my version, I have let my text stand in the part dealing with the conspiracies.

CHAPTER LII.

1043. THE Catilinarian conspiracy had been put down, and at the beginning of the new year (62) Antonius was free to slip away and continue his shameful career as the governor of Macedonia. Under the leadership of Cicero the civil government of Rome had to the general surprise asserted itself once more. It had ventured on bloodshed necessary for maintaining order, without depending upon the aid of a victorious general at the head of an army for the means of doing so. To men of hopeful temperament or blinded by virtuous pedantry it might seem that the working of the Republic was still not impossible. Difficulties might be smoothed over by judicious concessions, and corruptions in detail got rid of by firmness and partial reforms. But no thorough remodelling of the constitution on republican lines was seriously thought of; nor was it possible, for the force by which a beginning must be made was wholly lacking. Hence in the years that followed neither the eloquent and politic Cicero nor the stubborn incorruptible Cato could avail anything. They merely proved that the republican statesman was out of date. The return of Pompey could not be long delayed. That he might make himself supreme if he chose was obvious. If he did not do so, it became a question of the first importance what his position would be. It was a new and unforeseen strain on the Roman constitution that it was called upon to absorb a potential emperor. Pompey's six years in the East had made him more than ever unsuited to form one of a commonplace and jealous aristocracy, and he had probably no notion of the extent to which the relations of men and parties had changed during his absence. He can hardly have guessed that he would find neither *optimates* nor *populares* at his disposal, and that the attempt to stand aloof, dignified and dominant, would land him in the complications of political intrigue and end by making him the ally of Crassus and the tool of Caesar.

1044. Such knowledge of home affairs as could be got from letters he had in abundance. In particular he knew of the measures taken against the conspiracy, and saw that the unexpected vigilance and courage of Cicero was rendering unnecessary the services which he was himself most willing to offer.   For the Indispensable Man to land in Italy only to find that the state had been saved without his help, was a situation to be avoided if possible.   So he sent one of his officers, Q. Metellus Nepos, to Rome in time for the tribunician elections.   Metellus was to become tribune for 62, and his business was to agitate for the recall of Pompey to restore order.   Cato, it is said, met him close to Rome, and guessed that he was come for no good.   Giving up other plans, Cato at once stood for the tribunate himself.   Both were elected.   Even before they entered on office, the harangues of Nepos had begun to embarrass Cicero, and led him to appeal to Cato in his defence of Murena.   Once in office (10 Dec.) Nepos proposed that Pompey should be summoned to defend the state.   But the executions of the 5th December had already ruined the hopes of Catiline.   The agent could not carry out his instructions in the letter, but he resolved as far as he could to follow their spirit. If Pompey could not be brought in to filch away the credit of Cicero, as he had that of Crassus and Lucullus, perhaps it might serve much the same purpose if the acts of Cicero were held up as illegal.   When the consul laid down his office at the end of the year, he had to swear publicly that he had obeyed the laws.   If an outgoing consul had anything that he especially wanted to say to the people, this was his chance.   Cicero was not the man to lose it.   But Nepos refused to let him do more than take the formal oath.   He came forward and swore in a loud voice that he had saved the state.   Partial tradition adds that the whole meeting responded by affirming that he had sworn truly.   No doubt he was well cheered, partly for cleverly eluding the malice of the tribune: but it did not mean much.   The hostility of Metellus was a serious threat, for all knew that the conqueror of the East was in the background.   Nor was Metellus the only enemy of Cicero.   There were the relatives and friends of the men put to death, and the trials and condemnations of some of their accomplices added to these the friends of exiles.   Caesar himself, now praetor, was named by one informer, but the man was on other grounds suspected of foul play, and the matter dropped ; Cicero, when appealed to by Caesar, exonerated him.   In short, the year 62 began with bad omens for Cicero.   He had lost his hold on the 'popular' party, and depended on keeping the Senate and Knights in harmony.   The chagrin of Pompey more than outweighed the approval of Cato.   That Cato publicly called him the Father of his Country amid popular applause did not help him to defeat his enemies.   Nepos was still going about denouncing him for having put Roman citizens to death without trial, and even after the fall of Catiline still urging the recall of Pompey.

1045.   The competition for the great man's favour was now

extreme.   It was Caesar whose keen insight discovered the way to
secure it.   Pompey was greedy of compliments and unable to endure
rivalry.   Caesar began his year of praetorship by a clever move in the
religious department, which came naturally from him as chief pontiff.
The Capitoline temple had been rebuilt and dedicated by Catulus, but
never properly finished off.   Caesar found fault with this neglect, and
challenged Catulus to produce his accounts and shew how the public
money had been spent.   He proposed that the completion of the work
should be entrusted to Pompey.   Thus he ingeniously gained three
objects at once.   He weakened his respectable opponent Catulus, he
pleased Pompey by representing him as the one man to whom the
commonwealth looked for efficiency and by the prospective honour of
having his name recorded in the inscription as the restorer of the
temple, and he soothed any soreness that Pompey might feel in
reference to the pontifical election.   This proposal the strong opposition of the nobles caused him to drop, but its purpose had been
served.   Pompey was of course informed, and the reminder of the
jealousy of the nobles would not be lost on him.   Caesar also
supported the proposal for recalling Pompey, and thus forced the
Senate to resist it fiercely.   Cato as tribune blocked every attempt to
carry it.   Caesar and Nepos harangued meetings, and rioting and
bloodshed followed in the usual course.   The Senate now acted with
unwonted boldness, in which the hand of Cato is probably to be
traced.   We have two[1] versions of the story.   According to Dion, the
Senate passed the 'last decree,' empowering the consuls to use force.
Nepos had no means of resisting this, so he issued a formal protest
and fled to Pompey, regardless of the fact that as tribune he was
bound to residence in Rome.   This is not inconsistent with the version
of Suetonius[2], who says that Caesar supported Metellus in going on
with his seditious legislation in the teeth of his colleagues' veto, until
the pair of them were suspended from their official functions by a
decree of the Senate.   But Caesar went on with his juridical duties all
the same, till he found that armed force was going to be used, when
he laid aside the signs of office and withdrew for a time into private
life.   Soon a mob gathered and invited him to resume his official
station under their protection.   To this he would not lend himself,
and induced them to disperse quietly.   Hereupon the Senate, surprised
at his moderation, hastened to thank him and cancelled the suspensory
decree.

[1] Dion Cass. XXXVII 43.   See Cic. *ad fam.* v 2 § 9.
[2] Sueton. *Jul.* 15, 16.   We may recall the action of the Senate in the case of Saturninus
(§ 809) but the right of the Senate to act in this way is not clear.   In the present instance it
may perhaps be a corollary of the *senatusconsultum ultimum* loosely and variously reported
by the two writers.   In any case it is a suspension of function, not a deprivation of office.
See Madvig, *Verfassung und Verwaltung* I 304.

1046.   While Caesar had taken pains to shew how highly he valued the absent general, Cicero in the innocence of his heart had written to inform Pompey of his own achievements and was awaiting congratulations.   But that Eminent and would-be Indispensable Man took no pleasure in anything that gave the impression that people in Rome had contrived to do without him.   An official despatch, announcing the settlement of the East, was accompanied by a private letter to Cicero in which he avoided any expression of praise or sympathy. Cicero's reply[1] is pathetic in its timid expostulation.   His disappointment and uneasiness were evidently great.   He had served Pompey's interests well, and he plaintively lets out that he was hoping to enjoy a closer association with his hero, to play the Laelius to the great Africanus of the age.   It was a collision of two types of vanity, the light and generous appealing to the heavy and selfish.   The self-centred Pompey could not forgive the man who had had the bad taste to succeed in doing what he himself would have been willing to do. Cicero therefore took little by his humble remonstrance.   Caesar had shewn a proper regard for the feelings of a great man clumsily conscious of his own greatness.   He had contrived that when Pompey did return he should find in his real enemy a natural ally.   Caesar was content to seem for the present a satellite: Pompey was too shallow a judge to know that a man without vanity is dangerous.

1047.   Meanwhile it was no easy matter to carry on government in Rome.   We have seen that there was much disorder in the city.   The discredit of Caesar in the Senate and the threats of his enemies had so far alarmed the needy rabble for the safety of their favourite that they gathered round the Senate House in a menacing manner. Things appeared so serious that even Cato stooped to pacify the hungry mob with an extension[2] of the corn-doles, which laid a great additional burden on the treasury.   In the background of politics intrigue and mischief-making were busy.   Cicero warned Pompey that his old enemies were now his friends, since the news of his settlement of the East ; meaning no doubt Caesar and Crassus, who had failed in their designs on Egypt, and now thought it wise to glorify and court the great conqueror whose return was evidently near. Metellus Nepos had given his kinsman Metellus Celer, commanding in Cisalpine Gaul, highly coloured accounts of his own treatment by the Senate and the hostility of Cicero, and this produced a rude letter from Celer to the orator, and a soft answer in reply.   Nor were friendly relations between public men promoted by the prosecution of several Catilinarians in the earlier part of the year.   Cicero too did not improve his own position by everlasting references to his recent achievements, and the sneers of those who found his egotism a bore do

[1] Cic. *ad fam.* v 7.   [2] Plutarch *Caes.* 8, *Cato min.* 26.

not seem to have taught him wisdom. In the summer he was engaged on a case in which there was good excuse for dwelling on the affair of Catiline. P. Cornelius Sulla, one of the men elected consul in 66 and unseated for *ambitus*, was brought to trial[1] on charges of public violence (*vis*) connected with the conspiracies of Catiline. His colleague Autronius, and some of his own relatives, had been implicated in the design, and were in exile. Sulla's own conduct, particularly in gathering a body of gladiators, had been somewhat suspicious. But the evidence against him seems to have been indirect, and Cicero not only made a powerful speech in his defence, but asserted of his own knowledge that during the proceedings of the previous year nothing had turned up to inculpate his client. Sulla was acquitted. He was a very wealthy man, and at this time a creditor of Cicero. The great orator was buying[2] from Crassus a fine house on the Palatine, suited to his rank, and Sulla was one of the friends who advanced him large sums for the purpose. Cicero was habitually short of ready money. Another case undertaken by him in this year was of far more serious consequence to himself. The Greek poet Archias had passed for a Roman citizen ever since the legislation of 90 and 89 B.C. His domicile was at Heraclea in southern Italy, but he was a native of Antioch. He was now prosecuted under the Alien Act (*lex Papia*) of 65 for improper assumption of the franchise. The case[3] was evidently weak, and Cicero, who chiefly dilated on the literary merits of his client, had no difficulty in procuring an acquittal. But it was one of those cases, common in Rome, where the object was simply to annoy a political opponent, and where the person accused was not the person aimed at. Archias was under the protection of Lucullus, whom he had accompanied to the East, and whose exploits he sang. Lucullus was an enemy of Pompey, and doubtless bore a hand in the opposition to all proposals meant to gratify his rival. He was the person really attacked, and the real assailants were, not the insignificant accuser, but persons acting on the side of Pompey. We can hardly help suspecting that Caesar had some share in the business. Cicero had a difficult choice to make, but recent events had drawn him nearer to the section of genuine aristocrats of whom Lucullus was one, and away from the 'popular' leaders who were competing with him for the favour of Pompey. Moreover Archias had helped to guide the studies of Cicero in his youth, and above all had actually begun a poem on the glorious deeds of his consulship. But by his action in this case the orator was more deeply committed to the *optimates*, with

---

[1] See Reid's Introduction to the *pro Sulla*.
[2] Price over £30,000, Cic. *ad fam.* v 6 § 2.
[3] See Reid's Introduction to the *pro Archia*.

the disadvantage of being more moderate than his company and not really one of their leaders. He was more than ever parted from the *populares*, and the task of conciliating Pompey became at once more necessary and less possible. He was more than ever dependent on the Harmony of the Orders for retaining his public position, indeed for protection against the danger that menaced him. True, Cato was loyal, and strong in his unassailable virtue. But his unbending principles made Cato a rather awkward ally for an opportunist patriot. The great nobles were selfish, and the Knights ruled by considerations of gain. On the whole the prospects of the future were not reassuring.

1048. At the consular election this year (62) the chosen were M. Pupius Piso Calpurnianus and M. Valerius Messalla. The former, a bitter queer-tempered man but of some ability, was one of Pompey's men, sent over to represent his master. The election was even put off to suit his convenience, at Pompey's request. The latter was a noble of some standing, of whom Cicero thought highly. The most striking event in the latter part of the year was the famous scandal caused by P. Clodius. In December there was a nightly gathering of Roman matrons in the house of some leading magistrate to celebrate the mysterious rites of the Good Goddess. The Vestals took part in the proceedings, and every male was rigidly excluded. This year it was held in the house of Caesar, praetor and chief pontiff. Clodius was a lover of Caesar's wife Pompeia, and contrived to enter the house in female dress, in hope of reaching the lady, whose mother-in-law had been an obstacle to their intercourse. But instead of eluding Aurelia he was detected by a maid. The alarm was given, and the rites stopped, to be performed later without pollution. Of course the affair was the talk of Rome. The pontiffs pronounced it a sacrilege. Caesar, whose own infidelities[1] were notorious, was not inclined to make a fuss over the personal outrage, but as chief pontiff he was obliged to do something. So he divorced Pompeia, and prepared to let the matter drop. But religion could not be neglected. The rites of *Bona Dea* were a state function (*pro populo*), which even freethinkers preferred to have duly performed, while the superstitious masses viewed sacrilege with alarm. In January (61) the Senate took up the matter and instructed the consuls to propose a bill for holding an inquiry, with provisions for a specially selected jury. The consuls were divided, Messalla taking the serious view with Cato and others, Piso, who was in charge of the bill, being inclined to wreck the measure if possible. He was a friend of Clodius, and that dissolute

---

[1] Just at this time Pompey divorced his wife Mucia on the ground of an intrigue with Caesar during her husband's absence.

young Patrician had a good deal of influence with the nobles. What with these obstacles and the gangs of ruffians that were being got together, Cicero foresaw trouble. And the situation was rendered more delicate by the return of Pompey. He had dallied long, in hope that something would happen to place him in the coveted position of unquestioned supremacy without the use of force on his part. But things did not take that turn. He landed at Brundisium in December 62, and to the general surprise dismissed his army, to reassemble for the triumph in due course. He reached Rome in January 61. Now was the Senate's opportunity, for a hearty welcome and prompt approval of his acts in the East would surely have gone far to attach him to the nobility. He had really nothing in common with the popular party and its leaders. But the nobles were jealous of pre-eminence and mistrusted his intentions, and his bearing was not to their taste. Even in the Senate he was over-careful not to make himself cheap. Even Cicero, who was eager to stand well with him, was uneasy at his solemnity and reserve. So the nobles, either hostile like Lucullus, or punctilious like Cato, or preoccupied with other matters, missed their chance, and the natural champion of the republican aristocracy was left to be captured by Caesar.

1049. Attempts were of course made to draw from Pompey his opinion on recent affairs and present questions. He expressed respect for the Senate and approved its policy in terms too general to satisfy Cicero. Meanwhile the bill for the trial of Clodius was pressed on. Its opponents tried to get it thrown out in the Assembly by violence and by tampering with the voting-tickets. The Assembly had to be dismissed, and the Senate by a crushing majority instructed the consuls to see the bill through. A way of compromise was found by Hortensius. The clauses for a select jury were dropped, and the choice left to the usual chances of the lot. Then the measure was proposed by the very tribune who had hitherto opposed it. Hortensius and others thought that no jury could acquit Clodius. But after the allotment and challenges the jury finally empanelled was a bad one. Most of them could not afford to act honestly. Appearances were kept up during the preliminary stages of the trial, and conviction seemed certain, but when it came to voting Clodius was acquitted by 31 to 25 in the teeth of the evidence. Crassus had bought the verdict behind the scenes. It was scandalous, but the political bearing of the struggle was perhaps the most important part of it. Clodius was popular with the rabble, and Caesar would do nothing to help the other side. He professed ignorance, and explained the divorce of his wife by saying that it would not do to have her even suspected. Clodius put in an *alibi* as part of his defence. The prosecution called Cicero

as witness, who completely disproved this.   He had seen the accused
in Rome on the very day of the mysteries, only a short time before
they began.   From this time forth Clodius made up his mind to ruin
Cicero, and he was a dangerous enemy, who would stick at nothing.
Cicero was well aware that the rascal would never forgive him, but he
as yet underrated the force of Clodius.   He narrates with some pride
to Atticus[1] how he had cheered up the 'good' (*boni*, the senators of
his way of thinking) whom the result of the trial had left despondent.
He had thundered away at the infamy of the jurors, silenced their
apologists, disappointed the consul Piso of the rich province (Syria)
on which he had counted, faced Clodius himself in debate[2] and in an
exchange of repartees which on his own shewing was enough to have
irritated any man, let alone Clodius.   It was all very fine, but as it
happened it was not business.   The orator imagined that Pompey was
his good friend.   This was a delusion, and the serious fact was that
he had rashly provoked both Caesar and Crassus.

   1050.   The consular election was in sight, and Pompey was busy
spending money to buy one place for a creature of his own, L.
Afranius.   This man was elected together with Q. Metellus Celer.
Afranius was a dull soldier with none of the moral courage and
dexterity needed for politics.   He was a mere tool of Pompey, and
ineffective at that.   Celer, lately governor of Cisalpine Gaul, was of
the aristocratic party.   He was the unhappy husband of the notorious
Clodia, sister of P. Clodius.   The unpleasant misunderstanding
between him and Cicero had hardly cooled down as yet, but they
were soon friends again.   He had little to bind him to Pompey
beyond the fact of their family connexion, and now that the latter had
divorced his sister[3] Mucia he quickly became an opponent.   The
election had been somewhat delayed in order to find time for carrying
a new bribery law, containing[4] the strange provision that if a man
promised money, and did not pay it, he was to go unpunished, but if
he did pay it he was to go on paying a certain sum per Tribe for the
rest of his life.   This grotesque rule seems to be a despairing attempt
to check corruption automatically, by interesting the corruptible mob

---

   [1] Atticus returned to Rome in 65 and left again at the end of 62.   He was now residing
on his great estates in Epirus and employing his capital, in money-lending among other
things.   See Cic. *ad fam.* v 5, *ad Att.* 1 13 § 1.   The present letter is *ad Att.* 1 16.   The
confidential letters to Atticus now become numerous.
   [2] Of the speech *in Clodium et Curionem* only a few fragments remain, but there are some
good notes by the well-informed Scholiast of Bobbio.   How far the written speech agreed
with what Cicero actually said is rather doubtful.   See Cic. *ad Att.* III 12 § 2, 15 § 3.
   [3] Celer and his brother Nepos seem to have been Mucii by birth, adopted by a Metellus.
See Cic. *ad fam.* v 2 § 6.
   [4] So at least says Cic. *ad Att.* 1 16 § 13.   The tribune Lurco was the proposer.

in exacting a fine for its own corruption.   We are led to reflect on
the zeal for electoral purity which had been displayed by the Senate
in recent years.   Time was when they had been less eager for reform
in this direction.   The use of bribery had been on the whole in favour
of the rich nobility as against popular agitators.   But circumstances
had changed.   The aristocratic system was breaking up.   The rise of
eminent individuals, impatient of aristocratic equality, had not been
prevented by the legislation of Sulla, and the overthrow of his constitution had given a new life to the 'popular' party and its active
leaders.   Men of wealth, such as Crassus, were now finding their
support rather in the Assembly than in the Senate.   An immense
amount of capital was ready to be employed at any moment in
advancing the interests of ambitious individuals, who often found it
pay them better to run counter to the interests of the privileged
Order.   Moreover, simple bribery was not the only means of corruption.   It had now become usual to employ bands of armed men in
political strife.   The city swarmed with desperate ruffians, and it was
quite possible that after buying your voters you might not be able to
bring them to the poll in the teeth of a hostile army.   Altogether the
way of the ordinary noble was hard, unless he were content to become
the dependant of one of the great competitors for power.   Most of the
Roman nobles were still men of stouter fibre than to accept such a
position.   Hence they continued to make a fight for the aristocratic
Republic in which they found their honours and their hopes : hence,
as things were, they developed an objection to bribery.   There were
of course enlightened patriots who hated corruption for its own sake,
and saw that it must, if not checked, be the ruin of the Free State, the
government which was at least not a monarchy, the home of freedom
in thought word and deed, the centre of great and glorious traditions,
the *patria* to which they were bound alike by principle and sentiment.
But such men, of whom Cato was the chief, were few, and powerless if
not backed up by others of less vigorous type, and their efforts were
in the long run productive of no result.

1051.   When the trial of Clodius was over, Caesar went off to his
province, the Further[1] Spain.   He was deeply in debt, and his creditors
were pressing, for they did not want to lose sight of him in a far
country from which he might never return.   To quiet them he applied
to his good friend Crassus, who became security for an immense sum[2]
on his behalf.   He then slipped away with all speed, not waiting even
for the Senate to 'equip' (*ornare*) the province by the usual vote of

---

[1] Caesar in Spain.   Suetonius *Jul.* 18, Plutarch *Caes.* 11, 12, Cic. *pro Balbo* § 43 and
Reid's Introduction, Strabo III 5 § 3 (p. 169), Dion Cass. XXXVII 52, 53.
[2] Nearly £200,000.

money troops and staff. He had good reasons for being in a hurry, for he meant to return soon, and to use his governorship to such purpose that he might return with improved prospects. He took with him L. Cornelius Balbus of Gades, the man enfranchised by Pompey after the Sertorian war, as his chief of engineers. We know enough of his year in Spain to say that it was a time of great activity and that he achieved all his objects. But we have few details. A successful war was necessary to strengthen his claims to the consulship, and he found pretexts for campaigns in the West and North West, which were brilliantly successful. Money, also badly needed, he contrived to exact[1] in considerable quantity. Civil administration was not neglected, and in particular he dealt with the question of debt in a reasonable way, by assigning to the creditor $\frac{2}{3}$ of the debtor's yearly income until the debt was wiped out. Another undertaking, in the spirit of the best Roman policy, was the reform and improvement of the great commercial city of Gades, long bound to Rome by treaty. Caesar had known it in the days of his provincial quaestorship. Balbus now induced him to act as umpire in some internal disputes, and in some way to remodel the institutions of the city. He also got leave to extend its area, a step which added greatly to its prosperity. The favours of Caesar to Gades were not exhausted. His large imperial mind, free from Roman and Italian jealousy, could see clearly the benefits to be derived from the full development of the loyalty and resources of every part of the Roman world. Before the middle of the next year he had done what he meant to do. He had gained military experience in varied operations by land and sea, and had shewn his power of managing his men, whom he left contented with their rewards. He travelled back to Rome to be in time for the summer elections, with increased reputation and money in hand.

    1052. During his absence Pompey was left to find his way as best he might in the tangle of Roman politics. Soon after his return, having divorced Mucia, he tried to form a matrimonial alliance with the family of Cato, who was not to be captured by other means. But Cato declined the proposal, not wishing to be embarrassed by the connexion. With Cicero he had no difficulty in keeping on good terms. The orator made every effort to secure intimacy, but it does not appear that they became close friends. Cicero felt himself isolated. He missed the congenial company of Atticus, and his brother Quintus had gone to be governor of Asia. At the end of September[2] (61) Pompey celebrated his great triumph. It surpassed

---

[1] But he seems to have relieved the provincials of some imposts. See (Caes.) *bell. Hisp.* 42.

[2] Plutarch *Pomp.* 45, Appian *Mithr.* 116, 117, Dion Cass. XXXVI 2.

all previous exhibitions of the kind, particularly in the number of potentates and peoples whose conquest it recorded, in the immense area of land and sea over which his victories extended, in the number of captives notable either as members of royal families or as renowned leaders or as specimens of far-off races hardly known by name. Nor was the procession solely a record of conquest and destruction. The constructive extension of empire, the establishment of provinces and foundation of numerous cities, the prospective increase of imperial revenues, all found expression in the details of the splendid show. We have seen how deliberately Pompey had prepared for this event long beforehand, collecting suitable captives to be exhibited when the time came. His greed of fame was marked in relation to Crete. Metellus Creticus had captured the two chief Cretan leaders, and meant to shew them in his triumph, which did not take place until the year 62. But Pompey had procured a tribune to intervene, and the men were claimed for him on the pretext that their surrender was a transaction covered by his general inclusive powers. It was characteristically small-minded of him to grudge another man a little prize. There was one improvement in this triumph. None of the captives[1] paraded were put to death, or even led in chains. Another event of the year was the appointment of censors, but they seem to have done little or nothing beyond revising the roll of the Senate and letting some contracts. The news from Transalpine Gaul[2] is interesting in its relation to past and future events. It would appear that the envoys of the Allobroges had returned home rewarded and thanked for their services, but without gaining from the Senate any effective redress of their countrymen's grievances. The tribe rose in revolt and overran a considerable part of the province. The governor C. Pomptinus[3] succeeded with some difficulty in putting down the rising. But there was evidently unrest in Gaul and a prospect of trouble to come.

1053. These things however were not such as materially to influence the working of the Republic. The relation of Pompey to the Senate was the really important matter. He had two immediate objects, the confirmation of his Settlement of the East, and the provision of lands for allotment to his disbanded soldiers. The latter was indeed the raising of a new question. Pompey did not want to oust present landholders and plant garrisons of adherents in Italy after the example of Sulla. It was a form of pensioning, for which there existed no provision in the old Roman system. But the

---

[1] Mithradates was already dead.
[2] Dion Cass. XXXVII 47, 48, Livy ep. 103.
[3] He had been one of the praetors who arrested the envoys on the Mulvian bridge.

assumption that the citizen came from his farm at the call of duty, and returned to it if he survived the war, was long ago obsolete. Soldiering was a profession, and a profession that engrossed the energies of a man's best years of life.   Most of the minor occupations in which the old soldier of modern times ekes out a pension were closed to the discharged Roman veteran by the employment of slaves.   Slavery also degraded the labour of the artisan, and for a freeman to become an unskilled labourer, the workmate of barbarian bondmen, was too dreadful to be thought of.   Farming was practically the only honourable resource, and even a small farmer would expect to keep a slave or two as a part of his stock.   And now the relation of the veteran to his old commander was far closer than his relation to the state.   It was to Pompey that the army of the East was looking for a provision against old age.   For the moment they were not penniless.   Each foot-soldier had received a bounty[1] on discharge, and the lucky or thrifty ones had doubtless brought money home with them.   But these sums were melting away, and Pompey knew that he must press the matter forward, or the allotments would come too late.   There was money for buying land, for he had paid vast sums into the treasury, and the new yearly revenues were beginning to accrue.   If he had kept his army together, he might have dictated his own terms.   But he now met with stubborn opposition.   As for the confirmation of his acts, he required that the Senate should approve them as a whole.   In fact he regarded himself as having been a commissioner with full powers of final settlement in whatever questions might arise.   But by upsetting arrangements made by Lucullus, and by his high-handed treatment of Metellus Creticus, he had made enemies who were eager for a chance of humbling him. His pretentious reserve was offensive to the nobles, while the dismissal of his army left them free to thwart his wishes.   Cato was ready to support any movement against excessive power of individuals, and he with Lucullus and others insisted that the Senate should discuss the Pompeian settlement in detail, confirming or revising it point by point.   Pompey had expected a very different reception.   He had shewn (not for the last time) a lack of psychological insight, in supposing that the Roman nobles would yield to pretensions unsupported by overwhelming force.   Time went by, and the evidence of his utter helplessness only stiffened the opposition.   It was clear that his refusal to be a second Sulla, whatever its motive, had been a tactical blunder.

1054.   If Pompey had been more adroit, and less wrapped up in

---

[1] Between £50 and £60 of our money, cavalry and centurions of course considerably more.

his own dignity, there were two matters before the Senate at this time that might have enabled him to put pressure on the House. Both threatened to destroy that Harmony of the Orders, without which the recent revival of the Senate's power could never have taken place. First, the Senate had a bill prepared to deal with judicial corruption. If this became law, the Knights and *tribuni aerarii* who served on any jury would be liable to punishment for taking bribes, as senatorial members were by the letter of Sulla's law. The classes affected were indignant, and Cicero, to whom the Harmony of the Orders was the foundation of practical politics, tried to talk the House into giving up the project, but without success. He knew[1] that he had a bad case, but what was an opportunist patriot to do? Secondly, there was a shameless demand from the side of the capitalists. The syndicate that had bought the revenues of the province Asia for the next censorial period declared that in their eagerness to secure the contract they had made too high a bid. They coolly requested the Senate to cancel the contract. It was Crassus who egged them on to this step. Cicero, in fear of the probable estrangement of the Equestrian Order from the Senate, supported their claim. But through the opposition of Cato and others the matter dragged on till well into the next year, only to receive a settlement from a more dexterous and less scrupulous hand than that of Pompey.

1055. The year 60 opened with a number of unsettled questions pressing for solution and a complicated strife of interests. The tribune L. Flavius, a satellite of Pompey, came forward with an agrarian bill[2] for providing the desired allotments. Some of its clauses appear to have implied a disturbance of the land-settlement of Sulla, others to have carried it further by proposing to distribute the Etrurian land which he had confiscated without dispossessing the occupiers, others again to have dealt with the remaining public domains[3] which the Gracchi had not touched. But it also proposed to employ the revenues of the new eastern provinces for the next five years in the purchase of land for allotment. To this last part of the scheme Cicero lent his support, but even his wish to please Pompey could not reconcile him to the rest. The Senate was against the whole bill. A conflict of powers took place between the tribune and the new consul Metellus Celer. At last Pompey, seeing that he could not carry his point, called off his tribune, and the matter was dropped for the present. It was most likely an impracticable proposal. To

---

[1] Cic. *ad Att.* 1 17 § 8 (5 Dec. 61).
[2] Cic. *ad Att.* 1 18 § 6, 19 § 4, Dion Cass. XXXVII 50.
[3] This would surely be the Campanian land and not much besides.

improve the chances of carrying it, citizens generally, as well as Pompey's veterans, had been made eligible for allotments, but this might have given trouble when it came to carrying out the scheme. In any case the time was inopportune, for public interest was diverted from the matter by disquieting news[1] from Gaul. The Aedui, a tribe in alliance with Rome, had of late met with a crushing defeat at the hands of their neighbours the Sequani and Arverni, who had called in the help of Germans from beyond the Rhine. The Aedui had been compelled to become subjects of the Sequani and to undertake not to seek the aid of Rome. At the same time the Roman province was being raided by bands of Helvetii, who lived in what is now West Switzerland, and were a warlike and restless people, always exposed to the pressure of the German tribes beyond. Some part of this news now reached Rome and caused a good deal of uneasiness, as any movement of the northern peoples always did. By the middle of May a later report seems to have announced that things were quiet again[2], to the disappointment of Celer, who had drawn that province for the next year. Another measure of this time seems to have fared better than the land-bill. This was a proposal to abolish[3] all the dues payable at Italian ports. It is said to have been welcomed as a relief from the irritating attentions of the farmers of these imposts, to which, rather than to the amount, the trading classes objected. The proposer was the consul's brother Metellus Nepos, now praetor, but Pompey was probably at the back of it, for it called attention to the new revenues created by his conquests, without which no such relief would have been possible. Cicero had doubts as to the wisdom of this rash sacrifice of revenue. During the earlier months of this year the differences between the Senate and the Knights were dragging on, Cicero striving to compose them, Cato by his stiff-necked opposition widening the breach. Clodius too was not idle. He wanted to be tribune, as a means of settling his score against Cicero and other matters. Finding no other way of getting over the hindrance of Patrician birth, he was arranging for adoption into a Plebeian family. But the necessary formalities were governed by strict rules, and the chief pontiff, who could have seen the matter through, was not yet returned from Spain. Clodius could neither get a law passed to make Patricians eligible for the tribunate, nor a public abjuration of his Patrician quality recognized as valid. His

---

[1] Cic. *ad Att.* I 19 §§ 2—4, II I § 11. Compare Caesar *Gall.* I 31.

[2] Cic. *ad Att.* I 20 § 5. This may have been the work of the ambassadors sent from Rome, *ad Att.* I 19 § 2.

[3] Dion Cass. XXXVII 51. See Cic. *ad Att.* II 16 § 1, *ad Quint. frat.* I 1 § 33, and index under *portoria*.

cousin and brother-in-law the consul Celer contrived to prevent these illegalities, and for the present his designs on the tribunate had to wait.

1056. About the middle of the year, probably in June, a momentous change came over Roman politics with the return of Caesar. He had two immediate objects, a triumph and the consulship. He could not enter the city to stand for the latter without laying down his *imperium*, and with it his right to celebrate the former. He applied to the Senate for leave to be a candidate in absence, but the dispensation was not granted, being talked out by the obstructive Cato. Caesar soon made up his mind what to do: he threw up the triumph and came forward for the consulship. In this candidature he resorted to his old device of joining forces with another man. L. Lucceius found the money required, and Caesar the popularity. But the 'best men' resolved to provide Caesar with a colleague who would not be under his influence. By sheer force of money they brought in M. Calpurnius Bibulus, and even Cato condoned the bribery in such a cause. Bibulus was not only a determined aristocrat; he had an old grudge against Caesar from the time of their aedileship, when his purse, as now that of Lucceius, had been drained to win popular favour for his partner. But in these days the power of a consul was great or small in proportion as he had or had not the control of the unofficial and unrecognized forces that had become more and more the essential factors in Roman politics. Of these, military prestige and accumulated capital were two of the most important. Add these to Caesar's personal popularity and skill in dealing with the multitude, and there would be a combination that nothing could withstand. At this moment there existed an exceptional chance of forming such a combination. Pompey and Crassus were both just now disgusted with the Senate, and ready to lend an ear to any arrangement that appeared likely to serve their several ambitions. It is probable that Caesar had by letters and agents prepared the way beforehand for the masterly stroke which at once[1] followed his return. He adroitly made up the old quarrel of Pompey and Crassus, and induced them to enter into a coalition, secret for the present, with the object of using their joint power for the promotion of their several aims. They helped him to the consulship, that he might be able to further their interests. They were neither of them far-sighted, and neither seems to have had any inkling of the truth, that, while on the face of it Caesar was serving them, it was Caesar who was really turning their resources to account,

---

[1] Sueton. *Jul.* 19 seems to place it after the election and before Caesar's entry on office. This is surely improbable, so I have followed the mass of authorities.

and who stood to gain by the whole transaction. Some advances were made to Cicero, whose support might have saved a certain amount of trouble and friction, but on consideration the orator declined them. It is not likely that he would in any case have been admitted to the coalition as a confidential partner. The three were agreed in this, that each was fighting for his own hand. Cicero was for the Republic, and between his position and theirs was an impassable gulf. There was no way out of the dilemma which faced them all. Without supreme power there was no means of mending the Republic. Without ending the Republic there was no means of attaining supreme power. Another marked stage on the road to monarchy had been reached in the formation of the so-called First Triumvirate. Public official authority was ruled by a private unofficial junta. It only remained for the partners to fall out, and the monarch of the virtually existent monarchy would be revealed.

CHAPTER LIII.

1057. Caesar came into office as consul on the first of January 59 B.C. Rome now passed under a strong government, stronger than any government since the days of the second Punic war. A Republic still nominally existed, though to thoughtful patriots the difficulty of maintaining it was apparent. For the strength of the new government consisted in forces not recognized by the republican constitution, and in the event of collisions it was the law and practice of the constitution that must give way. We shall find the Senate overridden, the Assembly habitually coerced, the tribunate become a satellite office, to be muzzled or let loose according to the momentary convenience of the real holders of power. The magistrate in office has just so much power as the unofficial coalition allows him. The year is marked by the conflict of two strong-willed consuls, the complete predominance of the one, the complete suppression of the other. The supremacy of the so-called Triumvirs is the one great fact of the time, but that supremacy was, and could only be, a temporary stage. So long as these Three were bound together by a common interest, and so long as the real guidance of their policy was in the capable hands of Caesar, the arrangement might work. But interests were certain to diverge, and the growth of one member of the coalition was certain to dissolve it by the force of jealousy. Moreover it was impossible to fill up a place vacated by death. The death of Pompey or Caesar would have left Crassus powerless against the survivor. The death of Crassus would leave the other two face to face, and any new member coopted by them must become either the tool of one or the master of both. The peculiar situation which had led to the inclusion of Crassus could not be reproduced. Crassus had already made for himself a considerable position. Under the rule of the Triumvirs it was hardly possible for any other man to do the same, for the men who rose would be the nominees of the Coalition. No permanent solution of Roman problems was attained by organization of a strong unconstitutional government on cooperative principles: the rule of Three was a step to the rule of One. How far Caesar foresaw this, whether he did or did not consciously contrive the coalition as a means to this end, is a question to which different answers may be given.   It may suffice to say here that he was at least bent on reforming many things in the corrupt and feeble government of Rome, that he was able to look beyond Italy and view the empire as a whole, and that he was no dreamer.   It was useless to attempt any improvement of the present system by strictly constitutional means.   He had broken with the senatorial nobility.   He now as consul gave them one more chance, and they would not take it. Henceforth the breach was irreparable, and his career was inevitably bound up with the attainment of sovran power.

1058.   The first notable act of Caesar as consul was to provide for the publication[1] day by day of a record of the proceedings of both the Senate and the Assembly.   It was of course the *acta senatus* that were the important matter.   Hitherto the only official record was the copy of each decree or order actually passed by the House, attested by a number of members, and placed in the treasury. Memoranda of motions rejected or withdrawn, and other notes bearing on the debates, were commonly made by the magistrate presiding at any particular sitting, or rather for him by his secretaries. ·On special occasions he would dismiss these attendants and employ senators to take notes.   But the record thus kept was not official and public. It was a part of his private 'commentaries' or note-books, which contained also other matters beside senatorial proceedings.   Proceedings of sittings presided over by another magistrate would be in that magistrate's notes, also mixed up with foreign matter.   Each magistrate owned his own note-books, and took them home with him into private life.   What Caesar did was to arrange for the regular publication of a kind of official report[2] of all the *acta* in order as they occurred and to have them kept apart from irrelevant matters.   By what power he effected this change, we are not told.   It is most likely that he procured an order of the House itself to that effect, for members might well shrink from provoking so daring a politician to carry out his design in some other way.   The measure certainly exposed the working of the Senate more openly to the public gaze, and must have been unwelcome to many.   It was a sort of warning to senators that they would do wisely to concern themselves mainly with routine business.   Their day of greatness as directors of a mighty empire was indeed over, but the great council had its uses,

---

[1] Suetonius *Jul.* 20, *Aug.* 36.

[2] From this was soon developed as a private enterprise the gazette known as the *acta* (or *commentarii*) *rerum urbanarum*, a miscellaneous record of current events.   See Mayor on Juvenal VII 104, Mommsen *Staatsrecht*, index under *acta*.

and Caesar did not aim at its abolition.   The significance of his present move is shewn in the fact that Augustus, with whom it was a settled policy to conciliate the Senate, did away with the publication of its proceedings now introduced by Caesar.

1059.   In his first utterances before the Senate Caesar was studiously conciliatory.   He made overtures to Bibulus, expressing the hope that they might be able to forget old quarrels and work in harmony for the public good.   He had already given notice of a land-bill[1] of moderate scope, in which he avoided tampering with the valuable public estates (*ager Campanus* etc.) from which substantial revenues were drawn, and with the Etrurian lands[2] which Sulla had taken from Marian owners.   This bill he now laid before the Senate, with professions of his desire to secure the cooperation of the House in his legislation and of his readiness to accept amendments.   We are told that the main feature of the scheme was the proposal to apply the great sums accruing from the conquests of Pompey to the purchase of land from present owners[3] on equitable terms.   To pick holes in so harmless a project was hardly possible, yet we hear that Caesar could neither conciliate Bibulus nor win the confidence of the Senate.   To begin with, for a consul to propose a land-bill, instead of leaving the business to a tribune, was a novelty in itself suspicious.   And the ring of Roman aristocrats were not the men to be deceived by Caesar's show of moderation.   They knew that they must either be drawn into following Caesar on paths ever more and more difficult to retrace, or they must withstand him and go their own way.   And the choice could not be delayed ; if they meant to fight, the sooner they joined battle the better.   We can see now that they were bound to be beaten, but at the time this would not be evident.   Accordingly they resorted to adjournments and obstruction.   Cato in particular took the general ground that it was not the moment for unsettling changes, and in long rambling speeches wasted the time of the House.   No vote could be taken.   The consul ordered Cato into custody, but the best part of the House rose and followed the arrested member.   Caesar thought it wiser to release him, rather than have to face the odium of using force to the great Incorruptible.   But he dismissed the Senate with the warning that, as he found they would not work with him, he would be driven to work without them.   This was no idle threat prompted by ill temper.   He went on with his numerous legislative projects, paying no regard to the Senate, and laying bills before the Assembly direct.

[1] Dion Cass. xxxviii 1—6.
[2] Cic. *ad fam.* xiii 4.   See above § 1055 on the bill of Flavius in the preceding year. Cicero evidently was prepared to accept the present bill.
[3] The price offered was to be that at which the land stood valued in the censors' books.

The aristocrats had thus lost all chance of debating and modifying his measures. They could still try to procure their rejection. The chief weapons at their disposal were blocking, exercised by the other consul or by a tribune, and the hindrances of a formal religious character. But it was decidedly awkward that Caesar was the chief pontiff. And their own inherent weakness made a successful resistance impossible. They needed leaders at once active judicious and influential, and they had not got them. Catulus was dead[1], Lucullus was aging fast and not easily induced to leave his luxurious retirement. Metellus Celer died in the course of this year. The breach between the Senate and Knights, fatal to the power of the former, and the quarrel of the Senate with Pompey, had reduced Cicero to helplessness, and he passed a good part of the year in the country, engaged in literary work, querulous and despondent. Thus the active resistance to Caesar was mostly left to the initiative of Cato and Bibulus, who were both prepared to strain constitutional means of opposition to the utmost, but not to go beyond them. Behind them stood the main body of the Roman nobility, too many of whom, like Lucullus, were devoted to the enjoyment of ease in their town and country houses, and unwilling to face the storms of politics. Such men could not be relied on at a pinch, and the lazy 'fish-ponds brigade' (*piscinarii*, as Cicero calls them) were despised by no one more heartily than by Cato himself.

1060.   Caesar's first land-bill became law early in the year, perhaps in February. The twenty[2] commissioners to whom its execution was to be entrusted were not chosen till somewhat later. The circumstances in which the law was carried were highly significant. Finding that Bibulus would make no concession, Caesar openly threw himself upon the support of Pompey and Crassus. If official support was not to be had, it was time to shew the hitherto dissembled truth that men, not magistrates, were henceforth to dominate the politics of Rome. When speaking in public on behalf of the bill, he called on the two great men to give their opinions. Both expressed their approval of the measure. Caesar was resolved to carry it at all costs, and had therefore to reckon with the contingency of armed violence being used to defeat it. He turned to Pompey and asked him whether he would in that event give his succour to the movers. Pompey replied that if others took arms against the bill, so would he in its support. Such an utterance from a private citizen in a public meeting was unpre-

---

[1] He died in the winter of 61—60.

[2] Whether the *XX viri* were divided into sub-committees of five, or whether an inner board of five was to be the guiding power of the 20, are questions not important here. See Tyrrell on Cic. *ad Att.* II 7 § 4.

cedented, indeed inexcusable. But it served its purpose. None dared offer serious opposition in arms to the chief around whom his veterans would rally. But the odium of this curt reminder of the supremacy of the sword all fell on Pompey; the immediate political gain belonged to Caesar. The actual voting on the bill took place without any great fight. The veto of a tribune had to be set at naught and Bibulus to be driven from the place by the mob of discharged soldiers. But in these days a few broken heads were nothing. Of course even the minor violence of such a riot was unlawful. But the policy of the Senate from the days of the Gracchi had tended to make the constitution unworkable without occasional resort to force. And the appeal of the consul to Pompey for protection had certain analogies to the 'last decree' of the Senate. Both were at bottom usurpations of a power not positively conferred by law. Both could be justified only by the plea of supreme necessity. The vital question was whether such necessity had arisen. If there was reason to fear the employment of armed gangs on the senatorial side, it might reasonably be said to have arisen; and the emergency so created was one with which the Senate could not, from the nature of the case, be trusted to deal. The flagrant illegality of Caesar's conduct is not to be gathered from his proceedings in reference to this particular law, but from the acts of his consulship as a whole. He meant to carry a series of measures to further the designs of the Coalition. The Senate would not give way quietly, and he would not be thwarted. So the revolution took another stride when a consul spent his year of office in defying and intimidating the Senate.

1061. Bibulus tried to induce the House to declare the new law invalid, but the members did not dare to provoke a further conflict. Soon after they were called upon to face the question in another form. A clause[1] in the law, modelled on that of Saturninus, required all senators by a given date to swear to maintain it. Cato and one or two others at first declared that they would go into exile like Metellus Numidicus sooner than take the oath. It is said that Cicero dissuaded Cato from thus depriving his country of his services: at any rate they all ended by swearing. The clever management of Caesar was shewn in the appointment of the commissioners. He had expressly excluded himself, but Pompey and Crassus were both placed on the board, and of course there could be no doubt that they would guide its policy. Later in the year Cicero was invited to fill a seat vacated by death, but he declined the offer. We know nothing of any action taken by the commissioners under this law. The question as to the persons intended to benefit by land-allotments, and what was

---

[1] Dion Cass. XXXVIII 7, Plutarch *Cato min.* 32.

really done in the matter, will best be considered when we come to speak of Caesar's second law on the subject of land.

1062. Meanwhile there were other questions to be dealt with. One of these related to Egypt. We have seen that Caesar had designed to use that country as a base from which to hold in check the excessive power of Pompey. This design was now quite out of date. The worthless Ptolemy Auletes had vainly tried to procure recognition[1] from Pompey while the latter was in the East. But he was hated by his subjects, and was still endeavouring to strengthen his position by getting himself recognized as king. Pompey favoured his application. It was accompanied in the usual way by promises of money. But it seems that the matter did not progress, probably owing to the opposition of senators who hoped to extract bribes. Caesar soon settled it to Pompey's satisfaction. He carried a law recognizing Auletes as king and declaring him an ally and friend of the Roman people, and the Senate was compelled to pass an order to the same effect. For this accommodation the wretched king had to pay[2] an enormous sum. To raise it at once he had to resort to Roman financiers, a step which was the beginning of no small troubles for himself and others. Pompey being gratified, it was now the turn of Crassus. He was interested in the cause of the revenue-farmers who wanted their bargain for the dues of the province Asia to be cancelled. Caesar carried a law by which one third of the contract price was remitted. A scandalous job, no doubt, but not the first, perhaps not the worst, in the history of Roman finance. It transferred the sympathies of capitalists, already discontented with the Senate, to the Triumvirs. In particular it reconciled them to the revolutionary consul, at whom they had hitherto looked askance. We have observed that Caesar had a way of getting good value for money. On this occasion he contrived to gratify Crassus, to weaken the aristocrats, to win the favour of the Knights, and to make the state pay the whole cost of the transaction. The opposition of Cato had led the Senate into disaster. His high-minded pedantry had encouraged the House to evade the concession demanded, and Caesar had replied by taking the matter out of the Senate's hands. His policy was fitted rather for an Ideal State[3] than for the actual politics of corrupted Rome. His obstinacy constantly played into the hands of his adversaries, and rather hastened than delayed the fall of the

[1] According to Pliny *NH* XXXIII 136 he had spared no expense to support the operations of Pompey in Judaea.

[2] Nearly 6000 talents (say over a million pounds of our money) according to Sueton. *Jul.* 54.

[3] See Cic. *ad Att.* II 1 § 8.

Republic. By about the end of February Caesar had so completely got the upper hand in Rome that he could with ease carry through whatever legislation the interests of the coalition might require.

1063. While Caesar was thus breaking down opposition, and proving to the Senate that nothing could stay his progress, his satellites were not idle. They disregarded religious hindrances as recklessly as the chief pontiff himself. The tribune P. Vatinius and the praetor Q. Fufius Calenus (tribune in 61) carried laws dealing with procedure of the public courts, some time before the month of March. The chief point in the *lex Fufia*[1] was a provision that in taking the verdict of a jury the three divisions, Senators Knights and *tribuni aerarii*, should vote separately. Hitherto the joint voting, being secret, had enabled each section to lay the blame of a miscarriage of justice on the others. Henceforth the separate numbers[2] were known. So far as reform of machinery could do anything, the change seems to have been a good one. The *lex Vatinia*[3] dealt with the power of challenging jurors. Hitherto this power had been very limited, particularly in the case of accused persons not of senatorial rank. The new law made no distinction of rank, and gave to both the accuser and the accused the right to challenge the whole list of jurors once. This also may well have been a change for the better, but it would hardly tend to quicken procedure. The hand of Caesar is seen clearly enough in these measures. That he had a sincere desire to improve every part of the Roman administration his whole career amply proves. That the obsolete machinery of the Republic, if perversely worked, made all reform impossible, Bibulus and Cato were steadily engaged in proving. If anything was to be effected, it must be by gaining power boldly and by letting no formal scruples impede its use when gained. This was clearly the course that Caesar had resolved to take. Whether he was already aware that it could only lead to monarchy must remain a matter of opinion. At all events he was not prepared to let the law and custom of the constitution be for ever applied to perpetuate a state of clumsy misgovernment and corruption that was past all bearing.

1064. This law of Vatinius was not passed in time[4] to benefit a notorious offender who was brought to trial in March of this year. The criminal was Cicero's former colleague C. Antonius, who had returned in disgrace from his Macedonian governorship. He had of course been corrupt and extortionate: it was to fill his purse that he

---

[1] *iudiciaria.* See Orelli's onomasticon, and Du Mesnil's Introduction to Cic. *pro Flacco* §§ 35, 40.

[2] Asconius records them in several cases.

[3] Orelli's onomasticon, Cic. *in Vatin.*, especially § 27, *legem de alternis consiliis reiciendis.*

[4] Cicero declared that it was purposely delayed for this very reason.

had sought the province. But he had done worse than this. He had wantonly provoked the warlike peoples of the Danube country, hoping to earn a triumph. But his campaigning was a series of disasters. He came out of it with great losses, and left the prestige of Rome lowered in the eyes of the restless hordes who were always ready to give trouble on the northern frontier. His headquarters were said to have been a scene of licentiousness and disorderly living[1] such that no further explanation of the inefficiency of his army was needed. To any man burning to distinguish himself by prosecuting a criminal to conviction Antonius was a godsend. His past record, which counted for much in a Roman court, was exquisitely bad. His conduct in the affair of Catiline had made him hateful to all parties, whatever view they took of the conspiracy and its suppression. Of his accusers the most notable was M. Caelius Rufus[2], a young man of brilliant parts whom we know from his later connexion and correspondence with Cicero. No doubt Caesar had encouraged the prosecution. It was not easy to find any one willing to defend Antonius, and Cicero, who eventually undertook the case, did so with great reluctance. To abandon an old colleague would have been a rather extreme course, judged according to Roman sentiment. And after all he had himself an interest in the case. For there can be no doubt that the charge was one of *maiestas*[3] or treason. The question was whether by his public acts he had or had not impaired the essential greatness of Rome. To support the charge, not only his conduct as proconsul in Macedonia, but the utter infamy of his consulship, were exposed before the court. Cicero had bribed him to betray Catiline by resigning to him the province, and could hardly evade the obligation to defend him now. It was an unpleasant consequence of his own acts. Moreover, in pleading a bad case it was inevitable that he should appeal to general considerations, for of direct evidence to exculpate his client[4] he probably had little or none. We shall see that this necessity involved himself in serious trouble.

1065. Caesar had already made arrangements for a provincial government[5] after his year of consulship, and was busy preparing a second land-bill and other schemes. Meanwhile he was watching

---

[1] Quintilian IV 2 §§ 123—4 quotes a brilliant passage on this topic from the speech of Caelius.

[2] The character and career of this remarkable man are finely analysed by G. Boissier, *Cicéron et ses amis*. See also Fowler, *Social Life* pp. 127—32.

[3] I hold that this is the fact concealed under the muddled account of Dion Cass. XXXVIII 10. And the long note of Du Mesnil on Cic. *pro Flacco* § 5 seems to me conclusive.

[4] Antonius was condemned, and Catiline's friends, of whom Caelius had been one, treated the result as a triumph. See above § 1041.　　　　[5] See § 1067.

Cicero. Personally he liked the orator, but it was not his way to let people interfere with his plans. Cicero had at present very little influence, and we naturally ask why Caesar was so bent upon keeping him quiet. We must remember that Caesar was looking forward to a long absence from Rome, leaving Pompey and Crassus behind him. He well knew the characters of his two associates. If he thought it unwise to expose the vanity and jealousy of the one, and the untrustworthy nature of the other, to the temptations that Cicero might be able to offer, it is probable that he judged rightly. This is conjecture, but it does suggest a rational explanation of the impersonal hostility which led him to humiliate Cicero. Clodius was on the watch to pay off old scores, but he was not yet eligible for the tribunate. Cicero was living in fancied security. Caesar had not yet given his consent as chief pontiff to the adoption of Clodius. While the matter still hung fire, the trial of Antonius came on. Cicero, evidently at his wits' end to find a plea for his client, ventured to refer[1] to the unhappy state of public affairs. His remarks, reported by unfriendly witnesses, seemed to reflect unfavourably on the dominant coalition. Caesar saw that the orator was an incorrigible opponent, or at least required a sharp lesson to teach him compliance. That same afternoon he carried through the formal adoption[2] which made Clodius a Plebeian, and the augur whose presence was necessary at the ceremony was no other than Pompey himself. Here was warning enough. But Cicero, though disgusted, was not as yet seriously alarmed. He spent April and May in the country, and tried to persuade himself that his heart was in literature. It is true that Clodius was not yet tribune, and there were rumours that he was going to be sent out of the way on a trivial mission to Tigranes of Armenia. Perhaps he might have been sent, for he was a nuisance to all connected with him. But Cicero was still blind to his danger, and cherished endless delusions. He greedily welcomed every bit of gossip that told against the 'tyrants,' as he called the Triumvirs. Their coalition was by this time recognized as a permanent one, and various persons were shewing signs of restiveness under its yoke. One of these was C. Scribonius[3] Curio, son of the man who had defended Clodius, a youth of spirit. Clodius himself was said to be on bad terms with the mighty Three, and likely to attack them. Cicero drank in idle reports that the Three were now

---

[1] Cic. *de domo* § 41, Suetonius *Jul.* 20.

[2] In the form known as *adrogatio*, performed in *comitia curiata*. See *de domo* § 77, Gaius I §§ 97—107 with Poste's notes. The 30 curies of this ancient assembly were now formally represented by 30 lictors. The man who took Clodius for his son was some years younger than Clodius himself. In criticizing the proceeding two years after Cicero (*de domo* §§ 34—38) declared that it was illegal and void. But Caesar was then away in Gaul.

[3] This is the man who afterwards became an agent of Caesar.

unpopular—as if that mattered. Caesar had an armed bodyguard to ensure the peaceful reception of his measures, and besides, now that his province was assigned, he was openly raising an army. So long as the three partners held together, there was no power that could check them; grumbling was grumbling, and nothing more. Cicero was deceived by not having detected that the real head of the coalition was not Pompey but Caesar. Pompey was hesitating, and unwilling to accept his share of responsibility[1] for their common policy. The Republic, such as it was, stood in no danger from him. His aim was to be unquestionably the first man in it. Hence he cared what people said of him, and shrank from committing himself. Caesar was a reformer, to whom the approval of men interested in administrative abuses was a matter of indifference. Contemporary observers, Cicero included, seem to have been unable to see that the whole situation was changed when a man of clear mind and firm purpose had come to the front. Under the new control the only choice left was to submit or to be broken.

1066. The permanent nature of the compact between Caesar and his partners was illustrated by the new marriage arrangements made about this time. Both Caesar and Pompey had recently divorced wives. Caesar had a charming young daughter Julia, who was already betrothed to Q. Servilius Caepio. This engagement was now broken off, and the girl married to Pompey, to whom she proved a most affectionate wife. He was devoted to her, and the alliance with Caesar was strengthened by this tie, which lasted till Julia's death. Caepio, whose sister Servilia, mother of M. Brutus, had been suspected of an intrigue with Caesar, was provided for by marriage with Pompey's daughter, who herself was already betrothed to another. Caesar married Calpurnia, daughter of L. Calpurnius Piso Caesoninus, whom, together with A. Gabinius, the three partners had decided to make consul for the next year. These arrangements were naturally alarming to statesmen concerned in upholding the Republic. But it was vain for Cato to denounce this traffic with affairs of state in domestic transactions. The time for talking had gone by. Of any serious disagreement between the men in power there was at present no prospect whatever.

1067. The province destined for Caesar was chosen with care. In order to baulk his ambitions the Senate had assigned the most unimportant spheres[2] of duty to the consuls of 59 at the end of their

---

[1] See Cic. *ad Att.* II 16 § 2.

[2] *silvae callesque*, Suetonius *Jul.* 19. The charge of woodlands and country roads seems to be meant, strange duties, more suited to quaestors than consuls. See Cic. *pro Mur.* § 18. The matter is very obscure. See Index, *calles*.

year of office. This feeble attempt to hold him in check was set aside or ignored. A law carried through by Vatinius assigned him the combined province of Cisalpine Gaul and Illyricum. The former was a quiet district, fast developing in population and wealth. It was the best available recruiting-ground, and Caesar was already popular there. As to the exact status of the Roman dominions in Illyria we have no information. That there was some kind of organization[1] may be inferred from the existence of assize-districts (*conventus*). But no regular province of Illyricum was established as yet. Whether its combination with Cisalpine Gaul took place now for the first time, is not certain. Caesar was to be allowed three legions, and to have a free hand in the choice of his lieutenants. He was to be appointed for a term of five years, reckoned from the first of March[2] in the current year. Thus was created another of the great commands which heralded the coming Empire. Still it seemed small in comparison with that held by Pompey a few years before. But no sooner was this *lex Vatinia* passed than the Senate added the governorship of Transalpine Gaul and another legion. The proposal is said to have come from Pompey and Crassus, and to have been carried because members thought that, if they refused to grant it, the Assembly would do so. Which may be true. But the grant was only for a year, of course renewable, not for five years at once. Thus it followed the lines laid down by the *lex Sempronia*[3] of C. Gracchus, and the Senate kept in its own hands the power which Gracchus had left it. The Vatinian law, like the Gabinian and Manilian in favour of Pompey, was irregular. It dealt with matters strictly belonging to the Senate, not to the Assembly, and an irregularity more or less was nothing in this revolutionary age. The reserve of the Senate on the present occasion was destined to prove important at a later time. By another Vatinian law Caesar was authorized to add colonists to the town of Comum in the Transpadane part of his province, and to organize it on the plan of the old Latin Colonies, with Latin rights. This power he no doubt wished for to enable him to shew some favour to his old friends beyond the Po. Comum became officially *Novum Comum*. By his support of the policy embodied in these measures Pompey had furnished Caesar with the opportunities by the use of which the latter became his successful rival. Caesar could now proceed to form a devoted army, seasoned by campaigns for which

---

[1] See Marquardt *Stvw.* 1 218.

[2] This is perhaps the date of the *lex Vatinia* as Ferrero 1 290 suggests. It was the death of Metellus Celer that had caused the vacancy. His wife, the notorious Clodia, was suspected of having poisoned him.

[3] Cic. *ad fam.* 1 7 § 10, *de prov. cons.* § 36, and generally Lange *RA* III 290—1.

there was ample pretext, backed up by auxiliaries raised among the warlike peoples of the North, ready to go anywhere and do anything, ever responsive to its leader's call.

1068.   The price paid by Caesar for these opportunities seems to us, judging long after the events, absurdly small.   Some time early in the year he carried a law confirming in a body the acts of Pompey during his command in the East.   Thus an end was made of the senatorial opposition to the Great Man's will.   It was probably a good thing, but what Pompey gained by the transaction beyond the satisfaction of his honour is not very clear.   Any odium incurred would be his, for Caesar was still supposed to be the inferior partner, carrying out a bargain in good faith.   The violence with which Caesar overcame the opposition of Lucullus to this law was not a popular move.   Threatened with a prosecution, Lucullus, who had no taste for brawling, collapsed utterly.   He begged Caesar's pardon, and finally retired into private life a broken man.   The other item due to Pompey from Caesar was the provision of land-allotments for his discharged soldiers.   A law, chiefly for land-purchase, was as we have seen among the earlier measures of the year, and Pompey himself was one of the commission for executing it.   But it is evident either that the law was not working with sufficient speed or efficiency to satisfy its promoters, or that it was from the first meant to be only an instalment.   In April it was followed up by a second land-law, in which the proposals dreaded by Cicero and other conservative statesmen at last made their appearance.   The public estates in Campania[1] were to be cut up into allotments for distribution.   A serious sacrifice of revenue was inevitable, but this consideration, important in the eyes of those concerned with public finance, did not appeal to the necessitous multitude.   The opposition headed by Cato was firmly repressed by force, and the law carried, including a clause[2] requiring all candidates for office to swear that they would if elected do nothing to encourage any revision of the tenures created by the Julian laws.   The new law also conferred powers on the commissioners for founding colonies in the *ager Campanus*.   Under these powers Capua, so long a bone of contention, recovered local government[3] as a municipal town.   An attempt was also made to apply the same treatment to the neighbouring town of Casilinum[4] on the Volturnus, but this 'colony' seems not to have been a success.   It is clear

---

[1] The *ager Campanus* or territory of Capua, and the *campus Stellatis* in the same district. See map in § 310.   Not the land in Etruria.   According to Cic. *de lege agr.* § 84 the present tenants of the Campanian land were *optimi et aratores et milites* whom it was monstrous to' think of ejecting.

[2] Cic. *ad Att.* II 18 § 2.   [3] See Beloch's *Campanien* p. 306.

[4] Cic. *philipp.* II § 102, Beloch pp. 367—8.

however that a real effort was made to carry out the provisions of this law.   One point in connexion with it, the questions as to the persons benefited thereby, remains to be considered by itself.

1069.   The record of the law comes down to us in several versions.   Cicero, the contemporary witness, has only references[1] to it in his letters, which tell us little, and nothing at all on the point before us.   Suetonius[2] says that Caesar divided this land among about 20,000 citizens, fathers of at least three living children each. Velleius[3] gives the scope of the law as the 'division of the land among the Plebs,' and adds that about 20,000 citizens were planted there. Appian[4], mixing up Caesar's two agrarian laws, says that Caesar proposed to bestow the land on those citizens who were fathers of at least three children.   Thus he gained the favour of a great number, for it was found that the number of such persons was 20,000. Dion Cassius[5] says that the land was given to those who had three or more children.   So far we hear nothing about discharged veterans, but about poor citizens as such.   Yet it is certain that the law was carried to satisfy Pompey, and with Pompey's support, and also that his object was to provide for his old soldiers.   An anecdote in Plutarch[6] preserves a trace of this intention, and that veterans were settled on some part of the Campanian land is clear from a reference in a letter of Cicero[7] some years later.   To add to the tangle of evidence, we have a contemporary remark[8] from Cicero, that the land in question, at the rate of 10 *iugera* per man, would not be enough for more than 5000 men.   This may be a miscalculation, and is certainly the view of a strong opponent of the scheme.   When we try to extract a definite conclusion from the evidence, we find that we have to answer several questions with inadequate means of doing so. Never was a more annoying proof of our helplessness in the total lack of sound statistics.   The figure 20,000 may be taken as a round number.   It is not the number of settlers, but the class from which they were drawn, that is the real difficulty.

1070.   The first question is, of the two grounds of claim, military service and paternity, which was in effect the more important ?   For some forty years or more it had been becoming more and more the custom to enter upon military service as a means of livelihood, a profession commended by its variety and possibilities of gain.   It is very hard to believe that any large percentage of Pompey's veterans were at this time (59) fathers of three children born in wedlock.   The actual allotment of lands would fall in the next year (58), which

[1] Cic. *ad Att.* II 15, 16 §§ 1, 2, 17 § 1.   [2] Suet. *Jul.* 20.
[3] Vell. II 44 § 4.   [4] App. *civ.* II 10.   [5] Dion XXXVIII 7 § 3.
[6] Plut. *Cic.* 26.   [7] Cic. *ad Att.* XVI 8 § 1.   [8] Cic. *ad Att.* II 16 § 1.

would make a considerable difference. Even so it is hard to believe
that there were 20,000 of them qualified on both grounds. It is
possible, but we cannot regard it as an established fact. Then, in a
case of doubt, say between a veteran with one or two children and an
urban pauper with three or four, which would be preferred? Probably
the veteran, for the commission was under the influence of Pompey.
But here also we are left to guess. Again, there is the old puzzle as
to the demand for land. Was it widespread and serious? When
Cicero in 63 opposed the land-bill of Rullus, he thought it a telling
argument[1] to remind the city rabble of the pleasures and perquisites
of urban life, which they must sacrifice in order to embrace the
monotonous toils of agriculture. Such considerations had hardly lost
their force with the paupers of Rome. The veterans of Pompey may
have been more inclined to go back to the land, but it is most
unlikely that they would be disposed to do without slave-labour. We
hear of no provision for supplying the new colonists with slaves and
other stock. Most of the veterans seem to have been hanging about
Rome for about two years, and their savings were probably spent.
The men were doubtless of much the same type as the Sullan
colonists, and we know that these Campanian colonies were not a
success, for they were in decay, and were strengthened by new settlers,
after the great civil war. If we are to come to any sort of conclusion,
the following may be tentatively offered. The men to whom land
was allotted in Campania were mostly, if not all, veterans from the
armies of Pompey. It is not likely that all claims could be satisfied
within the limited area there available for allotment. In doubtful
cases preference was given according to a three-child standard of
paternity. That any great 'draining² of the dregs' of Rome took
place is not to be believed on the loose evidence of later writers. It
is much more likely that the real dregs of the city populace, largely
of servile extraction, were precisely the element that was left behind.

1071. In taking this view of the effect of Caesar's second land-
law certain remarks of Dion Cassius have been disregarded. Referring
to the moderation which made the first land-law so difficult to assail,
Dion says[3] 'for the mass of the citizens, being excessive, and in
consequence sorely troubled with seditions, turned to labour and
tillage. Most parts of Italy, which had been depopulated, were now
by way of being again inhabited. Thus there was found sustenance

---

[1] Cic. *de lege agr.* II § 71. He is speaking there especially of outlying malarious lands,
but the reminder of city privileges is the main point.
[2] Cic. *ad Att.* I 19 § 4. He is speaking there of his own amendments to the *lex Flavia* of
60. Compare his words in *de lege agr.* II § 70.
[3] Dion XXXVIII 1 §§ 2, 3.

enough, not only for those who had borne the burden of campaigns, but for all the rest also. And this was done without either exhausting the state treasury or putting the nobles to expense: indeed many gained additional honour and office thereby.' He goes on to describe the purchase-scheme of the first law. But we have seen reason to doubt the efficiency of that scheme, and it seems probable that Dion is rather giving us his impressions than recording facts. He wrote in the third century of the Empire, and his opinions on such a point cannot be authoritative. For nearly three quarters of a century legislators had with more or less sincerity been endeavouring to check the growth of pauperism and repopulate the country sides of Italy. Hitherto the movement had not been successful. Italy was and remained a land of large[1] estates, with the country seats of the wealthy dotted here and there in attractive spots. That any notable change for the better took place at the present time through the Julian laws is surely not to be believed. As to the 20,000, it is clear that men, heads of households, are meant. If we add a wife and three children to each, we get a total of 100,000, without allowing for a single slave. That a migration on anything like this scale actually took place, those may believe who will. The history of the Roman Republic is largely the history of the wealthier classes. It is in matters such as that we have been discussing that we become painfully conscious of the almost total lack of annals of the poor.

1072.   After the passing of this second land-law, the utter helplessness of all persons and parties before the power of the Coalition was manifest. Bibulus had made a stout resistance with the means at his disposal, but Caesar had now completely silenced him. Public opposition was crushed by force so overwhelming that we hear of no loss of life. Cato had been carried off to prison shouting defiance and calling vainly to the people to withstand the tyranny of the triumvirs. To save unpleasantness, one of Caesar's tribunes solemnly intervened to release him. Vainly did Bibulus attempt religious obstruction, giving notice of his intention to watch the heavens for signs, proclaiming special festivals, and issuing protests against illegalities. Loungers thronged to read his pungent utterances, but nobody ventured to do anything. Bibulus, shut up in his house, had by his action provided a pretext for the Senate to declare Caesar's laws invalid after he laid down office. But this procedure was out of date since the formation of the Coalition. Caesar would go out of office at the year's end, but he would not go out of power. One point however Bibulus did gain. He put off the

---

[1] It was the depopulation of Italy that gave such immense importance in this period to prosperous Cisalpine Gaul.

yearly elections from July to October, hoping no doubt that popular resentment, of which there were some indications, would issue in a political reaction and the defeat of the triumvirs' nominees. Caesar found it best to submit to the delay. Indeed it mattered little. People might chatter indignation and in the theatre applaud persons and passages that told against Pompey or Caesar. But there the opposition ended. If we may believe Cicero[1], writing in July, the Knights took part in these futile demonstrations, and the triumvirs thought fit to drop a hint that, if this sort of thing were persisted in, unpleasant results might follow. Did the Knights want to keep their reserved seats, and the populace their doles of corn? But Cicero, while declaring that nothing was now so 'popular' as to hate the so-called *populares*, had to confess that nothing could be done. Any real opposition could only lead to a general massacre. Yet among the three Rulers there was one whom their present despotic power did not satisfy. Pompey gave many signs of uneasiness. To have gained his immediate ends was pleasant, but he had never meant to lose his popularity. His wish was to be admired and cheerfully obeyed, and it hurt his self-complacency to find that people took no pride in obeying his orders. Cicero was watching, and reporting to Atticus, the great man's fall. The orator made fun of him under nicknames borrowed from oriental potentates, but was sincerely sorry to see that he had made a fool of himself. Meanwhile the edicts of Bibulus followed each other fast, and Pompey writhed under their sting. He was constantly reassuring Cicero as to the intentions of Clodius, who was now a candidate for the tribunate, and went about bragging of all he meant to do when in office. These assurances may have been sincere when uttered. But Pompey had no real control over the reckless Clodius. Even now Cicero had only occasional misgivings as to his danger. His popularity was reviving, and he thought himself safe with all the pick of Roman society at his back. But with politics he was utterly disgusted. In his dejection he mourned the virtual abolition of the Republic, and envied Catulus for not having lived to see it.

1073.   Cicero then devoted himself to advocacy and literature. But the intrigues of the time did not leave him at rest. In August, when he was busy with the defence of Flaccus, he was worried[2] by a base attack, the details of which are obscure. A certain L. Vettius, who had given information against persons suspected of complicity with Catiline, now tried to lure young Curio into a plot[3] for

[1] Cic. *ad Att.* II 19, 20.
[2] Perhaps alluded to in *pro Flacco* § 96.
[3] Vettius.   See Cic. *ad Att.* II 24, *pro Sestio* § 132, *in Vatin.* §§ 24—26, Sueton. *Jul.* 20,

murdering Pompey by the help of a gang of slaves. Curio told his father, who in his turn told Pompey. The matter was reported to the Senate. Vettius was sent for and questioned, when he made a pretended disclosure, implicating several persons in the design. Among them was Bibulus. It happened that circumstances shewed this accusation to be absurd, and his other revelations would not stand scrutiny, so the Senate ordered him into custody for the present. Next day Caesar brought him before a public meeting, when he made further disclosures, some of them not consistent with his previous utterances. He mentioned fresh names, among them that of Lucullus, and made an unmistakeable reference to Cicero. The man was evidently an infamous liar, and stupid at that. The purpose of this dirty business was pretty certainly to alarm Pompey. He had been uneasy of late, and seemed to be drawing nearer to Cicero, who was quite capable of leading him gently back into alliance with the aristocrats. This purpose had now been served, for it could not be difficult to persuade Pompey that he was of such importance as to deserve assassination. It remained to get rid of Vettius. A pretence was made of prosecuting him, for he had confessedly gone about with a dagger, and there was talk of his turning state-evidence and of further proceedings. But nothing came of this. He committed suicide in prison ; that is to say, each party insinuated that he had been made away with by the other side. Perhaps we may venture to acquit Cicero Lucullus Bibulus and the rest of that party. Suspicion must rest heavily on their opponents. The person who as usual profited by the informer's appearance and death was Caesar. We might lay the guilt on Vatinius, if we followed the direct allegations[1] of Cicero made a few years later. But by that time Cicero had learnt not to provoke Caesar himself. It matters little what view we take on the point. In any case we have in the affair of Vettius a little light on the life then led by public men in Rome.

1074. The trial of L. Valerius Flaccus for extortion in the province Asia is a striking illustration of the connexion of Roman politics with the abuses of provincial administration. It shews clearly that the subjects of Rome had practically no chance of obtaining redress of their grievances unless the classes represented on the juries had reasons of their own for wishing to punish the party accused. Flaccus was a man who had seen service in various parts of the Roman world. As praetor in 63 he had been concerned in the

Plutarch *Luc.* 42, Appian *civ.* II 12, Dion Cass. XXXVIII 9. There are several differences in these accounts. See also Dion XXXVII 41.
[1] Cic. *in Vatin.* § 15 (B.C. 56). See § 1120.

arrest of the Allobroges on the Mulvian bridge. In 62 he was governor of Asia. There can be no reasonable doubt that he was guilty of great extortion in the province, which was only just beginning to recover from the troubles and miseries of nearly thirty years. Yet he might have escaped prosecution, if he had not chanced to offend a Roman financier[1] who was doing business there. This man gathered evidence against Flaccus, and bided his time for revenge. In 61 Flaccus was succeeded in Asia by Q. Cicero, the queer-tempered brother of the orator, who sent him a great deal of good advice by letter. Cicero was a much better governor than his predecessor, and certainly abstained from doing some things that Flaccus had done. No doubt the contrast was pointed out by the prosecution with much stress, and therefore was slurred over in the defence. The enemy of Flaccus saw his chance in the political situation of 59. The charge was laid, the approval of Pompey secured. No doubt it was really a move of Caesar, who was busy chastising those who had borne a hand against Catiline. The charge was received early in the year. After a squabble over the right to be chief prosecutor, the collection of evidence in Asia would take a considerable time. Decrees of provincial cities had to be prepared, and delegates appointed to present them, and these with other witnesses forwarded to Rome, not to mention a mass of other documents. The actual trial seems to have come on in August. Cicero of course defended his former associate, and Hortensius was with him. He clearly understood that a reaction against his own policy in the matter of Catiline was at the bottom of these prosecutions, and that this reaction was one promoted for political reasons. He had not been able to save Antonius : with the case of A. Minucius Thermus[2] he had had better luck: he now put forth a mighty effort to win the acquittal of Flaccus.

1075. When we examine his speech for the defence, it is at once apparent that in relation to the actual charge of extortion he had no case. He dwelt on the good record of Flaccus in the public service elsewhere. He pointed out that the prosecution was essentially an attack on the interests of Rome as interpreted by himself and the jury, to whose class-feeling he dexterously appealed. He exerted himself to discredit the other side by imputing to them unfair conduct in getting up their case. He asserted the utter worthlessness of evidence furnished by the mongrel Greeks of Asia. Whether as a whole or taken city by city, their resolutions and decrees had no real

---

[1] C. Appuleius Decianus.   See Du Mesnil's Introd. to the *pro Flacco* § 15.
[2] Cic. *pro Flacco* § 98.   The speeches are lost.

value.   Their mass-meetings[1] would vote anything.   Individuals lived in the habitual practice of perjury.   How different was the dignified consistency of the Roman Senate, the serious sense of honour[2] and duty displayed by Roman citizens!   Moreover, it was certain that they hated Rome, and would swear anything to ruin a Roman.   As for account-books and other records brought to prove the exactions of Flaccus, he declared that the damning entries were forged.   On some particular charges, not to be thus summarily dismissed, he made but a lame defence.   Such was the matter[3] of ship-money, levíed by Flaccus on the pretext of a squadron to check piracy, and strange to say not accounted for in the official ledger. With another point he was better able to deal.   The scattered Jews[4] were in the habit of sending a yearly tribute to the Temple at Jerusalem.   It was exported in gold, and Flaccus had forbidden this export from Asia.   But the gold was forthcoming, and it suited Cicero's purpose to lay stress on a transaction by which his client had not profited.   He declared that this topic had been introduced for the benefit of the numerous Jews in Rome, of whom some were hanging about the court.   We learn from him incidentally that the Roman Jews stuck together and were a noisy troublesome element in public meetings.   There were also a few charges made on the complaint of Roman citizens.   To these the orator made what answer he could. It is probable that they were simply cases of rogues falling out, and that Flaccus was no worse than his opponents.   But the real answer to these, and to the accusations in general, was contained in the appeal to the jury[5] not to let the Catilinarian reaction triumph, not to condemn one who had maintained the cause of order and the rights of property, not to discourage patriotism.   This appeal came from the man who had risen to the primacy of the Roman bar by the glorious prosecution of Verres.

1076.   Cicero's brilliant speech, one of his most interesting pieces, was followed by the acquittal of Flaccus.   There was an end for the present of the hopes of the wretched provincials.   But at the same time it proved beyond a doubt that the orator was a man to be reckoned with, and that nothing but force could prevent his working to restore the shattered 'harmony of the Orders.'   We may be very sure that this would not suit the plans of Caesar, who was about to enter on a provincial governorship for a long term.   It is no rash guess that Cicero's forensic triumph weighed heavily with Caesar in deciding that there was nothing to be done but to get him out of

---

[1] *pro Flacco* §§ 15—19, a notable passage, giving a Roman view of Greek ἐκκλησίαι (*contiones*).   Compare *pro Sestio* §§ 125—127.

[2] *pro Flacco* §§ 9—12.   [3] *pro Flacco* §§ 27—33.

[4] *pro Flacco* §§ 66—69.   [5] *pro Flacco* §§ 94—99, very notable.

Rome.   Already he had been offered a vacant seat on the land-commission, a post under Caesar as *legatus* in Gaul, and an honorary mission (*libera legatio*) to travel on his own occasions.   He had refused them all.   He would not go quietly, yet go he must.   Caesar was driven to do what he had tried hard to avoid doing.   He unmuzzled Clodius.   But the orator, elated by his successes, and fancying that the friends who rallied round him could and would protect him, scorned his enemy's threats and was resolved to stand his ground.

1077.   In order to keep it separate from the legislation meant to satisfy the demands of powerful interests, the *lex Julia*[1] *repetundarum* has been left unnoticed hitherto, though it was probably passed earlier in the year.   It seems to have been a genuine attempt to improve the administration of the provinces.   Coming after a series of laws dealing with the same subject, it of course incorporated[2] a number of earlier enactments on various points.   But definitions were made clearer, and penalties more severe.   It restricted in various ways the free action of governors, particularly in respect of the power of making war, often assumed with bad results, as lately in the case of Antonius.   It also shortened procedure by limiting the time allowed for the speeches of counsel.   To guard against falsification of official accounts, it provided that, beside the copy placed in the Roman treasury, two others should be made, and kept in two of the cities of the province.   Other clauses provided for the safe custody of documents sent from a province for the purposes of a particular trial. The proceedings of accusers in gathering materials[3] for their case (too often an additional burden on the unhappy province) were also regulated by various limitations, such as a restriction of assistants (*comites*) to a moderate number.   The law was evidently a good one so far as it went.   Cicero afterwards praised it highly.   It long remained in force, supplemented by later interpretations, and made the subject of juristic[4] comment, down to the time of Justinian.   Yet it can hardly be said that the law put an end to extortion.   The corruption at Rome, the enormous expenses incurred in following an official career, forbade any such result.   Money had to be constantly streaming from the provinces to the centre, to decide who should come out to exact more money.   And the new law still took account of senators only.   The financiers, the source of half the mischief, remained exempt as before.

---

[1] See Orelli's onomasticon III, Du Mesnil's Introd. to *pro Flacco* §§ 37—40.

[2] See Cic. *pro Rabir. Post.* §§ 8, 9, *in Pisonem* §§ 50, 90.

[3] See *pro Flacco* §§ 13—15.

[4] Digest XLVIII, title 11 *de lege Julia repetundarum*.   The Digest or Pandects was published 533 A.D.

1078. The general effect of Caesar's consulship had been to weaken the power of the senatorial aristocrats. The process had long been going on, in spite of occasional small revivals and the great reaction of Sulla. But the constitution had hitherto been so far a reality that no popular leader could establish a working succession of magistrates following a coherent policy under the guidance of a leading mind. Speaking generally, the cessation of office meant a cessation of power. The coalition brought about by Caesar broke down this bulwark of the republican system. The unofficial power of the so-called Triumvirs was not such that it could be abdicated without grave public disorders, and possibly danger to the partners themselves. There was nothing to be resigned formally, and usurpation, however necessary, finds that its own continuance is the only alternative to anarchy. The remaining years of the nominal existence of the Republic were passed in the tideway of these grim alternatives. The immediate care of the Coalition was to see that the chief official posts should be filled for the next year by nominees of their own. They turned their attention mainly to the consulship and tribunate, for the control of these two offices could be made equivalent to the control of Rome. Gabinius and Piso, as already arranged, were made consuls, and a majority of the tribunes had also been secured. Among the latter was Clodius. He still affected an air of independence, perhaps not wholly assumed. But the notion that he might come forward as an opponent of the Coalition was either an idle dream of Cicero's, or at least an insincere suggestion too easily believed. That the election of Clodius meant no good to his beloved Republic, Cicero could see. But he could not see how near danger was to himself. He was lulled into security by the assurances of Pompey and Caesar, and by the promises of support that came to him from all sides. But he did not omit to prepare for a struggle that he believed to be inevitable. This struggle he evidently expected to take the form of a prosecution, and he counted on winning. Even in the event of a resort to force he had ample offers of effective help. The bearing of Gabinius and Piso was all he could wish. He felt that he could rely on several of the praetors-elect. So he writes[1] to his brother still in Asia. Yet the three Rulers had just given a clear sign that they meant to take a short way with opponents. A young man, C. Cato, rashly attempted to put Gabinius on his trial for corrupt practices at his election. The praetors, no doubt under orders, evaded the 'reception of the name' of the accused, and so foiled the attack. In indignation the youth denounced this burking of justice before a meeting, and called

[1] *ad Q. fratr.* 1 2 §§ 15, 16.

Pompey an 'unofficial dictator.' The ruffians who acted on behalf of the Triumvirs were within a very little of murdering him on the spot. As has been said above, a man had now to submit or to be crushed.

1079. All really important business had as usual been got over earlier in the year. After the elections in this October the time remaining was shorter than usual, and much broken by the great games. Caesar was no doubt much occupied with getting his army into shape. But the sequel shewed how fully he had thought out the political situation that he would leave behind him when he went to the North, and the means he had resolved to employ for keeping in touch with Rome from his headquarters in Gaul. The first indispensable condition of his plans was the removal of Cicero and Cato. With these two, alike irreconcileable, Pompey and Crassus were not able to cope by civilian methods, and it was no part of Caesar's game to provide his partners with armies. Therefore the serious matter of the last months of the year 59 was the maturing of the plans of Clodius, who was to play the leading part in the Caesarian drama of the coming year. By the 10th December, when he entered upon office, the plan of campaign was ready. He was to have a free hand. The new consuls were bound to support him, but they took care to exact a price. The provinces assigned them by the Senate were not suited to their ambitions. Clodius agreed to override this arrangement by a vote of the Assembly, giving Macedonia to Piso and Syria to Gabinius. This clinched the bargain, and it was now practically certain that Caesar at the end of his consulship would still be able by means of his agents to ensure the continuance of his revolutionary policy for at least another year.

1080. On entering office Clodius at once came forward with his programme. The senatorial aristocracy were to be so weakened that they could offer no effectual resistance to the designs of the tribune. By a corn-law abolishing the trivial payment[1] still demanded for the grain provided by the state, he secured the adhesion of the city mob. But the political efficiency of the mob was greatly increased by organization, so another law authorized the revival of the sham associations (*collegia*)[2] which the Senate had suppressed in 64 B.C. as a public danger. Thus, in well-defined bodies each headed by a 'master,' the paupers of Rome were formed into a street-army, ready to shout vote or break heads in support of their leader's policy. The religious hindrances which were used to hamper the action of

---

[1] For the wholesale manumission of slaves that followed see Dion Cass. XXXIX. 24.

[2] The expression of Dion Cassius XXXVIII 13 τὰ ἑταιρικὰ κολλήγια ἐπιχωρίως καλούμενα is a reminder of the somewhat similar spirit of the old ἑταιρεῖαι familiar to students of Greek politics.

demagogues had been lately set at nought by Caesar. Clodius now abolished this power of capricious obstruction, and thereby deprived the Senate of a cherished weapon. All days not marked as unlucky in the calendar were to be available for legislative Assemblies. No 'watching of the heavens' was to be allowed on such occasions, and even the tribune's right of *intercessio* was, if we may believe Cicero, so far barred. Finally, there was the question of membership of the Senate. The regular succession of new members provided by the twenty quaestors elected every year had practically taken away from the censors the power of filling up the House by arbitrary selection. But the power of expelling unworthy members still remained. True, the laxity of censors had long made such expulsions rare, and the office was on its last legs. But the power was valued by the nobles as an engine capable of use in favourable circumstances. We must remember that Caesar was going to be away from Rome for some time. In his absence it was quite possible that the office might be used to get rid of some of his partisans. To abolish the Senate was out of the question. Now that the Roman dominion was so great, the one deliberative body in the state was indispensable. But it was an object to prevent its being turned into a mere party conclave. Clodius therefore, doubtless under Caesar's direction, forbade the censors at any revision to strike a present senator off the roll, unless his fitness had been openly called in question by an accuser, and both censors agreed in condemning him. These conditions were seldom likely to be fulfilled. Thus the office, useful only in the hands of upright men with solid power behind them, lost the little remnant of its importance. For the moment there were senators who were not sorry to see it curtailed by the law of Clodius. Their seats were safe now, and with them that of Clodius himself.

1081. These four measures became law soon after the beginning of the new year (58), when Gabinius and Piso had come into office. Opposition was indeed futile. The new consuls were creatures of the triumvirs, and Caesar with his army watched proceedings from outside, so that there could be no hope of a successful resistance by force. The city was given over to Clodius and his gangs, for he had already revived the *collegia* without waiting for the passage of his law. Cicero made a feeble attempt to obstruct his legislation through the veto of a friendly tribune, L. Ninnius Quadratus. But Clodius would assuredly never have been checked by this constitutional means. Ninnius thought it best to accept the promise of Clodius, that he would not molest Cicero if his bills were allowed to pass, and withdrew his opposition. Clodius made no secret of the fact that he had the triumvirs at his back, and after he had carried through his first batch of laws he went ahead more boldly. He entrusted the administration of his corn-law to one Sextus Clodius, a dependant and perhaps a relative of his own. The wasteful largess went on, and the organization of the pauper rabble reached a pitch of perfection never before attained. In his speeches delivered after his restoration Cicero constantly asserts that slaves formed a large part of the ruffianly mobs on which the tribune relied, and there is no reason to doubt the main fact, coloured though it be by oratorical passion. Clodius had now got a firm footing, and proceeded to deal with Cicero and Cato in the ways agreed upon as appropriate to their several cases. The procedure adopted was ingenious. Three bills were brought forward. One enacted that Piso should succeed to Macedonia and Gabinius to Syria, and conferred on them exceptional powers in relation to the government of those provinces, jurisdiction over 'free' communities, discretionary power of making war, and so forth: it granted them exceptionally large allowances from the treasury, and in short opened up to them a prospect of enormous gains, with a possibility of cheap glory. This proposal the consuls were bound to support as the fulfilment of their bargain, though some at least of the provisions were contrary to the Julian law recently carried to prevent extortion. Clodius made it clear that the three bills must stand or fall together. Thus the greedy consuls were bound also to support the other two bills whether they liked it or not.

1082. The attack on Cicero was delivered without any mention of his name. A law in general terms outlawed any person who had or should hereafter put to death a Roman citizen uncondemned, that is without due trial and sentence. Everyone knew at whom this measure was aimed, though it was in form merely a continuation of the 'popular' party's policy, as expressed in the law of C. Gracchus reserving the right of appeal to the people, and reasserted in the impeachment of old Rabirius. The nerve and judgment of Cicero gave way under the strain of this obvious menace. He who had maintained that the Catilinarians were not *cives* but *hostes*, public enemies not entitled to the benefit of the laws of Rome, now stooped to extreme self-abasement in the effort to defeat the present bill. Such conduct only served to advertise the miserable truth that the orator had no real confidence in his ability to make good his former plea before an unfriendly court. And an unfriendly court he would have to face, if the bill became law and Clodius impeached him before the Assembly. He changed his raiment and went about appealing for help, but effecting nothing. Crassus had an old grudge against him. Pompey belied his hopes. Ever loth to take responsibility, the Eminent Man avoided Cicero all he could and shuffled meanly, pretending that, as the new consuls were now in office, he could not intervene without their instructions.   Caesar, in reply to a question from Clodius, reasserted his former opinion that the execution of the conspirators was an illegal act, but affected to desire that the matter should now be allowed to drop.   Clodius knew very well what this meant.   From the consuls no comfort was to be got.   Spurned by Gabinius, Cicero turned to Piso.   Cicero's story[1] is that Piso laid the responsibility on his colleague : Gabinius was deeply in debt, and could not afford to miss the chance of a rich province.   'We consuls' he said 'have, as you know by experience, to consider a colleague in the matter of a province.   It's no good asking us consuls to protect you : each must look out for himself.' That is, a bargain was a bargain, and Cicero had been sold.

1083.   Thus neatly had Caesar contrived to deliver the blow which Cicero's obstinacy had compelled him to inflict.   As usual, his agents and associates took the trouble and bore the odium, while he kept behind the scenes and blandly profited thereby.   It was not he that talked of marching his army upon Rome to put down resistance if necessary ; the threat came from Clodius.   But the presence of his army had a great effect in a quiet way.   It convinced Cicero's numerous friends that to aim at putting down Clodius and his gangs by calling on the wealthier classes throughout Italy to come to the rescue (slaves and all, of course,) was out of the range of practical politics.   There was no hope in a resort to open force, and other way there was none.   Hence, when Cicero took counsel with his supporters, they mostly advised flight.   Even Cato[2] is said to have come to this conclusion.   The staunchness of the man is not to be doubted, but he was, as we shall see, at this juncture in a peculiar position.   Duty, as he conceived it, was calling him away from Rome for some time, and to advise Cicero to stand his ground at all costs, while he himself would not be there to bear a hand in the coming struggle, was probably too easy a solution of the problem to suit the Stoic hero.   It was too like leaving his friend in the lurch.   And Cicero himself, looking back on this time, did not blame Cato.   He did blame the slack timidity of some who had given him faint-hearted advice, and to others, such as Hortensius, he imputed jealousy of his oratorical fame.   There were doubtless not a few persons in Rome who had been stung by the orator's references to them in his speeches,

---

[1] Cic. *in Pisonem* § 12.   The words need not be taken literally.

[2] Plutarch *Cato min.* 35, Dion Cass. XXXVIII 17.   I do not think that the passages of Cicero, *ad Att.* III 15 § 2, *ad fam.* XV 4 § 12, are really contrary to the above.   But see Mr Strachan-Davidson's *Cicero* p. 234.

or by witticisms at their expense, or by crushing retorts which they could not repay in kind.   Cicero had an unbridled tongue.   Cato had borne him no grudge for his ridicule of Stoicism ; but all were not Catos, and the disreputable and the dull could do very well without the jibes of Cicero.   The end of it was that Cicero had to abandon all that was dear to him and go, having grovelled before his enemies and false friends in vain.

1084.   The plan for getting Cato out of the way was not less cleverly managed.   The decay of the Lagid kingdom had already brought its affairs within the scope of Roman politics.   Rome held the Cyrenaic province once owned by the Ptolemies.   The base Auletes had bought his recognition as king of Egypt, and was now busy squeezing his wretched subjects to satisfy his Roman creditors. A brother of his ruled in Cyprus, the last remaining possession of the Lagids outside Egypt.   He was an inoffensive monarch, but Clodius bore him a grudge ; when in the East some years before, the young Roman had fallen into the hands of pirates, and the king of Cyprus had actually not found the money to ransom him.   For this economy he now paid dearly, by being turned into an excuse for employing Cato.   Clodius began by carrying a law declaring the island annexed to Rome.   He then insisted on the necessity of appointing a thoroughly trustworthy commissioner with large powers to carry out this annexation and see that the state was not defrauded of the moneys and other property now belonging to it.   Was not Cato obviously the man ?   Cato objected.   But Clodius would take no refusal.   It is clear that the Stoic was in an awkward fix.   He could not on his own principles[1] decline a duty laid upon him by the state. To refuse to recognize the authority of the Assembly packed and controlled by Clodius meant abdication of his own position as a republican statesman.   The Assembly might be no true exponent of the will of the Roman people, but at present there was no other.   At all events Clodius forced Cato to go, sorely against his will, and Cato was not a pliable man.   The above considerations may perhaps help to account for the success of his manœuvre.   To keep Cato's hands full, he was further entrusted with the duty of settling some disputes in the free city of Byzantium, involving the restoration of certain exiles.   In equipment the commissioner was stinted, but he seems to have been allowed ample time for his work.   Thus every care was taken to keep him busy as long as possible.   At the same time it was made more difficult for him in future to oppose the great commands, wide in scope and of long duration, against which he had hitherto

---

[1] His Stoicism was of the uncompromising orthodox type, not the moderate kind, adapted to the conditions of Roman life.   See § 659.

protested.   The Great Incorruptible was for the present effectually
shelved.

1085.   We need not dwell upon the efforts made by Knights and
senators to induce the consuls to stop the progress of Clodius, the
deputations repulsed, and the meetings dominated by the Clodian
gangs.   Nothing but a downright battle and a decisive victory could
have availed, and for this the ʻparty of orderʼ had only the will
without the strength.   Cicero saw that he must bow to the storm.
He dedicated a statue of Minerva in the Capitoline temple to record
the exile of the only genuine preserver of his ungrateful country, and
left Rome one day about the middle of March.   That same day
Clodius carried his batch of laws.   Very soon after this Caesar,
seeing the ground at last clear, started (none too soon) for his
province of Gaul.

1086.   Cicero's flight had simplified matters for Clodius.   He had
now only to charge Cicero with the offence retrospectively dealt with
by his general law, and to treat his non-appearance to answer the
charge as a proof of guilt.   This is what he appears to have done,
and to have followed it up by at once carrying a resolution of the
Commons which set forth as a fact that the accused had already
incurred the penalty of his past crime, and was already an outlaw,
whom all persons could receive only at their own serious risk, and
whom it was no murder to kill.   This declaration was on the lines[1] of
ancient precedent.   Nor was there anything outrageous in fixing a
ban-limit of 400 miles, within which distance of Italy he was
forbidden to remain.   The confiscation of his property was also no
novelty in the case of a man condemned by the popular tribunal.
The wrong done by Clodius was not so much in the laws he carried
as in the means by which he carried his laws and the brutality with
which he carried out the sentence extorted by those means.   He at
once destroyed Cicero's house on the Palatine, and devoted the site
to the erection of a temple of Liberty ; he even worried Cicero's wife
Terentia with threats of legal proceedings.   Above all he carried
a law forbidding under penalties any proposals for the exile's
restoration.   The matter of the ban-limit is obscure.   Some change
was made in the distance[2] named.   Whatever was the final figure, it
was so fixed as to exclude Cicero not only from Italy but from Sicily
and Melita as well.   His hope of finding a refuge among those whom

---

[1] See Livy XXV 4 §§ 9—11, XXVI 3 § 12, for the course followed in a *iudicium populi*.
Clodius did not prosecute Cicero in the standing court on a charge of *maiestas*.   The jurors
belonged to the upper classes, and would probably have voted for acquittal.

[2] According to Plutarch it was 500 miles from Italy (? from Rome) in the bill.   The
change is thought to have been to 400.   This at least was reckoned from Italy.   See Tyrrell
on Cic. *ad Att.* III 7 § 1.

he had served so well in the past was thus barred. In any case the governor of Sicily, though a friend, would not let him enter the province. We may ask why he did not go to Massalia, as others had done; perhaps the fact that Verres was there is reason enough. He made for Brundisium, meeting with much kindness on the way, and crossed the Adriatic at the end of April. Greece, particularly Athens, was a tempting resort for a man of letters, but here too the Father of his country was encountered by the obstacles created by his own eventful past. Catilinarian exiles were known to be there. So he went on eastwards from Dyrrachium, and at length found rest at Thessalonica about the end of May. Here he was most kindly received[1] by Cn. Plancius, quaestor to the then governor of Macedonia. But he was utterly wretched, and his letters during the time of his exile are full of despair. He regrets his flight from Rome and speaks bitterly of those who advised him to go. Accustomed to the public life of Rome, to bearing a prominent part in politics and being the leader of the bar, he was not only overwhelmed by his calamity but lost in new surroundings where his talents had no scope. The same temperament that under prosperity expanded in vanity and self-laudation shrank into utter dejection and self-reproach under the shock of his fall. He had meant to go on to Cyzicus, which was outside the zone of danger. But Plancius quietly saw to it that he was not molested at Thessalonica, and there he remained for the present. We will leave him and turn to Cato, whose mission is best described here, though he did not return to Rome for about two years.

1087. Cato was anxious to annex Cyprus peaceably, for Clodius had allowed him no force with which to put down resistance. So he waited awhile at Rhodes and sent a deputy on ahead to invite the wretched Ptolemy to submit quietly. The chief priesthood of the temple of Aphrodite at Paphos was one of those posts of dignity and ease that were found in the East, and on this preferment the king might retire. But for some reason Ptolemy preferred to poison himself, and there was nothing to do but to take possession. Cato then went off himself and settled affairs at Byzantium, sending his nephew Marcus Brutus to take over the royal treasures in Cyprus in readiness for his own coming. Brutus had been brought up under Cato's influence, and exposed to the best philosophic and literary culture of the day. He was a young man of the highest principle, as principles went. But he was a thorough Roman aristocrat, one of a class whose creed regarded the subject peoples as existing for the purpose of filling the purses of Romans. He seems to have been honest where

---

[1] Cic. *pro Plancio* §§ 95—100.

honesty appeared a duty ; at least we have no reason to think that he stole what had become Roman state property. But there was no doubt much to be got privately. To be first in the field on the virgin soil of a new province was a great temptation, and there can be no doubt that Brutus added to his means by various methods. He certainly opened profitable financial relations with Cypriotes, and settled down for some years in the East, engaged in employing his capital at ruinous interest and, in Cyprus at least, with horrible results. His incorruptible uncle discharged his duties with his usual thoroughness. The island became a part[1] of the province of Cilicia. The money collected is said to have amounted to 7000 talents (over £1,500,000). Cato made elaborate arrangements for the safe transport of all this specie to Rome, and had his accounts drawn up in duplicate. Very little money was lost on the voyage, but both copies[2] of the accounts perished by accident. Thus he was deprived of the one privilege—that of rebuking others by the contrast of his own perfection—which was to him ever a source of comfort in the discharge of an unwelcome duty. He did not return to Rome till the year 56.

[1] Marquardt *Stvw.* 1 382—3.   [2] See § 1122.

CHAPTER LIV

1088. THE Roman occupation of Spain had been a necessary move in the great struggle with Carthage. The occupation of the country between the Alps and the Pyrenees had been carried out in the first instance with a view to the retention of Spain. The province of Transalpine or Narbonese Gaul was in itself a rich and pleasant land, a highly profitable acquisition for Rome. A number of Romans had settled there, many others sojourned there for the purposes of trade or finance. Inevitable friction and wars had led to the gradual advance of the Roman frontier, till the province included the whole Rhone valley up to the lake of Geneva. In order to protect the territory of the republic with the least possible expenditure of blood and money, alliances with carefully selected peoples had ever been a chief department of Roman policy, and in Gaul as elsewhere Roman diplomacy was at work in advance of Roman arms. This policy had the disadvantage of involving Rome in the quarrels and embarrassments of peoples not under her control. It gave her enemies as well as friends; and it not only compelled her to take part with Gauls against Gauls, but also brought her into contact with the Germans. So long as the inner strength of Rome sufficed, the difficulties that arose beyond the frontiers were sooner or later solved by annexation. But the limits of Roman strength were now nearly reached. In a very few years the future boundaries to East and West were indicated by striking facts. Crassus had met with crushing disaster beyond the Euphrates, and Caesar had thought it wiser not to linger beyond the Rhine.

1089. The country comprised under the general name of Gaul extended to the Rhine the Alps and the Pyrenees. The feature of its physical geography that most concerns us is its accessibility in the parts far removed from the land-frontiers. Rivers flowing to the West or North-West, Garonne Loire Seine Maas and their tributaries, served to lead on those who entered it from the East or South to the rich lowlands of the West. The course of these streams had no doubt done much to determine the course of early migrations. By the time of Caesar their use as routes of trade was well established, and barges plied on most of the navigable rivers of Gaul. But we are concerned more especially with two rivers along which invaders could and did enter Gaul, working their way upstream into the highlands from which other waters issued to the West. Two such movements were in progress at the time of which we are speaking. Along the Rhone the Romans had now come to the critical point where Rhone and Saône unite and the latter river opens up access to the North. The importance of this point was perhaps as yet not fully understood. In a few years' time it was to be occupied by the famous city of Lugudunum, the headquarters of Roman power in Gaul, still great and famous under its modern name of Lyon. Meanwhile the German tribes had been busy in the North. Rivers have never been effective barriers, and the Rhine was no exception to the rule. Germans had crossed it to make raids, or even to settle, in northern Gaul, where large lowland tracts lay open to them. What was at this time a more serious movement was the advance of Germans up along the Rhine, and their entry into eastern Gaul. Looking back over the past, we can see that a collision between them and the Romans could hardly have been averted. The disunion and quarrels of the Gaulish states soon brought the intruders into direct conflict, the real issue involved in which has only been made clear by time. It was no less than the question who should be rulers in a conquered Gaul for about 400 years. If this question were to be decided in favour of Rome, some change making for efficiency would be necessary for the Roman government itself. The helplessness of that government needed no further demonstration. During Caesar's absence it was going from bad to worse. It could not do what it already had to do. It could never have dealt with such a problem as was created by Caesar's conquest of Gaul. A great statesman and general might conquer the country, but who was to go on guarding and ruling it ? A standing army was one of the first conditions for solving this problem, and a standing army required a standing master. Thus, while the direct issue at stake was the future mastery in Gaul, there was connected therewith the further issue of the future government of Rome. The overthrow of the effete Republic was effected by Caesar's imperial army, the weapon that he had forged and tempered in and for the conquest of Gaul.

1090. These great issues were of course hidden from the men of the time. Even Caesar himself, though he was probably looking forward to a career of conquest as chances might occur, can hardly have guessed that he would have to begin by a life-and-death struggle in defence of his province, and that events would lead him on from one step to another till he became master of the whole Roman world. Certain facts were known in Rome. The Aedui (or Haedui), who were allies of Rome, were calling for help in trouble. Their country, between[1] the Loire and the Saône, had on the West the great tribe of the Arverni, humbled by past defeats and hostile to Rome. To the East lay the Sequani, also a powerful tribe. We have already seen that the Sequani had called in the aid of Germans to defend them from the Aedui. To the combined forces of Arverni Sequani and Suebian Germans the Aedui succumbed. The Roman government did nothing to help their allies beyond sending[2] a futile embassy and passing a resolution that the governor of the province should as far as possible protect the allied peoples. But the Roman forces in the province were not increased so as to make effective action possible. The northern frontier was now open to invasion. Everything was allowed to drift, and the prestige of Rome in Gaul sank very low. Even among the Aedui many were for abandoning the Roman connexion which brought little profit and much loss. The tribes within the Roman border were discontented. The Allobroges had rebelled, and the suppression of their rising by Pomptinus (61 B.C.) had not left them happy. What saved the Roman province was the quarrel between the Gauls and their German allies. The Germans were victorious, and occupied a considerable district on the left bank of the Rhine. They were settling down there, meaning to stay, and their king Ariovist, already regarding himself as the first potentate in Gaul, was more likely to seek further conquests than to give up what he had won. Things looked very bad for the cause of Rome in this part of the world. But these were not the only grounds for anxiety. Rumour said that one of the great migrations[3] common in antiquity was about to take place. The whole people known as Helvetii were intending to find themselves new homes by passing through Gaul and taking possession of lands in the West. In their present territory, the western part of Switzerland, they had not room enough, and they were also molested by German neighbours from the North and East.

1091. The Helvetii are classed by Caesar[4] as *Galli*, and he tells

[1] The importance of this commanding position is well recognized by E. Demolins, *Les Français d'aujourdhui* p. 243. The Romans conversant with Gaul no doubt knew it.

[2] See above § 1055.

[3] How far Caesar's story, that the Helvetii, prompted by Orgetorix, meant to attempt the conquest of Gaul, is to be trusted, is very doubtful. But it was surely out of the question to sit still and let them pass into the country and add strength to the anti-Roman factions in the various tribes. The fact of the great migration was enough. The Cimbric war was not forgotten.

[4] *Caesar's conquest of Gaul*, by Mr T. Rice Holmes, is a work which has disposed of a portentous mass of vain theories and criticisms, to the relief of students. I wish to acknowledge great obligations to this erudite and luminous book. I have also consulted Desjardins, *Géographie de la Gaule Romaine*, on particular points. This too is a good book.

us that *Galli* (in the stricter sense) were the race who called themselves *Celtae*. But the population of Gaul as a whole evidently contained elements not now to be satisfactorily distinguished and classified by the scanty evidence at the disposal of modern ethnologists. The name *Gallia* meant several things in the time of Caesar. First, there was the *Gallia* in Italy, known as Cisalpine or Hither Gaul, the Gaul that wore the *toga*, Romanized in short. Then there was the Roman province of Transalpine or Narbonese or Further Gaul, the Gaul that still wore[1] the trews (*bracae*), in process of Romanization. Lastly there was the unconquered mass of the free tribes, commonly called the 'long-haired[2] Gaul' from the fashion of the race. Speaking of this last, Caesar classifies it under three heads. Between the Pyrenees and the Garonne were the Aquitani. From the Garonne to the Seine and Marne were the Celtae. Beyond these to the North and North-East lay the Belgae. The three aggregates thus marked out were distinguished from each other by differences of language customs and laws. From indications in Caesar and notices of other authorities, supplemented by archaeological researches, it is commonly inferred that the Aquitani in general had affinities with the ' Iberians' of Spain, possibly with the Ligurians also. The Celtae seem to have been a blend of a conquering 'Celtic' race with an earlier stock, on whom they had imposed their language. The Belgae[3] were said to have some Germans among them, but it is pretty certain that as a whole they were 'Celts.' Whether some of the tribes near the Rhine were actually of German race or not, is doubtful. Both Gauls and Germans are described to us as tall and light. It is probable that the earlier races, detected in the short dark people numerous in 'Celtic' Gaul and predominant in Aquitania, did not come to the front much in the time of Caesar. Even they were probably not all of one stock. It is hard to resist the conclusion of Mr Rice Holmes, that, 'when Caesar entered Gaul, the groups whom he called Belgae Celtae and Aquitani were each a medley of different races.'

1092. The people properly called Gauls or Celts had certain clearly marked characteristics. Such as the Romans had found them in Italy and in Asia Minor, such they found them in Further Gaul. Quick-witted, talkative, boastful, easily roused and easily depressed, they had none of the stolid patience that promotes combination and

---

[1] *bracata*, as opposed to *togata*.   [2] *comata*.

[3] It should be pointed out that Dion Cassius (probably following earlier writers) often uses the name Κελτοί of Germans. In XXXIX 49 he says expressly that it was used in very early times of the dwellers on both sides of the Rhine. The beginning of a clear distinction between Celts and Germans seems to date from Caesar. The distinction between Κελτοί and Γαλάται in Diodorus V 32 may be a trace of an earlier nomenclature, but it is hard to draw any conclusion from it, especially as the geography is most obscure.

is essential to discipline. Divided and subdivided in tribes clans (or whatever name we give them) the stronger groups tended to reduce the weaker to a state of dependence. Jealousies factions intrigues abounded among them. Particularist feelings were too strong to allow any tribe to submit cheerfully to sacrifices in a common cause, and any failure at once exposed a leader to the suspicion of treason. Their individual bravery was admired, but it was at its best in a furious onset: withstood and checked, their fiery valour was apt to cool. The Romans had long learnt to look them in the face, and in the wild disorder of mere slaughter-battle they were no match for the ruder barbarians of Germany. Civilization had made some progress, particularly in the tribes near the Roman frontier, but it would seem with dubious effects. Money had long been in use, but wealth was accumulated in a few hands, and the rich were too prone to gather round them debtors and other retainers, and such aggregations did not make for peace. A primitive age of kingship[1] seems, in most of the tribes at least, to have been followed by a kind of aristocratic system, under which the nobles, or 'knights' as Caesar calls them, held the real power, though magistrates (one in most tribes, if not in all,) were elected yearly with extensive powers. The influence of the priestly class, the Druids, was very great, but the relation of Druidism to the divinities whom the Romans identified with some of those in their own pantheon is most obscure. We know that to ceremonial it united dogma; the most famous tenet was that of the immortality and transmigration of souls. An Arch-Druid was at the head of the whole corporation, and a solemn assembly was held every year at a sacred place in the centre of Celtic Gaul. In this institution we find the only trace of any influence that might perhaps in more favourable circumstances have proved a germ of national union. But it fell upon evil times. The Romans regarded its mystery with suspicion and its human sacrifices with horror. Of its origin we know nothing. Caesar thought it an importation from Britain. But it is even uncertain whether it was a 'Celtic' system at all. At all events Druids and 'knights' between them engrossed all authority in the Gaulish tribes; the 'commons' were no more than a passive servile mass. We may say in general that what we know of their institutions does not point to either political cohesion or military efficiency. Vanity and the love of personal ornament went naturally with their deeply-marked social distinctions. The golden collar was a sign of the Gaulish noble in many lands. We have before noted their hoarding of the precious metal, which is said to have been found in considerable

---

[1] See the case of rival brothers in 218 B.C., above § 281.

quantities within the limits of Gaul itself. This gold was much of it destined to pass into the hand of Caesar and to affect the policy of Rome.

1093. For dealing with all the dangers that menaced the northern frontier Caesar was at the moment ill prepared. Only one of his legions was beyond the Alps; the other three were in winter quarters at Aquileia. But he had great resources at his back, on which he could and did draw as his necessities increased. In the first place, Cisalpine Gaul was the one progressive[1] and populous district of Italy. Neither the plantation-system of tillage nor the desolation of grazing-runs watched by slave-herdsmen had there ruined sound agriculture. The Roman element was strong there, and was blending well with the remnants of the conquered Gaulish tribes. It was now a province, but a province not likely to endure extortion such as drained the unhappy lands beyond the seas. In the hands of a popular governor its importance could hardly be overrated, and Caesar had as we have seen lost no chance of winning favour there. Nowhere else was there such a recruiting-ground for the legions. Caesar could thus raise great numbers of men, whom active service would soon convert into soldiers of the finest quality. For light troops he like other generals could draw on the outlying parts of the empire. Thus we find him employing Cretan bowmen, Balearic slingers, Spanish and Numidian horse, in his conquest of Gaul. As time went on he was able to use auxiliary forces of native Gauls, and in the later campaigns, as yet unforeseen, he found valuable material for his cavalry by hiring Germans. But it should be borne in mind from the first that it was the unfailing supply of moral force in Caesar himself that gave the tone and temper to his army. In the technical departments of the military art he was not without[2] experience. In the practical psychology which is the root of all great generalship he has probably never had an equal. It is because he could read the feelings of his adversaries and of his own men at the same time and with the same accuracy that he achieved things hardly credible. From his own 'commentaries' or record of the war in Gaul we may gather two characteristic traits which go far to explain his marvellous hold upon the confidence and affection of his troops. First, there was in him an extraordinary coolness and self-control, which inspired trust and enabled him to calm panic and avert disaster. This quality

---

[1] This progress was not confined to agriculture. The towns were flourishing. In his highly-coloured picture of Italian industries in this period Ferrero (II 134) is compelled to draw most of his examples from this district, technically not Italy at all.

[2] Not to mention his early service at Mitylene, he had seen campaigning in Spain. But he was not as yet a great general.

breathes in the sobriety of his narrative. Not less striking was his generosity. By this is not meant the vulgar appeal to self-interest in the way of lavish rewards, but the consistent readiness to recognize merit in officers or men. How competent and severe a critic he was it did not take them long to discover. All the more impressive was it when it appeared that he was eager to praise and loth to blame. This stands out clearly in detail in his book. The plain soldier-like records of individual acts[1] of daring or skill give us some notion of the spirit that prevailed in the ranks, of his heroic centurions, of his resourceful lieutenants. Such was the temper of the army that fought victoriously for eight years against enormous odds, the short men against the tall.

1094. No doubt the arms of the legionary were better than those of the Gaul. The *pilum* and the thrusting sword were as superior in practice to the long heavy cutting sword as they had been to the Macedonian pike in former days. Another advantage existed in Roman mechanical and engineering skill. Artificers (*fabri*) were attached to every legion, and every man carried, as part of his equipment, an axe and a spade. On the march the legionary bore an immense burden, but the camp, trenched and palisaded each afternoon, kept the force safe in a hostile country by night. The vast siege-works in attack or defence of posts, the bridges over the Rhine and other streams, the feats of shipbuilding on the Atlantic coast, were very important as operations of war. But none knew better than Caesar that their importance was not confined to their practical use. In dealing with Gauls and Germans the moral effect of wonder was a consideration of weight. The same is perhaps true to some extent of the artillery of the day, the *ballistae* and *catapultae*, both Greek inventions long adopted by the Romans. These few details must suffice here to give some notion of the means employed in enabling forces small in numbers and depending on high efficiency to overcome the resistance of a brave and numerous enemy. We must not forget the economical point of view. It took no more to feed a Roman soldier than to feed a Gaul, and his military value was several times greater. In a semi-civilized country, with imperfect means of communication, the question of supplies was a source of continual anxiety. To effect results with the smallest possible number of men (that is, mouths) was an object. And, if trained men were so valuable, it was not less an object to avoid throwing away their lives unnecessarily. To all such considerations the watchful industry of Caesar gave ceaseless attention. Lastly, it is well to point out that the campaigns of which

---

[1] To take one instance, turn out the passages referring to P. Sextius Baculus.

we are speaking were conducted in a country of which the Romans as yet knew very little even by report, and before the days of maps. How Caesar got together sufficient geographical knowledge to enable him, even with the help of guides, to move his troops with speed and certainty, and to form large plans of campaign, is by no means clear. The talent for exploring and surveying must have been highly developed both in himself and in many of his officers. Some of his information was certainly got from Roman traders who had visited the chief towns of Gaul. But this information cannot have sufficed for strategic purposes. It is also clear that he had an efficient staff of interpreters. Now and then we hear of service rendered by particular individuals in this department. But the surest proof is the way in which information was constantly got from prisoners. Nor was this done only in the case of Gauls ; in his first campaign he was able to learn[1] an important fact from captured Germans.

1095. The news of the misfortunes of the Aedui, of the settlement of Germans in Gaul, and of the intended migration of the Helvetii, had been received in Rome in the spring of the year 60. That the situation was serious was more or less understood, but no real attempt to face it was made till the following year. Caesar then procured for himself, as we have seen, the great command in the North, and succeeded to responsibilities and opportunities which the Senate was loth to see entrusted to any individual, most of all to Caesar. He set to work raising troops, and tried to stave off the German question for the present. Ariovist desired[2] to remain in quiet possession of his conquest, and the Romans had had enough of Teutonic invaders, for men remembered the perils of the Cimbric war. So the German king was declared by the Senate[3] a Friend of the Roman People, and this recognition delayed for a time the inevitable conflict. Meanwhile the preparations for the Helvetian migration were going on, stimulated by Orgetorix, one of their leading nobles. Orgetorix had great designs[4] for a Helvetian conquest of Gaul, and conspired with two others, who were to seize monarchic power in their states (Aedui and Sequani) at the same time as himself. The three kings were then to divide Gaul between them. But the Helvetii would none of it, and in the process of bringing him to justice the would-be usurper somehow met

---

[1] Caes. *Gall.* I 50.

[2] For the strange story of the 'Indians' driven by storms to Germany, and sent to Rome by Ariovist as a present to Metellus Celer in the year 60, see Pliny *NH* II 170.

[3] None of the authorities give the date of this act, but it seems to have been a move of Caesar's after his appointment to Gaul. Ariovist was not in 59 at war with the Aedui, so there was no real reason why Rome should not be on friendly terms with both.

[4] See note on § 1090.

his end. This affair did not stop[1] the Helvetii. In March 58 news came that they were actually on the move. It was time for Caesar to move also, if indeed it was not already too late. But he was now free to withdraw from Roman political life for a time. Clodius was now at work weakening the aristocratic party, and an attempt to call in question[2] his own acts as consul had ended in a vain squabble. So he posted off with all speed and on the eighth day reached the Rhone. He gave orders for all possible troops to be raised by a local levy in the province, and took what measures he could in the present emergency with the one legion at hand.

1096. The first problem for the Helvetii was how to get out of their country. Reckoning in the other tribes whom they had persuaded to join the expedition, they amounted[3] with women and children to 368,000 souls. They had burnt their towns and hamlets, and were taking with them meal for three months and much movable property, to carry which, and their weaker folk as well, a vast train of rude waggons was needed. From Genava (Geneva), their point of starting, there were two possible routes. On the north or right bank of the Rhone a narrow and barely practicable path between the river and the precipitous cliffs of the Jura led to the land of the Sequani. An easier way led by the left bank to the land of the Allobroges, who were known to hate their Roman masters and would not be likely to oppose the passage of the wanderers. At Genava there was a bridge. By this the Helvetii, who were on the right bank, decided to cross the Rhone and travel by the easier route. Caesar reached Genava just in time, and broke down the bridge. Still, the northern route was so very difficult for wheeled vehicles, that they sent envoys to Caesar, disclaiming all intention of doing damage to Roman subjects and asking his leave to march through the province. Caesar gave an evasive answer to gain time. Meanwhile he employed his men in fortifying the Roman bank of the river at all fordable points, and hurried up the new levies to reinforce the legion at the front. When the Helvetian envoys came by appointment for his final decision, he refused their request, and warned them against attempting to force the passage. This however they did, and were beaten off. They had now to make the best of the bad way, with a further disadvantage. They had committed an act of war, and given to Caesar the excuse which beyond doubt he desired. He meant to deal with them at

---

[1] Caesar (*Gall.* 1 5) records this without any expression of surprise. I cannot agree with Ferrero II 341.

[2] Suetonius *Jul.* 23. There was even a move to prosecute him and some of his subordinates after his departure, but the tribunes, aided by violence, brought it to nothing.

[3] See note on § 1097. We do not know that all these actually started.

once, while they were well within reach, not to let them settle down and be a continual source of trouble in the West. So he left the competent Labienus, the pick of his *legati*, in charge, and hastened back to the Cisalpine to bring up the main body of his army.

1097. How greatly the prestige of Rome had sunk in Gaul owing to the feeble policy of the Senate, is well illustrated by the way in which the Helvetii got leave to travel by the northern route. The Sequani did not wish for their presence—this was no doubt a very general feeling—and were only persuaded to grant a transit by the exertions of Dumnorix, the head of the anti-Roman faction among the Aedui, who was a son-in-law of the late Orgetorix and a sharer in his schemes. The Aedui were torn by party strife, and Divitiacus[1], the leader of the Roman interest, could hardly hold his own against Dumnorix. These two were brothers. However, the Helvetii got leave to pass, and slowly and painfully the lumbering caravan crawled along. Caesar had plenty of time[2] to cross the Alps, to mobilize his three legions at Aquileia, to raise and equip two more on his own responsibility, to conduct them all five across the Alps to the Rhone, and to catch up the enemy. Yet on this journey (his third in three months) over the mountain pass he was attacked by the highland tribes, and had to fight his way through. The Helvetii had got no further than to pass the Arar (Saône) into the country of the Aedui, and a fourth part of their force was still on the eastern side of that river. But the main body were ravaging the Aeduan lands, and a deputation was sent to Caesar to ask for help. Caesar had now all six legions with him. His cavalry was partly raised in the province, but it included an Aeduan contingent commanded by Dumnorix. He struck a blow at once. Marching by night, he surprised the Helvetian rearguard, cut down most of them and scattered the rest, then crossed the river and followed the main body of the enemy. An embassy now came from them offering to settle down quietly if he would assign them lands. But according to Caesar's account[3] they took a lofty tone, and he treated their menaces with scorn. So they moved on, and he followed at leisure. His cavalry hung upon their rear, but in a small mismanaged engagement met with a repulse, and the Aeduan horse were the first to run. Caesar's supplies were running short, for he had broken his communications by leaving the river. He now depended on his allies for food, and the Aeduan

---

[1] For his mission to Rome in 61 see Cic. *de divin.* 1 § 90.

[2] The enormous length of the 'trekking' caravan was of course a great point in his favour.

[3] Caesar was of course concerned to make his narrative favourable to himself, and we must always bear this tendency in mind. In this campaign we may trace a reproduction of the strategy of Marius against the Teutons.

excuses came in, but not the promised corn.   So he summoned the leading nobles of the tribe, the Vergobret or chief magistrate among them, and told them that this sort of thing would not do.   In the course of interviews he learnt that secret influence was at work to thwart official loyalty, and that Dumnorix was at the bottom of the treachery: the recent misconduct of the Aeduan contingent was also his doing.   Caesar spared his life as a favour to his brother Divitiacus, but gave him a sharp warning and had him watched.   The Helvetii were now not unwilling to fight.   Caesar was driven by want of supplies to turn aside from the pursuit in order to reach the granaries of the Aeduan town of Bibracte.   Hearing of this, the enemy attacked him on the march, but were defeated in a hard-fought battle.   The survivors, about 130,000 in all[1], managed to reach the country of the Lingones.   But Caesar warned that tribe[2] against helping them, and they had to surrender.   He accepted their submission, but 6000 of them tried to slip away afterwards and make for Germany.   These were at once hunted down and put to death.   The mass of the wanderers were sent back to their former homes; their function was to be to stop once more the gap left by their migration, and to keep the Germans out of Roman Gaul.   A contingent of Boii, who had joined the Helvetii, were allowed to stay at the wish of the Aedui, who found lands for them.   The number that returned home was 110,000. Caesar tells us that he got his figures from the tribe-rolls, written[3] in Greek characters, which were found in the Helvetian camp.   Of the 368,000 who had mustered at Genava for the journey 92,000 had been men able to bear arms.   Among a rude population the proportion of one in four is not incredible.   The mortality in the migration of a whole people was sure to be great, and we need not attempt an estimate of the number that perished by the sword.   The Helvetian trouble was ended.   It was no more than a striking episode, highly important because it completely altered the relation of Rome to the Celtic tribes.   After a period of drifting and dallying, it now appeared that the Roman power was going to play a leading part.   At all events here was a proconsul who had both the power and the will to expel intruders from Gaul.

1098.   News travelled fast from tribe to tribe, and soon delegates

---

[1] This is of course a guess-number.

[2] Caesar I 26 admits that his pursuit was delayed three days, to tend the wounded and bury the dead.   But his army could move far faster than the encumbered enemy.   In his book the Lingones always appear as friends of Rome.   From Dion Cass. xxxviii 33 § 6 it seems that they were already Roman allies.   The two versions agree, and the account given in Ferrero II 15 misrepresents the tradition.

[3] This is probably a trace of the elements of civilization that had penetrated southern Gaul from Massalia.   See Caes. *Gall.* VI 14 § 3.

of rank appeared at Caesar's headquarters from most parts of Gaul, to express joy and relief at the Helvetian overthrow. In a secret conference they unfolded to him the story of the unhappy past, how their own rivalries had led to the introduction of mercenary Germans, who had proved hard masters, and evidently meant to stay. Ariovist had already 120,000 with him, settled on land taken from Gauls, and a fresh swarm of 24,000 had lately joined him from beyond the Rhine. Where was this movement to stop? Now that Caesar was here with his victorious army, would he not ward off the German peril and save the Gauls from the necessity of migrating like the Helvetii in search of another home? Such is the colour given by Caesar to their appeal. We must remember that the delegates were no doubt sent by the Roman partisans in the several states, and also that Caesar had every motive to make the most of their invitation in his version of the affair, written as it was[1] to justify his forward policy against the carping of political opponents in Rome. The true grounds of his decision were, not the appeal of the Gauls at that moment, but the necessity of upholding the prestige of Rome and of protecting the Roman province and Italy as well. It was of no use to stop the Helvetian migration and then to leave an open door for successive hordes of Germans to come swarming over the Rhine. They would soon be at the gates of Italy, and the work of Marius would have to be done once more. So he sent envoys to Ariovist and proposed a conference. We need not follow the bickerings in detail. The aims of the two leaders were irreconcileable. The barbarian was not to be cajoled. For the 'friendship' of the Roman People he cared nothing, unless it meant that they recognized his rights won by conquest and left him unmolested to occupy lands and exact tribute in Gaul. Caesar required that there should be no further immigration of Germans, and that the Aedui should be left alone and all hostages restored. Of course the result was a deadlock. Meanwhile news came from the North that a great host of Suebi had appeared and were making preparations to cross the Rhine. Caesar had to make up his mind at once, or Ariovist would be strengthened by their accession. He shewed his understanding of Gaul and German alike by a bold decision. He arranged for the necessary supplies of food, and set out along the line of the Doubs, a tributary of the Saône, to settle matters with Ariovist at once.

1099. Any map in which the physical features of the country are given[2] will shew that the way by which the Roman and the German would naturally meet was the pass between the Jura and the Vosges.

---

[1] Probably in the year 51.
[2] See the excellent *Gallia* in the Müller-Grundy series.

The district held by Ariovist was the Alsatian country near Strass-burg. Caesar was in the land of the Sequani, whose chief town Vesontio (Besançon) it was important to occupy. He hurried on and seized it in time, and thus secured a strong base for his further advance. Here he formed a magazine and completed his com-missariat. The delay came near to wrecking his plans. The people of the town and the traders present had not recovered from the terror inspired by the Germans two or three years before. Ariovist had then carried all before him, and the Gauls now gave the most alarming description of the stature strength valour and ferocity of the German warriors. Caesar, like other Roman generals, had about him a number of young men of good family, nominally officers, but really amateurs who lacked fitness for civilian pursuits, and had a fancy to see something of military life. Such cadets were only accepted to oblige their influential friends. Here and there would be one who was wishing to serve a real apprenticeship; most of them had no great appetite for hardship and danger. These men were the first to take alarm at the chatter of the Gauls, but gradually the whole army were infected with panic. The scene in the camp is depicted by Caesar in a famous[1] passage. The pretexts for asking leave of absence, the secret lamentations, the long faces telling of dismay, the making of wills, are told in a few scornful sentences. Even the centurions, the very backbone of the army, lost heart in presence of the general dejection, and shook their heads over the prospect before them—the difficulties of the advance through the forests, and the chances of famine. Caesar was told that the men would not march, and indeed they were not fit to face an enemy. He called together his officers, including[2] all the centurions, and rated them soundly. Let them mind their own business. If Ariovist did not come to terms peaceably, there was no doubt but they could give these Germans another such lesson as the Cimbri had received from Marius. He meant to be master in his own camp. All was now ready, and the army had no grounds for fear or mistrust. In fact, things being as they were, he would put forward his plans and march the very next night. The tenth legion would at all events follow the call of duty: he would then see whether the rest were Roman soldiers or not.

1100. We need not describe the reaction that ensued. Having restored the nerve of his army, he set out as he had promised, and kept them on the move. So he crossed the watershed and entered

---

[1] Caes. *Gall.* I 39. There is no ground for doubting the truth of this picture, nor is the brief and loose version of Dion Cass. XXXVIII 35 inconsistent with it. For two conflicting views of Roman officers of this period see Ferrero II 23, 95—97.

[2] τοὺς ὑπάρχους καὶ τοὺς ὑπομείονας, says Dion.

the country sloping to the Rhine and its affluent the Ill.   The Germans were still in that neighbourhood.   A vain conference now took place between the two leaders.   Neither meant to give way. After much wrangling the Germans (so Caesar alleges) made a treacherous attack on his escort, and Caesar withdrew.   Then followed a characteristic episode.   Ariovist invited Caesar to another conference.   Caesar sent two men whom the barbarian had no excuse for treating badly, merely to hear and report what the king said.   But Ariovist in wrath seized and detained them as spies.   After this he broke up, and marched past Caesar's camp, hoping to cut off the Romans from their sources of supply.   Caesar could not force him to give battle, so he also marched past the enemy and regained touch with his supply-trains.   Then followed various manœuvres, till Caesar, learning from prisoners that the cause of the German delay was that the lucky day named by their prophetesses[1] was not yet come, advanced upon their camp.   This brought on a battle, in which Roman skill and steadiness at length prevailed.   The details[2] of the rout are uncertain.   Ariovist escaped beyond the Rhine, but the bulk of his host was destroyed.   Caesar had the luck to recover his two envoys still alive.   The news of the Roman victory sent the Suebians back into the wilds of Germany after losing a part of their force in the retreat by an attack of the Ubii, Germans also, who wanted to be rid of them.   So for the present there was peace along the Rhine.

1101.   The season for campaigning was not quite at an end, but Caesar had the affairs of a province to attend to, a province that extended from beyond the Adriatic to the frontier of Spain.   So he quartered his troops for the winter in the country of the Sequani, with Labienus in charge.   He then crossed the Alps for the fourth time this year and took in hand the administrative and judicial business of Cisalpine Gaul.

1102.   Now that no war was actually on foot in the North, it was only natural that independent Gauls should regard with some uneasiness the winter-quarters of the legions.   Why were they not within the Roman frontier?   Surely it could only mean that Caesar, having driven out other intruders, was preparing to intrude himself.   Helvetii and Germans were not wanted in Gaul; but neither were Romans. Roman rule even at its best implied a certain restraint on factious disorders and ambitious rivalries.   All the many restless elements in the Gaulish tribes loathed the notion of being 'brought into the shape of a province,' as the Romans phrased it.   The proconsul, busy with

---

[1] See Tacitus *Germ.* 8.

[2] Dion XXXVIII 48—50 gives one of his usual battle-pieces, worked up in the same sort of style as his inserted set speeches.   There is nothing to throw doubt on Caesar's story.

assizes and audiences in the Cisalpine, and keeping in touch with Roman politics, was probably not surprised to hear rumours of a general rising in contemplation among the Belgic tribes.   The reports were confirmed by despatches from Labienus.   He raised two more legions and sent them on into the Further province.   When the season opened he followed in person.   Inquiries among the border tribes shewed that the danger was pressing, so he saw to his commissariat and took the initiative, marching straight into the Belgian country.   The situation revealed by this movement was not unlike that which had been turned to account by the Romans in the early stages of their advance into Transalpine Gaul.   The friction between two powerful tribes led one of them, the Remi, to seek the friendship of Rome by way of strengthening themselves against their next neighbours, the Suessiones.   If the latter did not play so leading a part as the Arverni, the Remi were more consistently faithful to Rome than the Aedui.   Their territory, lying between the Maas Oise and Marne, and including most of the course of the Aisne, was a base of operations for the campaigns in Belgic Gaul.   From the Remi, who at once accepted the alliance and protectorate of Rome, Caesar leant that all the other Belgae were taking the field against him.   The Belgic confederacy included tribes still recognized as German. Tradition[1] spoke of an ancient immigration of conquering Germans, and most of the Belgae claimed descent from these conquerors.   But it would seem that these were merged in a Celtic majority and spoke a Celtic tongue, while those of Teutonic speech were certain tribes between the Rhine and Maas, in the upland forest district of the Ardennes.   Caesar was told to expect the forces levied to oppose him not to be much less than 300,000 men, but this was clearly not the whole fighting population.   Three great tribes, the Bellovaci and Suessiones to the West and Nervii to the North, were furnishing 160,000 between them.   The Belgae generally claimed to be the most warlike of the Gauls, and boasted that they alone had been able to stem the tide of the great Cimbro-Teuton invasion when it overran the rest of Gaul.   On the other hand it seems that disputes about the supreme command had already arisen and might occur again ; for the present Galba the king of the Suessiones was to command in chief. Caesar had eight legions, which with cavalry and light troops may have amounted to between 40,000 and 50,000 men.   He was also supported by a strong contingent of Aedui.   These last he ordered to move westwards and invade the country of the Bellovaci, hoping by this diversion to draw off the warriors of that tribe from the confederate army now advancing to meet him as he moved northwards.   The

---

[1] Caes. *Gall.* II 4.

defects of their organization seem to have made individual bravery quite ineffective. After a few minor operations the great Belgian host lost cohesion and retreated in disorder : Caesar's cavalry killed many in the pursuit, and one after another the chief towns fell into his hands. The Suessiones Bellovaci and Ambiani submitted to him, and he wisely granted them mild terms. His clemency to the Bellovaci was turned to the best account. In the name of the Aedui Divitiacus interceded for them. Caesar was thus able by one and the same concession to increase the prestige of the Aedui in Gaul and to strengthen the hands of the pro-Roman faction among the Aedui. The conquests thus easily made were of great strategic importance. Caesar had planted himself between the tribes of the eastern and northern Belgae on the one hand and the coast-tribes of Aremorica on the other. He could deal with them in detail at his own time. The conquest was of course hasty and incomplete, but he had gained a footing. It is to be observed that Samarobriva (Amiens), the chief town of the Ambiani, appears later as one of his chief military depots.

1103. But the campaign was by no means over. North and East of the Ambiani lay the Atrebates and Viromandui, tribes under the influence of the stronger Nervii, whose country lay beyond. These tribes reached from the Scheldt to the Maas, in what is now called Hainault and southern Brabant; through the middle of the district ran the Sabis (Sambre). The Nervii were a rough vigorous tribe, who eschewed the luxuries of civilization and allowed no traders to visit them. They claimed to be the bravest of the Belgae, and would make no terms with Rome. Caesar marched to find them, for he heard that they had placed their women and non-combatants in a safe retreat and were waiting for him in a position on the Sambre. There is no doubt that a piece of carelessness on his own part nearly involved him in a great disaster. The enemy surprised his main body (6 legions) while engaged in building the camp, and while the baggage-train with the other two legions was just coming up. A fierce and disorderly battle followed. Caesar honestly gives full credit to his officers and men, and lays special stress on the steadiness and intelligence of the rank and file. Thus defeat was averted, and the day ended in a decisive Roman victory. The Nervii fought bravely to the last, and the flower of the tribesmen perished on the field. The remnant of the tribe were admitted to surrender and taken under Roman protection. The display of clemency might tend to make other tribes more willing to submit. There was also a further point of policy. Any future molestation[1] of surrendered foes (*dediticii*) would furnish a valid pretext for chastising the offenders. Caesar was

---

[1] Caesar *Gall.* II 28 § 3, 32 § 2.

not the man wilfully to disregard the etiquette traditionally followed in Rome's foreign relations, and needlessly to set hostile tongues wagging in the Senate-house and the Forum.

1104. East of the Nervii again were the Aduatuci. This tribe were not of the old-established Belgae. They were said to be descended from a body of 6000 men whom the Cimbri and Teutoni had left behind[1] in charge of the property that they did not want to take with them on their further wanderings. Fifty years had gone by, and these survivors of the great migration had maintained their position and become a strong community. They had agreed to join the Nervii, but their contingent had come too late for the battle, and had returned home on hearing of the result. They did not venture to meet the Romans in the field, but concentrated all their strength on the defence of their chief fortress. But the mechanical and engineering skill which had already compelled the surrender of the western cities triumphed here also. The Aduatuci, astounded at the siege-works, made submission before the final assault. But they only gave up a part of their arms, and then, hoping that the Romans would now be off their guard, made a treacherous attack on them by night. They were driven back with heavy loss, and the protection promised them was now forfeited. Next day Caesar sold the whole population into slavery. Dealers were as usual following the army in search of investments. On this occasion the number accounted for was 53,000 head of human chattels.

1105. The growing confidence of Caesar, and his settled purpose of completing the conquest of Gaul, are clearly shewn in the campaign of this year. After his victory over the Nervii he had detached young P. Crassus with a single legion, and sent him to require the submission of the tribes in the far West, the parts then known by the general name of Aremorica, now Normandy and Brittany. Thus the effect of his recent victories was at once turned to account. For the moment the peoples of that seaboard, the Veneti and six other tribes, thought it best to acknowledge the sovranty of Rome. Caesar had at all events gained this formal advantage, that a real conquest would on Roman principles be quite natural and in order; resistance henceforth was technically[2] rebellion. His intentions were shewn by the way in which he placed the winter quarters of seven legions along the line of the Loire. This arrangement gave him the control of that important river, with facilities for shipbuilding and access to the outer sea close to the coast of the Veneti, the chief maritime people. It also cut off them and their neighbours from the hitherto unconquered

---

[1] Caes. *Gall.* II. 29, and § 785 above.
[2] Caes. *Gall.* III 10 § 2 *rebellio facta post deditionem.*

peoples of central Gaul. One legion and a body of cavalry were sent under Servius Sulpicius Galba to attempt an enterprise in another quarter. As the dominion of Rome was extended further to the North, it became desirable to secure a more convenient line of traffic to and from Italy by opening up an Alpine pass on a more direct line than that now in ordinary use (Mont Genèvre) far away to the South. Already traders were crossing by that now known as the Great St Bernard, but they were exposed to robbery and exorbitant tolls levied by the mountain tribes. Caesar had no doubt heard many complaints, and would gladly have opened up a safe and free passage by this route. But the expedition of Galba failed, chiefly because he had not a sufficient force. He tried to winter on the upper Rhone, but could not hold his ground. He fought his way out into the land of the Allobroges, but the conquest of the pass could not be taken in hand in the following spring.

1106. The achievements of the year 57 had been not less great from a military point of view than those of the preceding year. And they no longer consisted in the defence of the province and protection of allies, but in annexing to the Roman dominions a vast stretch of new country hitherto only known dimly by report. The news conveyed in Caesar's despatches made a profound impression in Rome, and the Senate decreed a public thanksgiving for the unprecedented period of 15 days. But while the mob made merry and the proconsul's agents took pains to keep alive their absent chief's political influence, he himself had more than enough to do in the winter months. He hurried back from the Loire to his work as governor of the Cisalpine, and found time for an official tour in Illyricum. He wanted to learn something of the country and visit the tribes in person. He says nothing of raising troops there, but we need not infer that he missed the chance of drawing auxiliaries from so warlike a race. From Illyricum he would return to the Cisalpine, and pick up a few threads of Roman politics. It was probably while there that he received news which shewed that his presence was urgently needed in the North.

1107. While the legions lay quiet in their winter camps the Aremorican tribes had had leisure to repent their prompt submission. The westernmost camp near the mouth of the Loire was in charge of young P. Crassus, who had distinguished himself greatly in both the late campaigns. Supplies were running short in the country round, so he sent out officers to collect food-stuffs among some of the tribes of the coast who had professed allegiance to Rome. The Veneti, who owned the chief harbours and most of the shipping of the Breton coast, and got no small profit out of the trade between Gaul and

Britain, were the first to seize the envoys of Crassus. Other tribes followed their lead. They were ready to restore the Roman officers in exchange for their own hostages in Roman hands. But they repudiated the sovranty of Rome, and banded themselves together for common action in defence of their freedom. News of this serious movement was sent off to Caesar. His reply was a comprehensive budget of orders. A fleet of war-ships was to be built on the Loire, ready for a naval campaign in the summer. Oarsmen were to be raised in the province[1] and trained to their work, and sailors and skippers procured. These orders were carried out in the early months of the year 56. The proconsul himself could not direct operations on the spot, being detained in Italy by business of even greater urgency. The true relation of the war in Gaul to the general course of Roman history will be made clearer if at this point we turn back for a while to review the state of things in Rome.

1108. In Rome things had quickly lapsed into confusion after the departure of Caesar. Pompey, solemn and irresolute, did nothing to keep order. Clodius soon began to set him at defiance, pursuing his own profit. He acted as the master of Rome, and sold his favours to the highest bidder. Even the young Tigranes, brought by Pompey from Armenia as a hostage, was enabled to escape by the connivance of Clodius, of course for a bribe. In a fight arising out of this affair, the gangs of Clodius got the upper hand, and the eminent Pompey had to shut himself up in his own house and leave the reckless tribune ruler of the street. Clodius next fell foul of the consul Gabinius, who tried to make head against him, but further rioting and the farce of 'consecrating' an opponent's goods, resorted to by both sides, were the only result. In the face of all this squabbling the aristocratic party took heart so far as to make some demonstrations of an ineffectual kind. But Clodius was able to go on carrying laws in the teeth of all opposition, obliging those who made it worth his while. Even Pompey's settlement of the East was not respected, for Clodius ventured to upset some of his arrangements in Galatia. And yet Pompey could, if he had chosen to exert himself, have put an end to this organized anarchy. Of Crassus[2] we hear nothing. There was never cordial alliance between the two, and Caesar was far away. Young P. Crassus was serving under him in Gaul. The important fact, that Caesar was more closely in touch with each of his two partners than either of them was with the other, may probably account for part of their ineffectiveness in his absence. It has been well said[3]

[1] Probably in Narbonese Gaul, but he does not say.   Caes. *Gall.* III 9.
[2] Probably he encouraged Clodius in secret.
[3] Tyrrell, *Cicero's Correspondence* II p. 34.

that it was a coalition which had never coalesced. In the two months after the departure of Caesar both constitutional government and the power of the usurpers seemed to have been reduced to nullity. Cicero's friends began to think it time to move for his recall. His brother Quintus had returned from his government of Asia. He had not been a popular governor, owing to his queer temper, but he had not enriched himself. There was however some talk of a prosecution, and he like his brother had financial troubles. But he and Atticus busied themselves to promote the orator's return, now that Clodius had fallen out with the Triumvirs. A friendly tribune raised the question in the Senate on the first of June, and the House passed a resolution in favour of Cicero's recall. But nothing came of this. Pompey too, disgusted with the insolence of Clodius, was beginning to look favourably on the proposal, but he hesitated as usual, and corresponded with Caesar. In October eight tribunes took up the matter, and even brought forward a bill, but Clodius blocked it, and this too was a failure. Meanwhile the exile was in misery, torn with alternate hopes and fears, at Thessalonica. There was indeed some hope when the elections for the next year (57) were safely over. They had gone well for his cause. One of the consuls elect, P. Cornelius Lentulus Spinther, was a friend, while the other, Q. Caecilius Metellus Nepos, formerly hostile, was no longer strongly opposed to Cicero, and indeed ended by supporting his recall. The new praetors and tribunes were also mostly in favour, though two of the latter were in the interest of Clodius. Two of those who supported Cicero were men of remarkable energy ; P. Sestius hurried off to Gaul[1] to see what he could do with Caesar, while T. Annius Milo was a bold turbulent being, eager to measure swords with Clodius.

1109. Clodius himself was not reelected tribune. It is not clear that he was a candidate. Anyhow he was no longer on terms with the Triumvirs. He ended his year of office by a wild attack upon Caesar and his Julian laws as being illegally carried in defiance of religion ; but the details of this affair are perhaps hardly to be taken on the authority[2] of Cicero. To follow out minutely the reported or conjectured opinions and actions of individuals in this question of Cicero's recall would only obscure the main points. The first important step was taken on the first of January 57, when the new consul Lentulus laid the matter before the Senate. His colleague Metellus declared his readiness to waive old animosities, and the tone of the House was as before practically unanimous in favour of restoration in some form or other. One view was that the proceedings of Clodius had been illegal and should be ignored ; Cicero should be invited to

---

[1] See Cic. *pro Sestio* § 71, a very curious passage.　　　[2] Cic. *de domo* § 40.

return, and nothing more need be done. It is obvious that this would have raised the question of the validity of the acts of Clodius other than those directed against Cicero. And by this time not a few persons would have acted on the assumption that those acts were valid. Pompey therefore with good reason urged that it was better to proceed directly by legislation expressly reinstating Cicero in his former position, and this view prevailed. But when, after several debates, a decree was passed to this effect, and a bill was introduced by a tribune at the end of January, it became clear that Clodius was still to be reckoned with. His armed gangs broke up the 'meeting of the Commons' by force, and in the free fight[1] that ensued the Forum ran with blood. Quintus Cicero was among the wounded. In short, the quiet coercion exercised by Caesar, in employing overwhelming force to carry his measures, was no longer available. The gangs of ruffians led by such men as Clodius were able to defeat other and weaker gangs, but would succumb to stronger ones. In a subsequent riot the tribune Sestius nearly lost his life. Milo now tried to prosecute Clodius on a charge of public violence (*vis*), but that worthy had still enough friends among the praetors and tribunes to prevent it. Nothing could be done by legal process in the present anarchy, so Milo and Sestius took the only practical step by engaging swordsmen, mostly slave gladiators, and competing for the guidance of public opinion. The months went by in a series of disturbances and street fights. Business was at a standstill, but bit by bit Milo gained ground. The process of meeting force by force was inevitably costly, but Milo seems to have had the help of sympathizers to a greater extent than Clodius. Pompey too was now beginning to exert himself. Though shunning the city brawls and often absent from Rome, he was still influential in Italy. He held office in the new 'colony' of Capua, and induced the local senate to pass a resolution in favour of Cicero. It was becoming clear that the recall of the exile was only a question of time. Whatever may have been the personal objections of Crassus, time had probably mitigated them, and his son Publius was a devoted admirer of Cicero. Caesar had a real liking for the orator; with him it was merely a matter of policy. He seems to have consented readily, always provided that Cicero would when restored give up his troublesome opposition. Some guarantee had to be found, and it was found in making Quintus Cicero give some sort of undertaking for the behaviour of his brother. The business now went through. The Senate began in June by passing one order to commend the exile to the good offices of all persons abroad, and another calling on citizens in Italy to mind and attend the Assembly

[1] Cic. *pro Sestio* §§ 75—8.

when the day of voting was fixed.   The opposition of Clodius and his supporters was broken down, and at last the decree, instructing the consul Lentulus to bring a bill before the Assembly of Centuries, was carried in a full House, Clodius alone opposing it.   The House also resolved that any attempt to hinder the holding of the Assembly on the day appointed would be the act of a public enemy.   Things had indeed changed.   After all Cicero was a popular man even in Rome, and the municipal element in Italy was strongly in his favour. Respectable voters rallied to the call from far and near, and on the fourth of August the bill for his restoration became law.

1110.   Cicero had been in exile about a year and three months. At the end of November 58 he thought it advisable to leave Thessalonica.   The new governor's troops were arriving in Macedonia and Piso himself was expected shortly.   But he did not move on to Cyzicus. He was evidently satisfied that he ran no danger of his life from the fact of his outlawry, and he was unable to resist the temptation to place himself nearer Rome, in more direct communication with his friends.   So he returned to Dyrrachium.   There he was within his 400 miles limit, but none molested him, and he could not only receive letters quickly but glean other news, for the stream of gossip-laden travellers[1] to Greece and the East was ever passing through the port. He took heart as prospects brightened, and ventured to cross over to Italy, landing at Brundisium on the fifth of August 57.   On the 8th he heard that the law for his restoration had been carried.   After this he made his way to Rome.   All the way he was greeted by crowds and met by deputations.   Brundisium had set the example, and all Italy seemed agog to welcome him.   His own accounts of this triumphal progress are more than satisfying, but perhaps not greatly exaggerated, for he did not reach Rome till the fourth of September. He had been driven out by the votes of a mob coerced by the ruffians of Clodius : a genuine expression of public opinion had effected—had been allowed to effect—his recall.   The scene of rejoicings in Rome (another of his favourite topics) was a fitting close to a journey that had been one long jubilee.   Everybody but Clodius and his intimates seemed to be his friend, and even Crassus came to meet him and laid his old grudges by.   It was more than native vanity in Cicero to which this grand reception appealed.   To be back again in the scene of his former triumphs and be once more a public man in his beloved city, the centre of the world, was a greater object than a momentary surfeit of glory.   Naturally he began life again (such is his own description of his return) with speeches, returning thanks[2] to Senate

---

[1] Catullus XXXVI 15 *Durrachium Adriae tabernam.*
[2] See *ad Att.* IV 1, and the speeches *post reditum.*   Doubt has been thrown on the

and People, and explaining to them what infinite credit they deserved for discovering that they could not get on without him.   But it did not take him long to find out that even those who had promoted his restoration were some of them not over-pleased to see him back, jealous of his position and his gifts that dimmed the lustre of their own.   Nor was the political situation so much changed as might appear at first sight.   The general enthusiasm displayed in the recall of Cicero might encourage the aristocrat party to hope for a revival of their power.   Now that Clodius was at loggerheads with the triumvirs, and Cicero restored in spite of him, their chance might seem to have come.   But the non-resident voters would soon disperse to their homes, and the place of the Roman People would be filled by the city mob once more.   The gangs of Clodius could only be held in check by the gangs of Milo.   The real power lay as before in the hands of the three partners, so long as they held together.   For the moment Pompey was the chief figure in Roman politics, and an occasion speedily presented itself for recognizing the fact.

IIII.   The harvests of the year 57 had not been bountiful, and just at the time of Cicero's return there was a difficulty in supplying Rome with corn.   The rabble became riotous, and Clodius declared that the dearth was all Cicero's fault, a visitation from heaven in disapproval of his recall.   The general view however seems to have been that a central control in strong hands was the thing needed, and the prompt success of Pompey in the war with the pirates indicated him as the right man for the charge.   The Senate took up the matter, and on Sept. 7 Cicero made a motion in favour of entrusting Pompey with full powers for the purpose.   The result was that an exceptional office was created.   Pompey was to have the *cura annonae* with proconsular power for five years throughout the empire.   He was allowed fifteen lieutenants.   Thus he was for the second time made ruler of the Mediterranean.   In this duty his talent for organization shewed itself as before.   Among his *legati* were the two Ciceros, and Quintus was for some time actually employed on the service under Pompey in Sardinia.   Difficulties were not overcome in a day, but the corn was procured and the mouths of the noisy multitude were stopped.   In the face of his success Clodius could only assert that, so far from Pompey being made controller to remove the scarcity of grain, grain had been held back in order to carry through the law for making Pompey controller.   But it was not only Clodius to whom the elevation of Pompey was

genuineness of these speeches.   The passage, in which he asserts (*ad quirites* § 18) that a bounteous corn-supply attests the favour of heaven in approval of his recall, is at least a strange utterance to be invented by a forger.

distasteful.   The aristocratic republicans had had enough of these great exceptional commissions.   They rightly judged that such measures boded no good to the Republic, and they were also jealous of the man.   No real reconciliation between Pompey and them had been effected.   A proposal had indeed been made[1] to grant him the entire control of the state treasury, to place at his disposal an army and a fleet, and to give him in every province a power overriding that of the several governors.   This open creation of an Emperor was probably withdrawn, at least not carried, but it may serve to shew what Pompey himself was more than willing to accept.   And Cicero too, though now drawing nearer to Pompey and still hoping to save the Republic by reuniting the great man with the Optimates, could not achieve any practical result on these lines.   The 'best men,' that is the great houses, were not minded to be dominated by Pompey or led by a 'new man' such as Cicero.   They did not see that in Pompey lay their only chance of escape from the supremacy of Caesar.   Caesar was away, Pompey was always offending them by his awkward solemnity and reserve.   Nor was Cicero in a happy mood for the function of a mediator.   In the long malady of hope deferred he had brewed a store of venom which he was now thirsting to discharge.   For quite two years after his return the language of his speeches is rich in violent and foul abuse of those who had been concerned in his banishment.   True, Roman custom allowed great license[2] in this respect.   But many of his hearers must have been wearied by these torrents of invective, and there were plenty of men in Rome, themselves victims of his ready witticisms, who would comment on his behaviour in no friendly sense.   So the orator soon began to feel[3] that the same people who had been willing to clip his wings were in no hurry to see them grow again.   Already while in exile he had felt doubts as to the wisdom of his former champion-ship of the cause of a selfish aristocracy.   What was he to do now? His patriotism urged him to uphold the Republic at all costs.   It was a pity that the Republicans, having no great leader, would not follow the man who had made such sacrifices for their sake.   But in heart he was still with them, and he did not leave them without a struggle.

1112.   In the law recalling Cicero the complete restoration of his former rights had been contemplated.   But there was still trouble about his house on the Palatine.   Clodius had pulled it down, con-secrated the site, and hoped that by erecting a monument to Liberty

[1] Cic. *ad Att.* IV 1 §§ 6, 7.
[2] See for instance the quotations in Ellis' note on Catullus XXIX 2.
[3] Cic. *ad Att.* IV 2 § 5.

thereon, and by alteration of adjacent buildings, he had dispossessed Cicero for ever. Religion and convenience alike barred restitution. But the orator fought for his house, maintaining the act of consecration to be illegal. At the end of September he pleaded his case before the court of the pontiffs. The pontiffs[1] ruled that, unless Clodius had been formally appointed to consecrate the site, his action was void and restitution admissible. The Senate followed this up by voting for restitution and for having the alterations of Clodius done away with. Clodius and a tribune who vetoed this on his behalf were overawed. No doubt the fact of Milo's forces in the background helped to quell the irrepressible mob-leader. The consuls were ordered to see the restoration carried out and to assess the damages due to Cicero as compensation. So far well, but the valuation of this town house, and of two of his country houses also destroyed, was in all three cases a sad disappointment. He put down the meanness of the valuers to the spite of those who did not wish to see him regain his lost position too quickly. And he was just now in one of his periods of financial difficulties. The rebuilding of his town house was accomplished, but not without fighting. Clodius attacked and put to flight the workmen, and the slopes of the Palatine were the scene of bloody affrays and regular assaults of houses; one day he set fire to Q. Cicero's house hard by. Milo had to be called in to protect the building operations. Such was law and order in Rome. Peaceful citizens, Cicero among them, found the streets unsafe, and things did not seem to be getting better. Meanwhile the elections for 56 had to be held. The aristocrats profited by the disorders of the time and carried off both consulships and a majority of the praetorships. But the chief contest arose over the election of aediles. Clodius, threatened by Milo with prosecution for public violence, sought office in order to bar proceedings. If the entry of the charge were accepted before the election, Clodius would be disqualified as a candidate. A warfare of tricks and intrigues ended to the advantage of Clodius. Metellus Nepos the present consul was his kinsman, and with his help the acceptance of the charge was deferred on a technical[2] pretext. Clodius became aedile for 56, but the election fell very late in the current year owing to the opposition of Milo. Milo had it is true strong support in the Senate, but the sitting in which the matter was debated was brought to an end by the threatening tumult of a Clodian mob, and the prosecution had to be dropped. Clodius had now another year to carry on his agitations. The only check was in the swordsmen of Milo, and it

[1] Caesar Pont. Max. was away.
[2] Cic. *ad Q. fratr.* II 1 § 2, Dion Cass. XXXIX 7.

began to be clear that the feud would only end with the death of one or both of these worthies. Cicero saw this clearly, and hoped for the best.

1113. A notable event of the year 57 was the affair of Ptolemy[1] Auletes. The exactions of the 'Piper' in order to pay off his Roman creditors drove his subjects to revolt, and the wretched creature fled from Alexandria to claim as an ally his restoration by the Romans. The Alexandrians had placed his eldest daughter on the throne. When they heard that the Piper was in Rome, they sent a numerous deputation (100, it is said) to entreat the Senate not to restore him. The Egyptian question gave rise to far-reaching intrigues, and filled a great space in Roman politics for months. Ptolemy had got the start, and Pompey, who wanted to be entrusted with the business, favoured him and even received him as a guest. If the prayer of the Alexandrians were granted, there would be nothing to do, and the great man was as bent upon getting a footing in Egypt as Caesar had been a few years before. The Piper, though in debt, had contrived to bring with him the ready money needed for commending his cause to Roman statesmen and for hiring agents. A good many of the hostile envoys never reached Rome, being (so it was rumoured) poisoned by the king's emissaries on the way. In September the Senate had decreed that Lentulus Spinther, who was to have Cilicia[2] for his province as proconsul, should see to the restoration of Auletes. It was notorious that bribery had been at work. There were now three party views in active competition. The Purist section, led by M. Favonius in the absence of his friend Cato, were for non-intervention, but took nothing by reopening the question. The Moderate section (if we may so call them) were for leaving the matter in the hands of Lentulus. Cicero took this view, and Pompey affected to support it. But Pompey's real wish was to be employed himself, and money was being raised by the king's chief agent to keep the Pompeian section strong in the House. Such was the tangle in January 56, when Lentulus had started for Cilicia, and the Piper had retired to watch opportunities at Ephesus. About the new year things were further complicated by a prodigy, which was seized upon to thwart the designs of Pompey. The Sibylline books were consulted and found to contain a passage allowing intervention in Egypt, but forbidding the employment of a 'multitude.' It was felt that without an army Pompey would not care to go, and an army the Senate did not mean him to have. The debates during January

---

[1] See Strabo XVII 1 § 11, Dion Cass. XXXIX 12—16. The matter is often referred to by Cicero in his letters of B.C. 57—56.

[2] Now including Cyprus, annexed by Cato.

produced several new[1] proposals, but no result. All turned on the question, Pompey or not Pompey? and the details are not important. Even a vote of the Senate forbidding the restoration altogether was vetoed some time in the spring of 56. So late as May we find Cicero writing[2] to Lentulus Spinther that Pompey had made this suggestion— 'let Lentulus restore order in Egypt with an army, and then restore the king without an army. There is no decree to stop that.' But the responsibility for a step sure to be judged by results rested wholly on Lentulus, and he knew better than to run the risk. And so, beyond its disturbing effect on Roman politics, nothing came of the Egyptian question for the present. It seems that one of the forces telling against Pompey's ambition was the jealousy of Crassus.

1114. At the beginning of 56 the confusion at Rome was indescribable. A proposal to recall Lentulus from Cilicia dragged on and came to nothing. In February Clodius impeached Milo before the Tribes. This also came to nothing, but Pompey's appearance on Milo's behalf was the occasion of a disgraceful scene. Rival mobs hooted and discharged foul abuse, and the followers of Clodius, trained to their part, chimed in with answers to their leader's questions, ridiculing and insulting Pompey. The latter was also attacked in the Senate by Gaius Cato, his old enemy, and the preparations for rioting were so manifest that he was in fear of his life. Crassus and others were understood to be backing up C. Cato and Clodius with money. Pompey therefore drew more closely to Milo, and summoned additional supporters from Picenum and the Gallic districts. So he and Milo contrived to weather the storm. The luckless Cicero had indeed fallen upon evil days. The aristocrats in the Senate were not sorry to use Clodius and his crew to weaken Pompey, and this of course made things worse for Cicero. But the orator at least found occupation in the law-courts. In February he defended L. Calpurnius Bestia on a charge of *ambitus*, and one of his greatest speeches still preserved was that delivered in March for P. Sestius, who had done and dared so much to effect his recall. The charge was one of public violence, but was essentially a party move to ruin an adversary of Clodius. A triumphant acquittal was the result. But Cicero was all through these months in a state of perplexity. The ties that bound him to the Optimates were growing weaker. He could not trust them. Soon after his return he confessed[3] that the 'good men' (*boni*, true republicans) were almost extinct. He could not well set up for himself on independent lines. Without a gang of swordsmen he would make himself ridiculous.

---

[1] Such as that Pompey should go and restore the king with a pair of lictors only.
[2] Cic. *ad fam.* 1 7 §§ 4—6.   [3] Cic. *ad Att.* IV 3 § 2.

No, for him there was no flaming in the van of great events. ' I am tired of surgery' he wrote[1] to Atticus 'and taking to a course of regimen.' But he could not keep on good terms with all parties, let him be ever so judicious. He had got to make a choice, and the further he drifted away from the republican aristocrats the nearer he found himself to the triumvirs, though sorely against his will. He had refused to work with them in the early days of the coalition. But the Three were now less united and seemed therefore less dangerous. Pompey was very irritating with his slowness and reserve. Still it was delightful to be once more on intimate terms with one whom he regarded as the head of the coalition, all the more as this connexion no longer necessitated submission to Crassus. He was gravitating to the side of the triumvirs, as Atticus, a shrewd time-serving judge, had advised. How he strove against this tendency, longing to think and act for himself, and how irresistible it was, soon appeared when a question arose on which he ventured to take a line of his own.

1115. On the 10th December 57 one of the new tribunes, P. Rutilius Lupus, raised the question[2] of the *ager Campanus* in the Senate. Evidently there was something wrong; probably the assignation of this land to Pompey's veterans had worked little if at all better[3] than the similar allotments of Sulla. The state had sacrificed the rents which under the old system of leases had been a mainstay of the treasury. And though there were now the new revenues from the East, expenses were also very great, what with grants in connexion with the corn-supply and the great sums voted to the governors of Macedonia Syria and Gaul. Whatever the details[4] of the trouble in Campania, Cicero was delighted to hear Lupus bringing up argument after argument that he had himself used against the bill of Rullus seven years before. Caesar had made a mess with his law for assigning the Campanian land, while Cicero's forecast was amply justified, and the great orator was innocent enough to think that this mattered. Lupus combined several hits at Caesar with appeals to Pompey. But Pompey was not there, being away on business of the corn-supply. No division was taken on that day, but Cn. Cornelius Lentulus Marcellinus, one of the consuls elect, entered a protest against debating the question in Pompey's absence.

---

[1] Cic. *ad Att.* IV 3 § 3 *ego diaeta curare incipio, chirurgiae taedet.*

[2] Cic. *ad Q. frat.* II 1 § 1.

[3] That something was working badly seems clear from a proposal (details unknown) of young Curio in the year 51. See Caelius in *ad fam.* VIII 10 § 4, Cic. *ad Att.* VII 7 § 6.

[4] It may be that the state-land had been assigned to little purpose, and that the question of continuing the process by purchasing private land was the point now in dispute.

The matter came up again[1] on the 5th April, just after a large sum (about £350,000) had been voted to Pompey for the purchase of corn. There was unusual excitement in the House, for funds were running low and corn was dear. Cicero took part in a very animated debate, evidently advocating a change of policy in the matter of the land. No decision was reached, but it was agreed to consider the question again in a full House on the 15th May. Pompey was present, and Cicero declares that he offered no objection to what had been said, in fact took it all quietly. He then left Rome for Africa and Sardinia on corn-business. But before May 15 a good deal had happened. Pompey had gone on from Sardinia to meet Caesar, and the whole political outlook underwent a magic change.

1116. When Caesar in the winter of 57—56 had got through his administrative business in Illyricum and Cisalpine Gaul, and had sent instructions for the formation of a fleet in readiness for next season's campaign, he was free to attend to Roman politics directly and with effect. He had kept himself well informed of the movements of the time, and he understood the position of his two partners better than they did themselves. Crassus was becoming restless. He wanted to play a larger part, and the distinguished career of his son in Gaul had rekindled in him the smouldering ambition of military renown. He had never liked either Cicero or Pompey, and the wide charge of the corn-supply had placed the latter in a position which roused the jealousy of Crassus. Pompey too was worried and ill at ease. He was hurt at the inadequate recognition of his merits, and blind to his own failings. Greedy of popularity, and prone to accept it as no more than his due, even with exceptional powers to match, he had received less powers than he coveted, while his popularity had died away. Meanwhile the republican nobles had gained ground and become bolder. Cato had either returned or was just returning from Cyprus. And now the news came that Cicero was beginning to tamper with the provisions of the Julian land-law. This was nothing less than an attack on the key of the triumvirs' position, as Cicero afterwards confessed. Caesar saw in a twinkling the importance of the move and the trouble that might arise from dallying. He seems to have heard of it in March, while he was at Ravenna conferring with Crassus. Already there was talk at Rome of recalling Caesar, and by the arrangement in force his command was to end in March 54. He knew, first, that two more campaigns were not enough for the conquest of Gaul; secondly, that if and when his Roman enemies attacked him he must look to himself, not to his two partners, for

[1] Cic. *ad Q. frat.* II 5 § 1.

protection; and thirdly, that he was not yet ready to face a civil war, if civil war were forced upon him. So he took Crassus with him to Luca[1] in northern Etruria, and sent for Pompey, who was easily able to join them by sea from Sardinia without having to cross the Apennine. The quiet country town was for a few days in April 56 the political centre of the Roman world. The news of the meeting spread fast. The revival of the coalition as a working agreement removed all possible doubts as to the real seat of power in the immediate future. Practical men hastened to Luca with an eye to their own interests. Plutarch tells us that there were assembled more than 200 senators. Among them were magistrates, and two provincial governors on their ways to Sardinia and Spain. In attendance on the official personages were 120 lictors. The three principals, thanks to the clear views of Caesar, backed up by his adroitness sympathy and personal charm, soon came to terms among themselves and made a division of the honours and preferments of the so-called Republic. Early in the next year Cicero refers[2] to the rumour that the names of the consuls for years and years to come were all recorded in a private note-book of Pompey. But the partners' own shares of the spoil were the main business of the famous conference.

1117. The reconciliation of Pompey and Crassus was the first necessity. Under Caesar's management community of interest soon got the better of jealousy and other causes of estrangement. At Rome all had gone badly, at Luca difficulties were smoothed. A comprehensive scheme of common policy would give the two bunglers what they wanted. In the conclave of the Three no friction could arise from Senate Assembly or annual Magistrates. Those republican organs would, when their cooperation was needed, work in obedience to an effective driving-power; and that power was present at Luca in the fact of the revived coalition. Pompey and Crassus each wanted an important province, a long term of command, and a powerful army. This was at once agreed upon, and probably in some detail, for votes of Senate or Assembly, not to mention the sacred decisions of the lot, might be taken for granted. The order of events was to be this. Pompey and Crassus were to be consuls together for the second time in 55, thus keeping out the aristocratic republican L. Domitius

---

[1] Suetonius *Jul.* 24 says that Luca was in Caesar's province. This I doubt, but the question is very obscure. The river Macra is supposed, rightly as I believe, to have been the boundary of Italy proper on this side at this time. If Luca was in the province, it was probably included by Sulla. Convenience was of course the reason for choosing the town now. Caesar was not the man to shrink from stepping a few miles outside his border for a few days. And there was nobody to stop him. Nissen, *Landeskunde* I 76, II 287—8, holds that Luca was in the province. See §§ 921, 1217.

[2] Cic. *ad Att.* IV 8b § 2.

Ahenobarbus, a determined opponent of the coalition, and preparing the way for their own succession to provinces. The province for Pompey was to be the two Spains, and it was probably also understood that he was to have a free hand in the employment of lieutenant-governors if and when he saw reason for remaining in Rome. Crassus was to have Syria, with the prospect of glory to be won in a Parthian war. There was it is true no Parthian war on foot, but the Parthians were said to be growing strong, and pacific scruples had no place at Luca. Both commands were to carry with them suitable armies, and Pompey at least was to be appointed for a term of five years. Caesar was to have his command prolonged for five years more, that is from March 54 to March 49. Plutarch says that the Three agreed to take matters in hand more vigorously. This is no doubt correct; what it meant was simply that no hindrances arising from the republican constitution were to be allowed to stand in the way of the real masters of Rome.

1118. The course of action by which the partners were to carry out their designs was also settled. It has the unmistakeable stamp of Caesar. We are told that Caesar promised to write to his friends in Rome and bid them support Pompey and Crassus for consuls, and also to grant furloughs to some of his soldiers to come and vote. The latter part of the promise is not quite clear. He could hardly give leave of absence to many men hundreds of miles away in northern Gaul, who were needed for field service in the summer and had to hold their winter camps in force when the season was over. Very few voters could be supplied from that quarter. If any considerable number[1] were sent to vote, it must surely have been from levies in the Cisalpine, not yet sent to the front. But it may be doubted whether much came of this promise of soldier-voters. We know that the elections were by deliberate obstruction[2] put off till very late in the year, which may possibly have been to give time for soldiers on leave to appear: but we also know that the year ended without an election. However this may have been, it was important to check or silence troublesome opponents. Cato was not to be frightened or bought. Clearly he must be thwarted in every possible way. Clodius had been troublesome to Pompey, and encouraged by Crassus. The change in the attitude of Clodius towards Pompey which shortly took place was probably a result of the revival of the coalition at Luca. In the case of Cicero there is no doubt as to the causes and effects. Pompey had

---

[1] The soldiers mentioned by Dion Cass. XXXIX 31 as having assisted at the election (early in 55) were a body conducted by young P. Crassus. I see no reason to suppose that there were many of them. It was their swords, not their votes, that were so useful.

[2] Lange *RA* III 328.

been intimate with him since his return, and had made no protest when he attacked Caesar's agrarian law. But the great man had now gained from Caesar the very concessions that the blind republicans had refused him. If Cicero was allowed to go on in this way, others would do the same. Domitius was already planning to deprive Caesar of Gaul. What if he were backed up by Cato, Bibulus, and the rest? This sort of thing would end no one could say where. So once more Pompey threw over[1] Cicero, and undertook to silence him. On his way back he told his *legatus* Q. Cicero that he had gone bail for his brother's future compliance with the policy of the coalition; if he did not seriously warn the orator to behave differently, he would himself have to pay for the indiscretion of his brother. Quintus lost no time in conveying the gist of this to Marcus. The effect was instantaneous. Cicero was reminded that his restoration had only been conceded through the consent of Caesar, and on the understanding that he was not to assail the acts of Caesar. There was no fear of his forgetting Clodius, who was still worrying him freely, and would like nothing better than to banish him again. Cicero made the best of a bad business. The debate on the Campanian land which stood adjourned[2] to the 15th May was never resumed.

1119. Having once abandoned his independent line of action in this matter, Cicero found that he must transfer his political allegiance to the side of the coalition. The aristocrats had been pleased enough to see him embroil himself[3] with the triumvirs, but they did not care for him, and would sacrifice nothing to protect him from attack. So he found cogent reasons for abandoning the party with which he had a real community of aims, and for following Pompey in his change of front. Pompey had ceased to carp at Caesar, and now made it his business to carry out the plans formed at Luca. Cicero, disgusted with his former associates, found himself bit by bit drawn on from acquiescence to advocacy. His letters betray his misgivings and lament his helplessness in the state of politics. But he could not endure to efface himself by retirement, so he had to go on, and long before the end of the year 56 he was safely lodged in the house of bondage. The transition was smoothed[4] by the ever dexterous hand of Caesar, whose letters and messages made the sensitive man feel himself appreciated as he would wish, and dissembled his submission. Old sympathies revived, and soon the statesman unhappy in Rome could plume himself on finding his letters of request and recommendation

---

[1] Cic. *ad fam.* I 9 §§ 8—12.
[2] Cic. *ad Q. frat.* II 6 § 2, a passage notable for its reticence.
[3] Cic. *ad fam.* I 9 § 10, *ad Att.* IV 5.
[4] The relations of Cicero and Caesar are ably discussed by G. Boissier, *Cicéron et ses amis.*

honoured at headquarters in Gaul. Caesar pleased him by reading his writings, even his indifferent poems. In connexion with this subject we may refer in advance to the promotion of the orator's brother to an important military post under Caesar. One of the results of the conference of Luca had been to open the eyes of enterprising men to the great prospects awaiting successful officers in the Gaulish war. Caesar had entertained the company magnificently. Not a few politicians had come away from the gathering with handsome retaining-fees. Familiar gossip with Caesar's staff no doubt convinced many that despatches had not exaggerated the greatness of victories already won, and that the opportunities of winning distinction, and perhaps of picking up some plunder, were greater than had occurred for many a day. The news soon spread, and many young men of good families were eager to make a campaign or two under a proconsul who was known to reward service and seemed to bring luck. Among those bitten with the fancy to serve in Caesar's military school was Quintus Cicero. In 54 we find Caesar taking him[1] as one of his *legati*. Marcus was delighted with Caesar's treatment of his brother, who gained no little credit in Gaul, as we shall see.

1120. To return for a moment to the position of Cicero before the conference of Luca. Earlier in that year, in his defence of Sestius, the orator came into collision with Caesar's satellite P. Vatinius. Vatinius in giving evidence for the prosecution provoked Cicero, who, as was allowed in the practice of Roman courts, turned upon him in a special speech of challenge (*interrogatio*) to destroy the value of his evidence. In the form of questioning he exposed the seamy side of Vatinius' public character with furious and malignant vehemence. It is one of his most abusive utterances, but it is to be noted that he makes a marked distinction between Vatinius and Caesar. One of the points made to discredit the witness is his vile presumption in fancying that he, the agent, might do things hardly to be tolerated even in his great principal. Cicero boasted that he had given the fellow a dressing, and silenced him. But the taunt of Vatinius had found its mark: that the rise of Caesar made Cicero fear to attack him in defending Sestius was an irritating truth. We need not dwell upon the continued feud with Clodius, in the course of which the occurrence of prodigies, and the report of the soothsayers (*haruspices*) to the Senate on their significance, led to further bickering. Among the breaches of religious propriety detected by the Haruspices were certain points which Clodius and Cicero turned against each

---

[1] For the story of Cicero's application on his brother's behalf, and the adventure of the letter, see *ad Q. fratr.* II 10 (12) §§ 4, 5.

other, and an edifying exchange of further abuse[1] was the result, with other equally trivial squabbles to follow.   A grand opportunity occurred in the defence of M. Caelius Rufus, brought to trial in this spring for public or criminal violence (*vis*).   The prosecution was a Clodian affair.   Caelius[2] had been a lover of the notorious Clodia, and her malice was now added to that of her brother.   Both Crassus and Cicero spoke for the defence, and an acquittal was secured.   There is much worth noting in this speech of Cicero, beyond the invectives against Clodius and Clodia, which are strong enough.   The accused had been intimate with Catiline, and the general excesses of his youth had been noticed unfavourably even in the dissolute society of Rome. The speaker handles the former of these topics with remarkable skill and delicacy: his treatment of the latter is a shameless masterpiece in palliation of youthful indiscretions.   The charge also alleged that Caelius had been concerned in certain affairs of poisoning, in particular the murder[3] of the philosopher Dion, head of the recent deputation from Alexandria.   The date of the speech for Caelius is uncertain, but it was probably early in the year.   Enough has been said to shew that life in Rome was full of excitement, for in the background of forensic activity the gangs of ruffians were still to the fore, and the anxiety as to supplies of grain was as yet not wholly allayed.

1121.   Things were somewhat quieter in the summer.   Food became more plentiful as Pompey's organization began to shew results, and Clodius had doubtless been warned to restrain his turbulence.   The driving power of the revived coalition (though the actual compact of Luca was at first a secret) set the wheels moving. The Senate voted Caesar money[4] for payment of the troops raised by him on his own authority, and allowed him to appoint the unusual number of ten *legati*.   Cicero had to support these proposals, and the House had to consent.   In June a debate took place on the fixing of provinces to be held in 54 by the consuls of 55.   These should by rights be elected in the course of the current summer (56), and their future provinces should according to the *lex Sempronia* of C. Gracchus (not always kept) be fixed before their election.   It was not as yet known that Pompey and Crassus meant to stand and be elected. Four provinces came under consideration.   Piso and Gabinius deserved to be recalled from Macedonia and Syria.   The former had misgoverned his province so shamefully that discontent within and inability to control barbarian raiders seriously endangered the interests

---

[1] That Cicero's speech *de haruspicum responso* is the edited copy of that actually delivered, I do not venture to affirm.   But I find it very difficult to attribute it to a forger.   It does not stand on a high level, I freely admit.

[2] For Caelius see Boissier, *Cicéron et ses amis*, and Tyrrell's *Correspondence of Cicero*, Introd. to vol. III.

[3] Cic. *pro Caelio* §§ 23, 54 foll.   [4] Cic. *ad fam.* I 7 § 10.

of Rome. The latter had been so busy with enriching himself that he had not duly respected the claims of Roman revenue-farmers to their share of the spoil. Servilius Isauricus proposed to name these two governorships for the new consuls. This Cicero[1] supported, eager to deal a blow at his two enemies, but proposed to send out praetorian governors, and so to recall Piso and Gabinius, not in January 54, but a year earlier. The other alternative was that favoured by the present consuls. Its aim was to check the dangerous growth of Caesar by withdrawing him from Gaul. But Caesar had both the Gaulish provinces. The Cisalpine, granted him by the Assembly, could not be taken from him before March 54, for there was no prospect of repealing the Vatinian law. But the Further province, with which the war was directly connected, was held from each January to the next by vote of the Senate. To take away this province was technically possible, but to do so would mean going back on the Senate's own policy, disapproving the advance of Caesar and the victories for which the House had voted special thanksgivings, and sending a new commander, not controlling the resources of the Cisalpine, to face the Gauls. And the Gauls, an old enemy dreaded for hundreds of years, now in a fair way to be pacified for ever,—was it wise to withdraw the general who had shewn his ability to make an end of the long-drawn struggle in favour of Rome? That these and other objections had weight was virtually admitted by some half-hearted speakers, who suggested a middle course, to name either Syria or Macedonia and either Hither or Further Gaul. But it was clear that, for the task before him, Caesar must have both Gauls or neither, and Cicero rightly opposed any such compromise. But he felt that he had to explain how it came about that he was upholding the cause of Caesar. The passage in which he justifies the reconciliation is ingenious and eloquent, but the plain truth was that on his side it meant submission. Caesar was now again his friend, but with a difference. He was Cicero's master. The orator had made his public[2] recantation, and the consciousness of his humiliation galled him sadly. His letters shew him either groaning over his submission, or justifying it by crying out upon the perfidy and jealousy of the aristocrats, which had brought him to this pass. It is not clear that the debate on the provinces ended with a decisive vote. But later we find that Piso was superseded, and Caesar retained the Gauls, while Gabinius was left in Syria for a further year, probably because it was destined for Crassus.

1122. In the spring of 56 Cato[3] had returned from his mission to

---

[1] See his speech *de provinciis consularibus.*

[2] On the whole I incline to think that a copy of this speech is the παλινῳδία referred to in *ad Att.* IV 5 § 1.

[3] Cato. See Plutarch *Cat. min.* 39, 40, Dion Cass. XXXIX 22, 23, Cic. *de prov. cons.* § 45, and § 1087 above.

the East. He gave himself airs in his usual perverse style, but the quantity of treasure that he paraded and handed over to the state chest was astonishing. He wanted to shew everybody what plain honesty meant, and leave them to draw inferences as to the common practice in such cases. But Roman society had got beyond profiting by good examples. Clodius soon began to worry him over his lost account-books and other matters, and shortly afterwards he found himself at loggerheads with Cicero. In one of his frequent squabbles with Clodius, the orator took occasion to assert that the whole tribunate of Clodius had been illegal, and his acts therefore invalid. Most people must have been weary of this oft-repeated and futile utterance. To Cato, just home from abroad, it may have been new. It struck him that his own commission rested on a Clodian law. He had done the dirty work unwillingly, but was vastly proud of the way in which he had done it. To have the confirmation of his acts delayed, possibly refused, through scruples about the adoption of Clodius three years ago, was too much even for the Stoic. The acts were his, and the scruples were not. So he took the side of Clodius, and maintained that, though his policy had been pernicious, his laws were valid. Cicero was angry, and for some time there was a marked coolness between these two eminent men. They were indeed now no longer in the same political camp. Just when Cicero had left the aristocratic republicans, the return of Cato gave renewed vigour to their counsels. They made much of Cato, who was ever ready to fight in the front of their cause and to take the knocks. Various honours were voted him, not to his mind. It was more to the point that he was to be supported in standing for the praetorship. There seems to have been some difficulty about this, probably owing to the date of his birthday. If this fell late in the year, then he would not reach the age for election till after the usual time of elections was past, and Cato was no man to accept special exemption from the ordinary rules. But, even as the consular provinces had been idly discussed in ignorance that the matter had been already settled at Luca, so now the republican leaders seem to have been ignorant that the triumvirs did not intend to let the elections be held at all in the current year. The present consuls, Lentulus Marcellinus and L. Marcius Philippus, were aristocrats. If either of them presided at the *comitia*, the whole power of the presiding officer would be used to defeat the scheme of the coalition. Under such conditions, Pompey and Crassus both being unpopular, and the gangs of swordsmen holding each other in check, the plan of the three partners might miscarry, and neither of the two on the spot was prepared to upset such a result by civil war. The end of it was that by means of subordinate agents Pompey and Crassus prevented any election of consuls or praetors in 56, and the

year 55 opened with an *interregnum*.   By that time Cato had turned
39 and was eligible.

1123.   The latter part of the year was not marked by great events
in Rome.   Cicero was fitting himself to his new position.   The
harness of the coalition galled him, but he could not deeply regret
having left his former selfish and disloyal allies.   A case soon occurred
in which he had to bear a leading part.   I have already spoken of
L. Cornelius Balbus of Gades, his enfranchisement by Pompey, and
his rise to influence in Rome.   He had for some time past been
serving Caesar, who quickly discerned his merits, in a confidential
capacity.   Not a few of the delicate negotiations of recent years had
been carried through by the agency of Balbus.   But in proportion as
he became the more valued by his employers, the more he became
obnoxious to their opponents.   It was as an agent of the triumvirs
that the successful Spaniard was now attacked.   He was brought to
trial[1] under the *lex Papia* of 65, accused of wrongfully usurping the
Roman citizenship.   Pompey Crassus and Cicero defended him with
success, and Balbus was a more important person than ever.   The
case seems to have involved much technical argument on the law and
practice of the constitution in reference to the franchise.   Cicero
appears to have had a good case, and it is possible that this may have
influenced the jury.

1124.   To conclude this chapter with the elections, the continued
obstruction[2] was evidently part of a definite plan, and it began to be
rumoured that Pompey and Crassus were aiming at a second consulship.   The consul Marcellinus at last questioned them plainly as to
their intentions, and got an evasive answer from Pompey, and a
hypocritical one from Crassus.   Suspicion soon became certainty.   But
when in January 55 the elections had to be held by an *interrex*, and
the two partners did not desire competitors, L. Domitius alone,
encouraged by his brother-in-law Cato, persisted in his candidature.
But an ambuscade of swordsmen put him and his following to flight,
and Pompey and Crassus became consuls as arranged.   The praetorian
election took place later, not before February.   Cato was a candidate,
and the partners' object was now to keep him out at all costs and get
Vatinius in.   A motion was made in the Senate that the praetors
when elected should for 60 days remain liable to prosecution for
corrupt practices.   This the new consuls would not put to the vote.
They made it clear that they meant to rule in defiance of everybody
and everything.   Their gangs of ruffians and the gold of Caesar did
the rest.   From this edifying spectacle let us turn again to the doings
of Caesar in Gaul.

---

[1] See Reid's Introduction to the *pro Balbo*.
[2] Cic. *ad Q. frat.* II 7, Plutarch *Pomp.* 51, *Cat. min.* 42, Dion Cass. XXXIX 30—32.

CHAPTER LV.

1125. WHEN the conference of Luca was over, the coalition once more effective, and measures taken to guide Roman politics in the way desired, Caesar lost no time in returning to the front. He found a fleet built in his ship-yards on the Loire, and a number of local craft were soon requisitioned among the tribes, Pictones and Santoni, who held the coast to the South. He meant to humble the Veneti and other rebels, and so to punish them as to convince the Gauls generally that to rebel after submission to Rome and lay hands on Roman envoys was a dangerous game. There was no telling how far the example of rebellion might spread while he was busy with the Veneti. Accordingly, while he conducted the main operations of the season himself, he resolved to send out some of his lieutenants with suitable detachments to make his power felt in other quarters. The trusty Labienus with a mounted force was to march eastwards, visiting the Remi and watching over the loyalty of the conquered Belgae. He was then to push on to the Treveri. He was to have an eye to the Germans, a body of whom were said to have been sent for by discontented Belgae, and to see that they did not pass the Rhine. Another force, under P. Crassus, consisting of both horse and foot, was ordered to the South and South-West. A combination of the Aquitanian tribes with those of central Gaul was to be prevented. It is probable that the safety of the prosperous Narbonese province, in which no army was stationed, was in Caesar's thoughts. A third and stronger detachment of three legions, under Q. Titurius Sabinus, was to operate against the northern Aremorican tribes on the seaboard of what is now north-eastern Brittany and Normandy. This movement was a diversion, to leave Caesar himself free to deal with the Veneti. The naval forces were concentrated and placed under the command of a young officer, Decimus Junius Brutus. But storms held the fleet for a time weather-bound in the mouth of the Loire, and Caesar could not wait. So he advanced into the Venetian territory and began his campaign by land.

1126. Time was precious, for operations had evidently been begun somewhat late this year (56), and progress was extremely difficult. The strongholds of the Veneti were generally fortified headlands, some of them actually islands at high water. In these places the population had taken refuge, and the open country had been emptied of supplies to victual them. If the Roman engineers made a fort accessible by means of a dam, the natives took ship and moved on to another post. Estuaries cut up the country and made effective movements by land impossible. In short all depended on the fleet, and the fleet on the weather. The native seamen had a great advantage in minute knowledge of the local waters, position of channels and shoals, anchorages, and so forth ; and also in long familiarity with the phenomena of the Atlantic tides. This last subject Caesar's skippers did indeed more or less master by careful observation, but they had to compete with the natives of a district which still breeds some of the ablest mariners of France. Not less important was the difference in the type of vessels composing the rival fleets. Brutus had with him some Gaulish ships, of which we have no detailed description, and on which it is clear that he did not greatly rely. But the bulk of his squadron were the vessels just built on the pattern used in the Mediterranean dockyards. They were galleys in which the motive power was chiefly supplied by oars, and for manoeuvring wholly so. To keep down the weight of the hulls, the framework of these galleys was as light as safety would permit, and the planking comparatively thin. Stability was gained by depth, and stiffness by depth of keel. This made them difficult to handle in shallow waters among reefs and banks. They wanted sea-room. At the same time they were not good sea-boats, owing to an insufficiency of free-board, and their low bows were unfit to face a heavy sea : nor were Mediterranean seamen as yet used to the waves of the Atlantic. Far other were ships of the Veneti. They were heavy sailing vessels of large size, built strongly of oak. Not only had they considerable free-board, but their high bow and stern, designed for service in rough waters, also formed towers for discharge of missiles. Their flat bottoms enabled them to take the ground without hurt and float again with the next tide ; against their stout sides the beaks of the Romans could do nothing. But the fleet was to these barbarians their military all. If it were taken or destroyed, the flower of their fighting men went with it, and without it their strongholds must inevitably succumb.

1127. Those who read with attention Caesar's simple story[1] will I think not deem it too much to say that this nautical episode is one of the very finest achievements recorded of even a Roman army. That military tribunes and centurions should take command of ships

[1] Caes. *Gall.* III 12—16.

of war in what Romans called 'our sea' was no new thing. But it was another matter to venture on seeking out and bringing to battle at such great disadvantage a fleet manned by seafaring people in their own home waters, the waters of the 'outer sea' or Ocean, regarded as the limit of the world. If anything went wrong with the Roman fleet, valour would be useless. The force on land could not help their comrades afloat, and they too would probably perish in a general rising of the Gauls. But we hear of no misgivings. When the weather got better, the admiral put out to sea and made for the Venetian coast to find and fight the enemy. The Veneti were not less eager for action, and the fight took place not far from shore, in full view of Caesar and his army. It was soon found that ramming was hopeless, and the exchange of javelins and other shot was all in favour of the loftier ships. The only hope was in destroying the mobility of the enemy's ships, and in boarding. An appliance had however been invented, consisting of a long pole with a sharp hooked knife at the end. With tools of this kind the Romans cut the slings that carried the yards of the heavy sails (made of hides) used by the Veneti. Down came yards and sails, the vessels lay like logs, and boarding-parties captured them one by one. After a time those still under sail took to flight. And then there fell a dead calm, and the whole fleet lay at the mercy of the Romans. Hardly any escaped, and this one battle ended the Venetian war. Fortune had again done great things for Caesar. The rash enterprise would surely have ended in another story if, instead of the wind dropping, it had come on to blow.

1128. On the submission of the Veneti, which quickly followed, Caesar carried out his intentions. He put to death all the members of their 'senate' or tribe-council, and sold the rest as slaves. Meanwhile the campaign of Sabinus had been not less successful. The rebellious tribes gathered in great force, and caution was necessary; but false information, supplied through a Gaulish emissary, tempted them to try and storm the Roman camp. Taken in both flanks by an unexpected sally, the barbarians were routed with immense slaughter. This disaster took the heart out of them, and the tribes, once more disunited, surrendered without delay. Crassus too had done well in the South-West. His legionary strength was small (12 cohorts) but he had a sufficient force of cavalry. He raised bodies of Gaulish auxiliaries, apparently not very trustworthy, and called out a number of Roman veterans settled in the cities of the province (Narbo, Carcaso, Tolosa), to give more stiffness to a miscellaneous army. The question of supplies as usual demanded great care. It was above all things necessary to avoid a reverse, for the record of Roman advance in Aquitania had hitherto not been particularly glorious, and a single defeat might now kindle a widespread rising. The natives called in help from Spain, including old warriors who had learnt something of Roman military methods in the service of Sertorius. But their attempts to cut the communications of Crassus were foiled, and when they built a regular camp the tribesmen had not the discipline needed to defend it. A vigorous attack in front was enough to make them neglect their rear, and the host scattered in flight was cut up by the cavalry. Nearly all the Aquitanian tribes at once accepted the sovranty of Rome.

1129. An expedition made by Caesar against the Morini and Menapii, coast-tribes dwelling further to the North between the Somme and Rhine, was less successful. The natives took refuge in the forests and harassed the invaders. Defeat made no impression on their obstinacy. The season was far spent, and a spell of bad weather made it necessary to withdraw the legions. So the campaign ended with laying waste lands and homesteads. The army was put into winter-quarters in the region between the Seine and Loire, where they could overawe the recently conquered tribes. Of the experiences of Labienus among the Belgae we have no account, so it may be assumed that nothing of importance occurred to thwart the objects of his mission. But there was serious trouble brewing beyond the Rhine. News reached Caesar while spending the winter months (56—55) in the Cisalpine which caused him to set out earlier than usual for the next season's work beyond the Alps.

1130. Gaul itself was quiet, but things had been going on in Germany the consequences of which were now felt in the Rhineland. The Suebi, of whom we have already heard, were a great confederation, said to be the strongest power in Germany. Fertile and warlike, they were always wanting elbow-room and winning it with the sword. Report said that the whole group consisted of 100 cantons (*pagi*) and that they were in the habit of putting into the field every year a host of 100,000 men. Those who served one year in arms spent the next year in raising food, while a fresh levy took their place. Their lands were held in common, and tillage was little developed. Milk and flesh were supplied by their flocks and herds, and by the produce of the chase; for they were great hunters. Their simple lives, great strength, scanty clothing, and power of enduring cold, made the Germans the terror of their neighbours; and the Suebi were the terror of other Germans. They had lately been pressing northwest-wards, and dislodged two weaker units, the Usipetes and Tencteri. Finding no other outlet, these tribes made their way to the lower Rhine in search of a new home, out of reach of the Suebi. At this time the position seems to have been as follows. The Suebi, dwelling in and about the Thuringian forest, had as western neighbours the Ubii, a strong tribe settled on the right bank of the Rhine. These Ubii they could not dislodge, but reduced them to a sort of tributary dependence. Lower down the river dwelt the Sugambri, and still further north was the district in which the Usipetes and Tencteri were for the time encamped, hoping to cross the stream and settle finally in Gaul. But the way was blocked by the Menapii, who extended so far eastwards that they held a strip of land on the German side of the Rhine. This outpost the Menapii withdrew when the migration became too pressing, and concentrated their efforts on defence of the river-frontier. A feigned retreat on the part of the crafty Germans tempted them to reoccupy their homesteads on the right bank. The enemy suddenly returned, surprised and slew the party detached from their main body, seized their boats, and effected the passage of the Rhine. The Menapii were driven westwards, and the wandering Germans took possession of their houses and lived on their food for the rest of this winter.

1131. Caesar knew the Gauls well enough to gauge the magnitude of the danger. Their fickle temper was not to be trusted. The only way to bind them to Rome was to prove to them that the Roman could and would drive out the German. When he returned to the front early in 55 he soon learnt that some of the tribes were already in communication with the invaders, and that the latter were on the move. They were now in the country of the Eburones and Condrusi (S.E. Belgium and thereabouts), tribes dependent on the Treveri, of whom Caesar already had his suspicions. So, while he concentrated his army, he summoned a meeting of Gaulish chiefs. He addressed them in a tone of confidence which he was far from feeling, but the impression of which it was important to convey, and ordered them to send in their several contingents of cavalry for the coming campaign. When all was ready he marched at once to meet the Germans. The geography of this campaign is more than usually obscure: its results are not in doubt and may be summarized as follows. A German embassy came to offer friendship on condition of their being allowed to settle in Gaul. They did not wish to be compelled to fight for a settlement, but this was not due to fear. They were afraid of nothing but the Suebi. In short, they were come to stay. This Caesar refused to allow. Out of Gaul they must go. But he added 'I have with me an embassy from the Ubii, who seek our protection against the Suebi; if you like to recross the Rhine into their country, I will arrange with them to find you lands.' The Germans replied by asking two days' delay to consider the matter, Caesar meanwhile to stay where he was.

But he, guessing that this was a ruse to gain time[1] for a mounted detachment to return from a raid, refused this condition and pushed on. The envoys again met him, asking to have three days time to get an answer from the Ubii, professing readiness to abide by that answer if favourable; and requested Caesar to restrain his advanced force of cavalry from acts of war in the meantime. To this he consented, though scenting the same trick as before, and sent forward orders to the desired effect.

1132. Shortly after this the cavalry (Gauls) came back in haste, a mob of demoralized fugitives. Of 5000 they had lost 74. Whether from a misunderstanding or (as Caesar makes out) from treachery, a body of 800 German horse had charged them when off their guard and driven them back in panic flight. To Caesar the most serious part of the business was the moral effect produced on his Gaulish allies. He resolved to fight the Germans without delay, before the mischief had time to work. Next morning all the chief Germans came to explain matters—and to try some new trick, if we believe[2] Caesar. He took a short way with the slippery barbarians. He seized the whole party, put his army in motion, and fell upon the main body all unsuspecting and bereft of their leaders. If Caesar's text be sound, their number, men women and children, was 430,000. Those who escaped the first rush of butchery were either cut down by the cavalry in flight or driven into a place[3] where two rivers met and drowned in the waters. No Roman was killed, and very few wounded. Caesar informed the chiefs whom he had arrested that they were now free to depart. But they, looking for no mercy at the hands of the Gauls whose lands they had plundered, replied that they preferred to stay with him, and he did not reduce them to slavery. It is necessary to tell this story here, though we have no German version to compare with that of Caesar. It illustrates the Roman point of view, and also the everlasting difficulty that men at different stages of civilization, with wholly different notions of honour and the nature of a compact, and dependent on interpreters for each other's meaning, had and still have in coming to terms. Nor must we forget the extreme peril of the Roman army, and the awful responsibility of the choice resting on Caesar. He soon made his choice, probably from the point of view that at the moment the only tolerable German was a dead German.

---

[1] Such is Caesar's account, perhaps not a fair one. *Gall.* IV 9.

[2] Caes. *Gall.* IV 13.

[3] Caesar *Gall.* IV 15 *ad confluentem Mosae et Rheni.* The prevailing opinion now seems to be that either *Mosa* here = *Mosella*, or that we should read *Mosellae* in the text. See the literature of this subject summarized and criticized by Mr Rice Holmes. Caesar's story is surely a gross misrepresentation.

We hear that the news of this affair was variously received in Rome. The Senate decreed honours for the victory; but it was proposed, if not carried, to send a commission to inquire into these wars of Caesar and report on the Gaulish question generally. Cato declared the right thing would be to deliver up Caesar to the barbarians. We must not impute this to humanity. It is far more likely that jealousy and party-spirit were the main motives. Nothing came of these discontents. In a city where the keeping of slaves as gladiators for hire was a recognized form of investment, and where political differences were now commonly settled with the sword, the mere massacre of a horde of barbarians would seem a trifle.

1133. While the news was travelling, Caesar was acting. He meant to stop German interference in Gaul. To produce the desired moral effect he must cross the Rhine and shew himself in Germany. This the Ubii invited him to do, and offered plenty of boats for the passage. He preferred to build a bridge over the river, so as to have the crossing under his own control, and to give a more striking demonstration of his power. His famous trestle-bridge, with its piles and struts, its ties and bearers and what not, was built by a devoted army in ten days, the felling of timber included, and the legions marched dryshod over the Rhine. The missing cavalry of the Usipetes and Tencteri, hearing of the slaughter of their tribesmen, had taken refuge with the Sugambri. To punish the latter for sheltering them, Caesar marched into the Sugambrian country and laid it waste. He did not hunt out the Suebi in their forests; that was not the work in hand. He had received envoys from various tribes, and had encouraged the Ubii, and other projects now called for his attention. So with a mind at present easy as to invasion from Germany he withdrew into Gaul and broke down the bridge.

1134. The season for military operations was not yet at an end, and Caesar thought he had time enough for a visit to Britain. Information about the island was very hard to get: the traders who did business with the Britons seldom got beyond the ports. That there was a connexion between the Britons and the Gauls was known, and he had reason to believe that this often extended to military aid. If he meant to carry out a thorough settlement of Gaul, he must learn what he could about Britain. It was a part of his problem, and Caesar therefore faced it. He marched his army into the country of the Morini, from which the passage was shortest, requisitioned local ships, and ordered up his last year's fleet to a rendezvous on the northern coast. An officer was sent over in a galley to get a general notion of the approaches to the island, but not much was learnt by this trip. His intentions got wind through traders, and envoys from some British tribes came over with offers of submission to Rome, no doubt in hope of inducing him to abandon his design.   He received them courteously, and sent back with them a Gaulish chief who at present enjoyed his confidence, to announce his coming and prepare the way for a Roman protectorate of Britain.   Before starting he was much relieved by the visit of an embassy from some of the Morini, who now accepted the sovranty of Rome.   He took with him only two legions; the rest he sent under Sabinus and L. Aurunculeius Cotta, to complete the conquest of the Morini and the Menapii beyond. The story of Caesar's passage and the difficulties of landing, the indecisive fighting that took place, the feigned submission of the Britons, the storm that did grave damage to the Roman fleet and how the ships were patched up for the return-voyage, the renewed fighting with the natives and their insincere submission again repeated, are matters interesting to read of, and have provoked a literature of controversy.   But they do not concern us here.   Suffice it that Caesar hastened back to the continent to escape equinoctial storms.   Only two of the British clans sent him their promised hostages, and further operations against refractory Morini were necessary before he could place his legions in winter quarters among the Belgae.   Caesar had made no conquest in Britain.   But the news of his expedition and his battles won in the far-off island produced an immense sensation in Rome.   The Senate had to order twenty days of public thanksgiving, and the possibilities of Britain in the way of gain and glory were a theme of gossip in Roman society.   Exaggerated reports made the enterprising and the greedy more than ever anxious to stand well with Caesar.   Caesar himself had not yet done with Britain.   He had learnt in what respects he could improve the model of his transports for a second expedition, and issued instructions for the purpose to the officers in charge of the depots.   Ropes were sent for from Spain.   So the legions were left to work as shipwrights during the winter, while the proconsul returned to his duties in the Cisalpine and Illyricum.

1135.   In this winter Caesar had a little trouble on the far eastern frontier of his vast province.   But the forays of a few restless borderers were no great matter, and a show of preparation to enforce his orders speedily restored quiet.   When he rejoined his army in the spring of 54, he found gratifying evidence of the zeal of officers and men.   The chief item of production was about 600 transports of the new model, low, broad, and propelled by oars.   There were also some war-galleys in the output of that winter.   It is to be remembered that some of the vessels at least had boats belonging to them, and gear of various kinds.   Oars alone must have been made in thousands. The old ships that remained were also over-hauled. A few vessels fitted out by private speculators, probably slave-dealers and the like, were to accompany the convoy. The concentration was to take place at the *portus Itius*, perhaps Wissant near cape Grisnez. This vast armada, built in an imperfectly conquered and little known country, under conditions of the greatest difficulty, may give us some notions of the handiness of Roman soldiers. And the men who had helped to build the ships took to the oar and rowed them—heavy transports—across the strait of Dover. Truly Caesar knew how to keep his men in condition and to get the most out of them. But he had other matters to attend to while the fleet was being got together, for there were ominous signs of discontent in Gaul. The Treveri in particular gave cause for uneasiness. No chiefs of theirs attended the conferences summoned by the proconsul, instructions sent them were disregarded, and it was reported that they were intriguing with Germans beyond the Rhine. Caesar could not start for Britain leaving so serious a danger neglected behind him. The great strength of the Treveri and their contact with the Germans forbade him to let the present unrest develope into rebellion. He marched promptly with a force of four legions and 800 horse to look into the matter. He found two chiefs contending for the first place in the tribe. Cingetorix declared himself loyal to Rome, Indutiomarus was the head of the 'national' party. The presence of Caesar strengthened the former so much that the latter offered submission, pretending that his anti-Roman attitude had been adopted in order to keep some check on the common people and prevent an outbreak. Caesar affected to accept this lame explanation, and took hostages for the good behaviour of Indutiomar. But by exerting all his influence to strengthen the position of Cingetorix among his tribesmen he mortally offended the rival leader, and the rage of Indutiomar, nursed in secret, was a cause of trouble at a later day.

1136. Disaffection was however not confined to the Treveri. Since the coming of Caesar the position of Gaulish chiefs[1] was not what it had been. A strong hand was over them, and they could

---

[1] It is quite true that Caesar mentions some cases of his recognizing certain men as chiefs (*reges*) in their several tribes, and that they suffered for his patronage. See IV 21, V 25, 54. But this does not prove any change in his general policy. His aim was to pacify the tribes, and he dealt with each according to circumstances. The assertion of Dumnorix (V 6) that Caesar had offered him the *regnum* of the Aedui was surely a lie. And it is clear that he did not now (V 4) make the pro-Roman leader *rex* of the Treveri. In VII 4 he tells us of the anti-Roman Vercingetorix that his own people the Arverni gave him the title of King. Clearly the age of tribal chiefs still lingered in Gaulish tradition. See § 1092. The *principes* often mentioned are the nobles.

no longer plot and squabble among themselves freely and go to ruin
their own way.   The tribesmen had to furnish contingents of cavalry,
while the hungry legions ate up quantities of corn raised by Gaulish
labour.   No wonder that Caesar suspected the loyalty of most of
the chiefs.   He had made up his mind to take them over with him
to Britain as hostages for the peace of Gaul.   None of these was
more suspect than the Aeduan Dumnorix, who had already given
much trouble and was now scheming further mischief.   Finding all
his excuses set aside, he tried to induce the other chiefs to combine
and refuse to embark.   Caesar heard of his machinations, and tried
hard to keep him in hand without resort to force.   Shortly after, the
wind shifted fair and the army was ordered on board.   All were
busy, and Dumnorix slipped away with his Aeduan troopers and
made for home.   Caesar stopped the embarkation, and sent a party
in chase, to bring him back or kill him.   He resisted and was cut
down; his men returned to Caesar.   So ended one of the most inveterate champions of 'Gaul for the Gauls.'

1137.   The second expedition to Britain was on a much larger
scale than that of the previous year.   To secure a landing on his
return, Caesar left Labienus behind with three legions and 2000 horse.
He took with him five legions and 2000 horse.   The whole armada
was more than 800 vessels, and the natives were so alarmed at the
sight that they suffered him to land unopposed.   Experiences repeated themselves in various ways.   For instance, the fleet again
suffered from a storm after the troops were landed and the campaign
begun.   Again the repairing of damaged ships consumed time and
labour.   Again the Roman was victorious when it came to fighting
in the open or storming British strongholds, but unable to achieve
any decisive result, owing to the superior mobility of the Britons.
This time however Caesar was able to stay some time in the island,
perhaps two or three months.   He penetrated beyond the Thames,
and received the submission of a number of tribes in the eastern
districts.   In Britain, as in Gaul, there were rival chiefs in some
tribes, and intertribal feuds.   The union of several tribes under the
leadership of Cassivellaunus was only a temporary confederacy to
resist the invader.   Caesar of course lost no chance of turning the
divisions of the natives to account.   But Cassivellaun was active and
watchful, and the Romans did not get back to their ships without
anxiety.   A rebellion took place in the parts of Kent, and the
naval station was attacked.   But Caesar had fortified it well before
marching up the country, and the garrison beat off the enemy.   On
this second expedition Caesar was able to learn a good deal about
Britain and the Britons, partly by inquiry, partly by observation.

What pains he took in the latter direction is shewn in the use of the water-clock[1] to measure the length of days and nights for comparison with similar measurements taken on the continent. He was in fact as much explorer as conqueror. In Britain, as in Gaul and Germany, his custom was to observe natural phenomena, the flora and fauna of the country, the food clothing institutions and habits of the natives. These things he recorded in brief notes for the information of Roman readers. The British war-chariot (*essedum*), and the four-wheeler (*petorritum*) of Gaul, found their way as models to Italy, and added new types to the variety of Italian vehicles. As for a conquest of Britain, Caesar was no nearer to it than before. He could not afford to winter there. A formal submission offered by Cassivellaun was perforce accepted, hostages taken, a yearly tribute to Rome agreed upon, and the British leader warned not to molest the tribes under Roman sovranty. But all this was make-believe. It might serve as pretext for another invasion, in case the opportunity occurred. But it did not occur, and no real conquest and occupation of Britain took place for nearly a hundred years. What did Caesar bring back with him to the mainland as the material reward of the skilled exertions of so many men? The answer[2] is—slaves.

1138. The letters of Cicero belonging to the years 54—53 are in great part either addressed to persons in and about the camp of Caesar (Caesar himself among them) or contain references to affairs in Gaul and Britain. They throw many side-lights on the state of things at headquarters, and reveal a scene such as no imagination could have divined. We have already noted that Cicero, on renewing friendly relations with Caesar, found himself able to push the fortunes of friends who sought preferment in connexion with the war in Gaul. The news of the first expedition to Britain only added to the number of applicants. At the end of 55 Cicero wrote on behalf of his brother. In the spring of 54 Quintus joined Caesar, who made him a *legatus* and took him to Britain on the second expedition. The nervous and irritable man seems to have had merits as an officer, for we shall find him shortly holding an important command. He was in favour with Caesar's prime agent Balbus, the man whom the orator had defended. The fate of Rome, decided in these momentous campaigns in the North, depended in no small degree upon the skill and energy of the capable Spaniard. Caesar could not afford to lose touch with Rome. His news must be correct and up to date, and his action not only prompt but well-advised. He maintained

---

[1] Caes. *Gall.* v 13.
[2] Caesar *BG* v 23 § 2 *captivorum magnum numerum*, Cic. *ad Att.* iv 16 § 7 (13), *ad Q. frat.* iii 9 § 4.

a regular mail-service, and neglected no means of keeping politics at Rome moving as he wished. Compliments and flatteries, loans and gifts, according to the characters of individuals whose cooperation was at any time needed, had to be scattered with a lavish but discreet hand. Favours at headquarters, such as those to Quintus Cicero, were only possible in a few cases; and Caesar, who was a man of his word, was also a keen man of business, and always managed to get value for his favours somehow or other. How highly he valued the support of Cicero is shewn by the pains he took to retain it. Among all his endless occupations he contrived to keep up a correspondence with the orator, and to charm him with delicate compliments and praise of his works. He honoured Cicero's letters of recommendation, and ended by lending him a considerable sum of money. But the amount of business transacted at headquarters must have been enormous. Military matters alone were enough for a first-rate man with a first-rate staff. But Caesar was governor of two old provinces, Narbonese and Cisalpine Gaul, not to mention Illyricum. However efficient his deputies might be, the administration of these must have necessitated occasional reference to the chief. Rome itself called for constant attention, and delicate negotiations could not always be carried on by letter. A trusty go-between, someone above the freedmen employed in ordinary concerns, was indispensable, and it was this duty in which the factotum Balbus proved his worth. Other useful helpers served Caesar in various ways, such as Matius in the social life at headquarters, and Oppius his agent in Rome, but Balbus was in touch with these and many more.

1139. The life in camp was not confined to a dreary round of military detail. When the day's work was done, intellectual interests of wider scope had their turn, and Caesar's dinner-table was no mean literary centre. Quintus Cicero found relief in composing tragedies. Caesar himself beguiled the tedium of long journeys over the Alps by writing a grammatical treatise. Now and then some man turned up at headquarters with a letter of introduction, and brought with him the last gossip of Rome. These visitors, mostly attracted by hopes of preferment, were not always easy to provide for. Such a case was that of C. Trebatius Testa, one of the men vouched for by Cicero. He was a distinguished jurist, with no bent for military life. In Caesar's camp there was no demand for advice in the niceties of the civil law or the services of a skilled draughtsman. So Trebatius soon pined for the Roman Forum, but was at the same time loth to give up the hopes of place and profit which had brought him to Gaul. Cicero had much ado to persuade him to stay on and wait for his chance. Caesar had no obvious post to offer him, and no spare time for interviews without result. Gradually Trebatius became more reconciled to his surroundings, and formed a friendship with Matius. But he never distinguished himself otherwise than as a lawyer, though he seems to have received some sort of appointment in connexion with the army.

1140. When Caesar returned from Britain, it was time to make his arrangements for the winter (54—53). This was a less simple matter than usual, for the harvest of 54 had been a short one, and to feed the legions it was necessary to draw upon the resources of a larger area. The winter camps were widely spread over Belgic Gaul. Of these we need only mention that under Labienus in the land of the Remi, set to watch the Treveri ; that of Q. Cicero among the Nervii ; and that of Sabinus and Cotta among the Eburones, who dwelt north of the Treveri in the region of the Maas. This last was a larger unit than the other two, comprising half a legion of seasoned troops and a whole legion of young soldiers recently raised in the Transpadane district. Two other legions, one in the North, one in the West in 'Celtic' Gaul, watched the Morini and the Aremorican tribes, and escaped the troubles of this winter. The headquarters of Caesar were at Samarobriva (the city of the Ambiani, now Amiens), and he kept his remaining three legions in that neighbourhood, well within call. The *legati* in command of these were L. Munatius Plancus, C. Trebonius, the actual proposer of the law by which the provincial arrangements made at Luca were carried out, and Caesar's quaestor M. Crassus, son of the triumvir. The last had not, like his more brilliant brother P. Crassus, gone to join his father in the East. Caesar tells us that, with the exception of the legion stationed in the West, no camp was more than 100 (Roman) miles from another. But that he felt anxious is clear, for he did not hurry off to his duties in the South as usual, but waited at Samarobriva till all the detachments should be reported settled in their quarters and their defences complete. He knew that a rebellious temper was developing in the tribes of Gaul under the pressure of the Roman occupation. And just at this time a tribal revolution occurred among the Carnutes, between the Seine and Loire. Their 'king' or chief was a noble whom Caesar had placed in power as a reward for service rendered. The opposite faction rose and murdered him. Conscious of their strength, these malcontents might lead the tribe into revolt. Caesar promptly sent Plancus with his legion to winter in the district and arrest the leaders of the outbreak. Soon he got news of all the legions being safe in their quarters. All now seemed quiet, but Caesar still delayed his departure for Italy.

1141. The first attempt at a rising occurred among the far-off

Eburones. The Maas-Mosel-Rhine region was full of inflammable elements. The Aduatuci, chastised in 57, were doubtless sulky; and the numerous small tribes in the neighbourhood were mostly clients of the Treveri or ready to follow their lead. Now the growing discontent in Gaul had strengthened the hands of Indutiomar and the 'national' party among the Treveri. It was Indutiomar who persuaded the chiefs of the Eburones to rise. To cut the story short, the Romans were induced by false information and treacherous promises to leave their fortified camp and set out to join one of the other legions. The Eburones waylaid and destroyed them on their march. Only a few stragglers found a way through the woods and brought the news of the disaster to Labienus. It appeared that Cotta had all along protested against acting on the enemy's advice; it was Sabinus, probably senior in rank to Cotta, whose nerve had given way, with this fatal result. For the present no news of the affair seems to have reached Caesar through Labienus. Perhaps the roads were beset by Gauls. Meanwhile Ambiorix the leader of the Eburones had raised the minor tribes around and marched into the Nervian country to overwhelm Q. Cicero. Cicero had not yet heard of the disaster of Sabinus, and he was now isolated, subject to ceaseless fierce assaults from a vast host of Gauls, and plied with the same false information and threats as had frightened Sabinus, whose fate he now learnt from the boasts of the enemy. The country round swarmed with Nervii and their allies; all his messengers to Caesar were caught; he himself was in weak health. But neither he nor his men spared themselves. Prodigies of labour skill and valour were performed; day after day went by, and still the camp held out. At last a Nervian refugee induced his slave by promise of his freedom to take a letter. The slave (a Gaul) got through, and so the first news reached Caesar. He at once called in M. Crassus and his legion to guard the great depot at Samarobriva. Crassus started at once; when he drew near, Caesar set out with the legion of Trebonius and 400 horse. Fabius and his legion were summoned to join him from the North, and did so on the march. Labienus was allowed to use his own judgment. He replied that it was too dangerous to move, and reported the disaster of Sabinus as described by the survivors. Speed was now everything. Caesar was only just in time. But he contrived to send news to Cicero of his coming, and his approach raised the siege. For himself, he outwitted the Gauls and routed them with great slaughter, pushed on to Cicero's camp, and praised him and his men as they deserved. Not one in ten had escaped unwounded. He was now able to compare his news of Sabinus' disaster with the accounts given by Gaulish prisoners.

1142. Caesar more than once refers to the speed with which news spread in Gaul. In this case he had joined Cicero about 3 P.M.; Labienus heard[1] of the victory before midnight in his camp some 60 Roman miles away. Indutiomar and a force of Treveri, who were on the point of attacking Labienus, also heard of it and fled. A contemplated attack on L. Roscius in the West by a great host of the Aremorican tribes was hurriedly abandoned for the same reason. But Gaul was full of unrest, and Caesar felt obliged to pass the winter at Samarobriva, keeping three legions close at hand. So great had been the effect of the disastrous affair of Sabinus. Caesar well knew that he had been within a very little of losing Gaul and of ending his own career. But he had not lost it, and he now used his efforts to intimidate disloyal chiefs. In most of Gaul he succeeded in preventing open rebellion. But a revolution among the Senones drove out the king, a nominee of Caesar, and the contumacious nobles would not render any account of their proceedings to the proconsul. There was reason to fear that most of the tribes only needed opportunity to revolt. The most inveterate foe of Rome was still the Treveran Indutiomar. Unable to induce the Germans to move, he contrived to raise his own tribe, and was said to have large plans for a rebellion in Central Gaul. But he had first to crush Labienus. In the attempt to do this he was outgeneralled and defeated with great slaughter, and himself perished. His allies, marching to join him, dispersed; and, though the Remi and Aedui were the only tribes really loyal to Rome, still Caesar for a little while had comparative peace in Gaul. But he had reason to look for a more serious rising, and resolved to daunt the malcontents by a display of Italian strength. He had lost about a legion and a half; he would make good the loss twice over. So he ordered his lieutenants in the Cisalpine to raise two new legions, and asked Pompey for the loan of a third. Pompey was now proconsul of Spain, but living in Rome and governing through *legati*. The death of Julia in 54 had broken the personal tie that bound the two men, but they were still on friendly terms. Pompey had a legion, raised in the Cisalpine, which he did not really want. This he now embodied and sent to Caesar.

1143. The death of Indutiomar only left the Treveran government in the hands of his friends, who went on with his plans, trying to hire mercenaries in Germany, and making a league with Ambiorix and his Eburones. All the tribes of the North and North-East were up in arms, and the Senones and Carnutes contumacious. There was no time to be lost. Caesar began by a sudden winter raid in the Nervian country. By laying waste their lands and carrying off cattle

[1] Caes. *Gall.* v 53.

and slaves he quieted them, and returned to hold his usual spring meeting of chiefs at Samarobriva.   But he found no response from Treveri Carnutes or Senones, and into the territory of these last he marched at once.   His promptitude forestalled an attempt to rally them in their tribal strongholds.   They had to submit, but were mildly treated.   Caesar was glad to listen to the intercession of the Aedui, on whom they were traditionally dependent, for he had his hands full elsewhere.   So too the Carnutes were let off easily as clients of the Remi.   Caesar now called in the tribal contingents of cavalry and set about the year's (53) campaign.   He meant to give the North and North-East a lesson that would keep them and their German allies quiet for many a day.   One main object was to destroy the troublesome Ambiorix.   Labienus in his camp among the Treveri was reinforced by two legions, while Caesar himself with five legions went to find and conquer the Menapii among their woods and fens. There was work for his engineers to do in getting at the retreats of an amphibious enemy, but it was done, and the Menapii, who had hitherto not offered to make terms with Caesar, now had their destiny explained to them by fire and sword and the carrying away of many into bondage. Thus the outlook of Roman civilization was enlarged, and a refuge closed to Ambiorix.   Meanwhile the Treveran rebels planned to overwhelm Labienus in his camp, but his two new legions now joined him, and the enemy waited for the coming of a German force.   By stale old tricks, which seem never to have lost their effect in dealing with Gauls, the Roman induced the Treveri to attack him at a disadvantage, and gave them a bloody and decisive beating.   The approaching Germans hurried back home without a battle, and the friends of Indutiomar went with them.   The pro-Roman Cingetorix was installed as chief of the tribe.   Caesar, marching south from his Menapian campaign, found order restored by Labienus.   But he felt it necessary to give the Germans another scare, and to cut off Ambiorix from a retreat eastwards.   He therefore built another bridge, somewhat higher up than the former one, and a second time took a Roman army over the Rhine.

1144.   The moral effect of this expedition, in checking the overflow of Germans into Gaul, was perhaps not dearly purchased at the cost of all this effort.   The material result was nothing.   In view of the unrest in Gaul, no risks could be run in Germany.   The Suebi could not be induced to attack him, and he dared not lead his army into the heart of the country, where supplies were almost certain to fail.   He renewed his relations with the Ubii, and in recrossing the river he only broke down the section of the bridge next the German bank.   The rest he left standing, and a guard to watch it, at least for a time.   He then turned upon the Eburones, and hoped at last to make an end of Ambiorix.   When he reached Aduatuca, the old station of Sabinus, he left there his baggage-train, his sick and convalescents, and one of his new legions, with Q. Cicero in command of the post.   He was to return himself in seven days.   Till then the troops were not to quit the camp.   Caesar now made a rapid march, overrunning and laying waste the Eburonian territory.   Ambiorix had narrowly escaped capture by a mounted column in advance. The small German tribes in the neighbourhood had promptly submitted.   It remained to destroy the whole tribe of the Eburones as a warning and a guarantee of local peace.   The difficulty of dealing with them was very great, for they were scattered in small bodies, hard to find and catch in a wild country, but well able to cut off stragglers.   Caesar therefore invited the tribes round about to come and share the plunder of the doomed people.   He meant to destroy them by famine, and to waste as few Roman lives as possible in doing so.   The news spread fast, and the robbers gathered to the spoil. Even the Sugambri heard of it, and a body of them, 2000 horsemen, came from beyond the Rhine.   Tempted by the prospect of a richer prey, they made a dash upon Aduatuca.   On the seventh day Cicero, wanting more supplies and worried by the impatience of his men, sent out a foraging party, and the Sugambri were just in time to deliver a dangerous attack on the weakened garrison.   Checked by the steady bravery of some invalid veterans, they turned upon the foragers, whom the noise of fighting had recalled to the camp.   Most of these were raw troops, and the Germans cut them up badly.   But there was no booty to be got in this way, and Caesar was coming. So the Sugambri presently drew off, picked up their Eburonian plunder, and carried it safely with them over the Rhine.   This adventure gives us a glimpse of the ways of the Rhinelanders in Caesar's time, and reminds us once more that as yet a standing army formed no part of the Roman system.   A new legion was raised and sent to the front with hardly any preparatory training to give it the cohesion which is an essential foundation of soldierly nerve.   Caesar had trusted to Cicero's obeying his orders as he had done on a former occasion.   Cicero's judgment had failed, and it was lucky the result was no worse.   That night Caesar returned according to promise. His advance-guard found the camp in a state of panic.   The raw recruits had made up their minds that Caesar and all his army were lost, and would not be convinced till they appeared.   Superstition, brooding over the ill luck of Aduatuca, had made them hysterical. Yet they were of the same stuff as other legions.

1145.   Fortune had played a queer game.   The Germans who came to loot the country of Ambiorix had ended by doing him a good turn. The chase of the rebel was now resumed, and the land of the Eburones searched and laid waste from end to end. But after hairbreadth escapes the fugitive at last got clear away. Caesar was now tired of this miserable campaign, and anxious to return to his duties in Italy. He withdrew to the chief town of the Remi, and held a great 'durbar' of chiefs. He inquired into the disaffection among the Senones and Carnutes and dealt out punishments. He then arranged the winter quarters of his 10 legions. Two were to watch the Treveri, two to take post among the Lingones. The remaining six were all to lie at the chief town of the Senones. This carried out and his magazines stocked, he was able to start for the Cisalpine. But his sojourn in his Italian province during the winter of 53—52 was a time of great uneasiness. The political broils long chronic in Rome had led to the murder of Clodius. To prevent sheer anarchy, the Senate had placed exceptional powers in the hands of Pompey, and called for a general levy of men of military age in Italy. It is true that a sort of order was restored and that no revolution took place at this time. But it must have been clear to Caesar from the first that the placing of Pompey at the head of affairs boded ill for the continuance of the coalition effected with so much thought and pains. Julia was dead, Crassus had perished in Parthia. Pompey was now neither bound by a domestic tie to Caesar, nor checked by a jealous partner. The two survivors were left in direct rivalry, and Caesar, whatever may have been his ambitions at this moment, knew that his rival at least was not to be trusted. But Caesar had strong reasons for not desiring a quarrel at present, and no doubt he flattered and conciliated Pompey in every way. Meanwhile he held a levy in the Cisalpine, ostensibly in accordance with the decree of the Senate, though that order only referred to what was technically Italy. He was likely to want more troops in Gaul, but on this occasion he did not embody them in new legions. They were a number of drafts to fill up the gaps in the old ones.

1146. News from Italy travelled fast through Gaul, and lost nothing on the way. The troubles in Rome were taken to prove that Caesar would be detained in Italy, and in the widespread discontent created by the sense of subjection the greater number of the tribes in central or 'Celtic' Gaul were ripe for revolt. While Caesar was busy south of the Alps, Gaulish chiefs were conspiring. They saw that it was important to bring about a rising so suddenly as to take Caesar by surprise and cut him off from his army. Suddenness could only be gained by secrecy; a great public gathering would be reported to Caesar, and bring him back post-haste to the front. The only way was for some tribe to break out, in the faith that others would at once follow their lead.   This the Carnutes undertook to do, and did. Their town of Cenabum (now Orléans) was an important place on the Loire.   It was a trade-centre, and had a bridge over the river.   Roman merchants were there, and a Roman officer of commissariat.   The conspirators fell upon these unawares and killed them at sunrise on the appointed day.   That night[1] the news reached the land of the Arverni, 160 Roman miles away, and was known all about among the tribes.   So effective were the rude means of transmission used in Gaul. The rebellion spread fast, but this was no guarantee against a speedy collapse.   Some unity was wanted, and could only be found in obedience to an able and persevering leader.   The rising of 52 was more serious than former risings because such a leader appeared, and because he not only attracted general support in ' Celtic' Gaul but retained great influence over his fickle countrymen for several months.

1147.   The great tribe of the Arverni had long ago learnt the power of Rome.   It is likely that among their mountains they saw less of Roman officials than the tribes of the lower country or those through whose territory Roman couriers travellers or troops were ever passing to and fro.   The leading nobles had no mind for taking part in a revolt.   When Vercingetorix, a young noble whose father had been put to death for monarchic designs, began to form a rebel conspiracy, they turned him out of Gergovia, their chief town.   He went on with his agitation, and all the discontented soon rallied to him. He reoccupied Gergovia in force and was acclaimed king of the Arverni.   He sent out envoys to a number of other tribes, who joined him and accepted him as commander in chief.   Acting on this authority, he took hostages from the confederate tribes and levied contingents, particularly cavalry.   He shrank from no severities to coerce waverers, and in a short time had formed a great Gaulish army to assert the liberty of Gaul.   The region in which he brought about this formidable combination may be roughly defined as including the Senones and Parisii on the Seine and the Cadurci bordering on the Garonne, and extending from the tribes on the western coast to his own mountains of Auvergne.   He had thus the bulk of central Gaul at his disposal, but only on Gaulish terms.   To conduct successful war with an army of clan-contingents has ever been found a task of peculiar difficulty, and the case of Vercingetorix was no exception. He was brave and loyal, and possessed the power of rousing a real enthusiasm among his followers; he saw the weak points of his countrymen, and tried to remedy them.   But he could never get a

[1] Caes. *Gall.* VII 3.

free hand in strategy. The true interest of the general confederacy and the immediate convenience of particular tribes often pointed different ways, and in the last resort the commander could only endeavour to persuade the part to make some sacrifice for the good of the whole. And the strength of particularist feeling among the Gaulish tribes made the position of the general Head a downright bed of thorns. Caesar was really master in his own camp, Vercingetorix was not. That the Gaul, under such conditions, made so gallant a stand against the Roman, proves him to have been a man of exceptional powers.

1148. His first steps shew what were the immediate needs of the insurgents, and throw light upon the state of feeling in Celtic Gaul. The Bituriges, a tribe between the Arverni and Carnutes, were dependants of the Aedui, and so as yet true to the Roman connexion, that is, publicly and officially. The sequel shewed that in these tribes also the rebellious ferment was working strongly. Vercingetorix invaded the Bituriges, and they (that is, their magistrates) called upon the Aedui for help. But the force despatched to their aid never passed the frontier: they returned home, alleging that only the discovery of intended treachery had saved them from being massacred by the Bituriges and Arverni combined. Who had been treacherous, was perhaps doubtful, but the Bituriges at once joined the rebellion. It was already too large a movement for Caesar's lieutenants to deal with in the absence of their chief, especially as the season for campaigning had not yet properly begun. And Vercingetorix sent a bold partisan to raise the southern tribes in the region of the Lot and Tarn, and so to threaten the northern frontier of the Narbonese province. Accordingly, when Caesar passed the Alps early in 52, the problem of how to reach his army was further complicated by the necessity of providing at once for the safety of the districts of Tolosa and Narbo. This he rapidly did by garrisons of local levies, and so effectively that the rebel forces did not dare to pass the border. To reach his army he carried out a daring manœuvre. At the head of his young troops he cut and dug his way over the snow-clad Cevennes, and broke into the upper Arvernian country. He had some cavalry with him, and proceeded to lay the land waste far and wide: the Arverni were taken by surprise, and their armed force was far away. Caesar was sure that this raid would recall Vercingetorix to the defence of his own people, as it did. Acting on this conviction, Caesar followed up this movement by another, and completed what was perhaps his greatest masterpiece of psychological strategy. Leaving young D. Brutus in charge, ostensibly for three days[1] only, he

---

[1] I take it that the instructions to Brutus were to occupy the enemy and, if Caesar did not

recrossed the mountains with all speed, and made for the Roman-Allobrogian city of Vienna (Vienne) on the Rhone. Here he found a fresh body of horse waiting for him according to orders. His first object was to reach his nearest legions, the two wintering among the Lingones. He chose the route west of the Rhone by way of the Aeduan country. Starting with this small escort (presumably Roman) he rode day and night, distrusting the intentions of the Aedui, and reached the two legions safely. He then called in the two legions from the Treveran frontier, and concentrated the whole army in and about Agedincum (Sens) the chief town of the Senones. Thus by speed and daring, above all by his insight into the feelings and motives of the Gauls, Caesar had in a few days completely changed the situation.

1149. On hearing of this sudden turn of affairs, Vercingetorix saw that he must strike a blow at once. He skilfully chose a weak point. In the angle between the Loire and the Allier were the remnant of Boii whom Caesar had allowed to settle there as clients of the Aedui when in the year 58 he sent the rest of the Helvetian host back to their own land. These Boii had not been settled in their present homes much more than five years, and their resources were as yet small. To crush them would be an object-lesson to others, not to rely on Roman protection. Their patrons the Aedui had not yet joined the rebellion, but Vercingetorix doubtless knew well that there was an anti-Roman faction among them. This faction, while making it difficult for the Aeduan chiefs to help the Boii, would be encouraged by a victory of the rebel forces, and the embarrassments of Caesar proportionately increased. Vercingetorix therefore invaded the land of the Boii and laid siege to their chief town Gorgobina. This move forced Caesar to begin his campaign at once under the disadvantage of exceptional difficulty in feeding his army. The trouble was chiefly one of transport, for the country was not yet opened up by solid Roman roads. The proper campaigning season, depending mainly on such considerations, was not yet begun, and to collect local supplies at the front was a long and dangerous business. He started from Agedincum with eight legions and some cavalry. Among the latter was a small body of Germans[1], which is worth noting. Caesar had evidently observed their military qualities, and he found them very useful: the horsemen of the Gauls were no match for them, and we have here the beginning of one of the vital facts of the Roman Empire, the service of German soldiers under the standards of Rome.

return in three days (he never meant to), to withdraw his men safely. These raw troops were afterwards forwarded to the depot at Agedincum. See Caesar *BG* VII 8, 9, 57.

[1] Caes. *Gall.* VII 13.

His line of march was not direct to the land of the Boii, but westwards, with the Carnutian city of Cenabum for his immediate objective. The massacre of Romans there had to be avenged ; and there was a bridge to be seized if possible, for on the borders of winter and spring the Loire was probably in flood.   The Carnutes were making leisurely arrangements for the defence of Cenabum, when the Roman army appeared sooner than expected.   The siege of Vellaunodunum on the way had only delayed Caesar for the inside of three days, and Cenabum was not ready.   An attempt to evacuate the town by night was detected, the legions broke in and carried the place with a rush. Few escaped, for the bridge and streets leading to it were quickly choked in the general stampede.   The town was looted and burnt. Caesar 'granted the booty to his soldiers,' a phrase which probably includes the proceeds of an auction of the captives.   He had at one stroke avenged the murder of Romans, won the passage of the Loire, and relieved the pressure on his Boian allies.   For the news of his movements caused Vercingetorix to break up from Gorgobina and march to meet him in the country of the Bituriges.   And this was no doubt what Caesar had intended.

1150.   After crossing the Loire, Caesar turned south-eastwards through the country of the Bituriges, making for their chief town Avaricum (Bourges).   On the way he took another town which the Gaulish army was just too late to rescue.   Vercingetorix well knew that a war of sieges would be all in favour of the Romans, for only a stronghold inaccessible to siege-works could defy their skill.   He now persuaded his unruly followers to change their method of warfare. They were to starve the Romans out of the land by destroying all surplus stores, burning their towns and hamlets, and cutting off Roman forage-parties and stragglers.   Deprived of corn and hay, the enemy would be driven to retreat.   This decree was carried out generally, but with a fatal exception ; at the passionate protest of the Bituriges it was agreed to spare Avaricum.   The town therefore had to be victualled and garrisoned, for Caesar was near.   Vercingetorix, aided by the good will of the people of the district, had a great advantage in scouting, and was able to inflict much hardship and loss on the Romans.   The siege of Avaricum demanded all the resources of the Roman engineers, and food, particularly farinaceous[1] stuffs, the mainstay of the Roman soldier, ran short in the camp.   Urgent messages to the Aedui and Boii produced little ; the former being lukewarm allies, and the latter having little to spare.   But Caesar records that the men bore their trials in a manner worthy of the great name of Rome, and for many days lived on the flesh of the beasts

[1] Caes. *Gall.* VII 17.

driven in by the foragers. They scorned all thought of giving up the siege, for they meant now to take satisfaction for the Romans treacherously slain at Cenabum. Some operations, unimportant in themselves, caused serious suspicion in the minds of the jealous Gauls that Vercingetorix was playing them false. But he had the address to regain his influence, as he deserved. Now however they insisted on sending 10,000 more men, so many from each tribe-contingent, into the beleaguered town. If we may believe Caesar, this step was partly prompted by jealousy; assuming that the defence was successful, it would not do to let the Bituriges have the whole credit. This may be true, for evidently mutual jealousy was first and last the main cause that prevented the making of a Gaulish nation.

1151. So the siege of Avaricum went on, both sides doing wonders of toil ingenuity and daring. But the Romans gained ground bit by bit, and at length the garrison resolved to escape by night. The women discovered their intention, and made such an uproar that the design could not be carried out. In the slackness and dejection that followed Caesar delivered an assault, and the town was taken. Out of about 40,000, men women and children, barely 800 men got away safely. The rest were butchered in a wild fury of wrath and revenge. This result was dexterously turned to account by Vercingetorix, and the silly Gauls, whose self-will had brought disaster on their cause, became somewhat more obedient to their leader. The spring was now beginning, and the difficulty of supplies was for the present solved by the stores captured in Avaricum. Caesar was therefore anxious to push on to the South and settle accounts with the Arverni in their own land. But Gaul was ever the seat of factions, and he was just now called in to act as umpire in a contested election among the Aedui. He could not leave them to fight it out, for the beaten party were certain to appeal to Vercingetorix. He could not hear the case at his headquarters, for Aeduan laws forbade the chief magistrate to pass their border while in office, and this was no time for slighting the tribal custom. So he moved eastward, crossed the river Elaver (Allier), and met the Aeduan disputants at their frontier town on the Loire. Inquiry shewed him that one of the claimants had been appointed in defiance of tribal rule and precedent, so he installed the other (who was the nominee of the Druids) as Vergobret, and read the company a lecture on the duty of concord and loyalty to Rome. He called for a strong contingent to guard his depots as he advanced, and made his plans for the next operations. To check rebellion in the region of the Seine, he gave Labienus half his cavalry and two legions; these with two now at Agedincum were to make up his force. With the other six Caesar started for Gergovia, marching on the eastern side of the Allier. Vercingetorix broke down all the bridges and attended him on the western bank. Caesar at last outwitted the Gaul and got his army across. Vercingetorix fell back upon Gergovia, and in a few days Caesar encamped before that fortress and found himself face to face with a problem to which he had not got the key.

1152.   We will not dwell on Caesar's operations (they never amounted to a siege) against this famous stronghold. To surprise it was hardly possible, for the whole country side would be on the alert to warn the garrison. Even with the aid of treachery success would have been extremely doubtful, and there was no prospect of treachery. All fortresses can be starved out, but Caesar, depending on the Aedui for his supplies and communications, was more likely to be blockaded than to blockade others. For the slow process of reducing Gergovia by hunger was certain to put a great strain on Aeduan loyalty to Rome; and, if the 'national' party got the upper hand, they had only to cut off the supplies of the Roman army to win the gratitude of their brother Gauls and forgiveness for their unpatriotic past. Siege works, the department in which the Romans were far superior, were practically impossible on the rocky heights of Gergovia. The dangerous position of Caesar was soon brought home to him by news from the rear. The Aedui were at last really deserting the Roman cause, and the new Vergobret was heading the movement. He had been bribed by Vercingetorix, and the belief that Caesar was at last caught in a trap made it easy for him to gain adherents. A tangle of intrigues followed, and the nobles loyal to Rome lost ground so much that they too began to waver. False information served to draw the multitude into revolt. The contingent sent to join Caesar was thus corrupted by its commander Litaviccus. It would simply have come and joined Vercingetorix, but Caesar, warned by an Aeduan friend, met them on the way with a strong force, proved to them that they had been deceived by lies, and took them along with him to Gergovia. But no great trust could be placed in such a corps. Litavic escaped and joined Vercingetorix. Caesar only got back just in time to save his camp, attacked by the enemy. The wretched Aedui at home, driven on by conspirators who had gone too far to draw back, swayed to and fro as new reports came in, till they were virtually in revolt. Caesar thought it best to temporize, so he dissembled his anger for the moment and affected to believe that the Aedui had their hearts in the right place after all. But in truth he now saw the extremity of his peril. The rising was evidently going to spread further yet. His problem now was how to extricate his army[1] from the mess into which his audacity had led it. Six rather

[1] His account (*Gall.* VII 43) makes this quite clear.

thin legions could hardly face all Gaul in arms, flushed with success. He must not appear to be running away, but he must reunite with Labienus. Till then he could make no effective stand.

1153. On the other hand Vercingetorix was not without his anxieties. In an endeavour to improve the defences of Gergovia he gave Caesar an opportunity of trying what could be done by a sudden assault. The attempt was made, but for various reasons it failed. Caesar then covered his intention of retreating by offering battle to the Gauls, but Vercingetorix would not be tempted out. In about three days after the repulse the Roman army was falling back upon the Aeduan country, where Caesar had established an important depot at Noviodunum (probably[1] Nevers) on the Loire. Troubles now gathered round him fast. Litavic had ridden with his Aeduan cavalry from Gergovia to raise his tribesmen in open rebellion. Caesar's Aeduan friends asked leave to go home also, on the plea of working for the Roman interest among the Aedui, and Caesar could not well refuse. But these men found the tribal authorities all committed to the rebellion, and themselves joined it, as they had probably all along meant to do. Caesar had unwisely left only a weak guard at Noviodunum, in charge of his Gaulish hostages, his military chest, great stores of corn, most of his baggage, and a great number of horses for remounts, bought in the markets of Italy and Spain. The rebels overpowered and massacred the guard and all the Roman financiers and other travellers found in the town. The hostages were handed over to the Aeduan Vergobret, the town burnt, the corn spoilt or carried off, the money and the horses shared as plunder. Mounted bands scoured the country, posts were established at points on the bank of the Loire, and the river itself was in flood. Caesar was now in greater danger than ever. He thought that the enemy wanted to prevent his crossing the Loire in hope that failure of supplies might drive him to make for the Narbonese province by way of the Cevennes. But he would not accept the disastrous alternative; he would not leave Labienus in the lurch. Eventually a ford was found, and the army safely got across. Caesar replenished his commissariat with Aeduan foodstuffs, and resumed his march to the North. Meanwhile Labienus had had no easy task. The news of Caesar's retreat from Gergovia had caused the rebellion to spread, and he was rather concerned to withdraw his own army safely than to carry on an extended campaign. But he was a good man of his trade, and his skill and nerve were equal to the need. By clever strategy he managed to defeat the enemy with great loss and brought his

---

[1] Certainly not Soissons, hundreds of miles away. Correct Ferrero II 116 by index to Teubner *Caesar*.

legions back to Agedincum. In a few days the concentration of the whole Roman army was complete.

1154. And now both sides prepared for the real tug of war on which hung the fate of Gaul. Even at Gergovia Vercingetorix had with him contingents from many tribes. The revolt of the Aedui gave a fresh impetus to the rising. All Celtic Gaul was up in arms with two exceptions; the Lingones hung back for some reason, and the Treveri were in difficulties with the Germans. Some Belgic tribes also joined the rebels, but the Remi were still faithful to Rome. The usual Gaulish jealousy appeared in an attempt of the Aeduan leaders to wrest the chief command from Vercingetorix. But a general congress held at their chief town Bibracte unanimously chose him as their commander. Gaul was conscious of having a real leader at last. The disgusted Aedui could not draw back now, and their wealth, accumulated under Roman protection, was at the disposal of others for the common cause. Vercingetorix now formed far-reaching plans. His own main army was strengthened by a large force of cavalry, and his operations were to be chiefly directed to cutting off Caesar's supplies. To this end he called upon all the confederate tribes to destroy all stores that might otherwise fall into Roman hands. His mounted columns would do the rest. But it is obvious that a strong base from which their raids could be directed would be a great convenience, and it is not unlikely that he occupied and partly fortified the post of Alesia for this purpose. The place was on a hill in the district held by the Mandubii, who seem to have been dependants of the Aedui, between them and the Lingones. But, while he hoped to make Caesar's position untenable, he had a scheme for invading the old Narbonese province[1] and destroying the Roman power in the South at the same time as he destroyed Caesar himself in the North. One insurgent force was to attack the part west of the Rhone at two points. Another was to operate against the Allobroges. The adhesion of this tribe he was especially anxious to secure, doubtless in order permanently to sever Caesar's communications with Italy, already interrupted. He therefore tried hard to win over the Allobroges to the national cause by negotiations. He offered them the headship of the Roman (Narbonese) province, he promised money to their chiefs; anything in short to gain them without resort to force. Surely they had reason enough to rue their past connexion with Rome.

1155. It would seem that not much came of the former part of this scheme, though the Helvii, a tribe subject to Rome between the Rhone and the Cevennes range, were defeated with heavy loss by

---

[1] Provision had been made for its defence. Caes. *Gall.* VII 65 § 1.

the insurgents. On the Allobroges no impression was made. They had grievances against Rome. But the prestige of a power that advances is ever great, and the lesson of Caesar's dealings with Helvetii and Germans was fresh in Allobrogian memories. Moreover it is in the highest degree probable that the administration of the province had been greatly improved in the hands of Caesar and his subordinates. The Allobroges were now offered a distinguished place in a system of free and united Gaul, but we may fairly guess that they did not trust the equity and stability of arrangements resting on the steadiness and good faith of their brother Gauls. They had submitted to Rome some 70 years ago, and were already to some extent Romanized. Their reply to Vercingetorix was to call out their forces and hold the frontier of the Rhone. But none the less the situation of Caesar was one of great peril, particularly owing to his weakness in cavalry. Roving bodies of Gaulish horse beset the ways and cut him off from his provinces, so that he could not draw succours from Italy. In these straits he turned[1] to the Germans. From the tribes beyond the Rhine whom he had brought to terms in former campaigns he now drew a mixed force, partly mounted, in part light-footed infantry, who fought among the horsemen after the manner of the Germans. So important did he think the mobility of these auxiliaries that he took the horses of Roman officers to mount them. The wiry little German ponies were not suited for the service required.

1156. Caesar now felt able to move. In order to open up communication with the province, he made for the country of the Sequani. As he was marching through the country of the Lingones Vercingetorix attacked him. The great army of central Gaul was gathered under an inspiring leader for a final effort. He pointed out to them that it was useless merely to force the Roman army to retreat. To destroy it was the only chance of preventing its return and reclaiming Gaul for the Gauls. But the actual result of much swearing and enthusiasm was disappointing. When attacked on the march, the legions stood firm, and the rout of some Gaulish horse by a charge of Caesar's Germans brought on a general panic in the mounted forces of Vercingetorix. He fell back on Alesia with a demoralized army. Caesar followed, and a survey of the position led him to give up the movement to the South and invest this stronghold. If he could hold his adversary fast in Alesia, the refuge might become a trap, and a solid victory might end the weary war. He had now with him ten legions, and the incorporation of the recruits, whom Labienus had picked up on his way through Age-

[1] Caes. *Gall.* VII 65, Dion Cass. XL 39.

dincum, had probably filled up most of the gaps in the ranks. His infantry may have amounted to something over 40,000 men. His cavalry consisted of some still loyal Gauls, useful at least in pursuit ; some Spaniards ; and, better than these, his German corps. In short he was far stronger than he had been at Gergovia, and the hill of Alesia, though too steep to give hopes of a successful assault, could very well be blockaded. The business required immense labour and tenacity, for relief would of course be attempted from outside, and to make and man a ring of siege-lines ten or eleven miles long, impenetrable from either side, was a colossal undertaking. The question of supplies was also troublesome, but less so than at Gergovia, for he had the faithful Lingones, not the faithless Aedui, on his rear. But Caesar knew that his men could not only fight well ; they would toil with pick and spade, with axe and hammer, and be cheerful on short rations. So the lines were planned out at once, trenches ramparts palisades entanglements towers redoubts, with camps for the cavalry on the lower parts of the ground. Seeing the works grow apace, Vercingetorix sent out his cavalry to stop the Roman progress, but after some success they were finally routed and cut up by the Germans. He saw only one thing to be done with them. Before the Roman investment was complete, he despatched them by night with urgent messages to the chiefs of their tribes in all parts of the country. He might at a pinch make his food last a little over 30 days, but only by shortening rations. He called upon them to raise every able-bodied man and hasten to rescue the 80,000[1] who with himself were risking their lives in the common cause of Gaul. When the cavalry was gone he seized all provisions, and the wretched Mandubii, to whom the town belonged, found themselves victims of the necessities of war.

1157. The assembled chiefs agreed to attempt the relief of Vercingetorix, but not to call out every available man. They did not know how to manage or feed so great a host. By contingents they raised an army, or rather a mob, of 250,000 foot and 8000 horse. Even in this supreme moment one tribe (Bellovaci) did not respond to the call, and squabbles about the command ended in the appointment of four generals. That this immense host can have been got together and brought to the scene of action in 30 days is incredible, and Caesar does not say so. By the time it appeared the corn in Alesia was all spent, and flesh very scarce. Vercingetorix drove the non-combatants out of the town, and it seems certain that they perished miserably in the open, for Caesar would not let them pass his lines or receive or relieve them on any terms. So the besieged

___
[1] This number is doubtful.

contrived to hold out for a few days more ; the expulsion of the Mandubii was cruel, but it was thought better than to put in practice a horrid proposal of cannibalism. At last the relieving army came in sight, full of boastful confidence. Assailed from within and without by forces outnumbering the defenders by eight to one, it could hardly be doubted that the Roman lines must be pierced, Caesar and his army be destroyed, and the Gauls be free—free, we may add, to work out their own ruin in their own way. Three fierce assaults were now delivered, and the last was very nearly successful. The details of these three days fighting, and of the siege operations in general, interesting though they are, cannot be given here. Suffice it that the struggle was worthy of the momentous issues at stake, and that the final repulse of the Gauls caused the survivors of the relieving army to disperse. Broken-spirited fugitives bore the tale of shattered hopes into every corner of the land.

1158. The unconditional surrender of Alesia naturally followed. Vercingetorix nobly offered to die by the hands of his own men, or to give himself up to Caesar, as might be best for his countrymen. The latter course was taken. Dion Cassius[1] says (on what authority is not clear) that he had once been on terms of friendship with Caesar, and now hoped for mercy on that ground, but that Caesar treated this fact as an aggravation of his offence. He was put in chains and forwarded to Rome to adorn the proconsul's triumph. This as we know was delayed by the course of events. The hero of Gaul lay in the Roman dungeon, while the civil war raged and Caesar became lord of the Roman world. In 46 the triumph took place, and the captive was exhibited. If we may believe Dion, he was then put to death in the old style, as Pontius the Samnite and Jugurtha the Numidian were before him. The remains of his army were for the present sorted out into two groups. Arvernian and Aeduan prisoners were kept as a means of extorting the speedy submission of their tribes. The rest were served out to the soldiers as slave-booty, to reward their splendid service. The two chief rebel tribes quickly made full submission, and between them received back about 20,000 captives. The favour shewn to these tribes, the stubborn arch-rebels and the faithless 'brethren of the Roman people,' was doubtless an instance of the old Roman policy of promoting disunion among subjects by inequality of treatment. Caesar decided to winter at the front once more, and made his headquarters in the Aeduan capital Bibracte. The legions were quartered in carefully chosen spots so as to overawe the tribes of central Gaul, and special

---

[1] Dion Cass. XL 41. I know no authority for saying that the chiefs in Alesia seized him and gave him to Caesar.

care was taken to protect the Remi against a possible attack of the refractory Bellovaci. The news of Caesar's campaign was again honoured in Rome by a thanksgiving of twenty days. But the winter of 52—51 was not a time of unbroken peace in Gaul. The proconsul had to take the field in order to put down local risings, first among the Bituriges, then among the Carnutes. Early in 51 a more serious rebellion in the North-West, in which a number of tribes headed by the Bellovaci took part, gave him a good deal of trouble. But this too was put down, and Caesar then made a devastating raid into the country of the Eburones in the North-East. This was to teach that restless tribe not to listen to the voice of Ambiorix, for that irrepressible chieftain still eluded capture. There was also trouble in the West, with which, so long as it was warfare in the open, Caesar's lieutenants dealt successfully. But those of the rebels who escaped made a last desperate stand in the stronghold of Uxellodunum, on the river Oltis (Lot). They held out so stoutly, and example was so dangerous, that Caesar had to go himself, and the place soon fell. He cut off the hands of the garrison and set them at large, by way of a lesson to Gauls in general, that those who had once become dependent allies of the Roman people were not at liberty to discard the boon.

1159. Meanwhile Labienus, despatched to chastise the ever troublesome Treveri, had cut up their cavalry, Germans and all, captured several anti-Roman leaders, and restored order in his workmanlike way. Various rebel chiefs in other parts of Gaul were either betrayed or surrendered to Caesar. One arch-rebel Carnutian was scourged till he fainted, and then beheaded. Caesar was loth to allow this, but the soldiers clamoured for it, regarding the man as the originator of the great rebellion in which they had suffered so much. What happened to the rest we do not know. The record of events in Gaul after the distribution of the legions for the winter of 52—51 is preserved in the eighth book of the *Gallic War*, which is an inferior continuation of Caesar's own seven books, written by his friend Hirtius. We may gather that after the suppression of the great rebellion a great deal of work remained to be done in the way of settling disputes and assigning punishments and rewards. This work was much interrupted by the smaller risings referred to above. Nor were the cares of Caesar confined to the lands that he had himself brought under the sovranty of Rome. In the summer of 52 a raid of Istrians had inflicted great losses on the flourishing town of Tergeste (Triest). The proconsul could not leave the Roman municipalities of the Cisalpine exposed to the incursions of mountaineers whom this raid would encourage. So he sent one legion over the

Alps as a precaution. But when late in the season of 51 quiet had been restored in Gaul, and he had paid a visit to Aquitania, the remaining legions had to be put in winter quarters. They were placed in central and northern Gaul, but the text accounts for ten legions. If there is no mistake, Caesar must have had eleven[1] legions under him at this time. He evidently felt that the Belgian tribes were those most needing attention as the close of his long term of government drew near. He fixed headquarters at Nemeto-cenna (Arras) the chief town of the Atrebates. The last little passage of guerrilla warfare occurred in this neighbourhood. Commius, an Atrebatian chief who had in the earlier years been a trusted ally and follower of Caesar, had for some time past gone over to the national cause, and had borne a leading part in the great rebellion. He was still in arms, and his mounted band gave no small annoyance. But he too was presently worn out by the activity of Caesar's cavalry, and made submission, only declining to surrender in person. He had nearly fallen a victim to the treacherous attempt of a Roman officer, and was resolved to keep out of the way of Romans for the future.

1160. Caesar had been appointed governor of the two Gallic provinces, the Cisalpine and the Narbonese. He had in eight years conquered the hitherto free Gaul, larger in area than his original provinces. By this conquest, however incomplete in some respects, he had at least given to Italy the only practical security against the old danger of Gaulish invasion. The new Gaul now lay quiet. For the moment it was really a part of his province. As proconsul at the head of an army he was responsible for keeping order and enforcing obedience. The settlement of disputes and the framing of administrative arrangements were in his hands. But his government was coming to an end, and there were clouds on the political horizon. In the ordinary course the report of the completed conquest should have led to the appointment of a senatorial commission for drawing up, under Caesar's chairmanship, a charter or organic statute (*lex provinciae*) to regulate the administration of the countries annexed. Or the recent precedent of Pompey might be followed, and the scheme of settlement be entrusted to the judgment of the proconsul alone. But Caesar well knew that the Senate would do neither of these things. They had far other designs ; their first object was to get him out of Gaul, and then to destroy him, and the jealousy of Pompey had enlisted the first man in Rome on their side. Whatever may have been the secret

---

[1] See *BG* VIII 24 § 3, 46 § 4, Rice Holmes pp. 782—3. The words of Suetonius *Jul.* 24 might be taken to imply that the Gaulish legion (*Alauda*), raised by Caesar among the Transalpine Gauls, was already in existence. But this is very uncertain.

ambitions of Caesar, we may at least be sure that he did not mean to submit tamely to be thrust down into the insecurities of a private station and handed over by his old enemies to the mercy of corrupt jurymen.   We have no right to charge him with desiring civil war. But he had surely for some time been aware that to civil war it would most likely come in the end, and for that event he was now prepared. He alone was master of a devoted veteran army.   But, whatever the immediate future might bring, it was on all grounds desirable that when he laid down his government he should leave behind him a Gaul pacified and willing to enjoy for the present a period of rest. The few sentences[1] in which Hirtius describes Caesar's policy after the conquest represent the work of a very busy winter at head-quarters.   He strove to avert the necessity for any more campaigns and to remove all discontents that might lead to a fresh rebellion when his back was turned.   He treated the tribes with courtesy and consideration, lavished rewards on the chiefs, and was careful not to impose new burdens.   From Velleius Suetonius and Dion Cassius we learn[2] that he treated the various tribes differently, as we might have inferred from precedent.   From some he exacted fines.   A moderate fixed tribute (*stipendium*) was required from most, if not from all. He seems to have left the tribe-system much as he found it, but some faithful allies, such as the Remi, were more independent than others, that is, a Roman governor would have no right to interfere in their affairs so long as they did what was required of them.   The position of the tribal units would be that of allies (*socii*) in various grades of privilege, and the Roman overlordship would be represented by the governor of the Narbonese province.   As the governor of Macedonia had authority over the Greek states, so the governor of *Gallia Narbonensis* would be High Commissioner for *Gallia Comata*.   One important obligation lay upon all the states of the 'long-haired' Gaul, as upon allies in general, the liability to furnish contingents to the armies of Rome.   Of this Caesar availed himself in the civil war, and the Gaulish tribesmen responded to the call.

1161.   All Caesar's arrangements were of course in a strict sense provisional, requiring confirmation as much or as little as Pompey's settlement of the East.   But the march of events superseded forms and scruples in the case of Gaul, and a regular provincial organization had to wait for the hand of Augustus.   Meanwhile a momentous financial revolution had silently changed the balance of political power in the Roman world.   The gold hoarded by long generations of Gauls had been wrung from them, and passed into circulation. Caesar's soldiers had been rewarded not only by marketable captives

[1] *BG* VIII 49.   [2] Vell. II 39, Suet. *Jul.* 25, Dion Cass. XL 43 § 3.

but by loot, and on special occasions[1] by presents of money. Centurions, military tribunes, and *legati*, had been well cared for[2] in their various degrees, for Caesar did not expect to get good service for nothing. The company at headquarters had shared the proconsul's bounties. Most of the purses filled during the war in Gaul were destined to be emptied again in Rome, and the pouring-out of this money had steadily increased the fame of Caesar. No doubt Caesar himself had all along taken the lion's share, not to hoard it, but to get value for it. He bought men, and so kept a constant check on hostile movements in Rome. And now that he knew the dangerous intrigues on foot to ruin him, he was more than ever compelled to look out for men who could serve his purpose and whose services were in the market. The winter of 51—50 came to an end, and his arrangements in Further Gaul were complete. Among other occupations, he had probably written out his seven books of the Gallic war from notes made year by year. This work[3] had now to be published without delay as a means of guiding public opinion in judging his achievements. At the opening of spring (50) he set out for the Cisalpine. His object as given by Hirtius was to canvass the Roman citizens in the municipal towns on behalf of his quaestor M. Antonius. Antony was gone to Rome to stand for a place among the augurs, and had been elected before Caesar's arrival. But the main object of his journey was surely to get more closely into touch with Roman politics and take measures on his own behalf. He took care to refresh his popularity with the municipal Romans, whom he had been prevented from visiting for now two winters. He was received with enthusiasm. At this time he probably published his Commentaries. But he did not stay long in Italy. The Further Gaul it is true was quiet, but what he had learnt of affairs in Rome may well have reminded him that in the last resort he had only his army to depend on, and that nothing was so likely to ruin his army as a prolonged

---

[1] *BG* VIII 4.

[2] For the notorious case of Mamurra see Pliny *NH* XXXVI 48, Ellis on Catullus 29. He served as *praefectus fabrum*. Labienus was one of those greatly enriched by the plunder of Gaul.

[3] I accept this as the main authority for the conquest of Gaul, to be used with caution, because written with a purpose, but on the whole trustworthy, and often conspicuously candid. The criticism of Asinius Pollio, cited by Sueton. *Jul.* 56, is too general to help us much. The notices of the Gallic war in Strabo, Dion Cassius, Plutarch, and Appian, so far as they are not derived from Caesar or Hirtius, may be drawn from Pollio's history. But I think their value is small, and believe that it has been rightly appraised by Mr Rice Holmes, who is singularly free from the perversity of many modern critics. That Caesar was still anxious to avoid a breach with Pompey is surely to be inferred from the references (*Gall.* VI 1, VII 6) to him. The unfavourable mention of Pompey is in VIII 52—55 (Hirtius). Cicero *Brutus* § 262 speaks warmly (B.C. 46) in praise of the style, and treats it not as history but as materials for history. This however does not amount to calling it impartial.

spell of dulness and inaction.   He hurried back to the North, and summoned all his legions to a rendezvous on the borders of the Treveri.   There he reviewed them, and solemnly performed the ceremony of purification (*lustratio*).   After this he kept them on the move, with a view to keep them in good health and efficiency. At this point, when all was now ready for facing the conflict which circumstances made inevitable, we may turn to see what had been going on in Rome and other parts of the Roman world.

1162.   NOTE ON TRIBE-NAMES IN GAUL.

It is matter of common observation that the progress of Roman conquest in Gaul is recorded in the marked difference of the names of towns.   In the South, the old Narbonese Province, the old Romanized town-name commonly survives in the modern one.   Such are *Arelate* (Arles), *Carcaso* (Carcassonne), *Massilia* (Marseille), *Narbo* (Narbonne), *Nemausus* (Nîmes), *Vienna* (Vienne), *Tolosa* (Toulouse), to give a few instances.   There are some in other parts, especially in the East, where the next advance of Romanization took place, such as *Genava* (Genève, Genf) and *Vesontio* (Besançon); but those elsewhere, such as *Burdigala* (Bordeaux), are rarer.

On the other hand in the *Gallia comata* conquered by Caesar the survival of the tribe-name in the town-name is normal.   Thus *oppidum Bellovacorum* is Beauvais, and the names of tribes remain, as *Redones* (Rennes), *Veneti* (Vannes), *Eburovices* (Evreux), *Treveri* (Trier, Trèves), *Lingones* (Langres), *Carnutes* (Chartres), *Lemovices* (Limoges), *Namnetes* (Nantes), *Mediomatrici* (Metz), *Turones* (Tours), an imperfect list.   In some cases Caesar gives us the old town-name of the place now known by the tribe-name.   These are

Town-name	Tribe-name	Modern name
Samarobriva	Ambiani	Amiens
Nemetocenna	Atrebates	Arras
Durocortorum	Remi	Reims
Agedincum	Senones	Sens
Lutetia	Parisii	Paris
Avaricum	Bituriges	Bourges
Noviodunum	Suessiones	Soissons

CHAPTER LVI.

ROMAN AFFAIRS FROM THE CONFERENCE OF LUCA TO THE OUTBREAK OF THE GREAT CIVIL WAR. 55—49 B.C.

1163. THE beginning[1] of the year 55 found Rome without consuls or praetors. The only important magistrates as yet elected were the tribunes, and of these only two out of ten were opponents of the Coalition policy. We have already seen that Pompey and Crassus carried their own election as consuls after an *interregnum*, and that in the election of praetors they brought in Vatinius and kept out Cato. Violence, religious obstruction, bribery,—everything, in short—was resorted to. At the election of aediles blood ran freely ; Pompey's gown was drenched with blood, and Julia swooned at the sight of it. Censors were elected early in the year, but no census[2] was carried out. All the republican machinery was clogged, and only allowed to work for the convenience of the real masters of Rome. The arrangements already agreed upon for provinces were now pushed through, and the opposition of Cato overcome by force. Crassus was to have Syria, Pompey[3] the two Spains, each for five years, and with wide powers of raising troops and waging war at discretion. The extension of Caesar's command was also provided for. Both Cato and Cicero are said to have warned Pompey that he was raising Caesar to a height from which he would not be able to dislodge him, but the self-satisfied man took no heed. In the case of Crassus it was no secret that he meant to attack the Parthians without any reasonable pretext, in order to place himself on a level with his two great military associates. Pompey does not appear to have divulged his real intention, which was to remain at the centre of affairs and govern his province through lieutenants. In short, the policy of the consuls was inconsistent with the continued existence of the Republic, which only

---

[1] Our chief authority for the events of this chapter is of course the correspondence of Cicero. Only a few of the more important references are given in the notes. The collection must be read as a whole.

[2] They did perform some functions, as in setting out new boundary-stones after the great flood in the spring of 54. Inscriptions in Wilmanns 845 and 845 a. Dion Cass. XXXIX 61.

[3] According to Plutarch and Appian, perhaps following Livy, Pompey was to have also Africa (Λιβύη), Crassus also Egypt or 'the country adjacent to Syria.' If there is any truth in these statements, it is probably this, that some special powers were granted them in these departments. Perhaps Λιβύη is not the Province Africa, but the client-kingdoms of Numidia and Mauretania. See Plut. *Cato min.* 43, Appian *civ.* II 18.

existed on sufferance. The republican nobles saw this clearly enough, and made what resistance they could. They found their best political weapon in the maintenance of gilds (*collegia*) and clubs (*sodalicia*), through which bribery and other means of influence could be organized and brought to bear. Clodius had given a new life to these unions, and in Caesar's absence it would seem that the aristocrats had captured them and turned them to account. The magistrates of 57 and 56 had been mainly men of their party, and the present recovery of power by the triumvirs had only been brought about by the clear and bold strategy—forcible usurpation—devised by Caesar at Luca.

1164. After all the laws that had been passed to improve the quality of juries and to put down corrupt practices at elections, further measures of the same kind were on the face of it absurd, in fact a mere confession of past failure without a prospect of future success. But we must remember that this kind of legislation only became chronic when the Republic was far advanced in decay, and that it was undertaken in hope of gaining a party advantage quite as much as of effecting a genuine reform. The same unwholesome motive is probably to be detected in the laws now carried by Pompey and Crassus in the few active months of their consulship. Pompey had several measures in hand, some of which he carried. Among these[1] the most important was the *lex iudiciaria,* in which he provided that in drawing up the yearly list of jurors a certain number should be taken from each of the 35 Tribes. Some further rules as to the property-qualification of jurors seem also to have been included in the law. Thus it was possible to form a jury for a particular case out of members of a few Tribes only. Now electoral corruption was carried out on an elaborate system, each agent having a certain number of voters assigned him to watch and bring to the poll. As voting went by Tribes (for Centuries were now only parts of Tribes) the little flock shepherded by each agent were naturally all voters in the same Tribe. No one dreamt of bribing all the 35 Tribes or all the Centuries: a majority was all that was needed. Therefore, by choosing a jury for a particular case out of members of Tribes that had not shared the liberality of the accused, it was possible to get a verdict from persons not prejudiced in his favour. This was the principle underlying the *lex Licinia*[2] *de sodaliciis* carried by Crassus. The prosecutor named

---

[1] For the Pompeian and Licinian laws see Holden's Introduction to Cic. *pro Plancio.* In §§ 30—31 he points out that the panel (*decuria*) of senators can hardly have been affected by the Tribe-rule.

[2] In the speech *pro Plancio* §§ 36—47 Cicero is at great pains to make out that the intention of the law (and of the Senate when the matter was discussed) was that the Tribes named should be those the accused was particularly charged with corrupting. But he carefully avoids saying that this was so stated either in the law or in a resolution of the House. It is

four Tribes, and the accused was allowed to challenge one. From those members of the remaining three Tribes whose names were on the *album iudicum* for the year the jurors were taken. No more need be said on the subject here. The point is that convictions were most difficult to secure, and that a great effort was made to secure them by removing the possibility of a friendly jury.

1165. The tension between the consuls and the Senate was evidently great, and the position of Cicero most awkward. His real sympathies were with Cato Bibulus and the various Marcelli and others who were the fighting leaders of the republican aristocracy. But he had to obey orders from his new masters, and the feeling of insincere dependence made him very unhappy. He passed a large part of the year in the country, and found solace in the composition of his work *de oratore*. The return of Piso from Macedonia gave him an opportunity of letting off some of his feelings. Piso was in disgrace, and ill-tempered, and let fall a remark in the Senate that irritated Cicero. The orator made this the excuse for a furious attack upon his old enemy. The speech *in Pisonem* is a specimen[1] of the unmeasured invective in which he was only too fond of indulging, but he took good care to avoid saying anything that would offend Pompey or Caesar. But if Cicero felt better after this discharge of venom, he had also the mortification of having to defend L. Caninius Gallus, one of Pompey's men, whom the senatorial opposition had brought to trial as a party move. It was hard to feel himself the triumvirs' hack; and the news from the East was not calculated to cheer him in his depression. His old enemy Gabinius was still governor of Syria, and in the course of this summer news came that he had taken an audacious step. In spite of all the debates on the Egyptian question, ending in a direct resolution forbidding the restoration of the worthless Auletes to the Alexandrian throne, it was announced that Gabinius had invaded Egypt, overthrown the existing government, and restored[2] the Piper by force of arms. Two points at least are certain in reference to this affair. The king had not received the help of a Roman governor and Roman troops for nothing, nor would Gabinius have dared to defy the Senate if he had not trusted that a power stronger than the Senate would see him safely through the perils of the law-courts. In fact he had received an enormous bribe,

clear that it was not. As for his attempt to make it appear so, without saying so, this is nothing but the artifice of counsel pleading a bad case. The ingenious process by which he arrives at his allegations is well analysed in Orelli's onomasticon III 208—9.

[1] The passage §§ 68—72 is a *locus classicus* describing the reception of Greek Epicurean theory in a Roman temperament.

[2] This is mentioned in Cic. *in Pison.* §§ 48—50. The fullest account is in Dion Cass. XXXIX 55—63.

and his action was undertaken in collusion with Pompey. It is said that he even gave up a Parthian campaign on which he had already started, simply in order to lose no time in earning the promised reward.   The scandal of this business was something quite out of the common, even in that corrupt age, and as the news leaked out there was general indignation.   But Cicero was no longer free to denounce the misdeeds of Gabinius. We shall see what happened in the next year. A public excitement in the autumn was the opening of the great theatre which Pompey had been building.   Hitherto temporary wooden erections had served the turn of the Roman public, but the new theatre was a permanent building of stone.   Splendid dramatic performances were held in it, and followed by other shows, particularly by a grand wild-beast-fight (*venatio*) in the Circus.   Hundreds of lions are said to have been slaughtered.   But the most brutal exhibition was a fight between 18 elephants and a body of armed men.   The poor beasts did not want to fight: they were tame, and looked on men as friends.   So when the men began to wound them they screamed in terror, and the sight was so revolting[1] that even the heartless mob of Rome was disgusted and clamoured to have the survivors spared.   Pompey, clumsy and tactless as ever in dealing with his fellow-citizens, seems to have gained little popularity by all his outlay.   Cicero looked upon the whole series of shows as an abomination and a bore.

1166.   In November Crassus, while still consul, set out[2] for the East. He should by rights have waited for the new year, but he was impatient.   He was 60, and there was no time to be lost.   Moreover, the doings of Gabinius made him wish to be on the spot.   He had had a grand reconciliation with Cicero, and dined[3] with him just before starting.   But the orator still thought him a rascal.   Indeed he was generally hated.   An impressive scene took place as he passed the city gate.   One of the two tribunes not nominees of the triumvirs waited for him there and solemnly laid on him the most potent curses at his disposal, accompanied by sacrifices to increase their efficacy. The sequel caused this scene to be recorded circumstantially, as a lesson to those who treated such things with levity.   So Crassus left Rome, never to return.   Pompey was now the sole representative of the coalition within reach, and to those on the spot he appeared the first man of the Roman world.   But his mysterious and shifty ways[4]

---

[1] Pliny *NH* VIII 21, Dion Cass. XXXIX 38.

[2] According to Dion Cass. XXXIX 39 the levy of troops this year caused great discontent, and even the opposition of some tribunes, particularly in the case of Crassus.

[3] Cic. *ad Att.* IV 13.   Compare *ad Fam.* V 8.

[4] See for instance Cic. *ad Att.* IV 9, *ad fam.* I 9 § 2.

were a constant source of weakness: to act with him was always embarrassing, and to be led by him was to feel the want of a leader. It is a sign of the times that we hear little of Clodius. His work was practically done. His importance had been largely due to his connexion with Caesar, and Caesar had no great use for him now. When he wrote to Caesar, Caesar did not answer[1] his letter. The political situation in general was full of uncertainty, drifting to anarchy. The republicans did not feel themselves beaten yet, and at the consular election this autumn L. Domitius Ahenobarbus, the determined enemy of the triumvirs, was successful. His colleague Appius Claudius Pulcher, a brother of P. Clodius, was backed by Pompey. He was one of the men who attended the conference of Luca, and Pompey's elder son had married his daughter. In the praetorships for 54 there was also a division of honours; among them was Cato. The election of curule aediles was interrupted by violence, and seems not to have been carried through[2] in the year 55 but at some time in 54.

1167. The new year came and Pompey ceased to be consul. He was now proconsul, governor of all Spain. But he was also still in special charge of the corn-supply, and he had no intention of leaving Rome. This combination of offices was strictly speaking unconstitutional, but the day of nice scruples was past. As proconsul with a military command in Spain he could not enter the city. But he remained in Italy, in defiance of all rule and precedent, fearing to lose his hold upon public affairs. Whether it were necessary to carry out some policy concerted with Caesar, or whether at times he began to think Caesar a rival to be watched, in either case he preferred to be near what he thought the centre of power. So he kept within reach, enjoying the company of his beloved Julia, whose health was now a cause of some anxiety. In Spain he had two *legati*, L. Afranius and M. Petreius, who were quite able to deal with a small rising that had lately occurred. The end of it was that he never went to Spain at all. Thus another well marked stage in the development of the Republic into an Empire was quietly reached. The process begun by reelections to office, continued by the election of Pompey himself to the consulship without holding the lower offices, extended by great commands over immense areas for a number of years, now began to shew its true tendency in a more definite form. The proconsul with headquarters in Italy, governing provinces by deputy year after year, was the very model of a Roman Emperor. Pompey was the chief creator of imperial precedents. But his quasi-imperial position was a vain thing as it stood, not so much because he was not the man to end the dying

---

[1] Cic. *ad Q. frat.* III 1 § 11 (in 54 B.C.).

[2] See Holden's Introd. to Cic. *pro Planc.* §§ 3, 5.

Republic, as because he was blind to the one dominant fact of the time. It was excusable to believe that the centre of power was still in Italy. But at the moment it was in Gaul. The provinces, including prosperous northern Italy, were far more important as centres of imperial power than Italy proper, the land south of the Rubicon, where the remaining free population was for the most part neither warlike nor industrial, and the parks and plantations of the rich consigned great districts to the care of slaves. But this truth was not revealed to men of that generation. The genius of Caesar alone detected it, at least in part. When he entered on a great public career, the end of which none could foresee, it was very soon clear that the dangers awaiting him were only to be overcome by the possession of superior strength. And in building up the needful strength he frankly recognized that it was not to be found in Italy.

1168. Before we pass to the internal movements and troubles of the year 54 in Rome, let us take a brief glance abroad. This was the year of the northern rising in Gaul, in which Quintus Cicero had been so near destruction and Sabinus and Cotta had perished. Young P. Crassus had left Caesar and followed his father to Syria, taking with him 1000 picked troopers, apparently Gauls. Caesar was obliging as ever, and nothing loth to earn approval, even in the far-off army of the East. Crassus himself had made the journey to his province with impatient haste, suffering some loss through carelessness on the way. When he reached Syria, he found the province in a very bad state owing to the misgovernment of Gabinius, but this does not seem to have given him much concern. A recent dynastic revolution had created a false impression of the weakness of Parthia. The new king Orodes offered no provocation, though the well-known designs of Gabinius had been a fair cause for resentment. But Crassus was resolved to have war, though he had not properly studied the necessary conditions of a Parthian campaign. For a pitched battle or the siege of walled cities he was no doubt sufficiently equipped. But to deal with a mobile enemy whose strength lay chiefly in mounted bowmen and lancers, followed by a camel-train bearing endless supplies of arrows, in vast expanses of sand where dust was everywhere and water scarce, was a task beyond the power of the legions. The blind ambition of Crassus was further excited by an exaggerated notion of Parthian wealth, though his own present riches were enormous. The general position of the kingdom was briefly as follows. The immense empire of Seleucus, formed out of the eastern conquests of Alexander, early began to lose its far eastern provinces. Among the most serious revolts was that of the Parthi, formerly one of the peoples subject to the great kings of Persia. The Parthian kingdom founded by Arsaces about the middle of the third century B.C. had survived many vicissitudes, growing on the whole as the power of the Seleucids in Syria decayed. The Parthians seem to have had the true oriental readiness to submit to an absolute ruler at home and to resent interference from abroad. The Arsacid kings had found a good number of Graeco-Macedonian cities established in the country at well-chosen spots, colonies planted by the great Alexander or his successor Seleucus. These were centres of trade, and maintained Greek arts and civilization, surrounded by wide stretches of open country over which the native barbarians roamed. The Arsacids were wise enough to encourage these cities, which added to the resources of their realm. They posed as protectors of the Greeks, and liked to have the title φιλέλλην on their coins. In spite of occasional disloyalty the cities seem to have retained their internal government under Greek constitutions. But there could be no genuine sympathy between them and their Eastern lords, all the more as the East was steadily gaining on the West and the Greeks felt the dissatisfaction inseparable from a losing cause.

1169. It was in the summer of 54 that Crassus passed the Euphrates and entered Mesopotamia. Following mainly the line of the river, he came upon some Greek cities, most of which submitted easily. He is said to have also overrun and laid waste a good deal of the country. This would be in the northern part of Mesopotamia, some of it probably in the district of Osrhoene. He found no enemy ready to resist him, but instead of pursuing his advantage he turned back to winter at Antioch, and put off the real campaign till the next year. Thus the Parthians had time to bring up their forces, and the people of the invaded districts to think over the situation. As for the 'Greeks,' Crassus had plundered one town and enslaved the people. His proceedings generally had not given much reason for preferring a Roman to a Parthian yoke. Avgar prince of Osrhoene had recently submitted to Pompey and been included in his settlement of the East. It would seem from the sequel that he had been turned into a deadly enemy by the silly brutality of Crassus. The winter was spent by the proconsul, not in training and organizing his forces for the coming campaign, but in taking stock of the remaining resources of Syria and Palestine with a view to confiscation. The hoards of precious metals in the temples were the chief object of his attention, in particular those of the temple[1] of Jerusalem. These sacred treasures, accumulations of the gifts of pious Jews scattered in many lands, were of immense value as bullion and prized also for reasons of sentiment. Pompey had spared them when he violated the Holy of Holies. Crassus now

---

[1] Josephus *Ant.* XIV 105—118, *bell. Jud.* I. 152—3, 179.

seized them, and contrived to give a peculiar blackness to the robbery by his perfidy. During the winter a Parthian embassy waited on him to complain of his unprovoked aggression and treat for peace. The overbearing Roman replied that he would discuss such matters at Seleuceia. This was the greatest of the Greek cities. It stood far down on the right bank of the Tigris. Over against it, not far from the left bank, was the palace-city of Ctesiphon, the capital of the Parthian monarchy. So far at least did Crassus reckon upon penetrating. The story is perhaps not free from the touches of a moralizing rhetoric, for Crassus was to after ages a classic example of the pride that goeth before a fall.

1170. Meanwhile Rome was a scene of worse confusion[1] than ever. The near presence of Pompey held in check the republican leaders, and produced an equilibrium of disorder. Intervals of comparative quiet were, as Cicero saw, not the signs of recuperative calm but of senile exhaustion. The Republic was dying. Quite early in the year some attack[2] was made on Crassus in the Senate, and Cicero, loyal to his present connexion, defended him in his absence. As the year went on, he had to give more and more proofs of subservience to his masters; C. Messius, one of Caesar's men, his old enemies Vatinius and Gabinius, and others too, had him for their counsel. The year was one of frequent trials[3] in courts that were, if possible, more corrupt than ever: Cicero, now far the first of the Roman bar, was in great demand. But he had little heart for public life. He found a melancholy interest in writing his work *de re publica*, dwelling on the merits of the Roman constitution as he conceived it to have been in its palmy days, while the Roman Commonwealth, the object of his patriotic devotion, was going to ruin before his eyes. He had no lack of other occupations, family affairs, commissions for his brother in Gaul, and so forth. His correspondence at this time was voluminous, but enigmatic utterances and frequent references to the necessity of caution shew his great uneasiness. In expressing gratification at his close relations with Pompey and Caesar he is not speaking from the heart. He still feared Clodius, needlessly. Clodius could not harm him, protected as he now was: but it was just the fact that he, Marcus Tullius, Father of his country, needed protection[4] in his own Rome and dared not move in politics without it, that made life bitter to Cicero. And the ever-disappointing slackness of Pompey was at

---

[1] A vivid contemporary picture may be found in Cicero's letters read continuously in order of time. Tyrrell Nos. 141—160, Shuckburgh's translation Nos. 140—159.

[2] Perhaps, as Lange *RA* III 354 thinks, in connexion with the friction between Gabinius and his successor. A speech *in Gabinium* is certainly referred to by Quintilian XI 1 § 73.

[3] See Cic. *ad Att.* IV 15 § 4.   [4] Cic. *ad Q. frat.* II 14 (15 b) § 2, 15 (16) § 2, III 5, 6.

this time bringing Cicero into a sort of dependence on Caesar, who had the happy knack of making him feel pleased with himself. The disturbances and scandals caused in this year by the candidates for the consulships of 53 were so serious, and pointed so clearly to a miscarriage of the elections, that there was some talk of making Pompey dictator to preside and see them through. It seems to have emanated[1] from one of Pompey's own satellites, and was probably a 'feeler' on behalf of the Great Man; but he of course affected to dislike the notion, and the Senate, hating the very name of a dictator, gladly ignored the hint.

1171. Electoral corruption had indeed now reached a point at which it could no longer become worse. The demand for ready money was so great that in July the current rate of interest[2] rose from $4°/_o$ to $8°/_o$. Meetings of Assemblies were being obstructed in every way, and the consuls grew nervous as to the completion of the formal arrangements necessary to enable them to take possession of the provinces assigned them. The powers of presiding officers at elections were such that candidates were eager to profit by their favour. So the present consuls[3] entered into an infamous compact (said to have been recorded in a written document) with two of the present candidates. The former bound themselves to promote the election of the latter. The latter undertook, if elected, to produce official witnesses to swear that they had been present at the completion of official formalities which had never taken place at all. They were to forfeit a sum of money in case they failed to deliver the stipulated perjury according to contract. The scheme was only wrecked by some difference behind the scenes. One of the candidates[4] (why, we know not,) suddenly blurted out the whole story in the Senate. After this the House passed an order for some sort of secret inquiry[5] into the proceedings of candidates, for prosecutions were clearly imminent. But the postponement of the election continued, and the year 53 began without consuls. Tribunes were elected, but a strange device was resorted to for preventing corruption. The candidates agreed to deposit each a sum of money with Cato, who was to decide whether any one of them had acted unfairly by the rest. Any one so condemned by Cato was to forfeit his deposit for division among the others. It was apparently understood that he would remain tribune

[1] Cic. *ad Q. frat.* III 8 §§ 4—6.

[2] Cic. *ad Q. frat.* II 14 (15 b) § 4, *ad Att.* IV 15 §§ 7, 8.

[3] Cic. *ad Att.* IV 17 § 2.

[4] C. Memmius, a man of bad character, to whom Lucretius addressed his poem. He had been an opponent of Caesar, but was now on his side, and backed by his partisans.

[5] For this *tacitum iudicium* see Cic. *ad Att.* IV 16 § 6 (17 § 3), and Plutarch *Cato min.* 44. (The latter mixes up the two sets of elections.) The effort to check bribery was most unpopular, and the plan fell through.

and not be exposed to a prosecution. The plan was calculated to save the purse of candidates, but bribery in the election of tribunes was always a minor matter, for the office did not lead on to a province,—which was now the main thing. The recognition of Cato as the representative of uprightness was a rude censure of the general corruption of jurors magistrates and public men. We are not surprised to hear[1] that the Stoic made enemies among the numerous persons to whom his honesty was a stumbling-block or a reproach.

1172. A few of the numerous trials held in this year must be briefly noticed. One non-political case gives us a glimpse of Italian local affairs, of which we seldom hear. The people of Reate, old clients of Cicero, had a dispute with their neighbours of Interamna. It was some question relative to the great drainage-tunnel by which the water of the Veline lake was carried off into the Nar, on which river Interamna stood. The case was heard by a consul and ten commissioners. In order to master the subject, the great orator paid a visit to Reate and went into the details on the spot. As he refers to the case with apparent pride, we may presume that he won it. The trial of P. Vatinius for electoral corruption through clubs (*sodalicia*) was the occasion of an exhibition of compliance with unwelcome orders on Cicero's part. Pompey had effected a reconciliation of a formal kind between the two men. Caesar made it a personal favour that Cicero should undertake the defence, so he had to do it and make the best of it in justifying himself[2] to an absent friend. Vatinius was acquitted, and so probably[3] (not certainly) was Cn. Plancius on a charge of the same kind. In defending him Cicero had the pleasant task of paying back the kindness of one who had stood his friend in the dark days of his exile. A trial[4] characteristic of the time was that of M. Aemilius Scaurus on a charge of extortion. He was the son of the old Scaurus who was in his day a notable figure, the typical solemn astute aristocrat of the last generation. He had as aedile in 58 provided shows of quite exceptional magnificence, and so incurred great debts. After his praetorship in 56 he had been governor of Sardinia, where he seems to have repaired his finances in the usual way. He was now a candidate for the consulship, and it was the support of his opponents that made the prosecution a serious matter. The case first came on in July, when the consular election had not yet been postponed, and when C. Claudius Pulcher, a brother of Appius the consul, was still understood to be a candidate and expected back from his province of Asia. Thus at first Scaurus had against him the official influence of a consul. But by the

[1] Plutarch *Cato min.* 44, 45.   [2] Cic. *ad fam.* 1 9 § 19.
[3] See Holden's Introd. to *pro Plancio*, § 34.
[4] See Cic. *pro Scauro*, partly preserved, and the very valuable notes of Asconius.

beginning of September a change had taken place. C. Claudius had been allowed to spend another year in Asia, and was no longer a candidate, so the hostility of Appius was greatly weakened. But the trial went on, and the presiding praetor in the court of *repetundae* was M. Cato. It was feared that private friendship with the chief prosecutor Triarius might induce Cato to favour a conviction, but the great Incorruptible[1] was just. The defence brought together some strange allies. In the exceptional number of six counsel we find Cicero, P. Clodius[2], and Hortensius. Among the nine consulars who headed the array of witnesses to character or 'intercessors' (*laudatores*) was Pompey. That Eminent Man was connected with the accused after a fashion. Scaurus had married Pompey's divorced wife Mucia, and had by her a son, the half-brother of Pompey's sons. The lady was a notorious character, and the whole affair distasteful to Pompey, who had early come to years of respectability. He supported Scaurus, but without warmth. From the remains of Cicero's speech we learn an interesting[3] detail. The prosecution had neglected to visit Sardinia and collect evidence on the spot. Of course Cicero made the most of this, as it was his business to do. But Asconius records the reason given to explain this neglect. With the consular election thought to be near, there was the risk that when the prosecutor returned Scaurus might be already consul-elect, and so beyond the reach of any charge (other than *ambitus* in the election): thus the evidence would have been collected in vain. Scaurus was triumphantly[4] acquitted. An attempt was even made to fasten the guilt of false accusation (*calumnia*) on the prosecutors, but this was a failure. So ended a trial which is at least highly instructive to a modern student of Roman history, though it can hardly have given much satisfaction to the Sards.

1173. It was about this time that Julia died. Pompey felt her loss deeply, but did not lose his interest in public affairs. The Roman mob would not be prevented from giving her a great public funeral. But she had been popular as Caesar's daughter rather than as Pompey's wife, and the signs of this feeling only served to ripen the latter's jealousy. The hand of Caesar was never long unfelt. One of the motives of the obstruction[5] that was delaying the consular elections was the wish to defer them till Caesar came for his winter assizes

---

[1] Cato did not lose the chance of asserting his singular personality. The weather was hot, and he presided in undress, having made out that this was a good old Roman style. Asconius and Plutarch.

[2] There were thus three Claudian brothers in various ways concerned in the case.

[3] Also that there was still a recognizable Phoenician element in Sardinia, at least in the coast-towns.

[4] On 2 September.   [5] Cic. *ad Q. frat.* III 2 § 3.

in Cisalpine Gaul.   But with this obstruction and the prospect of an *interregnum* Pompey was not inclined to quarrel: it all tended to increase his own importance.   The state of deadlock in Rome in these times is curiously illustrated by an isolated record in this year. The ex-praetor Pomptinus, who had defeated the rebel Allobroges in 61, had been waiting more than six years outside Rome claiming a triumph.   He now got it at last.   Servius Sulpicius Galba, who had served under him, was a praetor.   He carried through the necessary law by putting it to the vote before the day was officially begun. Thus he eluded the veto of a tribune.   So early in November Pomptinus held his triumph.   Cato and others tried to prevent[1] its taking place; Appius Claudius headed a party to protect it.   It is said that blood was shed in this paltry squabble.   What was to become of such a Rome as these glimpses reveal?

1174.   This year of disorder appropriately closes with the trials of Gabinius.   We have seen how he had not only oppressed but neglected his province.   Brigandage inland and a revival of piracy along the coast had caused widespread distress in Syria.   In February 54 a deputation from Tyre[2] complained to the Senate of their sufferings, while the representatives of the revenue-farmers laid the blame on Gabinius.   His intervention in Egypt was an open defiance of the Senate.   No law gave him power to leave his own province; indeed that step was, if we may trust[3] Cicero, directly forbidden by Sulla's law of *maiestas* and Caesar's law of *repetundae*.   But he is said to have acted for a bribe of 10,000 talents (about £2,350,000), and he relied on the protection of Pompey.   He returned to Italy in September, still giving out that he expected a triumph.   But he soon found that there was no prospect of this, for he was almost universally hated.   On Sept. 27 he slunk into the city[4] by night. The storm now burst upon him.   He was attacked in the Senate, and prosecutions for treason and extortion were at once set on foot. Cicero would have been delighted to undertake the former, but Pompey held him back.   He did however give some evidence against his old enemy, who was acquitted by the narrow majority of 38 to 32.   The scandal roused general indignation, but Pompey had succeeded so far: popular feeling was expressed by the condemnation of a wretched subordinate[5] of Gabinius on a wholly different charge. The trial under the law of *repetundae* came to an end in December. Pompey used all his efforts to save the accused.   He addressed a mass meeting outside the walls, and read out a letter from Caesar

---

[1] Cic. *ad Q. frat.* III 4 § 6, *Att.* IV 18 § 4 (16 § 12), Dion Cass. XXXIX 65.
[2] Cic. *ad Q. frat.* II 11 (13).   [3] Cic. *in Pisonem* § 50.
[4] Cic. *ad Q. frat.* III 1 § 24.   [5] Cic. *ad Att.* IV 18 § 4 (16 § 12).

on his behalf. He even sent a petition to the jury. Above all, he constrained Cicero to undertake the defence. The unhappy orator was not in a position to resist such pressure. He did his best, and his enemies called him 'turn-coat' more than ever. But it was all in vain. Gabinius is said to have economized[1] in his dealings with the jury, who did not feel justified in facing popular indignation at a cheap rate. Anyhow he was convicted, and cast in 10,000 talents damages. It is certain that no such sum was recovered. Gabinius went into exile. A corollary of his conviction was the trial of a certain C. Rabirius Postumus, a Roman knight who had got into sad difficulties by lending money to the plausible Ptolemy, and who had been driven to accept a post at Alexandria in order to watch his rash investment. He was alleged to have taken part in the affair of Gabinius, and was now, as the law directed, brought before the same jury in the hope of making him disgorge some of the plunder. Cicero[2] defended him also, and he was probably acquitted. But it is to be noted that, beside technical pleas and appeals to pity, the orator thought it worth while to lay stress on the fact that Caesar had generously come to the aid of this embarrassed speculator, and that he would be greatly distressed if the man were condemned. The result of the whole proceedings was in keeping with the general trend of events. Pompey had failed to protect his associate, and it is not surprising that Gabinius turned his hopes to Caesar, and earned his restoration as a Caesarian in the civil war. Cato as praetor had seen justice done. Cicero was thoroughly ashamed of himself, and to a man who loved, if ever man did, the sunshine of his own admiration this was a dreadful shock. He had foreseen[3] what would happen if he defended Gabinius, but he did it. He seems to have suppressed the speech, and endeavoured by silence to let the episode be forgotten.

1175. At the beginning of the year 53 the only magistrates in office were the tribunes. A series of *interregna* filled all the first half of the year, and this state of things carried with it the closing of the law-courts. To many the stagnation of public business was doubtless inconvenient, but the tribunes found themselves of such importance that they did not scruple to block the holding of the consular election. What with their obstruction and the failure of auspices, no consuls were elected till July. In the mean time there was much clashing of conflicting views as to what should be done to relieve the deadlock that could not go on for ever. Some of the

---

[1] Dion Cass. XXXIX 63.

[2] *pro Rabir. Post.*, a speech of which the present text is incomplete.

[3] Cic. *ad Att.* IV 18 § 3 (16 § 11), *ad Q. frat.* III 5 (6) §§ 4, 5.

tribunes were for returning to the old expedient of electing military tribunes with consular power, and urged that to have the chief magistracy held by a larger number of colleagues would be an improvement. Another proposal was to make Pompey dictator. Both plans recognized the failure of the consulship, but neither could be carried out, each party blocking the other. As usual, rioting and violence followed. Pompey had let matters get to this pass; he was willing to be called in to save the state, and meanwhile he had always the excuse of the corn-supply. When he thought the time ripe, he appeared before the city, and the Senate in despair voted him exceptional powers[1] to deal with the emergency. He accordingly provided for the maintenance of order at the Assembly of Centuries, and Cn. Domitius Calvinus and M. Valerius Messalla received the consulships for which they had paid months and months before. He saw that Cato would not let him be made dictator peaceably, and force was not his policy; but he had once more posed in his favourite character of the great Indispensable. The new consuls had at once to see to the election of the other regular magistrates for the rest of the year. This, with a certain amount of friction, was achieved. There were then the elections for 52 to be held. But, before any attempt could be made to hold them, the political situation, in particular the position of Pompey, was profoundly affected by grave news from the East.

1176. For his Parthian campaign of 53 Crassus had an army of about 40,000 men. His son Publius had joined him from Gaul. The infantry of seven legions formed the bulk of his force. The Armenian king, himself threatened by the Parthians, advised the proconsul to make his advance by way of Armenia and to keep to the high ground as much as possible, in order to avoid giving advantage to the enemy's cavalry. This meant in general following the line of the Tigris. But Crassus scorned his counsel, and passed the Euphrates into Mesopotamia as before. The ominous occurrences recorded in our tradition may at least serve to shew that the army had little confidence in its chief. Nervous and superstitious, the men saw prodigies in every chance word or deed. Soon treachery came in to verify forebodings; and Crassus, though an adept in the tricks of Roman finance, was no match for the subtleties of oriental guile. Avgar of Osrhoene joined him with a force and accompanied him some way along the Euphrates. Gradually he won the ear of Crassus, and induced him to leave the river and enter the Mesopotamian plain. Here the Parthians fell upon the helpless legions. Neither

---

[1] Either the *senatusconsultum ultimum* or something very like it. Plutarch *Pomp.* 54, Dion Cass. XL 45—6.

in open order nor in close masses could the Roman foot effect anything against the mounted bowmen and lancers of the enemy. Young
Crassus and most of his cavalry perished. The broken remains of
the army escaped to Carrhae, but in the retreat from Carrhae further
treacheries completed the tale of disaster. C. Cassius Longinus the
quaestor reached Syria with a small party, but Crassus himself was
lured to a conference with the Parthian general and killed. A considerable number of prisoners were captured and retained in the
service of the Parthian king. Plutarch has preserved the record of
a strange scene which illustrates the sort of Hellenism that enjoyed
the patronage of oriental courts. King Orodes had invaded Armenia
while his chief general was busy with Crassus. The Parthian and
Artavasdes the Armenian had come to terms and were celebrating
their alliance just at the time when the Parthian messengers arrived
with the news of their victory and the head of Crassus. Artavasdes,
who both spoke and wrote Greek, had some strolling players from
Asia Minor in attendance. Orodes too knew some Greek, and it was
thought appropriate to entertain him with a scene from the *Bacchae*
of Euripides,—that in which the frenzied Agave is carrying the head
of Pentheus. The head of Crassus was thrown down in the midst,
and the leading actor picked it up and delivered the lines in which
the maniac boasts of her prize. The horrid realism hit the taste of
the company. The thin layer of Greek culture covering essential
barbarism is worth noticing. The Orient was destined to become
more oriental, and the mongrel Greeks to become more Greek under
Roman protection; but the time was not yet. For the moment
Rome's prestige in the East was low indeed. But Cassius the
quaestor was a cool-headed and skilful soldier. He was now compelled to assume the command. The Parthians did not at first pass
the Euphrates, and when they did come Cassius managed to save
the chief cities and eventually to drive them out of Syria with loss.
We may forestall matters so far as to add that he kept the province
safe till the coming of the next governor, Bibulus. Bibulus adopted
the policy of fomenting the dynastic troubles which were ever
weakening the Parthian monarchy, and in 51 there was a sort of peace
between the two powers.

1177. The disaster of Carrhae was terrible enough to be remembered for itself. But what caused it to impress the Roman
mind and leave a deep mark in Roman literature was the train of
momentous consequences that could not all at once develope, still
less be understood. In foreign affairs the old Eastern Question now
definitely took the form of a Parthian problem, complicated with
that of Armenia, and was for centuries a worry to the Roman

Empire. Far more striking and immediate was its internal effect in letting loose the forces that were ready to complete the Roman Revolution. Nothing now stood between the two great rivals. A civil war was inevitable, for Pompey would not yield, and Caesar dared not. Hitherto the three·partners had ruled in defiance of the aristocrats who upheld the Republic, some from conviction, others as the system which afforded them the privilege of sharing among themselves the plunder of the subject world. But the coalition was broken by the death of Crassus, and between the two rivals the republicans had no difficulty in choosing. A true instinct told them that Caesar was the really dangerous man. Once his mind was made up, he would stop for nothing. Pompey, solemn and hesitating, had twice been the first man in Roman politics, and little or nothing had come of it. Accordingly the republicans, seeing more and more clearly that a great conflict was at hand, became more and more reconciled to the prospect of serving under Pompey when the time should come. Such a master might well turn out to be no master at all. Pompey on his part, as his own jealousy became more active and the conflict more certain, could see the advantage of having the Senate on his side. So the two forces steadily drew together, military prestige and the republican machinery : a formidable combination, but in sharing each other's strength they necessarily shared each other's weaknesses. From the first they were more or less at cross purposes, and indeed it could never be easy for the perverse candour of Cato and the ungainly dissimulation of Pompey to work in harmony.

1178. In the later months of 53 the election of curule magistrates for the next year was a pressing question. Milo was standing for the consulship. The republican nobles, and with them Cicero, were supporting him. The other two candidates, P. Plautius Hypsaeus and Q. Caecilius Metellus Scipio, were Pompey's men. For the praetorship Clodius was standing, and appealing to the numerous class of freedmen by a promised bill for enabling them to be enrolled and vote in any Tribe,—a very old story. Milo, regardless of Cicero's warnings, was spending vast sums on splendid shows and madly running into debt. He was therefore just now well provided with swordsmen. The now usual scenes of bribery and street fighting went on in full vigour. The Senate[1] was anxious to get the elections held, but was helpless. At this time (near the end of 53) we come upon a notice the importance of which does not appear at first sight. The Senate passed a resolution that in future consuls and praetors

---

[1] It was in a debate on the present deadlock that Clodius attacked Milo for falsely representing his financial position in his candidature, and Cicero delivered in defence his speech *de aere alieno Milonis.*

should not succeed to provinces immediately on going out of office, but after an interval[1] of five years. The reason assigned for this rule is that it would tend to relieve the strain of corrupt practices which was fast rendering all elections impossible. The real competition was not for the office but for the province to follow : if the two were parted by an interval, the present scandals would be less likely to occur. However this may be, it is clear that the rule would upset those contained in the laws of C. Gracchus and Sulla ; a law therefore would be necessary[2] to bring it into force. So for the present it remained an aspiration only. But it was the first draft of a change that brought a new and revolutionary principle into the Roman constitution. The pro-magistracy, hitherto regarded as a sort of continuation of the regular magistracy, was now to become regular and detached from that connexion. When a consul or praetor laid down his office, he was to pass five years without *imperium*. When he became proconsul or propraetor of a province, he would need to be deliberately reinvested with *imperium*, just as when he became consul after an interval following his praetorship. Now this change meant nothing less than the establishment of a new magistracy. And it would not only be new ; as the goal of an official career, it must rank above the old. Nor must we forget that this new creation really implied a recognition that provincial government was more important than home administration. Probably the movers of the scheme had no intention of recognizing anything of the kind, but circumstances do extort admissions more far-reaching than they seem at the moment to be. It was really the beginning of a change which came to its full expression under the Empire. The pro-magistracy of provincial governorships was destined to become imperial, while the Roman magistracies tended to become municipal.

1179. The beginning of the year 52 again found Rome without consuls or praetors. Even the appointment of an *interrex* was prevented by the tribune T. Munatius Plancus, who (as Asconius tells us) was acting in the interest of Pompey. Pompey, that is, was squeezing the Senate in order to compel them to take some step towards investing him with some more exceptional powers. So anarchy and general deadlock continued for a time, but eventually the appointment of a series of *interreges* was begun. The estrangement of Pompey from Caesar had recently been marked by his refusal[3]

[1] Dion Cass. XL 46. See below § 1185.

[2] Lange *RA* III 362. This matter is well discussed in Tyrrell and Purser's *Correspondence of Cicero* vol. III Addenda No. 7, where the various views of Mommsen are given, and the evidence set forth.

[3] Caesar had proposed that his grand-niece Octavia should be the successor of Julia. Sueton. *Jul.* 27, *Aug.* 4.

to renew their marriage-connexion. He had married Cornelia, the daughter of that Scipio who was standing for the consulship, and thus connected himself with a leading family of the republican aristocracy. The elections had still not been held, when all Rome was thrown into an uproar by news of the death of Clodius. Milo and he had both been travelling on the Appian way one day in the middle of January. Near Bovillae they met, each of course with a retinue of slaves, as was the custom. Milo's party were the stronger of the two. A quarrel brought on a fight, in which Clodius was wounded. He was carried into a tavern hard by, but dragged out and murdered by Milo's swordsmen. It was said that this was done at the order of Milo, who saw some gain in the death of Clodius but none at all in leaving him to recover and set on foot a criminal prosecution. Anyhow the corpse was brought into the city and exposed, among the wailing and rage of the mob. Next day it was shewn in the Forum; inflammatory speeches were delivered over it, till the crowd was mad with excitement. They carried it into the Senate-house and there burnt it on a pile of benches tables papers and whatever came handy. The House itself was set afire and burnt down; a public hall (*basilica Porcia*) adjoining it was much damaged. The mob then rushed off to attack, first the house of M. Aemilius Lepidus the *interrex*, then that of Milo, but were beaten off. They made a demonstration in favour of the two candidates rivals of Milo, and cheered Pompey as the man to be consul or dictator. But all this sound and fury presently died down, and the damage done by the fire roused a good deal of anger against the Clodian riffraff. So back came Milo and coolly went on with his canvass, openly buying voters wholesale. His friend the tribune M. Caelius gained him a hearing in a mass meeting, and spoke for him. The gist of their speeches was that Clodius had waylaid Milo, and that the latter had only acted in self-defence. Things had now come to such a pass that the Senate was compelled to do something. As yet there were no consuls and no prospect of any. So the House passed its 'last decree' investing the acting *interrex*, the tribunes, and Pompey, with the powers of martial law for the maintenance of order. The last, who as proconsul had full military[1] *imperium*, was authorized to raise troops throughout Italy, which he lost no time in doing. But he was in no hurry to bring on the election of consuls. Milo offered to withdraw his candidature if Pompey wished it, but Pompey declined to give any sign. The Roman people must freely settle its own business: in other words, the present deadlock was playing into Pompey's hand, and he would not spoil his own game.

[1] Not in Rome, of course. See Dion Cass. XL 49, 50.

1180. Meanwhile the relatives and friends of Clodius were exerting themselves to bring Milo to justice. They claimed to have his slaves surrendered for examination under torture. Milo replied that he owed his life to those who had fought for him, and that in gratitude he had given them their freedom. In the Senate indignant protests were made against his story of self-defence, and the House heard the widely-different Clodian version of the affray of Bovillae and its sequel. Thus the days went by in ineffectual bickerings. Late in February the insertion of an intercalary month, then the common expedient for correcting the disorder of the calendar, took place; and it was in this month that the slaves were demanded for torture. But it was clear that no progress could be made until some more regular government existed. A chief magistracy was a necessity. The Senate was not at all eager to take any step that would promote a prosecution of Milo, who was a kind of champion of the Republic. But they could not help themselves. Not only was there a renewal of the cry for Pompey to be made dictator; some tribunes and others were now beginning to talk of having Pompey and Caesar elected consuls, a much more distasteful alternative. So Bibulus and Cato put their heads together and carried a resolution that Pompey should be elected sole consul, with power to provide himself with a colleague after the lapse of two months. There was no precedent for this clumsy evasion of constitutional rule. But the jurist Servius Sulpicius Rufus, the acting *interrex*, carried out his instructions. Pompey thus received another grant of exceptional powers, not only by being sole consul, but by being consul and proconsul[1] at once, not to mention the commissionership of the corn-supply, which had not yet come to an end. Such were the shifts to which Cato and his fellow-republicans were driven in their struggle to keep the tottering Republic on its legs. Their desperate conservatism was one of the essential forces of revolution. For their readiness to sacrifice all constitutional scruples, if only they could keep out Caesar, was from the conservative republican point of view quite right: it was the choice of the lesser of two evils.

1181. Caesar had put down the Belgic rising, and in 53 had made good his losses by two new legions, and one borrowed from Pompey. In the winter of 53–52 he paid his usual visit to the Cisalpine. He was most anxious to keep on good terms with Pompey, and, if we may believe Suetonius[2], instructed the tribunes of his party to drop all suggestion of making him consul at once with his rival. He wished them rather to see to it that when his term of governorship expired he should be able to step into a second consulship at once. He wanted

---

[1] Moreover the legal ten years had not passed since his last consulship in 55.

[2] Suet. *Jul.* 26.

to be elected in 49 and hold office in 48.   In order to do this he must be allowed to stand for it in his absence.   His ten years ran out on the 1st March 49.   Even if he were not delayed till the end of 49 by the technical difficulties connected with the provision of his successor, the candidates in any year were well advanced in their canvass, and had bought their voters, before the first of March.   He knew that his enemies lay in wait for him, and hoped to ruin him by the votes of a jury, the moment he became a private citizen.   He was resolved to give them no chance of doing so: there must be no such interval as that on which they reckoned.   So his tribunes brought forward a bill to dispense him from the requirement of a personal candidature. Even Pompey favoured this solution, and disregarded the warnings[1] of Cicero, whose friend Caelius was ready as tribune to block the bill. If Pompey would give his advantage away like this, Cicero could do no more.   The orator was induced to visit Caesar[2] at Ravenna, and under the spell of the magician consented to persuade Caelius to support the bill.   So it came forward as a proposal of all ten tribunes and was passed into law.   Caesar had to hurry northwards to meet the great rebellion of all central Gaul, but he hoped he had removed the danger that threatened him in Rome.

1182.   ' The election of Pompey took place late in the intercalary month.   Before the first of March he had already begun a course of legislation some of which was destined to have serious consequences. Internal disorders were dealt with in two laws, one of which was a special temporary statute providing for the trial of persons concerned in the murder of Clodius and in the riotous proceedings that followed it.   With this *lex Pompeia de vi*, which did not supersede the general laws on the subject, was joined a new law against corrupt practices. Both laws introduced important changes in the direction of heavier penalties[3] and quicker procedure.   The former at least contained special provisions to secure a court capable of convicting the guilty. The president was to be a consular, duly elected for the purpose, and the preparation of a special list of jurors[4] was entrusted to Pompey. These measures did not pass unopposed.   The law against *ambitus* was so drafted as to include offences committed as far back as the year (70) of Pompey's first consulship.   Caesar's friends objected to it as including their principal's case (59), and no doubt many others were sincerely desirous not to question the past.   Cato was against retrospective legislation altogether,   But Pompey ridiculed the notion that

---

[1] Mayor on Cic. *philipp.* II § 24, Cic. *ad fam.* VI 6 § 5.   [2] Cic. *ad Att.* VII 1 § 4.

[3] For the objection of Caesar to this procedure see his remarks thereon.   Caes. *civ.* III 1 § 4.

[4] Thus he encroached on the sphere of praetorian duties, though he never held the praetorship.

Caesar, any more than himself, was threatened by the form of the law, and overcame the opposition. Against the *lex de vi* it was urged that a special trial of the offenders in question was needed, but neither a special law nor a special court; the existing law[1] was enough, if the Senate only took up the case and set the law in motion. This was the view of old Hortensius, but two resolute tribunes prevented the passing of any resolution that would have committed the House to oppose Pompey's bill, and the consul was free to proceed, so far as the Senate was concerned. Outside there were two tribunes, Caelius and another, threatening to block it, but a declaration from Pompey that he would at need employ armed force removed this obstacle. Rome was indeed at the feet of the master of the troops. Affecting to fear assassination at the hands of Milo and his ruffians, he kept adding to the forces under his own control, till he was in a position to decide exactly what should be allowed to be done in the city and what should not. Meanwhile several tribunes, particularly T. Munatius Plancus, were busy doing their best to make public every circumstance telling against Milo, and to create so general a belief in his guilt that it should be next to impossible for him to escape. They addressed public meetings in support of Pompey's bill. Cato and Cicero spoke against it, the latter defying even a threat of impeachment in the cause of Milo. But it became law before the end of March.

1183. Milo was now called upon to face no less than four prosecutions (1) for *vis* under the new law (2) for *ambitus* under the new law (3) for *vis* under the *lex Plautia* (4) for *sodalicia* under the *lex Licinia*. Of these the first was the only one of real importance. The enemies of Milo spared no efforts to ensure his condemnation. The mob was packed in threatening masses round the court, so that the defence had to appeal to Pompey for military protection. Plancus even addressed a meeting during the progress of the trial, and urged the people to be present in force when the votes of the jury were taken, and see that Milo did not slip through their fingers. The trial lasted from the 4th to the 8th of April. On the last day, when the jury had been finally chosen by the drawing of lots (81 in all), the speeches were delivered. Pompey had taken special precautions for the maintenance of order. The Forum and its approaches were strongly held by soldiers: he himself watched proceedings from a post hard by, surrounded by the bodyguard which the state of public affairs had lately given him an excuse for employing. The solemn pomp and circumstance of the arrangements was highly characteristic of Pompey. But the Clodian mob, if they could not use force to express their sympathies, could still shout, and when Cicero rose to deliver the

---

[1] *lex Plautia.*

only speech for the defence they received him with a howl of rage. The whole scene was too much for the orator's nerves; he lost the thread of his discourse and spoke feebly. After the speeches 30 jurors were withdrawn, 15 challenged by each side. The 51 remaining then voted, and found Milo guilty by a large[1] majority. He went into exile at Massalia. He was condemned on the other charges in his absence, but this did not matter to him. A number of other trials followed, on various charges with various results. In particular several Clodian partisans were condemned. But we cannot dwell on these minor matters. Cicero wrote a splendid oration to shew what he could have done for his client under more favourable conditions. He sent a copy to Milo, but that bravo, who had himself faced soldiers mob and jury with complete indifference, received it with a sneer. This is the speech that has come down to us: the broken utterance actually delivered was taken down by reporters, and existed in the time of Asconius. M. Brutus also produced an exercise in the form of a speech for Milo, justifying the homicide on the ground that it was for the public good, not as Cicero, who wisely adopted the plea of self-defence and made out Clodius to have been the aggressor.

1184. So ended the famous trial of Milo, one of those dramatic scenes to which later writers loved to refer. Politically it was important, because the republican aristocrats would gladly have rescued the criminal, and could not. Gossip even said that Cato, who was on the jury, had voted for acquittal. He at least made no secret of his opinion that the death of Clodius was a good riddance. But the precautions taken had made Milo's escape impossible. We can hardly help suspecting that Pompey was glad to see him removed from Rome. Milo was in the way. That Pompey was becoming more jealous of Caesar, and more anxious to secure the adhesion of the republicans, is certain. That these latter had lately regarded Milo as their champion made his banishment a convenience to Pompey. After this the Senate and the sole consul could more easily draw together, and they did. But the thoroughly unrepublican nature of his position was betrayed in various ways; the rules laid down for other men were not to bind him. To exclude undue influence from the law-courts was the first object of his recent legislation; he had even directly forbidden the testimonials (*laudationes*) customary hitherto. Yet when his father-in-law Scipio was accused of *ambitus* he sent for the whole body of select jurors and begged him off as a personal favour. When Plancus[2] soon after was charged with *vis*, he sent a written testimonial in his behalf. On this occasion he failed,

---

[1] 38 to 13. Asconius p. 53.

[2] Prosecuted by Cicero. For this case see Cic. *ad fam.* VII 2.

and Plancus went off to Caesar, the general refuge of men in trouble. For Scipio Pompey was able to provide; he took him as his colleague for the last five months of his consulship, for the helpless Assembly had only to obey its master's orders.   But the full extent to which the present powers of Pompey overrode the constitution of the Republic, and announced its fall, appeared in his legislation dealing with the magistracies and the succession to provinces.   We only know a few points in detail, but they are highly significant.

1185.   He took up the proposed rule requiring an interval of five years[1] between a magistracy and a provincial governorship, and passed it into law.   He also, in regulating the conditions of standing for office, enacted that a candidature in person was to be necessary.   He took no notice of the law of the ten tribunes exempting Caesar from this requirement, and thus indirectly repealed it.   To the complaints of Caesar's friends he paid no heed till after the new law was already carried.   But then, in order to avoid an open quarrel, he is said[2] to have inserted in the official copy a clause reserving the rights of any to whom special exemption should be granted by name.   This device, clumsy and illegal, took all effect out of the law.   The one certain result was that he had shewn his own hand.   Caesar was not blind, and he could now see the real disposition of Pompey towards himself. Pompey was already beginning to act disloyally towards his remaining partner, now that Crassus was gone.   But he wavered and drew back, because he was not yet prepared to fight.   The rule about the five years' interval also indirectly menaced the interests of Caesar.   It could only be carried out during the first five years of its operation by compelling ex-magistrates who had not yet held provincial governorships to take their turn now.   Probably there was a provision to this effect embodied in the law.   Certainly the Senate were empowered[3] to fix the length of each governor's term of office.   Now Caesar's term expired on the first of March 49, but according to the old practice he would not be actually relieved by a successor till the beginning of the next year.   Under the new rule the Senate could arrange to have him relieved at any time of the year.   He might thus find himself no longer proconsul and not yet consul.   He would then have to choose between voluntary exile and returning to Rome as a private citizen to face a storm of prosecutions; and to suppose that Caesar would submit to be tried like Milo by a court surrounded by Pompey's troops was simply absurd.   Yet Milo, if he had Pompey against him, was at least favoured by Cato and the republicans.   Both these forces would combine to effect the ruin of Caesar.   Such was the situation with

---

[1] Dion Cass. XL 56. See above § 1178.   [2] Suet. *Jul.* 28.
[3] See Tyrrell and Purser, *Corr. Cic.* vol. III Addenda No. 7.

which he had to deal after putting down the rising of Vercingetorix, and it was doubtless the main preoccupation of his mind. We have seen that he coolly took measures to strengthen his position and made ready to meet further developments.

1186. Meanwhile Pompey went on to make it clear that, whatever precautions were taken to check the growth of the power of individuals, they were not meant to apply in his own case. He procured an extension of his proconsulship for five more years, and the Senate voted him 1000 talents a year to maintain his troops. He still ruled Spain by deputy, and the power of appointing[1] various persons to active or nominal posts enabled him to oblige many by judicious patronage. As consul he had raised a considerable force in Italy. But it was not unlikely that an army would soon be wanted in the East. Cassius had done well with small means. In this year (52) he had beaten back a Parthian invasion, but Syria was clearly not safe, and even Cilicia was thought to be in some danger. For the moment nothing was done. A curious measure was carried in the latter part of the year by the consul Scipio. It repealed the law by which Clodius had sought to restrain the arbitrary action of censors. Thus they were once more nominally free to strike any man's name off the roll of senators or knights without waiting for somebody to bring a charge against him. But this restored to them the whole responsibility of their act, whether they struck a man off or left him on. Now the times were ill suited for revisory action of so personal a kind. To affix a stigma to all the unworthy was quite impossible; there were too many of them. To pick and choose would rouse animosities such as average censors would not face. To do nothing was to confess undignified impotence. So henceforth, says Dion[2], no man in his senses would stand for the office. Before we leave the year 52 we must remark that, thanks to the maintenance of order, consuls for 51 were elected in time to enter on office at the beginning of the year. The chosen were Servius Sulpicius Rufus the eminent jurist, a man of cautious moderation, chiefly concerned to avert the dangerous crisis to which public affairs were evidently tending, and M. Claudius Marcellus. The latter was a notable specimen of a convinced republican aristocrat, in character superior to many, but slow and generally ineffective. His importance at this juncture consisted mainly in his being a stubborn opponent of Caesar. These men had been elected in preference to Cato. The Incorruptible condescended to stand, but he would not court the voters, much less

---

[1] See Cic. *ad Att.* v 7.

[2] Dion Cass. XL 57. Lange points out that Scipio himself seems not to have been an immaculate character. Valer. Max. IX 1 § 8.

bribe them. He treated his rejection with ostentatious indifference, and never stood again.

1187. Caesar had been so closely engaged with the great Gaulish rebellion that he could not attend to affairs in Rome with his usual thoroughness. His partisans had evidently been weakened by being less fully in touch with their master. But the Roman populace were not allowed to forget their absent favourite. He had provided entertainments for them on a liberal scale in the funeral celebrations in honour of his lost daughter. And splendid public buildings, among them a public hall in the Forum (*basilica Julia*), were rising under the superintendence of his friends, of whom Cicero was one. It was a popular step to adorn the capital with some of the gold of Gaul. Private benefactions were not omitted, and the sequel shewed that things were so managed that he could resume effective touch as soon as his hands were free. But in view of coming dangers it was even more important that he should assure himself of his personal ascendency in his army and his provinces, and come to the conflict, if conflict there must be, as the undoubted master of devoted veterans and the solid resources of the North and West. Accordingly he took every opportunity of gratifying his soldiers, and it was probably at this time that he doubled their pay. It is also reasonably inferred that he promised to procure the full Roman franchise for the Transpadanes. He had long ago (in 67) encouraged them to press their claims, but they still had only the rights of 'Latins.' The *lex Vatinia* of 59 had given him certain limited powers of bestowing the Roman franchise on some of the citizens of Novum Comum at the time when that Latin colony[1] was enlarged. Of these powers he had made full use; some held that he had exceeded them. In raising legionary troops he had not scrupled to include Transpadanes, thus treating them as citizens. He was popular also in the Cispadane district, where Roman citizenship was the rule. Thus he had at his back the whole Cisalpine province, Italian (for the Celts were now practically Romanized) in all but a technical sense, and by far the most vigorous part of Italy. That he was hated by the Roman aristocrats, whom new citizens and Latins had little cause to love, was all to his credit in these parts. As for Transalpine Gaul, the one great name there was now that of Caesar. Once the forces of the rebellion were broken, his judicious treatment of the conquered tribes interested most of the remaining chiefs in the acceptance of peace under Roman overlordship, of which he was the representative. Many were ready to prove their new loyalty, and in

---

[1] For a case of a Greek colonist (there were a number of them) added to Comum by Caesar at Cicero's request see Cic. *ad fam.* XIII 35. For Comum see § 1067.

case of need Caesar well knew how to use them.   Suetonius[1] tells us in general terms that he contrived to do various favours to client kings and powerful cities in Italy and the provinces, disposing of the resources of the state without leave of the central government.   News of these doings found its way to Rome, and his enemies, alarmed by the indication of far-reaching designs, felt that there was no time to be lost.

1188.   Such was the situation at the beginning of the year 51.   It seems that Caesar, by letter or through his friends, had protested against any revocation of the leave granted him to stand for the consulship in his absence, and had requested the Senate to leave him in possession of his provinces till the end of 49.   This would, as we have said, have been in accordance with the practice[2] before the passing of the new Pompeian law, the practice in use at the time of Caesar's appointment.   The request was moderate, and his candidature for a second consulship was not in itself open to objection, for the statutory interval of ten years would have elapsed since his first consulship.   It was not Caesar in whose favour all the rules and precedents of the republican magistracy had been broken.   But Caesar had got to be destroyed, if the ring of republican aristocrats was to retain any hold of its power and perquisites.   So the republicans, egged on by Cato, secretly favoured by Pompey, moved on with Marcellus at their head to a conflict fraught with terrible consequences.   From this time onward republican scruples fell into the background.   The object was to get the better of Caesar at all costs; the republican party, save for Cato and a few fanatics, is not so much republican as anti-Caesarian. In April Marcellus summoned the Senate to discuss the situation. He made no direct motion but one condemning Caesar's bestowal of the franchise on colonists of Comum.   Vetoed by tribunes, this could only be recorded as an informal resolution.   But the consul spoke also[3] on the urgent need of providing a successor for Caesar.   This matter stood over for the present, and meanwhile the situation developed.   It was rumoured that the Transpadanes were being organized on the Roman municipal model.   True or not, this was enough to draw a retort from Marcellus.   Relying no doubt on the

---

[1] Suet. *Jul.* 27, 28.   We sadly miss details here.   He mentions Gaul Spain Asia and Greece.   It is probable that the case of Spain was the most important.   We know that he was in communication with that province, for he drew horses ropes etc. from thence.   And Pompey's main army was now there.   In the event of war it might well be worth while to have the goodwill of the local communities.   The king of Noricum or Noreia was probably one of the kings.   See Caesar *Gall.* I 53, *civ.* I 18.

[2] The classic treatise on the succession question is Mommsen, *die Rechtsfrage zwischen Caesar und dem Senat* (Breslau 1858).   But see the note § 1208 at the end of this chapter.

[3] Livy *epit.* 108, Suet. *Jul.* 28, Hirtius *Gall.* VIII 53.   Compare Caelius in *ad fam.* VIII 1 § 2 with VIII 2 § 2.

backing of Pompey, and urged by the more hot-headed republicans, he seized a citizen of Comum then present in Rome and found a pretext for scourging him. This blackguard act[1] was merely an assertion that the man was not a Roman citizen protected by the Porcian laws, in short a challenge to Caesar. The succession-question was again indirectly raised on July 22. Pompey had of late seemed inclined to proceed to Spain, and a vote of pay for his troops was before the House. In the course of discussion it came out that one of his legions was in Gaul. Questions were asked, and Pompey was worried into saying that he would withdraw it. He was also pressed for an opinion on the succession to Caesar, but he shuffled as usual, remarking[2] that all ought to obey the Senate. He was going to Ariminum, where he had a force of troops, and it was agreed to take the matter in hand as soon as he returned.

1189. Meanwhile the elections for the next year (50) were held. C. Claudius Marcellus and L. Aemilius Paullus were chosen[3] consuls. The former was a cousin of the present consul M. Marcellus, and under his influence, though married to Caesar's great-niece Octavia. He was an anti-Caesarian. So to all appearance was Paullus, but he had been acting for Caesar in the charge of some public works, and had himself been rebuilding the *basilica Aemilia*. He had therefore been fingering some of the gold of Gaul; how much, and with what result, some people were curious to know. Of the tribunes-elect nearly all were Caesarian. But the other side managed to get one of them condemned for bribery, and the hare-brained young aristocrat C. Scribonius Curio won the vacant place. But his extravagance, particularly in the costly exhibition of shows in honour of his deceased father, had involved him in debt so deeply that he was at his wits' end to find relief. Still he was as yet reckoned a safe anti-Caesarian. So too was Cicero's lively and cynical correspondent M. Caelius Rufus, who was elected a curule aedile. After the elections came a number of cases in the courts; among others that of the consul-elect Marcellus, who was tried for bribery and acquitted. Things were quieter in Rome, but the rise in the rate of interest seems to indicate some uneasiness beneath the surface. Late in the year the Senate passed an order that $12°/_{o}$ simple interest[4] should be the recognized rate. Fears were entertained by some that the stringency of the money-market might

---

[1] Cic. *ad Att.* v 11 § 2, Plut. *Caes.* 29, Appian *civ.* 11 § 26. If the man had held a magistracy he was by the 'Latin right' a Roman citizen, but there seems to have been some doubt on the point of fact. In any case, as Cicero saw, it was an out-of-date brutality to flog a Transpadane Latin.

[2] Caelius in Cic. *fam.* VIII 4 § 4.

[3] Defeating M. Calidius, the Caesarian candidate.

[4] Cic. *ad Att.* v 21 § 13.

cause repudiations and a collapse of credit, but this does not appear to have been the result.

1190.　　In the great succession-question no progress was made till the last day (29th) of September.　On the motion of M. Marcellus[1] it was agreed that the question of the consular provinces should be raised on the first of March in the next year (50) by the then consuls.　No other business was to be mixed up with it.　To secure a full House, all senators on the jury-list were to be relieved from any engagements in court, and the House was to go on holding an adjourned session, the legal obstacles (*lex Pupia*)[2] to sitting on lawful Assembly-days notwithstanding.　This proposal, aiming simply at the attainment of a decision, seems to have passed unopposed by tribunes.　There were however further motions; one to declare that any use of the power of *intercessio* to prevent a decision being reached on the occasion contemplated was contrary to the interest of the state; another to bind the House to take into consideration the claims of Caesar's soldiers to an honourable discharge; a third to mark out Cilicia and the eight[3] provinces now held by men of praetorian rank as propraetors, these nine, to be praetorian provinces.　All these proposals were vetoed, and accordingly were recorded as informal resolutions.　The first was a mere attempt to get rid of the tribunician veto in advance.　The second was meant to tamper with the loyalty of Caesar's veterans by suggesting hopes of reward at the state expense.　The third was a clever move to commit the Senate to interference with Caesar's tenure of the Gauls.　For the position was this.　There were in all 14 provinces.　If Cilicia (now held by Cicero) and eight others were to be ruled by ex-praetors, there would be five for ex-consuls.　These would be the two Spains, the two Gauls, and Syria.　Pompey had just had his tenure of the Spains renewed, so that these were not really in question.　There remained Syria (now held by Bibulus) and the Gauls.　Therefore, in assigning provinces to be held by ex-consuls in the year 49, it would be necessary to come to a decision about the Gauls, which would affect Caesar.　No wonder that these proposals were vetoed on Caesar's behalf.　From his point of view even the 1st March 50 was too soon to raise the question of his successor.　His reappointment by the law of Pompey and Crassus in 55 had taken place before the old succession-arrangements had been changed by the *lex Pompeia* of 52.　He claimed to be unaffected by the latter, and to remain governor until relieved in due course at the beginning of 48.　Then the time for considering his succession would according to the

---

[1] Caelius in Cic. *fam.* VIII 8.　　　　[2] See Lange *RA* III 191.

[3] The eight were, Sicily, Sardinia, Africa, Macedonia, Asia, Bithynia, Cyrene, Crete. I find this list agrees with that of Mommsen, *Rechtsfrage* p. 46.

old practice be not earlier than June 50. To fix the time for considering it in March rather than June was in effect to assume that the
vacancy would occur in the following March, and to imply that it
would be filled up as from that date by a fresh appointment. In
short, the republicans meant to apply the new *lex Pompeia* to Caesar's
case, and to get him out of his provinces before he could become
consul or even consul-elect. Here was an issue upon which no
accommodation was possible.

1191. Civil war was in the air. As in the earlier debates, the
consul Sulpicius deprecated the militant anti-Caesarian policy of his
colleague, and there is no doubt that the majority of the House desired
peace. If we may believe a Caesarian[1] authority, a division had been
even taken on a general motion of Marcellus (presumably to fix at
once the end of Caesar's term as 1st March 49), and the House had
passed to the order of the day. In any case the general effect of the
debate and the divisions was that the extreme partisans of both sides
had gone so far as to be virtually committed to going further. The
attitude of Pompey was characteristically halting. He posed as the
advocate of fair play. With a decision on the question of Caesar's
provinces before the 1st March he could have nothing to do, but
after that date he would not hesitate. Members were wanting a lead.
He was asked 'how if a tribune should then veto the decision?' He
replied that whether Caesar refused to obey the House, or procured a
tribune to block the passing of a decree, the contumacy would be the
same. Another member said 'but suppose he chooses to be consul
and keep his army as well.' 'You may as well suppose' retorted
Pompey 'that my son will choose to take a stick to his father's back.'
These utterances[2] had a marked effect on the hearers. There was
thought to be something behind. Either Pompey was already em-
broiled with Caesar, and so bound to support the republican leaders,
or Caesar was prepared to make important concessions, and Pompey
knew it. So the members took heart, little guessing that Pompey had
mistaken the vital facts of the situation, and that the blind was leading
the blind. Even Caelius, ever pluming himself on his freedom from
illusions, was satisfied that Curio, who would be tribune at the time of
the momentous decision, could be trusted to throw his whole strength
into opposing the claims of Caesar. The flighty wit did not know his
friend Curio, or himself.

1192. While Pompey, proconsul of the Spains and master of an
army in Italy as well, was talking of going out to his provincial

---

[1] Hirtius *bell. Gall.* VIII 53.

[2] See Caelius in Cic. *fam.* VIII 8 §§ 9, 10. I see no good ground for doubting his
report.

government but taking no steps to do so, his new law about governorships was bearing hardly upon others. Men of consular rank and
sufficient seniority had to be found for Syria and Cilicia, and the lot
assigned the former to Bibulus and the latter to Cicero. Both were
men of the city, and quitted Rome with the utmost reluctance. Each
was appointed for a year, but there was always the chance that circumstances might cause the term to be extended, a contingency the fear
of which was ever present to Cicero. The orator had lately been
much gratified by being chosen to fill the place in the college of
augurs vacant by the death of young P. Crassus. He had followed
up his treatise[1] on the Commonwealth by another on the Laws. He
was by way of being a Roman Plato as well as a Roman Demosthenes,
—so Roman indeed that he only dabbled in first principles and could
see little or nothing to improve in the laws and institutions of Rome in
what he regarded as her golden age. Never had he been less inclined[2]
to leave the great centre of great events, the scene of his triumphs
forensic and political, where he was immediately in touch with the
public to whom his manifold talents appealed. Even the prospect of
putting his high principles in practice by furnishing a model of good
government stirred in him no deep and lasting enthusiasm. The
exercise of immense power for the benefit of those subject to him was
a noble object in itself, but he had little appetite for employing his
virtues in what was to him a petty and uncongenial sphere. He would
be chiefly in contact with Roman officials and financiers on the one
hand and Greeks or Hellenized orientals on the other. Of the
probable behaviour of the former he had only too reasonable fears,
and for the latter, steeped in Greek though he was and owing so much
to the Greeks, he had at bottom the usual Roman contempt. He
knew much of the seamy side of both, but was destined to find that he
still had something to learn. He had in particular to learn by experience how hard was the path of a Roman governor who tried to be
just to the provincials and yet not to give mortal offence to the greedy
magnates of Rome. That he might have to take the field in command
of an army was hardly an objection, for it suggested the possibility of
what Cicero would dearly love, a triumph. Lieutenants of military
skill were to be had, and the new governor had at his disposal
C. Pomptinus his old associate, and his own brother Quintus, fresh
from the great war-school of Gaul. There was it is true some ground
for uneasiness in the weakness of the force under his command. He

---

[1] These works were the talk of Rome in 51 B.C. See Caelius in *ad fam.* VIII 1 § 5,
Schmidt, *Briefwechsel* pp. 11, 12.

[2] An excellent essay on Cicero's provincial government, with full references, is given in
Tyrrell and Purser's *Correspondence of Cicero* vol. III.

had only 12,000 legionaries and 2600 horse, and it was by no means certain that he might not have to face a Parthian invasion. To strengthen his army for a campaign he must draw auxiliaries from the client-kings, and it was a work of time and care to turn such levies into efficient soldiers. Moreover the vast size[1] of the province made administration a laborious task, and it included more than one mountainous district with the restless inhabitants of which trouble might at any moment arise. But it was vain to look for a fresh contingent of Roman troops. Neither the Senate nor Pompey was disposed to send abroad further forces at the present juncture; and in view of possible developments at home they were content to leave Rome's eastern possessions in jeopardy.

1193. Cicero was in his province for a year from the end of July 51. His correspondence of this period is very fully preserved, and no more interesting collection of genuine documents has come down to us from antiquity. His predecessor Appius Claudius, a brother of his old enemy P. Clodius, had bullied and fleeced the wretched provincials after the customary fashion of noble governors. But he was a man of influential connexions. Pompey's eldest son had just married his daughter. Cicero was very anxious not to have him for an enemy, and he wrote him a number of letters, mostly fulsome and insincere, in the hope of conciliating a man whom in confidence to a friend he describes as a wild beast. In his own direct relations with the subject communities of which the province was composed the new governor was able to practise the high principles approved by his conscience. He respected their rights, and especially that of local jurisdictions administering local law. He even inquired into local finances so far as to check what had ever been an abuse prevalent in the Greek world, the embezzlement of public funds by officials. He was easy of access and gracious to suitors, and not only above taking bribes himself but actively concerned to prevent corruption or incivility on the part of his subordinates. In this he flattered himself that he was successful, but he could not be everywhere at once, and before the end of his term he learnt that his instructions had not always been obeyed. Still he could always enjoy the simple admiration of his own purity. When driven to press an ill-used community to pay an iniquitous debt, he does not omit to tell us that nothing but his own abstinence from the usual exactions made it possible to find the money; 'it is out of your lordship's pocket' said the astonished orientals. But it has been well remarked that Cicero only records his own freedom

---

[1] Cilicia, Cyprus, Lycaonia, Isauria, Pamphylia, Pisidia, and three administrative districts of southern Phrygia. Beside this there was the duty of representing the Roman protectorate in client-kingdoms, particularly Cappadocia.

from the vices of oppression and extortion when he writes to intimate friends. He was not eager to call the attention of the republican nobility to a course of conduct in which the elder might see an implied censure of their doings in the past, the younger an uncongenial standard to which they in their turn might be expected to conform.

1194. The sad truth was that all the evil influences with which an honest governor came into conflict had their roots in the corruption of Rome, the Rome for which the virtuous Cicero was pining. Appius Claudius wanted the usual deputations to be sent to Rome in his honour, to express the gratitude of the province for the mild purity of his administration. Cicero found the wretched people so impoverished that they could not afford the cost of these missions. He tried hard to save them the expense, at least to keep it down to the legal amount prescribed by Sulla. But in the long run he had to wink at the abuse, and to minimize his own efforts at checking it, in order that he might be on terms with Claudius and his friends when he returned home. The heavy hand of Roman finance lay on the East, on client kings as well as on provincial cities. When the proconsul intervened in Cappadocia to protect king Ariobarzanes from a conspiracy, his work there was only begun. The king had been driven to borrow money during the troubles of his earlier years. He owed great sums to Pompey and Brutus, and it was Cicero's business not only to keep the debtor on his throne but to squeeze exorbitant interest out of him for these powerful creditors. Perhaps the most infamous[1] transaction with which Cicero had to deal was in Cyprus. We have seen that Brutus, when acting for his uncle Cato, had found openings for investing capital in the island on loan. The island was annexed, and Roman exactions made loans inevitable. Provincials had been forbidden by the *lex Gabinia* of 67 to borrow in Rome. But Brutus lent the money through agents and kept in the background. To cover the risks of a transaction not strictly legal he required exorbitant interest; on those terms he was prepared to let the capital lie. The debtors on the contrary wanted to pay off the capital and objected to the interest. A certain Scaptius appeared before Cicero, stated that the people of Salamis in Cyprus owed him money, and presented a letter from Brutus warmly recommending him to the proconsul's good offices. Cicero promised to help him in recovering the debt. Then Scaptius asked to be made a prefect. Now Cicero had made it a rule not to put official authority in the hands of anyone engaged in private business. Scaptius had to be content with his assurances of help. When Cicero had brought the parties face to face, he ordered the Salaminians to pay up, and cut short their complaints about Scaptius.

[1] Cic. *ad Att.* V 21, VI 1, 2.

At last he threatened to use compulsion. They then offered to pay, being able to do so through Cicero's refusal of the sum generally extorted by governors. Then came the reckoning of the amount due. Cicero in his edict[1] had declared that he would not recognize any higher rate of interest than 12%. This the Salaminians were ready to pay, but Scaptius claimed 48% as named in the bond. Cicero stood on his own edict. Scaptius then produced an order of the Senate passed in the year 56, specially instructing the governor of Cilicia to give judgment according to the terms of this bond. It turned out that the Senate had actually passed two orders in reference to this affair. So the influence of Brutus and his friends had been used to make the security good, while the rate of interest stood at 48% because it was assumed to be bad. Cicero took the ground that the Senate's action had legalized the debt, but could not override his decision fixing a 12% maximum for interest. Scaptius then tried to make out that the principal owing was 200 talents, but the Salaminians had no difficulty in shewing that 106 was the true figure. This sum Scaptius was not willing to accept, and they proposed to deposit it in a temple, after which the interest would cease to run. But the interest was of course the main thing; Scaptius begged the proconsul to let the matter stand over, and Cicero gave way. Thus the best a virtuous governor could do for his subjects was in the last resort to defer doing what he saw to be right, and leave a probably vicious successor free to do promptly what he knew to be wrong. It soon came out that Scaptius was a mere agent, and Brutus the real creditor. Cicero was both surprised and shocked by the discovery. In a second letter, now presented by Scaptius, Brutus, the model of cultivated virtue, the hope of the rising generation of Romans, not only confessed himself the lender but asked Cicero to make the man a prefect. Now Scaptius had been made prefect by Appius Claudius and granted a guard of cavalry. He had employed this force in financial operations, by blockading the senate of Salamis in their council house till five of them died of hunger and the rest presumably satisfied his demands. The affair was notorious, and Cicero's first official act had been to recall the troops. He now to his honour firmly refused to oblige Brutus. The melancholy thing is that he confidently looked for the approval of Atticus in his righteous conduct, and that Atticus was no better than the rest. Couldn't Cicero, he urged, let Scaptius have a little troop of horse—say fifty at most? This gave poor Cicero quite a turn. Was even Atticus, who had been charmed with the noble sentiments of his treatise *de re publica*, to tempt its author to go back on all his principles of right? Even so it was, and it is very doubtful

[1] See §§ 1373, 991, 638, 639.

whether Cato himself[1] would have given him any more moral support than the financier Atticus.

1195. Enough has been said in detail to indicate the perpetual embarrassments of Cicero in his governorship. Even abstinence from extortion was not necessarily a security against a prosecution. A case might be got up by enemies, false witness was no rarity, innocent men had been found guilty before now. To form a jury without including men interested directly or indirectly in provincial extortion was hardly possible. The same man[2] might urge a governor to wink at illegal exactions and then promote his condemnation under the law which he had been too scrupulous to break. The capitalists, whether noble senators or knights, hung together in matters of the purse, and in a civilization resting on slavery, when prisoners of war were driven in thousands to market, humanity in the treatment of subjects was a plant of slow growth. Moreover men of high character will ask another to do what they prefer not to do themselves. Cicero loathed the work of squeezing debtors on behalf of Roman magnates, and shirked it whenever he dared: yet he wrote[3] to the governor of Asia requesting him to do this very service for one Cluvius, who was really an agent of Pompey. It is hardly necessary to add that he kept on the best of terms with the revenue-farmers in his own province. By extorting nothing himself, and by checking the peculations of local rogues, he made the communities able to meet their liabilities, and by the offer[4] of enforcing the rule of 12°/₀ interest if payment were made by a certain date, not otherwise, he contrived to get most of the arrears cleared off. Thus he succeeded in satisfying the shareholders who had speculated in Cilician dues, and healed some of the wounds left by Appius, whose iniquitous decisions he spent much time in reversing. Military affairs also demanded some of the proconsul's care. In the summer of 51 he was troubled with rumours of the Parthian advance. He made what preparations he could with the help of the client kings, particularly Deiotarus of Galatia, and took no small credit to himself for his demonstration. Cassius drove the enemy out of Syria with loss, but Cicero grudged him the glory. Bibulus was not seriously annoyed by them when he took over that province, for dynastic strife kept them busy at home. Late in the year Cicero made a small campaign to punish some of the rebellious

[1] Messrs Tyrrell and Purser are rather hard on Cato, but I think we may safely go with them thus far.

[2] If on a jury, he might be challenged, but this would not make him less keen to use private influence.

[3] Cic. *ad fam.* XIII 56. See also XIII 9, 65. In one of these cases Mr Fowler, *Social Life* p. 78, thinks Cicero was a shareholder himself. This was in Bithynia.

[4] Cic. *ad Att.* VI 1 § 16.

hill-men in the border-district of mount Amanus. He besieged and took a stronghold named Pindenissus, gave the other booty to his troops, and sold his prisoners for the benefit of the treasury. The gallant general, whose efficient lieutenants had won him this victory, was duly saluted *imperator* by his army, and from this time he set his heart on a triumph. We may look forward so far as to point out that he never got it. Even the thanksgiving voted in his honour was carried against the opposition of Cato.

1196. Cicero's administration had been so pure and economical that even the allowance granted him by the Home government was not exhausted[1] when he left his province at the beginning of August 50, and he deposited another considerable balance in a bank at Ephesus. Cato himself could not have been more punctilious in accounting for all public moneys correctly. During his proconsulship he was a good deal troubled by private money-matters. Feeling himself drifting into hostility to Caesar on public grounds, he did not like being in debt to an opponent. He was also worried about the rumoured malpractices of his wife's steward Philotimus. His friend M. Caelius too was always pestering him to make the provincials catch panthers and forward them alive to Rome for his public shows, an importunity common enough, which Cicero was at pains to decline, the people being sufficiently burdened already. The fear of having his term prolonged through the insertion of a month early in 50 was happily averted; no intercalation took place, and the calendar was left to confusion. But the weary months were at last over, and he set out for home, glad to be rid of provincial boredom. He left the province in charge of his young and conceited quaestor C. Caelius Caldus, of whose unfitness for such a charge he was convinced, but it was the appointment most according to precedent and least likely to involve himself in blame if anything went wrong. In this as in everything Cicero had his eye on Rome. For his own part he was full of an innocent self-satisfaction. He would surely have been surprised to learn that his not having attempted permanently to improve the institutions of the country which he ruled would in a later age provoke[2] unfavourable comment. That his provincial government should ever be contrasted with that of Caesar, save as a model serving to bring out the defects of the latter, would have seemed incredible. Nor is the comparison fruitful in other respects: but it may justly remind us that we are here in the presence of two widely different ideals.

---

[1] Part of this surplus he left with his quaestor for current expenses, the rest he repaid into the treasury, to the disgust of his staff, who wanted to have it shared among them. *ad Att.* VII I § 6.

[2] Tyrrell and Purser vol. III pp. xvii, xxxvii.

The moral footing of Cicero's public life was in the past, that of Caesar in the future. To Cicero, hoping against hope that the Republic might yet overcome its corruptions, it seemed a sacred duty to strive for the preservation of what still remained. To Caesar, long convinced of the utter rottenness of the present system, under which the resources of the provinces were drained, not to strengthen Rome, but to gorge a few Romans with plunder, it could not seem a duty to uphold it. All hope that the Republic might reform itself was to him an idle dream. If such a work was to be undertaken, it must be by one possessing supreme continuous power. Even in a single province a governor holding office for a single year was in no position to effect lasting reforms; and the governors who strove to retain office for longer terms were almost without exception the very men whose conduct made reforms necessary. So long as the union of the governing and capitalist classes subsisted, nothing but sheer force could reorganize the Roman empire. That union it was Cicero's constant effort to consolidate. Things had now reached such a pass that either Caesar must destroy it, or it would destroy Caesar. That Cicero did not see very far into the causes of contemporary evils, that he could offer no real solution of the problems of the hour, is plain. But that he recoiled from Caesar's solution, the only one possible, was an excusable weakness, and one that may be imputed to him for righteousness by all who judge kindly the champions of lost causes.

1197. While Cicero was to little purpose doing his best according to his lights, in Rome the situation was developing. It was not that much happened in the actual passing of laws or decrees of the Senate. It was that the relations of public men to the one matter of first-rate importance (the succession-question) were secretly changing. Even those on the spot for some time knew or guessed little of what was going on behind the scenes. But, as they gradually became convinced that there was a point at which the concessions of either side must end without satisfying the other, one by one the more moderate men despaired of peace and made ready to appear as partisans in the coming struggle. In the latter part of the year 51 Caesar did a good stroke of business. He was determined not to let his enemies crush him, he had plenty of the gold of Gaul in hand, and most Roman public men had their price. He bought the consul-elect Paullus and the tribune-elect Curio. These were no doubt busy times for his trusty agent Balbus. With Caesar Paullus had been connected for some time, but he seems to have stood out for a high price. Curio got his debts paid, and the prospect of belonging to the winning side would count for something. Thus the republican party was assailed from within, for Curio was still trusted. He came forward in the character of a People's Man, and on entering office proposed a number of measures that were certain to be opposed and would thus give him a pretext for openly passing over to the Caesarian side. Of these the most striking were a bill for reopening[1] the old question of the Campanian land, and one for the annexation of Numidia. The first alarmed Pompey for fear lest the dispossession of his veterans should clear the ground for those of Caesar; in the second King Juba, a client of Pompey (who had placed his father Hiempsal on the throne), was attacked. Specious reasons were of course given for these proposals, but the republicans had no choice but to oppose them. Time was running short, for on the 1st March the debate on the succession-question was due, and the pontiffs refused to intercalate an extra month. Curio then gave notice of other bills, one of which seems to have dealt with the city corn-supply[2] in a sense even more favourable to the pauper mob than existing arrangements. It looks like an attempt to revive the old 'popular policy' of which Caesar had been the great exponent. And it is certain that in the political conflict of this year (50) the populace, somewhat suppressed of late, shewed marked sympathy with Curio as the champion of Caesar.

1198. We have now reached a stage at which it may fairly be said that all the moves[3] of the contending parties are nothing but insincere attempts of each side to make the other seem to be in the wrong. Neither really meant to give way; both played for vantage. The great debate of the 1st March was not brought to a conclusion. The consul Paullus adjourned it, and doubtless there was method in what some thought a mad freak. Enough had passed to shew that Pompey, though willing for the sake of seeming conciliatory to let the date of Caesar's resignation be deferred from 1st March 49 to the 13th November, was resolved not to let him step straight from his proconsulship into a second consulship. This would not meet the needs of Caesar, who would be prosecuted by his enemies in the interval. But it sounded moderate, and was meant[4] to shew up Curio, who had been addressing noisy meetings, as a mischief-maker. Curio continued his harangues, and laid the blame of the present quarrel on Pompey and the law passed by him in 55 extending Caesar's term. Thus he could affect to speak against Caesar while really supporting him against Pompey. The latter was in poor health

---

[1] See Caelius in Cic. *fam.* VIII 10 §§ 3, 4.

[2] Caelius in Cic. *fam.* VIII 6 § 5.

[3] It should be noted that the *fasces* and presidency were divided between the consuls thus. Paullus had Jan. March May July Sept. Nov.; Marcellus had Feb. Apr. June Aug. Oct. Dec. This is important in tracing the course of events.

[4] Caelius in *ad fam.* VIII 11 § 3.

at this time. In April he left Rome for Campania, where his illness[1] took a serious turn, and he lay for some time at Neapolis in danger of his life. Meanwhile the farce went on in the Senate. Curio's business was to make trouble, and anything served his turn. The debate on the thanksgiving for Cicero's victories was one occasion. He blocked the motion, but then gave way and let it pass, yielding to the urgent expostulation of Balbus, which was noted as a sign[2] that he had gone over to Caesar. He dropped his sham proposals, and devoted himself to opposing directly the motions for Caesar's recall. In reference to this there was now a third date[3] proposed, namely that he should retire on the 1st July and come at once to Rome and stand for the consulship. Of course this would not do, for it did not meet Caesar's difficulty. Curio therefore vetoed it, and declared that in the present crisis the only chance of peace lay in requiring both the rival chiefs to resign their commands and dismiss their armies. The tribune had an enthusiastic reception at the hands of the populace. But his solution was naturally unacceptable to the republicans. An attempt to put pressure on Curio, by a resolution of the House calling upon the other tribunes to induce their colleague to give way, was a failure. The House was not yet prepared to force on a rupture, and the motion was lost. So for the present there was a deadlock, which was all to the profit of Caesar. A letter from Pompey set things moving again. He offered to resign his own command before the expiration of his term if the Senate wished it, and repeated this profession when he returned to Rome. But Curio pointed out in popular harangues that this was a mere promise, and indeed no step seems to have been taken to give the proposal an official and irrevocable character. The mob would not listen to Cato; they were Caesarian, and applauded the contention of Curio, that the two chiefs should be treated alike.

1199. Before Pompey's return to Rome, the question of sending reinforcements to the East had been raised by an alarming despatch from Bibulus, who foretold another Parthian invasion. At the debate in May Curio prevented action being taken, but in June he gave way, and it was agreed that Caesar and Pompey should each be called upon to furnish a legion for the service. Pompey assigned as his share the legion lent to Caesar. Caesar returned it and sent another of his own. He was thus deprived of two legions at an awkward moment; but he took good care to give them a handsome largess at

---

[1] See Mayor on Juvenal x 283—6.

[2] Caelius in Cic. *fam.* VIII 11 §§ 2, 3.

[3] This is inferred from the words of Caesar *civ.* I 9, complaining (in Jan. 49) that the Pompeians had tried to drag him back to Rome *erepto semenstri imperio* (1st July 49 instead of 1st Jan. 48). See Cic. *ad fam.* XVI 12 § 3, Lange *RA* III 394.

parting and send them off in the best of humours. Until some arrangement was made for taking action in Syria, they were kept in Italy,
and the Parthian danger passed away. The Caesarian view was that
they had never been intended for the East. Caesar raised two new
legions in their place. Early in June the succession-question was
raised again by the consul C. Marcellus, who urged the Senate[1] to put
pressure on the tribunes (Curio) to cease blocking the proposed decree.
But the majority still feared to provoke a war, and a full House
refused to listen to anything of the kind. Soon after this it would
seem[2] that Pompey, still in poor health, returned to Rome and repeated his plausible offer in the Senate. Curio could not afford to
risk the possible effect of this proposal. He denounced it as insincere,
and called for a formal resignation carried out at once. He even
moved that, unless both Pompey and Caesar obeyed the order, both
should be declared public enemies and forces raised to compel
obedience. Nothing came of this as a motion, but Pompey once
more withdrew in wrath from Rome and sent to require the restoration of his legion lent to Caesar. In August the consular elections
for 49 resulted[3] in the defeat of Caesar's candidate Galba and the
return of two republicans, C. Claudius Marcellus and L. Cornelius
Lentulus Crus. The former was cousin of his namesake the present
consul and brother of the consul of 51. The latter was a man deeply
in debt, strongly anti-Caesarian. But in the college of tribunes two
of Caesar's men found places, M. Antonius and Q. Cassius. Antony
was also elected augur in September. The election of censors[4] had
been held earlier in the year. They were an untoward pair. Cicero's
old enemy L. Calpurnius Piso seems to have been pushed forward by
his son-in-law Caesar against his own wish. Appius Claudius Pulcher,
Cicero's predecessor in Cilicia, was father-in-law of Pompey's son, and
opposed to Caesar. Both had a record of trials and suspicious
acquittals in the public courts. Appius, a true headstrong Claudius,
set to work revising the lists of senators and knights, issuing edicts
against extravagance, to limit the holding of land (probably encumbered estates), the amount of debts, and so forth. Then he struck
a number of offenders[5] off the lists. He got up an unsavoury quarrel
with M. Caelius, who attached himself to Piso and began to shew
Caesarian tendencies. Piso sat still, while his colleague went on his
foolish way, driving man after man to seek comfort and support in

---

[1] Caelius in *ad fam.* VIII 13.

[2] If we are to trust Appian II 28.

[3] Hirtius *Gall.* VIII 50 seems to suggest that there was some foul play, probably referring
to Marcellus, who would be presiding officer.

[4] Caelius in *ad fam.* VIII 12, 14, Dion Cass. XL 63, Cic. *de divin.* I § 29.

[5] Sallust was one of these.

the camp of Caesar. Such were the last days of an office that had in its time been a characteristic organ of the great Republic. No complete census took place, but some of Rome's foul linen was exposed just when the existence of the Republic was menaced by the gathering storm.

1200. In September the situation was developing. After making his arrangements in Gaul, Caesar paid a hasty visit[1] to the Cisalpine. A rumour reached Rome that he was expecting four legions to reach Placentia by the 15th October. It was false, but it shews how closely his movements were watched, and how readily he was credited with violent designs by the nervous suspicion of republican extremists. There is no good reason to think that he wished for war. If he could but be safe to the end of the next year (49) and enter office as consul on the 1st January 48, he was well able[2] to deal with difficulties that might then arise. Pompey would either have gone to Spain or would once more be exposed to the judicious management of his rival, an influence which had hitherto never failed. But an accommodation between Pompey and Caesar was just what the extreme republicans in the Senate were determined to prevent. The great timid and wavering majority were not likely to clear the air by having an active policy of their own, while the Caesarian minority were ably led by Curio. Caesar was conciliatory. He sent the two legions demanded for a Parthian war. For this purpose they were no longer wanted, but they were kept under arms for the present at Capua. It was probably also by his orders that Curio ceased to block a vote of money to pay Pompey's troops, which he had been opposing. But to a keen observer[3] it was already clear that the two rivals were at a deadlock. Unless one or other of them went to face the Parthians, there would be a civil war. Caelius had to make up his mind what his own line of conduct was to be. He concluded that his duty as a good citizen was to hold by the aristocrats, the 'more respectable' side, so long as a peaceful solution was possible; but to take the stronger side in the event of war. That Caesar's forces were beyond comparison the stronger he had no doubt. Caelius judged the facts rightly. But the leading republicans were not likely of their own will to go on creating more of these great proconsular commands. If Pompey were sent to the East, they would be left at the mercy of Caesar. They preferred to keep him at home and use him in their own defence. This was all the more natural, as the enthusiastic reception of Caesar in the Cisalpine testified to his solid popularity in

---

[1] Hirtius *Gall.* VIII 50, 51, Cic. *ad Att.* VI 9 § 5, VII 1 § 1.

[2] As Pompey put it to Cicero (*Att.* VII 8 § 5) he would come *in possessionem rei publicae.*

[3] Caelius in *ad fam.* VIII 14 (24 Sept. according to Schmidt).

the district from which he drew most of his best troops. About the end of October Caesar hurried off to finish some of his arrangements in the Further Gaul, and in November he held a great review of his army in the North. He then saw to the winter-quarters of his eight legions, and did not return to the Cisalpine till December. Meanwhile he had left Labienus[1] in charge. Labienus had been the best and most trusted of his lieutenants, and had amassed a great fortune in Caesar's service. But the republican leaders were busy with secret attempts to detach him from his master. We may guess that some jealousy, combined with an ambition to take a higher social position in Roman life, disposed him to listen to their proposals. That he misjudged[2] Caesar's real strength is not likely. Hirtius says that Caesar knew of this tampering with Labienus and refused to withdraw his confidence: as to the Senate, his position was that, if the House were free to vote without constraint, his claims would be granted. That is, the majority were for peace at any price: stated thus, it was the simple truth. But in the middle of November the extremists received a fatal encouragement. The two legions required for the Parthian war arrived, and the officers in charge[3] spread unfavourable reports of Caesar's army. The veterans were weary of service and ripe for desertion. The falsehood was too easily believed, even by Pompey, and helped to create vain hopes that blunted energy.

1201.   In truth Caesar was not only able to rely on the efficiency and loyalty of his army: he had in Rome too a powerful following. We have noted his judicious purchases of influential or able politicians in a few special cases. But there were many others of less mark[4] whom he had won over by gifts or loans or other favours. He did not disdain to engage the good-will even of freedmen and slaves, if he saw them likely to be of use. In recent years his camp had been the resort of all men in trouble, many of them reckless fellows enough and damaged in their reputations, but at least bound by their interest to his cause. He was known as a good master, and therefore served by the best of agents, among whom Balbus was the chief. It is

[1] Hirtius *Gall.* VIII 52.

[2] His opinion cited in Cic. *ad Att.* VII 16 § 2 (28 Jan. 49) surely refers to the forces then in Italy. He may not have gauged the weakness of the forces under Pompey and the general apathy of Italy, having to depend on the representations of those who seduced him. See § 1210.

[3] Appian II 30 says that these officers had been sent by Pompey to take over the two legions, presumably at the frontier. If so, they would get their information from Caesar's officers. Plut. *Pomp.* 57, *Caes.* 29, implies that the information was meant to deceive. It may have been so. The effect may be traced in the vain confidence of Pompey on Dec. 25. See Cic. *ad Att.* VII 8 § 4.

[4] There was also no lack of waverers, such as those mentioned in Cic. *ad Att.* VII 3 § 3. See in general Suet. *Jul.* 27.

evident that during his years of absence he was regularly supplied with the most trustworthy information from Rome, where all intrigues were keenly watched, and gossip reported, on his behalf. Ever alive to the importance of moral effects, he played the game of legalities and apparent concessions with no more insincerity, and much more skill, than his enemies : and it should be observed that, if the Roman rabble was worthless, it was rather the republicans than Caesar to whom its presence was an embarrassment. Under the constitution this rabble was in the last resort the real sovran power. No means existed by which the true *populus Romanus*, the citizens living at a distance, sojourning abroad on business, or serving in the armies, could habitually give constitutional expression to their will. Their place was filled by the mongrel mob of the city, which therefore could not be ignored. Its riotous behaviour had been restrained by the measures taken in Pompey's sole consulship. In reading the records of these last years we are struck by its unusual silence. It was overawed by armed force. But whatever natural sympathies it still retained were with Caesar, certainly not with the republican nobles and Pompey. The real reason why the latter feared the return of Caesar to Rome as consul was the consciousness[1] that the Assembly would at once revive and override the Senate, and that the popular hero would become lord of Rome without the necessity of a civil war. Nor was any indulgence claimed in the demands of Caesar greater than, or indeed as great as, the exceptional privileges granted to Pompey. To remain in his province till relieved in due course at the end of the year 49 was in accordance with the old practice. To be a candidate in absence was no new thing, and Pompey had himself approved the decree exempting him from the restrictions imposed by recent laws. To step directly from proconsulship to consulship was a trifle compared with Pompey's holding both together. Moreover Caesar had gone through the course of public offices in regular order, and was now only seeking reelection to the consulship after the regular ten-years interval. Pompey had skipped the junior offices altogether, and had been consul twice (55 and 52) within four years.

1202. On the 24th November Cicero[2] reached Brundisium, and found the position of affairs in Italy even worse than the news received abroad had led him to expect. Caelius as well as Curio had now openly gone over to Caesar. Still, black though things looked, he began at once to try his hand as mediator in letters and interviews. The more he learnt, the more he was convinced that Caesar must be

---

[1] See Cic. *ad Att.* VII 3 § 5, 9 § 3.

[2] Cic. *ad Att.* VII 2—9, with dates fixed by Schmidt, give us Cicero's views up to the end of the year 50.

met by concessions, having been allowed to become so strong that it was now too late to meet him in the field. Cicero's talents as a statesman had led him to this sound conclusion, and indeed he had long ago warned Pompey that his connexion with Caesar was making the latter a dangerous rival. But the orator had no wish to quarrel with either. He was the friend of both, and had renewed his friendship with Caesar at the desire of Pompey himself. It now seemed that he would have to choose between the two, a most unwelcome dilemma. His principles and his past, not to mention his old attachment to Pompey, left no doubt that he would in the last resort take the side on which the republicans and Pompey were found in union. But it has been well said[1] that this union, so long desired by Cicero, only came about when it was too late, and he could see no hope for a cause in which there had been so much blundering. Peace, anything for peace, was his position: a war meant a conqueror, and a conqueror a tyrant. Hoping for the honour of a triumph, he could not enter Rome and speak in the Senate. So we find him in the country, chiefly at his Formian villa, watching with ever-growing distress the course of events. He had interviews with many people, some of them important, as we shall see. Meanwhile December came, the consular presidency for the month passed to Marcellus, and the last stage of the great struggle began. Marcellus opened fire, probably[2] on the 1st, denouncing Caesar as a brigand, and demanding that he should be declared a public enemy unless he resigned his Province (that is, his army) by a fixed date. Curio, backed by Antony and other Caesarians, maintained that the only fair and reasonable plan was for both the great chiefs to resign together. Out of the debate issued three motions. The consul first put the question whether a successor should be sent to Caesar. This was carried by an immense majority, and vetoed by Curio. Next, whether Pompey should be required to resign; this was rejected by a like majority. Then Curio insisted on having a motion for their simultaneous resignation put to the House. This was carried[3] by 370 to 22. It does not seem that a formal decree was passed, for the Pompeian tribune Furnius probably vetoed it. But Marcellus was furious at the faint-hearted attitude of the House, and said 'this vote means slavery to Caesar.' The triumphant Curio was received by the populace outside with demonstrations of joy. The above were public proceedings. In the background private

---

[1] Strachan-Davidson's *Cicero* p. 321.

[2] I think this has been established by Nissen in *Histor. Zeitschr.* XLVI p. 71.

[3] Appian II 30, Plut. *Pomp.* 58. We have no letter from Caelius describing this sitting. Perhaps he never wrote, for Cicero was now in Italy and getting plenty of news. The importance of Curio's action was immense, and the words of Lucan IV 819 hardly seem too strong.

negotiation went on, of which we get glimpses.   Early in December
Caesar returned to the Cisalpine.   On the 6th Hirtius reached Rome
with instructions for Balbus.   Balbus (acting for Caesar) arranged to
talk over matters with Scipio (Pompey's father-in-law) early next
morning.   But Hirtius started on his return journey without waiting
to hear the result of the interview.   By the 10th Pompey, who was at
or near Neapolis, had heard of this affair.   On that day Cicero visited
him, and learnt[1] that war was pretty certain.   The hurry of Hirtius
had confirmed his previous belief that Caesar was bent upon picking
a quarrel.   It is clear that as yet no irrevocable step had been taken,
so far as Pompey knew.   But in Rome things were moving.   We
must not forget that the extreme republicans had no firm trust in
Pompey, and had only combined with him in order to thwart Caesar.
There was always the fear that the two rivals might come to terms, in
which case there would be an end of the Republic as a system for the
profit of the noble clique.   Some bold stroke[2] was necessary, both to
overcome the timidity of the senatorial majority, and to commit
Pompey irrevocably to the championship of the republican cause in
the event of a resort to arms.

1203.   Marcellus did not hesitate.   On the 9th December[3], using
as pretext a rumour that Caesar was on the march for Rome, he again
urged the Senate to declare him a public enemy and authorize
Pompey to take command of the troops in Italy for defence of the
state.   A violent altercation with Curio followed.   The consul, unable
to carry his point, told the House that he meant to provide for the
public safety on his own responsibility.   He went off, accompanied
by the consuls-elect (his namesake and Lentulus), to Pompey, in
whose hand he placed a sword, and authorized him to take command
of the two legions (now moved from Capua to Luceria) and any other
troops available, to raise further forces, and to march against Caesar.
Pompey well knew that the consul was acting unconstitutionally, and
that to accept the commission was virtually war.   Nevertheless he did
accept it, probably[4] on the 13th December at Neapolis.   Meanwhile
Cicero had passed on to Cumae, and on the 16th reached his Formian

---

[1] Cic. *ad Att.* VII 4.

[2] Ferrero II 184 holds that an intrigue was being carried on by letter between Marcellus
and Pompey, and that the words of the latter to Cicero on Dec. 10 were uttered in knowledge
of the *coup d'état* contemplated in Rome.   This is certainly possible, but the assumption is
hardly necessary.

[3] Here I think Ferrero is right.   Our record clearly makes Curio the tribune, and the 9th
was his last day of office.

[4] Schmidt, *Briefwechsel* pp. 97, 98.   Plutarch Appian and Dion make Pompey to have
been in the outskirts of Rome, and I discard their statement reluctantly.   I think they have
confused the presence of Pompey in the suburbs with that on 1st Jan. and following days.

villa. The mad doings of Marcellus were now well known, and Cicero met a number of persons[1] who were as disgusted and alarmed as he was himself. For Pompey had gone to Luceria on the 14th and the breach of the constitution was a fact accomplished beyond recall. What was a good citizen to do? Cicero was in despair, but felt that his place would be to follow Pompey, the leader of the herd. Still, hoping nothing from an appeal to arms, he was in favour of almost any concession to preserve the peace. He found little reason[2] to believe in a general rally of all classes to the republican cause. The weakness of the Senate was and had been deplorable; they had let Curio defy them, and lost their chance against Caesar. The capitalist circles regarded only their own interest, and were now all for Caesar. The agricultural classes were solely concerned to avoid war at any price. A solid Italy, even a solid Rome, was not to be hoped for. Caesar had been allowed to gain so many points of vantage that it was now too late to withstand him with success. On the 25th Cicero had a conversation[3] with Pompey at Formiae, and found him resolved on war. He seemed confident of being a match for Caesar with the resources at his disposal, but thought that in face of his preparations Caesar would drop his claim to the consulship. Cicero was but partly reassured. Among the subjects of their talk was a reported harangue of Antony. Since the 10th December Antony had succeeded Curio in the capacity of Caesar's leading tribune, ready for obstructing[4] government measures. The news of Pompey's journey to Luceria reached Rome by the 20th. While the alarm caused by that step was fresh, Antony made (21 Dec.) a violent public speech against Pompey, abusive and menacing. If the man behaved like this, what would the master do? Pompey clearly meant war, and Cicero was left to worry over the fact that the money lent him by Caesar was still unpaid. The orator's gall broke out[5] in a fierce exposure of the hopelessness of the situation and the shamelessness of Caesar's claims. But this was only to relieve his feelings by pouring out his soul to Atticus.

1204. Caesar had been transacting some assize-business in the Cisalpine. By the 24th December he was at Ravenna, no doubt on purpose to be within reach of early news. About the 25th he was joined[6] by Curio, who had fled from Rome on the 21st, being no

---

[1] Cic. *ad Att.* VII 5 § 4 (16 Dec. Schmidt). The moral disadvantage to the republican cause is clearly brought out in this fact.

[2] Cic. *ad Att.* VII 7 § 5 (between 18 and 21 Dec.).

[3] Cic. *ad Att.* VII 8 (Dec. 25 or 26).

[4] A part of this lay in the use of tribunician power to hinder the levy of troops. Appian II 31, Plut. *Ant.* 5.

[5] Cic. *ad Att.* VIII 9 (Dec. 26 or 27).

[6] Schmidt, *Briefwechsel* pp. 98, 99.

longer secured by the sanctity of the tribunate.   Curio told him of
the steps taken by Marcellus and Pompey, and urged him to march
on Rome forthwith.   Caesar knew better.   He did not want civil war,
but the consulship for 48.   Though prepared for war if driven to bay,
he was not ready to fight at once.   The one legion at hand seems to
have been in winter quarters, the ten cohorts probably billeted in
several towns.   This legion (XIII) he at once ordered[1] to concentrate
at Ravenna, and sent off an express to summon two more (VIII and
XII) from Further Gaul.   The act of Pompey had from his point of
view created a state of war in Italy (*tumultus*) and precautions were
necessary.   Meanwhile he drew up a careful letter to the Senate, still
hoping to avert war, in which he reduced his claims to the minimum
consistent with his main object.   He had already through his agents
offered to give up the Further Gaul on the 1st March 49, provided he
might retain the Cisalpine with only two legions to the end of the
year : even this offer is said[2] to have been reduced later to Illyricum
with one legion.   But these concessions would, in the light of the
supposed disaffection of his troops, appear to be the outcome of
conscious weakness.   They had effected nothing.   He now took the
line of simple self-defence.   He recited his services to the state, and
refused to be given over helpless to the mercy of his enemies.   He
was ready to resign all his provinces and his army, provided Pompey
would do the same.   But he added that the refusal of these terms
would compel him to take measures for asserting his own rights and
the freedom of the Roman people.   In short, he had no fear of the
Assembly, if not coerced by Pompey's troops : with the Senate he
well knew that nothing would be so effectual as a threat.   As for the
constitution, it had been overridden by Marcellus and Pompey.   Some
versions of this letter[3] make Caesar offer to render an account of
all his acts and stand for office as a private citizen.   That is mere
verbiage.   Caesar surely knew that the Senate could not accept his
terms without throwing over Pompey, nor Pompey without throwing
over the Senate.   If they quarrelled (it is hard to believe that he hoped
for this), he, Caesar, was safe enough.   But they might stand firm,
and what then?   The Senate could only pass its 'last decree' by
overriding the certain veto of his tribunes.   If they did so, it could
not be helped : at least he would begin a war as a defender of constitutional rights.   Cleverly indeed had he manœuvred his enemies
into a false position.   The moral vantage was now safe in the hands
of one who knew, as few have ever known, how to use moral effects.

---

[1] Caes. *civ.* I 7 § 7.   [2] Suet. *Jul.* 29.
[3] See Appian II 32, Plut. *Pomp.* 59, *Caes.* 30, Dion Cass. XLI 1, 2, Cic. *ad fam.* XVI 11
§ 2 (Jan. 12), and for Caesar's own view *civ.* I 5, 9, 22.

With this ultimatum Curio set out very early on the 27th, and by travelling hard for three whole days reached Rome in time to hand it to the new consuls on the first of January, before the Senate had begun the business of the day. Lentulus was to preside at a sitting the momentous nature of which all men knew. The refusal of the consuls to let the letter be read was overcome by the persistence of the Caesarian tribunes, and Antony read it out, interrupted by indignant comments. The threat with which it ended was insolent, though indeed no more unconstitutional than the recent acts of the republican leaders. But the republicans were now at the head of affairs in Rome, while Caesar's small band could do nothing but obstruct. So Antony could get no hearing. Lentulus called upon the House to discuss the general interests of the state (*de re publica*) as was customary on the first day of the year, and refused to admit any motion arising directly out of the contents of the letter.

1205. The debate began with a declaration from Lentulus, meant to counteract the effect of Caesar's threat. He told members that, if they would speak out and give their opinions boldly, he would do his duty by Rome and them without fail. But if they took their cue from Caesar and tried to please him, then he, Lentulus, would look out for himself and pay no heed to the Senate: if others could fall back upon the friendship of Caesar, why, so[1] could he. Then followed Scipio, who assured them that Pompey was ready to do his duty by the state, provided the Senate backed him up; but, unless they acted promptly and firmly now, they must not look to him for help hereafter. All this was brave talk, but still some had misgivings. The slow-moving consular M. Marcellus thought it would be wiser not to come to a decision until the levy of troops was complete and the legions embodied; the House would then be at liberty to express its real views in a decree without constraint. M. Calidius, supported by M. Caelius, speaking from the Caesarian standpoint, proposed that Pompey should go to Spain and do away with all reason for war: the withdrawal of the two legions had alarmed Caesar; if Pompey did not mean to use them[2] for Caesar's ruin, why was he keeping them within reach of Rome? Lentulus in high wrath broke out against these proposals. That of Calidius was capable of being regarded as arising directly from Caesar's letter, and so not strictly[3] within the

---

[1] So Caesar *civ.* I 1 tells us. Lentulus was deep in debt (*ib.* 4 § 2). Caesar tried to buy him later, but somehow failed. Nissen well refers to Cic. *ad Att.* VIII 9 § 4, 11 § 5. See Tyrrell and Purser on *ad fam.* X 32.

[2] Probably an allusion to the troops on guard at the trial of Milo. See Suet. *Jul.* 50, where Cato's threat of a prosecution the moment Caesar had disbanded his army is mentioned in this very connexion.

[3] See Kraner on Caesar *civ.* I 2 § 5.

terms of the reference, and he refused to put it to the vote. Marcellus was so browbeaten by his invective that he dropped his motion. The consul did put the motion made now or earlier in the debate by Scipio. It ran, that a date[1] should be named by which Caesar was to give up his army, non-compliance with this order to be taken as an act of war. We hear that the tribunes stood out of the division, that Curio and Caelius voted No, while the rest of the House voted Yes. The violent men had made the waverers afraid to confess their fears, and drove them like a flock of sheep. The Senate was now morally committed to a civil war, but no decree passed. The Caesarian tribunes, Antony and Q. Cassius, put in their veto. Thereupon the consul invited opinions as to what steps should be taken to get the better of this obstruction. The House was in an angry mood after all its recent worrying by Curio and others, and we may believe Caesar that the tone of the speakers was severe. The most harsh and blood-thirsty suggestions were applauded.

1206. At sundown the sitting ended. Next day the resumed debate was fruitless. Antony revived the proposal that both the chiefs should resign at once. This was greeted with applause, but the consul would not put it to the vote. Nor in truth was it now a possible solution, for the House was determined to put no pressure on Pompey, and Pompey, who was now waiting at hand beyond the city precinct, had no intention of resigning voluntarily. But as yet the majority were too desirous of peace to override the obstruction of tribunes by passing the 'last decree.' In this serious deadlock it was unofficially agreed to wear mourning dress, a traditional mode of emphasizing the gravity of the situation. The 3rd and 4th were days lawful for Assemblies, so the Senate stood adjourned to the 5th. The interval was used by both sides. The republicans, encouraged by Pompey's presence, were busy putting pressure on waverers, and Caesar alleges[2] that a number of soldiers from the forces already raised were sent into the city. Antony made public the contents of Caesar's letter, and doubtless laid stress on the moderation displayed by the popular hero. On the 4th Cicero arrived outside the city, with his lictors and their *fasces* wreathed with bay. Though thirsting for a triumph, and charmed with his public reception (for many looked to him to find a way out of the deadlock), he at once began to work hard for peace. But he took his stand[3] on the fact of Caesar's candidature in absence having been legally granted by the Assembly with Pompey's express approval. This bargain must be carried out. We can see that this position implied consent to Caesar's demands (at

---

[1] Probably 1st July 49. Nissen p. 80, Schmidt p. 103.
[2] Caes. *civ.* I. 3.　　　　　　[3] Cic. *ad fam.* VI 6 §§ 5, 6 (end of Sept. 46).

least in their minimum form). Caesar must be able to step straight from proconsulship to consulship, without being exposed to the attacks of Cato and other enemies. In short it was an opportunist policy, and the republicans were not willing so to give up their case. Cicero also advised Pompey to go off to Spain and leave Caesar to be consul in his absence. Pompey was not strong, and he shewed signs of wavering, but he did not take this wise advice. Both Caesar and Cicero[1] tell us that there were a number of men who saw their own interest in a successful war. With Pompey committed to their cause they had such a chance as was not likely to recur. These men, deeply in debt, and convinced that Caesar's consulship would be fatal to their prospects of restoring their fortunes as governors abroad, overbore the counsel of Cicero. Flattery no doubt played its part in persuading the vain and nerve-stricken general. Yet it is almost certain[2] that he was aware that he might have to abandon the city, and probable that his plans of campaign already included the possibility of having to evacuate Italy. This was surely not what his bold advisers, among whom were Lentulus and Scipio, had in their minds. So the want of mutual understanding was weakening the republican leaders, while the cool and resolute man at Ravenna was free to play his game.

1207. On the 5th the Senate met again. Caesar says, perhaps truly, that care was taken to have the partisans of the consuls and Pompey present in full force. The House sat outside the city precinct, that Pompey and Cicero might attend. It seems that a further proposal was now officially made on behalf of Caesar. Simultaneous resignation had ceased to be a practical issue. The offer to be content with a reduced province and army was put forward, but on the point of holding this minimum till the end of 49, and being free to stand for the consulship in absence, there was and could be no yielding. And all was on condition that Pompey went to Spain. After all that had passed, this was not likely[3] to be accepted. Cicero spoke for it in vain. Lentulus and the men who saw that it meant their ruin would not hear of it. Cato would not make the public interests the subject of a bargain. Pompey had gone too far to draw back. Even now there were a few willing to try the effect of a mission to Ravenna. But the 5th and 6th went by without result, and the tension was extreme. No wonder, for the fear of a repetition of Sulla's exploits was in the minds of many. That the conqueror in a civil war would follow the precedents of murder and proscription

---

[1] See Cic. *ad fam.* IV 1 § 1 (April 49) *sero enim veneram; solus eram; rudis esse videbar in causa; incideram in hominum pugnandi cupidorum insanias*, and XVI 11 § 2.

[2] See Cic. *ad Att.* VII 8 § 5.　　　[3] Velleius II 49.

was a natural surmise. To one party Caesar appeared a bloodthirsty ogre; on the other hand Pompey had been a pupil of Sulla. And the ruined men on both sides were only too likely to regard victory as a means of enriching themselves at the expense of the vanquished. Now the resolution of the Senate on the first of January, suspended by the tribunes' veto, had to be made a valid decree in order to put Caesar formally in the wrong, and force him to act as the aggressor. To override the veto was only possible by passing the 'last decree,' declaring a state of siege, in fact suspending the constitution, and so placing the city, tribunes and all, under military law. And the majority of the House could only be induced to take this step under the influence of fear. Now that Pompey was fully committed to their cause, Lentulus and his party were able to urge that it was sheer madness to let the opportunity slip. Of course the most terrifying reports of Caesar's designs were circulated, and 'now or never' brought the senators to compliance at last. On the 7th the consul felt strong enough to force on the crisis. He announced that he meant to take a division on the 'last decree,' and he advised the obstructing tribunes to withdraw if they valued their safety. Antony protested against this as a violation of the sacred tribunate. After a dramatic scene[1] he withdrew, accompanied by Q. Cassius with Curio and Caelius, and the four set out for Ravenna in the disguise of slaves. The House passed the decree in the usual form, calling on the magistrates with the proconsuls present (Pompey and Cicero) to see that the commonwealth took no harm. It remained to carry out the policy thus finally adopted. Caesar at least could still maintain that his cause was that of the tribunate, and pose as the defender of the freedom of the Roman people.

1208. Note on the extension of Caesar's command by the law of Pompey and Crassus in 55 B.C.

Three articles in Lehmann and Kornemann's *Klio*, namely IV 76—87 and V 236—240 by O. Hirschfeld and V 107—116 by L. Holzapfel, are devoted to the question, what date was fixed by the law of 55 for the end of Caesar's term? The former puts it at 1st March 50, the latter maintains the old view of Mommsen that it was 1st March 49. According to Hirschfeld the general tradition that the extension was granted for five years, which is taken to mean from 1st March 54 to 1st March 49, is an error, and the three years given by Dion Cassius from his own calculation (compare XXXIX 33 with XLIV 43) is not a mere delusion, but a trace of a misunderstood truth. The contemporary evidence of the letters of Caelius and Cicero, passages of Caesar and Hirtius, etc., are held to bear out the view that the year in which Caesar wished to stand for the consulship was 50, not 49, so that he would hold it in 49, not 48. Of course this modifies our view of Pompey's conduct, though less so than might be expected. Ingenious and learned as these papers are, I confess that they

---

[1] Appian II 33, Caes. *civ.* I 5.

do not convince me. Niese in his *Grundriss der Römischen Geschichte* (1906) pp. 217—8 accepts the view of Hirschfeld. But I do not think that the second paper demolishes the doubts of Holzapfel. Some of Hirschfeld's explanations of passages seem forced, and I think it best for the present to abide by the older view. In particular, it is surely strange that the story of the five-years' extension granted in 55 should have obtained such currency if it were untrue. For Pollio's history was known and used by later writers, as Plutarch, *Pomp.* 51, *Caes.* 21, and Appian *civ.* ii 18, and Pollio was no servile Caesarian. I am rather disposed to agree with Nissen that the five-years' continuation of Caesar's governorship in 55 included all his provinces, and that the five years strictly speaking would end with 1st March 49. See Nissen's article, p. 56.

The very difficult chronology of events 51—49 B.C. has been most ably treated in the following works (1) an article by H. Nissen (*der Ausbruch des Bürgerkriegs* 49 *v. Chr.*) in Sybel's Historische Zeitschrift (1881 pp. 48—105), (2) *Der Briefwechsel des M. Tullius Cicero, etc.*, von O. E. Schmidt (Leipzig 1893). The latter corrects some details of the former. To both I am greatly indebted. It is only in connexion with the letters of Cicero that any trustworthy notion of the order of events can be gained. Livy's books are lost, and the abstracts of the later writers, meagre and loose, are wholly unsatisfactory from this point of view.

Note added in 1922. In *Journal of Philology*, No. 68 [1918] is an article by Dr Hardy on the evidence as to Caesar's legal position in Gaul. It is a searching exposure of the misuse of evidence by Hirschfeld and later [1913] by Judeich, and re-establishes the view of Mommsen.

CHAPTER LVII.

THE CIVIL WAR TO THE BATTLE OF THAPSUS. 49—46 B.C.

1209. WE are now come[1] to the great civil war, in which the Roman Republic, long since weakened by internal maladies, received its deathblow. Matters of purely military interest do not concern us, but it is well to bear in mind from the first that we have to deal with the military expression of great human facts. The higher strategy, operating mainly through moral effects, can only rest on a profound insight into human nature. This insight Caesar had shewn from the very beginning of his political career. In the conquest of Gaul he had become a great soldier, but the struggle now awaiting him was to be carried on under different conditions. A foreign people could be slaughtered or sold into slavery until such time as the remnant thought it better to accept the yoke of Rome. This treatment could not be applied to his Roman adversaries. He was compelled to aim at supreme power; his public career, perhaps his life, could be continued in no other way. But this supreme power must be in Rome. It presupposed a Roman empire in which he, Caesar, should be the embodiment of Roman will. From his point of view it was imperatively necessary to shed the least possible amount of blood, and to interfere with the liberties of the citizens in the least possible degree. These limiting conditions were evidently congenial to his temperament. But supreme power could now be won only by war, and the sooner this war was over the better for all parties. A long indecisive struggle could only end in general exhaustion, a result

---

[1] Authorities. Caesar's *Civil War* is to be read with suspicion as a partisan treatise, particularly where he offers an account of the motives of either side. But both he and the authors of the continuations are in respect of facts better evidence than the later writers. The loss of Livy's books 109—116 deprives us of a narrative which certainly put the Pompeian side of things more favourably. That it did not afford ground for a wholly different view of events from that I have taken, is I think a fair inference from the total failure of Lucan to make much of the deserts of Pompey and his cause. Lucan drew mainly from Livy. Of the late Greek writers, Appian is often demonstrably inaccurate, and Dion, though often useful as a compiler of facts, is a very dubious authority for reasons. Of the moderate contemporary narrative of Pollio only a few traces are preserved in the rare citations of later writers. Plutarch and Suetonius are useful from their own special points of view. It is hardly needful to speak particularly of Cicero, who is of course most important. He and his friends throw side-lights on numberles pointss.

which Caesar did his very best[1] to avoid. He had created an army with which he was able to deliver sharp strokes, and he proceeded to use it with appropriate vigour. He confounded his enemies by the speed which made Cicero[2] call him a 'prodigy,' and hardly less so by the mercy he shewed after his victories. He took extraordinary risks, hardly to be justified from a military standpoint, and in consequence suffered reverses. But political considerations necessarily enter into a civil war, and among the means of working upon the minds of men audacity and quick recovery from reverses are not the least. The fact of having the forces of rank and wealth arrayed against him was destined to cause trouble later, but during the war it gave him an advantage. He was the master of subordinates, many of them able men, and all bound to his cause by the certainty that to them defeat would mean death or ruin. His rival was hampered by the jealousies and intrigues of Roman nobles, self-satisfied and many of them incompetent, nearly all willing to criticize, few to obey. However alert and energetic Pompey might have been, it was impossible that he could in these respects be equal to Caesar. But the man himself was stale and his health impaired by sickness, no match for an adversary in fine training and with unshattered nerve. He knew how to handle an army, as Caesar found when he ventured to take liberties with the commander himself. But he had not provided himself with an army ready to take the field at once. His legions were either raw levies, or disaffected through attachment to Caesar, or far away in Spain. By the time he had got together a fighting force, half the world was already lost, discontent was rife at headquarters, and in the multitude of counsellors there was unwisdom. Caesar had also a great advantage in the clearness of his immediate aims. Both rivals knew that the rule of the aristocrats under the forms of a Republic was utterly corrupt, a cause of weakness to Rome and misery to her subjects. But there is no reason to think that Pompey had any further design than the recovery of his old position as the first man in an effete Republic, indispensable and paralysing. He was not prepared to mend or end it; Caesar saw that it was past mending, and was prepared to end it. Whether it was the more patriotic course to preside over inefficiency or to be an efficient autocrat, moralists may decide. The saying of Lucan, that the gods sided with the victor but Cato with the vanquished, contains an unwilling admission under its

---

[1] Cic. *ad fam.* IX 6 § 2, writing to Varro in 46 after Thapsus, confesses that the attitude of the Pompeians towards the war had been *cupere*, Caesar's *non timere*. Compare VI 6 § 6, *pro Marcello* § 15.

[2] *ad Att.* VIII 9 § 4 *sed hoc τέρας horribili vigilantia celeritate diligentia est.* Caesar in *ad Att.* IX 7 C, *haec nova sit ratio vincendi, ut misericordia et liberalitate nos muniamus.*

fierce antithesis. For the practical worth of the republican system in its degeneracy was just such as might commend itself to the perverse pedantry of the Roman Stoic. In any more human (or divine) judgment it must stand condemned. It is not necessary to worship Caesar: his work had got to be done.

1210. The declaration of war was at once followed by what might have been a serious discouragement. Labienus went over to the Pompeians. He had been Caesar's right-hand man in Gaul, and had been more uniformly successful in the field than his chief himself. He had lately acted as Caesar's deputy in the government of the Cisalpine. Labienus was received with open arms by the other side ; it is not clear that he was equally[1] trusted. Roman nobles could hardly be expected to put themselves under the command of a renegade who had played so important a part on the side of their opponents from the time (63) when he accused Rabirius till now. Socially he was not their equal, and he never held a leading position among the Pompeians. His desertion of Caesar was no doubt partly caused by a miscalculation[2] of chances, but there were probably other influences at work the clue to which is lost. When he reached Rome, this experienced soldier must have felt some misgivings. All was hurry and confusion, nothing ready. After the passing of the 'last decree,' the Senate met day by day to pass the necessary votes. Pompey still comforted them with assurances of the disaffection of Caesar's troops. A general levy throughout Italy was ordered. Arrangements were made for the succession to provinces, in particular Transalpine Gaul was declared a consular province, and allotted to L. Domitius Ahenobarbus (consul in 54), an obstinate conceited aristocrat, one of Caesar's bitterest enemies. Orders were sent out for the collection of stores of arms, and municipal towns were called upon to contribute money. Italy was divided into districts, each with a Roman official in command to oversee the preparations. Poor Cicero, who was still waiting outside Rome in hopes of a triumph, his lictors' *fasces* still decked with bay-leaves in honour of his little victories, was put in charge of a district including Campania. Capua was an important depot for the military levy, and the control of the southern coast was no small consideration, for from the first Pompey foresaw the probable need of a large fleet. But the general confusion and mismanagement around him soon disgusted Cicero, and he resigned his official command after holding it a few days. He stayed on by request of Pompey as a sort of confidential agent reporting to his chief. He was convinced of the folly of the war, and still hoped to

---

[1] See Cic. *ad Att.* VIII 2 § 3, *in Labieno parum est dignitatis.*
[2] That is, overrating Pompey's strength. See § 1200.

bring about a peace.   He suffered the agonies of alternate hope and despair, but he was loyal to the republicans, though he believed the cause desperate.

1211.   Caesar had forced his enemies to declare war, and the expulsion of the two tribunes gave him an excuse for posing as the innocent victim of aggressive violence.   He had with him at Ravenna only one full legion (13th) and a few cavalry.   But his legions beyond the Alps were ready[1] to march, and he sent orders for them to join him with all speed.   Meanwhile he addressed his men[2] on the spot, and persuaded them that the outrage on the tribunes left them no choice but to fight or to leave him to the mercy of his enemies.   In the latter event they would of course have given up all hope of further reward, for their master would be powerless.   They declared that they would stand by him and the tribunes.   To advance into Italy with only some 5300 men was a bold step, but this is what Caesar at once did.   He was certainly aware that he would not at first have to face any organized army, but we can hardly doubt that he was encouraged also by some knowledge of the state of feeling among the burgesses of the municipal towns.   The sequel clearly shewed that there was everywhere a party either Caesarian in sympathy or at least not disposed to resist Caesar.   The local senates and magistrates would probably be in general Pompeian, but Caesar's approach would embolden the poorer class to take their own line, and it is not easy to see why gratitude for the past or hope of future favours should induce them to risk their lives and goods in the cause of selfish Roman nobles who had left them unprotected to bear the brunt of Caesar's attack.   To them Caesar was as good a Roman as any, better than most; he had led the Roman 'popular' party; and, if past record went for anything, the party of Marius and Cinna, of Sulpicius and Carbo, had more claim on the sympathies of the country towns and hamlets than the party of the 'best men' who surrounded and encumbered Pompey.   Ariminum[3], the first town after passing the Rubicon, the border stream, was occupied without resistance on the 11th January. By the time the news of this had reached Rome, he had seized

---

[1] Some of them seem to have been already moved from their winter quarters so as to be within easy reach.   Certainly two joined him before the fall of Corfinium on 20th Feb.   Caesar *civ.* I 15, 18.   See § 1204.

[2] Livy and all authorities save Caesar place this address at Ariminum.   See in particular Orosius VI 15 § 2, borne out by Lucan.   This account is now generally accepted, but I am still in doubt, so have let Caesar's story stand.   At Ariminum he had only 5 cohorts.

[3] The exact chronology of Caesar's advance is matter of dispute.   To make him exhibit the tribunes and address his soldiers at Ravenna on Jan. 10 (*Class. Quarterly* I 224) is possible. But that he crossed the Rubicon (more than 30 miles off) that same night I cannot believe. For his further progress see Miss Peaks in *Class. Review* XVIII 346—9.   For my present purpose these points are not important.

Pisaurum Fanum and Ancona. A single cohort (about 500 men, probably less) was enough in each case to take over the place, and he soon withdrew them for further advance: garrisons were clearly not needed. Arretium[1] in Etruria surrendered to Antony, who was sent over the Apennine with five cohorts. Caesar now had a footing on both the great roads leading to Rome, and began to come upon detachments of Pompeian forces. Q. Minucius Thermus held Iguvium not far from the Flaminian road with five cohorts. But the Iguvines inclined to Caesar, so Thermus withdrew his men and ran away before Curio with three cohorts could reach him. In his retreat the recruits left him and went to their homes, while Curio was welcomed at Iguvium. Such was the state of things in northern Italy. No wonder Caesar felt able to move on boldly. He gathered in his scattered detachments and advanced upon Auximum. P. Attius Varus was holding the town for Pompey, and recruiting was going on in the neighbourhood; the district of Picenum had a Pompeian connexion since the days of the great Italian war. But the majority of the local burgesses[2] were willing to receive Caesar, and Varus evacuated the place in a hurry. Caesar's men caught him in retreat and brought on a small engagement, after which some of the Pompeian troops dispersed and the rest went over to Caesar. Varus escaped. The next town to welcome Caesar was Cingulum, which Labienus had turned into a Pompeian post. The people not only invited Caesar to come but furnished him recruits. Another of his legions (12th) joined him about this time. He now marched upon Asculum, where Cicero's friend Lentulus Spinther lay with ten cohorts. Spinther fell back like the rest, and lost most of his force by desertion. L. Vibullius Rufus took over the remainder, and with these and other levies and another party flying from Camerinum he made up a force with which he judiciously retired to Corfinium. At this stage of the war Caesar was master of Umbria and Picenum and had a footing in Etruria. He was meeting with no local opposition, and with their raw troops the Pompeian commanders could do nothing. He was gaining recruits, volunteers in good heart. He had with him two legions of veterans, and seven more, not to mention Gaulish and German horse, were on the march. Rumour magnified the non-Roman (Transpadane) and barbarian elements in his army, and Roman nobles, conscious of their own bloodthirsty intentions if victorious, proclaimed that the conqueror of Gaul was coming to Rome at the

---

[1] This was one of the places that had suffered much at the hands of Sulla.

[2] From Caesar *civ.* I 13 it appears that they put pressure on the local senate, who invited Varus to go away. For the temper of local burgesses further south see Cic. *ad Att.* VIII 13.

head of his northern savages bent on rapine and massacre. But of any such intention Caesar had given no sign.

1212. Meanwhile a negotiation had been going on of which we can form only a general idea, the dates being given differently according as we follow Cicero or Caesar. It appears that two envoys reached Caesar, probably in northern Umbria; Pompey had sent them on hearing of the occupation of Ariminum, but since that event other towns had been taken and the position materially altered. Pompey had left Rome soon after the 7th January, and was somewhere south of the city, busy with the attempt to form an army in a hurry. The main point of the envoy's message was (according to Caesar) a sort of lecture, urging on him the duty of making the interest of Rome his first object and of not letting a personal quarrel lead him into conduct hurtful to his country. In reply to what he considered a shallow trick to give him the appearance of unprovoked aggression, Caesar sent them back with a corresponding statement of his own spotless patriotism, of the wrongs inflicted on him, and finally of his present terms. These last were astounding in their moderation. He proposed[1] that Pompey should go to Spain, that both sides should disband their armies (that is, of course, in Italy), that recruiting should altogether cease, and the freedom of election be guaranteed. On these conditions he offered to hand over his provinces to the successors appointed, to come to Rome, and stand for the consulship in person. He added a request for a personal interview with Pompey, with a view to the settlement of minor details and exchange of guarantees. Yet in spite of all these concessions it is hardly likely that he seriously expected them to be accepted and the terms carried out. The request for an interview with Pompey was sure to rouse the suspicions of the leading nobles. They had had enough of such conferences. Nor would Pompey agree to go abroad after all that had happened, and leave Caesar master of Rome, as he would certainly be. Again, the proposal for disbandment was more plausible than genuine. In case of a quarrel arising after disbandment, Caesar could easily have recalled his veterans to arms, while the slack recruits of the Pompeians were likely to make a poor response. Had not Sulla disbanded his veterans, and died in his bed? However, such as the terms were, they were an ultimatum delivered by a victorious invader in full career, who did not wait for an answer, but pushed on. This was the vital fact, which the consuls and other leading nobles were too blind to see. They replied, after a meeting with Pompey[2] at Capua, that they accepted the terms on condition

[1] Caesar *civ.* I 9, Cic. *ad fam.* XVI 12.

[2] Caesar *civ.* I 10, Cic. *ad Att.* VII 14, *fam.* XVI 12. Caesar represents the 'towns' as being Ariminum only, which is fudge.

that Caesar should first evacuate the towns occupied by him in Italy, retire into his province, and disband his army. Once these conditions were carried out, Pompey would leave for Spain, and they would all return to Rome, where the Senate would see to the completion of the business. Caesar says that they refused to stop the levy of troops until Caesar had proved his sincerity in the above practical manner. In short, Caesar was coming on, and it was necessary to accept or refuse his terms at once. To bargain, that is to impose terms, was impossible while they were falling back in flurried impotence. As for gaining time, it was childish to act as if Caesar would be cheated of his advantage by so simple a trick. Now that there was war, it was his business to win, and he had not entered Italy to litigate or higgle. Moreover, no security was offered, no date was fixed, for Pompey's withdrawal to Spain, and Caesar, who was himself a man of his word, knew by experience that Pompey was not to be trusted. Naturally he refused to walk into the trap, and went on with his occupation of Picenum, as we have seen above.

1213. It has been said that this reply was sent from Capua. About the 17th January the alarm in Rome had reached its height. While the news of Caesar's advance caused a panic, Pompey summoned magistrates and senators to quit the city. His plan was for the present to transfer the seat of government to Capua, for he saw that he had not the means of holding Rome. It seems that a decree of the Senate was passed authorizing this step and approving the declaration of Pompey that he would[1] regard all who refused to obey the order as public enemies. It was an unconstitutional order, for the Assembly was left out of account; but the proclamation[2] of a *tumultus* or state of war in Italy might be held to cover the suspension of the constitution by the plea of emergency. So the consuls and most of the magistrates, the greater part of the senators, and many of the rich knights, fled from Rome : Cicero, outside with lictors (bay-leaves and all), moved southwards like the rest. He was generally at Formiae, but went to Capua and elsewhere on occasion. His friend Atticus, who had made up his mind not to join either side, remained in Rome. Cicero's letters to Atticus[3] at this time give a vivid picture of the state of things on the Pompeian side. Nothing had been foreseen and provided for. The changing news from day to day caused constant wavering and uncertainty of plans. There were military depots at Teanum Larinum Luceria and elsewhere, but at none of

---

[1] And indeed punish all towns that fell away to Caesar. Cic. *ad Att.* IX 10 § 2.

[2] On 14th Jan. after receipt of news of the fall of Ariminum, according to Schmidt, *Rheinisches Museum* 1892 p. 258.

[3] See *ad Att.* VII 13a, 14.

them a strong force, or the prospect of any. It soon appeared that men were unwilling to enlist. Even around the headquarters at Capua the Pompeian veterans settled in the district shewed no enthusiasm in the cause, and in Capua itself there was trouble. There was a school of 600 gladiators in the town, the property of Caesar. What was to be done with them? The stupid consul Lentulus Crus offered them their freedom and wanted to use them as cavalry, but others saw that, if this were allowed, there would be an end of recruiting in Italy. Pompey got out of the difficulty by making each of 300 heads of houses responsible for the safe custody of two of them. That this move made the cause more popular in the district is not likely. Moreover, the loyalty of the two legions withdrawn from Caesar was doubtful. It soon became an object to keep them out of the way of Caesar's army, for fear they should go over. Money too was badly needed. All there was in the treasury had been voted to Pompey, and the ordinary fund had been appropriated. But there was also a sort of sacred reserve (*aerarium sanctius*) in which certain shares of war-spoils and the $5°/_0$ manumission-duty had been accumulating for great emergencies (invasion) ever so long, perhaps since the second Punic war. In the hurry and alarm of the moment this fund had been left behind, and when, in February, Pompey instructed the consuls to go back and fetch it, they were afraid to run the risk. Some of the fugitives, as Cicero, were anxious as to the fate of relatives left behind in Rome, or vainly indignant at being compelled to desert the city at all. The arrival of Labienus and Caesar's father-in-law Piso cheered faint hearts for a while, but nothing came of it, and the hopes[1] of the desertion of Caesar by his army, and perhaps a rising of the Gauls in his rear, proved to be idle dreams. The movements of Pompey from place to place were often not easy to understand. The unhappy chief had more than enough to do. Italy was disappointing his expectations, and others, even the loyal Cicero, were disappointed in him. Yet he was surely doing his best; the legions that he took with him out of Italy shew that he and some at least of his officers had worked hard. But he had begun too late. If it was silly of Cicero in his letters to Atticus to rant and scold at Caesar, whose point of view he did not understand, he was quite right in insisting[2] that unreadiness ior war proved the necessity of peace. The talk of Pompey's going to Spain had come to nothing, and he had evidently at a very early stage begun to provide[3] for a very different contingency. He gathered a fleet oi ships at Brundisium, ready for the transport of

---

[1] Cic. *ad fam.* XVI 12 § 4.

[2] In *ad Att.* VII 15 § 2 he says that even Cato is now ready to submit.

[3] For his 'Themistoclean' policy compare Cic. *ad Att.* X 8 § 4 with VII 11 § 3.

an army. Not only was this port out of the way of the western voyage: his army for Spain was already there. In February it became clear that he expected to have to leave Italy for the East, a prospect which the fretful Cicero contemplated with mingled indignation and dismay.

1214. When Caesar had secured his footing in the interior of Picenum he returned to the coast road, occupied Firmum, and halted awhile to organize the deserters and volunteers who had joined him. South of him lay the mountainous country now called the Abruzzi, where dwelt the Vestini Marsi Paeligni and other small peoples of old Sabellian stock. The acquisition of Roman citizenship had probably made little difference to them. It was not a district of great estates, and the dalesmen had not lost the military qualities of their fathers. The heart of this district could be reached from the east by following up the river Aternus (Pescara), near which, some 35 miles inland, stood the town of Corfinium, the first capital of the insurgents in the great Italian war. South-east of it lay Sulmo, another Paelignian town, and further off to the west, near the lake Fucinus, was Alba, formerly a Latin colony, guarding the midland road to Rome. In this district the Pompeians had been busy: both to them and to Caesar it was of first-rate strategic importance. Domitius, Caesar's bitter enemy and intended successor in Gaul, was in command at Corfinium. Sulmo and Alba were held by other officers of rank. As Caesar drew near, Domitius was in doubt whether he could maintain[1] his position. The presence of a number of senators and other persons of quality at his headquarters was a great responsibility, but in view of the smallness of Caesar's army he finally decided to make a stand. In vain Pompey wrote to point out that Caesar would soon be reinforced, and to summon him back to form a junction in Apulia. The commander-in-chief had no means of enforcing his orders, and Domitius, conceited and obstinate, held on till it was too late. He wanted Pompey to march to his relief, and cut off Caesar, hemmed in between two armies. But Pompey had no troops that he could trust for such an operation, and wrote more urgently to recall Domitius. By the 14th February Caesar was before Corfinium. Domitius, with his own troops and other detachments that had joined him, seems to have had from 18 to 20 cohorts in the town. Caesar had at first two legions. The old story soon began again. The people of Sulmo sent to offer their adhesion; at present they were restrained by a Pompeian garrison. On the approach of Antony with a small force they at once

---

[1] Caesar *civ.* I 17 says that Domitius promised his men rewards in the form of land-allotments out of his own estates. Dion Cass. XLI 11 mentions that his wide lands were acquired in the time of Sulla's proscriptions.

went over to him, garrison and all. One of the Pompeian commanders was caught, and Caesar let him go free. Caesar was now joined by another (8th) legion, and newly-raised cohorts enough for two legions more, and with them a small body of horse sent by the king[1] of Noricum. He now formed a second camp on the other side of Corfinium. Retreat was no longer open to Domitius, but a letter from Pompey reached him, giving no hope of relief, and urging him to break out while he could and join the rest of their forces in Apulia. Caesar says that he concealed the fact from his men, calling on them to make a stout defence, as Pompey was coming. Meanwhile he made plans for slipping away with a few of his most important companions. His agitation betrayed the truth to the soldiers. Once convinced that he meant to leave them, they seized him, and delivered him and his noble friends, with themselves and the town, to Caesar. Caesar sent for all the persons of quality, senators, military tribunes, knights, councillors from local towns, and so forth, and reproved them for their conduct. Some of them had owed him a good turn. Then he let them go. He even allowed Domitius to take away a sum of about £48,000. The surrendered troops took the military oath to him, and were embodied as part of his own army. He was now in a hurry, for Corfinium had wasted seven days, and he was anxious to prevent Pompey from leaving Italy, or at least to make one more attempt to come to terms.

1215. Pompey had been at Luceria, able to effect nothing for want of trustworthy forces. There and at other Pompeian centres were parties of Roman nobles sneering and grumbling and getting in the way. The abandonment of Corfinium and the precious nobles in it filled them with fury. But Pompey had not acted lightly, and the loss of troops that he believed more trusty than his own was surely a great blow. There was nothing now to be done but to carry out at once the contemplated retreat to Brundisium. He called in all his forces save those despatched to Sardinia Sicily and Africa, and concentrated at that port before Caesar could reach him. His fleet was ready. Caesar followed by forced marches. On the way he caught one of Pompey's officers, through whom[2] he made one more attempt to open negotiations, in particular renewing his request for a personal interview. But the consuls and the bulk of the army had already sailed for Dyrrachium, and a repeated message only drew from Pompey the answer that in the absence of the consuls he could not treat for peace. Nor was this a mere evasion. Pompey's position

[1] See § 1187.
[2] So Caesar *civ.* I 24, 26. Another version in Cic. *ad Att.* IX 13a, where Pompey appears as making the first move.

depended on the adhesion of the republican nobles, jealous of him and of each other. Some were for war at all costs, rather from selfish than patriotic motives, while the more genuine patriots viewed him with mistrust as no less a potential autocrat[1] than Caesar himself. In short, it was only his submission to their interference that made him preferable to his rival. Caesar now tried to block the harbour-mouth so as to prevent the departure of Pompey with the rest of his force. In this attempt he failed, and had to be content with occupying Brundisium. Henceforth it was a Caesarian port, but the difficulty remained that ships were hard to procure, while fleets drawn from Egypt and Phoenicia, from Asia Minor and the islands, even from the Euxine, bore to Pompey the stores of the East and made him master of the sea. Italy had been left to its fate. Of the apathy of the country towns, whose burgesses in general cared for nothing[2] but their material interests, of the return of various persons of quality to Rome, disgusted with the Pompeians and reassured by Caesar's clemency, we hear in Cicero's letters. We learn also that the Pompeians already talked of starving Rome into submission. They held Sardinia Sicily Africa and the East, and could cut off supplies by sea. And when their turn came, and they recovered Italy, they promised themselves a recompense for present hardships in proscriptions and plunder of those who had stayed behind. Cicero himself knew not whether to go or stay. He knew that he would be wretched and useless in Epirus, but he was little better off at home. Caesar was all courtesy, writing himself and through Balbus to flatter the poor man and, if possible, to tempt him to return to Rome, where his presence would raise the standard of respectability. But the unhappy orator was more moved by the fear of what would be said of him in the Pompeian camp, where the 'best men' were already speaking ill of his absence. So he resisted blandishments, and waited about, lictors bay-leaves and all, till he saw a chance of following what he felt to be the call of honour. He even received[3] Caesar himself at Formiae on the 28th March, and stood firm on his principles in the face of Caesar's charm and Caesar's power. To forestall matters, he was a moral asset to either side, so Caesar had him watched[4], and he did not escape from Italy till June.

1216. Caesar did not dally in Brundisium ; he secured the town and gave orders for ships to be gradually collected there, and set out on his way to Rome. To recover the nearer sources of corn-supply was an urgent need. He sent out his lieutenants Valerius and Curio,

---

[1] See Cic. *ad Att.* x 7 § 1, 8 § 5.
[2] Cic. *ad Att.* VIII 13 § 2, 16 § 1.   [3] Cic. *ad Att.* IX 18.
[4] See Antony's warning letter, Cic. *ad Att.* x 8a, with Cic.'s own words x 8 § 10, and 10 §§ 1, 2, 3, 12 §§ 1, 2.

the former to Sardinia with one legion, the latter to Sicily with two in addition to the two formed out of the men taken at Corfinium and already despatched to the island. Curio was to rank as propraetor, and was instructed to invade Africa so soon as he had recovered Sicily. The position of Caesar was now this. He could not follow Pompey and his raw army to Epirus, but he lay between him and his seasoned army in Spain. The force landed at Dyrrachium would not be fit to fight for many a day. The Spanish legions were a real danger, and it would not do to leave them unbroken on his rear. He resolved to deal with them first, both for this reason and because the occupation of Spain would tend to promote continued quiet in Gaul. For the present he gave his remaining legions a short rest and went on to make arrangements at Rome. This duty had been forced upon him by the flight of his opponents. He could not stay at the centre himself, and materials for constructing a provisional government were hard to find. He arrived outside the city at the beginning of April. His tribunes, Antony and Q. Cassius, called together the remaining Senators, and he addressed them, defending his own conduct and impugning that of the Pompeians. He invited them to cooperate in carrying on the government, but explained that, in case they were afraid to bear a part, he would relieve them of the burden. Pompey was known to have said that to open negotiations was a proof of fear. Such was not his view. He proposed to send envoys to treat with Pompey: he felt strong enough to stand on justice and right. This was all very fine, but no envoys could be found willing to go. Men feared the parting threats of Pompey; another story says that they doubted the sincerity of Caesar. Days were wasted in futile nominations and refusals. Meanwhile he procured a vote granting him the reserve fund. But there were signs of obstruction. In particular, the tribune L. Metellus blocked the treasury door, and Caesar, sorely against his will, was compelled to take the money (about £3,450,000, it is said,) by force. This was an unpopular act, and he was annoyed[1] to mark signs of public discontent. So he hurried his departure. He left M. Aemilius Lepidus, a weak-kneed praetor who had returned to Rome, in charge of the city as city-prefect[2], and Antony as propraetor to command the troops in Italy. That he went away in anger seems certain; it was probably the knowledge of their master's irritation that led Curio and Caelius to speak and write in a menacing strain[3] about this time.

[1] Cic. *ad Att.* X 4 § 8, 8 § 6, *fam.* VIII 16 § 1.

[2] This was irregular, for only the consul or dictator had this old regal power of leaving such a deputy in his absence. Caesar was only proconsul.

[3] See Cic. *ad Att.* X 4 § 8, *fam.* VIII 16, and Caesar's own polite but serious letter, *Att.* X 8 b.

1217. A further annoyance awaited him on the way to Spain. The Greek city of Massalia, Rome's ancient and valuable ally, not only enjoyed freedom but ruled a considerable stretch of territory, to which Roman generals, among them both Pompey and Caesar, had in recent times made additions. The trade-connexions of the city were wide, and its influence in Gaul considerable. For a Roman commander invading Spain it was important to have a friendly Massalia at his back. For Caesar, to whom a quiet Gaul was a prime necessity, its good will was indispensable. But the Massaliots did not want to be drawn into a Roman civil war, and they declared themselves neutral. Neutrality however was, as usual, not the same as impartiality. Their leading men had been approached in the Pompeian interest, not without success. While professing neutrality, the government was embodying troops, collecting stores, and keeping the armouries and dockyards busy with preparations for the contingency of war. When Caesar appeared, they closed their gates and were deaf to his persuasions. But when Domitius, the hero of Corfinium, came with a small flotilla raised and manned on the Etrurian coast, they not only admitted him but gave him the command of their own forces. After this Caesar could only accept the challenge. He gave orders for galleys to be built at Arelate on the Rhone and the preparations for a siege to be made. He could not wait himself, so he left C. Trebonius to direct the operations in general, with D. Brutus, the naval hero of the Gallic war, in command of the fleet. Another of his tried lieutenants, C. Fabius, was sent forward to force the passage of the Pyrenees, and by the time Caesar had made all his arrangements at Massalia the way was open into Spain. Pompey, no doubt for good reasons, had divided that country into three[1] districts, each under a *legatus*. L. Afranius in the Hither Spain had three legions, M. Petreius in the West (Lusitania etc.) and M. Terentius Varro in the South had two each. The three had agreed on a common plan. Varro was to undertake the charge of Petreius' district as well as his own, that is, the whole of the Further Spain, while Petreius marched to join Afranius in the North. They had raised a large force among the natives, and occupied a strong position at Ilerda on the river Sicoris, a tributary of the Iber or Iberus (Ebro), where they awaited the coming of Caesar. When the two armies faced each other at Ilerda in the latter part of June they seem to have been fairly matched in effective strength. Nor were the Pompeian generals lacking in skill, but they were lieutenants responsible[2] to a distant chief. They evidently felt that their first business was not to

[1] A point to be noted, for this precedent was followed in the organization of Augustus.
[2] See the case of Varro, Caesar *civ.* II 17 § 2.

be beaten. Caesar was a principal, and ready to take any risk; nothing but a complete victory was of any use to him. Accordingly the operations on the two sides bore the stamp of a profound moral difference. Caesar was repulsed with loss in his first attack, then cut off by floods which broke his bridges and brought him to great extremities by the failure of supplies, and his only hope lay in the safe arrival of a convoy from Gaul, which the enemy were preparing to intercept. The manual skill of his handy men, often tried in Gaul, enabled him to build a new bridge by a piece of clever engineering. He was now able to save his own convoy and to harass the Pompeian foragers, and the inner difference of temper in two good armies was very soon exposed. There had been talk[1] of Pompey's being on the way to Spain, coming with legions by way of Mauretania. Wild fiction enough, it can have served little purpose, and now it was followed by a painful truth; some of the native communities were transferring their allegiance to Caesar. As the floods abated Caesar renewed his attacks. The Pompeians were deserted by some of their Spanish troops. They were not able to face the moral strain of this turn of affairs, so resolved to fall back upon central Spain, where the name of Pompey was great as the conqueror of Sertorius. It was now Caesar's object to catch them before they crossed the Ebro, and he won the race. Cut off in a place where they could not find water, they had to surrender. At one point in their retreat Caesar had had them completely at his mercy. To the indignation of his own men, eager to end matters with the sword, he had spared them then. He now, in the presence of both armies, explained that he had been forced into war by the malignity of the Pompeians, and that all he wanted was to make sure that this army of Spain, created to be used against himself, should be used against him no more. He required only that Afranius and Petreius should dismiss their troops on the way back[2] to Italy. All were to go free: no one was to return to Italy as a soldier of Pompey. This was duly carried out, and his grand object was attained. The best Pompeian army had ceased to exist. The men released from a hateful service were witnesses to his power and his clemency in thousands of Italian homes. No shedding of blood could have won him so great an advantage in the eyes of the Roman world as this splendid evidence of self-restraint. So ended a marvellous campaign of only forty days.

[1] Cicero (*ad Att.* x 6) heard a rumour that he was coming by way of Illyricum and Gaul. Cf. x 9 § 1.

[2] Caesar *civ.* I 86, 87, *ad flumen Varum.* The Var was probably at this time the western boundary of Italy or Cisalpine Gaul. The two names were now often confused, for the Cisalpine was felt to be really a part of Italy. See Mommsen in *CIL* v p. 902, Nissen, *Landeskunde* I 76—78, Lucan I 404.

1218.   It remained to deal with Varro.   The whole peninsula must be cleared of Pompeian forces, if Caesar was to be free to attend to other enterprises.   Varro appears in Caesar's story as a man above all things anxious to stand well with the winning side.   The occupation of Italy by Caesar led him to wait passively on events.   The early successes of his two colleagues at Ilerda set him to work making up for past slackness in the Pompeian cause.   To his two legions he added a strong force of local levies, he gathered supplies and raised a fleet, and exacted contributions of money, not even sparing the temple-treasures of Gades.   Cities and individuals suspected of Caesarian leanings were fined or coerced by garrisons.   When he was fully committed to the Pompeian cause, the news of Caesar's victory left him no choice but war.   He resolved to concentrate upon Gades and make a stout resistance with his back to the sea.   But Caesar was too quick for him.   Sending Q. Cassius[1] with two legions into Further Spain, he himself with a flying column made a dash upon Corduba, the chief Roman centre in the South.   Messengers hurried about the country with a notice summoning all the chief men of the local communities to meet him in that city.   The fabric of Pompeian authority at once began to collapse.   In Further Spain, where Caesar himself had served years before, his name was perhaps greater than that of Pompey.   His summons was obeyed.   Towns went over to him, and closed their gates against Varro or drove out the garrisons.   Even Gades declared for him, and its garrison held the city for Caesar.   One of Varro's two legions, which had been raised in the province, deserted him, and he was compelled to surrender.   Caesar quickly compensated those who had suffered loss for his sake, visited Gades and restored the temple-treasures, and left Cassius with four legions in charge of the province.   From Gades he returned by sea to Tarraco, the chief city of the Hither Spain, where he received deputations from the communities of that province.   He then proceeded by land to Massalia, where his presence was needed.   Here he heard of an event brought about by the news of Ilerda.   He had been named dictator by M. Lepidus, the praetor in charge at Rome.   A law had been carried to legalize[2] the procedure, which was of course quite irregular. But irregularities had long ceased to be surprising: it was a sign of the times.

1219.   The siege of Massalia had dragged on for three or four months, for it was now about the 9th September.   The defence had been most obstinate.   Great feats of engineering had been performed to little purpose.   Two naval actions had been fought, both to the

---

[1] This Cassius was a tribune and had no business to be out of Rome.
[2] Compare the nomination of Sulla by an Interrex.   See Cic. *ad Att.* IX 15 § 2.

advantage of the Romans, a notable fact, from which we may draw conclusions as to the state of fleets in this period, and the conditions[1] of maritime war.   Surrender was finally enforced by exhaustion and despair, for the besieged were suffering from pestilence and famine, and all hope of relief was gone.   Domitius got away to sea in a storm and once more escaped.   The Massaliots had to give up arms and ships, and pay a fine of money.   Caesar left them 'free,' that is, still enjoying their aristocratic Greek constitution and Greek laws.   At a later time he took away[2] most of their dependent territory.   The famous city sank into a quiet old age, as a centre of literary culture and pleasant residence.   For the present its brisk commercial life died down: Narbo, its Roman rival, was the chief trading port of southern Gaul[3] in the time of Augustus.   Caesar left two legions at Massalia and sent on the rest into Italy, and himself started for Rome.   Before we follow him there, we must pause a moment to consider how his lieutenants had fared in their enterprises for the capture of the corn-provinces.   Valerius had no trouble in Sardinia.   The Pompeian M. Cotta, expelled from the chief town by a popular rising, fled to Africa. In Sicily the Pompeian cause was represented by Cato, who had lately remarried his former wife Marcia, now widowed by the death of Hortensius, and left her for his sphere of duty.   He was doing his best[4] to put the island in a state of defence, raising troops in southern Italy to support the local levies, but he had no force at all fit to face the legions of Curio.   He would not shed blood for nothing, and the cause awoke no enthusiasm in Sicily, so he withdrew to Dyrrachium, cursing the folly of rushing into war unprepared.   Henceforth, says Plutarch, he was in favour of prolonging it, hoping that delay might lead to an accommodation and spare the Roman world much needless misery.   Sicily thus fell into the hands of Curio towards the end of April.   He appears to have spent about three months in the province, and to have set out for Africa in August, taking with him only the two doubtful legions pressed into Caesar's service after Corfinium, and a small body of horse.   P. Attius Varus, who commanded for the Pompeians in Africa, had but a weak force.   In making light of this adversary Curio was either ignorant or heedless of the important fact that behind him was the bitterly hostile power of the Numidian king. Juba was bound to Pompey as the patron of his father, and he had a special grudge against Curio[5] for having as tribune proposed to annex the kingdom.   This oversight was Curio's ruin.   Led on by some

---

[1] See note on § 245.   [2] See Marquardt *Stvw.* I 263.   [3] Strabo IV I § 12.
[4] He was not supported by the Pompeian fleet, of which Curio was reasonably afraid.   See Cic. *ad Att.* X 4 § 9, 7 § 3.
[5] Perhaps an old one against Caesar also.   See Suet. *Jul.* 71.

early successes against Varus, and further elated by good news from Spain, he ventured to advance some miles from his camp to attack what he believed to be only a part of the Numidian army. When the Romans were exhausted by heat and thirst, they were assailed and destroyed by the barbarian host. Even of the guard left in the camp few escaped to Sicily. Most of them surrendered to Varus, but Juba made him give them up, and killed them in cold blood, all but a few saved as specimens. By his force of character Curio had retained the wavering allegiance of his troops; by his rashness he lost them, and his own life too. Caesar does not omit to tell us that Juba lorded it over the Romans in Utica on the strength of his victory. He means[1] that the first result of a Caesarian defeat was the abasement of Roman citizens before a barbarian king.

1220. On his way to Rome Caesar had to deal with a mutiny. The ninth legion, which had fought well and sustained losses in Spain, were discontented, and broke out on reaching Placentia. Caesar was always indulgent to his men when not actually in face of an enemy, and it seems that the ninth were indignant at not being allowed to plunder or maltreat civilians. Here was a danger that must be met before the infection spread, and he met it boldly. The most probable account (we have none from himself) is that he gave them their discharge. This was not what they wanted, and they begged him to recall his decision. This he would only do on their delivering up the ringleaders, of whom he selected one in ten by lot, and put them to death. So discipline was restored, and the faithful ninth were destined to bear many a burden yet in Caesar's service. At Rome the new dictator assumed his office, but held it only 11 days. He meant to be consul in the coming year (48), and to conduct the next campaign as chief magistrate of Rome, shifting the legitimate authority, whatever that might be worth, from the side of Pompey to his own. He held the consular election and returned himself with P. Servilius Vatia Isauricus as his colleague. He also procured the election of his own men to the other offices; among the praetors was M. Caelius. He also filled up the vacancies in the sacred colleges, and held the Latin Festival, which the consuls in their hurried flight had neglected to do. He had for some time intended to redress the wrongs of those who had suffered for reasons of party-politics or under unjust laws. To do this in due order required the passing of new laws, for which purpose he had obedient tribunes at disposal. A law for restoring to the sons of Sulla's victims the right to stand for public office had perhaps been carried by Antony earlier in the year, after Caesar's flying visit to Rome in April. Another was now

---

[1] That the point was a telling one is shewn by Cic. *ad Att.* XI 7 § 3.

passed restoring all their rights to persons condemned under the Pompeian[1] laws of 52, the arrangements for the choice of jurors having from Caesar's point of view been unfair, and the trials held under the guard of Pompey's soldiers. Thus these, and possibly some few others likely to be useful, were relieved. But no general[2] restoration of exiles took place. Other laws dealt with the extension of the franchise, redeeming Caesar's promises both to the Transpadane 'Latins' and to the people of Gades in Spain. The whole Cisalpine was now made Roman, but still remained technically a Province. To meet various doubtful questions of jurisdiction arising out of this peculiar position, a further law[3] was probably put in preparation at this time and passed later, perhaps in Caesar's absence, containing suitable regulations. It may be that a measure for annexing the forfeited territory of Massalia was passed now or in the next year. A more urgent matter was the provision[4] of a temporary act for the relief of debtors and restoration of credit. The selling value of real property had fallen greatly in consequence of the civil war. Creditors were calling in their money, and unwilling to lend, while encumbered landlords could neither raise new loans nor discharge existing debts by selling their estates. There was also wild talk of a general cancelling of debts, which encouraged debtors to evade immediate payment. Caesar had no intention of the kind. His object was not to alarm the capitalists and discourage investment, but to get money back into circulation in the usual course as soon as possible. At the same time he must do something for the debtors: circumstances made a compromise necessary. He ordained[5] that interest already paid should be deducted from the capital, a concession which required the creditor to sacrifice about 25°/₀ of the sum lent. Moreover, to meet the scarcity of ready money, the creditor was compelled to accept the surrender of the debtor's estate in discharge of the debt so reduced. Machinery was provided for appointment of arbitrators empowered to fix the value at which the creditor in any particular case was bound to accept the debtor's goods. The valuation was to be the estimated selling price according to the state of the market before the war. It is said that Caesar went even further in his anxiety to bring money into circulation, by reviving an old statutory limitation of the amount (between £500 and £600) that a man might lawfully keep by him in specie. The motive is thus analysed—either pay-

[1] Caesar *civ.* III 1 § 4. See Cic. *ad Att.* X 4 § 8.   [2] Lange *RA* III 420.

[3] For this law, part of which is still preserved (*lex Rubria*), see Bruns, *Fontes* p. 91.

[4] Illustrated by Cic. *ad Att.* X 11, 15 § 4.

[5] Caesar, *civ.* III 1, 20, says *constituit*, Sueton. *Jul.* 42 *decrevit*, Cicero *de off.* II § 84 *perfecit*. See also Appian *civ.* II 48, Plut. *Caes.* 37, Dion Cass. XLI 37, 38.

ments in cash would be stimulated, or at least the holders of ready
money would be discovered, and induced by the risks of hoarding to
prefer investment. This move, it is added, was a popular one, and
the mob urged him to offer rewards to slaves for betraying their
masters' hoards. The cry served Caesar's turn (was it got up for the
purpose?), for he took the opportunity of repudiating with horror the
notion that he would ever place a citizen at the mercy of a slave-
informer. This sounds like a cheap and dramatic means of reassuring
the moneyed men, whom he did not want to frighten. What with the
recovery of $75°/_o$ of their capital, the total loss of which had been a
possible contingency, and the openings for investment in a time of
depression, we may surmise that these gentry were in a fair way to
emerge from the financial crisis without serious loss. As to the form
in which Caesar's present remedy was applied, Dion Cassius speaks of
a law. Appian, Plutarch, and the Latin writers, Caesar, Cicero,
Suetonius, do not. It may be that during his 11 days dictatorship he
issued an edict to the effect described, and afterwards (in 48, when
consul) had a statute passed to confirm and complete the work.
There was in later times a *lex Julia*[1] governing the discharge of
obligations by the transfer of the debtor's estate to the creditor, a
process called *cessio bonorum*. Whether the statute was due to Julius
Caesar or to Augustus, this important conception seems to have
found its way into the legal system through the remedial action of
Caesar at this time.

1221. Before leaving Rome, Caesar saw to the appointment of
new governors to the provinces in his power. He caused the Senate
to vote him some wide general powers when he ceased to be dictator
and was not yet consul, and further to make a declaration in reference
to African affairs. The Mauretanian chiefs Bocchus and Bogud were
honoured with the title of kings. They were meant to hold in check
Juba of Numidia, who was declared a public enemy. The Pompeians
had some excuse for regarding Caesar's Senate[2] as a mere Rump. As
the news from Spain had varied, men of Pompeian leanings had
ventured to shew their colours or had slipped away to Epirus. Those
now left could only register Caesar's will. Piso his father-in-law had
thought better of his flight and returned to Rome. He was all for
peace even now, but Servilius the consul-elect, who was to be at the
head of affairs during Caesar's absence, was for war. Caesar set out
for Brundisium in December. The prospect before him was not all
bright. Some of his twelve legions were already at the port, ready to
embark, the rest near by. He had a strong mounted force of Gauls

---

[1] Mentioned by Gaius III § 78, see Poste p. 347.
[2] *consessus senatorum* Cicero called it in April 49. *ad Att.* X 1 § 2, *fam.* IV 1 § 1.

(probably including Germans), but surely not 10,000 in number as texts of Appian say. But the ranks of his legions were thin. Losses in the West, the long exhausting march, exposure to autumnal malaria[1] in the fever-stricken Apulian coast-lands, all had been at work. The strength of his legions seems to have been in general about 3000 men. Nor had he enough ships to transport the whole army at once. At least two trips would be necessary, and the Pompeians were in great strength at sea. A chance success during the summer had cheered them. At the head of the Adriatic two lieutenants of Caesar were operating with a mixed force raised in the border district of Cisalpine Gaul and Illyricum. They were outnumbered and out-generalled by some of Pompey's officers and at last one of them, C. Antonius, brother of Marcus, was hemmed in on the island of Curicta and forced to surrender. His men had to take service with Pompey. One detachment died by each others' swords[2] rather than submit; they seem to have been some of Caesar's own devoted Transpadanes. The Pompeian army was now large, and its chief had had time to train it. He had with him nine legions, and Scipio, who had succeeded Bibulus, was bringing two more from Syria. The ranks were probably well filled, but the men of various quality. One legion, made up of the remains of Cicero's Cilician army, was a real corps of veterans. Three had been raised in the eastern provinces, and contained a number of old soldiers who had settled after their discharge in Macedonia or Crete. Some of these may have left their homes willingly to bear a hand in civil war, but surely not all. Five had been brought from Italy. These had taken their first lesson in the war-school of retreat and abandonment of their native land. Nor had they much to encourage them in the results of war elsewhere. Official reports might magnify the success in Africa; but it can hardly have been possible to conceal the truth, that the fine Pompeian army of Spain had ceased to exist. The prestige of victory was with Caesar's men, desperate fighters, used to bearing[3] cold and hunger as all in the day's work. Moreover Pompey had filled up his ranks by incorporating the men captured at Curicta in the legions, and also a large number raised in the states of Greece. In an enthusiastic army these elements might have been infected with the general feeling, but there is no reason to think that such was the result: the

---

[1] Caes. *civ.* III 2, Cic. *leg. agr.* II § 71.

[2] Livy epit. 110. The passage of Caesar relating this affair is lost, but he alludes to it. See Kraner on Caes. *civ.* III 8. Narrative, probably from Livy, in Lucan IV 402—581, Florus II 13 §§ 30—33.

[3] Caelius to Cicero in March 48 (*fam.* VIII 17) *nostri valde depugnare et facile algere et esurire consuerunt.*

moral temperature was too lukewarm.   On the other hand his auxiliary forces, foot and horse, bowmen and slingers, mercenaries or contingents furnished by kings and chiefs, were very numerous.   They were drawn from three continents.   Dardani and Macedonians, Bessi and other Thracians, came from Europe.   Asia sent Galatians Cappadocians Syrians and special light troops from Pontus Crete and Commagene.   Africa was strangely represented by a body of Gauls and Germans whom Gabinius had left at Alexandria as a royal bodyguard when he restored the Piper king.   To weld together these motley elements into an army of homogeneous discipline and true soldierly tone was impossible, at least in any time of respite that Caesar was likely to allow.   All were no doubt prepared to lend a hand in completing and enjoying a victory.   Few would doggedly fight on to make good early reverses, or endure the toils and hardships of a long campaign on behalf of a failing cause in which they had no vital interest.

1222.   While Pompey had thus got together great land-forces, and commanded the sea, the Roman magnates at his headquarters were as tiresome as ever.   Some were of course combatants ; he had indeed some Roman cavalry, chiefly made up of young nobles.   But the elder men, posing as the only genuine Senate, brought into camp an unwholesome element of debate.   Cato was not the man to be insubordinate, but he too talked.   We hear of him as persuading[1] Pompey and his council to pass a resolution against plundering provincial cities or killing Romans save in battle ; very pretty sentiments, but not likely to be remembered in case of victory, and a waste of time just when time was most precious.   In June Cicero came to join the company.   He had not been feeling well, and had gone through endless worries connected with the behaviour of his son and nephew, the confinement and poor health of his daughter, his own financial difficulties, doubts as to his own safety and consequent insincere[2] attempts to stand well with both sides, and consciousness that the victory of either side meant the fall of his darling Republic. We may add that he was bursting with suppressed oratory, and need not wonder that he relieved his feelings in sarcastic repartees[3] which raised a laugh but did not promote harmony.   Two are worth quoting. ' You're late in coming.'   ' Late ! nay, soon enough to find nothing

---

[1] Plutarch *Cato Min.* 53, *Pomp.* 65.   In the latter place he calls it a Senate (βουλή).   See the notes of Mommsen *Str.* III 925, 926, who remarks that the establishment of a regular Senate as depicted by Lucan v 7—65 is an invention.   But there is surely much truth in lines 13—14 *docuit populos venerabilis ordo non Magni partes sed Magnum in partibus esse.* See also Kraner on Caes. *civ.* III 16 § 4.

[2] See in particular the letter to Caelius, *fam.* II 16.

[3] Macrobius *Sat.* II 3 §§ 7, 8, Plut. *Cic.* 38.

ready.' And when in reference to Dolabella (who was a Caesarian) Pompey asked 'where's your son-in-law?' the nettled orator retorted 'with your father-in-law.' Life at headquarters was surely not a happy one, and in the background there was the never-ceasing anxiety about money. As more contingents came in, more money was needed, and it was only to be found by wholesale exaction of contributions from all the eastern provinces and client kings. A general squeezing[1] went on under the direction of Pompeian governors, and the demand for ready money at a time when general insecurity had forced up the rate of interest plunged numberless communities into debt. The revenue-farmers of Syria and Asia were required to pay over the sum due for the current year and outstanding arrears : they were also to advance as a loan the estimated valuation for the year following. By what extortions these gentry meant to recoup themselves for this outlay, the wretched provincials knew only too well. Even temple-treasures were not respected, and odd sums such as the balance banked by Cicero at Ephesus were requisitioned for the war-chest.

1223. For the winter of 49—48 Pompey seems to have quartered his army in various places. He was himself for a time in Macedonia, with headquarters at Thessalonica. Even if Caesar had returned from Spain, he was not expected to attempt the passage of the Adriatic till the coming spring. The great Pompeian fleet, distributed in more or less homogeneous squadrons under several officers, with Bibulus in general command, was left to watch the coast. Bibulus, like his chief, seems to have trusted too much to the deterrent perils of winter seafaring, and we must remember that a fair wind from Brundisium meant that, for the time it lasted, the coast about Dyrrachium was a lee shore. Still the position of Pompey was very strong. It ought to have been possible to prevent Caesar from landing in force on the coast of Epirus or Illyria. Unless he succeeded in doing this, he could hardly come to grips with the enemy at all. Once he got a footing, it would be easier for later convoys to join him. If he were prevented, his legions would be demoralized by the unaccustomed delay, and time would be given for the ripening of the discontent of which there were signs[2] in some parts of Italy. But as usual Caesar was too quick for his dull adversaries. On the 4th January 48 the consul sailed from Brundisium, and next day safely disembarked his force, seven thin legions and a few horse, on the coast of Epirus. He sent back his transports to fetch the rest, but Bibulus, now thoroughly roused, went in chase, captured

---

[1] See Caesar *civ*. III 3, 31—33, Tyrrell and Purser *Corr. of Cic.* IV, Introd. p. xlii.

[2] See Tyrrell and Purser IV, Introd. pp. xl, xlii, on the disaffection in Campania and elsewhere.

some 30 vessels, and wreaked his rage on them by burning them crews and all. At this point it is well to bear in mind that the winter was only just beginning. The Roman calendar was in great disorder owing to the pontiffs having lately neglected the needful intercalations. The civil year was about two months behind the solar year, and the 4th January 48 was properly 5th November 49. The naval patrolling of the Adriatic was no easy matter. Besides the landing of Caesar, the Pompeians had been beaten off with loss from Salonae on the Dalmatian coast. Bibulus, zealous but far from strong, did his best. From the naval headquarters at Corcyra to Curicta in the north he kept his squadrons on the alert, and for the present no more troops could reach Caesar. The part of the coast needing to be watched with special care was the stretch from the Acroceraunian headland northwards about as far as Lissus, the part belonging to the province of Macedonia. Caesar's aim was to occupy as much as possible of this coast, thus depriving Pompey of useful positions and Bibulus of some harbours of refuge in the winter weather. After landing, he set out at once for Oricum, which promptly surrendered to him. He was now consul, and the Pompeian officer in command could not induce either the Illyrian garrison or the townsfolk to resist the chief magistrate of Rome. He pushed on to Apollonia, where he was received in the same way. Inland towns soon followed the example of these two seaports. In a few days a large part of Epirus had sent to make submission. It was now a main object if possible to capture Dyrrachium, important both from its harbour and from its being the chief Pompeian depot for all military stores.

1224. Pompey was at this time on his way with a force from Thessalonica to the western seaboard, marching doubtless by the Egnatian road. While crossing the Candavian mountains, not having reached the point where the road forked, he was met by the news of Caesar's landing. The bearer was L. Vibullius Rufus, an officer whom Caesar had caught at Corfinium and again in Spain, and twice spared. He had been entrusted by Caesar with peace-proposals, which as stated by Caesar himself[1] sound sweetly accommodating. But when he reached Corcyra he was in no hurry to push on with his message to Thessalonica. He talked over the proposals with Bibulus and his company, and evidently met with little encouragement. These men were no fools. To make terms with Caesar now would leave him with a moral victory added to a material one. Unless they meant to submit, there was nothing to be done but to fight. While Rufus dallied at Corcyra, Caesar landed, and the situation was

---

[1] Caes. *civ.* III 10.

changed. Rufus posted off with all speed to bear the news to Pompey, but seems to have deferred the mention of Caesar's overtures. Pompey was amazed at Caesar's venture and hurried on his march, hoping to save Apollonia and the other seaports, but heard presently that he was too late. He then turned northwards and by marching day and night was just in time to save Dyrrachium. The alarm betrayed by his hurry was contagious. His local levies mostly slipped away to their homes, and his legions were in so nervous a state that Labienus came forward and renewed his military oath to Pompey, and induced officers and men to do the same. The armies now encamped facing each other with the river Apsus between them. Caesar only* waited for the rest of his forces to take the offensive, but at present there was no chance of a safe passage. He sent over orders to stop Q. Fufius Calenus, who commanded at Brundisium, from attempting it. By good luck the message arrived in time to prevent a step which would probably have led to the destruction of the whole convoy and the ruin of his cause. He was now encamped for the winter close to the enemy, and his chief trouble was to feed his troops. The country was not rich in corn, and supplies could not reach him by sea. But the Pompeian fleet was suffering great hardship in keeping up the winter blockade, being cut off from the land. Even fresh water had to be fetched from Corcyra, and this was not always possible. Their sufferings caused them to propose a conference. Caesar's own account of the matter is that this proposal was taken to imply that something was about to come of the mission of Rufus. He therefore met L. Scribonius Libo (acting for Bibulus), and soon discovered that there was no intention of treating for peace. It was a pretence made to procure a truce and access to the land. So nothing came of their meeting, and cruising in wintry weather soon proved fatal to the ailing Bibulus. No admiral was appointed to succeed him, and the commanders of squadrons acted independently. About this time Rufus broached the subject of his commission to Pompey and his chief advisers. Pompey would have none of it, seeing (what was the truth) that to disband armies and return to Rome now would place him in the position of one restored under Caesar's patronage. Still Caesar did not give up trying to reach an understanding. The men posted along the two sides of the Apsus held bank-to-bank conversations, as soldiers will, under a sort of tacit truce. This practice was so improved upon, that a Caesarian officer artfully appealed to the Pompeians to make an end of this horrible war by clamouring for giving a hearing to Caesar's proposals. It was found necessary to send Labienus to repudiate all notion of making terms, and to break up this informal conference by force. Such is the tale of Caesar.

1225. So the armies faced each other, waiting for the spring. In Italy Caesar's well-chosen colleagues, the consul Servilius and the city praetor C. Trebonius, managed affairs wisely. The latter carried out the new rules about debts with good sense and tact. But the praetor M. Caelius[1] was utterly disgusted to see things going so smoothly. Himself an embarrassed man, he had hoped for a general cancelling of debts, and wanted to find an outlet for his irregular energies in the situation that would be created by such a stroke of 'popular' policy. It seems to have been in the early spring that he began a course of demagogic action. He acted like a madman in the absence of his keeper. First, he publicly offered help to any who might invoke it, against the decisions of the city praetor. This was possible under the Roman system, for the division of spheres of duty did not in strict law extinguish the general power belonging to all colleagues. It was only custom that restrained the extreme application of the doctrine of *par potestas*. But all parties were so well satisfied with the rules as administered by Trebonius, that nobody would turn for help to a man distrusted like Caelius. He next gave notice of a bill to postpone payment of debts and abolish the claim for interest. This did not find favour, even with debtors; for the terms were thought less generous than Caesar's rule. He was becoming a nuisance, and the magistrates, headed by Servilius, set themselves against him. He then dropped the bill, and gave notice of two bills of a more extreme character, one to remit all rents of dwellings for the current year, the other a simple proposal for cancelling debts. At last he got together some sort of following, and drove Trebonius from the seat of justice at the head of a band of roughs. The Senate now authorized the consul to employ his superior power in preventing Caelius from taking any part in state affairs. Servilius made short work with him; resistance and buffoonery were of no avail. The man was now desperate. He sent for the reckless Milo. They were old friends, and had probably met lately at Massalia. Caesar had wisely not recalled Milo from exile. He came at the call of Caelius, and the pair set out for southern Italy, where they tried to rouse slaves and others in a sort of brigand rising. Both very soon perished. Sufficient precautions had been taken to render such wild enterprises hopeless. So ended two characteristic figures of the revolutionary age, and the Caesarian grasp of Italy was not loosened.

1226. Meanwhile the months went by, and Caesar could not afford to wait. Yet he was not strong enough to take the offensive with his present force. The Pompeians outnumbered him greatly,

---

[1] For the story of Caelius see his letter to Cicero, *fam.* VIII 17, Caesar *civ.* III 20—22, Velleius II 68, Dion Cass. XLII 22—25, Quintilian VI 3 § 25, X 1 § 115.

and Scipio with another army was coming to join them from the East. But his legions at Brundisium could not or did not come, and the abatement of the winter storms was likely to favour the Pompeian cruisers, who were able to use oars, while the Caesarian transports were merchant craft depending on sails and only effective in a breeze. At one time Libo had the happy thought that to blockade them in Brundisium would be simpler than to wait for them off the Illyrian coast. He seized the island at the mouth of the harbour, and for a moment held them in check. But Antony, who was now with Fufius and commanding the troops, managed to make his position untenable. Libo had to go, and the port was open once more. Still Antony did not come, and Caesar's situation was becoming perilous. He sent urgent orders that the passage was to be attempted with the first fair wind. He even tried to cross the Adriatic in an open boat[1] and fetch the legions himself, but was driven back by foul weather. At last about the beginning of April Antony put to sea with four legions (3 of veterans) and 800 horse. Two legions were left behind for want of ship-room. All now depended on the chapter of accidents, and the stars in their courses fought for Caesar. Becalmed off the Illyrian coast, the convoy seemed at the mercy of the Pompeian fleet, when a breeze sprang up and enabled them to make the harbour of Nymphaeum to the north of Dyrrachium. Only one shipload of recruits fell into the hands of the Pompeians, who promised to spare their lives and put them to death. Caesar records that a squadron of Rhodian ships chasing his transports were caught in a squall and wrecked on a shore commanded by his forces. His men rescued the survivors, and he set them free to make their way home. Antony sent back most of his ships to Brundisium to fetch the remaining troops, but this third trip was never made. The position was now this. Pompey, who had been a year and more east of the Adriatic without effecting anything remarkable, found himself between Antony on the north and Caesar on the south. His business was to prevent their junction ; if possible, to destroy Antony before Caesar could come up. Being able to move on inner lines, he had a good chance of doing this, and nearly did. But Antony, warned by friendly natives, stuck to his camp, and next day Caesar joined him. Pompey fell back to a position near Dyrrachium, and the first move in the game was won by Caesar.

1227. Caesar had now 11 legions and apparently about 1400 horse.

[1] This was the famous occasion when he is said to have cheered the boatman by telling him 'it's Caesar you've got on board.' The story, told by Valerius Maximus, Suetonius, Florus, Plutarch, Appian, Dion, and Lucan, seems to be true in the main, though highly coloured by Caesarian tradition. Caesar characteristically says nothing of it.

He was chiefly troubled by the scarcity of supplies. His next step was to detach three small forces, one in response to an invitation from Aetolia, another to back up his partisans in Thessaly, the third and largest to operate in Macedonia (where he had some prospect of local support) to prevent Scipio from joining Pompey. The two commanders of the smaller bodies were specially instructed to have an eye to procuring corn. Of the fortunes of these detachments we need only note that Scipio was kept employed and was not able to effect a junction with Pompey at Dyrrachium. The work of the next three or four months in the main theatre of war was one of the most extraordinary episodes recorded in military history. The Pompeian fleet began by attacking the ports of Oricum and Lissus : at both places Caesar had a few ships insufficiently guarded, which they either burnt or captured. Caesar was now cut off from Italy more completely than ever. He marched against Pompey, but could not force him to give battle. Next he contrived by a ruse to get between Pompey and Dyrrachium. He was not able to take the town, and an attempt made soon after to get in by night, with the aid of treachery from within, miscarried utterly. Pompey now took up a position near the town to the south-east. He could communicate with it freely by sea, and supplies could reach him. His adversary was in dreadful straits, and in spite of persistent efforts could hardly feed his men. Caesar now took the astounding resolution of blockading a well-fed army with a starving one. He began to build redoubts on the higher ground inland from Pompey's camp, and to connect them with a line of rampart. By carrying these works round to the sea on Pompey's further side he would hem him in on a small piece of coast. Then Pompey could no longer send out parties to intercept his provision-trains, and would himself soon run short of forage for his horses. Moreover he would appear to all the world to be afraid of fighting, and this would destroy his prestige, the prestige which had placed at his disposal the resources of the East. As Pompey was not prepared to stop the progress of the works by giving battle, his only course was to extend his own lines so far that the task of surrounding them would be very difficult, if not impossible, for Caesar with his smaller number of men. If it be true that Caesar was eventually forced to extend his circuit over a distance of about 14 English miles, the enterprise was indeed a marvellous one, for he had only about 22,000 men. He lays great stress on their cheerful endurance and firm resolve not to relax their grip of the Pompeian army. But the venture was in truth a desperate one. Even a second-rate army under a general who had seen his best days was not to be penned up like this by a smaller army for an indefinite time. Only such a man as Caesar would dare to run such a risk as was incurred by the hungry veterans who built and manned these long-drawn lines. The food of his men consisted mainly of roots and flesh; corn, the regular diet of the Roman soldier, was very scarce. But the year wore on, and there was some hope in the crops of the coming season. Meanwhile they were better off than their opponents in respect of water-supply. Caesar contrived to divert or waste the streams that flowed down to the Pompeian camp, and the wells dug to meet the necessities of the Pompeians were inconvenient, liable to dry up, and probably unwholesome. The health of their well-fed army was not all that could be wished, and the failure of their forage-supplies played havoc with their baggage-animals. Even the cavalry horses were in bad condition, and the carcases of dead beasts were noisome.

1228. We need not follow the details of the combats that took place from time to time, as the Pompeians tried to stop the extension of Caesar's lines or to pierce them at various points. Great feats of valour were performed. We hear of 120 holes being found in a centurion's shield, and 30,000 arrows being picked up in a Caesarian redoubt, after one of these fights. On the whole the men of Avaricum Alesia and Ilerda held their ground, however great the odds against which they had to contend at any point. The moral effect of the blockade was beginning to tell in various ways. A Caesarian officer with a small detached force found no difficulty in winning the adhesion of Thebes and other cities of central Greece, whatever it might be worth. Caesar even tried to open negotiations with Scipio, who was now in Macedonia. How far this move was seriously meant, we may doubt; he tells us that his emissary was at first well received, but presently dismissed, Favonius (Cato's friend) having intervened to stiffen the resolution of Scipio. An attempt to provoke Pompey into giving battle failed owing to his caution. Like his lieutenants at Ilerda, he was bent upon avoiding defeat. At this time he was particularly concerned to keep his cavalry efficient, and had found an outlet to some fresh grazing-ground. This Caesar discovered, and blocked the way, and the state of Pompey's horses became so pitiable that something had to be done. For to take the field without a mounted force was out of the question, all the more as he had to deal with an active enemy, and his legions had at present no experience of success. At this critical juncture he received unexpected aid. With Caesar's cavalry were two Gaulish officers, men of good family, who had long served under him and had been rewarded for good service. They were charged with cheating their men of pay and drawing pay for more men than were in the ranks. Caesar took no notice of the matter in public, but privately reprimanded them. The touchy Celts sulked, and resolved to desert, which they presently did, taking with them some other Gauls. Desertion from Caesar was a new thing, and they were welcomed. From these pilferers Pompey got the information that on Caesar's left, where the southern end of his lines abutted on the sea, the works were still in an incomplete state, quite unfit to resist a serious attack. He laid his plans with skill, delivered a sudden assault at daybreak, carried the unfinished works, and occupied a position beyond the line. Later in the day Caesar brought up more troops and tried to recover his lost ground. But Pompey's men were now flushed with the morning's victory, and the attempt to retrieve his failure only involved Caesar in downright defeat. Some of his troops lost their way in the confusion, and, when rout set in, the sight of their comrades in disordered flight caused the veterans of Gaul to turn and run. Pompey came up and completed their discomfiture, but did not follow up his success as he might have done by a more general attack. It was said that he feared an ambuscade; Caesar, who rallied his own men as best he could, remarked afterwards that if Pompey had known his business he might then and there have ended the war.

1229.   One thing at least was clear; the investment was broken, for the lines that had taken months to construct could no longer be held with advantage or safety. It seemed that all those efforts had been wasted. Caesar had lost about 1000 valuable men, and to all appearance he was a beaten man, whose destruction was only a question of time. It was just this persuasion that led the Pompeians to their doom. Pompey's young troops now fancied themselves invincible, and the noble gentlemen at his headquarters were fatally elated. Henceforth the caution of Pompey took a different colour in their eyes: if he was loth to give battle, he was not credited with judicious strategy, but with reluctance to end the war and descend from his position of supreme command. The general assurance of final victory seems to have been shared by the renegade Labienus, who proved his devotion to his new cause by murdering some of his old comrades who had been taken prisoners. Things were very different in Caesar's camp. He tells us himself of the rage of his men, which shewed itself in a more than ordinary devotion to duty and a grim determination to wipe out their disgrace. Later writers tell us that they even begged for military punishment. Caesar knew better than to stay and offer battle now. He was lenient but reproachful. His object was to let them cool down in new surroundings and recover their shattered nerve. So, while the Pompeians were rejoicing, and writing letters to announce their success abroad, he made his plans and withdrew his army in perfect order. Pursuit was at first attempted, but foiled, and soon given up. To decide upon the next strategic move was now an urgent matter, but for Pompey the decision was complicated by considerations of a political rather than strategic character. There had been talk of returning to Italy and seizing once more the control of the centre of government. This would mean the recovery of a moral advantage in the eyes of the world, and Caesar would not be able to prevent it. It might well mean also the recovery of Gaul and Spain. But it would certainly mean the abandonment of Scipio, and Pompey knew that to leave Scipio to be crushed by Caesar would damage his own reputation among the Roman nobles. Caesar also had to think of the safety of his lieutenant Cn. Domitius Calvinus, who was holding Scipio in check; but he was already master of Italy, and unencumbered by aristocratic criticism. He resolved to leave small garrisons at Apollonia Lissus and Oricum, and to march inland to join Calvinus. He guessed that by threatening Scipio he would draw Pompey also away from the coast into regions where food abounded, and hoped to force him to give battle on equal terms. He tells us that, if after all Pompey did make for Italy, he meant to come round upon him by way of Illyricum, picking up Calvinus (and of course crushing Scipio) to begin with. To this last desperate alternative he was not driven, for Pompey decided to join Scipio. Thus both main armies moved inland to join secondary forces, and both were in a hurry. But Pompey was able to use the Egnatian road, while Caesar, having to make a detour to Apollonia, was compelled to march by rude tracks through the great Pindus range and make for Thessaly.

1230. Calvinus had a near escape. Knowing nothing of the sudden change of plans, he had just moved to a place on the Egnatian road, right in the line of Pompey's advance. But his scouts fell in with some of Pompey's men, and from certain Gauls learnt the main facts. Calvinus hastened away southwards just in time, and got into touch with Caesar in the western corner of Thessaly. Caesar's march had not been made easier by the change of behaviour on the part of the people through whose country he passed. Exaggerated accounts of his defeat had made them unfriendly. But he got over the mountains at last, and came down upon the Thessalian border town of Gomphi. Here the effect of rumour appeared in the fact that admission was refused him, though some time before this the people had sought his favour. It was necessary to make an example, or other towns would do the same. So he set to work at once, carried the walls by storm, and gave over Gomphi to the fury of his men. A wild orgy followed, accompanied by horrid[1] scenes; but the

[1] Appian *civ.* II 64.

warning served its purpose, for the other Thessalian cities submitted
and were kindly treated, save Larissa. Larissa had been occupied
by Scipio, who waited for Pompey to come up. It was now about
the beginning of August, and Caesar's war-worn veterans refreshed
themselves with the corn and wine of Thessaly. He kept them on
the move, and the army regained its tone. Pompey had it is true
avoided the appearance of running away from Caesar, but his army,
though pleased to be in pursuit, could not be hurried along like their
opponents, who had practically no baggage. Cato had been left with
a force at Dyrrachium. The Stoic patriot hated the war and was
eager to stop the mutual slaughter of Romans at any cost. Now that
the Pompeian nobles felt confident of victory, his presence at the
front was unwelcome. It was even said that Pompey wished to be
rid of so unbending a republican. He was just the man for a position
of trust in the rear. Cicero, sick in body and mind, also did not join
the main army. Pompey's elder son Gnaeus was with the fleet. As
the army made its way to meet Caesar, the evil effects of restored
confidence made themselves felt. The chief himself, a far better
judge than the aristocrats in his company, was bent upon wearing
out his adversary, whose sources of supply must fail sooner or later.
Noble senators were longing to be back in Rome, in their congenial
surroundings of luxury office-seeking and intrigue, and free to take
vengeance[1] on their enemies. They were tired of being subordinate
to a permanent military chief, and Pompey was given the nickname
of Agamemnon. The poor man, clumsy hesitating and greedy of
public admiration from his youth up, was not the man to control
such persons as Domitius (the hero of Corfinium), Favonius (the
understudy of Cato), Lentulus Spinther and Lentulus Crus and many
more, when they clamoured for battle. Labienus the renegade joined
the chorus, declaring that Caesar had scarce any of his veterans left,
and leading the way in vowing 'Death or Victory.' Afranius, who
knew Caesar's quality, and had been for returning to Italy, was
silenced by the imputation of having betrayed his army in Spain.
What chance had a commander-in-chief, whose ruling foible was
a wish to please, surrounded as he was by such a crew as this?

1231.   The armies met in Thessaly near the city of Pharsalus[2].
Pompey had now made up his mind to fight, but some days passed

---

1 See Cicero's evidence, *ad Att.* XI 6 § 2, as to the *crudelitas* shewn in the talk at
headquarters near Dyrrachium.

2 Caesar himself never mentions the name, but only says 'the battle in Thessaly.' From
the other writers we learn that it was Old Pharsalus (*Palaepharsalus*) near which the battle
took place. For the form *Pharsalia* I know no earlier authority than Ovid *met.* XV 823.
See the full discussion of the site of the battle in the *Classical Quarterly* Oct. 1908 by
Mr Rice Holmes.

before he did so. Caesar repeatedly offered battle, and his men were now in the best of spirits. Meanwhile the Pompeian headquarters were a scene of rivalry and intrigues. The nobles were squabbling over the fruits of a victory not yet won. Caesar's place as chief pontiff was a special prize over which there was much brawling, and the fate of Caesarians and neutrals was freely discussed. Pompey explained the tactics by which he proposed to win the presumed victory. He was far stronger than Caesar in numbers, having about 45,000 Roman troops to Caesar's 22,000. Cavalry seem to be included in these numbers; Caesar had about 1000, Pompey about 7000. The proportion of Romans in the mounted ranks is not certain; the mass were probably Gauls or Germans, but Pompey at least had some young Romans of quality. There were evidently foreign bowmen, slingers, and other light troops, at least with Pompey. Pompey well knew that his legionaries were man for man no match for their adversaries in a stand-up fight. His plan was to use his superiority in cavalry to roll up Caesar's right wing, and then in the ensuing disorder to overwhelm the whole with his masses of infantry. It was tactically sound, no doubt; but Caesar had no great difficulty in divining it. He had strengthened his own few horsemen by picked men[1] trained to cooperate with them on foot, and the plan had worked well in practice. He also was prepared to keep a special reserve in hand to deal with this flank attack. Later writers edified their readers by describing the feelings of men as the day of battle drew near. It is not unlikely that it was a time of excitement and strain. Even the dullest wits must have known that the issue about to be decided was no ordinary one. As had been the case just before the outbreak of war, men dreamt strange dreams and saw, or thought they saw, strange phenomena, and drew various inferences as to the probable event. To omit all reference to such things is to ignore the power of superstitious fancy, to which masses of men, particularly soldiers and sailors, were and are prone. The battle took place on the 9th August. Pompey's cavalry, supported by a host of bowmen and slingers, made their expected attack on Caesar's right, drove in his weaker cavalry, and turned to assail the main line in flank. At once Caesar's reserve[2] cohorts, which had been kept out of sight, fell furiously upon the flank of the Pompeian cavalry, and so pressed home the charge that they broke and fled. The well-handled Caesarians had turned the flanking manœuvre back upon the enemy; next they made havoc among the light troops, and finally swung round and fell upon the Pompeian left rear. The Pompeian line now

---

[1] A German practice. See § 1155.

[2] Florus II 13 § 48, probably following Livy, says that these cohorts consisted of Germans.

began to give way, at first in good order, afterwards in confused flight. Caesar did all he could to stop the slaughter of Romans, and received kindly those who surrendered. Pompey left the field early, seeing that the day was lost, and took horse for Larissa when the Caesarians burst into his camp. Of the number of foreign auxiliaries killed no account was taken. Caesar put his own Roman losses at 200 rank and file and 30 centurions, the Pompeian at 15,000 killed[1] and 24,000 prisoners. We need not lay much stress upon doubtful figures. The great Pompeian army no longer existed. Among the ten Pompeian senators who fell was Domitius the hero of Corfinium. In their camp were found various appointments of luxury and great preparations for a feast in honour of the victory on which they had reckoned. The Roman aristocracy had fallen from the seat of power, and had omitted no circumstance that might enhance the tragedy of their defeat.

1232. In the battle of Pharsalus efficiency triumphed over numbers, yet it was not what is called a 'soldiers' battle.' Nor was it in respect of the commanders a victory of the professional over the amateur, for no man of the time was better able to handle an army than Pompey. We may call it the military expression of the coming political change. The one absolute chief, undistracted by irrelevant considerations and irresponsible meddling, could take risks, retrieve errors, and subordinate everything to the attainment of his end, without deference to the wishes of others. The head of an aristocratic clique could only gain a position of equal freedom by the firm suppression of his own supporters, a course for which Pompey was wholly unfitted. So he gave battle, against his own better judgment, and was beaten. The psychological strategy of Caesar in this campaign was based on a thorough understanding of his rival's embarrassments. But the situation created by his victory was from the nature of the case not a simple one. The removal of Pompey would not of itself suffice to put an end to the civil war. The Pompeian cause was ostensibly that of the Republic. Even if Pompey himself had fought his last battle, there were others; and to inspire them there was Cato still at large. If Pompey, though fully aware[2] of the importance of sea-power, had made too little use of his fleets, the sea was still in Pompeian hands, and to prevent the revival of their cause it was surely necessary for Caesar to gain control of the waters without delay. But there were considerations drawing him to another part of his task. The instant pursuit of

---

[1] Perhaps this includes wounded. Plutarch *Pomp.* 72 and Appian *civ.* II. 82 record that Pollio, who was present with Caesar, put the killed at 6000.

[2] See Cicero *ad Att.* X 8 § 4, a notable passage written in May 49.

Pompey seemed most urgent. This led him into the East, involved him in serious complications, and brought him into great danger. This danger surmounted, he had to deal with other eastern matters, in order not to leave the oriental provinces and potentates in any doubt as to their real master. And so time was given for the republican leaders to concentrate their forces in another part of the world and renew the war.

1233. The period, somewhat more than a year, following the battle of Pharsalus, comprises operations of which it is impossible to give a clear and connected account. The war went on in the form of detached conflicts carried on without cooperation or common plan, and we must briefly trace the course of events according to locality. The dispersal of the Pompeian leaders after the battle will give us a starting-point. The wiser of them made their way to Dyrrachium, where Cato was in command and their remaining land-forces were supported by the Adriatic fleet. Others had accompanied or followed Pompey, whose mental balance seems to have been utterly upset by disaster. He fled from Larissa to the Macedonian coast, then to Lesbos, where he met his wife and younger son. With them he sailed to Cilicia and Cyprus, hoping it was said to gain the support of the king of the Parthians. It was indeed a mad scheme, a counsel of despair, and quickly proved impossible. The news of his defeat had preceded him, and the fallen man had no friends. The Roman citizens in Syria gave notice that his party would not be admitted into Antioch, and the same line was taken by Rhodes and other Greek cities. Only one country in the East seemed open to him. Egypt was under the rule of children of the 'Piper' king. Now the restoration of the Piper had been carried out by Gabinius with the connivance of Pompey. Surely the present representatives of an illegitimate dynasty owed their father's patron a good turn. Pompey therefore made for Egypt in hope to secure at least protection, even if he could not win active support. The position there was just now complicated by a dynastic quarrel. Auletes had died in 51, leaving his kingdom to be shared by his elder son, Ptolemy Dionysus, with his elder daughter, who bore one of the names common among the princesses of the Macedonian royal houses, Cleopatra. Both she and her sister Arsinoe were persons of more spirit and character than either of the brothers. This was no new thing at the court of Alexandria, nor was the arrangement by which she became the wife of the brother whose throne she shared. She was now about 20 years of age, clever, masterful, and not inclined to submit to a boy-husband (about 13) or the eunuchs and other creatures of the court who controlled him. They therefore combined against her and drove her out of Egypt. Cleopatra raised an army to effect her restoration by force, and the two armies were facing each other near Pelusium, the fortress by the easternmost mouth of the Nile, at the time when Pompey's vessel appeared off that coast. Pompey sent messengers to claim the young king's protection, and the royal council had at once to decide what to do.

1234. The detailed accounts of the debate on this question may be untrustworthy, but the chief issues are clear enough. The first object of the king's advisers was to keep Egypt free from Roman interference, and themselves in possession of all real power. From this point of view to receive Pompey was impossible. To protect the vanquished was to provoke the victor. Nor was it certain that Pompey would or could remain in the position of a protected guest. The bulk of the Egyptian army consisted of mongrel mercenaries, runaway slaves and ruffians of all sorts, deserters fugitives robbers criminals, to whom the Lagid kingdom in its decay offered an asylum. The need of mutual protection gave them a strong corporate feeling, but they had no national or dynastic loyalty : their allegiance rested on the certainty of license and pay. Beside these there were the remainder of the Roman troops left behind by Gabinius seven years before as a guard for the restored king. Degenerate though they were, these had not wholly forgotten Roman traditions. Some of them had served under Pompey in his eastern wars, and might rally to their old commander if he were received in Egypt. Here was a risk to be avoided. On the other hand a simple refusal to receive Pompey would only shelve the danger for a moment. It would not satisfy Caesar, and would enrage Pompey, who might yet by some turn of fortune come to the front again. The conclusion was that Pompey must be put to death. This would really solve the problem, for it was of course assumed that Caesar would be delighted, and all other difficulties would cease. So a small party, including a Roman who had served as centurion in the pirates' war, were sent in a boat to invite him to land. He had gone too far to be able to refuse, and in the boat they murdered him. His head was cut off to be shewn to Caesar: it is said that a few old adherents gave his body a makeshift funeral. Such was the end of Pompey. He was just 58 years of age. For about 40 years he had been a leading figure in the Roman world ; for most of that time he had been the First Citizen, the man whose consent was generally sought to give effect to public acts. We have traced his career, and from time to time noted the weaknesses that marred it and that now brought it to a pitiful and feeble close. He was at his best in the campaigns of his earlier life, while strung up to the point of efficiency by immediate necessities of war. He had to look facts in the face and act with energy. But when he had earned the name of Great and entered on civil life, he could not keep his greatness in repair. Vanity and jealousy impaired his judgment, wavering and procrastination grew upon him like a disease. He could neither do what was necessary for keeping his primacy, nor endure a rival. So he drifted to ruin, the victim of slovenly delusions. He became a tool in the hands of Caesar, who rose at his expense. His later life was that of a solemn[1] dreamer, fancying that he still held a position which in truth was long since undermined. The civil war pitilessly exposed his weakness. As leader of the Roman aristocrats he was ridiculous, for he was neither their master nor their hero. As champion of the Republic he was equally ridiculous, for sincere republicans like Cato had no trust in his patriotism and self-denial. Mere military skill was not enough for civil war, and Pompey had no other qualification for the post of leader. He had never been a man of genius, and he was now stale. He could neither overcome his difficulties nor profit by his advantages, and the last scene of the tragic failure was of a piece with the rest.

1235. Caesar's decision to make the pursuit of Pompey his first object was doubtless based on what appeared to be good reasons. We can hardly challenge its wisdom. Yet the sequel seems to shew that in some at least of his calculations he was at fault. He certainly did not expect to be detained a whole year in the East, or to be for several months in dire straits at Alexandria. He was not the man deliberately to involve himself in tedious operations not directly bearing upon the civil war, while his real adversaries were recovering strength and hope, and while his cause was being mismanaged[2] in Italy and the West. Truth is, his rashness that succeeded so well against Pompey and the Roman aristocrats, whom he thoroughly understood, was less happily employed in the unfamiliar circumstances of Egypt.

1236. The battle of Pharsalus put an end to resistance in Greece. Athens in particular was pardoned for the sake of her past. As Caesar moved eastwards, he visited the province Asia. Here he left Domitius Calvinus in charge, granted some remission of taxes to the provincials exhausted by the recent exactions of the Pompeians, and hurried on. From reports that reached him he guessed that Pompey would make for Egypt, and accordingly sailed to Alexandria. He

---

[1] The bust at Copenhagen, said to be a portrait of Pompey, is at all events quite in character with what we know of him. A photograph of it is given in Th. Reinach's *Mithridate Eupator* p. 376. It is worth comparing with the Caesar of the British Museum.

[2] For the ill effects of the delay in Egypt see Cic. *ad Att.* XI 16, 17, 18, 25, *ad fam.* XV 15.

had with him only two legions, so reduced by casualties that their joint effective force was only 3200 men, and 800 horse.   He seems to have sailed from Rhodes: ten Rhodian war-ships formed an important part of his little armament.   He confesses that he entered upon this expedition in the belief that no serious opposition was to be expected. But misunderstandings began at once.   The presentation of Pompey's head did not, as was hoped, please him and induce him to refrain from meddling with the affairs of Egypt.   That he was disgusted, and sincerely disappointed at losing the opportunity of sparing his fallen rival, we need not doubt, though such a view would be unintelligible to those who had planned the murder.   To him on the other hand it seemed a natural and proper thing to land at Alexandria as Roman consul, representing the great imperial republic, the patron and protector of the Ptolemies.   His appearance with lictors and military escort roused the indignation of the Alexandrian populace.   Tumults ensued, and secret murders of Roman stragglers.   Things began to look black, for the insufficiency of his present force was rather calculated to provoke than to overawe the mob, and the attitude of the troops on duty in the city was openly menacing.   Still he was not seriously alarmed.   He sent to order some other legions, formed out of the Pompeians taken at Pharsalus, to join him from Asia.   To retreat from his present awkward situation was probably not consistent with his plans.   He gives as his reason for remaining the difficulty of withdrawing in the face of the north-west winds prevailing at this time of year.   But we learn from other[1] sources that he wanted money, and hoped to exact from the present rulers some at least of the large arrears still due from the late king on account of his restoration.   To whom this was due, and how Caesar proposed to claim it, we are not clearly informed ; that he meant to get money is quite likely.   Meanwhile he boldly took up the position that the dynastic dispute in Egypt was a matter for the sovran power to decide.   He called upon Ptolemy and Cleopatra to cease fighting for the crown and submit their differences to his arbitration as consul of Rome.   He pointed out that he was especially interested in the Egyptian question, because the recognition of the late king as rightful ruler and an ally of the Roman people had taken place at the time (59) of his former consulship.   At this point our record is very obscure, but it appears that somehow the young king was induced to place himself in Caesar's hands, and that Cleopatra at some stage in the proceedings presented herself in person.   The imagination of later writers ran riot in descriptions of her visit.   That her charms of person and manner captivated the amorous Roman is not to be

[1] Plutarch *Caes.* 48, Dion Cass. XLII 9.

doubted. He tried hard to find a way of settling the differences between her and her brother. The will of the late king was to be put in force. That is, Cleopatra was to be restored to an equal share of power with Ptolemy. It is even alleged[1] that he proposed to buy off the possible opposition of the younger members of the royal family by assigning to Arsinoe and the younger brother a similar joint kingdom in Cyprus. But Cyprus was now Roman territory, and the story may be a mere slander intended to lay stress on the arbitrary nature of Caesar's power.

1237. We hear that Ptolemy protested against the restoration of Cleopatra, and that a general rising in Alexandria was with difficulty averted for the moment. A far more serious danger arose from the advisers of the king, who were determined not to be set aside and placed at the mercy of Cleopatra without a struggle. Pothinus the chief eunuch had sent to fetch Achillas the Egyptian general with the army from Pelusium. This force was 20,000 strong, and was, as we have seen, largely composed of desperate characters to whom the assertion of Roman sovranty in Egypt was a most unwelcome prospect. Their arrival in Alexandria speedily changed the situation to one of open war. They had at their back not only the troops in garrison but the city populace. No more turbulent mob existed than that of Alexandria. Undisciplined and unfitted for battle in the open field, they were dangerous adversaries in street-fighting, for in the excitement of passion they became blindly daring. Skilled artificers were numerous, and Caesar could gain no advantage by superiority in engineering skill. The harbour-quarters swarmed with a seafaring population, and the Egyptian contingent of Pompey's fleet had returned home since his defeat in Thessaly. Caesar had now to contend against terrible odds under most unfavourable conditions. His opponents had a chance which they were eager to turn to account. If they could shut him up in a part of the city, and prevent supplies and reinforcements from reaching him by sea, there was hope that they might destroy him before a second army could come to his relief.

1238. To attempt a description of the struggle that now took place, involving topographical and other details which cannot be abridged intelligibly, would lead us too far from our subject. Fighting by land and water went on month after month with great obstinacy. Caesar and his men were often fighting not so much for victory as for life. He had come at the beginning of October 48, and he was not master of Alexandria till the end of March 47. His headquarters were in the royal palace, which covered a large stretch of ground

[1] Dion Cass. XLII 35.

on the northern side of the city. By barricades he turned a considerable part of this quarter into a defensible stronghold, from which the enemy were never able to eject him. Here he was in touch with the great outer harbour, the entrance to which from the sea was to the east of the island Pharos, and overlooked by the famous lighthouse at its north-eastern corner. The first attack was so fierce, and Caesar's forces so weak, that he only saved his communications with the sea by burning the ships in the royal dockyards. Had these fallen into the enemy's hands, they would have been able to blockade him. But soon after one of his Pompeian legions joined him. The struggle for the command of the sea continued. Caesar was forced to occupy Pharos, after which furious combats took place for the possession of a great artificial mole connecting the island with the mainland and dividing the two harbours. Here it was that he met with a disastrous repulse and was, himself for a time in extreme danger. Such were some of the more striking incidents in the so-called Alexandrine war. In all his varied experiences Caesar never had to deal with so many strange and unexpected difficulties as on this occasion. Psychology was at fault in the contest with an ingenious and enthusiastic enemy. Nothing but overwhelming physical force could make any impression on fanaticism such as theirs, and Caesar was all the while standing on his defence with insufficient forces. Though for some time he had both the young king and Cleopatra in his charge, a representative of the dynasty was arrayed against him. Arsinoe escaped and took her place at the head of the anti-Roman movement, and though she quarrelled with Achillas the general, and procured his murder, the vigour of the movement did not slacken. But Caesar still held out, and he seems never to have lost the confidence of his own men. His Roman troops did not fail him, and his little naval force, the Rhodians in particular, fought admirably. Towards the end of the war envoys came to negotiate for the release of the king and to suggest that hostilities might thus be brought to an end. Caesar for some reason[1] consented, but the youth when set free shewed no inclination to come to terms, and put himself at the head of the Egyptian forces. This matter is obscurely told. The absence of any reference to Cleopatra, whose claims Caesar had surely not set aside, perhaps may suggest a reason why he let Ptolemy go, and why Ptolemy at once joined the war-party.

1239. Relief came at last. A certain Mithradates of Pergamum, said to have been a natural son of the great king of Pontus, was among those whom Caesar had despatched to raise additional forces

[1] See *Bellum Alex.* 23, 24.

when he found himself committed to the Alexandrine war. This man set to work in Cilicia and Syria with great energy, and the local cities and chiefs actively supported his efforts. Now that Pompey was gone, no doubt they were glad to win the favour of Caesar. Mithradates raised a large and motley army, not inefficient, to judge from what followed. Among his various contingents was one of 3000 Jews. He entered Egypt by the eastern approach from Syria, and took the fortress of Pelusium by storm. An Egyptian force sent to stop him was utterly defeated. He advanced towards Alexandria, and a well-managed cooperation on the part of Caesar enabled the combined forces to attack and rout with great slaughter the main Egyptian army. The king perished in the flight, and the resistance of Alexandria was at an end. Caesar received the submission of the people with his habitual clemency. It was now about the end of March 47, but he seems to have stayed in Egypt three months more, in dalliance with the fascinating Cleopatra, it was said. An expedition up the Nile is said to have been one of their entertainments. But he did not omit to settle the affairs of the kingdom. The elder of the two Ptolemies being dead, Cleopatra was joined in the government with the younger, apparently on the same terms. But she was openly living with Caesar, who was understood to be the father of the son whom she bore soon after and named Caesarion. The question of a garrison to maintain order was settled by taking only one legion away with him, and leaving the rest behind. Among other matters it seems that he granted some favours to the Jews, who had formed an element in the Alexandrian population ever since the foundation of the city. We have seen that there were Jews in the relieving army, and the Jewish colony in Alexandria had probably borne no part in the war. They lived apart in a quarter of their own at the eastern end of the city. We must remember the connexion kept up by their scattered communities with the temple at Jerusalem ; the sacrilege of Pompey and the robbery of Crassus had enraged them, and they hoped, not in vain, to find a more sympathetic ruler in Caesar.

1240. Of the events that had been taking place while Caesar was in Egypt we must for the present speak only of those affecting the position in the East. The settlement of Asia Minor made by Pompey had been disturbed by an invasion too serious to be ignored. Pharnaces, the son and successor of Mithradates, had been left in possession of his father's Bosporan kingdom when the Pontic territories in Asia Minor were either made into Roman provinces or handed over to client-kings. The outbreak of the civil war had emboldened him to attempt the reconquest of his father's lost empire. Instead of joining Pompey, he invaded Pontus and the adjacent countries on his own account. There was for the moment nothing to stop him. He overran great part of Cappadocia, the kingdom of Ariobarzanes, and occupied the Lesser Armenia, which had been granted to the Galatian prince Deiotarus. Deiotarus had been with Pompey, but had submitted to Caesar after Pompey's defeat. He was to pay a money-fine, and this he could not do while deprived of territory and revenue. He applied to Calvinus, whom Caesar had left in charge of Asia, and Calvinus took the matter in hand. But just at this time two of the legions in Asia were summoned to Alexandria, and the governor had only one Roman legion at his disposal. He made up an army with two Galatian legions of Deiotarus and other miscellaneous troops hastily raised in Pontus Cilicia and Cappadocia. He rejected all proposals of Pharnaces, insisting on his evacuating the Lesser Armenia as well as Cappadocia, and marched up the country to enforce his orders. But Pharnaces, already encouraged by hearing that most of the Roman troops had been sent to join Caesar, presently got news of the serious trouble at Alexandria, and was in no mind to submit. A battle was fought, in which most of Calvinus' army was scattered or destroyed. He made his way back to Asia with a remnant, and Pharnaces was left master of the field. The king now occupied Pontus in true oriental fashion, confiscating the properties of Roman citizens and Pontic provincials, torturing and mutilating, and generally re-asserting possession of his father's realm. He seems to have passed the winter in Pontus (48—47) and to have meant to occupy Bithynia in the spring. But this design was checked by news that Asander, whom he had left at home as viceroy, had revolted, and when he set out to suppress this rebellion he was recalled by hearing that Alexandria had fallen and Caesar was coming.

1241. At the beginning of July Caesar sailed for Syria, and reached Antioch. He had with him one legion (6th), which was now reduced to less than 1000 men by the accidents of war. He was in a great hurry, for news from home shewed that his presence was most urgently needed in Rome and Italy. But he could not leave the East without restoring some sort of order, and until he had settled matters in Syria and Cilicia he could hardly march against Pharnaces. In Syria there was evidently a good deal to be done, and the 'few days' he is said[1] to have spent there must have been busy ones. But there was doubtless a general desire to stand well with the conqueror, and Caesar was a rapid worker, and inclined by temperament and interest to make things pleasant. We hear in general terms that he visited the principal cities, settling disputes and rewarding good service, and that he received all the chiefs of the numerous local principalities

[1] *Bellum Alex.* 66.

who came to declare their loyalty to the new representative of Rome. These princes were in effect a cheap defence of Rome's eastern frontier, and Caesar's powers of conciliation found a congenial task in encouraging them to perform their treaty obligations. We learn from Josephus[1] that he also did something for the patriots of Jerusalem. Hyrcanus, who had been left by Pompey in the office of High-Priest, had favoured the cooperation[2] of Jews in the campaign for the relief of Caesar. Caesar now recognized him in his position, and gratified Jewish sentiment by allowing the walls of Jerusalem, which had been dismantled by order of Pompey sixteen years before, to be restored. In short, the aim of Caesar was to leave all the cities and principalities included in the province of Syria contented and at rest. He then proceeded to Cilicia, where he acted in much the same manner, and from thence northwards to settle accounts with Pharnaces. On the way he had various matters to decide in Cappadocia, and some sort of army had to be got together. In this he made use of Deiotarus the Galatian, who came in person to receive Caesar's forgiveness and furnished troops. With this contingent, and the remains of the beaten army of Calvinus, a force was made up, small and mostly of doubtful efficiency. But he pushed on with his usual boldness, and came upon Pharnaces at Zela in Pontus. Negotiations had failed, for the king knew that Caesar was in a hurry to return to Rome, and hoped by delay to extort favourable terms. A battle was necessary, and a strategic blunder of Pharnaces[3] enabled Caesar to win a decisive victory. By this stroke the authority of Rome was reasserted in Asia Minor, and a new territorial settlement was necessary, on a principle of rewards and punishments. The chief feature of this rearrangement was the gift of a 'tetrarchy' in Galatia to Mithradates of Pergamum at the expense of Deiotarus. Caesar left two legions in Pontus: the remnant of the veteran Sixth were sent to Italy to receive their well-earned rewards. He now set out homewards as fast as the necessity of despatching business on the way would allow. The battle of Zela had been fought[4] on the 2nd August 47, and about the 24th September he reached Tarentum.

1242. We must now turn back to review briefly the course of events in other parts of the Roman world. And first let us take the

---

[1] Jos. *Ant.* XIV 137, 144.

[2] Hyrcanus was a weak creature, the tool of Antipater the Idumaean, whose policy it was to keep on good terms with the party in power in Rome.

[3] This was the battle afterwards described in the famous *veni vidi vici*. The words were probably displayed on a tablet or banner on the occasion of his triumph in B.C. 46 (Suet. *Jul.* 37), not sent as a letter to the Senate.

[4] This is known from the remains of ancient Fasti. It was the same day as the surrender at Ilerda in 49. See *CIL* I p. 324 and Mommsen's note p. 398.

regions affected by the presence of the Pompeian fleets commanding the Adriatic and Ionian seas. About the time of the battle of Pharsalus three important positions were held by Caesarian forces. M. Pomponius at Messana had a legion in the town and 35 war-vessels in the harbour, and at Vibo on the Italian coast was P. Sulpicius with a similar fleet. The command of the strait seemed secure. At Brundisium there was P. Vatinius, who had the legions which for want of transport had not been able to join Caesar, but little or no naval force. For many reasons it was desirable to keep hold of Illyricum, in particular because in the last resort Caesar might be driven to return to Italy by that route. Accordingly we learn that Q. Cornificius had been sent there with two legions. At all these three points there was fighting, which is of interest mainly as shewing how great was the strength of the Pompeian side. The loss of the army at Pharsalus by no means exhausted their resources. We shall presently come to their revival in Africa, and this revival took place though they had no great leader to direct combinations and improve the opportunities of maritime war.

1243. About the time of Pharsalus D. Laelius appeared off Brundisium with a Pompeian fleet, and made a lodgement on the island at the harbour mouth. No efforts of Vatinius could dislodge him, but on hearing of Pompey's defeat he withdrew. The Sicilian strait was visited by an eastern fleet under C. Cassius Longinus, the man who had held the Parthians at bay in Syria after the disaster of Crassus. His coming was a surprise, and he burnt the ships at Messana and came near to taking the town; some of the ships at Vibo were also destroyed. Here too the news from Thessaly brought relief, and Cassius sailed[1] away. The operations in the parts of Illyricum were on a larger scale. Since the capture of C. Antonius and his army in Curicta the hold of the Caesarians on these countries had been greatly weakened. Some towns in which the Roman element was strong were firmly loyal to Caesar, but some of the natives (such as the Dalmatians, who feared chastisement for a recent outrage,) were hostile, and ready to afford help to the Pompeians. In spite of this Cornificius managed to maintain himself, and by not attempting too much he was able to win several minor successes. Then came the battle of Pharsalus, after which M. Octavius with a strong Pompeian fleet appeared off the Liburno-Dalmatian coast. Still Cornificius, by the help of the maritime towns and the capture

---

[1] There seems to be no ground for supposing that he went off to the Hellespont and there fell in with Caesar. The story (Suet. *Jul.* 63, Appian *civ.* II 88, Dion Cass. XLII 6) is told of his brother Lucius, and is most improbable. The story referred to in Cic. *philipp.* II § 26 is obscure and doubtful.

of detached vessels from the enemy, contrived to hold his ground, but a new danger menaced him on the side of the land. A number of the fugitives from Pharsalus had made their way to the north and were entering Illyricum. So at least it was said, and Caesar, who was just setting out in pursuit of Pompey and anxious not to have the war renewed behind his back in Macedonia and Illyria, did not neglect the report. Among the exiles recalled to Italy was A. Gabinius, who had not as yet borne any part in the war. Caesar now sent him orders to take command of some newly-raised troops and proceed to Illyricum. He was to join forces with Cornificius, and hold the province at all costs. If advisable, he might even enter Macedonia; in any case the Pompeians must not be allowed to make head. Gabinius set out late in the year (48) and marched round the head of the Adriatic. In Illyricum he found himself short of supplies. The country was mostly bare and the people hostile. He was driven to attack towns and forts in order to feed his men. After suffering much from the inclemency of the weather, he was at last defeated in battle and lost most of his army. With the remnant he escaped to Salonae, where he died not long after. This failure gave Octavius hopes of winning the province. He was taking Caesarian posts one by one when Vatinius arrived from Brundisium in response to urgent appeals from Cornificius. Vatinius had great difficulty in fitting out a naval squadron, but his makeshift vessels had fighting crews of the best sort. There had been a kind of hospital-depot at Brundisium for the veterans who were left behind as invalids when Caesar sailed from Italy. Numbers of them were again fit for service, and this expedition was the very service for men more fitted perhaps to fight than to march. Ill health and the wintry sea did not stop Vatinius, who shewed himself a worthy lieutenant of Caesar. He quickly checked the career of Octavius, and in a naval action skilfully forced the fighting at close quarters. A good part of the Pompeian fleet was taken or sunk; Octavius fled southwards, eventually making for Africa. All the upper Adriatic was now clear, and Vatinius was able to leave Cornificius to restore order in Illyricum, and to sail back to Brundisium, having done a good piece of work with trifling loss. It may be well to remark here that the naval superiority of the Pompeians, which had never been used with vigour for combined operations, was declining fast. We know that both the Rhodian and the Egyptian squadrons left them after Pompey's defeat, and after the victory of Vatinius neither side appears as in unquestioned command of the sea.

1244. Meanwhile in the far West events were illustrating the boundless mischief that could be caused by the misdeeds of an ill-chosen subordinate out of reach of the master's control. We have seen that when he returned to Rome in 49 Caesar left Q. Cassius to govern the Further Spain. This man had been in Spain already. In 54—50 he was quaestor of Pompey, the non-resident governor, and had made himself so hated that an attempt was made upon his life. But at the beginning of 49, when he was tribune, he had served the cause of Caesar in the Senate, and afterwards accompanied him in the Spanish campaign. Thus he had great claims to a reward, and Caesar left him in charge with four legions. Southern Spain, the chief city of which was Corduba, was already considerably Romanized. Settlers from Italy had found a home there, ever since[1] the elder Scipio planted a settlement of invalids at Italica in the days of the Second Punic war. Intermarriage and convenience had reconciled Romans and natives, and these southern districts were normally peaceful. A string of prosperous towns lay along the line of the river Baetis (Guadalquivir), and in the hilly parts Roman enterprise had long been busy developing the mines. Latin was widely spoken; at Corduba there were poets who composed in Latin, though to Cicero's ear[2] their works seemed to lack the true Roman ring. The Lusitanian country to the north-west was less quiet and civilized. The long and bloody process of its conquest had left memories unfavourable to contentment. Still there appears to have been no rebellion there to justify severe measures. But when Caesar's back was turned Cassius set to work, and soon made his province a scene of confusion and trouble. He hoped to be able to work his will on Romans and provincials by granting largesses and indulgences to his soldiers, and by this means he corrupted the discipline of the legions. He made an expedition into Lusitania (why, we do not hear) and got himself saluted Imperator. He then settled down at Corduba for his assize (*conventus*), which was the occasion of an infamous campaign of exactions. He wanted money, and every means was used to extract it on any pretext from all sorts of people. Again there was a plot to assassinate him, and he added to his unpopularity by raising another legion and an expensive body of horse. Early in 48 he received orders from Caesar to cross over to Africa and operate against Juba, to prevent the king, who had destroyed Curio, from sending further help to the Pompeians. Cassius eagerly prepared to carry out these orders, but an attempt on his life took place at Corduba and left him laid up with wounds. He was expected to die, and great confusion followed. Some legions, in which local feeling was strong, accepted one of the conspirators as their leader. But Cassius recovered, and the legions were not yet ripe for mutiny. Some of the conspirators

[1] Appian *Hisp.* 38. [2] Cic. *pro Archia* § 26.

were put to death, others bought their lives from Cassius, who coolly made a handsome profit out of his escape.

1245. At this point, perhaps early in September, came news of the victory of Pharsalus. Cassius was not overpleased to find himself less necessary to Caesar, but he went on with his preparations, and also with his characteristic ways of finance. He wiped off his own debts by making his creditors record their payment, and wrung more money out of others. He called out men for service and made them pay for exemptions. But when he was nearly ready to start for Africa, and was busy with his final extortions, a real mutiny at last broke out. We cannot here follow the wearisome story in detail. Southern Spain was the scene of a half-suppressed civil war. All the troops were loyal to Caesar, but most of them detested Cassius. A misguided attempt to attach some of the mutineers to the Pompeian cause was an utter failure. Even Corduba was a centre of rebellion, but Caesarian. Cassius sent for help to the Mauretanian king Bogud, but neither his help nor that of a minority of the Spanish towns enabled the hated governor to recover his lost authority. The indecisive fighting was only put an end to by the arrival of M. Aemilius Lepidus, the proconsul of Hither Spain, with his army. Cassius had sent for him, but he was rather a mediator than a partisan. He evidently saw that Cassius was the cause of all the trouble, and took the line of supporting Marcellus, who was at the head of the loyal mutineers. One thing is clear, that months had been wasted in this mischievous and needless imbroglio, and that we have reached a point far on in the year 47. For we hear that soon after Lepidus had restored order, C. Trebonius arrived to take over the province. As he only reached Brundisium[1] from Antioch in the middle of August, he cannot have reached Corduba till September. Cassius at once took ship and sailed away, but was lost at sea on the voyage. There was an end of a bold rascal, but the consequences of his misdeeds were not so easily repaired.

1246. I have sketched the course of events in Italy down to the suppression of the mad enterprise of Caelius and Milo. The consul Servilius was at the head of the home government, and the general attitude one of waiting for news from the seat of war. The news of Pharsalus set the mob pulling down the statues of Pompey and Sulla, but no official action was taken till the report of Pompey's death was confirmed. Then Senate and Assembly rushed to heap honours and extraordinary powers on the conqueror. We hear of his being authorized to make war and peace, and to treat the Pompeians as he thought fit, without consulting Senate or People ; also to triumph

[1] Cic. *ad Att.* XI 20, *fam.* XV 21 § 2.

over king Juba for a victory which had yet to be won. He was to
have the right to stand for the consulship for the five ensuing years,
to nominate to all magistracies save those confined to Plebeians, and
to make appointments to all propraetorian governorships. This last
prerogative carried with it the repeal of the Pompeian law of 52, and
the retention of the old plan of the consuls drawing lots for the
proconsular provinces was only a nominal limitation of his absolute
power. Even the powers of the tribunate were conferred on him
(though a Patrician) in a new and comprehensive form. He was to
have the right to sit with the tribunes on their official bench, and to
rank as their equal in power. Thus he could legally block any
proposal that displeased him, including the candidature of an
unwelcome aspirant to plebeian offices. It was in short a legalized
tyranny, bestowed piecemeal with true Roman clumsiness. But all
this was not enough. He must be Dictator[1] a second time, and a
Dictator not merely for holding elections or any such limited function.
It seems that Servilius nominated him on much the same footing as
Sulla, without any specified limit of time. This was in October, when
Caesar was already entangled in the affairs of Egypt. At Alexandria
he entered on office as dictator, and named Antony as Master of the
Horse. Antony was not with him, but in Italy, having been sent
after Pharsalus to conduct back some of the veteran legions. They
were to be placed in quarters to await the return of Caesar and their
promised rewards. It was inevitable that a period of idle waiting
should demoralize these soldiers after their long active service, and as
months went by and they became more impatient their presence
added to the difficulty of maintaining order.

1247.   Such was the situation in Italy at the end of the year 48.
The consulship of Caesar and Servilius ended with the year, and
Caesar had made no provision for filling up the magistracies for the
next year. Senate and Assembly had abdicated most of their powers,
and the dictator was a fighting prisoner in the East. In Rome
Antony alone held curule office, and that not of a normal kind;
beside the Master of the Horse there were only the ten tribunes, and
the tribunate had never been a good working office suited for the
practical conduct of state affairs. For some months there was wild
confusion, and two tribunes were the chief promoters of disorder.
P. Cornelius Dolabella, Cicero's troublesome son-in-law, had not been
a success as a soldier. After Pharsalus he returned to Rome, became
a Plebeian, and was elected tribune. He now took up the policy in

---

[1] The masterly note of Mommsen on the dictatorships of Caesar (*CIL* vol. 1 pp. 451—3)
is the classic treatise on the subject. The epigraphic and numismatic evidence is there fully
discussed. See also his note on the inscription *CIL* 1 620 (Wilmanns 1108).

which M. Caelius had failed, of relieving debtors, and was opposed by L. Trebellius in the interest of the creditors. Cancelling of debts and remission of rents formed the programme of Dolabella, and the city was disturbed by rioting as the parties came to blows. The Senate voted that the question should be reserved for Caesar's decision, and called upon Antony and the eight tribunes to maintain order. But Antony had to leave Rome to pacify the discontented veterans, and the party-leaders paid no regard to the deputy whom he left in charge. So the disturbances went on. At the news of the fall of Alexandria there was a short spell of quiet, but when it was known that Caesar had on hand the war with Pharnaces the rioting began again. Antony affected to play a middle part, but first he favoured Dolabella and then Trebellius. The mobs got out of control, and the Senate had again to appeal to Antony, perhaps in the form of the 'last decree,' and Antony had to use his soldiers in earnest. In the fight which followed 800 men are said to have been killed. But the bills of Dolabella were blocked for the present, and men waited for the coming of Caesar.

1248. The news of Pharsalus was brought to Dyrrachium by Labienus about the middle of August 48. The Pompeians there evacuated the place in panic haste, and withdrew by sea to their naval headquarters at Corcyra. Cicero, ailing and despondent, was for submitting to the conqueror. Young Cn. Pompey would have killed him for a traitor, but Cato protected him. He and his brother retired to Patrae in Achaia, where they fell out and parted. The orator made his way to Brundisium in October, and there he stayed eleven months in utter misery and dejection, lictors bay-leaves and all. Questions arose as to whether he might stay in Italy, but Antony seems to have dealt kindly with him, and eventually excepted him by name from the general order against Pompeians. Vatinius too forgave old scores and treated him with much consideration. But he was distressed by a host of family troubles, and behind all there was the painful uncertainty as to the treatment that awaited him at the hands of Caesar. But Caesar reassured[1] him by letter, and on his return received him cordially. To win the adhesion of a man so distinguished and of so high a character in civil life was just what Caesar wanted. None knew better than he that most of his chief associates were men of dubious character and damaged reputation. They might serve his purpose in the war, but men of a more respectable type would be needed in the work of peace. To return to the Pompeians at Corcyra. They broke up and went different

---

[1] Cic. *pro Ligario* § 7. At the time of this speech (B.C. 46) Cicero had given up all hope of a triumph and dismissed his lictors.

ways. Scipio and others went to Africa, where their cause still
prevailed. Appian says that Cn. Pompey went to Spain, but this is
doubtful. Cato and a considerable party, after a vain attempt to
occupy the Peloponnesus, sailed towards Egypt, hoping to rejoin
Pompey, but were met by the news of his death; so most of them
went to Africa, others dispersed or took the handiest way of making
their submission to Caesar. Of these last Quintus Cicero was one;
he was pardoned by Caesar at Antioch. C. Cassius[1] seems to have
been another. Caesar knew his value as a soldier, and made him one
of his *legati*, and perhaps employed him in the campaign against
Pharnaces.

1249. Caesar arrived in Italy sooner than people expected, and
his presence at once put an end to political disorder. He had known
of the troubles in Italy, and hurried home to deal with them. He
was disgusted with the slackness of Antony, and it may be that he
even removed him from office. But in view of coming trouble with
the impatient veterans it was desirable to patch up matters in Rome.
He therefore excused the proceedings of Dolabella, and dealt with
the financial crisis in his own way. No general remission of debts
was granted, but the provisions of the Julian law of 49 for relief of
debtors were to be strictly carried out. In the matter of house-rents,
evidently a wide-felt difficulty calling for exceptional treatment, he
adopted the policy of Caelius and Dolabella. He carried a law
remitting rents for one year, but fixed an upper limit for the remission
of 2000 sesterces (nearly £20) in Rome and 500 (nearly £5) in the
rest of Italy, thus giving the poorer classes most of the benefit.
Another law was an attempt to revive credit by creating an artificial
demand for land. From our very imperfect record it would seem to
have enacted[2] that capitalists should have a proportion (perhaps ⅔)
of their capital invested in land, that is Italian land, and perhaps also
to have forbidden the mortgaging of landed estates beyond a certain
proportion of their market value. This might tend, if enforced, to
keep more ready money in circulation, and to diminish the number of
encumbered estates. There was also a prospect, possibly not left out
of account, that the wealthier classes might be more interested in the
welfare of rural Italy. That the governing class should be landowners
was an old traditional principle, and it did not die out with Caesar.
But such regulations were of course evaded; it was not possible to

---

[1] Dion Cass. XLII 13 states this, and it seems much the most probable account of the
surrender of Cassius (the future murderer of Caesar). See Cic. *ad fam.* VI 6 § 10 *Cassium
sibi legavit*, XV 15 § 3.

[2] Tacitus *ann.* VI 16, 17. See also Suet. *Tib.* 48, 49, and Pliny *epp.* VI 19 for an attempt
in the time of Trajan. Caesar had foreshadowed this legislation by an edict against hoarding
in the year 49, if Dion is to be trusted. See § 1220.

keep up the arbitrary guidance of capital. In the interest of peace and quiet it was desirable to put down the troublesome clubs or gilds (*collegia*) that had been suppressed in 64, and revived by Clodius. Caesar now again dissolved them by edict, authorizing some old or approved ones, among which was that of the Jews. There was also the matter of elections, though the year was far spent. To fill up the offices gave an air of regularity to his proceedings, and an opportunity of rewarding adherents. So Vatinius and Fufius Calenus were consuls for the remnant of the year, and the minor offices were assigned to others. The number of praetors was raised to ten, and additional places were provided in the chief sacred colleges, which were of course tenable for life. So means were found to gratify many ambitions cheaply. There were also many vacancies in the Senate. These Caesar filled up by promoting some knights and others of his partisans, among them a few of his trusty centurions. Some of his nominations were of course unpopular. But it is clear that his position was a very difficult one. He was in a great hurry, for the delay in the East had given the Pompeians time to collect great forces in Africa, while he had little leisure to prepare for a fresh campaign. He could not find money to reward adherents, for he was himself in urgent need of money to carry on the war. His requisitions in the East had probably not produced as much as he expected, and we now hear that he exacted forced loans from individuals and communities. It can only have been necessity that drove him to so odious a measure. We are told that he made an exception in the case of Atticus, being only too pleased that so wealthy a man, though at heart a Pompeian, had preserved an attitude of neutrality. It was probably with great reluctance that he ordered the properties of Pompey and others to be sold by auction, a proceeding which led to unpleasant consequences in two ways. It was an offence to patriotic sentiment. It also led to a special abuse. Some of Caesar's friends thought they saw an opening for a profitable job, by buying estates and then using their influence with the dictator to evade payment of the purchase-money. On the strength of this expectation they bid freely, and were genuinely indignant when Caesar, who had other views, insisted on the money being paid. A flagrant case[1] was that of Antony, who bought Pompey's house in Rome. The endeavours of Caesar to enforce payment, and of Antony to evade it, lasted for nearly two years, and led to a great coolness between them: in the end it seems that Caesar thought it best to forgive the debt.

1250. While Caesar was still in Rome, the impatience of the

---

[1] Cicero enlarges on this topic in the second *Philippic*, exaggerating, no doubt. But there is plenty of other authority. See the Halm-Mayor Introduction to the speech.

legions broke out into open mutiny. They had been ordered to proceed to Sicily in readiness for an African campaign, but they pelted the officer[1] who brought the order from Caesar in Asia, and refused to budge until the promises of money and lands, made before Pharsalus, were fulfilled. Another officer[2] was now sent to promise an extra largess of 1000 *denarii* (nearly £40) per man, and to conduct them to Sicily. He only saved his life by flight. They were tired of promises and wanted cash. They now marched on Rome. It is significant of the state of affairs that we hear of no prominent leader, nor of any anti-Caesarian partisan trying to turn their fury to account. Though mutinous, they were still Caesar's army; they dealt with him only, he only could deal with them. There was no real alternative to Caesar, and he faced the situation with his usual nerve. He appeared before them suddenly in the Field of Mars, and enquired what they wanted. They demanded their discharge. He at once discharged them, and assured them that he would satisfy all their just claims in full, with interest on moneys overdue, as soon as he returned from Africa to celebrate his triumph. But in addressing them as men already discharged he used the form of civil life, calling them 'citizens of Rome' (*quirites*), not 'soldiers' (*milites*), thus bringing it home to them that their military days were over. It was they who were now in a dilemma. To destroy Caesar was to destroy their hopes of reward. To accept discharge, and leave him to go to Africa without them, would answer their purpose no better. Either he would perish, and their hopes with him, or he would return with a new victorious army, an army whose claims to glory and reward would override their own. This was not what they wanted. They had no effective means of extorting ready money from a master who was proof against intimidation, and they were in no hurry to exchange the sword and *pilum* for the spade and plough. They begged to be forgiven, and with affected reluctance he consented to accept their service as volunteers. In short, he was master of them on his own terms. How he actually dealt with them is not certain. We have no contemporary evidence. Dion[3] says that he left behind in Italy the more orderly men, who were fitted for a rural life, and took to Africa only the more unruly. Thus he achieved two objects; he removed a turbulent and dangerous element from Italy, and used them up freely in Africa. This writer adds that Caesar, though a kindhearted man and indulgent, particularly to his soldiers, would not tolerate mutiny and was severe in his punishments. It is hard to say how far this

---

[1] P. Sulla, Cic. *ad Att.* XI 21 § 2, 22 § 2.   [2] Sallust.

[3] Dion Cass. XLII 52—55. Compare Plutarch *Caes.* 51, Suet. *Jul.* 70, Appian *civ.* II 92—94.

is a fair version of contemporary record, how far it is due to the interpretation of an author notorious for his malignity. That Caesar did make some selection, and perhaps even found land-allotments for a few favoured individuals, seems indicated by the brief references of Plutarch and Suetonius. This affair of the great mutiny, in which even the tenth legion bore a leading part, is a most important event in the history of the time, and it is a great pity that we are left in doubt as to what Caesar actually did.

1251. The preparations for the African campaign now went forward, but Caesar held the elections for the coming year (46) before leaving Rome. He remained dictator, but took the consulship as well, with M. Lepidus for colleague. In these times it mattered not that both were Patricians. Lepidus had made himself useful by restoring quiet in Spain, and had even been indulged with a triumph not earned by victory in battle. He was now to be at the head of the home government in Caesar's absence. Among the praetors was A. Hirtius. Of the arrangements for provincial governorships the most notable was the appointment of M. Junius Brutus to Cisalpine Gaul. He had been a strong Pompeian (or rather anti-Caesarian) like his uncle Cato. After Pharsalus he sought pardon, and was most kindly received by Caesar. He was now promoted to a post of the first importance, at the very time when Cato was in arms against Caesar in Africa. Caesar admired the intensity of his character, of which however sterling honour and loyalty seem to have formed[1] no part. As yet there was no proof that Caesar was trusting him too much: but in truth, among all the men, whether old adherents or forgiven adversaries, who surrounded the great dictator, none was less worthy of generous trust than this sham philosopher, self-conscious shallow solemn and vain. Having now settled the urgent matters of government, Caesar started for Africa in December 47. He reached Lilybaeum on the 17th, where his transports were ready, but only one legion of recruits and a small body of horse. Five other legions soon came up, and on the 25th he was at last able to put to sea. But only one of his six legions consisted of veterans, and he had only about 2600 cavalry. The other veteran legions were ordered to follow, but it was some time before they were able to join him.

1252. The Pompeian, or rather republican, leaders had had about a year and a half[2] to recover from the defeat in Thessaly, and they

---

[1] With the unfavourable estimate of Brutus given in Tyrrell and Purser vol. 6 I heartily agree. But he is said to have done well as governor of the Cisalpine. See Sandys on Cic. *Orator* § 34.

[2] See the remarks of Cicero (*ad fam.* XV 15) to C. Cassius, written in 47 before the return of Caesar.

had not been idle. Since the disaster of Curio they were masters of Africa. If king Juba was inclined to be domineering, he was at least heartily opposed to Caesar, and so they naturally concentrated on Africa and made use of the Numidian. Scipio brought a remnant of their forces from Greece, Cato led another by way of Cyrene; and these parties, joined to those already in Africa, made up a respectable army. Though deserted by many of their naval contingents, they still had a considerable fleet. If it was true that they now mustered ten legions, surely they must have been joined by a number of stray refugees from various parts. They had a great number of elephants, and endless swarms of cavalry and light troops, of which Numidia could furnish an inexhaustible supply: Juba could also put into the field four native legions trained on the Roman model. Their position was for the moment strengthened by measures which rendered difficult the subsistence of an invading army. Great quantities of corn had been stored in the fortified towns, and numbers of the farming population[1] had been pressed for military service. Hence the normal great crop of corn had not been raised in the season just past, and Caesar had to import most of his food-stuff, owing to the shortness of the local supply. Nor did the republican cause lack leaders. There were Scipio, Varus, Cato, Labienus, Afranius, Petreius, and others. The question was, who should command in chief. Varus had been longest on the spot, but his claim did not find favour. The moral force of the cause was represented by Cato, but the man of scruples was not the man for the business in hand, and he knew it. So he persuaded others to give the command to Scipio, who was above the rest in rank, and his loyal support enabled a general of very ordinary abilities to secure the obedience of more competent subordinates. Cato himself was put in charge of Utica, the capital of the Roman province. The people of this city were suspected of a leaning to Caesar, and it had been proposed to give it over to destruction and massacre to gratify the rage of Juba. This Cato managed to prevent, and he ruled the place firmly with general approval. He was not the Roman to humour the spite of a barbarian king, but over Scipio Juba had more power, and the uncertainties of his independent strategy were an embarrassment to the Roman leaders. One point in relation to Scipio is characteristic of the superstitions surviving in Roman armies; it was felt that in Africa Scipio was a name to bring good luck. Such was still the importance attached to omens, that Caesar, a freethinker but a practical man,

---

[1] *Bell. Afr.* 20 § 4 *stipendiarii aratores*. I take these to be natives, not the slave-labourers of Roman capitalists. In any case the mention of them suggests that there was a strong non-Roman element in Scipio's legions.

hunted up an obscure person of the name of Scipio and put him to the front when any movements were on foot. So far as omens went, one Scipio was as good as another, and the nervousness of ignorant soldiers was allayed. It is said also that in stepping ashore Caesar himself stumbled and fell. This was an omen of disaster, but he clutched a handful of earth and said 'Africa, I hold thee in my hand.' So ready was the wit of the chief pontiff to turn bad to good, so fully alive to the importance of moral effects.

1253. In order to get a clear notion of the situation in Africa we must also look further to the West. Beyond Numidia lay Mauretania, at this time ruled by two kings, Bocchus and Bogus or Bogud. We have seen that after the disaster of Curio in Africa pains were taken to win these princes to the Caesarian interest as a check to the power of Juba. The move seems to have been so far a success that they leant to Caesar's side, but the stimulus to effective action in the present crisis was supplied by a Roman adventurer, one of the strangest figures[1] of the revolutionary age. P. Sittius, a Roman knight engaged in financial speculations, had been suspected of complicity in the designs of Catiline. He seems to have done business on his own account, not on behalf of a syndicate, and to have operated with borrowed capital, raised on the security of estates in Italy. The scene of his ventures was Spain, and he soon sold his Italian land to clear off his debts, and devoted himself to business in the West. After the suppression of Catiline's conspiracy, Sittius visited Rome, and was threatened with prosecution. He did not wait to face the reactionary party then in power, but left for Spain, taking with him a band of fighting men, no doubt chosen out of the desperate characters abounding in Rome and Italy, ready for any risky enterprise sooner than patient industry. He had already been in Mauretania, doing business in royal loans, and to Mauretania he now returned at the head of a force strengthened by recruiting in Spain. For some years he took part in the dynastic quarrels that disturbed the kingdom, but seems not to have adhered permanently to either of the claimants. By giving the victory first to one then to the other he enjoyed the profitable position of umpire, and eventually some kind of settlement was reached, for we find both the sons of old Bocchus (Sulla's friend) on the throne, both apparently under the influence of Sittius. Sittius was not likely[2] to have any sympathy with the aristocratic party in the civil war. Kings and

---

[1] Sittius. Cic. *pro Sulla* §§ 56—59, Sallust *Cat.* 21 § 3, *Bellum Afr.* 25, 36, 48, 93, 95, 96, Appian *civ.* IV 54—56, Dion Cass. XLIII 3—12 *passim.* See below § 1257.

[2] P. Sulla, with whom Sittius had been connected, was now one of Caesar's chief lieutenants, and ex-Catilinarians would be sure to prefer Caesar.

king-maker alike were concerned to support Caesar against Juba and Scipio, and the Mauretanian kingdom was of great service to his cause.

1254. As in the case of the preceding campaigns, we will not dally over military details, of which we have a long and often confused record. The main points of interest are these. Caesar reached the African coast at the very end of the year 47, but with only a small part of his force, for the rest of the convoy were scattered. It was not easy to find a place for landing, for the enemy held the best ports. He landed near Hadrumetum, but was soon glad to move further south, where he occupied the Lesser Leptis, a town on the coast. After this his difficulties were chiefly in concentrating his scattered force, in feeding them, and in holding his ground against overwhelming odds. He was for some time in danger of utter destruction, but he managed to get through his first battle without disaster, and things began to turn in his favour. Deserters came in and gave him information, and means were found to protect his convoys of supplies. But he was confined to a very small patch of land, and it was only by building entrenched lines and free use of the artillery of the time that he kept the enemy at bay. Until his veteran legions arrived from Sicily he could not take the field, and the delay that ensued was a frightful strain on the nerve of his young troops. But Juba, on whom the republican leaders depended only too much, was drawn off to the defence of his own kingdom. The enterprising Sittius with a Mauretanian army had invaded it and even taken the capital city Cirta. The diversion caused by this inroad relieved Caesar. Moreover the Numidians and Gaetulians left with Scipio began to desert, and those of them who came over to Caesar were well received and employed in persuading their people to renounce allegiance to Juba. The name of Marius[1] was not forgotten, and Caesar was able to trade on the reputation of the conqueror of Jugurtha. It was also a help that Scipio and most of his colleagues had made themselves generally hated in the province of Africa. Their conduct is represented, probably with truth, as stupid and brutal, and it is not surprising that the provincials were ready to welcome the Caesarians whenever there was a reasonable hope that they could do so with safety. Nor was it to their advantage in the long run that they put to death Caesarians who fell into their hands. Their own men could not but reflect that even the clemency of Caesar might in time be provoked to reprisals; and if Scipio Labienus and others were fighting with halters round their necks, many of the rank and file were not. As time wore on, and convoys

[1] *Bellum Afr.* 32, 35, 56.

of supplies and the missing legions began to arrive, Caesar was able to adopt a more aggressive strategy, while the attention of Juba was further distracted by a Gaetulian rising. When the main armies faced each other, the moral forces of attraction came into play, and the stream of desertions steadily trickled into Caesar's lines. His prestige worked upon the foreigners: as for Romans, was he not more truly the representative of Rome than the Roman leaders who waited on the will of the barbarian Juba?

1255. We need not dwell on the indecisive operations, the trenchings and skirmishes that make the story of this campaign insufferably tedious. But it is well to note once more the general weakness and futility shewn in the naval departments. Naval inefficiency was a marked characteristic of the age. The predominance of Rome in the Mediterranean had made the maintenance of war-fleets superfluous. In Rhodes some naval tradition still lingered, but the island republic had long ceased to have a foreign policy of its own; it had been a shrunken and humble dependant for more than a hundred years, and second-rate professors, rather than first-rate sea-captains, were the chief glory even of Rhodes. In such a state of things Caesar was able to keep up his communications by sea, on which the success of his bold venture depended. But the extreme helplessness of his opponents, who never seriously interrupted the passage of his convoys, was probably the result of special causes at which we can only guess. Part of their fleet (only 30 small vessels) had at the beginning of the war gone on an expedition to the West under young Cn. Pompey. An attack on a Mauretanian town was made, and repulsed with loss. Pompey then made for the Balearic isles, and we hear no more of him and his squadron in this war. Probably the naval service was left in incompetent hands; such at least is the impression left by the notices of its doings. On land it is to be remarked that we hear of Gaulish and German cavalry employed on both sides. In a charge these troopers were more than a match for the Numidian light horse, of whom Scipio had great numbers. Caesar had to take special measures to make up for his comparative weakness in cavalry. But in this he succeeded, as in former campaigns, and his object now was to compel Scipio to fight a pitched battle and end the war. This for some time Scipio would not do, but on the 4th April Caesar suddenly moved and began to besiege the seaport town of Thapsus. Scipio could not abandon his garrison. He followed, and the battle at last took place. Caesar's men were eager for battle and in a savage temper. It is said that some of his veterans forced a trumpeter to sound the charge without orders. Caesar could not hold them in, and they fell on with irresistible fury. The republican army was quickly routed, their camp was carried with a rush, the cavalry and the leaders fled, and the foot were butchered wholesale in defiance of the entreaties of Caesar. The battle of Thapsus (6th April 46 B.C.) brought the African war to an end, for the other towns speedily submitted. The barbarities of Scipio's fugitive cavalry, and the mercy generally shewn by Caesar, fitly illustrated the closing scenes of a struggle useless and pitiful from first to last.

1256. The fate of a few of the republican leaders deserves a passing notice. The hero of that dark hour was Cato, who was true to his principles. He did his best to provide for the safety of the poor folks in Utica, and left them to make their peace with the conqueror, when he saw that they had no mind to resist. But for himself he had determined not to survive the Roman Republic, which he had loved and served to the utmost of his power and the best of his judgment, and which he believed to have now fought its last battle. He read the *Phaedo* of Plato, in which the philosopher's views on the immortality of the soul are put into the mouth of the dying Socrates. Then he calmly killed himself. To the Stoic suicide was a power held in reserve, the power of 'conducting himself out' of intolerable circumstances when all hope was at an end and his duty done. We have seen that as a statesman he was a failure. But as a moral force his character and his career left an impression on after generations deeper than that made by those of any other Roman. To contemporaries his merits might be a subject of controversy. Once the Empire was established, the worship of Cato became a fashion and a passion with all the bolder and loftier spirits who chafed under the restraints of the new order of things and sighed for an idealized past. The abominations of the Republic were forgotten, and Cato appeared as the champion whose heroism had dignified its fall, the martyr in a lost but worthy cause. So he passed into literature as one of its favourite topics, and was for centuries the subject of school-boy themes. The other leaders fared variously. Petreius fled with Juba, but the king's own subjects would not receive them, and the two died by their own or each other's hands. Afranius and Faustus Sulla were making for Spain, when they fell into the hands of Sittius and were somehow[1] put to death. Scipio and others tried to escape by sea, but were caught by a fleet belonging to Sittius, and so perished. Varus and Labienus succeeded in reaching Spain, where we shall meet them later with Gnaeus and Sextus the two sons of Pompey. To all appearance the republican cause had received its death-blow. There was for the moment little sign of further revival,

---

[1] According to one tradition, by Caesar's order.

nothing to foreshadow the appalling bloodshed that was yet to attend its final agonies.

1257. Before Caesar could return to Rome he had to set in order the affairs of Africa. A number of subordinate officers of the beaten party had fallen into his power. He spared their lives but sent all or most of them into exile. He annexed the kingdom of Numidia as a province, and this 'new Africa' remained thus a part of the Roman territory for some years. C. Sallustius Crispus, who had been useful in the war, was left in charge as proconsul. The future historian is said to have made a fortune there by extortion. But a part of the kingdom was given to Bocchus as a reward, and Cirta with its neighbourhood formed into a principality[1] for Sittius. This remarkable man organized a peculiar community there, settling his followers on the land and presiding over them till his death. In the old province of Africa the cities and the Roman landlords and business-men had to be punished for their support of the defeated side. This was done in the form of fines. Caesar well knew that he would need vast sums of money when he returned to Rome. These contributions were supplemented by the sale of property belonging to Juba and to Romans who had served under Scipio. On the 13th June he sailed for Sardinia. Here he fined a town for help given to his adversaries and sold the goods of a few individuals. He reached Rome towards the end of July. As he landed in Africa on the 28th December 47, and there had been an intercalary month inserted in February 46, he would seem to have been in Africa about 180 days.

---

[1] For Cirta under Sittius, his colony there, and the very exceptional position in which it stood as a *colonia* under the earlier Empire, see the article by Mommsen in *Hermes* I pp. 47—68. For the model of the confederation of Nuceria, followed by him in certain of his institutions, see Beloch, *Campanien* pp. 240—1.

CHAPTER LVIII.

FROM THE BATTLE OF THAPSUS TO THE DEATH OF CAESAR. 46—44 B.C.

1258. THE victorious campaign in Africa had immensely strengthened the position of Caesar. Materially, for the army of the republicans was beaten and dispersed, and morally, for the despair of Cato and the lack of respected leaders had left their cause deficient[1] in magnetic power. This time he did not return before he was expected, and the days of waiting for his arrival were far from pleasant to such men as Cicero[2], surrounded as they were by exultant Caesarians, and constrained to acquiesce in what could not give them joy. Naturally there was a fresh outbreak of public servility. The Senate led the way by voting a public thanksgiving for the unheard-of number of 40 days. Caesar's triumphs, already in preparation, were to include exceptional details, white horses to draw his car, and the attendance in force of the full number of lictors (48) used in his two dictatorships. He was to have a regular seat of office in the senate-house, between the consuls of the year, and always to give his opinion first. The right of presiding at the games in the circus was reserved for him, and a statue of him was to be erected with an inscription describing him as a demigod. These are the chief of the honours accepted by him; what those declined were like we can only guess. Such honorary distinctions served as a recognition of sovranty in the eye of the world. Whether it was wise to accept them we can hardly judge. More immediately important were the acts which conferred upon Caesar monarchic power, confirming and extending what had been already granted, until every part of the machinery of the state was placed under his control. Having the full *potestas tribunicia* without the limitations of the yearly office, he was supreme on the negative side. But on the positive side something might still be added to give popular sanction to his measures, particularly in the long-neglected department of the censorship. No doubt it was in response to a hint of his wishes that he was now made sole censor under the title[3] of 'guardian of manners and morals.' He was to

---

[1] Cicero *phil.* v § 26 truly says of civil war *quod opinione plerumque et fama gubernatur.*

[2] Cic. *ad fam.* IX 2 §§ 2—4.

[3] *praefectus moribus*, Cic. *ad fam.* IX 15 § 5, Suet. *Jul.* 76, Dion Cass. XLIII 14 § 4.

have the full powers of both censors and to exercise them for three years, double the usual term. This placed in his hands the census and all matters connected therewith, the composition of the Senate, the control of state contracts and other financial affairs, besides an undefined power of interfering with the habits of individuals. His second dictatorship still continued, and he held it on the Sullan footing till the end of this year (46). But we can understand that he was not unwilling to abandon the precedent of Sulla. A change was made in his tenure, to begin with the new year. He was to hold it as a yearly office, not indefinitely, but it was voted him for ten years ahead. Thus on the first of January he would in formal style be *dictator tertium designatus quartum*. We may add that he was now for the third time consul, and that he began the next year as consul for the fourth time and (after the precedent of Pompey) without a colleague. When we remember that he had long been chief pontiff, and that he was now a member of all the important sacred colleges, we see how unlikely it was that under his rule religious hindrances would be able to obstruct political action as they had often done in the past. He was also in charge of the calendar, and able, if he could find the time, to remedy the disorder of the Roman year.

1259. That we have reached the stage of virtual monarchy is clear enough. At this point we may briefly state two questions, and give them provisional answers. The full answers must remain to be implied in the narrative of Caesar's acts during the rest of his life. First, did Caesar intend to establish a permanent monarchy in Rome? Apparently he did. He is said to have delivered speeches after his return from Africa, reassuring Senate and people as to his intentions, and promising them a government not the unconstitutional and despotic rule of a master over slaves, but the mild paternal rule of a father over children. He would be their consul and dictator, not their Tyrant. But even the imagination of Dion[1] does not impute to him any suggestion of setting the Republic back upon its old footing, or anything like it. Secondly, did he contemplate retiring from the monarchy when established? Assuredly not. As things stood, no other man could possibly fill the place. Sulla had cleared the ground by his massacres and proscriptions, and then abdicated in favour of the Senate; with what result, time had shewn. Abdication was not for Caesar. However harshly we may judge his ambition from the point of view of patriotism, we must admit that his acceptance of the responsibility laid on him by events (his own acts included) was the part of a great though not faultless man. When contemporaries

[1] Dion Cass. XLIII 15—18.

thought him worse than Sulla, because he clung to autocratic power, they were unconsciously rendering him the highest praise.

1260. In August he celebrated his four triumphs on four separate days with intervals of a day between. Each of these processions had its own special equipment. First came the Gallic triumph, a genuine parade of victory over foreign foes. Vercingetorix, after six years in a Roman dungeon, was brought out, exhibited, and put to death. Why did the merciful Caesar countenance this old-fashioned brutality? Was it in order to call attention to the very different treatment dealt out to his Roman adversaries? There was surely some motive prompting him to this cold-blooded sacrifice of a stale victim. Next came the Egyptian. Arsinoe in chains was the striking and pitiful feature of this. After it the Pontic, with a tablet inscribed VENI VIDI VICI to signalize his speedy victory. Last of the four was the African, nominally over Juba. But people knew that the decisive battle had been a victory of Roman over Roman, and some parts of the exhibition are said to have recalled the fact. It was felt to be in bad taste, an outrage on Roman sentiment, committed, let us add, by the chief pontiff before the face of the Roman gods within the walls of Rome. A characteristic story has come down to us, illustrating Caesar's attitude towards popular superstitions. On the day of the first triumph the axle of his chariot broke and he had to finish the proceedings in another. This was of course ominous of evil to come. The dictator was not in the habit of regarding such signs. When he set out for Africa he had left Rome in defiance of the warnings of a soothsayer. But now he thought fit to abase himself in public by way of averting the divine jealousy. He made his approach to the Capitoline temple crawling on his knees up the steps, and so doubtless quieted the popular mind, perhaps his own also. For he, like Sulla, with a robust confidence in his own good luck, was ever a believer in the 'chapter of accidents' deified under the name of Fortune. In the processions the display of precious metals, money golden crowns etc., was enormous. Appian states it at more than £15,000,000 of our money. But it was wanted for the enormous charges to be met. The cost of the army is faintly to be guessed when we hear that the common soldiers received from £200 to £240 a head, and the centurions and higher officers twice and four times that sum. Each citizen had a bounty of about £4, and the ordinary doles of corn were supplemented for the occasion by extra distributions of corn and oil. All citizens present were entertained at a great feast, with stage-plays and other shows to follow. Splendid games, fights of gladiators, wild beasts (among them a novelty, the giraffe,) kept up the excitement into September. The funeral honours due to Caesar's daughter Julia gave an excuse for some of these events. There was also the temple of Venus Genetrix (mythical ancestress of the *Iulii*), the fulfilment of a vow made at Pharsalus, to be dedicated, and with it Caesar's new Forum, begun but not yet complete. A new extravagance was the exhibition of a sea-fight on a lake dug for the purpose in the Campus Martius. This seems to have been a very popular show, for in the imperial age we find Naumachiae a favourite form of entertainment. All this is worth notice, for it gives us some notion of the vast amount of slave-labour employed in the preparations and the frightful waste entailed by the effort to amuse an idle rabble at the expense of a subject world.

1261. Such doings in Rome of course attracted crowds from other parts of Italy. The common herd camped wherever they could. At the time of the shows people were crushed to death. Rome was mad. Excitement took strange forms. That a Roman knight should not only compose a farce but himself act in it was a lowering of Roman dignity. D. Laberius did so[1] under pressure from Caesar, who paid him for his complaisance. Worse was it that knights fought as gladiators; even a senator is said to have wanted to do the same, but the dictator drew the line at this. He had however already gone far enough in encouraging men of good position to disgrace themselves. The upper classes secretly resented these things as tending to level all in a common servitude to the autocrat. Nor was the lavish outlay on the appointments of the shows satisfactory to all spectators. Where was the need of silken awnings, the work of oriental looms, to keep off the blazing sun? So growled the soldiers, who would have been glad to have the wasted money to waste in their own way. Signs of unruliness appeared, and had to be sharply suppressed. All was not happy in Rome even during the carnival. And when it was over, and serious business began again, the entire concentration of power in Caesar's hands lay like a crushing weight on all patriots who had views of their own to which they could not give effect. To a man like Cicero it was torture to have to conceal his real sentiments. It mattered not that Caesar and Caesar's satellites treated him with the greatest consideration and respect, and that Caesar flattered his vanity by making a collection of his witty sayings. He was sick of political life. There was no scope for his energies, for all now depended on the caprice of one man. In the years 46 and 45 he only made three appearances as an orator, in each

---

[1] I agree with Tyrrell and Purser vol. v Introd. p. 17 in placing this scene in the *ludi* of 46, not 45. See their note on Cic. *ad fam.* XII 18.

case addressing Caesar, either to thank him for an act of grace or to plead on behalf of a fresh suppliant. In the letters of these years the feeling of oppression shews itself whenever he is writing to an intimate friend. In slightly varied phrases the current of querulousness flows, rising and falling according to the temper and circumstances of the moment. Sometimes he comforts himself with the assurance[1] that the Republic must revive ; Caesar can hardly help setting it in order again. At other times he sees more clearly that Caesar has not a free hand. The course of events, and the associates with whom he has to work, forbid him to restore the Republic. Cicero loathed the virtual monarchy with all his heart. He felt himself a slave, and writhed under his own contempt. And yet he was in a position of considerable influence, of which he did not scruple to make good use. His letters to friends in exile, and his efforts to procure their recall, are a bright spot in his dark history during these heavy years. His good offices were in great request generally. Letters of recommendation from him to provincial governors (who were all Caesar's men) seem to have been in demand as much as ever. When in Rome he saw plenty of society, for he was good company and welcomed as a guest. Nor could he help admitting the signal merits of the man who held the commonwealth in the hollow of his hand. Caesar's generosity and kindness, his fairness clemency industry and wisdom, are all attested by this unwilling witness. Nor again was he blind to the faults of the other side. With the savage sons[2] of Pompey and their desperate following he could have no real sympathy. Massacres and proscriptions were no policy for Cicero, yet it was anguish, bitter but unconfessed, to know that the only hope of amnesty rested on Caesar. No wonder that he turned to literary work. In these years 46—45 he produced a number of treatises[3], chiefly dealing with oratory and philosophy, and these, including the inquiries necessitated by their composition, gave him some relief. But this was after all no compensation for the old life, the triumphs of the senate-house and the Forum; at best it was an eking out[4] of utter wretchedness. In short, to be eminent on sufferance was a sorrow's crown of sorrow.

1262. No doubt the case of a man so sensitive as Cicero, to whom public activity was the thing that made life worth living, is an extreme one. No doubt the deep depression of Cicero was partly the

---

[1] See Tyrrell and Purser's remarks, vol. v Introd. p. 16. The slowly-fading hope of some sort of revival still leaves traces in the letters of the year 45. From *ad Att.* XIII 40 it seems that Brutus had some fancy of the kind even as late as Aug. 45.

[2] See the remarks of Cassius, *ad fam.* XV 19 § 4.

[3] The most important were the *Brutus* and *Orator* in 46, and the *Academica* and *de Finibus* in 45.

[4] Cic. *ad fam.* V 15 § 3 *propagatio miserrimi temporis.*

result of the domestic troubles that beset him in these years. His relations with Terentia had lately been strained, and at the end of 46 he divorced her. Early in 45 he married his own young ward Publilia for the sake of her dowry, being as usual in want of ready money; a connexion which did not turn out well, and soon led to a second divorce. The marriage of Tullia with Dolabella had to be ended in the same way. Early in 45, soon after her divorce, Tullia died, to Cicero's infinite grief. Marcus his son wanted to join Caesar's intended expedition to Spain, and was only prevented with difficulty. In 45 he was sent to study at Athens, where he at once became a sad drain on his father's purse. Nor was Cicero happy in his brother and nephew. He had quarrelled with Quintus the elder, and, when Caesar went to Spain, young Quintus used his position in camp to set the dictator against his own uncle. But Cicero could and did get over these troubles: what he could never get over was the slights that reminded him[1] of his present political nullity. There the shoe pinched cruelly. And if Cicero suffered so acutely from the feeling of helplessness, we may be sure that others too were galled, though in a less degree. And it was just some of the best men whom this feeling would affect most. Even those whom the conqueror had pardoned resented a clemency that had spared them only to be subjects, and the increasing isolation of Caesar had grave consequences. When the statues of Pompey, pulled down by the mob, were set up again by Caesar's order, Cicero remarked that by setting up Pompey's he was insuring the safety of his own. But Cicero and all convinced republicans would surely have been content to do without both. We must bear in mind that the atmosphere in which Caesar was living when he set about his far-reaching reforms was charged with insincere flattery which time and opportunity might and did develope into sincere hatred.

1263. The months spent by Caesar in Rome during the year 46 were indeed busy ones, and he must have employed an army of assistants. The discharge of old soldiers and provision of land-allotments was in itself a great undertaking, of which in the absence of statistics we can form but an imperfect notion. The principles of this assignation were (1) not to plant the settlers in continuous blocks, for fear of their proving as troublesome as the colonists of Sulla, (2) not to disturb the existing tenures. So they were incorporated in existing communities, not established in new colonies. Land-surveyors and allotment-commissioners had plenty to do, for the

---

[1] See Cic. *ad fam.* IX 15 § 4 (Sept. 46) where he says that his name had been put to decrees of the Senate, and even given as the mover, without his leave or knowledge.

work was begun at once, and was going on all the next year. We find references[1] to it in Cicero's letters. Though some persons were uneasy, it seems that private rights were respected and we hear of no serious complaints. This was probably due to the control of Caesar, who appointed the agents employed, and reserved the final decision of disputed points to himself. We have no list of the places in which the assignations were carried out, but stray references enable us to trace them[2] in various parts of Italy and in Cisalpine Gaul, more particularly in Campania. As to how it came about that a large quantity of land was available for the purpose, we are much in the dark. That some was bought seems certain, perhaps partly by the sale of waste lands unsuited for small holdings, and partly out of money still in Caesar's hands. The bulk of the confiscated estates seem to have been already sold. A few of the allotments under the Julian law of 59 may have reverted to the state in default of heirs, for that law forbade their sale, and the same rule[3] was followed now. Somehow land was found, and allotment took place, but the old difficulty of making soldiers into farmers remained as before.

1264. The possession of full censorial power, and the freedom to exercise it without restraint, enabled Caesar to take in hand a number[4] of much needed reforms. The doles of corn were an old abuse. It is said that this privilege was now enjoyed by 320,000 persons. To abolish this monstrous system of state-pauperism was impossible; it had gone on too long, and in a civilization based on slavery there was no hope of its automatic extinction through industrial development. Slavery only made the evil grow faster. To manumit a slave was a ready means of avoiding[5] the expense of his keep. Rome swarmed with freedmen, the cost of whose maintenance was to a great extent borne by the state in the form of a yearly outgoing for purchase of corn. And the facility with which an enemy could produce a famine in Rome, and weaken the government at its centre, had been well known since the time of Marius. Caesar cut down the number of corn-receivers to 150,000, doubtless after inquiries[6] carried out by trusty agents, probably a long business. Provision was made for a yearly revision of the corn-list and filling-up of death-vacancies

---

[1] Cic. *ad fam.* IX 17, XIII 4, 5, 7, 8.

[2] Detailed discussion in Zumpt *comm. epigraph.* I 304—8. **See Suet.** *Jul.* 38, 81, Appian *civ.* III 12, Nicolaus Damasc. *Caesar Aug.* c. 31 (*FHG* III 454—5), and the inscription from Capua *CIL* I 624 (Wilmanns 1436) with Mommsen's note.

[3] See Cic. *philipp.* v § 53, Appian *civ.* III 2, 7.

[4] See the convenient collection of *leges senatusconsulta decreta* in Kubler's Caesar vol. III (Teubner text).

[5] See Dion Cass. XXXIX 24.

[6] See especially Suet. *Jul.* 41. This proceeding was called *recensus.*

by lot.   As we read in Dion[1] that a great decline in the (citizen) population was noticeable in consequence of the numbers who had perished, and that Caesar granted privileges to fathers of large families, it has been thought that the new corn-rules may have been framed so as to encourage fertility.   But it was Caesar's aim to reduce the numbers of the urban mob, and the reference is perhaps rather to some measure designed to repopulate Italy.   In the census, which he undertook but did not live to complete, he set a notable precedent, very characteristic of his broad-minded views.   The practice had been to admit aliens (non-Italians) to the citizenship wholesale in one way only, through manumission of slaves.   The incorporation of foreigners on grounds of merit was rare, due either to the influence of a powerful patron, or to a claim established by service to the state, which often meant treason to their native country. Caesar admitted[2] medical practitioners and professional teachers, specialists and exponents of culture in various departments, to the Roman franchise, treating them as a class whom it was desirable to attract to Rome.   These men would all or nearly all be 'Greeks,' half-bred or pure.   To recognize them frankly was wise, for Rome needed intellectual influences, and Caesar knew the value of trained capacity in administrative work.   Under the coming Empire clever Greeks were destined to play a great part.

1265.   Some of Caesar's reforms were embodied in special laws, one of which was an attempt to check luxury, vain of course, like other sumptuary laws.   Another seems to have been designed to restore the free population of Italy by enacting[3] that stock farmers must employ at least one free man to every two slaves.   If carried out, this measure would greatly promote the security of the rural districts.   Slave-herdsmen were the backbone of brigandage, and the recent enterprise of Caelius and Milo had been undertaken with an eye to their support.   Another pressing matter was to improve the revenues of the state, which was giving up such public lands as yet remained to it, and needed a regular income.   Caesar restored the customs-duties on imports, which had been abolished in the year 60. The exact date of these laws or regulations is not certain.   But one remarkable statute, known as the *lex Iulia*[4] *municipalis*, the text of which is in part preserved, calls for particular notice.   It was probably passed at the beginning of 45, but must surely have been drafted in 46, before Caesar left for Spain.   Its known contents were

---

[1] Dion Cass. XLIII 25, Lange *RA* III 449.   [2] Suet. *Jul.* 42.
[3] So says Sueton. *Jul.* 42.   See Strachan-Davidson on Appian *civ.* I 8 § 2.
[4] For title see inscription from Padua (Wilmanns 2130).   For text, Bruns, *fontes*, Wordsworth, *Specimens*.   For date Cic. *ad fam.* VI 18.

briefly as follows. There were rules to govern the distribution of
corn in Rome, carefully guarding against the abuse of giving doles to
persons other than (a limited number chosen by lot from) those
placed on a select list. There were also rules for the cleansing and
upkeep of streets and lanes in the city and precincts, rules for wheeled
traffic, rules to prevent all encroachments on public ground, permanent
or temporary, but reserving the rights of persons acting for the public,
such as contractors for public works, erectors of stands and platforms,
clerks and state slaves, and the official conductors of religious
ceremonies. The powers and duties of the aediles and road-com-
missioners were left in full force as before. In general the effect
of these clauses was to enforce the liability of individual owners of
property to keep in order the rights of way on which their buildings
abutted, and to protect the public against their encroachments. So
far the statute dealt solely with the city of Rome and the precinct of
one mile all round it. After this it proceeded to lay down normal
rules for the self-government of municipalities, rules sufficiently
general to be applicable to the various types. The qualifications
for holding office or sitting in the local senate were prescribed, with
careful enumeration of causes of disqualification, such as the evasion
of military service, insolvency, conviction in a court of law, notoriously
disgraceful acts, and the practice of disreputable trades. There were
regulations for a municipal census to be held at the same time as
that in Rome and on the same model, with provision for the results
to be forwarded to Rome and a copy kept there. There was also
a clause providing a means of amending[1] local statutes in municipalities of a certain class, and a year was granted for the purpose.
But all these municipal matters, how came they to be included in the
same law as the urban regulations of Rome? Surely because Caesar
saw no good reason for keeping them separate. That he did so mix
up the affairs of the imperial city with those of its satellites the local
boroughs was surely, as Mommsen[2] holds, a sign of the spirit in which
he viewed the empire as a whole. To him, the champion of the
Transpadanes, the patron of Greeks, the tolerant friend of the Jews,
the war-chief of Gauls and Germans, the old conception of Rome
as the one centre, different in kind from all other cities, was no longer
a living creed. As Rome now included Italy, so she might in time
include the subject countries, and assuredly the mind of Caesar was

---

[1] § 30 in Bruns. The statutes are those approved by a commissioner sent from Rome
to one of the *municipia fundana*, which Mommsen holds to be provincial towns (in Spain etc.,
to which Caesar gave Latin rights. They would have accepted the Roman franchise, *jundi
facti*, see Reid on Cic. *pro Balbo* § 19.

[2] Mommsen *RH* IV 533 (Eng. trans.).

on the way to some such truly imperial design, though probably without at present forming any positive scheme. But we may trace the same tendency on its negative side in his desire to reduce the numbers of the Roman rabble, in his withdrawal of an exclusive Italian privilege by the reimposition of taxes on imports, perhaps also in his sumptuary legislation, for extravagant luxury was in the main both a cause and an effect of provincial extortion. That we do not hear of opposition to the dictator's policy is to be explained by the impossibility of opposing it with success. But that there was no lack of discontent may be inferred from the silly gossip[1] imputing to him the intention of leaving Rome in charge of some of his partisans and transferring the centre of government to Alexandria or Troy. The truth was that Rome as the corrupt mistress of a subject world had come to an end. Some one master, corrupt or not corrupt, was to rule the vast empire as an empire, with an eye to its well-being as a whole, were it only for his own interest. But that the imperial capital could be any other than Rome was in present circumstances an absurd notion, not in the least likely to commend itself to the clear and practical intellect of Caesar.

1266. There were also other matters dealt with in Julian laws, from which we may gather some knowledge of the points in which Caesar desired reform. It appears that the statutory penalties for crimes, particularly those of public violence and treason, were found insufficient to deter men from committing them. If prosecuted and convicted, they only suffered the inconveniences of exile ; they retained their properties. It was now enacted that they should forfeit 50 % of their property, and in cases of parricide the whole. This surely shews that the class of offenders aimed at were wealthy men whose crimes were carried out by a retinue of slaves. We cannot help thinking of Milo and the 'battle of Bovillae.' The constitution of the courts was also modified by doing away with the third *decuria* of jurors, that of the *tribuni aerarii*. The reason for this change from Caesar's point of view we do not know. Another measure may perhaps have given statutory form to his prohibition of new and mischievous *collegia*. Another consisted of a remarkable restriction on freedom of foreign travel. It is said to have forbidden any citizen between the ages of 20 and 40 to be out of Italy for more than three years on end, unless he were bound by the military oath (*sacramentum*): and further, no son of a senator might go abroad at all, unless he were on the staff of a magistrate in a military (*contubernalis*) or civil (*comes*) capacity. This is commonly spoken of as *lex Iulia militaris*, and no doubt it did bear on military service.

---

[1] Suet. *Jul.* 79, Nic. Damasc. *Caes. Aug.* 20.

But there were probably other reasons for checking the unlicensed movement of vagabond Romans. Such a man as Sittius had been useful, because he served the interest of Caesar at a pinch; but a Sittius on the other side was not to be desired. Moreover Romans travelling were apt to be a burden on the provincials, and a nuisance to any governor who tried to do his duty. It is to be noted that another *lex Iulia*[1] restricted the tenure of provincial governorships, in the case of ex-praetors to one year, in that of ex-consuls to two. The limitation was probably suggested by the way in which, ever since the time of Marius, long commands had weakened the stability of the central government. His own tenure of the Gauls was the last and most striking instance. He was now the central government himself, and stability was his aim. But his own time was now drawing to an end, and this and the preceding law were destined to record aspirations rather than to achieve results.

1267. We have already referred to the cool way in which, to the disgust of Cicero, decrees were drawn up in the name of the Senate. This liberty may not have been taken often, but once was too often to please the House. The relations between Caesar and the Senate were perhaps the most unfortunate part of the present situation. He fell into the habit of consulting only a few of the leading members, and sometimes a sort of inner Cabinet of his intimate friends. This was no doubt good for the despatch of business, and it was probably in part for this reason that the overworked dictator was glad to settle many matters without a debate in the full House. But with discontented critics he would not get the benefit of this excuse. Nor was the use to which he put his censorial power in filling vacancies approved by all. He had already in 47 introduced new members whom the nobles thought unworthy, and he now continued this policy, bringing in men who had been condemned in the courts and others suffering from the censorial stigma or victims of Sulla's proscriptions. These rehabilitations may have been generous and wise, but they were unsettling, and were sure to offend some. Caesar could not do away with the Senate, at least not unless he set up an undisguised military monarchy. This he had no intention of doing, as we see from the fact that he discharged his veterans and made no preparation for maintaining a standing army. But to allow the Senate to recover its old aristocratic character, and to remain in possession of the powers which the decay of the popular Assembly had enabled it to usurp, was not consistent with his plans. We must remember that the Assembly had long been wholly unfit to resume its lost powers. None knew this better than Caesar, who had first

[1] Lange *RA* III 456.

come to the front as a demagogue, using the Assembly as a tool. A strong aristocratic Senate, led by a few nobles jealous of their own importance, was certain to be embarrassing to a busy autocrat. Their views on imperial questions would generally be opposed to his. It was simpler to weaken the House by packing it with new members of a type not likely to coalesce readily with the remnant of old aristocratic cliques, and this policy, though it made him secret enemies, Caesar followed to the last. But the most decisive steps in this direction were not taken till the year 45, after his return from Spain.

1268. Of all the reforms of Caesar none was so unquestionably good or so lasting as the reform[1] of the calendar, ordained by him in his capacity of chief pontiff. There were in use two year-systems (*a*) the calendar-year, ordered by the pontiffs, by which the times of fixed festivals and the days available for transaction of public business could be ascertained, and (*b*) the magisterial year. The former by ancient custom began with March, and the two months January and February, the addition of which was ascribed to one or other of the Roman kings, came at the end of the year. The latter ever since 153 B.C. had begun with January. We need not go back further than the Republic in speaking of the number of days. The normal year allowed for 355 days only, but it was well known that this was too little for the solar year. Now the solar year must be observed, at least approximately, by all who till the soil. Accordingly the Roman farmers of early times followed a rough computation of their own, guided by the movements of the heavenly bodies, a system which we may call the year of seasons. The official year was conducted on a plan quite unsuited to their needs. The attempt to combine the principles of a lunar and a solar year was under the Republic carried out in the following clumsy manner. Tradition assigned the introduction of this plan to the Decemvirs of 450 B.C., and it seems to have been meant as an improvement on previous methods of correction. A cycle of four years[2] served as the basis. The first and third of the four had each 355 days only, in

---

[1] This account of the Calendar-reform is of course not complete, but only meant to illustrate the work of Caesar. The subject has a literature of its own, and a large one. Two convenient abstracts are in Marquardt *Stvw.* III 281—9, Lange *RA* III 451—2.

The chief passages in ancient writers bearing on the subject are Macrobius *Sat.* I 12—16, Censorinus 20, Suet. *Jul.* 40, *Aug.* 31, Appian *civ.* II 154, Plut. *Caes.* 59, Dion Cass. XLIII 26, XLVIII 33, Pliny *NH* XVIII §§ 207, 211, 212, Ammian Marc. XXVI 1 §§ 7—13, Solinus 1 31—47.

[2] Mommsen *Staatsr.* II 331—2, *Chronol.* 164—8 holds that this was derived from the Greek Olympiads. The *lustrum* too was designed to be a four-year period. It was not regularly kept, and became quinquennial through the prevalence of the later mode of reckoning. Caesar reverted to a four-year cycle in his calendar.

the second an intercalary month of 22 days was added, in the fourth one of 23 days. This plan, if regularly followed, added an average of $11\frac{1}{4}$ days to the year, and the average year of $366\frac{1}{4}$ days was about a day too long. How this error was corrected is not certain. What is certain is that intercalation was the pontiffs' business, and that they mismanaged it, whether from ignorance or carelessness, and in course of time from motives of corrupt complaisance or spite. Superstition also at times played a part. But the temptation to make their power felt by extending or curtailing the term of office of a friend or an enemy, by postponing or hastening the trial of an important case in the courts, by lengthening or shortening the period for which ·a contract was to run, was too much for the pontiffs. They did or did not intercalate as suited their own purposes, and the Roman year had in consequence become a monster of confusion, neither corresponding to the facts of nature nor adapted to the convenience of public life. Jobbery ruled it. In 51 Curio desired an intercalation, in 50 Cicero dreaded one: in neither year did it take place, for the prevailing interest was against it.

1269. It was not Caesar who discovered this scandal, but it was he who resolved to put an end to it. His plan was frankly to adopt the solar year as the year of Rome, and to make it begin with the first of January for all official purposes, taking care not to disturb religious prejudices by the change. So to 355 days he added ten, and provided that in every fourth year a day should be added to February[1] after the 24th day of the month. Thus the average year worked out at $365\frac{1}{4}$ days. The very small error still left was not remedied till 1582 A.D., but the Julian calendar thus amended is still that of the civilized world. It should be noted that in distributing the ten added days Caesar respected old scruples so far as possible. Odd numbers were deemed lucky. In the year as he found it every month save unlucky February had an odd number of days (29 or 31). To January Sextilis (Aug.) and December he added two days each, raising 29 to 31, to April June September and November one each, raising 29 to 30. March May Quintilis (Jul.) and October already had 31 days each, and a trace of this fact remained in the Julian calendar. In these four months the ancient divisions, the Nones and Ides, fell on the 7th and 15th days respectively, and they were left as before. But in the other months the corresponding dates were the 5th and 13th, and these were not disturbed though the months had

---

[1] For the date see Mommsen, *Chronol.* pp. 279—81. This was the traditional place for intercalation to come in. Feb. 24 was in Roman style the 6th day before the Kalends of March (A.D. VI KAL. MART.), and the new day was regarded as a repetition of this day (*bis sextum*).

been lengthened. Moreover the added days[1] were carefully inserted so as not to upset the traditional dates of festivals. The desire to combine a maximum of convenience with a minimum of disturbance is sufficiently obvious. The old intercalary month disappeared, and the Roman citizen now had a state-calendar suitable for all purposes. The new system was ultimately derived from Egypt, where the year of $365\frac{1}{4}$ days had long been known. In the preparation of his calendar Caesar employed specialists, in particular the Greek astronomer Sosigenes, said to have been an Alexandrian. When complete, he published it, and declared it binding on the state as from the Calends of the following January (45). This he did in an Edict issued, we may infer, in virtue of his power as Dictator. Meanwhile it had been necessary to provide for the transition[2] from the old system to the new. It was managed thus. The preceding year (47 B.C., 707 A.U.C.) ended as a calendar year with the last day of the intercalary month, the year 46 (708) began with the first of March. The next year (45 or 709) was to begin with the first of January for all purposes. The months from March to December inclusive accounted for 298 days under the old arrangement. Caesar added 67 days in the form of two months[3] (*intercalaris prior* and *posterior*), thus bringing up this March—December year to 365 days. The 67 days were exactly the number missing, and a normal year was thus produced before the new system came into force. But if the 80 days (Jan., Feb., intercal.) belonging to the calendar year 47 (707) but to the magisterial year 46 (708) were added to the 365, the total came to 445 days. By this process the conclusion was reached that Caesar made a year of 445 days, and we find it called *annus confusionis*[4] in a writer of the end of the fourth century A.D. This may be an echo of contemporary sneers, for there is evidence that Cicero made a sour jest on the constellations that duly appeared to date in compliance with the edict of Caesar. And it was true that Caesar's third consulship lasted 445 days. It remains to add that after Caesar's death the pontiffs again went wrong by putting in the extra day on the old Roman way of counting, by which 'every fourth year' was what we should call every third year; and this error had to be corrected by Augustus.

1270. While these reforms were being worked out, Caesar was receiving disquieting news from the West. When he last returned to

---

[1] The 10 added days were all marked F (*fastus*) in the new calendar, but not C (*comitialis*). Thus they were all available for business, but not for Assemblies. Macrob. I 14 § 12, Varro *de ling. Lat.* VI 29.

[2] Mommsen, *Chronol.* pp. 276—8.

[3] See Cic. *ad fam.* VI 14 § 2.

[4] Macrob. *Sat.* I 14 § 3, Plut. *Caes.* 59.

Rome he had sent C. Didius with his fleet to Spain, and hoped that with this support his governors there would be able to stifle the rebellion. But the misconduct of Q. Cassius had borne its natural fruit. The troops in the Further province mutinied and joined Labienus and Varus when they arrived from Africa, and Cn. Pompey was put at the head of the rising. The southern and western districts of the peninsula were dominated by the rebels, Caesar's lieutenants begged him to come, and he saw that he must go. He was weary of war, which with him was never more than a means to an end, an end that had for the present been attained, and it was with great reluctance that he prepared to interrupt his political work. Before he went, there were many matters to be settled if possible. Among these was the question of the exiles. Cicero and others were exerting themselves to procure the recall of republican friends, and among the pleaders for indulgence we hear of a youth[1] destined to leave a great mark on the history of Rome and the world. This was C. Octavius, son of Caesar's niece Atia. He was in favour with the dictator, and with excellent judgment used his influence to promote the recall of exiles. Thus he gained a reputation for a good heart, and shewed as a lad of 17 the tact and skill in turning opportunities to account which made him, as Octavian and Augustus, the practical builder of the Empire. No doubt Caesar was himself inclined to leniency, but the credit of any act of grace would be given rather to those who were thought to have mollified the autocrat than to the kindly autocrat himself.

1271. Of the cases in which indulgence was now granted, two are of particular interest, both from the special circumstances of each and from the reappearance of Cicero as an orator. One was that of M. Marcellus, consul in 51, the man who flogged the Transpadane and had been a bitter opponent of Caesar. In the Senate his cousin (consul in 50) and Caesar's father-in-law Piso pleaded for him, and the whole house rose to support their prayer. Caesar gave way gracefully; even the harsh Marcellus might return, if the Senate wished it. Cicero had meant to make no speeches while the Republic was in abeyance, but this magnanimity overcame him. He returned thanks[2] on behalf of the House. The fulsome praise and gratitude expressed in this oration (even in the version edited for publication), and the anxiety professed for the safety of the dictator's person, read strangely as the utterances of a man so discontented as Cicero. Yet they were not mere insincerities. They led up to a remarkable passage in which he expressed his own hopes, and enjoyed the pleasure of giving advice to Caesar. He pointed out that the glories

---

[1] Nic. Damasc. *Caes. Aug.* c. 8 (*FHG* III 430—1).

[2] Cic. *pro Marcello, ad fam.* IV 4.

of victory followed by mercy ought not to be an end but a beginning. The reform of the Republic, and its reestablishment on a sound footing, was the task awaiting the conqueror, the achievement which alone could win him not only present gratitude but an immortality of renown hereafter.   In short, Cicero had still some hope of a Republic voluntarily restored by Caesar.   That the lack of materials made this result impossible, however willing Caesar might be, was a conclusion less evident to the speaker then than it is to us now.   The case[1] of Q. Ligarius, one of the exiles pardoned in Africa, was less easily settled.   His offence was more recent.   A deputation visited Caesar at his house to petition for the recall of Ligarius, but in vain. Still Cicero thought he saw signs of yielding, and when a charge was brought against the exile he undertook his defence before a public court presided over by Caesar himself.   The speech *pro Ligario* was a brilliant success, for the dictator was so moved that he directed the acquittal of the accused and allowed him to return.   The forgiving disposition of Caesar was ever one of the most amiable features of his character.   And at this juncture, when he was anxious to leave contentment behind him in Rome, his interest also prompted him to forgiveness.   To enlist the ready tongue of Cicero in his praise was something gained.   It was not for nothing that Caesar's friend Balbus[2] was loud in praise of the speech for Ligarius and sent off a copy of it when published to Caesar in Spain.   There were no Opposition Journals, whose reluctant approval could be triumphantly cited by Government Organs; but to make much of the laudatory phrases of the great republican orator came to the same thing.

1272.   Rome was no doubt full of gossip, and one piece of scandal at least was of some importance.   Cleopatra came to Rome, on Caesar's invitation, it was said.   She brought her boy husband, and they lodged in Caesar's garden residence beyond the Tiber.   To infer a continuance of the amour begun in Alexandria was natural, nor was Roman society likely to be censorious from a purely moral point of view.   But unions with foreign women were not approved, and this was not merely a foreign woman but a queen.   When it was first whispered that Caesar meant to marry her, is not clear, but in time the suggestion took the form that he meant to be a king, with Alexandria for his royal capital.   This is not to be believed, but it was to Caesar's disadvantage that such a plan could be imputed to him, and we must not forget that imputations of aiming at regal power had for ages been at Rome the conventional preface to a public murder.   And we learn that the dictator insisted on having

[1] See Tyrrell and Purser IV Introd. p. 72, Quintilian XI 1 §§ 79, 80.
[2] Cic. *ad Att.* XIII 19 § 2.

the king and queen enrolled among the allies and friends of the Roman people, a step likely to be misrepresented and promote suspicion. Among the Roman nobles there was no lack of men ready to put a malign interpretation on every word or deed. This state of mind was no new thing. How stubborn and bitter Romans could be was well shewn in the cases of M. Marcellus and Q. Ligarius. Marcellus at first sulkily refused to accept rehabilitation. At length he yielded to the persuasion of friends, and left his retreat at Mitylene for Rome. On his way he met in the Piraeus a friend or client who killed him in a quarrel and then committed suicide. Ligarius did return, but gratitude did not prevent him from joining the conspiracy against the life of Caesar.

1273. In the arrangements made for provincial governorships one or two points require notice. Transalpine Gaul was left in charge of D. Brutus as before. None knew the province better. C. Vibius Pansa was to relieve M. Brutus in Cisalpine Gaul. P. Vatinius remained in Illyricum, and Sallust in New Africa, the annexed part of Numidia. For the government of Rome Caesar provided arbitrarily, not without good reasons, we may be sure. In 45 he would be in official style dictator for the third time. He now named Lepidus[1] his master of horse. Antony was at present in disgrace, and Lepidus was to be the formal head of the administration in the dictator's absence. But the real power lay with Caesar's trusty agents Balbus and Oppius. Lepidus held an election, in which Caesar was made consul for the fourth time, and without a colleague. The administrative departments of praetors aediles and quaestors were placed under *praefecti*, deputies appointed by Caesar in virtue of his wide general powers. All this may have been[2] in the interest of the public peace, but it was not a popular arrangement. Yet those on whom the autocracy lay most heavily were well aware[3] that no good was to be looked for from the possible success of the gang of desperadoes now heading the rebellion in Spain. Order and public prosperity rested on the control of the one strong master. The discontented men desired prosperity without a master, but in the circumstances of the time this aspiration was no better than crying for the moon.

1274. Caesar left Rome in December and, travelling with his usual speed, joined his army in Spain before he was expected. What troops he had is not clear, but he certainly had some of his

---

[1] Dion Cass. XLIII 33 says that Lepidus named himself *magister equitum*, unconstitutionally. Probably he read out a written commission from Caesar, who had gone to Spain.

[2] See Tyrrell and Purser v Introd. p. 20.

[3] See Cic. *fam.* VI 3, 4, XV 19 § 4, compared with *pro Marc.* §§ 17, 18.

veterans. Some of his old legions had been disbanded. It is natural to infer that those for whom land-allotments could not at once be provided had been kept under arms and sent on to the seat of war. The forces of the enemy were far more numerous, but a great part of them consisted of liberated slaves and native levies, inferior in discipline, and rather enjoying rebellion for its own sake than interested in the last struggle of the civil war. The pick of their army were the old Pompeian legions of Afranius[1] and Varro[2], with some refugees who had escaped from the African war, and some troops raised in the Roman towns of southern Spain. Both sides received auxiliaries from Mauretania. Bocchus sent help to the rebels, Bogud to Caesar; from which we may perhaps gather that the removal of P. Sittius to organize his new principality had caused the rivalry of the brothers to break out afresh. Caesar appears to have been better provided with cavalry than usual. The difficulties of the campaign were mainly those of finding shelter and supplies. He could not afford to wait, and the war had to be waged in the winter months. Following the enemy into southern Spain, he found most of the open country bare and the walled towns held by rebel garrisons. The accounts of the campaign are very confused, but it seems clear that it was carried on with great barbarity on both sides. Cn. Pompey was naturally brutal, and Caesar was driven to reprisals. The conduct of the slaves liberated and employed by the rebels was particularly atrocious. At first operations were indecisive, but some successes of Caesar led to a wavering in the towns, and the beginning of defections forced Pompey to accept the hazard of a pitched battle. It took place near a town called Munda, somewhere not far from Corduba. It was a stubborn fight, and tradition said that Caesar had to dismount and fight sword in hand. At last the forces of desperation gave way, and the exasperation of the Caesarians took its fill of butchery. Labienus and Varus fell fighting, Cn. Pompey escaped to Carteia and put to sea, but was obliged to land on another part of the coast, where he was killed. Sextus Pompey, who was in charge at Corduba, got away safe, to be a cause of trouble at a later day.

1275. The battle of Munda was fought on the 17th March B.C. 45. After it towns surrendered or were taken, and the Spanish rebellion died out. But Caesar stayed some time in the province, rewarding and punishing. Rebel towns lost some of their lands or had their quota of tribute raised. Others for their deserts received more territory or were granted certain immunities. Some received the Roman franchise after the precedent of Gades. Some were given

[1] Brought from Africa. *Bell. Hisp.* 7 § 4.
[2] Went over from Trebonius. See § 1245 above, and Kraner on Caes. *civ.* II 21.

the style of Roman *coloniae*, carrying with it a certain municipal rank. If we may believe the story[1] preserved by Dion, he made the favoured communities pay for these privileges. That he raised money by appropriating temple treasures and other exactions is credible enough. His readiness to grant the franchise is a symptom of his views as to the proper position of the provinces in the empire. While he was busy with this reconstructive work he was joined by the young Octavius, who had been ill, and now took an adventurous journey as soon as he was fit to travel. Caesar kept the youth with him, and formed a high opinion of his capacity, from which important consequences were to follow. Most of the business of this time was transacted at Hispalis (Seville) or on the way home at New Carthage. Caesar was back in Italy early in September. At his country place near Rome[2] he made his will, but did not enter the city till early in October. If we may trust Suetonius, the work of war and government had not occupied the whole of his time in Spain. Not to mention a poem entitled *Iter*, composed on his outward journey, he wrote a controversial treatise, the *Anticato* or 'Cato exposed,' intended to shew the faults and weaknesses of the republican hero, whose reputation was becoming troublesome. It was a counterblast to Cicero's *Laus Catonis*, and its literary merit considerable, but we may gather from a reference in Juvenal[3] that for a party pamphlet it was too long. But as a bloodless way of dealing with opponents it was characteristic of Caesar's methods, a striking contrast to the proscriptions and murders that had stained the past, and others that were yet to come.

1276. So Caesar returned to Rome for the last time, and Octavius with him. He had fought his last battle: the republicans had not. Since the news of Munda Senate and Assembly had been striving to outdo their previous servility in devising further honours to bestow on their master. Further powers there were none left to bestow, unless we reckon the right to hold the consulship for ten successive years, and to nominate even the plebeian magistrates, as extensions of his autocratic power. In effect he could already do these things. Nor were the right to the disposal of the moneys in the state chest, and the monopoly of the military *imperium*, anything more than the recognition of patent facts. He was already in full enjoyment of these powers, which Ilerda and Pharsalus had given him and Thapsus and Munda had confirmed. But the stream of honours flowed without ceasing till the springs of adulation ran dry. Fifty days thanksgiving,

---

[1] Dion Cass. XLIII 39.   [2] Suet. *Jul.* 83.

[3] Suet. *Jul.* 56, Juvenal VI 338. The book was preceded by a work of the same tendency by Hirtius. See Cic. *ad Att.* XII 45 § 3, 40 § 1, 41 § 4. Brutus and M. Fadius Gallus also wrote panegyrics on Cato.

yearly games[1] to commemorate his victory, distinctions of dress, some of them regal in their significance, the title of *Liberator*, the bestowal of the title *Imperator*, not as a military exceptional honour but as a first name (*praenomen*) to descend to his children, the right to a state-residence on the Palatine, built not on the common model but with a pediment or gable (*fastigium*) after the manner of temples,— these distinctions proclaimed the monarch and assigned him a palace. But this was not enough. An ivory figure of Caesar was to be paraded in procession to the Circus games. A statue of him was to be set up on the Capitol next to the figures traditionally representing the Roman kings, and another in the temple of Quirinus. Quirinus was traditionally identified with the mythical founder Romulus, assassinated and then deified. In May 45 Cicero, who was thoroughly sick of these proceedings, and saw the hope of a restored Republic passing away, wrote[2] to Atticus 'I had rather he shared the temple of Quirinus than that of Safety.' An ominous jest, within a year of its fulfilment as a prophecy. Later writers tell us that some (senators, that is,) who proposed or voted these honours did so deliberately with the hope of creating odium against the recipient, which is perhaps true. On the 20th or 21st Quintilis (July) Cicero[3] noted that at the *ludi victoriae Caesaris* the figure of Caesar was borne in the procession beside that of Victory, and that the people would not greet it with applause. Caesar was still abroad, but of course, with his agents in every post of authority, it was assumed that their consent to all these extravagances implied the approval of their master. Indeed when he returned he only declined a few of the voted honours, in particular the ten years' consulship, but he does not appear to have refused deification. To him it might well seem a small matter. A polytheistic system easily finds room for new divinities. The ancient religion of Rome itself regarded primarily *numina*, the manifestations of power in various modes, practically infinite, and the tendency to regard them as persons was at least largely derived from the anthropomorphism of Greece. Long ago the view that the gods were deified men had been popularized by Ennius. The East was the real home of this doctrine, and as an object-lesson there was Egypt, with its series of deified Ptolemies. With Julius Caesar began the deification of Roman emperors.

1277. After the return of Caesar from Spain we begin to detect

---

[1] The anniversaries of his great victories were also to be recognized as holidays.

[2] Cic. *ad Att.* XII 45 § 3 *eum σύνναον Quirini malo quam Salutis.* Cf. XIII 28 § 3. The statue bore the inscription DEO INVICTO.

[3] Cic. *ad Att.* XIII 44 § 1.

signs of a certain failure of judgment, which shews itself in acts[1] of omission and commission that proved him to be losing touch with public sentiment.   It was surely unwise to celebrate a triumph, even over Spain.   Spain was a Roman possession, and all men knew that the enemy conquered were simply Romans.   It was worse to allow his lieutenants Fabius and Pedius to triumph[2] *ex Hispania* soon after on their own account.   The African triumph had been painful enough, and three celebrations of the 'crowning mercy' of Munda were too much.   It was just those in whom patriotic feeling survived strongest to whom these triumphs were disgusting.   While we may admit that Caesar's head was somewhat turned by his present elevation, it is perhaps to the loneliness of his position that we should primarily attribute these ill-judged proceedings.   Balbus Oppius and others were friends, but also dependants, and now dependants more than ever.   He was now more than ever compelled to see with other men's eyes and to act on information furnished by men who, however honest, were his satellites, always tempted to dissemble unpleasant truths, and generally inferior to their master in far-sighted and penetrating judgment.   Moreover he was surrounded by a multitude of claims not easy to satisfy.   In order to give the pardoned Pompeians an interest in his government, he must give them a share of the important posts.   On the other hand it was necessary to gratify his own partisans, who were looking for immediate preferment. In departing from the simple methods of Sulla he had created for himself a new and embarrassing situation.   Mercy and the acceptance of responsibility had their drawbacks.   The former could be forgotten, while the latter concentrated all the forces of discontent against the autocrat alone.

1278.   Caesar now resigned his consulship, and had Q. Fabius Maximus and C. Trebonius elected consuls for the rest of the year. This provided for two claimants, but the arrangement was not a popular one, for it called attention to the degradation of a great historic office.   And at the end of the year, when Fabius died just before the close of his term, Caesar put in a successor for the vacant day or part of a day.   There were probably good formal reasons for the step, but not unnaturally it was made the occasion of sneers, and provoked[3] some of Cicero's bitterest jibes.   Other magistrates were also elected for the rest of the year, and the number raised in the

---

[1] See Suet. *Jul.* 78 for his irritation at a tribune who did not rise from the bench to greet him as he went past in his Spanish triumph.

[2] *ex Hispania* is the form in the *fasti triumphales.*

[3] Cic. *ad fam.* VII 30.

case of praetors (14) and quaestors (40). In the matter of the provincial governorships Caesar had for the present to make the new appointments for the year 44 provisionally. His schemes for a thorough reorganization of the empire could not be carried out at once. The most notable points in these arrangements were that D. Brutus was transferred to Cisalpine Gaul, that Vatinius was kept in Illyricum, and that Achaia remained (as it had done since the time of Pharsalus) under a separate governor, not subordinate to the Macedonian province under the form of a protectorate. The old Greece was clearly on its way to become in due form a Roman province. But the provincial arrangements now made were destined to be upset by the events of the coming year, and we need not dwell upon them. It has been well remarked[1] that a letter from Vatinius to Cicero on the 5th December 45 throws light on Caesar's firm control of his nominees. Vatinius had won successes in Dalmatia, and a thanksgiving had been voted in his honour. But he had to evacuate one of the captured towns, driven out by the severe weather. He begged Cicero to see that the affair was properly represented to Caesar, so that his apparent failure might be condoned. Caesar owed much to Vatinius, but the master was now in power, and his servants had to render account of their acts. Here was the practical beginning of that central control which was to become the essential feature in the Roman Empire.

1279. It was not the imperial acts of the great dictator, but his more despotic bearing, his readiness to take offence, and his unguarded utterances, passed on with malignant exaggeration by evil-disposed persons, that betrayed the degeneration that was going on in him, and tempted a band of malcontents to conspire against his life. Caesar was but mortal, and the long strain of many terrible years had told upon his constitution. An old tendency to epilepsy, which he seemed to have outgrown, had lately returned, and for an autocrat there was no rest. He had been ill in Spain. A year before he had been heard to say that he had lived long enough, and he was now weary and often ill-tempered. His isolation and the worry of business in Rome were too much for him, and he suffered from fits and dreams. Yet he was as ready as ever to forgive offences of the past. A number of the political exiles still abroad were freely pardoned and allowed to return with full rights, even to stand for office, and these select pardons seem to have been followed by a general amnesty. In one case, that of Cicero's friend A. Caecina, there was a private injury to be overlooked also. Caecina had published a most abusive attack on Caesar, but Caesar forgave him as he had forgiven[2]

[1] Tyrrell and Purser v Introd. p. 26.   [2] Suet. *Jul.* 73—75.

Memmius and Calvus for their attacks years before and repaid the lampoons of Catullus by inviting him to dinner. This lofty generosity was however viewed with jealous eyes by his own old partisans, who grudged their adversaries an equality with themselves, and served to ripen a growth of personal discontents. It is very likely that the last batch of excessive honours, those conferred on him after his last return to Rome, were deliberately intended by the movers and supporters to make the 'tyrant' odious. Such proposals as those for authorizing him to wear the triumphal robes on public occasions, to have the *fasces* of his lictors always decked with bays, for erecting statues of him in public places (temples etc.) not only in Rome but in the towns of Italy, for making his birthday a public holiday, and for giving him as a part of his after-name (*cognomen*) the title of 'Father of his country,' added to previous honours, only served to lower the dictator's subjects, not to raise the dictator. Of the vast schemes contemplated by Caesar we will speak below. But in voting the construction of new public buildings under Caesar's direction, destined to bear his name, the Senate hit upon a way of honouring him which was specially attractive to him in his present frame of mind. And two extensions of powers were of practical use in giving a legitimate character to his enterprises. First, his censorial power was made permanent by declaring him *praefectus morum* for life. This was convenient in connexion with the building and engineering department, the contracts in which were normally let by the censors. Secondly, the inviolability and right of *intercessio* were at present enjoyed by Caesar as possessing the tribunician[1] power already granted him. Some further grant was now made, apparently in the form of declaring him *sacrosanctus* in a wider sense. As we find the emperors, beginning with Augustus, possessing this inviolability not only within the sacred precinct (*pomerium*) but up to the mile-limit from the city walls, and interpreting it as extending all through the empire, it is probable that the substance of the new grant was something of the same kind.

1280. Before we turn to the official acts of Caesar in Rome during the last months of the year 45 it will be well to look at the vast projects[2] attributed to him both in Italy and abroad. Exaggeration there probably is, but the tradition is in the main quite credible, and it gives us a view of his grand imperial ideas. Some of the

---

[1] That the *intercessio* of a tribune was valid as against the military *imperium* within the *pomerium*, but not up to the mile-limit, seems to have been an ancient rule. See Mommsen, *Staatsrecht* I 64—70, II 844. Lange *RA* III 470 speaks too positively on the evidence, which is very loose. It is thought (Mommsen *Str.* II 684) that Caesar also received a general power as proconsul throughout the empire.

[2] Lange *RA* III 468—9.

programme, but by no means all, may have been suggested by the career of the great Alexander, an influence that had never ceased to work on enterprising conquerors. Italy was to be the scene of colossal[1] undertakings. A great road was to be driven through the Apennine range, giving Rome more direct communication with the Adriatic. The lake Fucinus was to be drained, and the Pomptine marshes as well. In connexion with the latter work a new channel was to be dug for the Tiber, discharging into the sea at Terracina. But the old harbour of Rome at Ostia was to remain and to be improved by building breakwaters and clearing away the banks of silt[2] that were choking the mouth. The new cut to Terracina was perhaps meant chiefly to be a canal for drainage. The capital was of course not to be neglected. The *pomerium* was to be enlarged, and with it the city. He had already added to the public buildings of Rome, and now proposed to undertake[3] a comprehensive scheme of reconstruction, including a splendid temple of Mars, a theatre partly cut in the side of the Capitoline, a new Senate-House, and other works. Some changes in the Forum, such as the removal of the platform (*rostra*), were actually carried out. But the most far-reaching part of the plan was that for treating the *campus Martius* as building-sites and providing instead of it a new Campus beyond the river, a design which would surely have implied the building of one or more new bridges. Nor were matters of a less material kind forgotten. Caesar intended to form two great public libraries, a Greek and a Latin, and the duty of superintending the purchase and arrangement of books was to be entrusted to Varro, the most learned of Romans, whom he had pardoned. Perhaps none of his designs was grander than that of legal reform. He appears to have contemplated a Digest of the law as it stood, reducing its unwieldy bulk by cutting out superfluities. This would surely have been followed by legislation to supplement and amend it and eventually to produce a scientific code. He would have had no lack of skilled jurists to see through whatever was necessary and possible. It is thought that Ofilius[4] was to have been his chief agent. But the death of Caesar put an end to the design, and the work was not seriously taken in hand till the time of Justinian.

[1] Suet. *Jul.* 44.

[2] Plut. *Caes.* 58 τὰ τυφλὰ καὶ δύσορμα. Not 'rocks' (Long) but Tiber-silt, such as has choked the later works of Claudius and Trajan.

[3] It is now generally held that the change by which the buildings in the Forum were made to conform to the lie of the ground was a part of Caesar's scheme. The ancient orientation was guided by the sun, and so followed approximately the points of the compass, as recent excavations have shewn.

[4] Suet. *Jul.* 44. See Roby, Introduction to Justinian's *Digest* chapter viii, especially page 115.

1281.   We have seen that Caesar devoted much attention to the provinces, and that he had already, by granting the Roman franchise to communities outside Italy, given indications of an intention to extend the citizenship of Rome over a wider area.   But for any large plans of organizing the empire more detailed information was necessary.   He projected an imperial census, which would doubtless have furnished statistics of population and the property of individuals, probably also the public revenues of the several communities.   As a first step he ordered a general survey, which was actually begun before his death.   It was an important part of his imperial policy that he designed a large scheme of colonies to be planted in the provinces.   It was intended to meet several needs at once.   To find suitable plots of land in Italy for all the discharged soldiers was probably impossible.   The restriction placed on the corn-doles would leave a great part of the Roman populace without means of sub-sistence.   The Romanizing of the provinces, and the prospect of further extension of the franchise, would be advanced by planting communities of Romans as centres from which Roman civilization would gradually spread.   And outside Italy the state had domains at disposal, as for instance in the territory forfeited by Massalia, a most attractive land in a strategic position of great importance. There were also the sites of Carthage and Corinth.   The fear that had doomed them to desolation had long passed away, but the advantages of position remained.   East and West furnished other suitable sites for colonies.   Accordingly Caesar procured an extension of his colonizing powers by a new law[1] authorizing him to found settlements abroad, not of soldiers only but of other citizens as well, and it is said that he was prepared to provide for 80,000 citizens in this way.   The scheme was most seriously meant, and a beginning made[2] in southern Gaul, but this like other plans was interrupted by his death.   Still preparations had been so fully made that some colonies at least were in process of foundation in the year 44 and the model charter[3] (*lex*) of one of them is in great part preserved.   Some of the proposed foundations were afterwards carried out by Augustus. One of Caesar's great engineering schemes was a canal through the isthmus of Corinth, and he had already selected a chief engineer for the work.   This waited for accomplishment till our own day, when the changed conditions of navigation have rendered it superfluous.

1282.   But the complete restoration of peace was necessary before the organization of the empire could be thoroughly taken in hand.

---

[1] Lange *RA* III 473.   [2] See Marquardt *Stvw.* I pp. 263—4.
[3] The *lex coloniae Genetivae Iuliae* for the colony at Urso (Osuña) in southern Spain.   In Bruns *Fontes* p. 110 foll.

A small local rising of the Bellovaci in Belgian Gaul had been put down by D. Brutus in 46. It was not the north-western parts that were just now causing anxiety, but the north-eastern and eastern frontiers. The rude peoples beyond the Danube had long been in the habit of invading the lands to the south, and had on occasion given much trouble to the governors of Macedonia. Since the fall of Mithradates the general policy of Rome had been to maintain relations with the Thracian princes, who with their warlike subjects formed a screen protecting the Roman province to a considerable extent. Only a strip of the seaboard was in Roman possession, through which ran the road to the Hellespont. The Thracians of the Hinterland were free, and it was not Rome's interest to let them be conquered by the northern barbarians. Shortly before this time[1] these barbarous Getae or Daci had been greatly strengthened by union under an able and vigorous king, Burebistas by name, and they were now threatening the whole Balkan country. This was a danger not to be neglected, and Caesar would no doubt have dealt with the Getae who crossed the Danube as he had dealt with the Germans who crossed the Rhine. But this cloud for the present passed away. Burebistas was murdered, and the powerful Getic kingdom fell to pieces. More distant, but more persistent, was the danger from Parthia, the form in which the eternal Eastern Question was destined to appear for centuries to come. Ever since the disaster of Crassus the Parthians had been restless, and aggressive when opportunity offered, and Syria was just now in a state such as to provoke invasion. In 47, when on his way to meet Pharnaces, Caesar left his relative Sextus Julius Caesar in charge of the province. During the African war a Pompeian officer, Q. Caecilius Bassus, who was in Syria, fomented a mutiny among Sextus Caesar's troops and brought about his murder. Bassus was soon placed in a difficulty, for after Thapsus he was nothing but a rebel. He obtained help from an Arabian prince, and invited the support of the Parthian king. As yet the Parthians had not done much, but there was every likelihood that an invasion in force would soon take place, and Syria be lost. Caesar had sent out a governor with three legions to recover the province, but without success. The governor of Bithynia had to be sent with additional forces to help the governor of Syria. Evidently there was a real need for the master's presence to restore order and provide for the security of the eastern frontier. In procuring a declaration of war against the Parthians Caesar acted with good reason; if the duty of avenging Crassus was put forward, it was only a natural appeal to Roman pride. Preparations for dealing effectively with the Eastern Question were made on

[1] Strabo VII 3 § 11 (pp. 303—4).

a large scale. Great armies were mustered and trained in Greece and Macedonia, ready for the coming campaign. Young Octavius was sent over to Apollonia to continue his studies and gain experience while keeping in touch with the legions. Meanwhile some of Caesar's friends induced the custodians of the so-called Sibylline books to search them for some utterance bearing on the present situation. Early in the next year (44) the rumour spread that a discovery had been made; none but a king could conquer the Parthians. This of course served to confirm the impression that the dictator meant to make himself king of Rome. It seems that imagination was busy imputing to him schemes of wild ambition. Plutarch has preserved the gossip that Caesar designed, after conquering the Parthians, to sweep round by way of the Caspian and the Caucasus to the north of the Euxine, then to overrun Germany, and return to Italy through Gaul. Such may well have been the chatter of Roman dinner-tables, for there was no really interesting topic of conversation but Caesar.

1283. Among the most significant of Caesar's acts was the revision of the Senate. Hitherto he had never had time to deal with this matter comprehensively, though he had put some new members into the House. His present changes were thorough enough, and were evidently aimed at bringing that body into harmony with his system of government. He struck off the roll[1] some who had been found guilty on charges of *repetundae*, from which we may perhaps infer that he was determined to enforce obedience to all regulations bearing on provincial administration. But he enrolled a large number of new members, bringing the total, it is said, up to 900. Among them were soldiers, sons of freedmen, and even Gauls to whom he had given the Roman franchise. Lampoons, and the rather feeble waggery of 'don't shew a new senator the way to the House,' were called forth by this levelling policy, which was not calculated to please either the old senators or the rabble. But such a strong infusion of new blood was no doubt intended to paralyse the nobles who usually took the lead in the Senate, and keep them out of mischief during his long absence. With the degrees of rank (ex-consuls first, and so on,) he dealt arbitrarily, promoting men whom he wished to favour, and thus giving them precedence in the right of speech. Another measure, which seems to have been unprecedented in historical times, was the deliberate creation of new Patricians. For certain purposes, chiefly priesthoods, Patricians were required, and the number of genuine Patrician houses was now very small. Caesar

---

[1] Suet. *Jul.* 43. We must remember that the law now in force was his own *lex Julia* of 59, a statute dealing with many offences other than simple extortion. How these *convicti* had got back to Rome, Suetonius does not say. I suspect the cases were few.

settled this matter[1] simply. He had a law passed to authorize a fresh creation, and carried it out as chief pontiff. Among the new Patricians was young Octavius, whom he had adopted by his will.

1284. Caesar had absorbed the powers of all the highest magistrates. Even the judicial functions of the praetors were assumed by him when it suited his purpose to preside in court. We have seen him on the bench at the trial of Ligarius. In these last months he appears to have done the same on several occasions. According to Dion, his conduct gave rise to the scandal that he took money for directing acquittals. We need not believe this story, but it is no doubt true that he wanted money for numberless purposes. Auctions of confiscated properties were still going on, and it is said that sites belonging to the state were also put upon the market. But the most notable case was the trial of the Galatian king Deiotarus, heard by Caesar in his own house. Deiotarus was suspected of disloyal intentions during the African war, when there were rumours of the defeat of Caesar, and this was probably the reason why the present charge was brought to a hearing. In 47, after the defeat of Pharnaces, Caesar left him his throne but took away some of his territories after an inquiry in which M. Brutus had pleaded the king's cause. He was now charged with having at that time laid a plot to assassinate Caesar. The witnesses in support of this charge were apparently not worthy of credit, and the real danger of Deiotarus was that Caesar wanted an excuse to get rid of a chieftain whom he mistrusted, and (we may add) whose dominions might form the centre of a rebellion while he was himself engaged with the Parthian war. The king was not present in person, but Cicero undertook his defence. All his skill and flattery of Caesar only succeeded so far[2] as to induce the dictator to put off his final decision. The whole trial was a striking assertion of arbitrary power, for the Senate do not seem to have had any voice in the matter at any stage, though it was so closely connected with external policy. This aspect of it was not likely to escape notice, with so many persons still hankering after the lost joys of senatorial misrule. How Caesar appeared to republicans who met him in private life, we may gather from a letter of Cicero[3] written in December. Cicero was in his villa at Puteoli, when the dictator, travelling with a bodyguard of 2000 soldiers, came to visit L. Marcius Philippus, whose country place was close by.

[1] Dion Cass. XLIII 47, Suet. *Jul.* 41, and Nipperdey on Tac. *Ann.* XI 25. The process, known as *adlectio*, bore some analogy to adoption. The grandfather of Octavius was not even a senator, but of respectable equestrian family. If we may believe the speech of Calenus in Dion XLVI 22 § 3, Cicero was one of these new Patricians.

[2] This is inferred from Cic. *philipp.* II §§ 93—5.

[3] Cic. *ad Att.* XIII 52.

The next day he dined with Cicero, who laid himself out to receive the great man worthily. All passed off well and conversation flowed freely, but the orator noted that serious topics (politics) were avoided. Of literary talk there was plenty, doubtless of the best, and Caesar enjoyed it. But to be made to feel his insignificance as a statesman was a bitter pill to Cicero. Early in the year he had tried to carry out a project of addressing an elaborate letter of advice to Caesar, placing his wide political experience at the service of the conqueror. While Caesar was in Spain he submitted his draft to the criticism[1] of Balbus and Oppius, who knew their master's views. They suggested so many modifications that Cicero preferred to drop the project altogether, rather than send an expurgated and pointless composition. No wonder that the vain and sensitive man was hurt by the avoidance of political topics at the dinner in December. No wonder he told Atticus that the honour of entertaining such a guest was one that he was in no hurry to repeat. Now, if such was the attitude of Caesar towards Cicero, whom he was sincerely anxious to please, what slights would he not inflict on persons for whose goodwill he cared less?

1285. We now come to the elections for the year 44, which were held in December. Caesar had had a law passed, by which he was authorized to nominate both the consuls and half the other magistrates. This arrangement seems to have extended to the appointments for three years ahead, but these were never completely carried out. In any case the pretence of restoring free election in some degree was an idle show. The Assembly dared not elect a candidate disapproved by Caesar. A further increase in the number of posts was also made. There were to be 16 praetors and 6 aediles. The two new *aediles Ceriales* were to have the charge of the corn-supply. Among the minor offices, the commissioners of police and coinage (*tresviri capitales* and *monetales*) were raised from three to four in each case. For the year 44 Caesar had himself elected consul for the fifth time. As his colleague he took Antony, who was now restored to favour, and had probably been forgiven his outstanding debt. The most remarkable thing however was the choice of M. Brutus and C. Cassius as praetors, followed by their appointment to the two posts of chief dignity, the 'urban' and 'alien' praetorships. So fully did Caesar trust his pardoned adversaries. For himself, he continued to hold the dictatorship, and began the year 44 as *dictator quartum*

---

[1] Cic. *ad Att.* XIII 27. In the next letter (28) he lets out the truth that he saw an analogy between Caesar and Alexander. This point was probably made in the letter, as notoriously pleasing to Caesar.

consul quintum. But early in the year, probably[1] in February, he laid down the dictatorship as a yearly office and accepted it as an office for life. This left no doubt as to his intention of retaining autocratic power. We may also trace the design of founding a Julian dynasty in the steps taken to bring young Octavius to the front. He was now 18, and had already been made a pontiff, and left in charge of Rome as city-prefect at the time of the Latin festival on the Alban mount. Thus he was already a public character. Caesar now as dictator had the post of *magister equitum* to fill up. He nominated Lepidus for the time being, but arranged that on his departure for the Parthian war Octavius was to succeed to the place, thus becoming the second man in the whole Roman world. The will by which Caesar had adopted him was in the custody of the chief Vestal virgin, but its contents were not generally known, and the full meaning of the promotion of Octavius was perhaps hardly clear to contemporary observers during Caesar's life. Among the men whom Caesar wished to reward was Dolabella, whose service in Africa and Spain had cancelled his previous troublesome behaviour. The plan was that he should resign the consulship, and Dolabella become the colleague of Antony. But these two were rivals, and Antony was reckless enough to interrupt the election by declaring a flaw in the auspices, as he could in his capacity of augur. So Dolabella was not consul till after the death of Caesar. Two sound Caesarians, A. Hirtius and C. Vibius Pansa, both men with long records of service, were elected consuls for the next (43) year.

1286. Caesar was no doubt prodigiously busy with his preparations for the eastern expedition, but the Senate had leisure for voting him more honours, positively the very last in his lifetime. With servile persistence, not unmingled with malignity, they rang the changes on the two main notions of royalty and divinity. All his future acts were by anticipation declared valid, and an oath to uphold them was to be taken by magistrates entering on office. Public prayers, a festival in his honour, a temple to be shared by him with the goddess Clementia, under the care of a special priest (*flamen*), and the change of the name of a month, *Quintilis* becoming *Iulius*, are all that we need mention here. It is more important to notice details of his conduct in which we can see a foreshadowing of the end that was soon to come. A scene in the Forum seems to have made an impression on contemporaries. Caesar was busy there giving directions for some of the works of reconstruction, when the Senate in a body approached him to announce that certain honours had just been voted him. He was so preoccupied that he did not rise from his

[1] Between 25 Jan. and 15 Feb. Henzen in *Ephem. Epigraph.* II 285.

seat to receive them. He afterwards gave out that he had been unwell, but the excuse did not satisfy the senators, who could grovel and yet take themselves seriously. And while wrath was growing venomous in the minds of some, and gratitude decaying in many, he chose to dismiss his bodyguard[1], despite the warnings of faithful friends. A guard of senators and knights had been offered for the protection of his sacred person. This he refused, and it is said that the proposal was a successful ruse to induce him to dismiss his praetorians and leave himself open to attack. Suetonius, probably referring to this time, says that Caesar knew of secret gatherings held at night, but took no further notice of them than to publish the fact of his knowledge. Anything more unlike the traditional Tyrant could hardly be conceived. But by this time there were men actually conspiring against him, and therefore interested in engaging public sympathy by representing him as aiming at regal power and ready at any moment to take even the title of King. Accordingly it was arranged that on public occasions he should be greeted as King by voices from the crowd ; and when he declared in reply that he was not King but Caesar, attention was directed to the lukewarmness of his repudiation. This criticism may or may not have been fair, but it was not without effect. Soon there came a quarrel with two of the tribunes. A crown had been placed upon a statue of Caesar. The two tribunes removed it, and gave out that Caesar did not wish for it. Caesar was annoyed, as he might well be, for their action left him neither the crown nor the credit of a spontaneous refusal. Then came the Latin festival, and as he rode back from Alba he was saluted as King. The tribunes[2] arrested the men who first started the cry, and are said to have meant to bring them to trial. Caesar had repudiated the salute, but he could stand this sort of thing no longer. He employed another tribune to attack them in the Senate, and hurried through measures for their removal from office. No doubt they were acting in concert with persons actually conspiring against the dictator, and their object had been to provoke him into some arbitrary use of power. After all his clemency, it did not look well when the autocrat passed from indulgence to severity. Yet it was his very unwillingness to shed blood that enabled men to plague him without risking their lives. No man would have dared so to provoke a Sulla. This affair took place about the beginning of February, and played into the hand of the conspirators. Not long after, the elections for 43 were held, and it leaked out that among the voting-tablets several were found inscribed with the names not of

[1] They were Spaniards, according to Suet. *Jul.* 86.
[2] Dion Cass. XLIV 9, 10.

Caesar's nominees but of the deposed tribunes. Busy scandal whispered that one of Caesar's men was shortly, after his departure, going to bring in a bill to empower him to marry as many wives as he chose, with the view of securing a natural heir. This probably pointed to queen Cleopatra, and was connected with the other story of his intention to settle at Alexandria. Then came the famous episode of the Lupercalia on the 15th February, when the crown was repeatedly offered him by Antony before all the throng assembled for the festival. Caesar declined it, and the people cheered. He sent the crown to be offered to Capitoline Jove. But it was said, truly or not, that he had refused it with a bad grace, really wishing for it. And, if Cicero[1] is to be believed, he ordered a record of his refusal to be made.

1287. Who first thought of assassinating Caesar we do not know. The man who formed the conspiracy was C. Cassius, a pardoned Pompeian, who owed his life and his present praetorship to Caesar. He seems to have been a man of bilious temperament, constitutionally prone to magnify slights and nurse bitterness. The presence of such a man was all-important at this moment. He bore a grudge against Caesar for being his master, and any grievance, however trivial, was enough to make him wish the master put out of the way. He learnt from others in their unguarded moments that they too found the omnipotence of Caesar galling, and bit by bit drew together a band of malcontents, all men of position, all sighing for 'liberty,' the liberty to misgovern the Roman world, the privilege of republican aristocrats, which Caesar had taken away and evidently did not mean to restore. But sympathy and actual conspiracy were very different things, and in order to develope the former into the latter there was need of some person of respectability to serve as a figure-head and give a serious air to the plot. The obvious man for the post was M. Brutus. He was Cato's nephew, and pretended[2] to be a descendant of the Liberator Brutus, famed for his share in the expulsion of the Tarquins, whose statue stood in the Capitol. His solemnity and intensity had given him a weight far beyond his real merits in a society so generally reckless and selfishly indifferent as that of contemporary Rome. We have seen that in financial matters he was a hard and usurious speculator, but the men who admired him were not squeamish critics, and had either done or looked forward to doing the same. If Brutus could be induced to take the business in hand as a matter of principle, his mere pedantry was a guarantee that he would not back out of it, and others would be ready to follow. He was first approached by broad hints conveyed in anonymous appeals scribbled on the base

---

[1] Cic. *philipp.* II § 87.   [2] Cic. *ad Att.* XIII 40.

of the Liberator's statue or left to catch his eye when he took his seat in court as praetor. Then he was privately sounded, and bit by bit led to think that it was his hereditary moral duty to join in murdering the benefactor whose confidence he had enjoyed for more than three years. That Rome should be waiting for him to lead appealed to his vanity. With this aid, principle overcame scruples, and he threw himself heart and soul into the treacherous design. Cassius had been jealous of Brutus, who stood above him in Caesar's favour, but he laid aside his jealousy to win Brutus to his purpose, and he had his reward. More than sixty men in all were eventually partners in the plot. Among them were such Caesarians as D. Brutus the governor of Cisalpine Gaul, C. Trebonius the governor of Asia, and L. Tillius Cimber, just appointed to Bithynia. Of ex-Pompeians we may note Q. Ligarius, who owed everything to Caesar's mercy, Cn. Domitius Ahenobarbus son of Caesar's bitter adversary, and L. Pontius Aquila, the tribune of 45 who had refused to greet the Spanish triumph. Where so many persons were concerned, it was unlikely that their secret should be safely kept. That some plot against the dictator was on foot was soon whispered in Rome, and the usual signs and prodigies were in evidence, awaiting their interpretation by events. But nothing seems to have leaked out so as to become really public. Care was taken not to draw unsuitable men into the conspiracy. Thus Cicero was left out, not being thought to have the nerve for such a business. The case of Antony was discussed, but he too was not solicited, for he was mistrusted, not without reason. It was then proposed to kill him, but Brutus drew the line at a precautionary murder of convenience. The day for action was at length fixed for the Ides (15th) of March and the place was to be the Senate-House. On that day the motion for granting Caesar the formal title of King for the purpose of the Parthian war was to be put to the vote. The dramatic fitness of the occasion was calculated to appeal to Brutus, inflated with Greek theories of the duty of tyrannicide, and moreover there was manifest danger in delay. The rest of the story—Calpurnia's dream, the forebodings to which Caesar would not listen, the written information which he would not read, and all the details of this greatest of historic tragedies, down to the moment when the glorious victim fell dead at the foot of a statue of Pompey,—this is a part of the world's literature, familiar to all peoples.

1288. There is perhaps no subject on which historians have differed more widely than the estimate of Caesar and his work. The amount of material at hand for forming a judgment is very large. But, if we omit the utterances of later writers writing in fear of the

Emperors who regarded themselves as his successors, the mass of the tradition relative to Caesar speaks from a republican point of view. His clemency, his courage, his genius, his personal charm, were facts which no malignity could deny, yet Roman sentiment is not unfairly summed up in the verdict of Suetonius[1], that the evidence against him is on the whole enough to justify his murder. This is merely a way of saying that he was guilty of treason to his country. If we hold that Caesar alone overthrew the Republic, which by acceptance of office he was virtually pledged to uphold, we may concur in this judgment. But if this is the impression conveyed by the foregoing narrative, the fault is that of the writer and not of the facts. Under the influence of deep-seated causes, mainly economic and social, the Roman republic had been going to ruin for more than a hundred years. When Caesar entered public life, inefficiency and misgovernment had reached such a pitch that some great change was inevitable. The constitution, gradually formed of old in and for very different circumstances, provided no machinery for effective reforms, supposing reforms to have been otherwise possible. Already for a brief moment it had been suspended under the supremacy of Sulla, and its formal restoration was a failure. In Caesar's time it was not possible to assail inefficiency without assailing privilege. The two were inseparable, and whoever put down senatorial misrule must become an autocrat, whether he wished it or not. That political issues could now only be decided by the sword was not the fault, or even the discovery, of Caesar. He took things as he found them, indeed he only resorted to military methods when political methods had failed. At what stage in his career he made up his mind to play for supreme power in some form, is a problem that will be solved to their own satisfaction by different judges in different ways. That the bitter hostility of enemies who sought his ruin had a great influence upon his conduct, admits no doubt. That he was dissolute in his private life, and unscrupulous as a political agitator, does not distinguish him from the average public men of the age. In his sanity, his clear appreciation of facts, his contempt for shams, his creative genius, he stands alone. To us, looking back over more than nineteen centuries, it is of minor interest to inquire whether Caesar was blameworthy from this or that point of view. The fact of prime importance is that there was no practical alternative to monarchy in some form or other, and no possible monarch so wise hard-working just large-minded and sympathetic as Caesar. We need only compare him with Pompey. It is but in a very limited sense that Pompey can be called amiable. That he was vain and unwise is beyond all doubt.

[1] Suet. *Jul.* 76.

Dreaming of impossible ideals, he was apt to misjudge situations and be too late for opportunities, and those who put their trust in him found him a broken reed. That he did not aim at overthrowing the Republic, may be counted to him for a virtue, but a negative virtue, more evident to those who profited by his self-restraint than to a student coldly viewing his career as a portion of the past. That he did play an effective part in the Roman revolution has been proved above. Indeed, of all the individuals who contributed to the overthrow of a worn-out system, none more surely or more blindly brought about its fall than the solemn waverer who could neither do without power nor make up his mind to use it.

1289.   We shall do well ever to bear in mind that the great civil war was merely a stage in the revolution, and that the conqueror was not primarily a soldier, but one who began as a politician and ended as a statesman. It was not for nothing that, while Crassus and Pompey were both pupils of Sulla, Caesar traced his political pedigree back through Marius and Cinna to the Gracchi. Even the age of the Punic wars had produced Flaminius and Varro. We have traced the growth of contrasts and conflicts, as the free farmer gave place to the slave, the city drained the country, the citizen ceased to be necessarily a soldier, the rich heaped up riches while the poor became paupers, the Roman oppressed the Ally till the Ally turned upon the Roman, and the enfranchised Italian shared as a Roman the plunder of the subject peoples. We have seen that under the republican constitution, with its yearly magistrates and its Assemblies that could only express the popular will under conditions of transitory excitement, no steady movement of progress could be kept up by political methods. What was done was done by violence, even by the sword. Old rural life was not restored in Italy, and indeed could not be. With the immense social change that economic changes and imperial expansion had brought about, the spread of luxury and the race for wealth, the old moral forces that alone made the Roman constitution workable had departed never to return. Roman citizens for the most part either sought their fortunes abroad in exploiting the provinces, or took shares in financial and trading ventures and watched their investments at home. The greedy capitalist, great or small, was now the typical Roman; even the pauper lived on the provinces, fed at the expense of the state, and entertained by candidates for office, to whom he sold his vote to enable them to recover their outlay and something more. Wild extravagance and occasional failure of enterprises left numbers of men burdened with debt and ready to support any movement that would facilitate repudiation, regardless of the shock to public credit. Inefficiency marked all the acts of the government. Gaul and Spain, Numidia and Asia Minor, had witnessed mismanagement and corruption to an extent hardly to be imagined, and on the water pirate fleets defied the mistress of the Mediterranean world. The painful cry for some sort of efficiency was ever rising, but no serious step was taken to attain it till things were so bad as to jeopardise the purse or person of the capitalists. This was too much; the financial interest supported the demagogue of the moment, the direction of affairs was temporarily wrested from the senatorial nobility, until the present danger was overcome, and they resumed their power, weaker and more corrupt after each interruption. On transitory waves of popular impatience Marius and Pompey had risen to an eminence for which the Roman constitution did not provide, but for the normal evils that beset the state neither they nor Sulla's reactionary interlude had found a remedy. Then came Caesar, the true child of the revolutionary age, in whom the pent-up forces of discontent found their representative, and under whom they passed to the only logical conclusion. His whole career was conditioned by the history of the past and the circumstances of the present, as that of any leader must be. As demagogue and soldier he so broke the power of the Roman aristocrats that it could never be revived effectively again. The skill and versatility with which he met difficulties as they arose were all his own. Perhaps nothing shews how thoroughly he understood the times more clearly than his relations with the men of money. He was probably the most reckless borrower in Rome, certainly unsurpassed in the use of other men's money for his own ends: once in power, he did all that could be done to calm the sensitive nerves of capital. Of such a man in such an age it is enough to say that the world has seen no better autocrat. Some monarchy—tyranny, if you will,—there had to be. The past had made legality impossible, and in Caesar illegality was amply justified.

1290. It has been said that Caesar was the true child of this revolutionary age. The economic causes that had long been at work, undermining the old fabric of the commonwealth, had from the first been strengthened and quickened in their operation by foreign (chiefly Greek) influences of an intellectual and moral character. In no man were these influences more thoroughly incarnated than in Caesar. The sceptical spirit, the attitude of the seeker, at its best in scientific inquiry, but in affairs of state apt to underestimate the practical obstacles to the prompt attainment of logical results, was the grand contribution of the Greek mind to the development of the human race. Side by side with this was a frank recognition, based on experience, of the power of chance in all human affairs. The old

Roman godhead[1] *Fortuna* seems to have been primarily a power of
Good Luck, for whose favour a man contracted in the old legal
fashion by the flawless performance of the proper rites. In the
Greek notion of Fortune (τύχη) mere chance was the prevailing
element; the goddess was more an impersonation of the incalculable,
and this view of Fortune, whether derived from Greek sources or not,
had tended to become dominant in Italy also. In Caesar we not
only see the scientific spirit actively at work, but a not less thoroughgoing reliance on the chapter of accidents. No man ever made more
allowance for the operation of forces beyond his foresight or control.
Even in his narratives he candidly admits that again and again
disaster was averted by a lucky chance. In war his business was
to win, not to flatter his own vanity; the way to victory lay through
sound appreciation of facts, not through delusions as to the infallibility
of his own judgment. Let us now apply the foregoing considerations
to Caesar as a statesman. That he saw below the surface of things,
and understood the needs of the time, better than his contemporaries,
is surely not to be denied. This must be set down to what has been
called the scientific side of his character and intellectual equipment.
He cleared away rubbish with a vigorous hand, and laid foundations
for the inevitable structure which he did not live to erect. The irony
of fate decreed that he should fall beneath the daggers of men whom
he had spared and promoted. This was the fruit of a temper naturally
kind, encouraged in the practice of mercy by the influence of the
later Greek philosophy which had long been gradually softening the
old hardness of Roman fibre. Yet Caesar was a Roman of Romans,
a Patrician; that is, descended in the male line from one of the
houses recognized as belonging to the ancient nobility of birth.
Intellectually and socially an aristocrat, a blend of the choicest
Graeco-Roman elements, he had the privilege of looking the part
to perfection. Tall and slim of person, handsome in face, his appearance (of which he was ever careful) was somewhat marred by partial
baldness in his later years. It is said that in order to hide this defect
he gladly accepted[2] the offered right to wear a wreath of bay. His
wiry strength bore him through the toil of arduous journeys and
campaigns. He often marched on foot with his men, and his men
were no malingerers. Soldiers, like women, worshipped him. His
sobriety in private life, and indifference to pleasures of the table, were
remarked in a gluttonous and wine-bibbing age. His friend Oppius

---

[1] See Preller, *Röm. Mythol.* x § 1 (vol. II p. 179). The matured view of Fortune appears
in the famous passage, Pliny *NH* II §§ 22—27.

[2] Like Agathocles, Diodorus xx 54.

recorded[1] that at a dinner where the olive oil served was not in good condition, and the other guests declined it, Caesar took it, and asked for a second helping, not to hurt the feelings of his host.   That, of all who bore a hand in overthrowing the Republic, Caesar was the only sober one, was one of Cato's surly growls.   Moderation was clearly the key-note of his conduct, and we may probably infer that this was true of him not only in relation to meat and drink but also in the matter of vices over which Roman scandal-mongers gloated and which public opinion but half-heartedly condemned.

1291.   To represent Caesar as a pure heroic figure with scarcely a trace of blemish, and his death as the martyrdom of an unselfish patriot cruelly misunderstood, would be to indulge a passion for hero-worship till it ends in caricature.   Nor is it a sound appreciation of his place in history that would regard him as a mere adventurer consumed by ambition, cleverly extricating himself from a series of difficulties by a policy of unscrupulous opportunism.   Ambitious he was, or he would have aimed at nothing; versatile, or he would have achieved nothing.   But from first to last he was the opponent of the republican aristocrats.   They soon recognized in him a dangerous enemy, and their attempts to destroy him forced him to destroy them. But this destruction was not thorough.   It took away their power but not their lives.   Though their chief leaders had perished in the war, enough republicans were left to encourage each other in the hope of recovering with the dagger what they had lost by the sword. Against this peril Caesar took no precautions.   Was this the result of miscalculation, of over-confidence, or of weary indifference?   It is perhaps safest to guess that all three had a share in it.   It is said that, when warned to beware of Brutus, he replied that Brutus (in whom he saw a coming man) would wait for his skin, that is, would wait for his death in the course of nature.   Another of his reported sayings was that the preservation of his life was more in the interest of the commonwealth than his own.   And on the evening before his murder, when conversation turned upon the best way of dying, it was recalled that he said 'to die quickly without a warning.'   All these touches are in full harmony with the rest of his life and character. We see him not self-centred or nervous, but serenely brave.   Such as he was when as a youth he won a civic crown at the siege of Mitylene, such as he was when he pleaded for the lives of the Catilinarians at the risk of his own, even such, a man of steely mettle with no fears and few scruples, he was to the end.

[1] Suet. *Jul.* 53.   In short, Caesar was a man polite beyond the average of Roman gentlemen, in an age when the standard of urbanity was high.   See Fowler, *Social Life*, pp. 106, 124.

BOOK VIII

THE LAST STRUGGLES AND THE TRANSITION TO THE EMPIRE

CHAPTER LIX

FAILURE OF THE ATTEMPT TO RESTORE THE REPUBLIC.
44—42 B.C.

1292. How far the recklessness with which Caesar had exposed himself to assassination was due to an insufficient perception of his danger, how far to sheer weariness and a resolve to face the danger however great, we shall never know. As to the position of his murderers immediately after his death there is no doubt whatever. The only practical justification for the removal of the man in whom the forces of the state were centred was to have a clearly-defined policy, capable of being carried out at once, so that without delay or hitch the commonwealth might pursue its course under new direction. But the only definite aim of the conspirators was a negative one, the destruction of Caesar. This presented itself as the removal of a Tyrant, and underlying it was the assumption that this act was equivalent to the abolition of the Tyranny. Evidently those who thought of the sequel at all were content to believe that the time-honoured organs cf the Republic, Senate Assembly and Magistrates, would at once begin to work effectively, and the Roman aristocrats regain the possession of all the privileges and perquisites of which the great autocrat had deprived them. To the idealizing patriotism of Brutus such an assumption was natural. The clearer judgment of Cassius was probably clouded for the moment by his passionate absorption in the details on which the success of the conspiracy depended. A serious debate on the course to be adopted after the murder would have led to differences of opinion, to delay, possibly to treachery and detection of the plot. In any case Caesar would probably have got away safely to the East, and previous attempts to upset his arrangements in his absence had been utter failures. So Brutus, who represented the moral force of the conspiracy, was left, with all his shallow philosophy, to lead it, and the murderers found themselves alone with the corpse of Caesar and uncertain what to do next. Those who took part in the murder[1] were but a small number. The mass of the senators, who were not privy to the plot, had fled.

1293. The death of Caesar at once raised three very urgent questions. Was the Republic still alive? If not, could it be revived? If not, who was to be master of the Roman world? The first was soon negatived by the attempt to answer the second in the affirmative, an attempt which cost the lives of Cicero and many more, and finally ended in 42 with the defeat of the republicans at Philippi. The third was only answered thirteen years later (in 31), when the cause of Octavian triumphed at Actium.

1294. Our subject is the story of the Roman Republic, and the details of this period of confusion concern us only so far as they serve to throw light on the past and enable us to test the soundness of our views. For the events of the period we have copious evidence, contemporary and later, often contradictory, sometimes incredible, nearly always of a violently partisan character. The loss of the history of Pollio and the later books of Livy deprives us of what were perhaps the best connected narratives, though the value of the former is uncertain. The relations of the surviving authorities to each other, their comparative value, their various tendencies, and their sources of information, have been critically examined by[2] Schwartz. Their generally partisan nature is clearly proved, and the discussion deals with many points of the greatest interest to those who study this complicated period in detail. Here I can only touch briefly on a few of the main conclusions. The desire of the emperor Augustus to place the acts of his earlier life in a favourable light found direct expression, not only in the famous autobiographical manifesto[3] in which he finally summed up the events of his career, but in other writings now lost. Chief among these was a book of Memoirs carried down to 24 B.C., in which he gave his account of his doings as C. Octavius and C. Julius Caesar Octavianus. This, which may be called the official version, is undoubtedly the source of many details that have come down to us. It was used by Velleius and Suetonius with some independence, but its influence is probably to be traced generally in the narrative of Dion Cassius and (to judge from the epitomators) in that of his predecessor Livy. Its views appear in the work of Nicolaus of Damascus, in a form bordering

[1] Evidently not all the conspirators. The number of wounds counted was 23, and about 60 men were in the plot.

[2] E. Schwartz in *Hermes* XXXIII 185—244, a most valuable essay, though perhaps sometimes pushing reconstruction too far.

[3] The so-called *Monumentum Ancyranum.*

on caricature. In this version, as is only natural, Antony is shewn at a disadvantage. Plutarch, probably influenced largely by writings of Brutus and his following, is less unfavourable to Antony, less favourable to Octavian and incidentally to Cicero. But the Antonian point of view is found mainly in Appian. The misdating and misrepresentation of facts, combined with the acceptance of downright fictions, are so striking that he has even been thought[1] to have followed some unknown writer, the author of a Defence of Antony. This is however no more than an ingenious conjecture. The conduct of Cicero in this last stormy period of his life has been (and probably will be) variously judged. As an authority for facts pure and simple his letters are of course most valuable, particularly those to Atticus. But everything appears as coloured by the passion or prejudice of the moment; and in some cases[2] (as in writing to Antony) his utterances are signally insincere. In his Philippic speeches, among all the furious invective and arguments too often unfair and sophistical, much may be gleaned. His hatred of Antony was genuine enough, but, once an open breach became inevitable, he depicted his enemy in terms to which no importance need be attached. His varying relations to Brutus and Octavian are only to be traced satisfactorily in the letters, particularly in those which passed between him and Brutus in the year 43. It may be said of the surviving authorities in general that they present confused distorted and mutually inconsistent pictures of the chief figures and their several policies. An attempt to extract the truth from such a tangle, and to combine the salient points in a brief narrative, is one in which the best intentions may completely fail.

1295. On the 15th March the conspirators, bloody daggers and all, appeared in public and called the people to rise and take up their freedom recovered by the tyrant's death. Meeting little or no response, they occupied the Capitol. Some senators and others joined them; among these was Cicero, whose help, now the murder was done, they were particularly anxious to secure. During the 16th the consul Antony and Lepidus, who had been Master of Horse to the slain dictator, had time to collect themselves. The latter had a legion on the spot, and Antony was the person to whom the numerous discharged veterans still in the city naturally looked for a lead. The conspirators had no such forces at their back. If it came to blows, they had a body of trained gladiators at disposal, and every Roman of wealth and position had his escort of sturdy slaves. They again tried vainly to raise the mob, and to gain the

---

[1] Schwartz, pp. 231—4.
[2] See Cic. *ad Att.* XIV 13 with 13 *a* and 13 *b*.

adhesion of Antony and Lepidus. Antony indeed proceeded from the first with great caution. No one as yet knew what support the murderers might receive. His position as representing the Caesarian interest was confirmed by the action of Caesar's widow Calpurnia. She handed over to him all the dictator's memoranda and ready money. Antony was not blind to the vast possibilities that this trust afforded him, and in no mind to throw them away by a false step. On the 17th a meeting of the Senate was held. The majority of the House was in favour of the murderers, but it was already seen that they had nothing to hope from an immediate resort to force. And they were all the more disposed to compromise, many of them having an interest in the arrangements made in advance by the 'tyrant' in favour of themselves or their friends. In the debate Cicero, who knew his audience, made and carried a motion for a general amnesty. But in its final form the resolution contained a clause expressly confirming the validity of the dictator's acts, apparently without distinguishing between his intentions already known and those which the examination of his papers might presently disclose. It was also agreed that his will should be opened and read in public, and that he should receive the honour of a public funeral. Thus the action of the murderers was stultified, for Caesar's usurpation was implicitly condoned, and the 'tyrant' to whom so many owed so much was declared to have been no tyrant at all. As in the case of Scipio Aemilianus, no attempt was to be made to bring the murderers to justice; and in the present case their identity was not a matter of any doubt. Clearly the first move in the game had been won by Antony. He had made sure of Lepidus by promising him the succession to Caesar as chief pontiff, and had detached Dolabella from the republicans by withdrawing opposition to his succession to the consulship. The conspirators were induced to leave the Capitol, taking hostages for their safety. Brutus and Cassius dined with Lepidus and Antony, and the inevitable conflict was ushered in by a hollow truce.

1296. Meanwhile the soldiers and the mob were uneasy at the loss of Caesar, and the discharged veterans who were waiting for their land-allotments were wanting to know whether the promises made them were going to be kept or not. It was to little purpose that Brutus quieted their apprehensions in a reassuring speech, and that Cicero spoke in justification of the Senate's decision to have no inquiry into the murder. Whatever had been gained by these efforts was more than undone by the reading of Caesar's will and the events of the funeral. It appeared that he had left his gardens beyond the Tiber as a public park, and to every Roman citizen a present of nearly

£3 of our money.   His chief heir was his great-nephew C. Octavius, who took ¾ of the estate, the remaining ¼ going to two other relatives, and Octavius was adopted as his son.   In the usual way he named 'second heirs' to succeed in case of the failure of the first heirs. Among these latter was Decimus Brutus.   All knew that this man had come to the front as a trusted lieutenant of Caesar and had been well rewarded for his services.   The possible event of the birth of a posthumous son by Calpurnia was not forgotten, and guardians were duly named for that contingency.   Among them were several of the murderers.   Popular indignation was intense.   How artfully Antony took advantage of the situation, and inflamed the rage of the excited populace, the burning of the body in the Forum, and the tumults that followed, do not need description here.   The lives of the murderers were in danger, and they sought safety in hiding or flight.   The republican cause was thus left to be upheld in Rome by men who had not borne a hand in the murder themselves, however much they might approve it and be willing to profit by the deed.   Their party in the Senate now consisted of its weaker elements only, either the men of less standing and importance, or men whose enthusiasm judgment or nerve had been deemed unequal to the perils of the conspiracy.   On the other hand there was a Caesarian minority, already recovering from its alarm under the skilful leadership of Antony, and not hampered by any obligation to attempt the revival of the old republican system.   No doubt there were also many members not committed to either of these parties.   In the crisis of the moment and the uncertainty of coming developments, the general spirit prevalent among the senators was undoubtedly a sincere regard to their own interests and personal safety.   Any party that scored a success was sure to gain adherents so long as its prestige lasted, and the lack of any consistent policy in the Senate had a powerful influence in shaping the miserable sequel.

1297.   It was the policy of Antony not to provoke an immediate conflict, but to strengthen his own position, and he was not the man to be over-scrupulous as to the means.   We hear that he checked the eagerness of Lepidus for revenge on the assassins: that could wait. Meanwhile he soothed the republican nobles by consulting some of them on the steps to be taken next.   He proposed the perpetual abolition of the dictatorship, which the House readily voted.   It was a cheap way of winning their favour, for all must have known that what was abolished could be restored.   Cicero declares that he also allowed a decree to be passed by which the publication of grants of privileges on the strength of Caesar's memoranda was forbidden. This attempt to recall the general confirmation of Caesar's acts is

perhaps not fairly reported.   If such an order was passed, Antony
soon shewed that he meant to treat it with contempt.   But he gained
further credit as a 'good citizen' by vigorously suppressing riots in
the city and putting to death the ringleader, a Greek impostor who
pretended to be a descendant of Marius.   This was in April.   Meanwhile Antony had been turning over Caesar's papers and preparing
to make a profitable use of them.   He took into his service a certain
Faberius, who had been a secretary of the dictator, with whose help
he extracted and edited their contents.   In the process he seems
to have resorted to forgery, producing documents to authorize the
restoration of exiles, grants of citizenship, and immunity from taxation, confirmation of kings in subject principalities, anything in short
for which a bribe could be exacted.   If we may believe Cicero, his
forgeries were on a colossal scale.   Certainly he was in great need of
money, and he found a pretext for laying hands on a large sum
belonging to the state, deposited in the temple of Ops.   Dolabella,
now in full function as consul, was bought off with a share, and
Antony pursued his course unchecked.   It has been thought[1] that, in
order to give himself a free hand in these lawless proceedings, he
carried a law allowing him the fullest discretion.   This is possible,
but not certain.   Dolabella[2] followed up the suppression of the sham
Marius by putting down further disorders, executing slave-rioters,
and destroying a column erected in honour of Caesar on the spot
where his body had been burnt.   Antony did not interfere: indeed
such futile demonstrations of the Caesarian mob were only hindrances
to his own plans.   If the murderers and their republican sympathizers
were to be effectively dealt with, this was not the way to begin.   The
Senate approved these vigorous measures.   The mob resented them,
and Antony found in their menacing attitude an excuse for enlisting a
bodyguard, with the consent it is said of the Senate.   This he gradually
raised to 6000 men, all picked soldiers.

1298.   It should be mentioned in passing that Cleopatra, who had
been sojourning in Rome, left for Alexandria[3] soon after Caesar's
death.   More important than the flight of the queen was the arrival
of C. Octavius in Italy.   The youth, not yet 19 years of age, had
received the news of his great-uncle's murder while at Apollonia.
About the middle of April he crossed the Adriatic.   By the 18th

---

[1] Lange, *RA* III 494.   The conjecture is plausible, but the passages cited as evidence
hardly amount to proof.

[2] That the profligate and unprincipled Dolabella was in any serious sense a champion of
the Republic, I see no reason to believe.   When Cicero praised his action, the wish was
father to the thought.

[3] I do not think that Cicero's words in *ad Att.* XV 15 § 2 (13 June) imply that she was
still in Rome.   She had agents there.

he was in Campania, fully informed as to the course of events, and bent upon taking up his perilous inheritance and succeeding to the name of Caesar. From this intention he was not diverted by the misgivings of his mother and the earnest dissuasion of his stepfather L. Marcius Philippus. He was not prepared to efface himself by a complete abdication, and the early ripeness of his judgment was shewn in declining a middle course offering less advantages and no less danger than a bold one. In Campania Cicero met him and was charmed with his respectful behaviour. True, he was surrounded by men hostile to the republicans, and Cicero feared their influence; but he flattered the vanity of the old consular, who entertained no suspicions of one whom he regarded as a boy.

1299. The absence of Cicero from Rome was not due to satisfaction with the turn things had taken. For a few days his exultation over the glorious deed of the Ides of March threw all else into the shade. But he very soon began to see that the removal of the 'tyrant' had not put an end to the tyranny and restored the Republic. It was an absurd situation[1] that, after easily ridding themselves of an autocrat, men should be bound by his designs, the slaves of his note-books, genuine or not. But such was the fact, and as the days went by Cicero became more and more conscious that his beloved Republic was no longer a reality. The blunders that had been made proved that even the Senate could not be trusted, and outside the Senate there was nothing. Early in April he left Rome, moving southwards. It is characteristic of the men and the times that his friend Atticus, keeping aloof from politics and making himself useful to all sorts of people, lived safely in or near Rome all through this troubled period, and was Cicero's chief source of news whenever the orator withdrew from the centre of affairs. Meanwhile Cicero, though delighted with the violence of Dolabella, was becoming ever more depressed at hearing of the growing power of Antony and the impotence of the 'heroes.' Brutus and Cassius were both praetors, and should have been on duty in Rome. But they dared not shew themselves in the city, and the Senate with Antony's approval granted them leave of absence for a time. Trebonius had slunk away to take possession of his province of Asia, Decimus Brutus to Cisalpine Gaul; their appointments were part of Caesar's acts. The likelihood of a civil war was one of Cicero's more reasonable fears. In Syria the Pompeian Bassus was still holding his ground against the lieutenants of Caesar. In southern Spain Sextus Pompey was making head, and news soon came that he had defeated the Caesarian governor Asinius Pollio and was practically master of the

[1] See in particular *ad Att.* XIV 6 § 2 (12 April), *ad fam.* XII 1 (to Cassius, 3 May).

Further province. He had a fleet, and held command of the sea. It was rumoured that Antony meant to turn D. Brutus out of Cisalpine Gaul, and this would surely lead to war. But the republican cause was on the face of it hopelessly weak for lack of armies. The forces abroad were commanded by nominees of the late dictator. We can see how much depended on the attitude of these leaders in case matters came to an open rupture. Would any of them be induced by interest or sympathy to support the republicans? if so, could they carry their soldiers with them? To Antony the progress of Sextus Pompey was evidently the matter most needing serious attention. He persuaded Lepidus to go to his province of Hither Spain and to treat for an accommodation with Sextus, offering him the complete restitution of his civic rights and compensation for his losses in the confiscation of his father's property. Thus this danger was staved off for the time.

1300. It was not less important to keep Caesar's discharged veterans in a good humour. Antony therefore went to Capua and took in hand the settlement of a 'colony' in that neighbourhood. It was said, probably with truth, that he arranged to have them supplied with arms so as to be ready for embodiment at short notice. This, and the talk of other Caesarians, convinced Cicero that war was in contemplation. And it was painful to reflect that in a war between the present combatants there would be no room[1] for any man of mark in politics as a neutral. Toleration and mercy had perished with Caesar. Antony was soon drawn back to Rome by the news of Octavius. The 'boy' had reached the city at the end of April, and lost no time in claiming his inheritance. He announced that he would discharge the liabilities created by the dictator's will. Thus he was winning the favour of the multitude, while by his singular tact and discretion he was teaching the Caesarians to take him seriously. To Antony, who did not lack enemies, his presence was most unwelcome. He claimed the fortune left by Caesar. Antony had had it and spent it, and declined to pay. Octavius then sold his own properties, and with this money and loans from friends he made a start with the payment of legacies, thereby greatly strengthening his position. He also celebrated some games in Caesar's honour to commemorate the victory of Pharsalus. Clearly a dangerous rival to Antony was now on the spot. The disadvantage of youth, sure to diminish with time, was more than compensated by the advantage of temperament. From the excesses on which Antony was expending a robust constitution Octavius was debarred by delicate health. Both were opportunist, but the opportunism of the younger man was

---

[1] Cic. *ad Att.* XIV 17 § 6 (3 May), 22 § 2 (14 May).

directed by a far-sighted judgment and habitual self-control, gifts in which the elder had little share. In the use of resources the two presented a striking contrast to the end of their days. The passionate and often generous Antony was ever ready to squander whatever came into his hands, and to get little in return. Octavius did everything with a definite object in view, spending included: and there is all the difference in the world between fitful liberality and scientific investment. The friction now developed by the dispute over Caesar's estate lasted for some months. Octavius went on his way undeterred by the opposition of Antony. But the formal completion of his adoption was delayed till the latter part of Sextilis (August) 43, though he was publicly referred to as *Caesar* long before that date.

1301. It was now a prime object with Antony to get the provincial governments for the coming year (43) settled in accordance with his interest. A meeting of the Senate was fixed for the first of June, the usual time for dealing with this business. The present position[1] was briefly this. Two provinces were held by ex-consuls, Asia by Trebonius, Hither Spain and Narbonese Gaul by Lepidus. These would not be vacant till 42. The rest, held by ex-praetors or on a propraetorian tenure of one year, according to the Julian law in force, had to be filled up. Caesar had designed Macedonia for Antony, and Syria for Dolabella. In the ordinary course they would as consuls have succeeded to these provinces for the years 43 and 42. But Antony had not studied the career of his great master for nothing. He too desired a longer tenure[2] than two years. Caesar's long term in Gaul had enabled him to provide for his own safety, and had armed him for contingencies. Moreover for watching events and taking advantage of opportunities the best position by far was the Cisalpine. Add to it the Further or Transalpine Gaul, and the holder would be in a fair way to command the destinies of the Roman world. By the end of April it had been rumoured that Antony intended to take the Gauls himself, and to make the Senate grant both him and Dolabella a term of government longer than that allowed by the law. It was true, but in a short time he began to doubt the policy of leaving the decision to the Senate. We must remember that the departure of D. Brutus to take possession of the Cisalpine and the appearance of Octavius in Rome had altered

[1] See Schwartz, *Hermes* XXXIII 185—190, 226—7.

[2] Schwartz acutely points out that, if matters followed a normal course, Brutus and Cassius, now praetors, might be consuls in 41. Then they would succeed to consular provinces for the two years 40 and 39. If Antony now secured a term of six years, his government would not come to an end before theirs. This eminently Caesarian calculation may, I admit, have dictated part of Antony's policy in the affair of the provinces.

the situation. Antony inclined to follow another of Caesar's precedents, and gain his end by a vote of the Assembly, that is by a law. As the first of June drew near, this design leaked out, but there was no means of preventing it. His bodyguard gave him an irresistible power in the city, and the old soldiers who came swarming in were at present wholly at his disposal. So on June 1st the Assembly voted the two Gauls to him, and Syria to Dolabella, each for a term of six years including the current year. By this law he got an excuse for ejecting D. Brutus, and apparently also the command of four legions at present in Macedonia, raised by Caesar for the Parthian war. He at the same time finally committed Dolabella to act with him against the republicans. The position of Antony seemed to be stronger than ever. He controlled his colleague; of his brothers, Gaius was praetor, and Lucius tribune. The Senate was overawed by his military following, and the more earnest republicans did not attend its meeting. But it was on the support of the veterans that his power mainly rested, and the veterans were not supporting him for nothing. If their allegiance were transferred to another leader, the power of Antony would be severely shaken.

1302. In reading Cicero's correspondence during May and the early part of June nothing strikes one more than the helpless uncertainty and mistrust that was paralysing the chief republicans. The consuls-designate for 43, Hirtius and Pansa, had been Caesarians, but were both behaving and expressing themselves moderately, and it was hoped that they might be induced to cooperate with the loyal (republican) party. Cicero was employed to sound them and try to win their help. But the guarded replies of Hirtius only shewed that it was premature to rely on them. Cicero was himself wishing to procure a permission to travel at the public cost (a *legatio*) in order to have a decent excuse for quitting Italy. He had now no wife or daughter, his son was at Athens, and his nephew Quintus was a satellite of Antony. He was by this completely disillusioned as to any positive gain having resulted from Caesar's murder. He saw that his 'heroes' had blundered, and knew not what next to do. Brutus and Cassius were hanging about not far from Rome, but afraid to return to their urban duties for fear of the veterans flocking there. They issued an edict in which they took great credit to themselves for not having tried to disturb the peace of Italy. In truth they had not the means of doing so with effect. They even went so far as to write to Antony, inquiring whether it would be safe for them to appear in the city on the first of June. All this was solemn trifling. In assuring the consul of their peaceful and patriotic intentions they were ignoring the vital fact that Rome was under the rule of force, and that force at present in the hands of Antony. It was a pitiful confession of weakness or rather nullity, that Brutus did not venture to preside in person at the games[1] which it was his duty to conduct as city-praetor. He gained no popularity by his outlay, and Antony's brother Gaius presided in his stead. But before this a shrewd blow had been dealt at the two chief 'heroes.' On the 5th June Antony held a meeting of the Senate, in which provinces were assigned to Brutus and Cassius for the next year, probably[2] Crete and Cyrene. The intention was to get them out of the way during the year 43 by placing them in unimportant posts. But there was the rest of the current year to be provided for. This was done by appointing them to the charge[3] of procuring corn for the city, not with wide general powers as in the case of Pompey, but assigning them limited districts, Asia to Brutus, Sicily to Cassius. The two were furious at this cynical and insidious patronage, and at first resolved to decline it. Cicero[4] could only calm them so far as to prevent a flat refusal. A seeming acquiescence was indeed necessary, for their position in Italy was now one of impotence and danger, and the commission offered a means of escape to the East. Only in the East could they hope to obtain the command of resources for the great struggle in which the effort to restore the Republic was likely to involve them. The West was held by Antony and Lepidus. For the present there was nothing to be hoped from young Pompey, and Antony was preparing to turn D. Brutus out of Cisalpine Gaul. In their helpless rage the two leaders cursed the folly of Decimus, who had been exercising his troops in expeditions against Alpine tribes instead of marching to put down the growing power of Antony. Cicero too thought it a blunder, but not so gross as that of sparing Antony on the Ides of March. Thus the most earnest republicans were not only outgeneralled by their adversaries but depressed by a painful consciousness of each other's incapacity. Brutus, with his usual solemn airs, announced that he would proceed to Asia. Cassius would not go to Sicily. Cicero had not yet openly broken even with Antony, and had just been gratified by Dolabella with an appointment as one of his *legati*. Thus he too accepted the patronage of the Caesarian consuls. Nay more, he had even, to oblige Atticus, been exerting his influence with them (that is with Antony) on behalf of

---

[1] The *ludi Apollinares* on the 7th *Quintilis*, now first officially styled *Julius* to Cicero's disgust. Cic. *ad Att.* XVI 1 § 1, 4 § 1.

[2] Crete and Bithynia, according to Dion Cass. XLVII 21.

[3] Earlier in the year the failure of the corn-supply in Rome had been feared, probably because of the uncertainty about Sextus Pompey and his fleet, and Antony had seized the supplies on the spot as a precaution. Cic. *ad Att.* XIV 3 (9 April).

[4] Cic. *ad Att.* XV 9, 10, 11, 12.

the people of Buthrotum[1] in Epirus. Caesar had proposed to deprive them of some of their lands and settle a colony of veterans there. This infliction their neighbour Atticus, whose castle and estate lay hard by, was anxious to spare them, and Cicero could not refuse to do his best. He wrote to Dolabella in support of their petition, and it was successful. The matter had been dragging on for months, and troubles did not end with the consuls' decision. Its importance in connexion with our present topic is that Cicero could ask a favour of Antony while deploring the omission of his murder. Such was in political relations the moral code of the best contemporary representative of republican virtue, the man whose dearest ambition was to 'put the constitution on a sound footing.' Meanwhile, among all the worries of the time, his pen was ever busy. This year he produced a number[2] of treatises, several of which still survive, and this activity continued, while he shifted from place to place, till September, when he appeared once more in his favourite character as an orator. But for the present he was preparing to leave Italy, all the more readily because of the likelihood of war. In June it began to be rumoured that young Pompey had declined the offers of Antony and Lepidus and was coming with his forces from the West.

1303. And yet Cicero[3] was very loth to go. What he really wanted was to get back to public life in Rome. Even in the latter part of June we find him asserting[4] a serious wish to keep up his 'old-established friendship with Antony, which had never been interrupted by a quarrel.' Not long before, he had expressed a high opinion[5] of young Octavius, whom he begins to call Octavian, and entertained some hope that he would turn out to be well disposed to Brutus and Cassius and the 'heroes' generally. But he saw that this depended on his being kept apart from Antony. If the absent Cicero could think thus, we may fairly suppose that people in Rome might some of them think the same. A conflict of interests between the young heir of Caesar and Caesar's powerful marshal was devoutly to be wished by all good republicans. Meanwhile it is interesting

---

[1] Cicero's letters from April to July contain frequent references to this matter. See in particular *ad Att.* XIV 17 § 2, XV 29, XVI 1 § 2, 16 a—f. It was really a part of the confirmation of Caesar's acts, for Caesar had revoked the sentence before he 'happened to die suddenly' as Cicero puts it.

[2] The Tusculan Disputations, *de Deorum Natura, de Divinatione, de Fato, Cato Maior, Laelius, de Officiis.* Among those lost was the *de Gloria*, of which he seems to have thought highly.

[3] Cic. *ad Att.* XV 18, 25, *Phil.* I § 6, *ad Att.* XVI 6 § 2.

[4] Cic. *ad fam.* XVI 23 (to Tiro in Rome). Was this meant to be repeated so as to reach Antony?

[5] Cic. *ad Att.* XV 12 § 2 (10 June).

to note that, while public affairs were in a perilous state, ripening in fact for an atrocious civil war, the business of private life was going on without serious hindrance. Men were borrowing and lending, receiving and paying (or not paying, like Dolabella, who still had not refunded all Tullia's dowry): courts were sitting, lawsuits proceeding or pending, legal issues still engaging the attention of jurists. Traces[1] of all such matters meet us in Cicero's letters, though he was not in Rome. His own financial affairs, in their usual muddle, were among the plagues of the patient Atticus. Marriages, divorces, building enterprises, sales of properties and so forth, were in progress, not to mention the intrigues to prevent this or that person's estate from being confiscated to provide lands for clamorous veterans. The 'acts of Caesar' were all the time being exploited by Antony, and the bribes exacted for various accommodations (such as the purchase of regal rights by Deiotarus) probably contributed to some extent to keep up the movement of ready money. When Cicero actually set sail from Pompeii on the 17th July, he meant to return to Rome about the end of the year. His intercourse with Brutus during the last ten days had taught him how shallow poor-spirited helpless and hesitating the man really was. To the last Brutus was indulging idle hopes[2] that his costly shows would restore him to the favour of the Roman populace, and pave the way for his return to public life. Cicero knew better. In grim scorn he confessed the truth, that the Roman people used their hands, not for defence of the Republic, but for applause. So he left Pompeii with sad forebodings, and wrote to Atticus that he was leaving behind him peace only to come back to war. He looked forward to seeing his son at Athens. But the prospect of the voyage was not pleasant. To avoid meeting the legions expected from Macedonia he had given up the short passage by way of Brundisium, and it was rumoured that pirates were beginning once more to infest the seas. And he had lately received information which made civil war almost a certainty. Young Pompey had been gaining ground in Spain, and had now sent an ultimatum to the consuls, demanding (in addition to the offers already made him) the restitution of his own father's house, now held by Antony, and the disbandment of all military forces.

1304. Cicero then sailed on the 17th July, and coasted along by Velia and Vibo to the Sicilian strait. He got as far as Syracuse, but when he tried to bear away for Greece he was driven back by foul winds to a spot near Rhegium. Here he received important news[3],

---

[1] See the interesting letter *ad fam.* VII 21, on a case in which Brutus (Q. Caepio) had as City praetor earlier in the year made a provisional order.

[2] Cic. *ad Att.* XVI 5, 4, 2.   [3] Cic. *ad Att.* XVI 7.

about the 7th August.   An open quarrel between Antony and Brutus and Cassius was being carried on by public manifestos (*edicta*) and letters.   On the part of the republicans these demonstrations were futile, having no force behind them.   But they were trying to beat up senators of rank to attend a meeting of the House on the 1st September.   They even indulged a hope that Antony would give way, and an accommodation be effected whereby it would be possible for republican partisans to return to Rome.   In that case Cicero's absence would provoke criticism.   He at once changed his plans.   On the 17th August he was back at Velia, where he met Brutus, and before the end of the month he was at Tusculum.   Yet he did not as yet look forward to renewing his active political life.   Things were not looking well.   An attempt to oppose Antony in a meeting of the Senate on the 1st August had failed for want of support.   Meanwhile a tightness had come over the money-market, as capitalists became affected by the shadow of impending war.   The time was at hand when Cicero would be drawn into the conflict, and play his last great stroke for the republican cause.   It was fast becoming clear that a breach with Antony was inevitable, but for the present it had not occurred.   And ever since Caesar's death he had been on friendly terms with some of the best of Caesar's adherents, such as Balbus Oppius and Matius.   That they should lament the loss of their great master, seemed to Cicero a proper and honourable feeling.   He was free[1] from the intolerant arrogance which prompted Brutus and his circle to proclaim that a tear shed for Caesar was treason to the Republic.   Such was the narrow-minded bitterness of the 'heroes' whose praises the orator thought it his duty to sing.

1305.   We must turn back to glance at the doings of Antony. The appearance of Octavius (whom we will now call Octavian) on the scene was an embarrassment, for the young man would not be denied.   In vain the consul declared that the estate of Caesar was public property; the heir still asserted his claim, and we have seen that he stuck at no sacrifice to begin paying off the legacies charged on the estate.   He was conciliating the republicans, and the hindrances and slights offered him by Antony could not prevent him from gaining ground.   At the beginning of June an attempt was made to check Antony's corrupt dealing with the 'acts of Caesar' by manipulation of the papers in his possession.   A decree of the Senate had entrusted the revision of these memoranda to the two consuls acting with a committee.   If we may believe[2] Cicero, Antony had acted by himself, paying no regard to the order.   Now a law was

---

[1] See Cic. *ad fam.* XI 27, 28.
[2] Cic. *Phil.* II § 100, *ad Att.* XVI 16 b § 8, c § 11.

passed to enforce it, but Antony seems not to have been effectively checked thereby. In truth nothing could stop him but force. His veteran bodyguard would back him up as against the republicans, whom they suspected of wishing to deprive them of their promised or hoped-for rewards: as against Octavian, this was not so certain, for they looked with favour upon Caesar's heir. Octavian, pretending to be well disposed to the republicans, was to them a valuable asset. Antony thought it time to bring more forces upon the ground, and presently sent orders for the four available legions to be fetched from Macedonia. Meanwhile he tried to strengthen his position by a fresh[1] land-law. The details are obscure, but it appears to have called in question the title of present holders to various lands in Italy (perhaps estates bought under recent confiscations), and even to have treated as suitable for allotment the as yet undrained Pomptine marshes. It appointed a commission of seven to carry out its provisions, and it was the action of these seven[2] that alarmed Cicero for the safety of his Tusculan property. Not only veterans, but poor citizens, were to profit by this measure, and senators of known republican leanings were the chief sufferers. In the months of July and August the government was completely in the hands of Antony and his two brothers. He even contemplated having censors elected, and designed his disreputable uncle, Cicero's old colleague, for the office, but thought better of the plan and dropped it. Meanwhile his un-popularity was growing, and he tried to regain lost ground by two legislative[3] projects, both of which ran counter to the legislation of Caesar. One of them restored the third panel (*decuria*) of juries, which Caesar had abolished, and provided that it should consist of centurions. Thus the military element as such was introduced even into the public courts. The other granted to persons condemned for public violence or treason (*vis* or *maiestas*) the right of appeal to the Assembly. This was flagrantly inconsistent with the whole system of the public courts, which acted as the delegates of the Roman people. The decisions of these *quaestiones perpetuae* had been regarded as final for more than 100 years. To break with an established principle, approved and confirmed by the laws of Sulla and Caesar, was a reckless proposal, and could only operate to give the persons in power at any moment a more assured immunity from punishment than that already provided by the corruption of juries. These laws seem not to have been actually passed before September.

1306. If Cicero had entertained any hope that Antony would

---

[1] Carried early in June, in defiance of signs from heaven. See Lange *RA* III 503.

[2] The three Antonii, Dolabella, and three others, all dependants of Antony.

[3] See Lange *RA* III 505. The chief reference is Cic. *Phil.* I §§ 19—23.

now give way and come to terms with the republicans, he was soon undeceived. He entered Rome on 31st August, but did not attend the meeting of the Senate on the first of September. He gave out that he was tired after his long journey, but reluctance to face Antony and appear as the aggressor in an unequal conflict had probably as much to do with his absence as the fatigue of travelling in an Italian summer. The chief business before the House was a proposal of Antony's, that in all public thanksgivings an extra day should be added for offerings to the deified Caesar. The proposal was objectionable from the standpoint of the laws of religion; a monstrosity, according to Cicero. But such objections were out of date, and it was carried. In his speech Antony commented on the absence of Cicero, whose relations with Brutus and Cassius he well knew, and whom he wished to compel, now that he was back in Rome, openly to shew his colours. He threatened that, if the old consular persisted in abstention, he would try what force could do. Next day the Senate met again. Antony was not present. On this occasion Cicero[1] spoke, criticizing the policy of Antony, but abstaining from personal abuse. He contrasted some of his earlier and more constitutional acts with his later and more revolutionary proceedings, his use of Caesar's notebooks, his nullification of Caesar's laws. To maintain order in the city, to abolish the dictatorship, was well enough: but arbitrary government, the mere rule of fear, was a very different thing, and the two new proposed laws would if carried simply destroy the whole working of the public courts. Would Romans endure this sort of thing? He could only point to what had happened in the case of Caesar. The orator took care to approve the confirmation of the dictator's acts—his genuine acts—and to praise as much as he could of the proceedings of the present consuls. But the conciliatory tone of parts of this speech (to judge from the edited version) did not in practice amount to much. Antony could only break off all relations with so manifest an opponent, and he did. He called a meeting of the Senate for the 19th September, for which he carefully prepared a speech. In this speech he denounced Cicero, reviewing in no measured terms the great orator's whole political career, in which there were only too many actions that lent themselves to invective from an adversary's point of view. His object doubtless was to convince the members that it was both dangerous and unwise to follow the lead of such a man; for no one was so able as Cicero to stir up the wavering senators and head what might prove a troublesome opposition. Cicero[2] feared, perhaps with reason, that Antony

---

[1] The so-called 'First *Philippic*.'
[2] See his letters at this time, *fam.* X 1—3, XII 2, 3, 23.

would procure his murder, but remained in Rome till the middle of October. He was preparing a reply to the consul's virulent invective, and meanwhile taking stock of the situation. One of his conclusions evidently was that, if the Republic was ever again to become a reality, it could only be through the loyal support of the provincial governors commanding armies. We get a glimpse of the considerations he thought likely to promote such loyalty. He tells Plancus, governor of Further Gaul, that he will do wisely to rest all his hopes of future preferment on the 'best settlement[1] of the constitution,' that is of course the restoration of the aristocratic Republic. To Cornificius in Africa he offers indignant sympathy on his approaching supersession by a governor of strong Caesarian views, and fears that he is taking the slight too quietly. In short, he is appealing to motives not likely to prevail if at any time they should conflict with self-interest or personal safety.

1307. At the end of September Brutus sailed for Greece, and Cassius soon followed. They were bent on taking possession of the East before the coming of Dolabella, and the chief republicans were eager for news of the success of an enterprise on which the future of their cause so greatly depended. Of leading republicans Cicero mentions several who were either out of Rome or afraid at present to appear in the Senate. They were only five beside Cicero himself. Still it was something to have five men of high station to whom he might look for some support in leading the House if a chance came. And things were beginning to move. Octavian had avoided openly breaking with Antony, but they were really on hostile terms. To all deeply-committed Caesarians it seemed essential that Caesar's murderers should be punished, amnesty or no amnesty. Antony and Octavian both were understood to desire this, but the former had certainly acted as though he were more concerned to succeed the late autocrat than to avenge him. Octavian managed to give the Caesarians the impression that he was more in earnest, while privately allaying republican suspicions by his moderation. On the 2nd October a hostile tribune called upon Antony to declare his intentions before a public meeting. He could not evade the challenge, and admitted that he meant to punish the murderers. According to Cicero, he was very ill received by the meeting. Perhaps we may fairly guess that the growing influence of Octavian was lessening the fear of Antony. A few days after this the report was spread that assassins had attempted the consul's life, and that they had been employed by Octavian. Cicero tells[2] us that the knowing aristocrats believed the

---

[1] *ex optimo reipublicae statu, ad fam.* X 3 § 2.

[2] Cic. *ad fam.* XII 23 § 2. The confession in *Phil.* III § 19 is thought to refer to this

story and approved the design, but that Antony, knowing himself to be generally hated, did not venture to take any public action (*rem proferre*) in the matter. The rabble treated it as a charge made up by Antony to discredit Octavian, and they were probably right. The young man's agents were tampering with some of the veterans in the consul's bodyguard, and Antony was uneasy, not without reason. On the 9th October he left Rome to meet the four legions now landed at Brundisium. If he could secure them and bring them back with him to Rome, he would be undisputed master of the situation. But he had not reckoned with the address and determination of Octavian, who at once set out on a tour to raise a force of veterans in the Campanian colonies. He took the chief necessary, money, no doubt partly furnished by those who hoped to find in him a counterpoise to Antony. He quickly raised a force strong enough to be taken seriously. Early in November he was busy organizing them at Capua, and the recruiting was proceeding well. Meanwhile his emissaries had been at work among the troops at Brundisium. Antony had a bad reception there. He offered them a largess of 100 *denarii* a head, but they no doubt knew that Octavian was giving 500 to his men. Antony tried to restore discipline by executing some of the disaffected centurions, but only increased the disaffection. He started for Rome with the Gaulish legion *Alauda*[1], and left the others to follow. He reached the city about the middle of November, but found Octavian already there at the head of about 10,000 men. These however could hardly be called an army. Nor were they yet prepared to act openly against the consul. According to Appian, most of them deserted their leader for a time. At all events he had much difficulty in using them to give effect to his policy. To avenge Caesar, and uphold the Caesarian military government, were the chief things from their point of view; why they should take part in a quarrel between Octavian and Antony they did not see. But the situation was soon changed by the news that one of Antony's four legions had left the line of march along the northern coast road, had occupied Alba[2], and declared for Octavian. This was the *Martia*. The fourth quickly followed their example. Octavian did not make the mistake of ignoring the Senate, of which he meant to make use in

---

affair. Of the later writers, Seneca and Suetonius believed the story, Velleius, Nicolaus, and Appian, rejected it. It is hard to say what line Plutarch (*Ant.* 16) or his authority took. Appian (*civ.* III 39) argues that it was not at this time Octavian's true interest to make away with Antony, which is not convincing.

[1] This legion, so named from their crests (a lark), was not one of the four, and had probably been brought from Rome. The four were II, IV, XXXV, and *Martia*.

[2] Opinions have differed, but I think that this Alba was the old fortress-colony on the lake Fucinus.

the conflict with Antony. He had been in constant communication with Cicero while he was busy in the South, and professed himself ready to act with and through the Senate. He tried to induce the orator to come to Rome and lead the House, disclaiming the design of avenging Caesar. But for the present Cicero hung back, mistrusting the effect of such an alliance, eager though he was to destroy Antony. The young heir had been well received in the city. But an utterance of his, in which he laid stress on his position as Caesar's successor, was alarming[1] to a loyal republican, and the prudent Atticus was all for waiting to see how things would turn out. Octavian moved his force into Etruria, where he formed a depot at Arretium. He raised more troops, veterans and young recruits, and formed an effective army. Antony had brought his still faithful legions to Tibur, but found it necessary to visit them and confirm their obedience by largesses. Indeed the one constant feature of military life at this time was the ceaseless outlay of money to satisfy for a moment the demands of the greedy soldiery. At Alba he could not get a hearing, for the men hated him and were in the pay of Octavian. On the 28th November he was in Rome. He hurried a lot of business[2] through the Senate, in particular the allotment of provinces to be held by the ex-praetors in the following year. Macedonia fell to his brother Gaius. After this he mobilized his forces and pushed northwards to Ariminum. He was now more in his element at the head of an army in the field. His object was to drive D. Brutus out of the Cisalpine, and take possession of his province before Octavian's army was ready and other forces raised to prevent his design.

1308. The departure of Antony left the republicans free to move, provided they could command a sufficient armed force to justify action. This was only to be found in one way, by coalescing with Octavian. The young man (now 19) was willing enough. The help of the leading republicans would give the coalition a strong majority in the Senate, and enable him to appear as the armed representative of Rome. The Senate was also willing. They indeed could not help themselves, nor was it as yet seriously suspected that, in using Caesar's heir to oppose Antony, they were giving themselves over into the hands of a far more able and irresistible master than Antony was or could be. Cicero reached Rome on the 9th December, by this time fully committed to the conflict on the result of which he staked his life. He had been composing the most ferocious of political pamphlets, his so-called Second *Philippic*, written in the form of a speech in reply to Antony's invective on September 19. Submitted

---

[1] Cic. *ad Att.* XVI 15 § 3. For Cicero's own misgivings see 14 §§ 1, 2.
[2] The news of the defection of the fourth legion reached him during this sitting.

to intimate friends for criticism and polished with loving care to whet and envenom every sting, it was and is admitted to be the classic masterpiece of Roman rhetoric. Whatever injured vanity, the bitterness of political antagonism, and the discharge of a hatred deliberately nursed and lashed into reckless fury, could inspire, was presented with matchless vigour by the greatest living master of literary form. He published it after Antony had left for the North. Roman society found it good reading. But of the many who gloated over its fierce personalities and chuckled as they caught the force of its brilliant points—and the career of Antony certainly lent itself to such treatment—few, we may be sure, were ready to make any great sacrifice for the republican cause, fewer still to risk their heads with Cicero. Applause was cheap, and Cicero greedy of literary fame. But the die was now cast, and he returned to public life bent on restoring the Republic and on making full use of Caesar's heir to make an end of Caesarism. That the 'boy' was capable of using the worn-out machinery of the constitution just so far as suited his own purposes, and wily enough to make a veteran statesman his tool, was as yet hidden from Cicero by his own vanity. The bargain was struck, and in that bargain the last chance of reviving the Republic was bought and sold.

1309. The first of January 43 was now approaching, when the state, at present hampered by the absence of both consuls, would have Hirtius and Pansa as its official heads. Of the trustworthiness of these men and their fitness for such responsibility grave doubts had been felt, and were still felt by some. Hirtius was in poor health. But whatever their weaknesses and vices they seem to have been now heartily sick of Antony. And there was now an actual state of war, and it was impossible to sit idly waiting for the new year. Accordingly we find Cicero writing to provincial governors, to confirm the loyalty of these men with armies, particularly the shifty Plancus in Further Gaul. To D. Brutus he wrote urging him to stand firm in the Cisalpine, and not to wait for the approval of the Senate, which would be publicly voted as soon as the removal of present fears enabled the House to act. The great truth, that the Republic (that is, the means of restoring it) lay in the provinces, had been confessed[1] by him soon after Caesar's death. He now called upon Decimus to free the commonwealth from the tyrant Antony, to carry through the work begun : not the Roman state alone, but all the peoples of the [Roman] world, were looking to him for this. The reference to the subject races is striking in this connexion. No doubt the provincials generally took some interest in the fate of Rome. But the warlike

---

[1] Cic. *ad fam.* XI 5, 7 (December 44), see also XV 20 § 2 (April).

sighed for freedom, and the most submissive had assuredly no pre-possession in favour of the corrupt tyranny of Roman aristocrats coupled with the pitiless exactions of Roman financiers. That the abuses were an integral part of the aristocratic republican system was a plain fact, obstinately ignored by Cicero to the last. In another point his ardent wishes led him into self-deception. Many country towns had received Octavian well, and furnished him with young recruits. When Octavian joined hands with the Senate, the orator talked himself, and perhaps others, into the belief[1] that the subsequent recruiting was the outcome of genuine attachment to the republican system. The course of events sadly belied this theory. Some real feeling of the kind there doubtless was, but it would be through and from men of the well-to-do classes that Cicero would hear of it. Of the feelings of the poorer citizens he is not a satisfactory witness. Other motives were the unpopularity of Antony, the popularity of Octavian, and consciousness of the fact that in times of trouble none were so well able to promote their own interest as those who bore the sword. The spirit of the adventurer had become more and more the spirit of Roman troops ever since the second Punic war. It had been the spirit of the mercenary ever since the reforms of Marius, and could not be suddenly changed now. It was idle to indulge such a hope: as idle as the hope 'that the Roman people[2] would at last shew the spirit of their fathers.'

1310. With the 10th December the new tribunes came into office. On the 20th they called a meeting of the Senate, in which Cicero[3] denounced Antony as a public enemy and lauded Octavian as the loyal saviour of the state. He warmly praised the conduct of the two legions that had been won over to their side, and carried a resolution (a) calling upon the consuls-elect to see that the House should be able to meet in safety on the 1st January, (b) commending D. Brutus and approving his manifesto of intention to hold the province and resist Antony, (c) instructing the present governors of provinces, in particular[4] D. Brutus and L. Plancus, to continue at their posts until relieved by decree of the Senate, (d) voting the thanks of the House to Octavian and the two legions as the loyal champions of Roman freedom, (e) instructing the consuls-elect to lose no time in providing for the effective expression of the public gratitude. Thus

---

[1] To what lengths this infatuation afterwards led him may be seen in *Phil.* XI § 39, where he prefers young troops to veterans (March 43). See § 1314.

[2] Cic. *ad fam.* XII 22 § 2 (to Cornificius in Africa, Dec. 44).

[3] Third *Philippic*. For his own confession, that he had uphill work to rouse the members to a bold policy, see *ad fam.* X 28 (Feb. 43). On this day he laid the foundations of a Republic, he says X 25 § 2 (March).

[4] These two had been designated by Caesar for the consulships of 42.

he not only carried the House with him in defiance of Antony, but indirectly annulled the allotment of provinces for 43, lately made under Antony's direction. He followed up this step by addressing[1] a public meeting, explaining the situation, justifying the policy of the Senate, and calling on all citizens to support it. At last Cicero was to all appearance the first man in Rome, guiding the central government of the vast imperial Republic. But in truth he was as the impassioned nurse of one sick unto death and virtually dead, calling on the sick man to rise and exert vital forces that had left him to return no more. The palsy of the Republic was final. Even in the only part still feebly capable of conscious action, in the Senate, there was a minority led by Q. Fufius Calenus, a strong Caesarian, not afraid to oppose Cicero, and certain to attract the votes of waverers in any hour of doubt and difficulty. We may well admire the pluck and nervous energy displayed by the veteran statesman in doing what he thought his duty to his country at all costs. His bitter hatred of Antony could not blind him to his own danger. But it was not for a contemporary patriot, devoted to the Republic as he conceived it, to see and tamely to confess that the crisis of its fate was past. Of all the persons at this moment concerned in public affairs the only one to profit by the policy of Cicero was Octavian.

1311. Meanwhile the news from the North was grave. Antony had entered the Cisalpine, driving before him the outlying forces of D. Brutus, who fell back upon the fortress-colony of Mutina. There he stood at bay. His troops were no match for Antony's veterans, and Antony invested the town, keeping another force for the present in Bononia. War had begun. On the first of January (43) the Senate met under the new consuls. The debate did not reach a final vote till the 4th. Calenus found support for a proposal to send an embassy to Antony before proceeding to extremities, and to warn him out of the Cisalpine. Cicero replied[2] in a vehement speech, arguing that the vote of the 20th December had virtually pronounced Antony a public enemy, and for the best of reasons. He protested against the delay that an embassy would bring, to the damage of their cause. He proposed honours and rewards to D. Brutus and his men, and to all who had deserted or should desert Antony. He moved that Octavian should have the rank of propraetor as though he had been appointed in the ordinary way; he would thus have the *imperium* necessary for the command of troops in the service of the state. That the young Caesar was in the service of the state was manifest; that he would never cease to be its faithful defender,

---

[1] Fourth *Philippic*.

[2] Fifth *Philippic*, followed by the Sixth, an address to the people.

the old consular pledged his own word. This and other honours were voted to Octavian, and he was commissioned to act with the consuls in the war. The proposal to declare Antony an enemy in due form was stopped by the intervention of a tribune. And the partisans of Calenus worked upon the weak nerves of senators behind the scenes, and brought the whole matter to a weak conclusion. The embassy was voted. The envoys were to order Antony to quit the Cisalpine and submit to the will of the Senate, but to keep 200 miles from Rome: if he refused, they were to declare war. The consuls were to raise an army at once, to be ready for events. They set to work in haste, and Cicero[1] asserted that no compulsory levy was needed, for all came forward as volunteers, so great was the enthusiasm in Italy. But Antony was not the man to be frightened by such menaces, or to accept such terms. One of the three ambassadors died on the journey. Antony, who had now a tight grip of Mutina, received the others, and sent them back with insolent counter-proposals of his own. He was willing to give up his claim to the Cisalpine and content himself with the Further Gaul for the next five years, but only on condition of receiving six more legions, and of the confirmation of the decrees laws grants, in short of all the acts of his administration, which Cicero and his followers were eager to undo. Early in February this reply was debated in the Senate, and a state of war in Italy (*tumultus*) was decreed. Cicero insisted[2] that it was really a foreign war (*bellum*) of the most atrocious kind, and drew a vivid picture of the murders and confiscations that would attend the victory of Antony and his ruffians thirsting for spoils. It was no time for any show of irresolution, by which the general enthusiasm of Italy would be damped. He was all for peace, but a real sound peace, which could now be attained only by present war carried on with vigour. He lashed the base cowardice[3] and disloyalty of certain of his fellow consulars, to whom the state looked for light and leading, and found none. He moved that an amnesty and rewards be voted to those who deserted Antony or did good service otherwise. Antony was now in the position[4] of a public enemy. He was meanwhile pressing the siege of Mutina, and the supply of food in the town was running low.

1312. We must now turn for a moment to see what was going on in other parts of the Roman world. From the beginning of the

---

[1] Cic. *ad fam.* XI 8 § 2.

[2] Eighth *Philippic*. The seventh was a speech of general encouragement to persevere.

[3] See also *ad fam.* XII 4, 5, X 28.

[4] Not yet formally declared such. For details, raising of money by subscriptions and economies, annulling certain laws, the general donning of the military dress (*sagum*), etc., see Tyrrell and Purser, VI 34.

year Cicero had continued to correspond with provincial governors of his acquaintance, impressing upon them their duty to the Republic and the honours that would await their loyal services, and making the best of the prospects of the cause. The Senate too was alive to the importance of these governors, and they were officially invited to declare their loyalty and strengthen the hands of the Home government. We will first look to the West and North. Pollio in the Further Spain had been a Caesarian, but he was no Antonian. A moderate man of critical temper, he preferred a Republic to an autocracy. But he was cut off from the rest by the huge province of Lepidus, who was more than suspected of inclining to support Antony. He could only be sure of getting letters if forwarded by sea. And he was not disposed to make a great effort with no reasonable prospect of success. Lepidus, in Hither Spain and Narbonese Gaul, had been gratified by honours[1] decreed him in November last, and had found a connexion with Antony serviceable hitherto. He probably mistrusted the republicans led by Cicero. He wrote plausibly, advising a cessation of hostilities. But peace just now was all in the interest of Antony. L. Plancus in Further Gaul was a rogue, caring only for his own advantage. He made fine professions in guarded language, and as time went on he was more and more inclined to find grounds of offence with the republicans, in order to be able at need to desert them with some excuse. He had a powerful army, as he took care to inform the Senate late in March. But it was in vain that Cicero appealed to him to cross the Alps and rescue D. Brutus. Let us now turn to the East. Macedonia[2] was held in the year 44 by Q. Hortensius, son of the orator. The province had been destined by Caesar for M. Antony, but we have seen how the latter took the Gauls instead, and in November transferred it to his brother Gaius. Vatinius was in Illyricum. C. Trebonius had Asia for 44 and 43. Tillius Cimber had Bithynia. L. Statius Murcus was governor of Syria. Q. Marcius Crispus had a province, most probably Cilicia. Syria had been procured for Dolabella by Antony, and Dolabella had gone to take possession of it, passing through Asia on the way. Brutus and Cassius had left Italy and were bent upon raising forces in the East to uphold the republican cause; Brutus was in the first instance to secure Macedonia, Cassius Syria. To these provinces they had no legal claim, and the minor provinces which had been assigned to them in June (44) they ignored as unsuited to their design. We

[1] A *supplicatio* in honour of his negotiation with Sextus Pompey.
[2] I am here accepting the conclusions of Schwartz in the article (*Hermes* XXXIII) referred to above.

have seen that on the 20th December the Senate had instructed present governors to hold their provinces for the present, but we shall see that this order, if received, was not of much effect. The problem before Brutus and Cassius was how to win over the Roman armies in the eastern provinces. This once done, they could raise further troops from the Romans settled in the East, and could rely on the support of the client-princes in that part of the empire. Cavalry, bowmen, and light troops generally, were to be had in plenty. Infantry could be found among the Thracians and other warlike races, and money and stores to pay and feed a large army could be wrung from the long-suffering Asiatics. The naval resources of the East were much greater than those of the West, and Cassius had already the nucleus of a fleet, commanded by his brother Lucius. All in short depended on their reception by the provincial governors; and the provincial governors, however willing they had been to serve under their former master Caesar, could not as yet appreciate the growing importance of Octavian, and were not at all likely to accept readily the supremacy of Antony. The enterprise of Brutus and Cassius was therefore not so desperate as it might at first sight appear to us. The governors, all members of the Senate, could hardly be unwilling to see that body restored to power, and Brutus and Cassius might (and surely did) claim to represent the real wishes of the senatorial majority. They had at their back a considerable moral force, the effect of which must not be underrated.

1313. Brutus spent some time at Athens, now a sort of University town, where young Romans went to improve their minds by attending the schools of philosophy. But he was making ready for war, and among the youths who hung about the Professors' lecture-rooms he found some willing to follow him. He wanted intelligent officers, no doubt. Two of these lads were Cicero's son Marcus, and Q. Horatius Flaccus, the son of a respectable freedman. While at Athens he was treating with the governors of provinces near, to good purpose, as the sequel proved. Fortune favoured him. He induced the commander of some Roman ships to surrender the whole squadron. Quaestors[1] returning to Rome from Asia and Syria handed over to him a large sum of public money. He picked up some of Pompey's old soldiers, still lingering in Greece, intercepted and brought over some cavalry on their way to join Dolabella in Asia Minor, and seized a large depot of arms at Demetrias, stored there by Caesar's order for his Parthian war. He entered Macedonia, and Hortensius at once handed over to him both province and army. The surrender

[1] One now, the other probably later. See Tyrrell and Purser on *ad Brutum* I 11 (No. 850).

of Vatinius soon followed, for Brutus pushed over the mountains in wintry weather (Feb. 43), and Vatinius[1] seems to have made no resistance. Gaius Antonius, who claimed Macedonia, could make no head against the forces of Brutus. He was eventually deserted by his troops, who went over to Brutus like the rest. All the Balkan peninsula was now held by the republicans with a strong army. In the further East Cassius had been not less successful. He too had got some public money in Asia, and hurried on to Syria. Murcus and Crispus were besieging the Pompeian Bassus in Apamea. They handed over their armies to Cassius, and the soldiers of Bassus[2] soon forced their ₍chief to do the same. By about the beginning of March Cassius was supreme in the province where he had made his military reputation. His first concern now was to exact money, which he did. But his good luck was not yet ended. A lieutenant of Dolabella had been sent to Egypt to bring up the troops stationed there in pay of the Ptolemaic queen Cleopatra. What with the men left there by Caesar in 47, and the Pompeian and other refugees, there were four legions. On his way through Syria, to meet Dolabella in Cilicia, this commander fell in with Cassius, who was greatly superior in force. So he too had to surrender, and early in May Cassius was at the head of 11 or 12 legions. The greater part of the Roman East was already in the power of the republicans. On the other side, Dolabella had entered Asia at the beginning of the year (43). He overcame and captured Trebonius, and put him to death, it was said with great barbarity. But his forces were small, and in face of the growing strength of Cassius his prospects were bad.

1314. The exact chronology of events in Rome is not to be recovered, but it is clear that the Senate was very busy, and Cicero very active, in the month of March. The news of the successes of Brutus led to a sharp debate. Calenus moved to decree the deposition of Brutus, and urged that, if they wanted to keep the veterans loyal, they had better not offend them by honouring the chief of Caesar's murderers. Cicero in reply could not[3] stand on the ground of legal right, for Brutus had none. He argued from expediency, pointed out the immense services of Brutus, with which the Republic could not afford to dispense in the present crisis. He called upon the Senate not to let its whole policy be dictated by the supposed wishes of the veterans who, he remarked, were marching to the rescue of D. Brutus.

---

[1] His men left him, according to Dion Cass. XLVII 21 § 6.

[2] It is remarkable that the ex-Pompeian was the only one unwilling to surrender to Cassius. See Cic. *ad fam.* XII 12 § 3 *misere noluit.*

[3] Tenth *Philippic.* The ninth was in support of a proposal for honours to the great jurist Servius Sulpicius, lately deceased on his way to Mutina as ambassador.

But if Marcus was under ban as Caesar's murderer, so too was Decimus. Cicero moved that Brutus should be thanked and recognized as holder of a general command embracing Macedonia Illyricum and Greece, with full power to use public moneys, to raise loans, and levy supplies, and instructed (a significant point) to keep his forces as near as possible to Italy. This was carried. Clearly the good news had strengthened Cicero's following. It seemed that, even if Mutina should fall, an invasion under Brutus would turn the scale in favour of the republican cause. But the elation of the moment blinded Cicero to one important consideration. If he was charmed with the success of Brutus, there were others, at present acting with him, to whom that success was less welcome. The restoration of the Republic by an army commanded by the chief of Caesar's murderers would bring to an end the ambitions of Caesar's heir. And if Cicero could urge that the veterans had no ground for fearing that Caesar's acts would be annulled in the event of a republican victory, the veterans might well reply that for the maintenance of their privileges they had rather trust to Octavian. To protest against undue deference to these rough soldiers had a free and noble sound. That it had not been expedient, time was to shew. And Octavian was not one to miss the significance of what had happened. He still adhered to the republicans as against Antony, but was coolly playing a game; his own, not that of Cicero. Soon after this a second step in the same direction was taken. On hearing of the conduct of Dolabella in Asia, the Senate voted him a public enemy. This raised the question of Syria. Cicero[1] declared that Dolabella had acted as Antony would act were he not held in check. He too must be put down, and Cassius was obviously the man to do it. But Cicero's motion for giving Syria to Cassius, with a general superior command over the further eastern provinces, and instructions to put down Dolabella, was defeated. Calenus, supported by the consul Pansa, induced the House to decree that Asia and Syria should be allotted to the present consuls, when they had done with the war in the North. Cicero's objections to this course were sound enough, but the Senate, from whatever motive, ignored them. It was on this occasion that, referring again to the veterans, he was unwise enough to stake his hopes on the newly-enlisted volunteers and the enthusiasm of Italy. He preferred the young soldiers to the old, who had seen their best days. Many of his hearers must have shrugged their shoulders at this wild talk. Beaten in the Senate, Cicero addressed the people[2] in a vehement harangue, which he says

[1] Eleventh *Philippic.* Cicero does not even pretend that Cassius had any legal claim to Syria.   [2] Not preserved. See *ad fam.* XII 7.

was very well received.   In one point the orator was right: he said that Cassius would take the law into his own hands, and we have seen that he did.

1315.   By the end of February Hirtius and Octavian were posted on the line of the Aemilian road between Ariminum and Bononia. The latter place, important as commanding the junction of the Cassian[1] road with the Aemilian, was still held by Antony, whom they did not venture to attack, most of their forces being raw recruits. The relief of Mutina seemed far off, and the weakening effect of anxiety upon the nerves of men was soon evident in Rome.   It was proposed to send another embassy to treat with Antony: among five names that of Cicero was one.   The scheme was absurd, and Cicero, who seems to have let it pass unopposed, next day expressed his repentance[2] and succeeded in getting it withdrawn.   About the middle of March Pansa left Rome for the seat of war.   Soon after this letters arrived from Lepidus and Plancus.   Both these governors recommended peace.   But in truth things had gone too far for a pacification: one side or other must submit.   From Cicero's replies[3] to private letters it is clear that he and his republican followers were not satisfied with these two men.   We have only Cicero's speech[4] at the end of a long adjourned debate, in which he supported a motion thanking Lepidus, but reserving for the Senate the question of war or peace.   This seems to have been carried.   The most striking part of the speech is that in which the orator proves the impossibility of coming to terms with Antony.   This he did by taking a letter[5] which had just been received, addressed by Antony to Hirtius and Octavian.   He read it out clause by clause, with running criticisms. As a piece of debating, this was doubtless most effective.   But the letter, read as a whole, proves to us, if proof were needed, that Antony understood the present situation, with all its secret conflict of irreconcileable interests, better than Cicero.   He was defiant enough, but he took care to hint at a private compact with Lepidus and a policy shared with Plancus.   And he cleverly pointed out that Hirtius, and even more Octavian, were playing the game of a party that was using them both for its own purposes.   Whether they defeated him or he them, the survivors would be at the mercy of what was no less than the old Pompeian gang over again, this time led by Cicero. Let Hirtius and Octavian look to themselves.   To combine with

---

[1] That is, its continuation by the *via Flaminia* of 187 B.C.   See § 562.
[2] Twelfth *Philippic*.   [3] Cic. *ad fam.* X 6, 27.
[4] Thirteenth *Philippic*.
[5] Wisely included, in continuous form, in Shuckburgh's translation of Cicero's *Letters*, vol. IV pp. 189—192.

himself against their common enemies was the true policy. This letter gives us a means of appreciating the real talents of Antony when braced by military needs and not fuddled by debauch. Surely it was read by Hirtius in a spirit very different from that of Cicero; that Octavian laid it to heart we cannot reasonably doubt. But it contained no offer sufficient to detach Octavian from the cause in which he was at present engaged. Antony was not really humbled, but still fighting for his own hand, so the operations for the relief of Mutina went on. At this juncture the restless Sextus Pompey began once more to concern himself with Roman affairs. He wrote from Massalia offering his services to the Senate, and Cicero ended his criticism of Antony by moving a warm vote of thanks to this welcome ally.

1316. Early in April a despatch came from Plancus, who now (but still with a certain cautious reserve) posed[1] as a loyal governor, only anxious to keep his province obedient and contented, to strengthen and train his forces, and to use them for the good of the Republic. He would not imitate the rash example of D. Brutus. Cicero, who either believed or affected to believe these professions sincere, succeeded in carrying a vote of thanks and honours to Plancus on the 9th April. But the debate had lasted three days, and the obstructive opposition of P. Servilius, a tiresome republican, backed up by a tribune, had exposed the inner weakness of Cicero's party. It was a crisis when they could ill afford to be fastidious, but even now, after all these years of revolution, these men were willing to embarrass their leader with technical scruples. At the last moment the arrival of the news of the complete success of Cassius in Syria had enabled Cicero to get his motion carried. And now all were waiting impatiently for news of a battle in the North. It was well known that famine had made the relief or fall of Mutina a question of days. How entirely attention had lately been engrossed by this department may be inferred from the proceedings of a military adventurer in Italy. P. Ventidius[2], who had served under Caesar and was a partisan of Antony, actually raised two legions in the South, and on his way northwards a third in Picenum. He avoided the republican armies by crossing the Apennine, and joined Antony later when in retreat at a most opportune moment. It is an astounding story, but there is no good reason to doubt the main facts.

---

[1] Plancus had now learnt that Antony had claimed his province of Further Gaul, and was displeased. Jullien cited by Tyrrell and Purser, VI 41. See Cic. *ad fam.* X 8, 12, *ad Brutum* II 2.

[2] He was from Picenum, and had when a child been taken prisoner in the great Italian war. For his wonderful career see Dion Cass. XLIII 51, Gellius XV 4.

1317. And now at length the war in the Cisalpine took a decisive turn. The pressure of Hirtius and Octavian compelled Antony to evacuate Bononia, and the arrival of Pansa made it necessary for him to check their advance. On the 15th April a battle[1] was fought between Bononia and Mutina, on the line of the main road. The veterans on both sides did most of the fighting, and lost heavily. Antony had the best of it so far, but Hirtius fell upon him as he retired on Mutina, and routed his wearied army with great slaughter. The strength of his cavalry (foreign) enabled Antony to escape. On this day Pansa was severely wounded. The part of Octavian was confined to the repulse of an attack on his camp. Such was the battle of Forum Gallorum. On the 21st another battle was fought close to Mutina, in which Antony was utterly beaten. He withdrew in disorderly flight, and Mutina was relieved. But Hirtius fell in the hour of victory, and in a few days Pansa died of his wound. Two general officers only were left to command the armies of the Republic on the spot: D. Brutus, Caesar's murderer, whose men were weak with hunger or dying from a sudden change to over-feeding, and Caesar's heir, to whom, since the death of both consuls, three armies were looking for orders. For military reasons it was most important to pursue and destroy the beaten army of Antony, who was flying to the West, and whom another defeat would render harmless. But nothing was done. D. Brutus was in no condition to start at once. Octavian held aloof, and would do nothing to help him. So Antony escaped. It remained to be seen what view the Senate would take of the situation, and in particular how they would deal with the young man whom fortune had just placed in so commanding a position. Now, while fighting was going on in the North, in Rome things were in a bad way. Rumours of defeat were circulated, and found some belief, perhaps in connexion with alarm caused by news of the march of Ventidius. It was also suggested that Cicero was intending to seize supreme power. He was for a time in some danger, but a friendly tribune spoke in his defence. The news of the battle of Forum Gallorum led to enthusiastic demonstrations in his honour. He was the hero of the hour. Next day (21 April) it was proposed in the Senate that the garb of peace should be resumed. Cicero[2] wisely opposed the change, and induced the House to wait till they heard of the relief of Mutina. But he supported the motion for a public thanksgiving, all the more gladly as this clearly implied that Antony and his men were public enemies. He proposed honours for the fallen of their own armies; rewards for the living, to be shared

---

[1] See Galba's letter in Cic. *fam.* X 30, Tyrrell and Purser VI 42—3.

[2] Fourteenth *Philippic*, his last extant speech.

by relatives of the dead.   Soon came the news of the second battle
and the relief of Mutina, and on the 26th the formal decree declaring
the Antonians *hostes* was actually passed.   The elation of victory
overcame caution, and the republican[1] majority voted honours and
rewards with unguarded joy.   Their real sentiments were shewn in
the marked distinction made between the two surviving commanders.
D. Brutus was voted a triumph, with other honours some of which
were unprecedented.   Octavian was to have only the minor triumph
(*ovatio*).   The difference was presently emphasized by assigning the
armies of the fallen consuls to D. Brutus, with orders to follow up
Antony and end the war.   That this arrangement was something
more than a recognition of the claims of seniority, was evident from
the other decrees[2] passed at the same time.   The recent offer of
Sextus Pompey was accepted, and he was appointed commander
of the naval forces, with charge of the coasts.   Cassius too was
entrusted with the duty of crushing Dolabella, and formally appointed
governor of Syria, with a wide general authority in all the provinces
of the further East.

   1318.   By these orders, and others of less importance, the Senate
had shewn its hand.   The republicans led by Cicero fancied that the
danger was past, and they might safely carry out their real wishes.
In shelving Octavian, who had saved them from Antony, and in
promoting the murderers and open enemies of Caesar, they did that
which only the existence of the Republic as a working reality could
make effectual.   And the Republic of which Cicero had 'laid the
foundations' with much ·eloquence had no real vitality whatever.
Even if Octavian had been sincerely devoted to the republican cause,
he was now warned that he must depend on himself, if he did not
mean to let his public career be brought to an end.   That was the
certain result, if talking and voting were to rule the course of events.
But the young man knew that the civil organs of the Republic, the
Senate and the so-called Roman People, were merely shadows bearing great names.   The real power lay with the masters of armies.
As for the prestige conferred by high office, it had ceased to matter
much; and it so happened that both the consuls were dead, and
technical difficulties[3] stood in the way of a speedy election of their
successors.   Thus the constitutional machine, such as it was, was
hampered by exceptional bad luck.   Octavian waited and watched,
and the republicans blindly played into his hand.   They believed

---

[1] Dion Cass. XLVI 39 says that they passed a decree restricting the tenure of offices to
the old period of one year.   This shews the reality of the attempt to restore the Republic.
[2] 27th April.   Cic. *ad Brut.* I 5 § 1.
[3] See Tyrrell and Purser on Cic. *ad Brut.* I 5 § 4.

Antony to be in a worse plight than he really was, and D. Brutus to be pursuing him at the head of a large and efficient army. They summoned Lepidus and Plancus from beyond the Alps to close in upon the flying enemy and complete the victory of the Republic. Of the certainty of final success they had no doubt, and turned to carry out the degradation of Octavian. They sent a deputation with an official report of recent decrees relative to rewards. These rewards[1] were not the same for all, but designed to create jealousies and divisions, and the announcement was to be made to the soldiers direct, not communicated to the general in the usual way. Octavian took good care that the envoys should have a warm reception from the indignant legionaries, and the affair only served to attach the soldiers more closely to him and make them more suspicious of orders from Rome. And the military situation in the North was far from being such as Cicero and his friends supposed. Antony had fled in disorder, but with two days start, and at a pinch there was no better commander than he. D. Brutus had at first no transport, being only just escaped from a long siege. The troops he got together were either sickly men from Mutina or raw recruits. The veteran corps of the two consular armies would have nothing to do with him, and Octavian, secure in their allegiance to himself, found pretexts for refusing to cooperate in the pursuit. Ventidius and his three strong legions crossed the Apennine unmolested, and joined Antony at Vada Sabatia near Genua. From thence it was easy to reach the province of Lepidus, and what Lepidus did we shall presently see. In truth Octavian had no wish to destroy Antony, and the latter was now humbled enough to incline him to accept terms. To Cicero and the fanatical republicans Antony was an outlaw, but not so to Octavian, who allowed captured Antonians to rejoin him, and gave other indications of goodwill. And so the efforts of D. Brutus were foiled and wasted. All through the month of May and the first days of June the unhappy man was doing his best with insufficient means. In vain he wrote begging for reinforcements, for money, for M. Brutus to be summoned with all speed from Macedonia. Nothing came, and his position soon became one of great danger. But he was given to understand that the men in Rome thought him wanting in vigour and were disappointed not to hear of better results. The failure was, as he knew and pointed out, the fault of Octavian. He thought at first that the young general was hindered by the unruliness of his troops. How completely the republicans misjudged the power and intentions of Octavian may be seen from the fact that at the end of May Cicero[2] could write to

---

[1] See Velleius II 62 §§ 4, 5, Dion Cass. XLVI 40, 41, Appian *civ.* III 86.

[2] Cic. *ad fam.* XI 14. He mentioned that the legions in Africa had been sent for.

Decimus, admitting that things were going ill, and saying that he too was in favour of sending for Marcus and his army, and of keeping Octavian to protect Italy. Meanwhile, as if the 'boy' had not already had warning and provocation enough, the Senate were appointing ten commissioners to revise the acts of Antony's consulship. All manner of questions were likely to be raised, among them that of the land-allotments. Octavian was not to be one of the ten, and his veterans were angered, fearing that their interests would suffer. And the young Caesar himself had laid to heart a recently reported[1] saying of Cicero. The orator had expressed his view[2] of how to deal with Octavian, 'we must praise him, honour him, and hoist him.' In the third word was a double meaning, 'elevate' or 'get rid of' him. The ill-timed jest betrayed the insincerity of the compliments hitherto lavished by Cicero on a youth about whom he was just beginning to feel a little anxious, a youth who neither forgot nor forgave.

1319. We must turn to Lepidus and Plancus. The latter professed stout loyalty, and seems really to have preferred a Republic, at least to the rule of Antony. He and Cicero exchanged many letters during the anxious months of May June and July. Plancus knew better than to act on all Cicero's exhortations or to accept his over-hopeful views of the situation. He saw that more remained to be done than men in Rome fancied, and was resolved not to ruin himself by attempting a hopeless task. He mistrusted the intentions of Lepidus, and said that he was doing his best to keep him from combining with Antony. He declared that some of his own troops were not to be trusted, still less those of Lepidus. Lepidus indeed was suspected by everybody: even Cicero could do nothing but hope for the best. On the 29th May Lepidus joined Antony. He had allowed the latter to approach, doubtless under a secret agreement, and intercourse between the two armies soon gave him a pretext for asserting that a mutiny of his men had forced him to go over to the enemy. He had taken this step to promote peace[3] and stop bloodshed. So the weak and shifty chief pontiff had shewn his colours at last. Plancus, who had advanced his army to the border of his province, watching events, had now good reason for retiring, being unable to cope with the forces united against him. But the design of Antony, who now completely dominated Lepidus, was not to control by forcible pressure the governor of Further Gaul. Other plans were in contemplation. Neither Cicero nor Plancus, nor even D. Brutus, was aware of two important facts which were destined to

[1] *ad fam.* XI 20, 21, Velleius II 62 § 6.
[2] *laudandum, ornandum, tollendum.*
[3] See his hypocritical letter in Cic. *ad fam.* X 35.

rule the subsequent course of events. First, that Octavian was in treaty with Antony and Lepidus. Secondly, that Marcus Brutus had quite made up his mind not to invade Italy in support of the republican cause. In ignorance of these facts the Senate declared Lepidus a public enemy, and hoped that with Octavian's strong army, with two legions expected from Africa, and with the coming of Brutus, they were still more than a match for their outlawed enemies.

1320. It is time to speak of the influences that led Brutus to so momentous a decision. His successes in Macedonia and Illyricum had been striking, but they could not do much towards reestablishing the Republic, if the provisional republican government were allowed to fall. His presence was sorely needed in Italy, more perhaps than he at first recognized. But, after the death of both consuls, when the war took a bad turn, and Cicero wanted forces able and willing to give effect to his policy, why did not Brutus come? The truth is, there was a fatal disagreement[1] between him and Cicero. From the first he had greatly disliked the acceptance of the help of Octavian, and the honours conferred on the heir of the 'tyrant' had irritated him beyond endurance. In his narrow-minded conceit he fancied that he at a distance could judge policy and possibilities better than[2] the opportunist Cicero on the spot. In the middle of April the two were in correspondence not of a harmonious kind. C. Antonius, the defeated claimant of Macedonia, was a prisoner in the hands of Brutus. What was to be done with him? Keep him, said Cicero, as security for the life of Decimus. On the 13th a letter from Brutus, with one from C. Antonius, was read in the Senate. To the astonishment of all, Brutus referred to his prisoner in mild terms, and even allowed him to style himself *proconsul*. The inner meaning of this was a puzzle: some argued that the letter of Brutus was a forgery. The pitiful truth was that this model of true republicanism was not unwilling to come to terms with Antony, whose brother was from this point of view a valuable asset. Cicero wrote blaming Brutus for leaning to clemency and talking of peace. Real peace could only be gained by victory in war, and slavery to Antony had only been averted by the timely aid of Octavian. The three brothers Antony were in the same position as Dolabella. The only choice was between destroying them or being destroyed by them. And so the correspondence continued, Cicero warning Brutus of the danger attending a

---

[1] The question of the genuineness of the Brutus-Cicero correspondence is admirably discussed in Tyrrell and Purser vol. VI. I believe with them that only the two letters *Brut.* I 16, 17, are reasonably doubted.

[2] See his own words *Philippic* XI § 27.

weak policy, and confessing that Octavian had hitherto been the saviour of their cause.   The victories that relieved Mutina raised Cicero's confidence so that he ceased for a time to call for help from Brutus, but he still thirsted for the destruction of C. Antonius and Dolabella, while Brutus raised scruples as to killing his prisoner without orders from the Senate, and began to criticize[1] the policy of Cicero.   In particular he objected to the honours bestowed on Octavian.   The young man must not be pushed forward so as to become dangerous.   Brutus seems to have believed the rumour that Cicero was going to stand for the consulship with Octavian for colleague, and plainly shewed his disgust.   This was in the middle of May : soon after we find that he left the Adriatic coast and moved into Macedonia.   He was still on friendly terms with Cicero, and felt entitled to ask favours of him.   Cicero could venture to do the same. But Brutus was now far away.   And by the end of May things were looking very bad for the republicans in the North.   Decimus was clearly in extreme danger, and Octavian would not budge.   In June and July Cicero was in terrible anxiety, writing to cheer Decimus with hopes of the coming of Marcus, and to Marcus (and to Cassius also) appealing for help before it was too late.   Too late it probably was already, even had Brutus come with all speed.   But he did not want to come.   Native obstinacy and philosophic pedantry would alike disincline him to change his plans: he was disgusted with Cicero's conduct as he understood or misunderstood it: but there was another influence also at work, an influence illustrating the nature of that Roman aristocracy whose virtues had made the Republic, and whose vices had contributed to its fall.

1321.   This influence was that of a family connexion.   Lepidus and Cassius had married two half-sisters of Brutus.   Among the Roman nobles these marriage-connexions were generally a matter of careful calculation.   In spite of frequent divorces and much marital infidelity, the fact of the connexion constituted a bond which social habit made it difficult to ignore.   Cicero himself had found it hard to break finally with Dolabella, whose bad character he knew and loathed, and whose treatment of his beloved Tullia had been infamous. The same case reminds us of the financial side of these transactions. Cicero was at his wits end to recover Tullia's dowry.   To refund that of the divorced Terentia cost him much embarrassment, and his marrying and divorcing Publilia was a money-matter from beginning to end.   A hundred years before, the extreme 'closeness' of the Romans where money was concerned had been noted by Polybius,

---

[1] If the two letters, *Brut.* 1 16, 17, are genuine, he descended to bitter ranting, addressed both to Cicero and to Atticus.

and this remark was called forth in speaking of dowries. Nor was the greedy capitalist Brutus the man to overlook the financial point of view. Accordingly, while Cicero was writing in June to impress upon him the dangers gathering round the Republic, and piteously appealing to him for immediate help, Brutus saw the situation differently. That things were in a very bad way, that even Cicero no longer felt sure of Octavian, that the young man was demanding the consulship, and so on, merely convinced him that, if D. Brutus (as Cicero said) had bungled, the chief bungler had been Cicero himself. We may guess that to hurry from Macedonia now was open to serious objections. If he arrived in time, a very doubtful contest would await him. If he came too late, it was far from unlikely that his army would go over to the anti-republican majority whom it would find in possession of Italy, and his own death, and the ruin of his cause, would follow. Neither he nor Cicero made sufficient allowance for each other's difficulties. But if Brutus, for whatever reason, failed Cicero in time of need, the outlawry of Lepidus caused him no small concern. In July, when Cicero's one remaining hope was in the long looked-for succour from the East, what he received from Brutus was an urgent request to protect the family of Lepidus. The outlaw's property was forfeited to the state: his wife and children would probably be held as hostages. The reply of Cicero at first was that the law must take its course. But he soon after admitted that he was doing all he could to spare the family. In his last despairing cry to Brutus he even tries to move that self-satisfied pedantic uncle by the plea 'come and protect them yourself.' Here the correspondence ended, and the writers went their ways apart, each to his doom. Cicero had humbled himself so far as to explain and justify his policy on the plea of necessity, an unavailing and doubtless unwelcome self-abasement, nearly the last sacrifice that he was to make for Rome.

1322. The voluntary deadlock in the North lasted through June and July. Before the middle of June D. Brutus had effected his junction with Plancus. They had between them 13 or 14 legions, but only four of veterans, and it was doubtful whether the loyalty of all could be relied on. Money was needed, and as time went by the need became more pressing. Antony and Lepidus also waited. They were at least as strong as their opponents, probably stronger, but delay was doing more for them than battles. Emissaries conveyed lavish offers of bounty to the camp of Plancus, offers which could of course only be made good by the winning side. And the soldiers of the revolutionary age were men who had taken to arms as a profession. For orders and for rewards they looked to their generals. Military life habituated them to the need of having a definite individual to obey and to trust. If a commander professed to obey the Senate, it was for the Senate to reward his troops freely and promptly. Otherwise what was the good of the Republic to a soldier? The glories of office, with a provincial governorship to follow, might commend the old system to patriot nobles, but they were far beyond the reach of the rank and file. Now the provisional government headed by Cicero was practically bankrupt. An attempt to revive the old plan of war-loan (*tributum*), after a disuse of 125 years, produced but a trifling sum, and a confession of extreme necessity was not the way to draw contributions from the rich, who in Rome as elsewhere had mostly thriven by selfishness. The Senate could not appease the military appetite with cash, and the promises of a large body would be more easily broken or evaded than those of an individual whose responsibility was personal. Thus the lack of ready money paralysed the Senate, and probably drove the government to look round for casual sources of irregular gain, such as confiscation of the property of Lepidus. But confiscations, to be of any use for satisfying the soldiery, would have had to be on a vast scale, which was impossible. The policy of Antony therefore was to sit still, to keep in communication with Octavian, and to let discontent sap the loyalty of the republican armies.

1323. About the beginning of August the long suspense came to an end. Octavian sent a deputation of centurions and other soldiers to Rome, to demand the prompt payment of their promised bounties and the consulship for himself. The men knew their business, and added a demand for the repeal of Antony's outlawry. Evidently Octavian and Antony were in league, and the only practicable course was to obey their orders. But the republicans were either blind to the facts of the situation or felt that they had gone too far to draw back now. The Senate refused or evaded the other demands. As to the consulship, they had already offered him the titular distinctions of a consular, foolishly imagining that the young man could be put off with toys. This offer being spurned, it seems that they offered to make him eligible for the praetorship. Yet in June Cicero had known that there was a popular movement, promoted by Caesarian agents, for making Octavian consul. To refuse to admit his candidature now was sheer madness. But no concession was made, and the deputation withdrew with ominous threats. Their return inflamed the indignation of the army, and Octavian with eight legions and horse and foreign auxiliaries, probably not less than 40,000 men in all, marched on Rome. What exactly the Senate did on hearing of his approach is not certain. It is said that at first they sent money[1] in hope to stop the advance of the army by payment of the promised bounties, that they offered him the consulship, and made other concessions. But it was all too late now. Cicero had kept out of the way, but at the very last appeared again to head a reaction of despair. A fresh message was sent to forbid the army to come to Rome, and the two legions just arrived from Africa, with one left in the city by Pansa, were placed on guard. But in truth no defence was possible with such forces, and the population doubtless knew that there was no prospect of relief from outside. The coming of Octavian was the signal for a crowd to pour out of the city and welcome him, and for the three legions to join him. It is said[2] that Cicero was admitted to an interview and pleaded for himself on the ground that he had supported Octavian's claim to the consulship. But this, if true, was too late, and the old man was dismissed with a sneer. There is also a story that two legions were said to have deserted Octavian in righteous indignation at his proceedings, that the senators hurried to the House only to learn that the rumour was false, upon which they dispersed, Cicero flying in a litter. Be this as it may, the last hope had perished. Cicero for the last time left Rome for Tusculum. The Republic of which he had 'laid the foundations' had collapsed. The republican cause was still represented by Brutus and Cassius and their armies and fleets in the East. In the West nothing was left but to submit to the new masters without delay.

1324. In Rome the alarm and flurry of the last few days soon subsided. Affairs were now directed by one who had begun by making himself irresistible, and who proceeded to legalize his position coolly and deliberately, with the least possible departure from precedent. He was determined to be consul. Not to mention other advantages, the consulship would place him in a stronger position for dealing with Antony and Lepidus, whose inferior he did not mean to be. The constitutional difficulties which had hindered the election of successors to Hirtius and Pansa were overcome by a new device. The acting city-praetor held an election of two commissioners with consular powers for election purposes. These *duoviri* then held the election of consuls. Octavian withdrew from the city during the election, in order forsooth not to interfere with the people's freedom. He had provided that his colleague should be his relative Q. Pedius, one of his co-heirs under the late dictator's will. On the 19th August[3]

---

[1] How much, and whence raised, neither Appian *civ.* III 88—90 nor Dion Cass. XLVI 44 tells us.

[2] Appian *civ.* III 92. He follows authorities very hostile to Cicero.

[3] Octavian was not 20 until Sept. 23.

they entered on their office.   The soldiers had already been quieted by payment of the promised bounties.   It is said that public moneys had fallen into the conqueror's hands, and supplied the means.   How there came to be so large a sum[1] as to suffice for the purpose is not explained.   The first step now taken was to complete the formalities of adoption.   This done, Octavian was legally C. Julius Caesar, and he at once paid off the outstanding legacies left by the dictator, these also, if we are to believe Dion[2], out of public moneys.   Appian tells us that one reason for the exact completion of his adoption was that it established him in the position of *patronus* to Caesar's numerous freedmen, many of whom were rich.   The outlawry of Dolabella was revoked, his defeat and death not yet being known.   It was now the turn of Caesar's murderers.   A law carried by Pedius set up a special court for the trial of all concerned in the murder, either directly, or indirectly by joining the actual assassins.   Under this *lex Pedia* a number were at once prosecuted and punished with outlawry and confiscation of goods.   Rewards quickened the zeal of accusers, and the jurors knew better than to acquit the accused, most of whom did not appear.   It was noted that one juror voted to acquit Brutus.   For the moment this rash man escaped, but, having served the purpose of illustrating Octavian's clemency, he perished in the following proscription.   Among the condemned was Sextus Pompey, who had nothing to do with the murder and had been in Spain at the time.   But it was desired that he, like Brutus and Cassius, should be an outlaw, whom any man might kill at any moment.   Among the accusers we hear of a young man destined to play a great part in coming years, M. Vipsanius Agrippa, who had been with Octavian at Apollonia and accompanied him to Italy.

1325.   Caesar's heir was now chief magistrate of the Roman state.   That he had gained his position by force was no new thing.   That he had defied the law of the constitution, by becoming consul 23 years too soon, was only after the example of Pompey.   In point of form the Republic remained, for the Latin phrase *res publica* did not, like most Greek political terms, necessarily connote a special form of government.   The general notion of a free self-governing community had now left the famous words, never to return.   Henceforth they mean 'the State,' the common interests, public affairs, and the like, save when some writer employs them with peculiar stress[3]

---

[1] Compare Cic. *ad Brut.* 1 18 § 5 with the passages cited by Gardthausen, *Augustus* II 3 note 10.

[2] Dion Cass. XLVI 48, Appian *civ.* III 94.

[3] See for instance Tacitus *hist.* I 1 *inscitia rei publicae ut alienae*, IV 38, *ann.* I 3 *quotusquisque reliquus qui rem publicam vidisset?* Compare *hist.* I 16, and note the passages

in a pungent reference to the past. The grim irony of history was at this point strikingly exemplified. The Senate met and passed orders instructing the young consul to levy more troops, and entrusting him with the defence of Rome and the conduct of the war against Antony and Lepidus. They placed the army of D. Brutus under his orders. As he had come with eight legions, and three more had joined him, his Roman infantry alone would thus amount to about 17 legions, not including his foreign auxiliaries and any troops he might choose to raise besides. The Senate could not help themselves, and no doubt there were still many who cherished a hope that after all things might turn out favourably for the republican interest. It was known that Brutus and Cassius had now armies the joint strength of which was far superior to the forces of Octavian. The latter were hardly a match for those controlled by Antony. If then Antony and Octavian fought for the mastery of Italy and the West, the weakened victor might succumb to the armies of the East, and the old Republic be restored again. But considerations probably present to the minds of senators at this juncture were certainly not overlooked by Octavian. Combination with Brutus and Cassius was out of the question: indeed he had already made this clear by the proceedings under the Pedian law. Only one solution of his present difficulties was possible consistently with his own designs. Brutus and Cassius must be destroyed, and this was only possible with Antony's help. He saw that he must come to a full understanding with Antony. For this move previous approaches had prepared the way, but it remained to be seen whether Antony was yet disposed to form a coalition on equal terms. So Octavian slowly marched back to the North, while Pedius was inducing the Senate to revoke the outlawry of Antony and Lepidus. On hearing that this was done, he wrote to them with congratulations and offers of help. Antony needed none. It was now September, and the news from Rome had effected a great change beyond the Alps. Waverers no longer hesitated to save themselves by abandoning a lost cause. Pollio, who had marched up from Spain, and Plancus in the Further Gaul, had made submission to Antony. D. Brutus, deserted by Plancus and afterwards by his own troops, tried vainly to escape to the East, and was eventually put to death by a Gaulish chief. Antony replied to the young Caesar in a friendly tone, but his strength was now so great as to inspire misgivings. After leaving a lieutenant with six legions in Gaul, he was able to enter Italy at the head of 17 legions and 10,000 horse. He advanced to Mutina, and Lepidus arranged a meeting with Octavian, who was

ann. I 7, XI 23, XVI 22, where the adjective *vetus* is added. For the use of *res publica* by Augustus see Mommsen on the *Monumentum Ancyranum* VI 14 (34).

strongly posted at Bononia.   At a chosen spot in the neighbourhood
the three met under careful precautions to secure safety for each and
privacy for all.

1326.   Their interest required them to lay aside their enmities
and act together.   Two days discussion sufficed to settle all necessary
details.   On the third day Octavian as consul announced the main
result to the army.   It had been agreed that they should assume
joint responsibility for setting the commonwealth in order, under the
title of *triumviri rei publicae constituendae*, in other words arbitrary
power.   The present predominance of Antony betrayed itself in the
arrangement that Octavian should resign the consulship, and Ventidius
hold it for the rest of the current year.   For the next year (42)
Lepidus was to be consul, remaining in Italy with three legions,
handing over the rest of his army to his two partners, who were to
march with twenty legions apiece to put down Brutus and Cassius
and recover the eastern provinces.   The West was divided as follows.
Lepidus kept his present province with addition of the southern
Spain lately held by Pollio.   Antony had the Cisalpine and the
Further Gaul.   To Octavian fell Africa Sardinia Sicily and the lesser
islands.   Here also Antony came off best.   His share included the
districts best able to furnish recruits.   Lepidus was to be allowed
to govern his provinces through lieutenants while he ruled Italy.
This gave him a great show of power, or rather dignity, but its effect
was that he, as formerly Pompey, was not easily able to become
dangerous.   The share of Octavian had marked disadvantages.   Africa
and the islands were not yet in the hands of the triumvirs: to hold
these scattered provinces, he must first win them.   Moreover, to win
and hold them he must command the sea, and this at a time when
Brutus and Cassius already had a strong navy, and Sextus Pompey
was joining them with his privateers.   And yet the astute youth had
gained what was more important for him than a more eligible sphere
of immediate influence.   He was to command an equal army by the
side of a general of experience and repute, a man whose foibles he
well knew, foibles which Caesar's heir, with the prestige of Caesar's
name, might turn to account.   The claims of the armies were of
course not forgotten.   Magistrates were designated in advance for
five years to come, and leading officers thus rewarded.   To the
soldiers generally great bounties were promised, in particular 18 of
the finest towns[1] of Italy as 'colonies'; that is, they would be
authorized to provide for themselves there, by ejecting any present
possessors who stood in the way.   Italy in short was to be treated

---

[1] Appian *civ.* IV 3 says that among the 18 were Capua Rhegium Venusia Beneventum
Nuceria Ariminum Vibo.   See IV 86 and § 1338 below.

as a conquered country, in which the civil population had forfeited their rights. After all the military colonies planted about Italy ever since the time of Sulla, and the general failure of soldiers as farmers, how did the new scheme differ from earlier ones? It appears to have been aimed at the wealthy class in the towns. It has been above suggested that it was the republican views of these men that in all probability deluded Cicero into believing in the 'loyalty' of the towns of Italy. Rough soldiers, drawn from a poorer class, were now to turn these fat burghers out of their pleasant houses and gardens.

1327. The assembled armies were delighted with the programme. The union of the three chiefs was exactly what they wanted. They even urged that it should be further cemented by a family alliance. The step-daughter[1] of Antony, Clodia, should be betrothed to the young Caesar. This was agreed to. There was however another item in the terms of the partnership, not included in the public announcement. In order to secure themselves, and to procure the vast sums of money needed for satisfying present claims and for the coming war in the East, they had decided upon a proscription. We need not stay to inquire into the shares of the three partners respectively in this horrid business. From their point of view it was necessary. The clemency of Julius Caesar had been a failure, and in the present crisis there was no room for scruples. So they drew up a list of persons whose removal would leave any republican reaction impossible for want of leaders, and whose estates would provide the needful funds. Of course private hatreds claimed their victims, and the most illustrious victim was Cicero. His name was on a small select list sent in advance with orders to put these men to death at once. The story of Cicero's end need not be told here. After a miserable time of waiting, with hope ever growing fainter, he faced certain death bravely, and offered his neck to the slayer. With his oratorical and literary gifts, and the personal charm of which we have such abundant evidence, we are not here concerned. As to his public career, recent years have seen a decided reaction against the unfavourable judgment of Mommsen. This reaction has in my opinion gone too far. A statesman is to be excused if circumstances make him an opportunist. But if his opportunism be combined with a state of mind in which the wish is father to the thought, and with bitter personal and party antipathies, he must be content to take the consequences. That Cicero's political life was marred by grievous inconsistencies and delusions, can hardly be denied. His wondrous intellectual facility made a change of parts

---

[1] Daughter of Fulvia by her former husband Clodius. See Suet. *Aug.* 62 with Shuckburgh's note.

easy to him. In politics this was no unmixed advantage. But in one respect he was more than consistent. As a 'new man,' he worshipped hereditary rank; as a member of the Equestrian Order by birth, he was not blind to the claims of capital. To promote the harmony of rank and wealth, senators and knights, was his one constant political ideal. He could see that the cooperation of these classes only took effect as a partnership in gross misgovernment, extortion, and corruption of every kind. Keeping his own hands clean, he was ever ready to connive at the iniquities of others. Party motives or professional ambitions might lead him now and then to expose a great criminal, but far the greater part of his energies was devoted to screening infamous offenders. It was not only his eloquence but his respectability that he placed at the service of the governing class. To judge him by the standard of modern counsel is utterly misleading. The personality of the pleader was of infinite importance at the Roman Bar. In the Senate it was of course even more so. Yet it is certain that Cicero over and over again spoke in favour of courses that he did not really approve on their merits. Whatever was least likely to weaken the aristocratic government and the alliance of rank and wealth, that he supported. The tragedy of his public life unfolded itself in its latest scenes, when he came forward boldly as the champion of an aristocracy that had once deserted him and had never loved him, and laid down his life in their cause. The man who had clamoured for the blood of the three Antonies had barred all claim to forgiveness in that cruel age. But posterity did not forget that Octavian's consent had been given to his murder. All historians have remarked that the writers of the Augustan age[1] are in general silent on the subject of Cicero. It was in truth not easy to refer to him without offending the ruler of the Roman world by recalling an act that had stained that ruler's early days; and the plea of necessity had grown weak by lapse of time.

1328. The triumvirs did not hurry to Rome. They entered the city late in November, and by that time had prepared a long black-list of victims, in which were included some even of their own relatives. All was done deliberately and in order. On the 27th November the tribune P. Titius carried a law giving practically absolute power to

---

[1] Livy of course could not avoid it. His account of Cicero's end, and a remarkably fair-minded appreciation of his career and merits, have been preserved as extracts by the elder Seneca. The post-Augustan writers were not under the same restraint. But it is to be noted that Velleius II 66 (under Tiberius) is hostile to Antony as much as friendly to Cicero, and that Lucan VII 62 foll. (under Nero, and full of the idealizing republican tradition) only brings in the great orator as enforcing bad advice by his eloquence. The sixth *suasoria* of the elder Seneca, written under Tiberius, is very interesting as shewing how quickly the fame of Cicero revived after the death of Augustus. See below § 1371

the three partners, nominally for five years from the 1st January 42. This made their coalition a formal act of state, not an informal combination like that of Crassus Pompey and Caesar. The *lex Titia* was for the time the constitution of Rome. Octavian laid down his consulship. Both places were now vacant, for Pedius, after great exertions to quiet the alarm caused by the preliminary death-list, was carried off by a sudden illness. C. Albius Carrinas a Caesarian officer was made consul with P. Ventidius Bassus for the rest of the year. We need not dwell on the irregularities committed in connexion with these and other appointments. The really important business was the proscription, and it was organized with thoroughness. The Republic was not to be restored; there was to be no mistake about it this time. Rewards were offered to any, free or slave, who procured the murder of one proscribed, and, to allay all fears of future retribution, it was added[1] that no names of persons receiving blood-money should be recorded in the public accounts. Those who harboured or aided the escape of the destined victims were liable to be proscribed themselves, and rewards were offered to those who betrayed them. We have what professes to be a Greek translation[2] of the edict in which the hideous intention of the three rulers was publicly announced. Other references to it shew that it is at least substantially correct. With pitiless logic it exposes the advantage treacherously taken of Caesar's clemency, and declares the necessity of the present severities in order to end once for all the miseries of civil war. The destruction of Brutus and Cassius was to follow, and to effect this the representatives of Rome must not leave a host of enemies behind them. The triumvirs claimed that after all they were more merciful than Sulla. There would be no irregular massacre. The soldiers, though justly angry at the outlawries and insults lately decreed against the armies, would be kept in hand, and only slaughter according to orders. A list of 130 senators and many knights followed, to which additions were subsequently made. It is said that in all about 300 senators and 2000 knights were thus sentenced to death and forfeiture of property. It was business, for, allowing liberally for the influences of fear and revenge, the essential fact of the proscription was the confiscation of riches, wrung from a plundered world, to enable the new masters to take possession of the dominions of Rome. We need not doubt the terror that the announcement caused. To add to the shock, Pedius is said[3] to have given out in good faith that the

---

[1] This was an improvement on Sulla's methods, for some of the Sullan ruffians had been punished afterwards.

[2] Appian *civ.* IV 8—11.

[3] See Appian *civ.* IV 6, Suet. *Aug.* 27.

preliminary list of 17 names was final. And when the truth came out, the hope of finality was deferred again by an utterance of Octavian in the Senate. Lepidus had expressed sorrow for the past and held out prospects of mercy for the future. The young Caesar's comment was that, while he had agreed to stay the proscription, he reserved his freedom of action later on.

1329. The harrowing scenes and agony of this awful time do not lack their record. In particular, Appian[1] gives a selection of tragic stories, taken from the works of earlier writers, enough to sate any reader's appetite for horrors. It was as in the time of Sulla, only worse. Society fell to pieces under the strain, for none knew whom to trust Unnatural sons and wives there were to help on the bloody work, with cases of self-sacrificing devotion to afford contrasts. Debtors seized the chance to rid themselves of creditors, and the covetous and malicious to supplant the owners of desirable properties or gratify some cherished grudge. At such a crisis the domestic slave was master of his owner's fate; yet there were not wanting instances of faithful bondmen who not only spurned the offer of freedom and money, but who risked and even laid down their own lives in the endeavour to save their lords. Some evaded murder by suicide, some were the victims of mistaken identity. In spite of attempts to keep the soldier-butchers in hand, orders were some-times exceeded, and persons not proscribed were simply sacrificed to military greed. Antony's wife Fulvia was notorious for hunting down her enemies. The triumvir himself, naturally a pleasure-loving easy-going man, had no love of murder[2] for murder's sake, but he had always a disreputable set of boon-companions round him. Of his own doings we hear that he proscribed old Verres. Verres had retained some of his Sicilian plunder, in particular some fine Corinthian bronze vases. Antony had seen them, no doubt during his sojourn at Massalia, and coveted them, but the old connoisseur would not part with them. So Antony put him on the death-list, and Verres met death manfully, having outlived Cicero after all. Cicero's brother Quintus, and his son with him, were among the well-known victims. And yet, thorough though the proscription was, a number of the doomed managed to escape, some to join Brutus and Cassius, more

---

[1] Appian *civ.* IV 17—51. An interesting case was that of a wealthy old Samnite of 80, a hero of the great Italian war. He gave away all his goods, and burnt his house with himself in it. The learned Varro, already spared by Caesar, was one of those concealed by a faithful friend, and escaped. For the case of Q. Lucretius Vespillo, saved by his wife and slaves, see Gardthausen I p. 140, II 55—6, where part of the funeral *laudatio* of Turia, preserved in an inscription, is given, and Fowler in *Classical Review* XIX 261—6.

[2] Dion Cass. XLVII 7, 8 charges Antony with pitiless cruelty and enlarges on the clemency of the young Caesar. I believe the other tradition.

to Sextus Pompey who commanded the sea and had occupied Sicily. And perhaps no fact of the time is more striking than the safety of the wealthy Atticus. That far-sighted man had studied with scientific exactness the conditions of survival in a revolutionary age, and had concluded that there was no better investment than the established character of a Friend in Need. For about 40 years he had been watching opportunities, always on good terms with the present holders of power, to whom his approval was welcome, all the more because untainted by servility. Meanwhile he was ever ready to help friends among the party at present down, thus earning their gratitude in the event of their rise to power. His latest deal[1] had been a sequel of Caesar's murder. He was the best of friends with Brutus, and willing privately to be his banker if needed. But he would not join a syndicate of financiers to provide funds for the republican cause. When Brutus had to fly from Italy, it was another matter. Then Atticus sent him a present of about £1000, and soon after this a remittance of about £3000 when he was in Epirus. When the republicans led by Cicero were holding Rome, it was Atticus who shielded the family of Antony and provided for their escape from danger. So the proscription found him only alarmed lest he might suffer for his friendship with Cicero and Brutus. But Antony protected him. In the days of blood, when heads of senators and knights were being brought in, identified, paid for, and some of them (as that of Cicero) stuck up by the Rostra in the Forum, Atticus was not only safe himself but able to save others. His estate in Epirus gave shelter and support to many refugees. After Philippi he continued to comfort and aid those on whom a lost cause had brought distress or ruin, but lived on terms of friendship with the new rulers till his death ten years later. It is not our business here to inquire[2] whether the intimate friend of Cicero stained an honourable and useful career by a too ready acceptance of intimacy with the slayers, and by too brief a mourning for the slain. It is enough to note that, even in the period of fierce conflict and merciless bloodshed that ended the Roman Republic, such a man as Atticus could live wealthy and unharmed to the age of 77 and die in peace.

1330. Death or flight soon removed the persons proscribed, but the sale of estates was less successful. Many possible buyers were shy of calling attention to the fact of their having ready money at disposal, and lack of competition kept prices low. The triumvirs found themselves short[3] of their expectations by an enormous sum.

---

[1] See Corn. Nepos *Att.* 8—11. [2] See Boissier, *Cicéron et ses amis*, p. 165.
[3] Appian *civ.* IV 31 ἐνέδει μυριάδων ἔτι δισμυρίων, drachmas, no doubt. Roughly about £8,000,000.

So they decided to tax wealthy ladies, and required a number of the richest to make returns of their properties for the purpose, with penalties for false returns. There was precedent for such taxation of women for war-expenses in the finance of the old Servian constitution. But it had long been in disuse, and the present attempt led to a great demonstration on the part of the indignant ladies. They beset the tribunal of the triumvirs, and Hortensia, daughter of the great orator, made a speech[1] on their behalf, protesting against the taxation of those ineligible for public office and manifestly not responsible (not being voters) for any of the acts that were now meeting with punishment. And, of all the persons on whom at this time the exactions of the new rulers pressed, the women alone seem to have gained some abatement of the extreme demand. The list of those required to make returns was reduced from 1400 to 400. But money[2] had to be found, and that without delay. So censors were appointed for the year 42, not with any real intention of holding a regular census, but to inquire into the means of citizens and impose further taxes. We hear of the revival[3] of customs-dues in Italy, a carrying-out or extension of their renewal by Caesar. Also of an appropriation of a year's rent (or estimated yearly value) of houses throughout Italy, and 50% of the yearly return from landed estates. Slave-owners were required to furnish slaves to man the fleet ordered for the coming war, and a tax of about £1 per head was to be paid on all slaves. Add to this the burden of keeping soldiers billeted on the Italian towns, and some faint notion of the general distress may be conceived. For all power was now in the hands of the triumvirs, and exercised[4] in detail by their creatures, men who were in most cases certain to abuse it. Properties sold below their value fell largely to military men, who dared to bid for them, and partial officials winked at the evil deeds of soldiers who were making the most of their time before they were again sent to the front. Doubtless individuals here and there escaped the various exactions by favour of persons in authority. But the general aspect of affairs was a gigantic scene of spoliation, and the unfairly-burdened citizen had no means of redress[5] in the universal terror of the sword.

1331. These horrors did not come upon Caesar's murderers, who

---

[1] Quintil. 1 1 § 6, Valer. Max. VIII 3 § 3, App. *civ.* IV 32—34.

[2] Plutarch *Ant.* 21 says that the triumvirs even seized moneys deposited with the Vestal virgins.

[3] References in Lange *RA* III 554, Gardthausen I pp. 140—1, II p. 57.

[4] Antony's freedman Hipparchus was one who amassed great riches at this time.

[5] Valer. Max. VI 2 § 12 tells how the great lawyer Cascellius marked the illegality of the whole proceeding by refusing to draw pleadings (*formulae*) on behalf of the grantees of the lands seized by the triumvirs. Roby *Intr. to Justin.* p. cxxi.

had been condemned under the Pedian law. Most of them were alive and at large, but not within reach; their fate hung on the fortune of war. The victims of the proscription were for the most part unconscious of their danger. While the business proceeded, the triumvirs were organizing their government, dealing with the magistracies arbitrarily, and arranging the provincial governorships for the coming year. The consuls for 42 were Plancus[1] and Lepidus. Before taking office, at the end of December 43, they both celebrated triumphs, Plancus for some small successes in Gaul, Lepidus for having negotiated with Sextus Pompey and quieted Spain. The consummation of the political revolution was illustrated by the steps taken to place Julius Caesar among the gods of Rome. Octavian[2] dedicated the spot where the dictator's body had been burnt, and erected there a temple in honour of his memory, the *aedes divi Iuli* of which the remains have been excavated. It was ordained also that on the first day of each new year all should solemnly swear to the maintenance of his acts, and that his birthday should for ever be a holiday, and the Ides of March a black day. This last observance was not long[3] kept up, for Augustus the emperor did not like it. No detail was more significant than that relative to family funerals. The mask (*imago*) of Julius was not to be borne in procession with those of other ancestors. Its proper place was to be among the images of the gods when these were publicly paraded. The final step was taken in a *lex Rufrena* of 42, which gave legislative sanction to Caesar's divinity, and henceforth he was officially *divus Iulius*. The succession of the triumvirs to the autocratic power of Caesar, and the absence of any intention to restore the Republic, appeared clearly in their treatment of the coinage[4]. In Caesar's last days the obsequious Senate had issued coins bearing on them the head of the dictator. The 'image and superscription' had been and still is the symbol of supreme power, and coins stamped with the head of a living person, instead of that of the goddess *Roma*, were a practical recognition of the end of the free Republic. The triumvirs[5] were not slow to follow the precedent. Beginning with representations symbolizing scenes in the mythical traditions of their respective houses (*Aemilii Antonii Iulii*), they presently introduced their own heads on the obverse side of the new pieces, and the custom was never afterwards dropped. Monarchy might, and long did, wear a disguise: its asser-

---

[1] Plancus had been nominated by Caesar with D. Brutus for this year.
[2] See Mommsen on *Mon. Ancyr.* IV 2.
[3] Gardthausen I p. 133. See Dion Cass. XLVII 18.
[4] See Mommsen, *Staatsrecht*, II 687, 706, 789, Gardthausen I 132.
[5] A few specimens are given in Mr G. F. Hill's *Historical Roman Coins*, Nos. 72, 73, 74.

tion on the coinage remained. But the nullity of the senior partner soon betrayed the truth that the triumvirate was a rule of two, not of three, and the officers of the mint recognized this by ceasing to coin pieces with the head of Lepidus.

1332. Preparations for the coming war in the East were going on, and we must now return to the progress of Brutus and Cassius, against whom these were directed. After leaving the Adriatic sea-board Brutus had been busy in Macedonia. He enlisted Macedonians and organized them in legions, and made a campaign in Thrace, where he chastised rebellious natives and raised auxiliary forces. He employed his increased strength in gaining full control of the province Asia, and managed to get together a considerable fleet. Immense sums of money were of course needed for his enterprise, and he procured them by the usual means of requisition and appropriation. As a Roman general he had the right of coining for the purposes of his command. His refusal to recognize the triumvirate as the lawful government of Rome was presently marked by the appearance of his head[1] on some of the pieces issued by him. Cassius had shut up Dolabella in Laodicea on the Syrian coast. His strong army and fleet made escape impossible, and Dolabella was driven to suicide. Cassius meant to invade Egypt, where queen Cleopatra was taking the other side, but news of the preparations of the triumvirs called him to cooperate with Brutus in Asia Minor. He plundered Tarsus in revenge for its reception of Dolabella, deposed Ariobarzanes king of Cappadocia, and generally established his authority in those parts, while he secured his rear by a friendly understanding with the Parthians. Meanwhile Brutus had won over old Deiotarus the Galatian. All Asia Minor was now in the hands of the republican leaders, save only the independent Lycian League and the republic of Rhodes. Time pressed, for it was known that the first detachment of the Caesarian forces was already on its way. But at a conference in Smyrna it was agreed that the resistance of these two communities should be overcome before advancing to meet the enemy in Macedonia. Brutus pacified Lycia, after one stubborn city had been taken. Cassius also conquered Rhodes, after a naval battle in which Rhodian skill proved unable to contend with the number and size of his ships. Both commanders carried off all the public and private money they could find, and then exacted ten years' tribute in advance from the provincials of Asia. The two then met again at Sardis to arrange

---

[1] Dion Cass. XLVII 25 § 3, Appian *civ.* IV 75. That his action was a violation of republican rules is pointed out by Mommsen *Str.* II 707. The case of Sex. Pompey is different, for he posed as on the same footing as the triumvirs, not as a republican proconsul. Some specimens of the coinage of Brutus are given by Mr Hill, Nos. 68—71.

their plan of campaign. Their armies were immensely strong in numbers, and for the most part fit for war. The plunder of the East had filled their war-chests, and the command of the sea secured their commissariat so long as they kept in touch with the fleets. In these respects they certainly had an advantage over their opponents, but they suffered from the disadvantage of standing on the defensive instead of delivering the attack. Moreover they were an ill-assorted pair. The ill-timed scruples and pompous rectitude of Brutus were enough to provoke any plain man, let alone the bitter and jealous Cassius, devoted to the main object, victory, with venomous thoroughness. They quarrelled, but made it up again, and worked together as best they could. But even Cassius was no match for Antony as a general when that pleasure-loving soldier was on his mettle, and Antony was just now at his best. Still more marked was the superiority of Octavian to Brutus. His interest was at present the same as Antony's, and he was certain to follow it without letting any scruple or jealousy mar their concert. But the final struggle did not take place till the autumn (42), and we must turn westward to note the events that occurred there and prevented an earlier decision.

1333. It proved to be no simple matter for Octavian to take possession of his provinces. In the old province Africa the senatorial governor Cornificius would not budge without the Senate's orders. When the new master ordered him to hand over his province to the Caesarian Sextius, governor of the New Africa (Numidia), he refused to obey. In the war which ensued he was at first successful, but in the end Sextius, supported by a Numidian prince, was the victor, and Cornificius lost his province and his life. Far more serious was the state of things in Sicily. The condemnation of Sextus Pompey under the Pedian law, though he had had nothing to do with Caesar's murder, of course put an end to his command of the Roman fleet, and warned him to shift for himself. This he speedily did. He got together a few ships, which soon grew into a formidable fleet. His fierce pugnacious temper was well known, and robbers, runaway slaves, refugees from the proscription, broken men and desperadoes of all sorts, flocked to him. He cut off corn-ships, made the ports of Italy unsafe, and was the pirate-ruler of the western Mediterranean. The position and resources of Sicily made it a convenient naval base. Sextus landed there, and in a short time was master of the whole island. His headquarters were a place of refuge for the proscribed, many of whom he either ransomed by outbidding the blood-money offered for their heads or helped to escape by means of his ships cruising off the Italian coast. His success drew to him such numbers of skilled seamen and slaves willing to serve at the oar, that his fleet became the most efficient of all the naval forces of the time. Octavian sent an army and checked his descents upon southern Italy. But an attempt[1] to pass the strait and drive him out of Sicily was a miserable failure. Meanwhile the triumvirs wanted all their strength for the eastern war, and the freebooter had to be left in possession while Antony and Octavian set out to do battle with Brutus and Cassius.

1334. In the campaign that led to the battles of Philippi nothing is more remarkable than the recurrence of certain phenomena closely resembling those of the campaign of Pharsalus. The futility of most of the naval operations is in both cases equally striking. In both cases the defeated army suffered from the interference of amateur judgment with expert strategy: in other words, the representatives of republican principles were at a moral disadvantage for fighting purposes as compared with the representatives of arbitrary power. This is more obvious in the case of Pharsalus, but the effect was hardly less damaging in that of Philippi. We can see now that it was to the interest of the republicans to wait and to use their naval superiority in preventing the enemy's forces from crossing the Adriatic, in intercepting their supplies, and in embarrassing the masters of Rome by depriving the city of corn and so creating unrest in their rear. An effective cooperation with Sextus Pompey would have enabled them to sweep all Caesarian squadrons from the seas. But any such far-reaching plan of combined naval warfare would have called for much patience, and it would not have been easy to explain the delay satisfactorily to the armies. Once the soldiers began to suspect that their chiefs had lost confidence in their strength, and the game was up. As has been well pointed[2] out, the Roman instinct was for settling the issues in a pitched battle. We may add that the naval forces were almost entirely non-Roman. The prejudices of the Roman combatants could not be ignored; and the rank and file of the legions were not men likely to await the development of a more far-sighted strategy, sustained by a reasoned belief in the better prospect of final victory. Republican principles were a comfort to Brutus, and in a less degree to Cassius also. A few catch-words were all that would reach the common soldier, and this was not enough to support him under a continued moral strain. We must judge the plan actually adopted by the standard of the above con-

---

[1] According to Appian *civ.* IV 86 Octavian was himself present, and sailed away to join Antony at Brundisium. But the strait was held by the fleet of Sextus, and he had to make a voyage all round Sicily.

[2] Gardthausen I 167.

siderations.   Early in 42 the fleet of Cassius was most of it sent under L. Statius Murcus to cruise off Taenarum in the Peloponnese.   Its first duty was to cut off an Egyptian fleet which Cleopatra was sending to aid the Caesarians, and prevent its junction with the ships of Octavian.   The Egyptian armada was broken up by a storm. Murcus then sailed for Brundisium, to stop the passage of the enemy's convoys.   But this he was not able to do.   The weather favoured the passage of transports under sail, and the remaining legions were safely carried across the Adriatic in two trips.   Cassius sent more ships to support Murcus, and the operations of the fleet caused no small annoyance to the triumvirs by interrupting communications with Italy.   Later in the war a convoy was destroyed and a whole legion perished, but on the general fortunes of the struggle these doings had no effect.

1335.   The armies gathered at Sardis were glad to learn that they were to march to the Hellespont and fight it out in Macedonia. The fleet of Brutus lay at Abydos, growing in size as the later contingents came in.   After ferrying the armies across the strait, it was to operate in support of the land-forces, keeping in touch with them as they moved along the Thracian and Macedonian seaboard. No serious mishap occurred.   The advanced divisions sent forward by Antony to check their progress were either constrained to fall back, outflanked by the fleet, or eluded by a difficult detour inland. So they reached the town of Philippi, near which they posted themselves astride of the great Egnatian road, the main land-route from Dyrrachium to the Hellespont.   Their position, covered by a line of works in front, could not be turned, for on the right Brutus touched the mountains, and the flank of Cassius on the left was protected by a swamp between him and the sea.   Not only was the position very strong for defence: their fleet kept up communication with their chief magazines in Thasos, and ensured the regular supply of food.   Their opponents had to advance through a country not rich in corn, and the transport of provisions for a large army was a difficult matter.   It was clearly the interest of Antony to force on a battle without delay, that of Cassius to wait and let hunger do its work.   Both saw this. Cassius indeed had from the first disliked a plan of campaign tending to a pitched battle, and now did his best to delay it.   Octavian was in weak health, and lay sick for a time at Dyrrachium while his army went on, but he managed to follow in time to be present at the battle.

1336.   The accounts of the first battle of Philippi vary: that of Appian is probably the best.   It seems that Antony tried to turn the lines of Cassius by running a dyke through the swamp, which

Cassius met with a counter-dyke. When the latter had drawn off a large part of his men to this work, Antony delivered a sudden assault upon his lines and took his camp. The success of Antony was considerable, but not decisive; he could not hold what he had won, and withdrew his men. Meanwhile Brutus was victorious on the republican right. It is said that Cassius had allowed him the best troops of their army. Seeing that fighting was in progress on their left, the soldiers of Brutus fell on without orders, and defeated the army of Octavian with comparative ease, taking their camp. But they too were withdrawn. So far the republicans had not fared badly, and their losses were thought to be much less than those of the Caesarians. But the worst was to come. The nerve of Cassius was shaken by his defeat, and a misunderstanding led him to think that Brutus was also beaten. He killed himself in despair, and with him the cause of the Republic perished. This battle seems to have been fought late in October. The numbers on the two sides were about equal. The triumvirs had after all not been able to bring more than 19 full legions to the front against 19 of their opponents, not quite so full. But the latter had more numerous cavalry and auxiliary forces, all foreign, as indeed some of the legionaries on both sides probably were. Twenty days of waiting followed. Antony moved to get between Brutus and the sea, but could not break his line of communications. On the contrary he was himself in great distress for want of supplies. Winter was coming on. But about the middle of November the discontent in the camp of Brutus overcame his better judgment and forced him to hazard all in a second battle. His men were some of them old Caesarians, and even the lavish bounty distributed after the first battle left him still uncertain whether he could rely on their loyalty. He made promises of Greek cities to be plundered by his men in the event of victory. But he knew that it was a mistake to fight at all. The death of Cassius had not only caused much disheartenment. It had a bad effect on discipline. Officers had perhaps good reason for fearing the results of delay. Instead of calming their men and supporting the judgment of their commander, they took the easier course of putting pressure on Brutus. And Brutus, no longer backed by the military experience of Cassius, had not the strength of mind to stand firm. The weakness of the republican system, when tried in civil war, once more appeared, and headquarters became a centre of debate. The presence of proscribed refugees assuredly did not promote counsels of cool wisdom or subordination; and the principles of Brutus made it difficult for him to assert an arbitrary power. So the clamours of the impatient soldiers, rendered over-confident by the result of the former engagement, prevailed, and Brutus, overruled as Pompey had been in Thessaly, offered battle. After a desperate struggle the republican army gave way. Brutus himself, and others for whom there could be no hope of mercy, died by their own hands or the help of friends, and the last chance of restoring the Republic was at an end. In or after this battle many of the chief republicans perished. Of those who fell alive into the victors' hands some were put to death. One or two were spared by Antony, but the colder Octavian is said to have been merciless. Among those who escaped were M. Valerius Messalla, one of the proscribed, who refused to take command of the remains of the beaten army and protract a hopeless struggle ; young Marcus Cicero ; and Horace, who lived to sing of his own flight from the stricken field. These all sooner or later made their submission and prospered under the new government in various ways. The mass of the soldiers of Brutus, about 14,000 according to Appian, surrendered and were pardoned and added to the armies of the triumvirs. The fleet in the Adriatic, true to its piratic character, still for a time gave trouble, and was even reinforced after Philippi by another miscellaneous squadron raised in Rhodes and other eastern ports. Part of it under Murcus presently joined Sextus Pompey. The rest, under Cn. Domitius Ahenobarbus, was an annoyance to the triumvirs for a while longer. But these are small matters. The great issue was decided at Philippi. The only question now was who the master or masters of the Roman world were to be.

1337. Our story of the Roman Republic is therefore at an end, for with the establishment of the Empire we are not concerned. But it is hardly possible to avoid touching however briefly on the sequel of Philippi so far as it bears upon the condition of Italy. The Italy of Augustus was a weary land. Peace, a lasting peace, was the one common interest, the only hope of a gradual recovery from the wasting miseries of the past. These miseries reached their height in the period following Philippi, and are part of the phenomena that attended the final overthrow of the Republic.

Cisalpine Gaul[1] at last ceased to be a Province, and henceforth the Alps were officially the northern boundary of Italy. Thus the intention of Caesar was carried out. In consequence of Philippi the true position of Lepidus in the imperial firm was openly recognized. He was made to take a back place, and in 41 he lost his great nominal sphere of government and had to be content with Africa, which neither of his partners wanted just then. Antony had fairly earned whatever prize was to be had. He took the further East, and went to his ruin. We need not follow his regal progress. One of his

---

[1] Dion Cass. XLVIII 12 § 5.

chief functions was to wring more money from the already exhausted provincials and client-princes. The need of great sums in Italy, for paying off the troops and settling matters generally, was most urgent; and it was part of his bargain with Octavian that he should remit money for these purposes, for it was only in the East that it could be found. Antony was a generous and not unkindly man, but it was not in him to keep a firm hand over the worthless and greedy creatures who surrounded him. His favourites extorted more money than he ordered, but what with their pilfering and his own extravagance there is reason to think that the sums remitted to Rome fell far short of expectation. Meanwhile he brought home to the oriental mind the fact that the days of senatorial rule were over. Nothing was needed to introduce monarchy to the peoples of the East, and Antony's splendour and amours with royal mistresses were quite in order. As King of kings, dispensing rewards and punishments and assigning thrones, or even posing as a divinity, he was in accord with the traditions of Alexander's Successors, particularly the house of Seleucus. But his task was easy and his reception corrupting, and in becoming the slave of Cleopatra he sacrificed the imperial prospects offered by his daring and military skill.

1338. Octavian returned to Italy. To him had fallen the post of difficulty, indeed of danger. The reduction of the armies had left on his hands the appalling task of satisfying the discharged veterans, estimated at about 170,000 men. In the absence of statistics it is not possible to form more than a general notion of the problem. For instance, we do not know with any accuracy the composition of the disbanded legions. We do know that Julius Caesar[1] enlisted Gauls Germans and Spaniards. That this was not for the cavalry only, appears from such facts as the existence of a Gaulish legion (the ‘Larks,’ probably including Germans) and the *vernaculae* or ‘home-bred’ legions of whom we hear in Spain. When we read of legions raised in the provinces, we may well suspect that the ranks were not exclusively filled by Roman citizens of Italian origin. Brutus raised whole legions of Macedonians. In short, the military needs of a great empire engaged in civil wars had led to no small relaxation of old rules that were out of date. That there was a considerable barbarian[2] element even in the legions of the line can hardly be doubted, and it is not likely that the claims of the foreign cavalry could in all cases be ignored　Now the planting of military colonists in districts of

---

[1] In 44 Antony had a special bodyguard of Syrian bowmen, Augustus afterwards one of Germans.

[2] See Vergil *bucol.* 1 70—1 *impius haec tam culta novalia miles habebit, barbarus has segetes?*

Italy had hitherto been most unwelcome to the old inhabitants; the inclusion of barbarians would only make matters worse. There was also from the first the awkward question, where the necessary lands were to be found. The soldiers wanted allotments in Italy, and it was impossible to refuse them. The triumvirs had promised them 18 towns[1] in Italy to despoil or occupy. Of those 16 were still on the list, but the territories of these 16 would only provide but a small part of what was required. Moreover they protested against being singled out to bear a burden which, supposing it unavoidable, could not with justice be imposed on them alone. And indeed facts were too strong for the limitation to be maintained. It was clear that all Italy (including the Cisalpine) must be involved. Naturally the blow fell heaviest on communities which had in any way incurred the disfavour[2] of the new rulers. Some contrived to buy exemption by payments of money. For the government was in sore straits for money. Pay and bounties were due to the disbanded veterans, and the treasury was empty. It was therefore impossible to acquire the needful lands by purchase or to compensate ejected occupiers. A general expropriation took place under most cruel conditions, and vast numbers of men who depended on the land for their livelihood, as owners or free cultivators or both, were at one stroke reduced to beggary. Those who lived on their farms lost their homes, and few would be able to win patrons by their literary gifts and make themselves a new position, as did Vergil Horace and Propertius, all victims[3] of the wholesale robbery of this time. Nor is it likely that the burden was equally distributed. The soldiers liked to be settled not as scattered individuals but in blocks, corps by corps, and the insufficiency of the territory of one town sometimes led to the seizure of adjoining[4] lands, to gratify the military whim. Most of the dispossessed had no choice but either to seek their fortunes abroad or to migrate to Rome and increase the idle mob, already too numerous. The cases in which[5] the free yeoman and the intruding soldier came to terms, the former staying on as cultivator (*colonus*), while the latter shared the profits, shew the transaction on a more favourable side. But we have no reason to think that there were many such cases. On the other hand we hear[6] that resistance was offered, and that in

[1] Rhegium and Vibo had been exempted, as their help was needed in the war with Sex. Pompey. See § 1326.

[2] The case of Cremona is in the Cisalpine. For Patavium see Macrob. *Sat.* I 11 § 22, and compare Velleius II 76 § 2.

[3] See Horace *epist.* II 2 49—52, Propertius IV (v) 1 129—130. The words of Tibullus (I 1 19—44) do not say that he lost land in this way, but it is probable.

[4] See Verg. *bucol.* IX 28 *Mantua vae miserae nimium vicina Cremonae, georg.* II 198, and the passages cited in full from commentators in Gardthausen II pp. 89, 90.

[5] See Horace *Sat.* II 2 112—136.   [6] Dion Cass. XLVIII 9.

some places there was fighting, of course to little purpose. Probably the commonest experience was that of Vergil, who escaped the violence of a ruffian by flight. And the action of the government, in itself cruel enough, was made worse by the insolence and greed of the veterans. The eyes of the commissioners employed could not be in all places at once, and there is no doubt that their own proceedings were summary. The interruption of tillage, caused by so widespread a disturbance of the population settled on the land, helped to aggravate the general distress, and this at a time when Rome itself, the refuge of many, was threatened with famine. For the cruisers of Sextus Pompey were on the alert, and the coming of the corn-ships was uncertain.

1339. Even if Octavian had been left free to carry out this economic revolution[1] with a reasonable care to avoid the infliction of unnecessary hardship, he could scarcely have done much to alleviate the sufferings of the innocent. It was the soldier's hour, and the events of the civil wars, ending in a proscription employing soldiers as butchers, had tended to make the Roman warrior a brute. On at least one occasion Octavian's own life was in danger from military violence. But a sinister influence was at work to make things if possible worse. Antony's abominable wife Fulvia was in Rome. She and her confederates raised the cry that all the popularity arising from the distribution of land to the veterans must not be appropriated by Octavian. The friends of Antony must have a share in the work, or the absent would be forgotten. Octavian had to give way to this demand, and we hear that a horrid competition was set up, the Antonians outbidding the young Caesar in encouraging the soldiers to worse feats of iniquity. But perhaps the saddest part of the whole proceeding was that this gigantic wrong was perpetrated in defiance[2] of the teaching of experience. For surely it was by this time well known that men whose lives had been spent in alternations of toil and idleness, hardship and debauchery, were never likely to settle down into the watchful patience, the loving care, the monotonous drudgery, required in successful tillers of the soil. It has been well remarked also that, whereas the confiscations of the proscription had fallen upon rich men who had happened to take, or be accused of taking, the side of the beaten party, traitors by virtue of defeat, the present ruin fell mainly upon men of small means, who had borne no part in the civil war. So the best and soundest element in the population of Italy were driven from the land. After the long operation

---

[1] Details are collected in Gardthausen II 88—93.

[2] It seems that among the districts affected were Campania and Etruria. Even the oft-colonized Capua again received settlers. Dion Cass. XLIX 14 § 5.

of unfavourable economic conditions, after the failure of the movement initiated by the Gracchi, after years of misguided fitful legislation, after the military 'colonies' of Sulla and his imitators, the small farmers left in Italy were no doubt far less numerous than they should have been, than they had been in the good old times. The present measures made a clean sweep of most of those remaining, and the failure of the soldiers who displaced them prepared the way for the extension of great landed estates in the imperial age. Even if Italy had been conquered by a foreign enemy, the land could hardly have changed hands more completely. Of course it was only the best land that was suited for the present purpose, land that derived most of its value from the skill and labour spent on it in the past. It was not merely the confiscation of surface-areas. It was a brutally plain announcement that the sword was now supreme, and that the citizen farmer had no security that he would reap the fruits of his own industry. Imagination cannot picture a more fatal calamity than this.

1340. To narrate the series of public events which marked the establishment of the new monarchy and the union of the empire under a single ruler is not the business of this book. The outbreak of war in Italy, ending with the siege of Perusia, the war with Sextus Pompey, the final discarding of Lepidus, the quarrel of Octavian and Antony, patched up for a time but ending in the overthrow of the latter,—these matters are clearly part of the story of the Empire. How Antony threw away his splendid chances is a worthy subject of human interest, and a theme for the moralist and dramatist. It only remains to sketch in outline what became of the three essential parts of the republican constitution in the wonderful mechanism of the Augustan Empire. The Magistracy remained. But the powers of the chief magistracies were extracted and conferred on one and the same person in a more permanent form, eventually for life. Thus the holder of a state office was overshadowed by the constant presence of one whose official powers, nominally equal with his own, were in other departments equal with those of other officers, and did not come to an end with an office held only for a year at most. The tribunate, with all its noisy traditions, was silenced before the holder of the perpetual *tribunicia potestas*. The consulship was a great honour, but its power was gone. The tribunician power could prevent independent action of the consul's *imperium* in Rome, while his full military *imperium* abroad had ceased. That all-important authority was concentrated in the hands of the one ruler, who had the *imperium* of a proconsul extending over the whole empire and overriding all local *imperia* of provincial governors. All the military forces were subject to him, and to him they swore obedience. In virtue of these and other supplementary powers he was unquestionably the first man in the state, and it was as 'first man' (*princeps*) that the cautious Octavian, now the 'revered' (*augustus*), chose to express his preeminence, rather than by the title of King. The Senate too remained. It suited the policy of Augustus to make the Senate a formal partner in the government, and even to leave it the control of the most peaceful provinces of the empire, of course not without watching the doings of the House and having in his tribunician veto the means of holding it in check. But the guidance of external policy, the most important department of its functions in the days of the Republic, had passed from the Senate, and the consciousness of lost power long rankled in the minds of many. The warmer and bolder spirits sighed for more scope, and fondly idealized the old system. These aspirations, which are writ large in the post-Augustan literature, created a vain Opposition[1], the chief effect of which was to irritate and alarm some Emperors: and in course of time the Senate, defenceless and occasionally persecuted, lost most of the real power left it by Augustus. As for the Assembly, it continued to meet for election and legislation. But this was a mere form; all it could do was to act by leave or order of the real master, and imperial legislation soon came to be transacted by decrees of the Senate. To confer the *potestas tribunicia* on a new Emperor was the chief function of the Assembly that had once been the sovran power in the state, and whose support had in later days started Julius Caesar on his public career. It had served its turn, and it had long ceased to be the mouthpiece of the Roman people. The real Roman people were either the citizens in the legions or those settled or travelling in pursuit of their business, not only in Italy but in all parts of the Roman world. It was high time that the mongrel rabble of Rome should lose the right to misrepresent the will of the whole people. And it was quite clear that the military system of the later Republic must undergo a thorough reform. An army was necessary. To protect and rule the empire from Rome as a centre, it must be a standing army, quartered near the frontiers and capable of speedy mobilization. On these lines Augustus reorganized the imperial forces, in this respect completely ignoring the disorderly traditions of the past. Thus he introduced order where order was most needed. In future it was for no good purpose that Roman armies appeared in Italy. The system of Augustus at least kept foreign enemies out of the empire; and the sorely-tried Italian land, if more and more ceasing to produce her own defenders, enjoyed after the battle of Actium a century of welcome peace.

[1] This subject is brilliantly treated in G. Boissier's *L'Opposition sous les Césars*.

CHAPTER LX.

LITERATURE AND JURISPRUDENCE AS ILLUSTRATING THE LIFE OF THE REVOLUTIONARY PERIOD.

1341. I propose to conclude this story with a series of short essays, reviewing the state of things in Rome Italy and the empire generally, and endeavouring to shew under what conditions the new monarchy of Augustus was established. To avoid some repetition seems hardly possible. The different topics are too closely connected for treatment in rigidly separate compartments. Nor is it easy to avoid looking far into the sequel, if we are to grasp what the fall of the Republic really meant. I have tried to compress both repetitions and forecasts so far as is consistent with making my view clear. Therefore a number of highly interesting details are omitted, either as having been already referred to in the course of the narrative, or as having too slight a connexion with the subject.

It is not possible to omit from our consideration the literature of the revolutionary period, of which no small portion has come down to us. The writings of authors of whom we have only a few fragmentary lines, however interesting these may be, hardly concern us here. It is the surviving works (no doubt, speaking generally, the most important) that we have to consider, as throwing light on the condition of Roman society in a generation of which the elder men had seen Marius and Sulla, while some of the younger lived to see Octavian receive the title of *Augustus*. The struggle to keep alive the effete Republic, the collision of the civil war, Caesar's autocracy, the vain attempt to revive the Republic, the final necessity of submission to the master of the legions,—these rough outlines are enough to remind us of the long agony of Rome. From Sulla to Augustus was about fifty years, and in this space of time nearly all the writings referred to in the following sections were produced, as well as the other works (chiefly Cicero's speeches and letters) constantly referred to above. To give some life to our picture of the times it is necessary to observe what things were of interest to educated men during this period of strain and stress. The cases of Varro Lucretius and Catullus are peculiarly instructive, and the continued growth of jurisprudence in an age of disorder compels us to look at Roman life on a side that, in tracing the course of revolution, we might be tempted to forget.

Rhetorica ad Herennium.

1342. Various writers of whom it is not necessary to speak here have left only fragments, to which reference has been made on occasion in previous chapters. There is however one important work of the Sullan period preserved whole, which we can hardly ignore. This is the treatise on rhetoric[1] addressed to Herennius. It was probably written not long after the death of Marius in 86. The author was almost certainly one Cornificius, but he is not as yet satisfactorily identified with any known person of the name. Its importance may be summarized as follows. As a practical Art of Rhetoric it is rated highly by competent judges, and its writer was no mere copyist of Greek originals. It proves that rhetorical training in Latin had, in spite of the edict[2] of the censors of 92, become thoroughly established in Rome when Cicero was a young man. Cicero had himself studied the work and borrowed from it in his book *de inventione*. The examples used to illustrate precepts are very numerous. Some are drawn from the practice of orators, no doubt reminiscences of well-known speeches, but the greater number are supposed cases made up by the writer himself, an innovation[3] which he is at great pains to justify. Roman history and Roman life are the sources of most of his material, and this is all the more important as he was a strong partisan and often uses examples that betray his hostility to the aristocratic party. We thus get now and then illustrations of points of view otherwise unknown to us. References in former chapters will shew that the *Rhetorica ad Herennium* has been found useful in the period for which we have such meagre authorities, that from the Gracchi to Sulla.

Cicero.

1343. So much has been already said of Cicero that we need not dwell long on him here. We have constantly had to refer to his letters and speeches as contemporary evidence less or more trustworthy according as he has or has not an object to serve at the moment. His published speeches are a part of the pamphlet-literature of the day. In regard to his verse-compositions[4] it is to be noted that, in spite of his lack of poetic gifts, he performed no small service to Roman poetry. Like most versifiers of the time, he began

---

[1] Well discussed and analysed in Wilkins' Introd. to Cic. *de orat.* pp. 51—64.
[2] See above § 826.   [3] *ad Herenn.* IV §§ 1—10.
[4] See note of J. B. Mayor on Cic. *de nat. deorum* II § 104.

by translating from the Greek. Part of his Latin version of the astronomical poems of Aratus survives. He afterwards wrote original heroic poems, the most important of which were that on his consulship and that on his own times, others on Marius and a glorification of the conquests of Caesar. It can hardly be denied that Cicero marks an advance in technical skill. His lines are heavy and somewhat monotonous, but with a certain stateliness of movement. As an experiment in verse-building they mark a distinct step in the process of discovering the possibilities of the Latin hexameter. His translations from Greek dramatists need not detain us. According to the younger Pliny[1], he threw off light and indecorous trifles in verse, as others did; but this was probably a clumsy attempt to follow the prevailing mode. His facility in prose-composition was prodigious, and he felt able to write about anything. The loss of his historical works, one of them an account of his own consulship in Greek, is not greatly to be deplored. Of other subjects in which he dabbled we may mention civil law and augury. He was not a profound student, but in one subject at least he was a great authority. Of the permanent value of his rhetorical works there can be no doubt. If he is inferior to his Greek predecessors in scientific treatment of the theory of rhetoric, his unrivalled experience makes him a sound practical critic and adviser. All this group of his works, with one small exception[2], belong to the later years of his life: the *de oratore*, written in 55 at the height of his powers and before the civil war, is one of his master-pieces. Of great historical importance is the *Brutus*, a critical sketch of Roman orators and the growth of Roman oratory from the earliest times to its culmination in Cicero himself. Written in 46, its tone is affected by the depression[3] arising from the civil war, more particularly by the feeling that the voice of the free orator is silenced in the din of arms. But he settles down to give a full account of what was in fact far the most prolific branch of the republican literature. It is in this work that he gives a sympathetic description of the rise and decline[4] of his great rival Hortensius, and a remarkable appreciation of Caesar[5] as speaker writer and language-reformer. But Cicero is not wholly absorbed in weighing the merits of a number of individuals; he contrives to bring in here, as in his other rhetorical treatises, his own views of the many things needful for the training of the complete orator. Not to speak of the management of voice and gesture, or the study of great models, the two most vital needs are, immense industry in acquiring general knowledge and fully

---

[1] Pliny *epist.* v 3 § 6.
[2] *de inventione*, a work of his youth.
[3] *Brutus* §§ 1—23, 329—31.
[4] *Brutus* §§ 229—31, 301—29.
[5] *Brutus* §§ 251—62.

developing the mental powers, and the formation of a good and pure Latin style. This last was a pet hobby of Cicero, and it was a ground on which Caesar and he could meet and enjoy mutual admiration. They both held that a man should speak and write so as to make it easy to understand him and a pleasure to hear or read him. The taste of both was opposed to new-fangled or old-fashioned expressions, and disgusted by the affectation of such mannerisms. Their standard was the Latin used in good society, divested of mere colloquialisms, and moulded into periods of the length suited to the sense and constructed in accordance with the rules of grammar. The language once purified, there remained the question how to use it. And here Cicero cannot help referring to the battle of the styles[1] then being waged in literary circles, a matter of which he treats more fully elsewhere. To put the matter briefly, there were three competing ideals. The 'Asiatic' school, whose chief representative had been Hortensius, allowed themselves a free use of ornament and mannerisms, which inevitably tended to redundancy and bombast. They were directly opposed by the new 'Attic' school, led by Calvus, who aimed[2] at a classic simplicity, which tended to become too cold and dry for the essentially popular function of oratory. Between these two extremes stood Cicero and his followers. Cicero like the rest accepted Greek models as a standard. But he well knew the difference between the languages, and sought to solve the problem before him, not by transplanting a ready-made style from the one to the other, but by finding out what style best fitted the purest Latin. The 'Asiatics' he set aside as un-Roman, but he studied the Attic orators in a larger spirit than the 'Attics.' With him it was a question something like a rule-of-three sum—how shall we in good Latin produce the same effect on Romans as the great Attic orators did in good Greek on Athenians? This is not the place to discuss his solution of the problem. We know the striking success that attended his efforts. Whatever we may think of Cicero's other achievements, it is a fact that he created a standard style of Latin prose suited alike for speeches and treatises, and that he so used it for both purposes as to provoke and render vain all future rivalry.

1344. It remains to speak of his philosophical writings in relation to the time and the aims of the writer. It is generally admitted that Cicero was not a philosopher by nature, and that his earlier studies of philosophy were undertaken as a part of the mental training by which he differentiated himself from contemporary speakers of inferior

---

[1] This subject will be found admirably treated in Sandys' Introd. to Cicero's *Orator*.
[2] For an unfavourable judgment of Calvus see Tacitus *dial.* 21.

equipment. His philosophical treatises[1] belong to his last years of sorrow and depression. They were produced in a great hurry. He saw that the Republic was overthrown, and in the years 46—44 until the Ides of March no hope of its restoration had appeared. So he sojourned in his villas, and turned feverishly to literature: he tried hard to persuade himself that here was his true vocation, when in truth he was seeking an anodyne. Already in the years 56—52, when the first triumvirate had suspended the action of free political life, he had found relief in occupation[2] of this kind, and even it seems looked forward to a prospect of dealing with questions other[3] than those then engaging him at some later time. But he was surely dreaming of these projects as the leisurely pursuits of an honoured old age, not as a means of distracting his mind in a second period of far greater disappointment and misery. The latter experience was nevertheless his lot. So in the space of less than three years he produced[4], beside five works on oratory, the whole of his treatises on ethical and religious subjects, an astounding mass. Three points only can be considered here, his aim in writing such books, his position as an expounder of philosophy, and the method on which he worked. First, Cicero aimed at enlightening the average Roman who was not thoroughly at home in Greek (especially in the technical Greek of philosophers) by presenting Greek thought in a Latin dress[5] of the best quality. He did not aim at propounding a new system of his own, but at providing a mental stimulus for his countrymen, of course indicating his own preference of one view to another. He felt bound to justify himself[6] in Roman eyes for handling such un-Roman subjects at all. His own earlier choice among the Greek Schools had led him to the so-called New Academy. Taken educationally, the attitude of this school might well commend itself to one bent on winning distinction as an orator. It was a readiness to hear conflicting opinions, and to choose that which seemed most probable. It required no unqualified assent to any proposition as absolutely and finally true. Thus it asserted human fallibility, and the absence of embarrassing dogma was a good preparation for a life to be spent in handling probabilities and suggesting doubts. Cicero never abjured the New Academy, but in later life leant to the so-called Old Academy, in name a revival of the school founded

---

[1] The relations of Cicero to philosophy are excellently discussed in Reid's Introd. to the *Academica*. But when it is said (p. 6) that Cicero was before all things a man of letters we must not imply that Cicero himself thought so. This seems to be admitted later (p. 23).

[2] *de oratore, de re publica, de legibus.*   [3] *de legibus* I §§ 52—5. See Reid p. 7.

[4] List in Teuffel-Schwabe §§ 182—4.

[5] A good illustration of his difficulties in creating a terminology is *de finibus* III §§ 51—7.

[6] Reid p. 23.

by Plato, in reality a blend of the views of several schools, combined by one of his teachers at Athens, Antiochus of Ascalon In this there was a strong Stoic[1] element, and it is not to be wondered at that, in addressing a Roman public with whom the sects most in favour were the Stoic and the Epicurean, Cicero should shew clearly his antipathy to the latter. Though constitutionally inclined to hesitate, in this decision he did not waver. In order to sketch his position generally we must bear in mind that the great aim of Greek philosophy had long been the discovery of a basis for practical morality, an 'art of living.' Also that there were two fundamentally different ways of dealing with the popular religion, now no longer taken seriously by educated men. And these two ways in theology led from the conclusions reached in two widely different systems of physics, one of which recognized a divine government of the universe, while the other did not. The two ways led to widely different views of the true position of Man in the universe, and on the choice between these views[2] depended the conclusions to be received as to the Chief Good for Man, in other words the standard of human happiness. The position of Cicero was that of an Academic critic of Epicurean Stoic and other doctrines, and without doubt he was strongly biassed by his Roman conceptions of public duty. In his eyes the acquiescence enjoined by Epicureanism simply put it out of court. The mechanical physics repelled him, the agnostic theology did away with a Providence, the ethics disgusted him as being an unmanly system of impotent despair. On the other side, he was far too human to be attracted by the formal logic of the Stoics, which might suit the temper of a Cato, but to a Cicero seemed barren and perverse. Nor could he accept their physical theories save as a well-meant effort to attain truth. But with their Pantheism, which extended a divine presence[3] and providential government to every corner of the universe, and with the inspiring ethical system linked to this sublime theology, Cicero had a great and growing sympathy. He never became a professed Stoic. His temper and training shewed him too many objections for that. But the fact of his warm appreciation of the merits of the lofty Stoic morality has its own place in the dark story of the Republic's fall. As he saw that the course of events had fatally narrowed the sphere of oratory, so he had a foreboding of a time in which Romans of birth

---

[1] In the de officiis Cicero drew mainly from Posidonius, the great Stoic philosopher of the period.

[2] de finibus bonorum et malorum (on the summum bonum), Tusculanae disputationes (on happiness).

[3] The belief of the Stoics in divination was a great stumbling-block to Cicero, though he was a member of the College of Augurs.

and education, finding their former political activity repressed[1] by autocratic power, would need some other interests to employ their thoughts. The revolution in states he accepted from Plato as Nature's law for human societies. Rome had reached the stage of transition to monarchy. It would seem that in responding once more to the calls of public life after the death of Caesar he had at first little hope of 'recovering the Republic.' And the spirit of this passage agrees very well with the tone of his letters written at the time when the arbitrary doings of Antony had filled him with disappointment.

1345. As to the method on which Cicero worked, it was in the main that of free translation or adaptation from the Greek. For the most part he followed one guide[2] at a time, and his authorities were chiefly writers of comparatively recent date and not always satisfactory guides. That some at least of his shortcomings as a writer on philosophy were due to too faithful reproduction of errors found in the books before him at this or that time has been pointed out by an able judge. But his own superficiality in this department must bear some of the blame. To get the matter into a Latin form was the most urgent need, all the more perhaps as Lucretius was in the field before him. His attacks on the Epicurean system are suggestive of a fear that it might gain ground among Romans, and in the case of one of his latest treatises good reason has been shewn for believing[3] that he wrote with direct reference to Lucretius. That the philosophical works of Cicero are dressed up as dialogues is due to imitation of Greek usage. But his model is the dialogue of later writers, in which the characters in turn generally discourse at length, not the subtle and dramatic question and answer usually employed by his beloved Plato. He did not attempt too much in Latin; the instrument was new. His determination to reach the Roman mind is shewn in the illustrations freely introduced to point a moral. For Romans the concrete had always a strong attraction, and Cicero knew better than to be sparing of instances; these he drew from Roman history[3] and Roman life whenever he could find suitable ones. Let me add one word on the general tone of Cicero as theologian and moralist. With all his weaknesses and flaws, there hangs about him a certain atmosphere of goodness and nobility which gives to many passages a comforting and even tonic effect. He was bearing up under terrible depression. That he cared more for his country than for his own life

---

[1] See *de divinatione* II §§ 4—7.   [2] See Reid pp. 24—5.

[2] J. B. Mayor, Introd. to *de natura deorum*, vol. III pp. x—xiii, where Cicero's distinction between *religio* and *superstitio* is discussed. Whether in insisting on the social nature of man in *de re publ.* I § 39 he has an eye to Lucretius, who traces social union to physical needs only, I cannot say. There is nothing in the dates to preclude it.

[3] See Holden, Introd. to *de officiis*.

the immediate sequel was to prove. So the real man peeps out behind
the superficial copyist. This is surely a main reason why these later
works of his have been admired, not only by his own countrymen,
but by Christian writers down to the present day.

Caesar.

1346. Of Caesar[1] too there is little to be said here. As an orator
we know him only by repute. But Cicero's favourable judgment of
his speeches is sufficient evidence of their merits, and it is supported
by that of Quintilian. The latter lays stress upon the force (*vis*)
of his oratory, and the style of his *commentarii* agrees very well with
this opinion. No doubt the talent of Caesar was shewn in enforcing
views rather than in appealing to emotional feelings. Tacitus[2] thought
less highly of his speeches, but remarked that his genius found its
sphere of action mainly in other departments of life. We have seen
that he composed in verse, but this was a casual relaxation. To the
political pamphlet-literature of the day he contributed the *Anticato*,
and he wrote a grammatical treatise, the *de analogia*. He was deeply
interested in questions of language, and we have already noted his
sympathy with Cicero in the effort to develope a pure[3] and lucid
Latin prose style. Compared with Cicero, he seems to have differed
in so far as he wrote with at least equal clearness and force but
with less colour. As an authority for facts his value has been very
variously judged. We are tempted to believe all his statements,
partly by his position as a contemporary witness conversant with
the matters of which he writes, partly by his apparently self-restrained
and ingenuous manner. His freedom from personal vanity saved
him from boasting, and his generous appreciation of the skill and
valour of those serving under him insensibly draws us over to his
side. But that he did represent events and motives in a light favourable to himself is not to be doubted. Some modern critics have
therefore undertaken to rewrite the story, not only of the civil war,
but also of the Gallic campaigns, on anti-Caesarian lines. By piecing
together stray notices preserved in later writers, and assuming that
these are both correctly reported and rightly understood, ingenuity
has sufficiently justified an attitude of caution in receiving the story
as told by Caesar. Whether future criticism will approve the reconstructed narrative proposed as a substitute for the alleged misrepre-

---

[1] See in general Sueton. *Jul.* 55, 56.

[2] Tac. *dial.* 21 (an early work). In *annals* XIII 3 he calls Caesar *summis oratoribus aemulus.*

[3] Gellius I 10 § 4 has preserved his advice to writers, to steer clear of an unusual word as they would a rock.

sentations of Caesar, I will not attempt to pronounce. To me it seems that in removing some difficulties the amended version only creates others, and I have therefore preferred to accept Caesar's story as in the main true. Wherever I saw legitimate ground for doubting his candour, I have tried to make it plain that his testimony is not admitted without reserve, and in a few cases have rejected it. It should always be remembered that his Commentaries were written in the intervals of manifold occupations, and minor errors should not hastily be imputed to ill faith.

The accounts of his last year in Gaul by Hirtius, and of the post-Pharsalian campaigns in the civil war by unknown writers, are useful as contemporary records written from the Caesarian point of view. Taken in order of the events, their literary merit steadily sinks, and the writers have none of the wide grasp and happy clearness of their master. But this does not lessen their merit as witnesses. Like the letters of some of Cicero's correspondents, they may give some notion of the average fairly-educated men's use of Latin. The Latin of Cicero and Caesar was most certainly the language of a few.

Varro.

1347. Among the remarkable men of the generation that saw the fall of the Republic there is perhaps none more worthy of particular notice than Marcus Terentius Varro. Born 116 B.C. in the Sabine[1] country, and not dying till 27 B.C., his life overlapped that of Cicero at both ends. He is apt to receive insufficient attention from students of Roman history, for his brilliant contemporary attracts readers, and the letters of Cicero are a running commentary on events of the time, a lively document such as scarce any other age can shew. Moreover it has been the fate of Varro to be known largely, perhaps chiefly, through the judgments of scholars upon whom the warm vivacity of Cicero has cast its spell. The grim efficiency of Varro has assuredly suffered by an unconscious bias arising from an unfair comparison. In respect of achievement the man of Reate was quite as great as the man of Arpinum. Both took part in public life, both were great writers. But to Cicero public life was the life of the Senate-house and the Forum. To lead and to persuade was his ambition, oratorical triumphs his glory. When he took to writing treatises, it was generally a sign that for the time he felt unable to appear with advantage on the public stage. Writing was then a consolation, but it was not his chosen sphere of activity. To Varro public life was departmental duty. After filling a minor office he became tribune, aedile, and

---

[1] For his simple home-training in early youth see Fowler, *Social Life* p. 177.

eventually praetor; the troubles of the times were no doubt the cause of his never reaching the consulship. But his military service under Pompey against Sertorius, and later (67) against the pirates, gained him the confidence of his chief, and we find him in 59 a commissioner for land-assignations under Caesar's agrarian law. In 49 he was *legatus* of Pompey in southern Spain. After Ilerda he was forced to submit to Caesar. It is probable that he had not much taste for civil war. Caesar pardoned him, and afterwards gave him the charge of organizing the great library with which the imperial capital was to be equipped. He was still a republican at heart, but his submission to Caesar seems to have been sincere. He could work under a master, and he was probably a man of few delusions. After the Ides of March he was in sympathy with the republicans, but we do not find him taking a leading -part. Scholars have pointed out[1] that even now his friendly relations with Cicero never reached the stage of warm intimacy. The orator found him cold distant and critical. But we need not look far for an explanation of his unresponsive attitude. The volatile effusiveness and vanity of Cicero could hardly be congenial to Varro. Mutual admiration was not in the great student's line, and the man of persuasion soon jarred upon the man of fact. It is idle to blame either for the effect of an incompatibility of temperament which neither could help. Varro was a man of property, and as such was proscribed by Antony. But he found protectors, and escaped, not without loss of books and lands. He was afterwards protected by Octavian, and passed his later years in the production of treatises the fruit of immense research. He is justly called the most learned of the Romans, but it is not merely on the ground of his learning that his career and character concern us here. Of all the republican types that meet us in the revolutionary period, none foreshadows the position of competent and industrious men under the Imperial government so clearly as Varro. While we cannot refuse to admire the devotion of such men as Cato and Cicero to the cause of the Republic, which to them was patriotism, we need not depreciate the conduct of those who loyally accepted the change of system, when once that change, in truth inevitable, was accomplished. They too served their country in their own way. A type such as that of Cicero could never be reproduced. The would-be imitators of Cato might risk their own lives and create dramatic situations; the effect of their protests was only to provoke repression and confirm the power of Emperors. It was the function of men more nearly approaching the Varronian model, content to be efficient and industrious in a secondary position, to preserve for Romans a share

---

[1] See Tyrrell and Purser, Introduction to vol. IV of Cicero's correspondence.

of authority, and rescue something from the grasp of courtiers and imperial freedmen. There were not a few who performed this unassuming public service both in civil and military duties, but none with more usefulness and consistency than the elder Pliny, whose life and work bear a close resemblance to those of Varro.

1348. An account of the known facts relative to the writings of Varro must be sought in histories of Roman Literature. It is enough here to say that he was the author of 74 different works, some of them long and abstruse. From the first he seems to have been an antiquary, but in the earlier part of his life he put forth a great number of occasional pieces in verse or prose or mixed, in which he gave vent to his views on the morals habits and current opinions of what he regarded as a degenerate age. Of these *saturae*[1] *Menippeae* nearly 600 fragments survive, mostly quoted by later grammarians to illustrate points of linguistic usage. Some of these incidentally throw light on the ways of Roman society in his day, and the picture is not a flattering one, naturally. He saw round him a corrupt and luxurious world, gluttonous and profligate, where men were greedily jostling each other in the race for wealth, in which competition was a raging disease and the big fishes ate up the small. Respect for parents had well-nigh ceased, and needed to be preached anew, while experience shewed the futility of sumptuary laws. Laws, dealing with offences in general terms, could do nothing : in practice it rested with men to give them effect, and the favour that acquitted the guilty, the spite that condemned the innocent, were no part of the statute law. Insincerity and roguery were rampant ; good men might be admired, but their examples were not copied. In short, the practice of Roman society was even worse than its principles. No abomination but had some Professor to justify it, for philosophy ran into endless absurdities, and the orgies and initiations of foreign cults were the bane of Rome. What with barren women and the wastage of pestilence and war, deaths were outnumbering births. As for the men, what sort of progeny could be expected from them ? they were not chosen, as a mule-breeder would choose a jackass. In a horrid scene of demoralization and crime, with wasteful slaves eating their masters out of house and home, with demagogy and bribery in possession of the Forum and the courts, it is not strange that Varro refers to the revolutionary changes of the times and the calamity of civil war. He was fully persuaded of the superiority of the ancient ways. When people lived in dwellings of unbaked brick, simple in their diet and habits, religious and law-abiding, then

---

[1] Edited by Bücheler with his *Petronius*, and Seneca's skit *de morte Claudii*, from which we may perhaps get some notion of these works of prose and verse mixed.

Rome was Rome indeed.   As a man versed in all the culture of his time, he was no stranger to the power of music and poetry, and he appears to have been much interested in promoting the improvement of Roman dining in respect of tasteful appointments, well chosen company, and rational talk on uncontentious topics.   But the social liberties taken by ladies of the new school in dress and bearing were to him indecent and matter of disgust.

1349.   The above picture of Roman society about 60—45 B.C. is composed of selections from the more intelligible fragments.   It will be seen that the materials are much the same as those which have been used by satirists in all ages, and that Varro like other writers, dissatisfied with their own times and somewhat prone to idealize the past, probably shut his eyes to the better features of the present. But it cannot be denied that most if not all of the charges brought by him are borne out by other evidence.   It is a pity that we have not one of these compositions in a complete form, to shew us how he treated these multifarious topics.   We may perhaps regard the *saturae* rather as satirical pamphlets than as formal Satires in the sense derived from our reading of Horace and Juvenal.   The word *sermones* 'talks,' used by Horace, might have fitted them well.   Of Varro's other writings in verse we know practically nothing.   His orations seem to have been written pamphlets.   But the great bulk of his prose writings consisted of serious works in various departments of knowledge and inquiry.   Some were philosophical essays or dialogues.   As to his views, we know that he belonged to the school of the earlier Academics: the all-enfeebling doubt and uncertainty of the New Academy[1] was distasteful to him.   As a student interested in all branches of investigation, he had surely much affinity with the Peripatetics.   To search for facts and attain positive results was evidently his master-passion, and he wrote to communicate knowledge to others, without much concern for elegance of style or pursuit of literary fame.   But the Peripatetic school of later times supplied little in the way of philosophic creed.   Since the days of Aristotle and Theophrastus its chief product[2] had been the special treatises mostly the fruit of the workshop of learning at Alexandria.   Varro's subjects included History ancient and contemporary, antiquities political religious genealogical and literary.   Some of his works dealt with chronology, topography, the history of Roman civilization, and

---

[1] See Reid's Introduction to Cicero's *Academica* pp. 48—51, Augustin *de civitate Dei* XIX 1—3.   Reid pp. 10—17 points out that this was the so-called Old Academy, a revival due to Antiochus of Ascalon, containing Stoic Platonic and Peripatetic elements.

[2] In Varro's time Ethics, very near the Stoic, were the staple of decayed Peripateticism. Varro was greatly influenced by the Stoic Posidonius.

the niceties of senatorial procedure. We hear of a collection of biographies of famous men, Greek and Roman, the text of which was illustrated with portraits (*imagines*): of a great work called *disciplinae*, a sort of encyclopaedia of the liberal arts: of special treatises on various sciences, mensuration, geography and navigation, the civil law, grammar and philology, and others besides. In most of these works he undoubtedly followed chiefly Greek authorities or Greek models. But he was, as we shall see, a genuine inquirer, not a mere copyist, somewhat pedantic and formal, occasionally fanciful. That he hoped to enlarge the views of after generations by handing down his knowledge, we have his own authority[1] for believing. He was not mistaken in thinking that posterity would make use of his labours. Not only is he cited freely by the elder Pliny Gellius Macrobius and others. His works served as a quarry to which those desirous of ready-made erudition resorted. Their massive character has no doubt told against their chances of survival. Of his work on the Latin language we have a considerable portion. Its chief importance consists in the number of incidental details which throw light on the obscure institutions of early Rome. Readers of such books as Mommsen's *Staatsrecht* are continually brought into contact with this valuable relic of Varro's scholarship. The one work preserved to us entire is fortunately the treatise of rural industries[2] (*res rusticae*). From this we are able to get some authoritative information on that most important subject, the state of rural Italy. It is only necessary to preface a brief account of the work by remarking that what the author says is sometimes not more significant than what he does not say.

1350. The treatise is divided into three books, the first on tillage of the soil (*agri cultura*), the second on flocks and herds, with other animals employed on a farm (*res pecuaria*), the third on the keeping of what we may call fancy-animals for profit (*villaticae pastiones*). Of these occupations he points out that the first is historically a later development than the second. The third is comparatively recent, and is mainly concerned with satisfying the demands of modern luxury by producing dainties for the Roman market. Varro wrote this work in 37 B.C. in his 80th year. It is cast somewhat carelessly into the form of a dialogue between himself and some friends who were authorities on various parts of the subject. The sources from which he draws[3] are three. First, his own experience in managing his own estates, and his observation in general. Secondly, reading.

---

[1] *de re rustica* I I § 3.
[2] There is a good little description of the treatise by A. Riecke (Stuttgart 1861).
[3] *RR.* I I § 11.

He refers repeatedly to his Roman forerunners, Cato, Saserna, and others. Of Greek writers he gives a long list, in which we may note particularly Xenophon Aristotle and Theophrastus, and a Greek translation of the Punic treatise of Mago. Thirdly, information gained from practical men (*periti*) by word of mouth. He is formally precise in defining the scope of his work. With industries such[1] as potteries mines quarries and the like he has nothing to do, any more than with keeping an inn, which might be a paying concern on a farm near a high road. In choosing the site for a *villa* he insists strongly on general considerations, such as a healthy spot with a good aspect and water-supply[2], soil fertile but if possible various in quality, ready access to markets, and a neighbourhood not infested by robbers. He also makes it quite clear that his ideal *villa* is a country house and farm of the old-fashioned type. The modern 'place in the country' with fine decorations but no farm, a seat[3] to which the noble owner paid flying visits, and where he entertained a few friends with dainties got down from Rome, is not for Varro. All through, whether growing crops or pasturing herds or fattening snails and dormice, Varro has his eye to profit. Does it pay? is his first and last question in considering an enterprise. Old Cato himself was not more hostile to waste in any form, and he enjoins minute precautions against the inroads of vermin. Storage is carefully designed, in order that the produce of the farm may not have to be sold in haste on a glutted market. The utmost importance is attached to sanitation. Drainage both of land and farmstead must be kept in thorough working order. Granaries and other store-rooms should be well ventilated; cleanliness must reign everywhere, and all live stock be constantly supplied with fresh water, to avoid losses by disease. Like Cato, he insists on preserving a due proportion[4] in land and buildings. The various departments of the farmstead should be on a larger or smaller scale according to the relative quantities of produce in each, which will vary in different localities. Enough has been said to shew that Varro treats his subject thoroughly, perhaps as thoroughly as was possible before the great advances made with the help of modern science, particularly chemistry. And Varro was too much of a Roman to forget the legal side of all business transactions. This comes out in a striking manner when he refers to the purchase of live stock. The forms of valid transfer and guarantee of soundness

---

[1] I 2 §§ 22, 23.

[2] I 12 § 2 he speaks of minute animals, too small for the eye to detect, bred in marshy spots, which get into the human body and are the cause of troublesome ailments. This Mr Jones in his essay on *Malaria* p. 66 cites as evidence of that malady in Varro's time.

[3] I 59, III 2. Compare Lucretius III 1060—7.　　　　　　　　　　[4] I 11.

were not exactly the same in the case of different animals, so he is at pains to furnish the reader with the correct formulas used in the several cases, as recognized in the Roman courts. The Roman love of prescribed rules, doubtless congenial to Varro, appears in his Farmer's Calendar. Eight divisions, of $1\frac{1}{2}$ month each, make up the Farmer's Year. A schedule of these, with the work assigned to each, should be posted up in the farm-house as a reminder to the bailiff. Of course the exact observance of these rules was an ideal, carried out so far as weather[1] permitted.

1351, The agriculture of Varro includes grain-crops, wheat beans barley spelt and so forth; green-crops for grazing and for hay; fruit-crops[2], vines olives apples pears figs nuts etc.; garden vegetables (*legumina*), not a very important item; wood for fuel buildings fences implements etc., including trees grown for shade and osiers for basket-work. The various operations connected with these products are discussed fully with a keen eye to profit. For instance, gleaning after reaping is only to be undertaken if it will pay, and pressed grape skins are to be wetted and pressed again; the *lora* or 'seconds' will do for the farm-hands. This last was an old provision, recognized by Cato. It may be remarked that Varro does not mention many varieties of the several species of plants. When he comes to stock-keeping he has much more to say on this head. This department includes sheep goats pigs oxen asses horses mules, also dogs shepherds and stockmen. Attention is called to famous breeds of home or foreign origin; he points out that the noted asses of Arcadia are rivalled by those of his native Reate. For the treatment of sick beasts prescriptions are to be copied in note-books, of which the bailiff and the head-shepherd each have one. The various duties connected with the live stock are detailed, but we need only refer to that which in Varro's time was more important than it is now, namely the protection of domesticated animals, the young in particular, from wolves and birds of prey. We learn that in passing from lowland winter pastures to the highlands in summer the flocks and herds sometimes traversed great distances. Thus from Apulia they were driven not only into Samnium but even to the Sabine hills. They travelled by rough country paths (*calles*)[3], evidently recognized rights of way (*publicae*), where it was bad going (*difficultas*), and the way to the runs sometimes led through woods. When the run or grazing-ground (*saltus*) was reached, the perils of

---

[1] See Lucretius v 213—7.

[2] Among them the pomegranate (*malus Punica*) and the cherry (I 39 § 2) a recent importation from the East by Lucullus (Pliny *NH.* xv 102). Dates (*palmulae*) seem not to have ripened in Italy, so the fruit must have been imported. See I 67, II 1 § 27.

[3] II 2 § 10, 9 § 16, 10 §§ 1, 3, III 17 § 9.

wild beasts[1] and robbers remained. The *magister pecoris* must have under him powerful dogs and slave-herdsmen sturdy and well-armed. We see also that some at least of the wild upland pastures were still state-property, let to speculative middlemen who collected the grazing-tax (*scriptura*). To them declaration[2] of the number of beasts must be made, to avoid the legal penalties of evasion (*ad publicanum profitentur*). Of one animal, the horse, a word must be said. Horses were not kept for farm-work, but bred for sale, also for the production of mules. The horse was used in war, and for transport on the roads, also in Rome for chariot-racing. It is clear from Varro's remarks on the teeth and other evidence of age, that horse-dealing already had its peculiar perils. He tells us also that most of the development of veterinary[3] skill had taken place in connexion with diseases of the horse, so that in Greek 'horse-leech' ($i\pi\pi i a\tau\rho o s$) simply meant a 'Vet.' Of the slave we will speak below.

1352. It was however unhappily true that the profits of agriculture and stock-farming proper were not great, considering labour skill risks and capital sunk. So in the third book Varro begins by groaning over the vain luxury of his degenerate age, town-life, monstrous extravagance, and so forth, and at once proceeds to accept these latter-day abominations as a fact to be exploited for profit. Rome is ever feasting, what with triumphal entertainments, banquets of gilds (*collegia*), and other occasions of guzzling. The man who is ready to execute a large order at short notice can rely on splendid returns from keeping and fattening for market (1) birds (2) minor quadrupeds (3) fish. Of these some are bred on the place, others, such as migrant birds (quails etc.), are caught wild. He refers to many species of birds, of which we may note in particular the pea-fowl (very[4] profitable), pigeons, turtle-doves, barn-door fowl, geese, and ducks. So much for the *aviarium* (new style, $\delta\rho\nu\iota\theta\omega\nu$). In the paddock-preserve, *leporarium* (new style, $\theta\eta\rho o\tau\rho o\phi\epsilon\hat{\iota}o\nu$) were kept all manner of marketable beasts, wild goats and swine, hares, rabbits, and so forth, with separate enclosures for edible snails and dormice. All these were fattened for table. The rage for fish, not only as an article of diet, but as pets, is well known[5] from the references of Cicero

---

[1] Compare Lucretius v 39—42. In 1386—7 the poet lays stress upon the impressive loneliness of this up-country.

[2] II 1 § 16. See Cic. *ad Att.* II 15 § 4. For Sicily see Cic. *II in Verr.* II §§ 169—171, III § 167.

[3] II 7 § 16.

[4] The birds fetched about £2 each for the table, the eggs about 4s. It was Hortensius the orator who brought the *pavo* into fashion as food.

[5] See Pliny *NH.* IX 168—73. Oyster-beds seem to have been made to pay, even before 90 B.C.

to the *piscinarii* who idled away their time over their fish-ponds instead of attending to politics. The Luculli and Hortensius were notorious instances. The marine ponds, chiefly in the fashionable neighbourhood of Baiae and Puteoli, were a source of vast extravagance; great incomes were wasted[1] on them. Varro has no patience with this sort of thing. To him the humble fresh-water tank, fed by a running stream, is the only sort worthy the attention of a practical man, but of this he says very little. A department not strictly connected with luxury is the time-honoured industry of bee-keeping. This he discusses[2] in detail in a most interesting chapter. On his farm it would be the special charge of a *mellarius*. But he points out that it could be made very profitable on a quite small holding entirely devoted thereto, and cites a case of two brothers who had served under his command in Spain. These men inherited a small farm-house and one *iugerum* (say ⅝ of an acre) of land, which they planted with flowers suited to bees, and year by year gained a good and steady income[3] from their enterprise. Of this subject Varro shews minute study, and characteristically does not forget to comment on the geometrical significance of the hexagonal cells.

1353. Nothing strikes the reader of Varro's work more than the frequent references to the products and usages of other lands. The horizon of the student husbandman had been immensely widened since the days of old Cato. New species of plants and animals were being introduced into Italy, and the knowledge of new processes and foreign experience was leading to a more enlightened management[4] of estates. This development was partly due to the extension of landholding by Romans in the provinces. A good instance is the case of Atticus, who had great estates in Epirus. Varro often refers to him, and he appears as one of the speakers. But a great deal was the result of recent wars. Lucullus and Pompey had opened up vast regions of the East, lands of ancient civilization, and oppression and extortion were not the only fruits of conquest. The readiness of Romans to learn from other peoples had been remarked by Polybius, and it was as active as ever. We have seen Caesar recording his observations on the flora and fauna, the habits and husbandry, of new countries on both sides of the Rhine. No wonder that in the hands of Varro the subject begins to receive a scientific treatment for the benefit of Italy. He had himself been an observer in Gaul and Spain,

---

[1] Compare the case of the estate which did not pay its expenses, Catullus CXIV.

[2] III 16.

[3] III 16 §§ 10, 11. The sum named in Keil's text, *dena millia sestertia*, is incredible to me. The number is surely wrong.

[4] For improvement of crops by scientific farming see Lucretius I 208—14, V 206—17, 1367—9.

and records not a few particulars.   From him we learn that the curing
of bacon and hams was a speciality of Gaul[1], and that there was a
brisk trade in them for the Roman market.   But, among his collections
of facts and his serious method, he often betrays the limitations of his
time in the queer relics of old superstitions and the traditional wonders[2]
that he repeats.   He gives us the story that bees can be spontaneously
produced from the rotting carcase of an ox, familiar to readers of
Vergil.   He tries to relieve his seriousness with occasional jokes, but
with generally bovine effect.   His best[3] is one perhaps as old as the
Republic, but neatly turned.

1354.   We have now to consider the system of husbandry
contemplated by Varro from a more general point of view.   What
picture does it give us of Italian farming in the last years of the
Republic?   In what relation does it stand to the system of small
farms on the one hand, and the system of great plantations on the
other?   Does it suggest a general improvement or a decline, and in
what respects?   The answer, so far as we can find it, comes out more
particularly in his discussion[4] of the labour-question.   The labour
employed, he says, is that of slaves or free men or both.   Free labour
is either that of the small farmer who tills his own land with the help
of his family, or that of the wage-earner (*mercennarius*) employed for
some of the more important operations, such as the vintage and hay-
harvest.   A subdivision of the latter class is formed by men who owe
money (*obaerarii*) and work off the debt by service.   Numbers of these
semi-bondmen are still to be met with in Asia Egypt and Illyricum.
It seems implied that they had died out in Italy, and the immense
armies of Varro's time will sufficiently explain why.   Of free labour
in general he holds that it pays to employ it (*utilius*) for two special
kinds of work (1) in the cultivation of malarious[5] land (*gravia loca*)
(2) in work of more than common importance (*maiora*) even on healthy
ground.   That is, the free labourer is a more intelligent worker than

[1] Belgic Gaul, according to Strabo IV 4 § 3.

[2] One of his strangest stories is that of the stallion who resented being made an Oedipus,
II 7 § 9.

[3] III 17 § 4 (of some pet fish) *hos pisces nemo cocus in ius vocare audet.*

[4] I 17.   It is remarkable that Vergil in his *Georgics* ignores slave-labour.   Surely this is
one of many signs that his precepts record aspirations rather than present facts.   The
robustus fossor of II 264 may be merely a *mercennarius*.   In I 507 he says *squalent abductis
arva colonis*, lapsing for a moment into the facts of the revolutionary age.   Vergil himself
came from the Cisalpine, where there is reason to think that slavery was of a mild type.   See
§ 663.   Seneca *ep.* 86 § 15 says of Vergil *non quid verissime sed quid decentissime diceretur
aspexit, nec agricolas docere voluit sed legentes delectare.*

[5] For an exact economic parallel see Olmsted's *Journey in the seaboard Slave-states*
1853—4, new edition 1904 pp 11, 100—1, on the use of Irishmen instead of negroes
for ditching and draining unhealthy ground.

the slave, while his sickness or death involves no loss of the master's capital. In connexion with this subject we may note what he says[1] of special skilled labour. The apothecary (*medicus*), the fuller, the manual artisan (*faber*), are specimens of workers whose help is needed at certain times on the farm. To buy such skilled men and keep them on the place is out of the question unless the farm and its staff are on a large scale. If one of these costly specialists dies, you stand to lose a year's income from the estate. For there were no Insurance companies. Hence the custom of tenant-farmers (*coloni*)[2] is to depend on occasional help in these departments from men who go their rounds[3] (*anniversarii*) and can be called in. Even if you can well afford to keep such men, it is doubtful policy to have them kicking their heels in idleness (*ambulet feriata*) on working days, instead of helping to make the farm pay. For of course your *familia rustica* cannot be allowed to stray off the place. Only three persons can be granted this liberty; the bailiff (*vilicus*) and his assistant, and the store-steward (*promus*). All are slaves, and the bailiff must be punished if any unlicensed breaking of bounds takes place. The upper slaves may have privileges and perquisites, which they will be loth to lose. In short, despite the passing reference to small farmers[4] (of whom he gives us no reason to think them numerous) and to free labour (evidently a very limited quantity), the husbandry of Varro is essentially slave-husbandry. He points out the unwisdom of keeping too many of the same nationality, for fear[5] of combinations. The overseers (*praefecti*) should be encouraged by letting them acquire something for themselves (*peculium*), a sort of rudimentary pension-system of great antiquity, and by allowing them to form unions with female slaves. This attaches them to the place, and the young of slaves have their value. With judicious care a slave-establishment may be governed with little or no use of the lash. In treating of flocks and herds he recurs[6] to the breeding-question. Even the herdsmen on duty in the hill-pastures should have able-bodied females to keep house for them. Child-birth is nothing to women leading such a life. They are none of your frail Roman ladies. As for buying[7] slaves, the methods of acquiring full right of property in

---

[1] I 16 §§ 4, 5.

[2] For *coloni* of this period see Cic. *pro Caecina* § 94, *pro Cluent.* §§ 175, 182, *II in Verr.* III § 55.

[3] Such as the *pharmacopola circumforaneus* mentioned by Cic. *pro Cluent.* § 40. These, I take it, are free, some at least probably freedmen.

[4] If we may believe Cic. *II in Verr.* III §§ 27, 120, there were a considerable number of small farmers in Sicily, whom Verres ruined. But the evidence of an *ex parte* orator is poor authority.

[5] His expression (I 17 § 5) for slave-mutinies is *offensiones domesticae.*

[6] II 10 §§ 6—9.   [7] II 10 §§ 4, 5.

a human chattel are clearly laid down in Roman law, but you must see that you get only those sound and warranted free from vice. And the bailiff and head stock-man at least must be able to read.

1355. The model estate of Varro is certainly much nearer to the great plantation worked by slave-gangs than to the small holding supposed to have been normal in early times. It is a *latifundium*, and a rich man, unwilling to risk all on the yearly fortunes of climate and soil in one district of Italy, might (and some did) own estates of manageable size in several different districts, or (as many did) abroad. There is nothing in Varro's work to hold out any prospect of reviving the old race of sturdy Italian yeomen whose solid virtues had enabled the clumsy and ill-designed Republic to overcome rival powers and become the mistress of the ancient world. A more scientific husbandry might be an economic gain. It was less wasteful, not to say less perilous, than the crude and brutal system of the earlier *latifundia* that roused the indignation of the Gracchi. As compared with the small holdings of olden time, the big capitalist commanded more knowledge, better appliances, and had the most profitable species of seeds and stock at his disposal. But, if we assume that there was an economic gain, such as would nowadays be paraded in statistics shewing a higher average return in proportion to costs of production per acre,—a bold assumption—this is a very different thing from a benefit to the community at large. The gains from tillage and stock-keeping tended to be concentrated in the hands of a few, and to be spent by those few in ways which further corrupted genuine rural industry. When Varro wrote, the economic revolution that set in after the second Punic war had not been seriously stayed by agrarian legislation, and any improvement that may have been achieved in places had been more than annulled by the consequences of civil wars. Varro in effect simply takes things as he finds them: he is willing, practical man, to see fortunes made by rearing peafowl or snails for the gourmands of Rome. This was conscious acquiescence in evil, not a message of hope. When he speaks[1] of Italy as cultivated throughout (*tota*) in a manner superior to the cultivation of any other country, he says what must be taken relatively and judged by the side of his other utterances. Elsewhere[2] he bitterly laments the crowding of people into cities, where the hands that should have tilled and reaped had no better occupation than to applaud the shows, while the corn and wine that Italy could have produced were

---

[1] I 2 §§ 3, 4. Vergil *georg.* II 136—176 is curiously reticent on the subject of actual achievement in Italian agriculture. Mr Fowler, *Social Life* p. 93, takes Varro's remark more literally than I do.

[2] II *praefatio*.

imported wholesale from abroad. Such was not the ideal or the practice of the Romans of old, who knew that a sound agricultural population was the one trusty basis and bulwark of a state. Country life, he says again, is older than town life, for 'god made[1] the country, but man made the town.' Whether this view represents a vital truth in the history of civilization or not, is not our business to inquire. It is enough to point out that the alternative, often delusive, suggested by theorists in modern times, namely that a displaced rustic should find other employment[2] in town life, hardly applied to Italy in the days of Varro. The porter, the policeman, the navvy, the drayman, the scavenger, the unskilled labourer in the building and other trades, stand for occupations that in Rome were either non-existent or mainly if not wholly carried on by slaves. Therefore the degradation resulting from the migration of country folk into cities was more extreme than anything in modern experience. The blight of slavery made impossible any rational solution of labour-problems: all the Empire could do was to organize an unwholesome peace in Rome by permanent endowment of the unemployed. The picture we get of Italy is that of a country sharply divided into arable districts and open wastes of grazing land, with here and there a woodland patch, a country in which it was never very far from an area of high cultivation to the wild uplands where there was no force to maintain order, and where the wolf and the brigand were encountered by private enterprise alone.

1356. Such is the evidence we get from Varro as to the state of Italy. Incidentally he also throws some light on the state of Rome itself. This comes in the setting of the dialogue, which he can hardly have wished to seem unreal. The scene is first laid in a temple[3], on the inner wall of which was painted a map of Italy. At the end of the first book the company breaks up on news of a murder. The assassin had eluded detection in the crowd, and was understood to have stabbed the wrong man by mistake. Alas, such is life, was the reflexion of the party, but what can you expect in Rome? The scene of the second book is not known, owing probably to a lacuna in the text. A summons to a sacrifice[4] threatens to call away some of the party, but the duty is deferred. In the third book an election of aediles is going on, and the company turn to account the delays[5] of the proceedings by conversing in the building (*villa publica*) on the edge of the Campus Martius used by the censors at a census and for other purposes. Their talk is interrupted[6] by the

---

[1] III 1 § 4 *divina natura dedit agros, ars humana aedificavit urbes.*
[2] See § 1397.
[3] I 2 § 1. Temple of *Tellus* in the Subura.
[4] II *praef.* § 6, 8 § 1, 11 § 12.
[5] III 2 §§ 1—5. Cf. Livy IV 22 § 7.
[6] III 5 § 18, 17 § 10.

sound of shouting. It appears that an election-agent had just been caught in the act of slipping forged ballot-tickets into the box. The book ends with a sound of cheering, and compliments to their successful candidate. It is interesting to get a few touches of life in Rome from so matter-of-fact a man as Varro, and to note that they are quite consistent with the pictures of other writers. Among all the fuss and formality that still remained, corruption and anarchy are quietly assumed as normal phenomena in the capital of the civilized world.

Lucretius.

1357. Of the personal history of the poet Lucretius[1] we know practically nothing; for, if we accept the tradition of his madness, it must be only in a limited sense. If his power of sustained argument and sublime treatment of a mighty theme were indeed the outcome of lucid intervals, the fact is astounding. How the tradition arose, we do not know; we do know that many of his contemporaries were fully capable of misunderstanding such a man. That he went out of his mind at the last is quite credible. In his poem the intensity of his temperament and the loftiness of his genius are alike un-mistakeable, and it is evident that he worked under conditions of wear and tear beyond the experience of ordinary writers. His full name[2] is traditionally given as Titus Lucretius Carus, and it has been thought that he was of servile origin, descended from a former slave of some member of the Lucretian house. If this be true, the extremely Roman spirit that breathes in his poem, and his bold strictures on the aims and habits of the Roman society of his day, are all the more remarkable. They fit in far better with the view that he was a Roman of quality, convinced that the times were out of joint, and unable to restrain the expression of his conviction. The generally received dates place the life of Lucretius 96—55 B.C. He would thus be able to remember the end of Marius and the bloody clearances of Sulla. As a young man he had seen the Sullan system overthrown, and the revolution advance another stage; the new forces, wealth in the person of Crassus, military renown in that of Pompey, taking possession of the Roman state. He had witnessed the combination of forces effected by Caesar in 71, and the coalition of the three partners in 60, by which the normal working of the Republic was paralysed. The Sertorian war, the rising of Spartacus, the affair

[1] See Munro's *Introduction*, Sellar's *Roman Poets of the Republic*, Teuffel-Schwabe, *History of Roman Literature* § 203.

[2] The engraved gem supposed to give his portrait is reproduced on the title-page of Munro's edition.

of Catiline, the rise and fall of Lucullus, the various fortunes of Cicero, the doings of Cato and Clodius, to him were contemporary history, and he lived to hear news[1] of Caesar's annexations in Gaul. But Lucretius, living in a time of stir and strain, was so far as we know a mere spectator of public events, deeply concerned for the welfare of his country but taking no part in the jars and conflicts of the age. His work was the poem on the 'nature of things' (the Universe, as we might say,) in six books, which it seems certain had not received the final touches at the time of his death. Tradition[2] says that it was published under the editorship of Cicero, which may be true. It is not likely that Cicero did more than see it through the copying-room (perhaps that of Atticus), or rather employ Tiro to do so. There is no reason to suspect him of improving it, for which let us be thankful. The poem is addressed to one Memmius, apparently the man with whom Catullus was disgusted, and whose public career was more noisy than consistent. But dedications were then in vogue, as we know from Cicero's efforts to wring one out of Varro, and the name of a worthless man was immortalized. Lucretius is mentioned once by Cicero. His only other contemporary recognition is that Nepos refers to him and Catullus as the best poets of the time. Later writers such as Ovid and Statius speak of him in high terms. But the highest of the ancient praises is the profound influence[3] of Lucretius on the poetic development of Vergil.

1358. We have more than once noted the Roman readiness to learn from other peoples. This nowhere appears more clearly than in the region of thought. In borrowing from their Greek masters they were largely guided by their own marked preference for the positive and practical, and the Greek schools most influential at Rome were those whose systems were most directly applicable to conduct of life. Hair-splitting distinctions and hesitation were suited only to few, and those men of wide reading and fluid temperament. To the average Roman of education theory was valuable as leading rather to dogma than to doubt. Thus it was, as we have seen, the Epicurean and Stoic schools that took the strongest hold of society in Rome, appealing to very different types of mind and character. The relations of these two systems respectively to the popular religion were marked by an important difference. The Stoics absorbed all particular divinities into one supreme godhead, called by various

---

[1] The reference to *Brittanni* in VI 1106 can hardly be an echo of Caesar's expedition to Britain in 55.

[2] See Munro's Introduction to Lucr., and Tyrrell's note on Cic. *ad Q. frat.* II 9 (11) § 4. To insert *non* in that passage is abominable. For the reminiscences of Cicero's *Aratea* in the *de rerum natura*, see Munro on V 619.

[3] See Sellar's *Virgil*.

names, who is both matter and force, the substance and efficient cause of all that really exists, coextensive and identical with the universe. This amounted to a patronizing adaptation of the polytheistic theology in the form of pantheism, and involved no open breach with the religious institutions of the state. It simply explained away the multitudinous gods in whose existence and powers educated men, under the influence of Greek scepticism, had ceased to believe. The Epicureans dealt more plainly with the popular pantheon. Scepticism had left nothing but vulgar superstition, and to this superstition, obscurantist and enfeebling, they traced most of the evils that beset human life. The remedy of Epicurus was to concede to the gods an existence in some ethereal heaven, a life of unruffled calm, but to deny them any interest or concern in the affairs of mankind, in short any part or power in the motions of the universe. The one real power was Nature, working by eternal laws, the operation of which was not to be averted or checked by the appeals of sacrifice or prayer. Divine it might be, but to speak of this power as a God in any received sense was unmeaning. The fundamental difference between the two schools from this point of view was that the Stoics embraced the notion of supreme Will, while the Epicureans were content with immutable Law. The logical outcome of the former was a rigid conception of individual duty, favourable to moral dignity, but liable to foster an arrogant intolerant spirit. The latter led rather to a conviction of individual powerlessness, ending in acquiescent submission to the inevitable, which was assuredly productive of unwholesome effects in the weaker natures. The moral systems of both schools were closely connected with their physical theories of the universe. The difference in their attitude towards public life is well illustrated by Cato and Lucretius. Both were profoundly impressed by the degeneration of government and the failure of the Republic, shewn in the rise of individuals to unconstitutional power. Cato threw himself into the strife of politics, and vainly fought to stay the stream of inevitable tendency. Lucretius, no less a fanatic than Cato, no less intensely Roman, set himself to combat evil by an impassioned appeal to reason and the truths of nature as understood by Epicurus. But the chance of guiding Roman society by an appeal to reason, if it had ever existed, was now at least gone by. Of the noisy pugnacity of Cato we have seen enough. Let us see how the genius and zeal of Lucretius approached the momentous questions of the hour.

1359. Pleasure, in the refined sense of Epicurus, was the one unconditional good, rightly and instinctively followed by mankind[1]

11 172 *dux vitae dia voluptas.*

as the motive and rule of conduct.   The highest pleasure is attended by no pain other than a preceding consciousness of want.   The lowest consists in gratifying appetites such that the attendant pain outweighs the pleasure.   It is a fundamental condition of human happiness to avoid whatever tends to disturb our mental repose.   We must therefore follow the guidance of Nature rightly understood, and avoid the creation of artificial cravings.   The real wants of man are very small, and Nature provides satisfaction in abundance.   Inordinate desires, says[1] Lucretius, are the root of all the mischief that good patriots are deploring to-day.   Extravagant luxury and display breed an unhealthy competition, a race for wealth and for the power that secures and increases it.   Jealousy and greed are rampant, all scruples are laid aside in the scramble for preeminence.   The growth of violence soon developes this into a struggle for supremacy, which means civil war with all its horrors.   The most sacred ties of blood and friendship are broken, and mutual confidence destroyed, in an atmosphere of self-seeking and treason.   The prospect of failure leads men to despairing suicide.   And yet, after all the bloodshed and wrong, success brings no real happiness to the victors.   The risen tyrant lives among the perils created by the very process of his own elevation.   A peaceful submission[2] to the force of circumstances is a far surer road to bliss.   Now, where shall we find a cure for these terrible evils?   Surely we cannot wish to see all that has been gained in the past progress of civilization lost by the blindness of human folly.   We must appeal to human reason.   The malady is deep-seated, for the poison has long been at work; but, if men can only be induced to listen, the gospel of Epicurus will afford an antidote.   First and foremost, the baneful influence of superstition[3] must be utterly destroyed.   How can you convert men to rational views when their minds are prepossessed with the absurd delusions of the popular mythology?   These delusions are the inevitable result of the general ignorance of physical laws.   They arise from the misinterpretation of natural phenomena, and to the right understanding of the order of Nature the system of Epicurus alone affords the key.

1360.   Thus the way to repose of mind and rational joy in life lies through a sound and full appreciation of the laws that govern the universe.   This once attained, man will see the necessity of acquiescing in what he can neither alter nor elude, and the acceptance of facts will set him free from his present slavery to idle dreams.   Lucretius therefore expounds to his reader the atomic philosophy

---

[1] See II 7—54, III 59—86, 995—1002, V 1117—9, 1412—35.

[2] V 1120—35.

[3] See I 62—158, and other passages too numerous for reference here.

as developed by Epicurus from the earlier system of Democritus and explains the course of nature according to its principles. The details of this ingenious theory are a part of the history of philosophy. Suffice it to say here that in observation and explanation of natural phenomena it went far, probably as far as human faculties could go before the invention of the telescope microscope and other instruments, and before the development of chemistry and physics opened up more exact methods of experiment. The spirit of the old Atomists was scientific. But for ascertaining facts they had to rely on the very fallible evidence of unaided senses, and misapprehended facts interpreted[1] by guessing however acute inevitably led to erroneous conclusions. Sometimes the error shewed itself in the form of an assumption out of keeping with the principles of the system, an inconsistency which rival schools[2] were not loth to expose. But after all it was perhaps the least arbitrary of the ancient physical theories, and its firm grasp of the idea of Infinity was a majestic feature of the system, rendering it peculiarly fit for poetic treatment. This treatment could only be successfully applied by an enthusiast able and willing to lighten and vivify by his genius and art the somewhat dull and arid discussion of controversial points. Now it was just in this respect that Lucretius rendered signal service to his cause. It was not only from reading that he gathered the earnestness which breathes throughout his poem. His deep convictions were the result of his own observations also, and the warmth with which he presses his convictions on the reader was a powerful and much-needed auxiliary to a philosophic system only too apt to encourage a selfish apathy in its disciples and quench zeal in ordinary citizens. Here at least was an apostle of temperance whose heart burned within him to give utterance to a message which he held to be in the highest sense divine. This message is for men, and he sets himself to draw men's attention by the unsparing exercise of his sympathetic and imaginative powers. Wonder admiration loathing scorn and curiosity are pressed into his service as he expounds the nature of things and the true position of man in the universe. Human affection and the ways of children engage his sympathies, but he has some left for the brute creation; for the cow that vainly seeks her lost calf, for the bitch that fondles her puppies. No Latin writer brings before us so many vivid pictures of things animate and inanimate, homely scenes, sights and sounds of every day, as Lucretius; and he draws his pictures not only from the country side but from the streets of Rome.

1361.   In nature two things alone exist, Atoms and Void. Our

---

[1] Alternative hypotheses were freely admitted in doubtful cases. v 729—30, vi 703—11
[2] See for instance Cic. *de finibus* I §§ 18—20.

senses are our sole means of learning facts. Yet neither atoms nor void are directly perceived by the senses as separate existences. But from the sense of touch, for instance from feeling the wind, we learn that something invisible exists and is in motion. By a process of inference we conclude that this something must be material (else how could we feel it?) and that it is not solid (for how then could it move?). This brings us to the master-conception of solid Atoms moving in a yielding environment, which can only be Void. With our eyes once opened to this truth, we soon see that we have in it the only possible solution of the problem of the universe. Everything that exists is made up of atoms and void. Atoms are themselves in-destructible. They have no such qualities as sense colour etc., but they are of various shapes. From their combinations in and with void are produced the things we see hear feel and so forth. Their quantity is infinite, but their varieties of shape finite. There is no such thing as annihilation, only dissolution, of which death, decay, and the general wastage of things, which we detect in result but not in process, are instances. The atoms released when a body is dissolved do not perish with that body, but pass on to form parts of other combinations. Thus one thing by its death gives birth to other things: life and death are but phases of the same great order of nature, a process to which there can be no end. In this scheme of nature there is no room for any divine interference. The phenomena traditionally supposed to be produced by the action of the gods are, when coolly considered, quite inconsistent with such a supposition. Nor is it respectful to attribute to divine agency the creation of a world in which the intelligent observer can detect such glaring imperfections. The theory of a . make-shift creation through the fortuitous concourse of atoms is open to no such objection. So the Epicurean leaves his unreal gods in undisturbed enjoyment of a meaningless bliss in their calm region of aether. But he has still to find an initiative force to account for the beginning of all things. What first set the atoms in motion? To answer this question he has to assume an independent force, in short a First Cause, and to attribute to atoms a power of diverging from the straight lines[1] in which it is their tendency to fall; for without this power they would never meet and combine. Thus the dismissal of the gods only amounts to this, that the First Cause is not to be called supernatural. Epicurus could not explain the mystery of creation, nor as yet can we. But Lucretius was satisfied with the theory, and called on his

---

[1] We should note that though gravitation to a centre is denied (I 1052—113) and there is no lowest point (*imum* II 90) in the sum of things (which is infinite), yet a downward motion is assumed.

readers to accept it as the basis of belief. What then is the place of man in the order of nature, where life and death are the alternations of a never-ending series, and atoms, however set in motion, wage without ceasing[1] an elemental war?

1362. Man, says Lucretius, is body and soul[2] in union. Body and soul are alike corporeal, alike mortal. Neither can live apart from the other; even as wine or frankincense are inseparable from their respective scents. Old age and disease, swooning-fits and intoxication, affect them both. So death ends them both; their component atoms go to form other units, all portions of the great sum of things; what we call death is merely a stage in a rearrangement that is always going on. If the soul were immortal, surely it would have some memory of its former existence in other bodies, but it has not. Surely it would not view its approaching dissolution with shrinking reluctance, as nevertheless we know it does; it would make no more ado about quitting the body than the snake does about sloughing his skin. What then is there to fear in death? Once dead, we have no existence, and therefore no sensation. The pictures of an after-world with its gruesome punishments are idle myths, the creations of diseased fancy. Man is bound to accept with a good grace what is after all only the common lot awaiting the world in which he lives. Not the All, the universe. The Epicurean comfort offered to atomic Man is that heaven and earth will pass away, but atoms and void will not pass away. Earth indeed, according to Lucretius, is not[3] of vastly ancient origin, and she already shews unmistakeable signs of old age. The spontaneous fertility of her youth is worn out; the crops that she once gave freely are now hardly raised with much toil. Man, feeble Man, whose birth and death are alike scenes[4] of anguish, has no choice but to recognize his own helplessness. His proper course is to enjoy wisely such life as Nature grants him, to follow rational pleasure and avoid painful reaction, to acquiesce peacefully in the order that has made him and will unmake him in due time.

1363. To many minds it would seem that the Epicurean creed offers but a chilly consolation in face of its generally pessimistic view of this present world. Yet it had no small following[5] in Rome. Of the men who came to the front in the last part of this stormy period C. Cassius was a professed Epicurean. His attitude towards public life was evidently very different from that of Lucretius, but it does not appear that in planning the murder of Caesar he was actuated by

---

[1] I 573—4, V 380—95.   [2] The subject of book III.
[3] V 330—1, II 1148—74.   [4] II 576—80, V 222—7.
[5] See Zeller's *Stoics Epicureans and Sceptics*, page 390, Eng. tr., Horace *Sat.* I 5 101—3.

motives of personal ambition. Atticus was in practice an Epicurean, but not a declared adherent of the school: he was probably not satisfied with the theories, and arrived at his practical conclusions by a somewhat different road. But to Lucretius the system of his choice is a gospel that arouses enthusiasm, not merely a theory that requires assent. When he denounces vain superstition, his scorn and sarcasm[1] are worthy of Isaiah exposing the folly of idolatry, or Elijah mocking the prophets of Baal. When he traces the effect of false assumptions in the perverted aims of men, the misguided lives of ambition luxury and morbid restlessness, he catches the lofty tone of an inspired preacher and breaks into a sublime appeal, perhaps the finest passage[2] of Roman literature. But of all his powerful utterances none is more striking, or more significant of the author as the observant critic of a disordered age, than his review[3] of the love-passion. Led in the course of his argument to discuss the physical facts of generation that underlay this subject, he was impelled to go further and deal directly with what from his point of view was a grave social evil. The tradition of Roman society in regard to sexual relations had been a simple one. Marriage with a view to offspring was the ideal, fairly well realized on the whole, but less fully since the invasion of Greek influences. Into the special temptations presented by slave-owning we need not enter. It was not in this direction that our poet found the material for censure. His anathema fell on love of the new style, an all-absorbing passion bearing no relation to marriage, or even discouraging family ties. In an age that produced Clodia and Catullus, not to mention others, Lucretius probably found plenty of actual examples to authenticate his picture of the fashionable craze for wild amours. We need not dwell on it further here than to indicate the gist of his objection to the passion. It is that it destroys all chance of leading a rational and dignified life. Indulgence only confirms its power, until a man becomes a perfect slave to it. He is the victim of delusions, the absurdity of which, set out by the poet with satirical force, is apparent to every onlooker. He is tortured by the absence or indifference of a charmer whose charms are in most cases the mere creations of his own imagination. He obeys her every whim, and (this is a very Roman touch) he squanders on her the fortune earned by his thrifty ancestors. His duties are all neglected, and people look upon him as a man gone wrong. Such is the love-sick man[4] (*miser*), to whom for all his sacrifices no peace or satisfaction ever come. The pleasure he pursues

---

[1] See in particular v 1194—1217, vi 378—422.
[2] iii 830—1094.   [3] In book iv.
[4] Compare the use of *perire*=to be in love, Catull. xlv 5 etc.

is one grievously alloyed with pains; he knows no more repose[1] than Tityos in the myth, torn by vultures. Whatever true enjoyment there is in love falls rather to the man who keeps his head (*sanus*), and does not become its slave. Even a plain woman may be an amiable companion for life, and habit insensibly breeds affection, as dropping water wears away the stone.

1364. Such in brief outline is the teaching of Lucretius when he sets himself to apply Epicurean principles for the benefit of Roman society, to lead men to pursue happiness by attaining repose of mind. That he had before him more or less clearly and consciously cases supplied by the careers of contemporaries, is no very daring guess. But he does not spoil his types by turning them into portraits. Touches here and there may be found that would fit the cases of many of those who played noteworthy parts in the revolutionary age. But this is all. He is too much of a Roman satirist not to have a leaning to the concrete, too much of a philosopher not to analyse and combine the personal traits into the typical. It was not that men of his time feared to indulge in personalities; the necessity for such caution was not yet come. But numberless remarks betray the position of Lucretius as 'taking notes' among the social turmoil of the day. Thus in tracing the progress of civilization and origin of law he points out that violence is made to recoil[2] on those who employ it, and the wild fury of anger checked by the salutary restraint of fear. When commenting on the uses of adversity in removing the mask of pretence and exposing the real man, he illustrates[3] his text by the case of banishment, and with a few bold strokes depicts the exile in a foreign land turning despairingly to the gods for aid, in a state of utter moral collapse. He is not blind (in such an age he could not be) to àll the pomp and circumstance of war, but the carnage of battles, the sufferings and horrors, make deeper impression on his mind. He sees too how weak and vain after all are these pompous exhibitions of human power when brought face to face with the irresistible forces of Nature. One of his most contemptuous passages[4] is that in which he shews us the great commander with his legions and elephants on board ship, caught in a storm, imploring the mercy of heaven in abject panic, and often ending in disaster none the less for all his prayers. That he expresses[5] a longing for wars to be brought to an end is fully consistent with his general principles, but in this aspiration he was probably not peculiar. Before Lucretius died, numbers of men were doubtless longing for a period of profound

---

[1] III 992—4.   [2] V 1152—5.
[3] III 48—54.   [4] V 1226—35.
[5] I 29, 30. Compare V 999, 1000, II 40—53.

peace; vainly, for no party was as yet prepared to give way, and jarring ambitions had to run their course. He complains bitterly that it was hard to stick to the business in hand[1] (*hoc agere*), to perform his task of expounding the nature of things for men's enlightenment, in a time of such distraction. His scornful reference[2] to the power of wealth may seem a commonplace of satirists of every age, but it is surely none the less sincere. And when he speaks of the extravagant splendours of the theatre, the orator bawling himself hoarse, the bodily and mental signs of drunkenness, the deceptive arts of ladies' toilet, and so forth, he is drawing from life. In discussing the specific characteristics of animals, he is led to consider the various characters of men, and to remark[3] the very slight degree in which they can be modified by education. Of the refractory persistence of inherited characteristics the Rome of Lucretius would doubtless supply numberless examples When treating[4] of sexual incompatibility, he is speaking of what he must have known to be made a ground of divorce, and indeed this is the solution suggested by the context.

1365. We are regarding Lucretius as a man of his time, as an observer and critic of Roman life in the last days of the Republic. Space fails me to record his numerous references to trades and professions, to machines and tools, to the traffic of the streets, and other matters of daily life. Nothing comes amiss to him for illustration of his theme. Nor can we dwell on the consciousness of his duty as a poet[5] to make the dry truths of philosophy palatable to readers by investing his message with the Muses' charm. To reach the lazy unphilosophic mind he even allows himself the conventional use of mythological language. These vanities are a concession to popular prejudice. For himself, though filled with joy in his task, and inspired by the pride of a pioneer, he bows before the majestic discoveries[6] of Epicurus with reverential awe. Cicero's great series of works interpreting Greek philosophy in Latin prose had not yet appeared, and Lucretius had painful misgivings[7] as to the possibility of conveying abstract thought in his native tongue. But the poems of early Greek thinkers, Empedocles Parmenides and Xenophanes, supplied a stimulus and a model. For Latin verse composition of the kind he had some sort of precedent[8] in Ennius, who had handled some difficult topics, such as the transmigration of souls. So Lucretius

---

[1] I 41. Compare 142—5, IV 969—70.

[2] v 1113—6, 1273—5.   [3] III 307—15.

[4] IV 1248—56.   [5] See in particular I 921—50.

[6] III 28—30. In v 8 he calls him a god.

[7] I 136—45, III 260.

[8] I 117—26. The poets of the new school despised Ennius.

did his best. It was evidently no easy matter to render abstruse
Greek speculations in a Latin diction which, though pure classical
and strong, was more archaic than that of the best contemporary
literature. His success as a poet under such conditions was an extraordinary feat. What bore him along was his enthusiasm and his
deep love of nature. His touch is never so firm and true, his flashes
of light never so vivid as when he refers to the natural phenomena
on which he had pondered. Learning from books he had in plenty,
and like Varro he refers freely to the flora and fauna of foreign lands,
the strange things that need explanation, wonderful springs and
mephitic caverns ; nor does he forget those old puzzles, the periodic
trade-winds of the eastern Mediterranean and the problem of the
Nile. But we get our clearest notion of the living Lucretius when
we find him discussing the fallacies of vision, perspective effects,
reflexions in mirrors, echoes, the sea-water made brackish by filtering
through sand, the dampness that comes from sea-air to cloths hung
out to dry, hurricanes, clouds, the rainbow, thunder and lightning
(two sorts), heat and cold, frost and thaw, the ways of liquid and
viscous fluids, smoke, sparks, exhalations, the causes of sweetness
sourness roughness smoothness heaviness lightness and qualities
generally. It is not that he explains the phenomena rightly, but
that he is so thoroughly at home with them. The above topics are
selected from a much larger number that could be named : the man
must have been ever on the watch, asking himself questions. Appeals
to experience occur all through the poem. He has observed the blind
man's sensitive touch, the persistence of a ruling passion in a sleeper's
dreams, the various digestive and nutritive affinities, often so marked
that what is one animal's meat is another's poison. Observations
such as these and many more are surely not the mere fruits of reading worked into his argument with a view to effect. Lucretius,
however mistaken in his explanations, is always a genuine recorder
of things as he saw them. That he sometimes repeats an absurd
story[1] in good faith is no wonder in the then state of knowledge.
That he spoke in vain to the men of his own time is merely another
of the many ironies that meet us in the story of the later Republic.
A few years after he had dismissed the gods to insignificance, Caesar
was added to their number, Augustus was building new temples, and
reviving the observances of religion on a magnificent scale. A new
generation of poets, among them men of real genius, were hailing
this revival as the return of a golden age, and preaching piety to
order. But in modern times the influences that stood in the way
of Lucretius have died away and the great Roman poet has come

[1] See IV 710—21.

to his own.   In the story of republican Rome there are many elements
of tragedy not to be ignored by those to whom human interest is
worth a thought.   Pathetic indeed is the situation of the man who,
distressed beyond measure at the evil plight of his country, still found
his deepest feelings stirred by the beauties of nature, the bloom of
flowers, the song of birds, the majesty of sea and stars, the stillness
of night and the freshness of the early morning.

Catullus.

1366.   It is fortunate that we have preserved to us the collection
of 116 occasional poems known as the Book[1] of C. Valerius Catullus.
Otherwise we should have to depend on Cicero Lucretius and Varro
almost entirely for contemporary notes on the gay life of Roman
society.   None of these three is quite a satisfactory witness.   Cicero's
apology for early dissipation in his speech for M. Caelius stands out
as giving somewhat of the current morality of the 'fast' youth of
Rome.   The utterances of political party-spirit, invective, or satire,
must be received with caution.   But in Catullus the young Man-
about-Town speaks for himself, and that plainly.   Catullus was born
at Verona of a family, Roman no doubt, established in that town and
possessed of considerable means.   His father was on terms of friendship with Caesar.   The Transpadane part of Cisalpine Gaul was one
of the most prosperous districts of what was virtually Italy.   It was
thoroughly[2] Roman, though the population generally had not yet
received the franchise.   Vergil (born 70 B.C.) was a native of the same
district, which produced many men of talent.   Among the literary
men was Cornelius Nepos the contemporary and friend of Catullus.
Catullus lived about 87—54 B.C.   Rome was the centre to which all
young men of wit and spirit were drawn, and to Rome Catullus went,
when perhaps about 17 years of age.   We can well believe that he
was an attractive youth, and he was evidently not socially cramped
for want of money.   He soon found his way in the gay world, and
the fashionable diversion of love-making landed him in the toils of
an overpowering passion.   The Lesbia of Catullus was almost certainly
none other than the fascinating Clodia, the notorious sister of Cicero's
enemy P. Clodius.   She was older than Catullus, and now at the
height of her charms.   An extreme type of the 'emancipated' woman
of the day, she scorned a dull husband (Q. Caecilius Metellus Celer,

---

[1] Probably he did not write much more.   We hear of a love-incantation, Pliny *NH.*
xxviii § 19.

[2] The Latin spoken there was of course not quite up to Roman standards.   See Cic.
Brutus §§ 171—2.   A favourite word of Catullus is *basia* (kisses) said to be of Gaulish
origin.

consul in 60), and kept a number of other men dangling after her, among them the brilliant and unprincipled[1] M. Caelius Rufus, of whom we have often spoken above. In 59 Metellus died, and rumour charged Clodia with having poisoned him. The widow, wealthy, witty, versed in all modern accomplishments, in particular a finished dancer of the new style, now lived a dissolute life in open defiance of the proprieties. It was a fatal devotion to this woman that was the ruin of Catullus. To her he was but a charming youth, whose talent she was well able to appreciate, and whom she was very willing to enrol among her wanton followers. To his warm-hearted warm-blooded temperament such a thing as a half-passion was impossible. For years he was her slave, and went through the trying experiences of the *miser* or victim of love, elated by occasional favours, tormented by jealousy, or driven to despair by indifference and disdain. He did not overcome his infatuation till shortly before his death. But, though his life was disordered by his attachment to a worthless woman, he had room for other feelings. The loss of a much-loved brother, who died far away[2] in the Troad, plunged him into the deepest grief. Some years after (in 57), Memmius, whose acquaintance he had made, was governor of Bithynia, and Catullus accompanied him as one of his staff (*cohors*). Young Romans of quality were in the habit of accepting such appointments with the object of seeing a little life in the provinces, with no clearly-defined duties and a good chance of picking up a few crumbs for themselves. This last consideration probably appealed to Catullus, who had been extravagant like others. In any case he was by this time weary of a life of idle dissipation. But he had not forgotten his brother, and took the opportunity of visiting his grave. Memmius however disappointed any hopes he may have had of enriching himself in Bithynia. The province, never very opulent, had suffered much from wars and governors, and Catullus was indignant[3] that the present propraetor kept what pickings there were to himself, and neglected the interests of his suite. Whatever may be the truth of this accusation, it is certain that Catullus quarrelled with Memmius and immortalized his disgust in lines of exemplary coarseness. In 56 he broke away from the connexion. He did not however return to Italy direct, but went on a cruise[4] in a yacht among the cities and islands of the Aegean. Thence he came home to his native Verona and to his villa on the peninsula of Sirmio jutting out into lake Benacus, a beautiful spot of which he was very fond, but which he soon left for Rome. There he was among friends once more, but things had changed for the

---

[1] See Tyrrell and Purser vol. III Introduction.   [2] LXV, LXVIII 19—26, CI.
[3] X, XXVIII.   [4] XLVI, IV.

worse. Lesbia was more shamelessly profligate than ever. All hopes of a requited passion were over, but the poor attempts of Catullus to shew indifference in scandalous verses do not serve to conceal his pain. Moreover public affairs were not going as Catullus wished. His connexion lay in fashionable circles, and the bulk of the upper classes were uneasy under the usurpation of the so-called First Triumvirate. The skill of Caesar had lately revived the failing coalition, and the conference of Luca was weighing on the minds of men whose interests were bound up with the maintenance of the Republic. Catullus would seem to have detected that the real danger to the old constitution lay in Caesar, especially in Caesar's influence on Pompey. Accordingly we find him no longer concerned solely with the loves and hates of a gay private life. Among the lampoons of his last years one of the most notable[1] is his attack on Caesar and Pompey. Indignation at the enrichment of Caesar's satellite Mamurra furnished the occasion for a poem characteristically vehement and gross enough to attract considerable attention. Was it to glut the greed of a disreputable spendthrift that Caesar and Pompey had usurped power? Was the gold of Gaul and Britain to be put to such infamous uses? Caesar was of course the real object of attack. But somehow a reconciliation was brought about; it was not Caesar's way to quarrel, and he probably knew better than to take the poet very seriously. Catullus soon after produced a remarkable ode[2] in which he referred admiringly to the achievements of Caesar in the far North-West.

1367. In the political differences of the time it is clear that the sympathies of the poet were with the republicans. But it is as illustrating the tone of the upper circles of Roman society in the relations of private life that we get most light from Catullus. We must not suppose that all were as dissolute and vicious as the grossness of his language might at first sight lead us to believe. But things were very bad, and the coarse names and foul imputations in which he freely indulges are a sign of the times. Catullus was far too clever to write as he wrote, had the abominations to which he refers been incredible or even very rare. Mere dull pointless abuse was not in his vein. But his words are surely not always to be taken in a literal sense. To what lengths even public utterances could go we know from the speeches of Cicero, and fragments of other orators shew that Cicero was no exception. Poets outdid the orators in indecent frankness. A good instance[3] is C. Licinius Calvus, the great friend

---

[1] XXIX. Compare LII, LIV, LVII, XCIII, CXIV, CXV.
[2] XI.
[3] See index to Quintilian, and commentators on Horace *Sat.* I 10 19.

of Catullus, and often coupled with him.   His few fragments[1] shew
that he wrote in much the same style, and with the same freedom.
He was also an orator, and his speech in prosecution of Vatinius was
doubtless a good specimen[2] of the plain speaking practised in the
Roman courts.   The right to say anything of anybody without too
close a regard for facts was a cherished prerogative of Roman citizens.
It was carried to monstrous lengths in the revolutionary age, and the
speakers and writers of the Empire, galled by their own limitations,
looked back with regret[3] and sighed for the unbridled bluntness of
republican times.

1368.   But the social pictures of Catullus are not confined to the
harlotry and unsavoury vices of Rome.   The minor social crimes and
misdemeanours are often assailed with bitter sarcasm.   We hear of a
guest who stole a valuable napkin or doyly[4] from the dinner-table,
and other thefts of the same kind, such as those of the pilferers who
loitered about the baths and stole the property of bathers.   The man
who grins to shew his white teeth[5] is warned to give over advertising
the filthy means by which that whiteness is notoriously procured.
The man who says *chommoda* for *commoda*[6] and so on is ridiculed
for his misuse of aspirates.   Above all, the plague of bad writers[7]
stirs the poet's wrath.   The men who invite you to dinner in order
to inflict on you[8] their wretched compositions are in particular a social
pest.   But, while he gives us a sort of Dunciad in detachments by
his references to these literary pretenders, he speaks in warm terms[9]
of the works of his own friends.   As all are lost, we can form no
opinion as to the fairness of his judgments.   In one case at least his
condemnation is supported[10] by the criticism of Cicero.   Among the
men of letters to whom he addressed poems[11] are Hortensius and
Cicero, but his intimate friends were mostly younger and less eminent
men.   Some at least of these were like himself natives of the Cisalpine.
He was very fond of his own district, as we see from various pieces,
particularly the famous lines in which[12] he hailed the lovely and restful
Sirmio on his return from the East.   He refers to the gossip and
scandals of municipal[13] life.   One of his best poems sets forth the
folly of a townsman of Verona who neglected to keep an eye on the

---

[1] Baehrens' *fragmenta poetarum Latinorum* pp. 320—2.
[2] LIII, XIV.   For Calvus as orator see Sandys' Introd. to Cicero's *Orator* pp. xlvi, xlvii.
[3] See Mayor on Juvenal I, especially 151—4.
[4] XII, XXV, XXXIII.   [5] XXXIX, XXXVII 20.
[6] LXXXIV, Quintilian I 5 § 20.   [7] XIV, XXII, XXXVI, XCV, CV.
[8] XXII, XLIV.   [9] I, XXXV, L, XCV.
[10] See Tyrrell and Purser on Cic. *ad Att.* VII 17 § 2.
[11] LXV, XLIX.   [12] XXXI.
[13] C, XVII.

diversions of his young and skittish wife. Evidently the well-to-do society of Cisalpine towns was following the lead of the naughty world of Rome. But in Verona Catullus not only missed his literary circle. At Rome he had his own books[1] around him, and access to other libraries. He was a great reader, and profoundly influenced by the Greek poets. We have one or two specimens of his direct translations[2] from the Greek, probably the work of his earlier years. Other pieces are certainly imitations or echoes[3] of Greek originals, though by no means copies. Like many of his contemporaries, he seems at first to have admired the learned poetry[4] of the Alexandrian school. While still under this influence he produced[5] his *Peleus and Thetis*, a poem in about 400 hexameter lines, his longest work. It contains echoes of Homer, but it is really a miniature Epic on the model of Alexandria. But he was too bright a being to confine himself to such artificial literary food. His true affinities were with the early Greek lyric poets, who wrote from the heart, and whose loves and personal hatreds were congenial to his own feelings. It was the stimulus got from these writers that helped Catullus to find his proper vocation. Short pieces, in which the impulse of the moment is pointedly and warmly expressed, are the field in which his fresh and fitful genius displays itself most happily. The latter-day poets of the Republic produced short pieces to suit the taste of gay society, which could enjoy wit but was easily bored. Of this new school Catullus was the most brilliant representative. His love of variety shewed itself in the number of different Greek metres to which he boldly adapted the less pliable Latin tongue. Some of these were forms of peculiar delicacy, and the success of his experiments is one of the most striking phenomena of Roman literature. Horace Statius Petronius Martial and others might afterwards by restrictive polishing give to some of these metres a finish outwardly more in keeping with the character of the language, but their work could never be so fresh and their style so vigorous as that of their republican forerunner. The metre in which Catullus moves least gracefully is the hexameter. Transplanted by Ennius, ennobled by Lucretius, this measure still awaited the deft harmonies of Vergil. Yet Vergil's occasional echoes of the *Peleus and Thetis* prove that he found in that poem something to admire.

1369. It is as the mouthpiece of love and hate, friendship and

---

[1] LXVIII 33—40. [2] LI, LXVI.

[3] Such as XXXIV (hymn to Diana), LXIII (*Attis*).

[4] For imitators of the Alexandrians, Callimachus, Euphorion etc., see Cicero *Tusc.* III § 45, where he calls them *cantores Euphorionis*, Baehrens' *fragm.* pp. 317—30.

[5] LXIV. See Cicero *ad Att.* VII 2 § 1, and Sandys on Cic. *Orator* § 161.

disillusionment[1], joy and disgust, that Catullus appeals to the reader. No other Roman poet is so natural, so unreservedly human. In an age of seething passions he blurts out anything—anything. Out it comes, in language forcible and idiomatic, but often not fashioned on the strictest grammatical models. Some of his most vivid passages gain not a little from the use of phrases and constructions belonging rather to conversational[2] Latin than to the correct literary dialect as developed by Cicero and Caesar. But this informality does not impair his elegance. He excels in pretty trifles[3], such as the lines to Lesbia's pet sparrow and on its death, those on his yacht, and a sportive invitation to a friend. But he is most at home in an atmosphere of mutual passion[4], endless kisses, and so forth. His epigrams too, though somewhat rough, are often pointed and strong. In some of them his grossness reaches its utmost limits, but he always gives the impression that he wrote filthily just because he had something to say which unhappily chanced to be filthy. He did not revel in obscenity as if it were the soul of wit. Much has rightly been forgiven to one who recklessly exposed his own weakness. Many of those among whom he lived no doubt shared his failings and did worse than he. After all, he was a man, though not exactly a good one, and Roman society in the last days of the Republic was of a manlier and less degenerate type than in the quieter times to come.

Nepos.

1370. Of Cornelius Nepos, the friend of his fellow Transpadane Catullus and of Cicero, little need be said here. He was a voluminous writer, but all that concerns us is the fact of his addiction to biography. We may regard him as a representative of the highly-respectable element in Roman literature, though he too wrote amatory poems in his lighter moments. As a moralist he shared the common Roman preference of the concrete to the abstract. In his hands history became very decidedly biographical, and examples rather than precepts the apparatus of enlightenment. He did not confine himself to Roman history, but drew freely from the traditions of Greek and other foreign worthies. These he placed in comparison with those of eminent Romans. His use of authorities was defective and his style and treatment not faultless. We have in his remains only second-rate work from a second-rate man. He was a good deal influenced by Varro, but in no sense a rival. His most important

---

[1] LVIII.   [2] X, XII, XVII, will illustrate this.
[3] II, III, IV, XIII.
[4] Such as V, VII, XLV (Acme and Septimius), LXI (epithalamium).

surviving work[1] is his Life of Atticus, in which he writes from his own knowledge. Atticus (born 109, died 32 B.C.) was ten years or more the senior of Nepos, who survived him. The fault of this biography is that the author's uncritical admiration makes it a mere panegyric. What was in fact a lifelong policy of 'hedging' to secure his own safety in an age of fierce party-struggles, appears to Nepos not only consummate prudence but consummate virtue. We can hardly accept the portrait as faithful to life, but the work contains many interesting details which there is no reason to doubt, some of which throw light on the inner history of the period. He was immensely proud of his long intimacy with the prince of neutrals, and seems to have held much the same position in politics, that of a man who preferred the Republic but would incur no danger for its sake. In Quintilian's list of Roman writers the name of Nepos does not appear.

Pollio.

1371. The writings of C. Asinius Pollio[2] (76 B.C.—5 A.D.) were mostly composed after the fall of the Republic. But his history of the civil war was important as dealing with great events in which as a young man he had borne a part. The Asinii came from the Marrucinian country, and were a family of considerable repute. Of his public career we have often had occasion to speak. He was one of the most remarkable figures of the period of transition. In his boyhood known to Catullus, who seems to have detected his talents, and a correspondent of Cicero in his riper years, he lived to be a patron of Vergil and Horace, and to have no small influence on the literary fashions of the Empire. His poems are lost. As an orator he was eminent, but the cramping effect of the fall of the Republic was soon felt in this department, and it was as a critic and historian, and as a promoter of learning and art, that he was most distinguished in his later years. When Caesar's project for public libraries was resumed under Octavian, it was Pollio[3] by whom the first of them was founded. It was he also who first started the practice of inviting friends to come and hear him read[4] aloud portions of his works. From this grew the recitations[5] to large mixed audiences, which became a social nuisance in Rome, but in the absence of political interests served to provide some occupation for idle minds. As a

---

[1] First published in the lifetime of Atticus. Chapters 19—22 were added later.
[2] Included here, though his works are lost, because of his special importance.
[3] Pliny *NH.* VII § 115, XXXV § 10.   [4] Seneca *controv.* IV *praef.* § 2.
[5] See Mayor's Juvenal, index ' *recitations.*'

critic he was severe and not always fair. He found fault[1] with Sallust, in particular for the use of obsolete words and over-bold metaphors: but it seems that he was himself guilty of archaism. He was a leader of the reaction[2] against the style of Cicero. His own is described as dry hard and unpleasing. His unsympathetic nature comes out in his judgments of Cicero, whom in a published speech he represented as having begged his life from Antony and being prepared to disown and burn his Philippics. This malignity towards the dead he did not repeat in his history, but in summing up his judgment admitted Cicero's greatness in grudging terms, hardly to be called praise. This seems to have been his normal attitude, the detection of flaws rather than the generous recognition of merits. The elder Seneca cites many instances of his criticisms of the rhetoricians of the day, nearly all unfavourable: and Suetonius[3] records his censure of Caesar's Commentaries as careless and inaccurate. But he does not appear to have charged his old master with deliberate perversion of truth in his own interest, and on the part of a sour critic like Pollio the omission may pass for something on Caesar's side. Pollio's reputation as a historian is on the whole good. He was at all events not a violently partisan writer. He gave a moderate figure for the Pompeian losses at Pharsalus, and he spoke well of Brutus and Cassius. That his impartiality was closely connected with jealousy may be fairly guessed from the story[4] that, when a reciting poet referred to the loss of Cicero as the death-blow of Roman oratory, Pollio took it as a personal slight, and left the room in a huff. The available evidence seems on the whole to justify the general conclusion that he was a painstaking and critical writer who aimed at impartiality, but that his opinions were often biassed by strong personal feelings sometimes amounting to downright perversity

Sallust.

1372. We have several times had occasion to speak of C. Sallustius Crispus (86—35 B.C.). We have seen him expelled from the Senate by the censors in 50, and noted his services to Caesar in the civil war, his government of the 'new African' province in Numidia, and his extortions there. Like many of Caesar's men,

---

[1] Suetonius *de grammaticis* § 10. It was he that detected *Patavinitas* in Livy's style, Quintil. 1 5 § 56, VIII 1 § 3.

[2] See H. Peter's fragm. *Histor. Rom.* pp. 262—5, and index to Kiessling's edition of the elder Seneca.

[3] Suet. *Jul.* 56.

[4] Seneca *suasor* VI §§ 26, 27. It is interesting to note that there were poets who ventured to praise Cicero even in the time of Augustus. But these were not the men standing high in Imperial favour. See above § 1327.

he had lived a scandalous life, and regained his position through Caesar's favour. After Caesar's death he seems to have retired from public life. He was now very wealthy, and his house with its splendid grounds[1] was one of the sights of Rome. Like Varro, he came from the Sabine country; his birthplace was Amiternum. In his retirement he found occupation as a writer of Roman history, treated in episodes[2] or compartments—first the story of the Catilinarian conspiracy, then that of the Jugurthine war, and lastly a larger work, his '*Historiae.*' Of this last work, which nominally began with the year 78, but contained also matters previous to Sulla's death, we have only[3] fragments; he appears not to have carried it down later than the year 67. Sallust is interesting to us on two grounds. With him begins the series of Roman historians to whom the form and principles of their composition were as important as the accuracy of their narrative, and much more important than research. He went to Greek literature for his models, and was more particularly the follower and would-be rival of Thucydides. Accordingly his works were remarkable for dramatic qualities. He took immense pains with the speeches put into the mouths of his various characters in various circumstances, striving to give to each speaker sentiments appropriate to the occasion and the man. This method of developing the action of the piece is closely connected with the frequent and often acute analysis of motives, with pithy reflexions on the present and past, and maxims of general application. In short, Sallust posed as a historical moralist, and later writers did not omit to point out that his own career had hardly entitled him to come forward as a severe critic of others. It is true that in this respect he only did what others[4] had done. But a considerable license may be allowed to orators and poets. Even with the loose Roman notions on the subject of history, in which moralizing and partisanship played a leading part, the professed historian could hardly be judged by quite so lenient a standard. We must not be misled by Sallust's protestations of perfect impartiality, though it may be admitted that he did not confine himself to stating a case for the side to which he leant. This however is perhaps mainly the effect of art. For instance, in representing the movement of Catiline as the outcome of causes long operative, in recognizing the degeneracy of its supporters, the services of Cicero, the bold severity of Cato, he puts himself in a better position for

[1] The famous *horti Sallustiani* on the rising ground north of the Quirinal hill, outside the city wall, afterwards owned by the Emperors. See Tacitus *ann.* XIII 47, *hist.* III 82.

[2] *Catil.* 4 § 2 *carptim.*

[3] Edited by Maurenbrecher (Leipsic 1891) so as to bring out their importance.

[4] He himself noted the inconsistency of Sulla in posing as a legislative reformer of morals. See *hist. fragm.* I 61 M.

laying stress on the cool moderation of Caesar and for exonerating him from complicity in the conspiracy. So too in the *Jugurtha*; by duly appreciating the merits of Metellus[1] he leaves himself free to do full justice to Marius. But that he was really without bias cannot fairly be maintained. The worthlessness of the republican nobles, and the degradation of Roman government in their hands, are his essential preoccupation, and it is this that gives vital unity to his writings. Among his luxurious surroundings, Sallust, a true child of his age, bemoaned its degeneracy, and looked back with regret (perhaps not wholly affected) on the past glories of Rome. To him, as to other observers, the displacement of the small farmers[2] and the decay of agriculture over a large part of Italy were public calamities, and he laid most of the blame on the greed and corruption of the rich It was quite in harmony with the character of his views that he expressed them in a deliberately archaic style. Both his sentences and his vocabulary bear witness to his imitation of earlier writers such as Sisenna and the elder Cato. The developed periods of Cicero and Caesar present a striking contrast to the 'Sallustian brevity' noticed by Quintilian. Both as historian and as stylist Sallust has been very variously judged by various critics from his own time till now. As an authority we must admit that he is not faultless. His chronology is often obscure, at times certainly wrong. But to say this is not to say that his views of what was to him the recent past are erroneous. Our judgment of them must depend on the side we take in relation to the great issues of the revolutionary age, and it is best to say so plainly. For my part, though I have no leaning to Caesarism on its merits, the organized anarchy and corruption of senatorial government in its latter days seems worse than the new monarchy to which the efforts of the 'popular' agitators, good or bad, inevitably led. To admire the courage and resolution of those who laid down their lives in defence of the republican system, preferring it with all its faults to the rule of an autocrat, is not enough to justify us in approving a bad cause. Nor should we be too eager to discredit the utterances of the winning side because we find it largely backed by men of bad character and selfish aims. Making allowance for the impossibility of discussing recent times[3] with perfect freedom from bias, I believe the narratives of Sallust, where he is not concerned to defend Caesar, to be on the whole fair and true. The most striking instance of candour is his confession of contempt for agriculture[4] and

---

[1] Also of Sulla. See Summers' Introd. to Sall. *Jug.* pp. xv, xvi.

[2] *Catil.* 11 § 4, *Jug.* 41 § 8, *hist. fragm.* I 11, 12.

[3] For his *Catiline* see above § 762.

[4] *Catil.* 4 § 1 *non fuit consilium socordia atque desidia bonum otium conterere, neque vero agrum colundo aut venando servilibus officiis intentum aetatem agere.*

rural life. Well aware as he was that the decline of agriculture and the decline of the commonwealth were closely connected, he has no hesitation in announcing that he does not mean to waste his retirement on such mean pursuits. He had given up politics for history. But it is clear that to him, as to Catullus and others, the centre of the world was Rome.

Jurisprudence.

1373. Intellectual activity in all departments was characteristic of the revolutionary age, and among political disorders and general unrest no subject was more steadily pursued than Law. This was of course the Roman civil law, for the 'public' or criminal courts, in which the leading orators found a suitable field for the display of their talents, were chiefly concerned with questions of fact. The old civil law as laid down in the crude and general language of the Twelve Tables had in course of time been supplemented and modified in various ways, as has been pointed out on occasion above. Something had been done by legislation[1], but far more by interpretation. The latter process, at first conducted by the pontiffs, had gradually led to the rise of a class of professional jurists not necessarily members of the pontifical college, though the old connexion between the two was by no means severed. To devise the means by which old and ill-defined legal principles could be so extended as to cover new cases, and rightful claims no longer thwarted by verbal quibbles, was the great work of the jurists, and on the whole a steady advance had been made. But the opinions and inventions of these private specialists could only derive force and validity from official sanction. If the city-praetor announced in his yearly Edict that he would adopt a particular suggestion, and extend the application of some legal remedy to cases to which it had heretofore not been deemed to apply (as by modifying the wording of a formula to state an issue differently) the change held good for his year of office. If then his successors adopted the change, in a few years it became a part of the legal system, with all the force of precedent at its back. In this way the views of great jurists gradually became operative. But it was also possible to cite the opinion of an eminent lawyer on the points of law involved in a particular case, and to produce him in court as an expert in support of a contention. And a praetor, himself generally no authority on technical points, could hardly help being influenced by a preponderance of specialist opinion on one side or the other. Then

---

[1] For instance see index to Greenidge's *Legal Procedure* under *lex Aquilia, Furia, Publilia, Calpurnia, Pinaria, Silia, Plaetoria*, etc., and §§ 634, 649, 651, 1220, above.

the particular form in which he finally referred the case to a *iudex*[1]
for decision on the points of fact would, if it contained any novelty,
create a precedent to which future litigants might refer.   And so bit
by bit grew up the complicated system existing in the time of Cicero.
Moreover praetors were in the habit of fortifying themselves with the
advice of chosen assessors, who sat by the magistrate on his *tribunal*.
They were said to be *in consilio*; the employment of a *consilium* was
a regular feature of Roman life, public or private, even in family
affairs.   Thus the amount of expert assistance available in the civil
courts was very large.   The *iuris consultus* was in a position to lay
many people under obligations.   The profession was an honourable
one, but it was only a form of private enterprise.   There was as yet
no state-recognition of qualified individuals, and no scale of fees.
Presents there doubtless were, but the effective remuneration consisted
in the popularity gained, by which the attainment of high office was
made easy.   Among the intellectual occupations of Romans none
was so beneficial in promoting a high moral standard as the study
of Law.   Of the many Greek influences at work in the Rome of the
later Republic, some very bad, the most elevating was Stoicism.   It
appealed to the stronger and nobler characters, and tended to develope
Roman hardness on its better side; in some cases[2] too much so.
With the mental attitude of the lawyer its formal logic and positive
ethics gave it a special affinity.   Hence most of the great lawyers
became adherents of the Stoic school.   And the minds of such men,
ever engaged in problems of right and wrong, ever brought face to
face with the difficulty of reconciling the spirit and letter of the law,
could not help tending on the whole towards equitable[3] improvement.
But the lawyer-Stoics not only did good service as legal reformers.
Stoic principles enjoined the mastery of all disturbing passions, and
we cannot doubt that their influence on men of high standing promoted a just and impartial administration.   Not only in the courts
of law, but wherever[4] that influence could make itself felt.   It was
not for nothing that the brightest spot in provincial government
under the Republic was the administration of Asia by Scaevola and

---

[1] I have not thought it necessary to encumber this brief sketch with details such as the
reference of certain cases to *recuperatores*, or the court of the *centumviri*.   The former have
been spoken of above (see index), the chief authority for the latter under the Republic is
Cic. *de orat.* I §§ 173—80.

[2] Such as the younger Cato and his friend Favonius.

[3] See Maine's *Ancient Law* c. III on the growth of Roman Equity.   The gradual recognition of rules prevailing among all peoples (*ius gentium*), and their incorporation in the
Roman legal system, no doubt began in the edicts of *praetores peregrini*.   The views of
philosophers supplied a later stimulus.

[4] And therefore seldom in the provinces, where administration was corrupted by weak and
greedy governors and by the influence of Roman financiers.   See § 991, 638, 639, 1194, 1195.

Rutilius, both Stoic lawyers. In the corrupt Rome of the revolutionary age, while politics were a scene of venality and violence, while religion was mostly trickery, while the public courts were as infamous as partiality and bribery could make them, and while literature was recording the abominations of private life among the upper classes, the civil law-courts were the soundest department of the state. Business interests, and whatever still remained of healthy public opinion, cooperated to uphold so useful an institution and rescue it from the prevailing corruption. Its chief dangers were internally from fraud and false evidence, externally from the interruptions of public disorders and civil war. With the former the courts dealt as best they could; the latter came to an end with the establishment of the Empire, and the improvement of civil procedure and scientific development of the law went on unimpeded.

1374. We are not here concerned with the history of technical Roman law. But it is proper to observe the marked difference between the political and legal institutions of Rome, and the way in which that difference recorded itself in the sequel. The political constitution was that of a city-state, and was wholly unfitted for the government of a vast empire. I have traced the long process of decay in which that unfitness became more and more manifest, and have pointed out that the system contained within itself no means of constitutional and thorough reform. Thus a revolution was necessary. The wonder is that the Roman Republic, the greatest experiment of the ancient world, lasted so long. But, as it had grown slowly, so it fell by degrees. It survived the passing tyranny of Sulla, the awkward predominance of Pompey. The frank autocracy of Caesar overthrew it, and the failure of the attempted revival only led to the Augustan Principate, an autocracy muffled in fictions. The civil law grew by interpretation adapting it slowly but surely to the growing complexity of daily needs, and the course of events tended to keep the direction of its development in good hands. And so, when political interest had died down and free public speaking was out of date; when government, though better, was mechanical, and the curse of uninspiring idleness lay heavy upon rich and poor alike; when literature was ceasing to be the utterance of feeling, and declining through the over-cultivation of the arts of expression; still the civil law continued to develope, and the supply of great jurists[1] did not fail. This eminently Roman institution in short owed its vigorous continuity to its practical usefulness and its capacity for change. Beside the ancient *ius civile* grew up the *ius praetorium*,

---

[1] See *Digest* 1 2 §§ 35 foll., and Roby's Introduction.

created by the edicts[1] of a long succession of praetors, an admirably elastic system; and thus a very little statute-law went a very long way.

1375.   The topics that chiefly engaged the attention of lawyers in Cicero's time were for the most part those familiar to all civilized societies.   Such were sales transfers and contractual obligations; the rights of ownership and possession; the law of trusts dowries guardianships partnerships and agencies; the law of successions, intestate or testamentary, including the drawing of wills so as to give effect to the intentions of the testator, and the claims of kindred according to Roman rules.   A characteristically Roman detail was the matter of the *sacra*, rites the performance of which was an obligation often attached to estates.   In course of time these became an onerous nuisance.   Ingenious lawyers were called in to devise means of evading the obligation, and the tombs of ancestors long forgotten were left to shift for themselves.   The law relative to the status of persons was also more important in Rome than in a modern state.   The existence of slavery introduced various complications, in particular the class of freedmen, to whom special rules applied.   For instance, when a freedman died intestate, his *patronus* succeeded to his estate. We have already seen that the emancipation of women was proceeding fast; this was mainly effected by the devices invented by the lawyers.   The means by which Roman citizenship could be legally acquired, the forms of adoption, the various methods of manumission, all remind us of the differences of status recognized by Roman law.

1376.   It remains to mention briefly a few of the eminent jurists[2] who flourished in the last period of the Republic, and to indicate one or two points illustrative of their activity.   First comes Q. Mucius Scaevola the chief pontiff, murdered by the Marians in 82 B.C.   He was one of a family of lawyers.   Cicero had been one of his pupils, for the study of civil law[3] up to a certain point was of importance to an orator who intended to plead in the courts.   That he leant to conservatism of a somewhat narrow type, is shewn by his action as consul in 95, when he took part in rejecting the claims of the Italian Allies, and by some recorded facts relative to his pleadings in court. But he was a man of high character, and was noted for his consistent

---

[1] Cicero *pro Caec.* § 33, *Digest* I 1 § 7 *ius praetorium est quod praetores introduxerunt adiuvandi vel supplendi vel corrigendi iuris civilis gratia propter utilitatem publicam.* See Poste on Gaius 1 § 6.

[2] See Roby's Introduction to Justinian's *Digest* pp. ci—cxxiii.   Their fragments are collected in Huschke's *Jurisp. anteiustiniana* and Bremer's *Jurisp. antehadriana.*

[3] See the opinions put into the mouth of the orator Crassus, Cic. *de orat.* 1 §§ 166—200, and the reply of Antonius §§ 234—45, with Wilkins' notes.

efforts to promote good faith in all dealings between man and man.
Thus he was fond of introducing the words *ex fide bona* into legal
formulae, and it was by drawing up his provincial edict on these
lines, and acting upon the principle thus laid down, that he incurred
the hatred of the Roman financiers in Asia. He also devised a means
of removing certain difficulties that arose in connexion with wills in
which the testator had made bequests on conditions which from the
nature of the case could not be literally fulfilled. Another great
lawyer was Scaevola's famous *legatus* P. Rutilius Rufus, whose career
was cut short by exile. He was a pronounced reformer. His general
aspirations are shewn in his attempt to procure some limitation[1] of
the height of buildings in the streets of Rome, already a public
danger. He improved the arrangements for satisfying the claims
of creditors out of the estates of debtors, and restricted the rights
of patrons as against their freedmen. C. Aquilius Gallus was a rich
man of high character, remarkable for his exclusive interest in legal
questions. Of his virtues and juristic skill we have a flattering picture[2]
drawn by Cicero, whom he was helping with advice in a difficult
case. Beside other technical improvements in drafting legal forms,
he was celebrated as having invented a means of making fraud[3]
(*dolus malus*) a ground for action at law. Servius Sulpicius Rufus,
Cicero's friend, has often been mentioned above. He was consul
in 51, but politics were not his forte. Though he was a good orator,
literature and systematic jurisprudence were his chief claims to distinction. A pupil of Aquilius, and himself the teacher of many
pupils, he was remarkable for the great number of his legal writings.
According to Cicero[4], he brought to bear on legal subjects a thorough
training in logic, and his skill in analysis, distinctions, and sound
generalizations, enabled him to bring system into what had been
hitherto chaotic. Thus he gave an impetus to the production of
treatises on law from a broader point' of view. Among his pupils
was Ofilius the legal assistant of Caesar, who also left a number
of treatises of repute dealing with many subjects of the first importance. In particular he seems to have given great attention to the
praetor's edict and improved it in some way. His connexion with
Caesar leaves no doubt that he was a thoroughgoing reformer.
C. Trebatius Testa, a Roman knight like Ofilius, has appeared above
as a friend of Cicero, who recommended him to Caesar. He wrote
on wills and other topics of civil law. He outlived the change of
government, and lived to be a legal authority under Augustus and

---

[1] Sueton. *Aug.* 89, Strabo v 3 § 7 (p. 235), Mayor on Juvenal III 269.
[2] Cic. *pro Caec.* §§ 77—8.   [3] See J. B. Mayor on Cic. *de nat. deor.* III § 74.
[4] Cic. *Brutus* §§ 152—3.

a friend of Horace. The definition of legal terms, dealt with by all jurists more or less, seems to have been the department with which C. Aelius Gallus chiefly concerned himself.

1377. This selection of a few names of men distinguished in the jurisprudence of their time may bring home to us the good work that was being done quietly behind the scene of distraction and disorder on which we have been dwelling only too long. Of these men, Scaevola Rutilius and Sulpicius reached · the consulship. These three, and Aquilius also, held praetorships. But it would seem that none of them, save probably Rutilius[1], held the posts of *praetor urbanus* or *peregrinus*. If this be correct, the fact will indicate that it was not as praetors, but as advisers, that the jurists for the most part forwarded the development of the civil law. The man of proved professional skill enjoyed a permanent influence such as no vote of the Assembly could confer. His authority did not depend upon the accident of holding a yearly office, and it was a standing proof that there was still plenty of commonsense in Rome.

---

[1] For Rutilius see Gaius IV § 35, Roby p. cii.

CHAPTER LXI.

REVIEW OF THE REVOLUTIONARY PERIOD AND THE CONDI-
TIONS AT THE TIME OF TRANSITION TO THE EMPIRE.

Hellenism and Specialization.

1378. IN considering the changes that had come over Roman life since the times of Aemilius Paullus, the elder Cato, and Scipio Aemilianus, we cannot but observe the greatly increased influence of Hellenism. What had then been the privilege of a few enlightened households was now common property in the upper ranks of society. Education was now chiefly in the hands of Greek teachers. Such a man as Marius was already at a disadvantage from not being up to date. In general we may trace a tendency to adopt Greek methods, and therefore towards specialization. A good instance is that of medicine. Old Cato had warned his son against Greek practitioners, and considered his own traditional remedies (charms etc. included) far more wholesome than their new-fangled therapeutics. Medical practice in Rome was now completely Greek and in the hands[1] of Greeks. Its vocabulary was Greek, a technical language the growth of centuries, though a few Latin terms[2] still held their ground. The travelling quack[3] (*pharmacopola*) seems to have been known even in old Cato's time; he was now a well-known figure in the country towns. The same process is to be noted in other departments. The differentiation of the soldier and the farmer had long been going on. The lawyer was becoming separate from the pontiff, and the successful general was seldom an orator of mark. In all these pursuits the influence of Hellenism had more and more made itself felt. Greek search for principles, Greek rationalism, Greek special treatises, were victorious over Roman tradition, and the old Roman training by apprenticeship was slowly dying. In military life it lingered on in the custom of taking young men of quality, attached to headquarters, to make a campaign as cadets studying under a master. And in this department a revival took place through the organization of the defence of the empire initiated by Augustus. But the tendency of the later Republic, so long as the senatorial aristocracy held power,

---

[1] A good instance is the physician Craterus, Cic. *ad Att.* XII 13 § 1. See below § 1396.
[2] Such as *febris, tussis, gravedo, tormina.*   [3] Jordan's *Cato*, p. 58. See above § 1354.

was rather the other way. We find inexperienced men placed by political interest in command of armies with disastrous results, and Marius is represented[1] as referring scornfully to them as gaining office first and reading up the subject afterwards in Greek military handbooks. In oratory the change was more marked. Young men still attached themselves to famous pleaders and watched their practice in public meetings and at the bar, but a technical training in rhetoric was much more common than in the earlier period, and was found conducive to success. In the education of the well-to-do classes[2] the old home-training was a less important factor, and it was the custom to send boys (in charge of a slave *paedagogus*) to one of the schools kept by men of letters (*grammatici*), of which there were now many in Rome. There they received a literary training, and generally passed on to a professor of style and speech (*rhetor*), who trained them in the arts of composition and delivery. Rhetorical exercises or 'declamations' on set themes were a chief feature of this course, and some men kept up the practice in their riper years. Greek teachers and Greek methods were all the fashion, and Cicero, zealous for practical oratory and eager to push Latin on to literary equality with Greek, was uneasy at the slavish and unintelligent imitation of Greek models, and came forward as leader of a reaction. The excessively rhetorical character now given to the higher education had serious consequences. So long as there was life left in the Republic, the great mass of trained speakers could find a vent for their energies in public harangues or in senatorial debates, or in the time-honoured warfare of prosecution and defence in the 'public' courts. But under the Empire the free license of political speech and political allusion was inevitably checked, while the rhetorical schools were busier than ever. Declamations became a regular department of literature, and all literature became tainted with a rhetorical tone, a forced straining after effect, which only hurried on its decline. But what were unemployed orators to do?

1379. If oratory had reached a stage very different from the rude commonsense method of old Cato, we have seen that Stoicism had begun to work upon jurisprudence. In Rome changes suggested by experience were realized slowly, and it was an important movement when the Stoic creed took possession of the jurists and made them more willing to become artists in equity. Agriculture too felt the same specializing influence, as is pointed out above in discussing the

---

[1] By Sallust in *Jug.* 85 § 12, probably repeating a tradition. For the study of military history see Reid on Cic. *Acad.* II § 2. Cicero wrongly speaks there of Lucullus as *rei militaris rudis*.

[2] See in particular Horace *Sat.* 1 6 71—88.

work of Varro. And the organization of all businesses and trades seems to have become very minute and highly specialized, under Greek influences. Banking and finance in particular had been carried to wonderful perfection. Perhaps the most striking detail is the highly developed system of exchange by which it was made easy to remit money from one part of the empire to another. This was often complicated by the various coinages in use, particularly in the eastern provinces. In a large remittance it was very important to get the draft cashed in the local currency at a favourable rate. But these delicate operations were thoroughly understood, for the management of money had been a leading interest to Romans from very early times. So when the expansion of empire opened up a wide field for financial activity the opportunity was quickly grasped. The old notion that the business of a money-lender (*faenerator*) was disreputable died out under the allurements of gain, and even senators indirectly employed their capital in provincial ventures through the medium of syndicates or private agents, mostly freedmen or Roman knights. For conducting the immense volume of financial and mercantile business, and for transferring sums to and from the public chest, the bills of exchange (*permutationes*)[1] were a great convenience, in fact indispensable. The development in detail was derived from the commercial experience of the Hellenized East. Everything was now done on a large scale, and in consequence more things were done by contract, for instance[2] the undertaking of funerals. Even in agriculture contractors were sometimes called in to supply gangs of temporary labourers (free or slave) in a season of pressure such as the harvesting of crops.

1380. While specialization was increasing in private enterprise, the lack of it was making havoc of the public administration both at home and abroad. We have seen that the public courts were not presided over by judges trained in law, but by praetors elected under a system which was becoming more and more corrupt. Any legal advice they might choose to employ was given by jurists on their own authority. In the criminal courts there was no summing-up, and even an honest juror could be bewildered by clever counsel, who purposely obscured the issues, unchecked by the fear of exposure. And the same praetor who presided in court without special qualification passed on in due course to be governor of a province, the supreme head of its administration both civil and military, being very likely equally unfitted for both. His staff might be more competent than he; it was just as likely that they would be less so, whether appointed

---

[1] See for instance Cic. *ad fam.* III 5 § 4, II 17 §§ 4, 7.
[2] See Marquardt, *Privatleben* p. 383.

by lot or by his own choice. The virtuous Scaevola or Cicero would look out for good men and try to keep them to their duty. A Verres would take care to surround himself with villains. We need not go into further detail. The individuals of the aristocratic class from which magistrates were drawn had far too much power placed in their hands by succeeding to provincial office. There was no effective control over them, no official salary, no trained civil service under them, no public opinion at home for which they need care, so long as they did not stand in the way of other Romans bent on enriching themselves by any means fair or foul. That there was no consideration of special fitness for public duties in appointing men to administrative posts was a deep-seated disease of the republican system. Only when some great danger or distress menaced Rome and Italy was it possible to get the right man put in the right place, as Marius to beat off invaders from the north, and Pompey to put down piracy and save the people's food. In such crises the combined forces of the financiers and the mob could overcome the opposition of the senatorial nobility, and invest an individual with necessary but unconstitutional powers. After the crisis was over the effort died out and the nobles resumed their sway, but each revival found them weaker and the government more inefficient and corrupt. All modern historians of Rome can see that the constitution, developed to meet the needs of a city-state with small territory, had long ceased to meet those of a great imperial state. To contemporaries this failure presented itself in the simple concrete form of the danger from aggrandisement of individuals. This was what Cicero and Cato feared. Sulla had abdicated, Pompey had effaced himself, but some one of firmer mould and clearer purpose would appear ; when Pompey was again pushed to the front, it became gradually manifest that the individual seriously threatening the Republic was not Pompey but the man at work behind the scenes. When the aristocrats at last prepared to do battle for their power and perquisites, it was too late. They would not create an efficient administrative system, and they fell, not ignobly, but deservedly. The first work of the new monarchy was to put an end to anarchy and organize the administration of the empire.

1381. If the eastern Hellenistic world suffered under the evil government of its republican conquerors, many of its ablest men at least found some compensation in the discovery of a grand market for their talents. With the failure of Mithradates, the extinction of the Seleucid monarchy, and the ever-growing dependence of Egypt on Rome, it was now certain that there could be only one great centre of life, imperial life, in the countries fringing the Mediterranean. It was also well known, no doubt, that money tended to the imperial centre; and money is a magnet to enterprise. Greeks of ability had long been well received in Rome, and the Romeward stream of adventurers now began to flow freely. Of the success of Greek teachers and professional specialists I have spoken elsewhere, but one remarkable phenomenon calls for a few words by itself. This is the common practice of keeping a Greek man of culture as a sort of retainer or permanent guest in the house, partly for the sake of his company and conversation, partly with a view to advertisement. A philosopher could keep his noble host abreast of the current thought of the age, a writer in verse or prose could trumpet his exploits to a wider public[1] than Latin could reach. The relation between the patron and his protected friend was well understood. In the time of the younger Scipio, his entertainment of Panaetius and Polybius was an exceptional thing. In Cicero's time it was quite common. As Mommsen[2] remarks, the house of Lucullus was a rendezvous for Greek men of letters, but there were plenty of others less notable. Even the reserved and awkward Pompey had his Theophanes. Mahaffy[3] well points out that Caesar differed from other leading Romans in this respect. In this as in other matters the cool insight of Caesar marks him off from weaker men. He was under no delusions as to the true value of the 'sentimental Hellenism' of the domestic Professors and their admirers such as Brutus. But that the Hellenistic world deserved better treatment from dominant Rome none recognized more frankly than he, nor had anyone a more thorough practical appreciation of the merits of Greek specialists. At the same time, great though the influence of Greeks was in Rome, there was a strong undercurrent of prejudice against them as fawning and slippery. Among the minor financiers and the vulgar generally it was not judicious to appear too fond of Greek ways or too much steeped in Greek culture. As an advocate, Cicero[4] could affect ignorance of such things, and even turn the adoption of Greek habits against an opponent, when it suited his purpose. If his Sicilian witnesses against Verres were highly respectable men, he paints the Asiatics appearing against his client Flaccus as supple rascals ready to swear anything. It is a clearer exposure of his own views when he complains of their untrustworthiness in his letters. And indeed it was true of the Greeks, as of some other gifted peoples, that the moral qualities were not their strong point. Nor does their cross-breeding with eastern races seem to have produced a satisfactory type of character. And the vulgar Romans, of whom there were many, were quite capable of

---

[1] Cic. *pro Archia*, especially § 23

[2] *RH.*, Eng. tr. IV 604.

[3] *Silver Age of the Greek World*, cc. VII, VIII.

[4] Cic. II *in Verr.* IV § 5.

applying high standards to others while overlooking their own defects.

Religion and mysticism.

1382. Religious and mystical movements can only be touched on here so far as they indicate the moral confusion of the age and the spread of foreign influences. From the earliest times it had been the Roman custom to take over the gods of the conquered. Thus for instance the worship of *Juppiter Latiaris* on the Alban mount and of *Juno Sospita* at Lanuvium passed into the keeping of Rome. The transplanting of an alien cult to Rome was another matter, but we find the worship of the 'Great Mother' brought into the city in the stress of the second Punic war. In the course of the second century B.C. three main tendencies may be detected. First, the more complete identification of native divinities with Greek, and the more definitely anthropomorphic conception of Deity resulting therefrom. Secondly, the rationalistic movement, which sapped the religious beliefs of educated men without removing the superstitions of the ignorant. Thirdly, the more decided conversion of religion into a political engine worked by the aristocracy for their own ends. The century following the destruction of Carthage and Corinth (say 145 to 45 B.C.) saw the conquest of the East and the rapid spread of Hellenistic influences in Rome. The importation of eastern cults in a more or less Greek dress was inevitable. Excitement and ritual observances appealed to thousands whom the theories and dogmas of philosophers could not touch, particularly to women; and the emancipation of women was rendering them a more and more important element in social life. Moreover the constant stream of aliens pouring into Rome was adding to the number of those on whom the state-religion had not even the sentimental claim of tradition, and to whom mysteries, orgies, secret associations, alternations of self-restraint and self-indulgence, were congenial. No wonder the movement spread and affected the lower classes. The Senate was no longer strong enough to put it down with a high hand, as it had the Bacchanalia in 186. Smart Society took it coolly enough, and in the time of Lucretius and Catullus we find the worship of the Great Idaean Mother[1], with her eunuch-priests and wild carnival, in full swing, referred to as an ordinary phenomenon. Beside this was the importation of Egyptian gods in the forms understood at Alexandria. The worship of Isis and Osiris or Sarapis had long been spreading in the Mediterranean countries, and seems to have entered Italy from the South. Puteoli with its trading population was a convenient station on the way to

[1] Lucret. II 598—628, Catull. LXIII (Attis). Preller *Röm. Myth.* II 387.

Rome, being the chief port for the commerce with Egypt. But the Roman nobles were as a class interested in maintaining the religion of the state for political reasons, and the gods of the Nile were not allowed[1] to settle in the city without a struggle. Things had indeed gone pretty far when an attempt was made in 58 B.C. to set up altars to Egyptian gods on the Capitoline hill near the temple of Jove. For the time the invasion was repelled, and the altars destroyed, in spite of Clodius and his mob. But the movement was not stopped ; in 53 private shrines had to be destroyed, and in 50 a consul had himself to deal the first blow in demolition, so great was the superstitious awe among the common people. But it was not only the lower orders that were affected : the *demi-monde*[2], a sure index of fashion, inclined that way. These worships were well understood to promote licentiousness among the gay ladies of the Augustan age, and the same was probably the case now. A man like Cicero[3] might doubt the efficacy of the cures said to be revealed by Sarapis in dreams : to the thoughtless and the vulgar belief was easy, and doubtless stimulated by priestly imposture. In this age, as often, scepticism and credulity met.

1383. That in previous chapters reference has so seldom been made to the occurrence of prodigies, phenomena supposed to have foretold notable events, is simply due to a desire not to obscure the narrative with a mass of very wearisome detail. Our records supply any quantity of such matter. That a superstitious belief in such things was quite common is certain. Epicurean agnosticism was powerless against it, and the Stoic belief in divination gave a certain respectability to popular prejudice. We have seen that two men so different as Marius and Sulla were both profoundly superstitious, and the coarse recklessness of Crassus in disregarding official curses and warning signs of disaster seems to have made no small impression on his contemporaries. In connexion with this subject we cannot omit to mention P. Nigidius Figulus[4], one of the strangest characters of the age, the Roman representative of what passed for a revival of Pythagoreanism. Faint traditions of Pythagoras and his famous brotherhood lingered in southern Italy. Antiquaries had striven to find a

---

[1] See Preller *R. Myth.* II 378—9, J. B. Mayor on Cic. *de nat. deor.* III § 47. In 42 the triumvirs undertook to build a temple to Isis and Sarapis, but it seems to have been in the Campus, not within the city.

[2] Catull. x 26.

[3] Cic. *de divin.* II § 123. The fragments of Varro's satire *Eumenides* indicate that he held this superstition up to ridicule.

[4] See Teuffel-Schwabe § 170, Ueberweg *Hist. Philos.* Eng. trans. I 233, Tyrrell and Purser vol. IV Introd., Mahaffy *Silver Age* pp. 105, 218. The remarks of the last on Mommsen's description of Figulus are most just.

connexion between the Greek sage and the shadowy figure of the legendary Numa, second king of Rome and founder of religious institutions.   Anything savouring of transcendental mysticism was easily attributed to Pythagoras, of whom wondrous little was and is known : the gross imposture of the so-called 'books of Numa' (181 B.C.) has been spoken of above.   Into the causes and full significance of the present 'revival' we cannot inquire here.   I think it is rightly traced to Alexandria.   It seems to have been a movement of much the same kind as is nowadays called Theosophy, an attempt to elude at once both a discredited Theology and an unsatisfying Rationalism.   It dealt in prophecy and divination, and cloudy fancies of eastern origin ; it was probably mixed up with a good deal of more or less conscious imposture.   Figulus himself was a friend[1] of Cicero, who thought (or at least spoke) very highly of his judgment and advice.   In public life he was a consistent aristocrat, took sides with Pompey in the civil war, and died in exile.   He had a great reputation for learning of a recondite and fanciful kind.   A perverse grammarian, to judge from the citations of Gellius, his chief interest seems to have been in astrology and in zoology as a repertory of marvels. Pliny[2] often cites him as authority for astounding statements.   Lucan, probably echoing Livy, introduces him as discussing the celestial portents that accompanied the outbreak of the civil war.   Suetonius tells us that when a son was born to C. Octavius and Atia in 63 Figulus cast his horoscope and announced that the infant was destined to be the master of the world.   It is at least clear that this strange devotee of things mysterious and abnormal attracted the attention of many, and was respected in social circles far removed from the vulgar.   He was something more than a pedant and a dreamer.   I know of no reason to think that he was insincere.   Scientific knowledge was not yet far enough advanced to expose what was apparently the truth, that he was a living encyclopaedia of errors.

Rome and Roman life.

1384.   Of the total number of the population resident in Rome we can form no satisfactory estimate.   Many ingenious and learned attempts have been made to reach a probable result, and the question has been approached from many different points of view.   A recent inquirer[3] arrives at a conclusion which is at least less wild than those

---

[1] See Cic. *pro Sulla* § 42, *Timaeus* § 1, *ad Q. frat.* I 2 § 16, *ad Att.* II 2 § 3, VII 24, and especially the letter of comfort, *ad fam.* IV 13, in B.C. 46.   Also Plutarch *Cic.* 20, *an seni gerenda resp.* 27.

[2] Pliny *NH.* index, Lucan I 639—672, Sueton. *Aug.* 94.

[3] Beloch, *Bevölkerung* pp. 392—412.   He gives the estimates of earlier inquirers.

of most of his predecessors. He holds that the population of the
city in the first three centuries of the Empire was generally about
800,000. He guesses it in the time of Sulla at 400,000 or less. Considering that women, children, slaves, and free aliens, are all included
in this estimate, it is perhaps rather too low than too high. It assumes
that in about 80 B.C., when the spread of houses outside the Servian wall
was only beginning, the population was not more than half as large as it
was (say) 150 years later, when there were considerable suburbs. But,
as it is quite impossible to guess how many people were displaced by
the clearances made to provide for the vast buildings of the imperial
age, it is also impossible to guess what proportion of the new quarters
was occupied by persons other than those dislodged from the old ones.
It is certain that in Cicero's time[1] a very large part of the city
consisted of mean narrow streets. Sites were too valuable, and the
demand for accommodation too great, to allow the old-fashioned type
of low houses to continue. Rebuilding had evidently been going on
for some time, and the extra accommodation needed was obtained by
raising the height of buildings. The process was as we have seen
hastened by fires. The practice now was to rebuild in the form of
great blocks[2] (*insulae*), constructed with the utmost economy of space,
and to let them out in flats[3] or chambers to poor tenants. This plan
was found to pay well, but no doubt it led to overcrowding, perhaps
far worse than we can imagine. And with a view to profit only the
cheapest materials were used in building these tenement-blocks. The
ground floor[4] was of unbaked brick, the old-fashioned material, liable
to perish from damp. It was too heavy and too weak to be used for
high building, so the upper storeys were of wood and plaster, flimsy
constructions for the most part, particularly the partitions between
the rooms. The flat roofs of oriental pattern, not unknown in
modern Rome, could not be employed by reason of their weight.
But a roof of Roman tiles was heavy enough to make the whole
structure top-heavy, and any settlement or failing below was likely to
cause a disastrous collapse. Fire was not the only danger. In the
year 54 an exceptional flood[5] of the Tiber did immense damage. All
the low-lying parts of the city were covered deep with water, beasts

---

[1] Cic. *de lege agraria* II § 96. Much evidence on the subject of Roman streets in
Mayor on Juvenal III 269. See Catullus XXIII 9.

[2] Cic. *ad Att.* XV 17 § 1, 20 § 4, XVI 1 § 5, etc.

[3] The term *insulae* was used of these also. Other names were *cenacula, habitationes,* and
meritoria.

[4] Vitruvius, writing under Augustus, II 8 §§ 16—20 speaks of better materials on the
ground-floor. This seems to have been an improvement dictated by experience, such as
that of the flood of 54.

[5] Dion Cass. XXXIX 61, 63, Cic. *ad Q. frat.* III 7. See note on § 1163.

drowned, corn spoilt in granaries. Worst of all, the walls of sun-dried brick gave way and houses came crashing down, not without loss of life. We must remember that most of the tenement-houses crammed with the poor were on the low ground. From Cicero we learn that the flood even damaged properties belonging to men of position. But the houses of the rich were mostly out of reach of the waters.

1385. Such calamities were in great measure due to preventable causes, and the scandalous neglect of the republican government had to be repaired by Augustus. He organized a fire-brigade (*vigiles*), and issued a by-law[1] limiting the height of houses to 70 Roman feet. He had the bed of the Tiber cleared of accumulated rubbish, and removed the private walls which had been suffered to check the natural flow of the stream. But his successors had plenty left for them to do. Fires[2] in particular were an ever-recurring source of trouble, as was natural in such combustible buildings, unprovided with chimney-flues. The lodgings of the poor were no doubt very uncomfortable both in hot and cold weather. But the importance of the *insulae* in the last years of the Republic is seen in their recognition by Caesar[3] as convenient units of population. In his revision of the list of those entitled to corn, he ordered the inquiry to be made *vicatim*, that is by groups of houses[4] (*vici*, not quite = streets), and got his information through the landlords of blocks (*per dominos insularum*). The general appearance of the city can hardly have been improved as these crazy stacks of tenements took the place of the humbler dwellings of earlier days, and the discharge of refuse and potsherds from above was perhaps already almost as great a nuisance as it was in the time of Juvenal. The appliances for dealing with fires were probably very primitive in the time of the Republic. Water would have to be carried by hand from the nearest supply-station, for we must not suppose that it was laid on to the poor men's lodgings. There were now four aqueducts pouring water into the city, the *Appia* (313 B.C.), the *Anio vetus* (270 B.C.), the *Marcia* (144 B.C.), and the *Tepula* (127 B.C.). In this department too the last period of the Republic was a time of slackness. That a further supply was needed is indicated by the great waterworks of Augustus and later Emperors. Not only was the population increasing, but the growth of baths naturally increased the demand per head. And we know that the water in the aqueducts did not all reach its desti-

---

[1] Suet. *Aug.* 30, Dion Cass. LV 26 §§ 4, 5, Strabo V 3 § 7 (p. 235).

[2] See Mayor on Juv. III 6, 190—222, XIV 305, Suet. *Aug.* 28, and the account of the re-building under Nero, Tac. *ann.* XV 43.

[3] Suet. *Jul.* 41, *Aug.* 40.

[4] Marquardt, *Stvw.* I 7—8.

nation in the basins and fountains of Rome.   It was notorious[1] that
the channels and pipes were tapped and water drawn off for private
purposes without leave.   The carelessness or connivance of republican officials was to blame for this fraud, and under Augustus
stringent regulations were made to prevent it.   The main streets
were paved with blocks of lava (*silex*) neatly fitted together : side
streets and foot-walks with softer stone squared.   Driving in vehicles
was only allowed within the city as an exceptional privilege, reserved
for consuls, triumphal processions, and priests on great occasions.
The use of the slave-borne litter (*lectica*) seems to have brought the
old driving-privilege of Roman ladies to an end, and men of wealth
used this conveyance freely.   Of course all heavy materials for
building had to be brought in drays, but this traffic was probably
now as afterwards restricted to the early hours of the morning.   The
jostling throng in the narrow streets doubtless made noise enough at
all times.   The clatter of feet would be absent, as the shoes had no
heels, but there was much shouting, and the cries of hawkers vending
their wares, and slaves clearing the way for their owners, contributed
largely to the din.

   1386.   It is not to be wondered at that there were no windows on
the ground floor of houses, looking on the street.   In the houses of the
rich, which were never built up[2] to a great height, the solid front with
its one door guarded by a porter was an essential feature of the
design.   Though the increase of wealth and luxury had led to the
erection of splendid mansions, unknown to the simplicity of earlier
days, the old principle of privacy was retained.   The house was built
in courts, and the rooms looked inwards.   Though the absolute power
of the Father was no longer in practice so autocratic as it had been of
old, the Roman household was still a little kingdom, and there was
no question as to who was its head.   The Family was a well-defined
independent unit, and the jealous resistance to all external influences[3]
was instinctively expressed in the seclusion of its dwelling.   The
houses of the Roman nobles were now for the most part placed on
the hills.   The Palatine in particular was a favourite spot, looking
down as it did on the Forum and facing the Capitoline with its public
buildings.   Convenience and health were equally considered in the
choice of such sites, and it was a great comfort to escape at will the
turmoil of the crowded streets.   From his quasi-royal residence the

---

   [1] See for instance Cic. *ad fam.* VIII 6 § 4, Pliny *NH.* XXXI 42.
   [2] There was at least sometimes an upper storey to these *domus*, but it was evidently not
a choice part of the house.   Cicero offers his upper floor as sick-room for a slave of Atticus,
ad Att. XII 10.
   [3] For the decay of Roman home life shewn from the history of the Roman house see
Mr W. W. Fowler in *Proceedings of the Classical Association* 1907.

noble head descended to take part in public affairs, to attend a sitting
of the Senate, to appear in court as a supporter of some party in a
trial, to do business with his banker, or to canvass for office with
the help of a special name-slave (*nomenclator*) who enabled him to
address unknown and otherwise (to him) insignificant voters by their
proper names. The whole life of such a man had a flavour of
dignified patronage, and it was only natural that the Roman nobility
in general should view with extreme jealousy the rise of individuals
to exceptional power. All their surroundings tended to foster aristocratic sentiment, and the wealth on which their power materially
rested was mainly acquired in the government of provinces. An
autocrat would lower their proud position, and it was hardly less
certain that he would curtail their emoluments. Hence their stubborn
opposition to the establishment of the Empire. No modern analogy
is sufficiently striking to bring home to us all the circumstances that
combined to give the republican nobles a sense of their own vast
importance. The mere presence of obsequious freedmen, bound by
law to render certain service to their patron, and eager to win his
favour by exceeding the requirements of law and custom, was of
itself a constant reminder of greatness. The freedmen of the later
Republic took the place of the clients of earlier days. The nobility
were of course no longer a nobility of blood, but they were as greedy of
power as the Patricians had been of old, and they were not the *de jure*
lords of a small community but the *de facto* rulers of a mighty empire.

1387. It might have been expected that the immense sums of
money poured into Rome since she had destroyed her rivals and
become a great imperial power would have led to the execution of
public works far surpassing the humbler efforts of earlier days. Such
however was not the case. While the mansions of the nobles were
steadily growing in size and splendour, the public buildings of the
revolutionary period were few and not of first-rate importance. One
aqueduct (127 B.C.) may be reckoned. The reconstruction of bridges
in stone made some progress, but was very slow. There were only
the old *pons sublicius* and the *Aemilius*; the latter, begun in 179, did
not receive its arches complete till 142. To these were added the two
short bridges connecting the opposite banks of the river by way of
the island, the *pons Fabricius* in 62 and the *Cestius* probably in 46.
On the great Flaminian road to the North, about two miles from
Rome, the *pons Mulvius* was rebuilt in stone 109 B.C. The growth of
the Transtiberine city belongs to a later time, and villas and gardens
seem to have occupied most of the suburban ground on this side. Of
public halls (*basilicae*) the only new building in this period was the
Opimia, erected in 121 by L. Opimius who destroyed C. Gracchus and

built the temple of *Concordia* hard by.   Like the earlier basilicas, *Porcia* and *Aemilia*, it stood on the north of the Forum, under the Capitoline citadel, close to the old meeting-place (*comitium*) and near the old senate-house.   The public buildings in this part of the city must have been awkwardly crowded together, and it is no wonder that the great fire at the funeral of Clodius in 52 did extensive damage. In 50 the *basilica Aemilia* was rebuilt.   But the cramped space at disposal gave no room for grand designs.   When Julius Caesar planned his great *basilica Julia* in 46, he chose a site on the south-west side of the Forum.   But its completion (on an even larger scale) was reserved for Augustus.   The erection of arches to commemorate triumphs had begun soon after the second Punic war.   In this period we have the *fornix Fabianus*[1], set up in honour of the victory of Q. Fabius in 121 over the Arverni and Allobroges in Gaul.   It stood on or by the Sacred Way at the eastern end of the Forum.   A notable event in the architectural history of this period was the building of a permanent theatre in stone.   The conservatism of the old-Roman school had confined enterprise in this department to temporary erections of wood.   But the cost of putting up and taking down such structures must have been enormous, and the decorations and awnings to give the audience shade rendered this one of the most extreme forms of extravagance.   In 58 M. Aemilius Scaurus is said to have surpassed all previous feats of the kind by erecting a temporary theatre of the most splendid materials, capable of seating 80,000 people.   In 50 the notorious Curio[2] outdid this, at least as a feat of engineering.   He built two wooden theatres, each of which could be turned round bodily, revolving on a pivot.   These were so placed back to back that after serving as theatres they could be turned face to face and form a single amphitheatre, suitable for any spectacle that appealed to the eye only.   Meanwhile Pompey had overcome opposition and erected in 55 his permanent stone theatre, which included a temple of Venus Victrix.   But the Circus continued to be the place for races and other non-dramatic shows until the amphitheatre too became a permanent building[3] devoted to fights of gladiators or wild beasts in the time of the Empire.   We may pause to remark that it had already come to this, that the Roman populace found its serious interests in cheap corn and demoralizing shows.   The Circus, still apparently an enclosed race-course only fitted up with wooden stands, was perhaps not much changed from its earlier state.

---

[1] It was restored about B.C. 56. Some of the inscriptions on it are known (Wilmanns 610) and are of great interest.

[2] See Pliny *NH.* XXXVI §§ 116—120.

[3] In Campania earlier than in Rome.   Marquardt *Stvw.* III 556.

1388. It is strange, but apparently true, that the regular place for gladiatorial shows was still the Forum. The space available was very small, and the temporary wooden stands must have taken up a good part of it. Hence the competition for seats was keen, and to provide them was a favourite way of gratifying useful voters. As a mere place of public resort the Forum was quite inadequate, and to enlarge the accommodation, and at the same time to beautify the city, was for the next 150 years an occupation of the Emperors. Already in the last age of the Republic parts of the *campus Martius* were built over or enclosed for public purposes. A few temples stood there, and two colonnades (*porticus*). Pompey built his theatre there. The enclosure known as *circus Flaminius* dated from about 220 B.C. But the most important step taken beyond the walls was the transference of all elections[1] to the Campus, the Tribe-Assembly and the *concilium plebis* thus following the precedent of the *comitia centuriata*. The spaces marked out for the voting-groups probably began to take a permanent form, and Julius Caesar designed built enclosures for the purpose, a work carried out by Agrippa when popular elections had ceased to have any real meaning. These *saepta* or *ovilia* were on the western side of the great north road, close to the *villa publica*, a building said[2] to have been erected in 435 B.C., but probably reconstructed since that date. The tendency to spread in this direction is to be noted, for the whole Campus was included in the new wall of the third century A.D., and it was the site of medieval Rome. The business-centre was as heretofore in and about the Forum. Wherever a convenient corner could be found, shops and stalls were set up, and the offices of bankers and money-changers were a most important feature of the scene, clustering especially round certain arcades[3] known as the *Iani*. In these *tabernae argentariae* the money-transactions of Rome took place, and the amount of business was now enormous. That the increase of banking-establishments had tended to reduce the space available in the narrow Forum can hardly be doubted.

1389. Enough has been said to shew that the city was far from being a magnificent capital worthy of a mighty empire. The money drawn from the provinces to Rome had mostly come into private hands. The public treasury was never full enough to meet exceptional demands for long, and the yearly loss on corn was a constant drain. And the nobles spent their money on their own luxury and splendour.

---

[1] Not legislative Assemblies, which seem to have been held in the Forum. See Mommsen *Str.* III pp. 382—3.

[2] Livy IV 22. See § 1356.

[3] See Marquardt *Stvw.* II 65, Palmer on Horace *Sat.* II 3 18, Wilkins on *epist.* I 1 54.

Their public outlay was in the form of wasteful shows and bounties. So public works were few, and existing temples falling into decay: it was more important to please voters than to do honour to the gods. The coming of an imperial master changed all this.   It was not for nothing that Horace, singing as the court-poet of a new era, called attention[1] to the personal extravagance and selfish neglect of public duty in recent times, and pointed to the example of the Romans of old, whose conduct had been just the reverse.   It was the policy of Augustus to represent his efforts to adorn the imperial capital as a recurrence to the nobler ways of the distant past.   He not only himself spent prodigious sums on new works, but repaired or rebuilt 82 temples, and stirred up his courtiers to do likewise.   In his later days he was able to boast[2] that he had taken over a Rome of sun-baked brick (*latericiam*) and was leaving it a Rome of marble.   This was his practical comment on the wasteful iniquities of the republican system in its degenerate days.   It was really an execution on a grand scale of the unfulfilled purposes of Julius Caesar.   Of one class of monuments the Rome of the revolutionary age had plenty.   Portrait-statues early found favour, and the influx of Greek artists had doubtless improved their quality; but it was portraiture in durable materials that was the main attraction, ministering as it did to family pride. There were of course a number of statues, gods or ideal figures, valuable as works of art, the spoils of the Greek world.   Of these many were private property, and served to adorn the palaces of wealthy nobles.   But in public places the quantity of figures[3] must have been prodigious.   Not to mention the temples, the images in which were often ancient works in wood or terra-cotta, open spaces, such as the yard of the Capitol, the Comitium, the Forum, and so forth, were full of statues of one sort or other.   A theatre, an arch, a basilica, the Rostra, anything, served as an excuse for setting up statues.   For the decoration of private gardens they were in demand, both in Rome and in the country, and the manufacture of statues, and the importation of copies of famous originals, went on freely.   Statue-dealing[4] was a flourishing business.   If some of the figures turned out wholesale did not satisfy the cultivated taste of educated men, other customers were to be found, less fastidious.   That the difference between good and bad taste was recognized by a good many, seems indicated by Pompey's getting Atticus[5] to superintend this part of the

---

[1] Hor. *carm.* II 15, compared with 18 and parts of III 1 and 6.

[2] Suet. *Aug.* 28, 29, *Mon. Ancyr.* cc. 19—21.

[3] For the attempt o⸍ censors in 158 B.C. to check the excess of these erections see Pliny *NH.* XXXIV 30.

[4] See Cic. *ad fam.* VII 23, XIII 2.   [5] Cic. *ad Att.* IV 9 § 1.

decoration of his theatre.   But the use of statues for commemorative purposes was marred by a barbarous philistinism.   Degenerate Athens had set the example of putting new heads on old figures[1] and false titles on the pedestals, in order to gratify the vanity of powerful patrons, and the abuse easily spread to Rome.   Inscriptions therefore were not always to be trusted, and Roman nobles, proud to see the statue of an ancestor publicly attesting their family glories, could make strange blunders[2] as to the career and identity of their hero. Pictures, which Cicero characteristically preferred[3] for decorative purposes, were also common, scenes of battle, mythology, and maps ; the walls[4] of temples and colonnades were the places for those of them that were shewn in public, but many (probably the greater number) were in private mansions.   Of the collectors of works of art none were more conspicuous[5] than Hortensius and Lucullus, but there were not a few others, and great prices were paid for choice examples of famous masters.   But it was mainly the adornment of private houses in town and country that stimulated this market.   The adornment of the city was the work of the Empire.

Italy and local institutions.

1390.   It is only possible to speak very briefly here of the change that came over Italy in consequence of the great Italian war.   Before that upheaval there were in Italy

A.   Roman citizens, living

(a) in and about Rome.

(b) in the citizen colonies.

(c) in country districts, without town-centres equipped with local governments, law being administered by *praefecti* sent from Rome on circuit.

(d) as individuals, in the Latin towns, having mostly acquired the Roman franchise under the terms of the ' Latin right.' Probably also a few in non-Latin Allied states, who had received the grant of *civitas* as a personal favour.

B.   Allies.

(a) Latins of a few old Latin towns.

(b) Latins of the Latin colonies.

---

[1] Cic. *ad Att.* VI 1 § 26, Plutarch *Ant.* 60.   For the prevalence of this practice in Rhodes see pp. 155, 277—8, of Mahaffy's *Silver Age of the Greek World*.

[2] Cic. *ad Att.* VI 1 §§ 17, 18.   [3] Cic. *ad fam.* VII 23 § 3.

[4] Pliny *NH.* XXXV 17—25, 113—5.

[5] See Pliny *NH.* XXXIV 48, XXXV 125—7, 136.

(*c*) Ordinary Allies, attached to Rome on various terms according to their several treaties.

The fundamental distinction between these two classes lay in the recognition of the former as part and parcel of the Roman state. Whatever local administrative institutions there were among them were merely matters of convenience, not of right. They belonged to the Roman Tribes, and the Tribes were only conceivable as parts of a whole. The individual citizens in theory shared both the privileges and the burdens of the Roman franchise : in practice we have seen that the tendency had for a long time been to claim the privileges and evade the burdens more and more. The latter class on the other hand were in theory independent[1] communities, that is, enjoying self-government in their internal affairs, under their own laws administered by their own magistrates. Against this advantage there was to be set their complete subordination to Rome in external affairs, with the continuous increase of military burdens involved in that subordination, and the communal isolation by which it was secured. The growing pride of the Romans marked the inferiority of the Allies, and the inevitable collision at last took place, with the result that the remains of the two great forces had to be finally united. The blending was not accomplished without further friction and bloodshed, as we saw above. The point to be kept in view here is that it was a blending of two masses of population differing from each other in their political organization. The old citizens, however scattered, simply belonged to Rome. In Rome their rights and duties centred, and to them the whole notion of local autonomy was quite a secondary and undeveloped thing. The new citizens, henceforth to be the equals of the old, came into the union with a past of local autonomies behind them. To compel them to give up their local institutions was not possible. Nor was it desirable. Communities of citizens could not be ruled by governors sent from Rome, like provincials ; nor was it the traditional policy of Rome to meddle with local politics beyond the favouring of aristocratic parties in states with which she had dealings. Therefore, while the citizens of a former Allied state became citizens of Rome, the township retained its local government. The citizen existed there in a double capacity, holding a franchise within a franchise. His general rights were those of a *civis Romanus*. But distance would prevent him from habitually appearing in Rome as a voter, and surely the majority took no active part in Roman politics. Local interests engaged most of the attention of the citizens of the

---

[1] Those enjoying most independence could receive Roman exiles. After the enfranchisement of Italy this was no longer possible.

country towns, and Roman elections and imperial legislation only drew to the capital a few country voters.

1391.   The result of the great war had been that a large number of communities enjoying local governments were within a very few years incorporated with Rome.   But this resumption of a long-neglected process was on very different lines from those followed of old. Formerly a community was generally incorporated on an inferior[1] footing, its members being reckoned as Romans but not enrolled in the Tribes.   Conditions varied, but the 'public rights,' the participation in state-life, was in all cases denied to these half-citizens, 'citizens without right of voting' as they are often called.   They shared the burdens of the full citizens and were accordingly called *municipes*, and their townships *municipia*.   The term *municipium* seems at first to have connoted inferiority, in fact subjection, but the admission of the half-citizens to the full franchise gradually changed its meaning in practice.   Now the Allies were admitted wholesale[2] to the full franchise at once, without passing through any probationary stage. All about Italy appeared communities which, though now consisting of Roman citizens, managed their internal affairs as before under local constitutions.   They were *municipia* in the later sense[3] of the term, and were so styled.   It was only natural that the addition of all these to the Roman total should have some effect on the local organization of the old citizens.   It led indeed to a great extension of local governments.   In districts where there had been no town-centre, and a Roman *praefectus* had administered justice as required, the new tendency was to recognize one of the hamlets as a town[4] and make it the centre of local self-government for the group.   So Italy became parcelled out among a number of municipalities, as we find it in the time of Cicero.   The old names *colonia* and *praefectura* were in use, as connoting the original status of particular towns, but all were virtually *municipia*, and the usual adjective for 'local' as opposed to 'imperial' was *municipalis*.   It was in these Boroughs, as we may call them, that the strength of Italy now lay.   Some flourished, others did not, but in general there was considerable life in them. The normal type of constitution was a sort of miniature copy of Rome, with a senate magistrates and assembly ; but there were varieties, especially in the number and title of the chief magistrates, to

---

[1] The so-called *cives sine suffragio.*

[2] One of the most notable of the new *municipia* was Neapolis, which retained many Greek institutions and used Greek as the official language.   See Beloch's *Campanien.*   It became a favourite retreat for quiet cultivated Romans.   Vergil was one.

[3] See Mommsen, *Staatsrecht* vol. III, chapter on Municipalrecht.

[4] Hence, as Mommsen points out, *praefecturae* appear as a class of town-communities after the great war.

detail which here would only serve to obscure the main facts.   There can be no doubt that in practice the affairs of the Boroughs were dominated by aristocracies of wealth, as selfish and greedy as the nobles in the capital.   The ways of Rome were aped by the country towns, and, if we may trust Cicero[1], some of the municipal families achieved a great proficiency in crime.

1392.   Each Borough then was a corporate unit with a life of its own, and at the same time a part of an all-containing Roman whole. Beside its local territory held as communal[2] or individual property, it could in its corporate capacity derive revenues from holding and letting lands[3] in the provinces, and these rents were sometimes a very important item in the local budget.   Disputes now and then occurred between neighbouring municipalities, especially on such subjects as boundaries[4] and water-rights: in a case of the latter kind we find a commission[5] headed by a consul appointed to settle it, and Cicero retained on behalf of one of the parties.   This may remind us that the Italian Boroughs, just as the provincial communities, found it worth their while to keep up a connexion[6] with some influential personage in Rome.   He watched the interests of the Borough as its *patronus*, and saw to any business in which his clients were concerned. But this connexion was unofficial ; he did not act as their representative, but as a Roman noble anxious to see that a certain community did not suffer wrong.   Such connexions were kept up by the upper class in the municipalities, and tended to link together the aristocratic elements throughout the peninsula.   It was this solidarity that encouraged Cicero to rely on the support[7] of the *municipia* in his struggle against Antony, and to perish vainly in the cause of the nobles ; this that furnished the excuse for the far-reaching proscriptions of the triumvirs.   We must not however suppose that the Roman nobility had sincerely abated anything of their former pride. In moments of elation or pique the truth came out.   Even in the last agony of the Republic men could still depreciate Octavian[8] as one of a municipal equestrian family, and Cicero, himself by birth *municipalis eques*, could in 55 taunt Piso (an ex-consul like himself) with his municipal birthplace[9] Placentia and speak of him as no better than a

---

[1] See the *pro Roscio Amerino* and *pro Cluentio*.

[2] This is quite different from *ager publicus* the domain-land of the Roman state.

[3] See'Cic. *ad fam.* XII 7, 11, Velleius II 81 § 1.

[4] The form of settling boundaries is well illustrated by the case of the award in a Ligurian case 117 B.C.   Inscription at Genoa, Wilmanns 872.

[5] Cic. *ad Att.* IV 15 § 5, Varro *RR.* III 2 § 3.

[6] Cic. *ad Att.* IV 15 § 5, *in Pison.* § 25, *phil.* II § 107.

[7] Cic. *phil.* VII § 23.   [8] Cic. *phil.* III §§ 15, 16, XIV §§ 9, 10.

[9] Cic. *in Pison.* §§ 14, 34, 53, 62, 67.

Gaul. 'On the other hand there was no lack of local patriotism. Most citizens had now two[1] fatherlands. There was 'our town,' the *patria naturae* or *loci*, the *patria quae genuit*, in relation to which a man was *ortu Tusculanus Arpinas Venusinus* or whatever his place of origin might be. There was also Rome, the *patria civitatis* or *iuris*, the *patria quae excepit*, the *patria communis* of all *municipes*, to belong to which marked a man off from the outer world as *Romanus*, not less so than the Patrician of ancient Roman blood. Whether this condition of twofold allegiance was or was not[2] exceptional among Roman citizens before the great Italian war, it soon after became common, and in the time of Cicero's public life it was not the exception but the rule.

1393. How defective our records are is shewn by the fact of our having no account of this notable change in process. Yet there is no doubt about it. Cicero could even venture to remind the Senate[3] that most of them belonged to *municipia*, and this at a time when he was in great need of their support. The normal position now was that a man was a Roman citizen in virtue of being a citizen of a Borough-town. Mommsen has shewn that the change necessitated a certain amount of rearrangement in the assignation of Tribes, but this interesting matter is too technical to admit a brief statement, and the political bearing of the change is sufficiently evident without it. We find it the rule that citizens of the same municipal unit, when they go to Rome as voters, vote in the same Tribe. Only we must not take this to mean that all registered citizens of (say) Ariminum or Venusia habitually went to Rome and took part in the Assemblies. What was now possessed by the local burgesses in their capacity of Roman citizens was the right to exercise the privilege of voting, not the means of doing so.

1394. It remains to mention a few details that throw light on the general state of Italy. Since the changes of Sulla the regular course was for the consuls of the year to stay in Rome, or at least in Italy. They were the heads of the Home administration. If a local question arose in the country, a consul was entrusted with the settlement of it. But the want of a properly organized police was severely felt in unsettled times. At the end of the year 50 a friend of Cicero's was wounded and robbed[4] by foot-pads near Rome on the Appian way. Brigandage in country districts was never put down for long ; Varro takes it into account as an ordinary risk of rural life. After the suppression of Spartacus and Catiline the remains of their bands,

---

[1] See the notable passage Cic. *de legibus* II § 5.
[2] Mommsen holds that it was.   [3] Cic. *phil.* III § 15.
[4] Cic. *ad Att.* VII 9 § 1.

joined no doubt by runaway slaves, gave trouble[1] for years, and we
have seen the ease with which M. Caelius raised a robber band in
southern Italy during the absence of Caesar. Indeed for about fifty
years (say 80—30 B.C.) the country was never free from the presence
of discontented men seeking redress or revenge, and the outbreaks of
which we hear probably give us a very faint notion of the insecurity
that prevailed. Disputes between neighbouring occupiers were in
some parts carried on with open resort to force. Of the two cases[2]
dealt with in surviving speeches of Cicero, one took place in the South
near Thurii, the other in Etruria, both bad neighbourhoods. But the
main roads must have been generally safe, or the incessant courier-
traffic could not have gone on as it did. Wealthy travellers were
guarded by their slave escort. We get a glimpse of the abominations
that occurred in the dark corners of the land in the work of Augustus.
When he addressed himself to restore order[3] in Italy, he had not only
to put down bands of brigands (*grassatores*), who had increased
greatly during the disorders of civil wars, but to remedy a hideous
abuse in connexion with the slave-gangs on big estates. He found that
it had become a practice to seize travellers, freemen as well as slaves,
and confine them in the slave-pens, incorporating them with the
existing gangs. Evidently the supply of additional labour was
welcomed, and no questions asked. This evil, as well as brigandage,
the new emperor did his best to put down. But the detention of
persons[4] kidnapped (*suppressi*) on plantations was an abuse too well
established to be finally got rid of by a single effort. The refreshment
of travellers on the roads between towns was provided by roadside
inns[5], which were generally set up by owners of estates near, who
found this a convenient means for disposing of some of their produce
at a profit. Owners of distant country houses sometimes kept up
small night-quarters (*deversoria*) of their own, where they (or by leave
a friend) could break a journey. The number of country seats
scattered about in the pleasant parts of Italy was prodigious, and in
course of time *villa* came to mean a park and mansion, whether it
included a farm or not. In the autumn, when those who could afford
it left the city, the wealthy Romans transferred their luxury to
country seats, and the distraction of callers could even there be a
nuisance to a man of letters, as Cicero had reason to know. Rural

---

[1] Sueton. *Aug.* 3 with Shuckburgh's note.   [2] *pro Tullio, pro Caecina.*
[3] Suet. *Aug.* 32.
[4] We find legal remedies against *suppressores* of free persons mentioned in the later jurisprudence. See *Iulii Paulli sentent.* v 6 § 14, *Digest* XLVIII 15 § 6, with XLIII 29, XLVII 2
§ 83.
[5] *tabernae deversoriae* or *tabernae* simply. See on Varro § 1350.

town-councils, of whose little ways[1] a great man from Rome could make fun, sometimes found a distinguished neighbour a trouble[2] if he were inclined to be quarrelsome. Arable land in Italy was in Cicero's time practically all held as private property. The *ager Campanus* was the only part still remaining state-property, and we have seen that it also was assigned to veterans by the end of this period. A great deal of pasture land was also in private hands, but we still hear of *ager publicus* after all the agrarian legislation that had taken place from the Gracchi onwards. Upland pastures[3] are doubtless meant; and they may still have been extensive in some districts, for instance in Samnium after the bloody clearances of Sulla. It is of importance to note the change in the land-question during this period. It begins with the Gracchan movement for planting the poor on public land resumed and allotted by the state. The failure of this only confirmed and intensified old evils. It ends with the confiscations of private land and the cruel displacement of farmers to make room for soldiers. Of malaria[4] we hear little directly, but enough to shew that the Roman Campagna, the coast district of Apulia, and some parts elsewhere, were affected by this scourge, which seems to have been on the increase. Nor do we hear of a series of great plagues such as devastated Rome itself in earlier times. To Cicero the site of the city seemed well-chosen, partly because of the numerous springs found there : but it is likely that the better health of the people was due to the supply of purer water through the aqueducts,

Slaves, freemen, and the Roman mob.

1395. It seems wearisome to be ever harping on the matter of slavery. It is generally allowed to have been the economic substructure[5] of Graeco-Roman civilization. Whatever doubts had at one time been raised as to the morality of human bondage, neither statesmen nor philosophers proposed to abolish it. We have met with glaring instances of its evil effects. But it is necessary to say something of it here in general terms from the standpoint of its effect on the position of the poorer freemen. It has been remarked above that of the poor citizens we know practically nothing. We hear of them

---

[1] Cic. *ad fam.* VII 1 § 3.   [2] Cic. *ad Att.* IV 7 § 3.

[3] See on Varro § 1351. From Suet. *Dom.* 9 it seems that there were odd remainders (*subsiciva*) of unallotted land even in Domitian's time.

[4] See Cic. *de republ.* II § 11, *de lege agrar.* II § 71, Caesar *civ.* III 2. The draining of the Pomptine marshes was not carried out. In *ad Att.* XII 10 Cicero hints at the possibility of something ἐπιδήμιον on the Quirinal hill.

[5] See W. L. Newman, Introd. to *Ar. Pol.* p. 125, on the non-Hellenic elements presupposed in Aristotle's theory of the state.

only in the mass as worked upon by demagogues seeking power, as being feasted, entertained with shows, courted, bribed, brought up to the ballot-box Tribe by Tribe, and organized in gilds and associations to facilitate their management by agents. Above all, we hear of the ruinous arrangements for providing them with cheap food at the cost of the state. That the formation of an idle mob in Rome can be traced back to the economic revolution in the second century B.C., is fairly certain. Thus the great estates and the wholesale slave-husbandry were the causes of its origin. But it seems that the mob of the Gracchan period still consisted largely of the country-born, and was not as yet to any great extent recruited from the slave-population. They were able to combine for a time at least with the rustic voters who attended to support the Gracchi. Marius in his time still found in the streets of Rome a good recruiting-ground ; but, when afterwards he came to blows with Sulla, he called the slaves to arms. Probably the mob already contained a strong freedman-element, after the manumissions of the last 40 years. The proscription of Sulla no doubt added greatly to this servile element. His own *Cornelii* were a striking example of the process by which the citizen body in its political capacity was being turned into a mongrel mass, and Roman blood and Roman traditions gradually dying out. When we get to Cicero's consulship, we find the orator able to defeat an agrarian law, mainly by appealing to the prepossessions of the Roman rabble in favour of urban life. To Caesar the city mob was simply a political tool, and in the critical times of his rise to power the Assemblies were dominated by the use or fear of force. These brief outlines, and the circumstances of which they remind us, may serve to suggest that the degradation of what passed for the *populus Romanus* in Assemblies was going on continuously. It is amazing that Brutus should for a moment have fancied that any serious reaction in favour of a Republic could come out of such a body.

1396. Now the responsibility for the degradation of the resident *populus* lay in the first instance on the very nobles whose power it was eventually used to overthrow. Land-grabbing filled Rome with discontented poor citizens, and the use of influence bribery and force combined to render the Assemblies wholly unfit to represent the people's will. And slavery was at the root of both these evils. Of *latifundia* and rural slavery we have said enough. In the city there were several classes of slaves. Of those in the service of the state[1] (*servi publici*) we need not speak. Those in private ownership may be put in two groups. First, those kept for profit. Such were the

---

[1] For instance those employed in connexion with the waterworks, sewers, scavenging, the mint etc. This class existed everywhere. For Sicily see Cic. II *in Verr.* III §§ 86—89.

gangs employed by contractors for building and other public or
private works; artisans employed in trades, manufacturing such
articles as were made in Rome, or hired out to those in need of their
services; among them were stage-artists gladiators and all manner of
labourers employed in connexion with the public shows. The total
number of these must have been enormous. In the building trades
alone there was a great opening for the speculators in skilled labour,
of whom Crassus[1] was a specimen.   Fires, accidental or caused by
street-fighting, were frequent, and Crassus not only bought up sites
cheap, but building-slaves also.   Then he made a profit both on the
sites and on the hire of the slaves whom he let out to speculative
builders: he did not rebuild at his own risk.   Secondly, there were
the domestic slaves, very numerous and with endless varieties of
function.   All men of means had some: to have no slave[2] meant
sheer poverty.   All the wealthy had many: in some cases the *familia
domestica*[3] ran to hundreds.   Stalwart knaves were in request to act as
door-keepers, to carry their master and mistress in their litters, to clear
the way in crowded streets, and to act as a bodyguard.   The service
of the toilet, male and female, was becoming a serious matter in
fashionable houses.   Beside the valet and the lady's-maid were the
tutor (*paedagogus*) and the nurse, who had charge of the children.
The service of the kitchen and the table employed numbers: a good
cook or a handsome waiter fetched high prices.   Men with large
correspondence[4] were obliged to keep couriers (*tabellarii*) to deliver
their letters.   This occupation alone must have required thousands of
slaves, for letters were constantly passing to and from all parts of the
Roman world.   The courier-slaves, entrusted with important duties,
must have been well treated, and much travel would tend to quicken
their wits: the poor freeman had no such chance of seeing the world.
Then there were the literary slaves, who read aloud to the master,
wrote from dictation, made copies, kept his accounts, and his books, if
he had a library.   Atticus carried this department so far as to keep a
large staff of trained writers engaged in producing copies of books.
He was in fact the chief publisher of the day.   Out of a private
convenience there was thus developed a trade.   Some of the rich were
lucky enough to buy a slave skilled in medicine.   If so, he could be
turned to profit for his lord's benefit.   But the best of the medical and

---

[1] Plutarch *Crass.* 2.   Among his other enterprises as a slave-speculator mining is
mentioned.   It seems that almost any kind of trained slave could be hired from Crassus.

[2] See Ellis on Catullus XXIII.

[3] Marquardt, *Privatleben* p. 156, well points out that the totals of 10,000 or 20,000 must
include the *familiae rusticae.*

[4] In particular the *publicani* concerned in provincial speculations.

surgical practice in Rome fell to Greek adventurers[1] who came with their assistants (slaves or freedmen) to make their fortune in the capital.

1397. Speaking generally, the domestic slaves seem to have been a contented class. They were not overworked, and they were allowed to acquire and save for themselves on a small scale. This small *peculium* was a practical guarantee of good behaviour. The slave looked to his owner for the gift of freedom some day, and for present indulgences. And he had endless opportunities of winning favour. The master often became unable to do without him. Cicero was annoyed at his brother's dependence on his slave Statius, and doubtless there were many cases of the kind. These obedient and adroit bondmen, mostly drawn from the Greek or half-Greek peoples, saved their masters a vast deal of trouble, and were therefore getting the practical details of private and public business into their hands. The influential slave was already an important person, and gave himself great airs in dealing with people in general. The system suited both master and slave, and it was the interest of both to keep the poor freeman of Italian birth in the background. Thus the indigent citizen, however willing he might be to perform useful duties and by efficient service to improve his position, found the path of such advancement barred. The man of property through whose hands private and public business passed found it most convenient to be the owner of his confidential subordinates, who could be punished or sold at will and could give him no trouble by their scruples or independence. As the industrial labour-market was spoilt by the competition of slave-labour, so was the market for clerks and agents, save in the case of agencies requiring appearance in court, for which citizen-rights were necessary. And the stigma[2] attached to labour, the curse of all slave-holding societies, was a bar to all improvement. Men are ruled by the notions current in their age and country, and there was as yet no general consciousness that slavery was both morally and economically wrong. We do hear of an attempt[3] to enforce by law the employment of a minimum percentage of free labourers in rural work. But we have no reason to think that this rule was ever operative. There was no army of inspectors to see it carried out; and what the prospects of free labour in the country were at the time of

---

[1] The most famous practitioner of this period was the Bithynian Asclepiades, a rhetorician turned doctor. See Cic. *de orat.* I § 62, Pliny *NH.* VII 124, XXVI 12—17. Celsus *de medicina* often refers to this remarkable man.

[2] The contempt felt for wage-earners, retail-dealers, etc. is sufficiently illustrated by Cic. *de orat.* I §§ 83, 263, *Brutus* §§ 257, 297, *ad Att.* VII 2 § 8, *Tusc.* V § 104, *de offic.* I §§ 150, 151. See § 1355 above.

[3] See above § 1265.

the fall of the Republic the evidence of Varro[1] shews only too well. The vain attempt died away, and the military settlements of the revolutionary period would in any case have ended it. Bad farmers the veterans might be, but no one would have dared to dictate to them. Moreover legislation was the function of the Assembly, and the Assembly was becoming less and less a Roman body. There was, as we have seen[2] above, every inducement to owners of slave-property to get rid of their human chattels when their best years were past and the return on the capital sunk so diminished that the slave was no longer worth his keep. By giving him freedom he became a freedman-citizen, entitled to the privilege[3] of cheap or gratuitous corn. Thus the cost of his maintenance fell chiefly on the state, and with his little savings he could do very well in a humble way. There were of course many reasons[4] for manumission, but it is highly probable that this facility for transferring a private burden to the public treasury often turned the scale in cases of doubt. Now every freedman entered on the register of a Tribe helped to strengthen the alien element in that group, and the laxity of the revolutionary age was unable or unwilling to confine them to the four city Tribes. Their influence in voting steadily grew, and with it the influence of their former lords, to whom as their *patroni* they still owed a peculiar loyalty. If this process had been allowed to go on unchecked, in no long time the rich, aided also by bribery, might have held the Assemblies in the hollow of their hand. Even rioting was in their favour at first, for the rich man's slaves bore a share in a free fight, on the pretext of defending their master. But the split between the senators and knights revived the 'popular' party and brought Pompey, Crassus, and afterwards Caesar, to the front. The senatorial nobility never really recovered the ground then lost, let Cicero do what he might to reunite the wealthy Orders. Under the cool and cynical guidance of the rising Caesar sufficient force was employed to coerce the Assembly whenever any project of importance was in hand. From the overawing of the aristocrats by armies in 71 to the gladiators of Clodius was no great step, but it meant that slave-swordsmen determined the public acts of the Roman People by shedding Roman blood in the Roman streets. So the disease had run its course. The rich and their slaves had destroyed all that was left of the popular element in the Roman constitution. It only remained for those who had taken the sword against the Gracchi themselves to perish by the sword.

---

[1] See above §§ 1354, 1355.   [2] See §§ 661, 1264.

[3] See Dion Cass. XXXIX 24, Dionys. Hal. IV 24.

[4] For some bad ones see Cic. *pro Caelio* § 68, Asconius Introd. to the *pro Milone*, Gaius I 47.

1398. While it is certain that the number of freedmen in Rome was increasing all through the revolutionary period, it is less clear how matters stood in regard to migration from other parts of Italy. That we hear[1] of the attendance at Assemblies being very thin at the time when Clodius was dominating Rome, may be merely a proof of abstention due to terrorism combined with the growing apathy which Cicero often laments. But there is some reason to think that the stream of migration into Rome was no longer flowing in any great volume since the time of Sulla. Some of the landholders ejected to make room for his soldiers did come to the city, but we have no reason to suppose that many did so. It is certain that many remained near their old homes. After Sulla had come to terms with the Italians and all Italy enjoyed the Roman franchise, one great cause of general discontent had been removed. The municipal towns (each with its considerable territory) had an opportunity to regain their vigour in a period of comparative rest. The risings of Lepidus (77) and of Catiline only affected the suffering district of Etruria, and that perhaps not very severely. The bulk of Italy only suffered from the slave-war of Spartacus (73—71). It would seem that some revival of agriculture took place in the following twenty years, and this would aid the prosperity of the towns. On this supposition we are better able to understand the great number of troops raised in Italy at the time of the civil war. The vast armies of which we read were not wholly barbarian, or recruited in the Romanized Cisalpine, or by the enrolment of freedmen and slaves, though all these contingents were considerable. On the whole, though the evidence is miserably indirect and meagre, I am inclined to think that migration of the poorer citizens to Rome was small during the last thirty years of the Republic, and that this falling-off contributed to increase the relative strength of the alien and servile element in the Roman mob. There is probably much truth in the constant complaints of Cicero that the *collegia* revived by Clodius were packed with slaves, and the breaking-up of these sham gilds could not prevent evasive reorganization under somewhat modified forms. From a modern point of view it is hard to understand how the poor freemen could put up with a practice so much to their own disadvantage. We do not indeed hear that they liked it; but the only serious objection to sharing their privileges with others is (so far as I know) found in the opposition of the city populace to the extension of the franchise before the great Italian war. To form any clear notion of the comparative numbers of free and slave labourers in the time of Cicero is hopeless. There seem to have been free artisans (*fabri*), and

---

[1] Cic. *pro Sestio* § 109.

general expressions such as 'workmen' (*operarii*) may include both classes.   Porters (*baiuli*) and oarsmen (*remiges*) are also doubtful, but we know that freemen were loth to carry burdens or toil at the oar.   The 'hired man' (*mercennarius*)[1] is a free wage-earner, but it was as easy to hire a slave from his owner as a freeman from himself.   Many small shopkeepers no doubt were free-born (*ingenui*), but many were freedmen (*libertini*), and slaves set up in business by and for the benefit of their owners[2] were to be found, more particularly in trades beneath the dignity of a noble Roman.

1399.   From these considerations I venture to conclude that during the revolutionary period the Roman populace was rapidly changing its character, all the faster as time went on.   A hundred years later Lucan[3] spoke of Rome as no longer thronged by real native citizens but filled with the dregs of the world.   The process was then complete, and votes of Assemblies had long ceased to confer power.   The last state of the falling Republic had come very near to this pitiful consummation.   It was only necessary to suppress riotous disorder, and peace dawned upon a ready-made proletariate of mongrels, living on public and private charity, serving no purpose but to applaud the races of the circus and the bloodshed of the amphitheatre.   This proletariate wealth and luxury, based on a foul economic system, had created, and it was a matter of the first necessity that a clique of rich and extravagant nobles should no longer be allowed to exploit the misery of the subject world for their own profit.   For the strength of the empire now lay in the provinces, and an Emperor was needed to turn it to account.   To the provinces the establishment of a single supreme ruler was a priceless boon.   In Rome the Emperors had to keep a sharp eye upon the remaining nobles, and to feed the idle populace.   Their real interests lay in the vast provincial dominions, and the history of the Empire was the history of the diminishing importance of Rome.

The Empire and the transition to monarchy.

1400.   To form some notion of the situation created by the fall of the Roman Republic, and the task awaiting the new government, we must enumerate the countries included in its dominions under their modern names.   These are France, a strip of modern Germany and Switzerland, nearly all Spain and Portugal, Tunis, Tripoli, the islands

---

[1] See Cic. *de off.* I § 41, Seneca *de benef.* III 22.
[2] See Marquardt, *Privatleben* pp. 159—62.
[3] Lucan VII 404—5 *nulloque frequentem cive suo Romam sed mundi faece repletam.*

of Corsica Sardinia Sicily Crete Cyprus and the Archipelago, Dalmatia, Greece, Turkey in Europe[1] and most of that in Asia. Such was the range of the Provinces. Besides these there were many lands subject to Roman influence or acknowledging the overlordship of the Republic. Such were the Netherlands, where the Batavians furnished good soldiers, Morocco and Algiers (the latter was for a time a Province), Egypt, and a number of dependent principalities in Syria Asia Minor and Thrace. In the centre of this subject or dependent world lay the imperial land of Italy, from which all powers emanated, and to which the profits of empire were drawn. And now the government under which these vast dominions had been acquired had completely broken down, not through pressure from without, but through revolution within. Civil wars, proscriptions, and economic disturbances, continued for two generations, had left in Rome and Italy what looked like irremediable chaos and exhaustion. Demoralized armies were clamouring for rewards and rest. Their demands could not be refused, but the supply of land-allotments did not suffice, even with the cruel ejection of present holders, and the treasury was empty. Yet in spite of all this disorganization and misery the empire did not fall to pieces, composed though it was of so many peoples, varying widely in nationality language customs and traditions, and attached to the central power by no economic or sentimental tie. Caesar, who overthrew the Republic, the man of great imperial ideas, was murdered before he could establish a regular monarchy in the Republic's stead, and 13 years of trouble and strain ensued before the battle of Actium again placed the sovran power in a single hand. The empire was still there, waiting for the master to be assigned it by the fortune of war. The old Republic had in short done solid work as an imperial power, had done it clumsily and fitfully, at first reluctantly, of late willingly, but at least so far thoroughly that it lasted as no work at all comparable in scale had ever lasted before. If Rome had shed much blood and levied much tribute, other great powers had done the same in the past; any other that might arise was likely to do the same in the future. And on the whole Rome had kept faith with her allies. In the earlier period of conquest a great difficulty had been found in accustoming subject allies to the precise formalities and legal interpretation of treaty-obligations, which were dear to the Roman mind. This difficulty had become less as the dominion of Rome spread and the necessity of obedience superseded argument. On the whole too the policy of Rome had been fairly consistent; as it became more masterful, it

---

[1] Nearly all its present (1907) area. The Thracian tribes, though humbled in recent years, were not yet formed into a province.

also became more intelligible. The extortions and cruelties that stained provincial government in the later Republic were the work of individuals. The fault of the central power was its inability to control them. If that central power could be strengthened, surely its own interest would impel it to reform abuses that were no necessary part of the imperial system, and were eating away the resources of the empire. By any such change the provincials would be the first to profit, and accordingly they were interested in the approach of a settlement that could not be brought about until an Emperor was found. Provinces and client-princes alike knew that they could not stand alone. Rival powers had completely disappeared from the Mediterranean world. How exclusively the might and majesty of Rome filled the political horizon in those days, the submissive waiting of the subject peoples may shew, but to allow its due weight to the fact in looking back over many centuries is perhaps beyond the power of imagination.

1401. Thus the fallen Republic left the world disposed to wait for a reconstitution of the Roman government, rather than to break up into small independent units, each striving to hold its own against the jealousy and encroachment of others. But this waiting could not have gone on for ever. Once let the subjects be convinced that their imperial mistress could no longer protect them, and they would no longer have let her rule them. Once let them break loose from Rome, and Italy had not the strength to reconquer them. The power of Rome already rested on moral force, a prestige generated by a long career of success: if this imperial asset was not to be sacrificed, there was no time to be lost. There was urgent need of security from without, of peace order continuity confidence and solvency within. And the fate of Caesar's prematurely logical imperialism was a warning that whatever was to be done must be done with the least possible show of departure from republican precedent. To review these needs briefly may give us some notion of the tangled situation with which the heir of Caesar was left to deal.

1402. If the empire was to be free for recovery and development within, it was necessary that it should be secure from invasion. The frontiers must be fixed and defended. But frontier defence could not be carried on under the haphazard military system of the Republic. Peace must now be ensured, and armies no longer left to become the instrument of ambitious generals. Nor must they be allowed to disturb the repose of Italy. There must be a standing army, posted on or near the frontiers, at points where it could guarantee the security required. And regular provision must be made for the maintenance of men discharged after a term of regular service.

The state must no longer be at the mercy of its own disbanded armies. Moreover it was necessary that this army should have one master. The Senate had fully proved itself unable to direct military affairs. And the army of the new model would have to be largely drawn from the provinces. Accordingly we find that Augustus set himself to meet all these requirements, and the success of his system on the whole was remarkable. But the effort to find a scientific frontier to the North was very costly, and in part a failure.

1403. For every purpose, from the disbanding of the old armies to the improvements urgently needed in every department of state, vast sums of money were required, and this in the form[1] of a steady income. This money the provinces were quite able to supply, if only they were freed from the wasteful exactions of governors and their staffs, and in some cases from the not less iniquitous blood-sucking of tax-farmers and usurers. With a revival of legitimate trade an immense increase of wealth was certain ; it was only necessary to restore confidence, particularly in the eastern provinces, drained as these were by the extortions of the Pompeians, of Brutus and Cassius, and lastly of Antony. Confidence could only be restored by continuity of sound administration. Therefore the corrupt and feeble management of the Senate must be mended or ended. The governors of provinces must not be licensed brigands in the form of temporary despots, but servants of the state, paid salaries and forbidden to plunder. An effective control must be kept over these officials, and the system of letting out the collection of state-dues to middlemen be brought to an end. How Augustus dealt with these necessities, and started the Empire on lines along which it moved without material change for about 300 years, is part of the Imperial history.

1404. But the legacy of the Republic consisted not only in things that must be done. There were also the peculiarly difficult conditions under which all this reorganization had to be carried out. Though wars proscriptions suicides and banishment had thinned the ranks of the Senate, that body still existed, and in it was to be found whatever knowledge of affairs and experience of government still remained. The new master could not afford to destroy it, and in order to work with it he must manage it by methods different from the frank autocracy of Julius Caesar. There was also the Equestrian Order, not an organized body like the Senate, but bound together by common financial interests, and sure to resent any reform by which their exploitation of provincial resources would be checked. How to utilize both Senate and Knights so as to keep both classes employed, controlling both while degrading neither, was the problem before

---

[1] The first pressure was much relieved by the Egyptian treasure seized at Alexandria.

Augustus, and his solution of it is admitted to be one of the greatest masterpieces of political history.   Probably no other solution was possible, and it is to be noted that the new system rested on a principle long established in Roman life.   Make-believe was deeply rooted in Roman institutions, and in posing as a first-citizen (*princeps*) on whom a grateful country had bestowed a number of separate powers which strange to say enabled him to enforce his will at all points, whenever he saw fit to do so, Augustus was merely developing an old principle to meet new conditions.   His proconsular *imperium* gave him supremacy abroad, and he ruled the frontier provinces directly through his deputies, thus having the armies under his control.   This was merely an extension of the powers previously granted to Pompey Caesar and Lepidus, to Antony and himself.   His *tribunicia potestas* gave him the means of controlling the Senate, not to mention the futile Assembly and any Magistrate who might be troublesome.   This too was merely an extension of old official powers, while continuous reelection to a yearly office (for he was not tribune) was scrupulously avoided.   On the positive side he could always initiate proposals like a Gracchus : on the negative side he could always block proceedings like a Curio.

1405.   Armed with powers of which these two were the vital essence, the *princeps* could reconstitute the sovran power on a new basis[1] while ostentatiously affecting to preserve the old.   In make-believe the Republic was still there.   Assembly Senate and Magistrates were there.   And yet all men knew that nothing could really be done without the Master's leave, for the power of initiative had departed.   The creation of Augustus was a machine made up of old parts slightly modified and ingeniously fitted together, with the hidden driving-power turned on and off by a single controlling hand.   It took him many years and many experiments to bring it to its final form.   We are not here concerned to follow out its development under his successors, how its defects were in course of time disclosed and how, when worn out, it was superseded by a monarchy of absolute oriental type.   The long duration of the Principate is the best attestation of its founder's foresight.   Nor need we enter into the details of his reconstructive work further than to point out the cleverness with which he treated the problem of the Senate and Knights.   He brought both Orders into connexion with military judicial and administrative duties, but arranged a separate career for each.   But the two Orders were not without coordination; for

---

[1] A very clear account of the work of Augustus is given in Bury's *Student's Roman Empire*. The classic work on the subject is that of Gardthausen cited above. Boissier's book *l'Opposition sous les Césars* is a brilliant picture of the early Empire from this point of view.

instance, the son of a senator was a Knight until the age of 2⁵
the Emperor could raise a Knight to the Senate in suitable
The chief convenience of this division of careers was that it enⱥ━━━
the Emperor to employ Equestrian officers in posts of less dignity
but more importance directly under his own control. Thus members
of the Senate were prevented from monopolizing the administrative
work of the empire, and the new Equestrian official class formed a
counterpoise to the formerly dominant Order. With the loss of
the financial opportunities enjoyed and abused under the Republic
the capitalist class had to be content, to the relief of the subject
peoples. It is true that all oppression and extortion was not at once
brought to an end. But the improvement was certainly great, particularly in those provinces reserved to the Emperor, where the new
methods of tax-collecting were at once introduced, and where
governors left in office for longer periods were directly responsible to
a single head. The Senate was less prompt and efficient in managing
its share of the provinces. But Augustus interfered with them as
little as possible in this department. Rome too and Italy were left
under the administrative supervision of the Senate and consuls. But
experience proved their insufficiency, and in the end the Emperor was
compelled to take over much of the administration through subordinates of his own. In the matter of the state-religion it was
obviously convenient that he should himself be chief pontiff, all the
more as he was bent upon a revival of the ancient worships. But
here too his cautious respect for precedent prevailed. Lepidus had
been deposed from his position as triumvir, essentially an irregular
one, but he was left in possession of the chief pontificate, a post
regularly held for life, and Augustus only succeeded him on his death
in 12 B.C. So too with the bodyguard, which in the latter days of the
Republic had become a normal accompaniment of military command.
He maintained a picked corps of 9000 men, raised in Italy, but only
brought a few of them into the city, where as commander-in-chief of
the army he had his headquarters (*praetorium*). It was Tiberius who
concentrated these praetorian cohorts in Rome and enabled them to
make themselves felt in the disposal of the Empire.

These few outlines are enough to make clear the point with which
alone we are concerned,—that the Principate was artfully built out of
old republican materials so as to disguise the real completeness of the
change that took place. It was necessary to say thus much, for the
fact that the Republic was not swept away, but converted, is no unimportant feature of its long and wonderful story.

1406. It is well to give one or two specimens of the way in which
Augustus appeared as a determined reformer, and, as in the matter of

public works, passed a practical censure on the neglect and corruption of the republican government. The practice of granting to individuals free licenses to travel on their own business or pleasure abroad as though on public duty (*legationes liberae*) was a source of endless abuse and a great burden on the provincials who were required to furnish conveyances. In place of this irregular system he established a posting-service on the main roads under imperial control, which, organized on a military model, developed later into a regular Imperial Post. This was carefully guarded from abuse by strict regulations, and the improvement of communications throughout the empire was a great help in administration, for it promoted the development of a regular Civil Service and strengthened the central government. In the social and moral sphere he endeavoured to bring about a much-needed reform. We have seen something of the deep corruption of domestic life in the last age of the Republic among the upper classes. It was not merely gay society that treated the marriage-tie with shameless laxity. When a Cicero and a Cato had so little delicacy in matters[1] of marriage and divorce, what could be expected from the dissolute majority? The circles in which Caesar Clodius Gabinius Dolabella Antony and Catullus moved were evidently utterly profligate. The women were as bad as the men. Clodia and Fulvia are specimens enough. Fast life and families did not go together, and childlessness, no longer a misfortune but a privilege, was becoming common. Civil wars and proscriptions tended to encourage it, and Augustus saw in it a serious danger. But the legislation by which he strove to promote fertility and discourage wilful barrenness, through a system of rewards and punishments, was hardly a success. He produced more outward decorum, it is true. But the inner reform of family life could not be effected by law: it was not merely the result of wars and violent deaths that we meet with so different a set of names among the public characters of the Empire. The great old houses, at least in the direct lines, had for the most part died out.

1407.   Whether Democracy working through representative institutions provides a force capable of reinvigorating exhausted peoples, is a question the full answer to which the present generation will perhaps hardly see. But we may already hazard the guess that any achievement of this kind will be rather the fruit of a change of spirit than a change of machinery. We are now slowly learning that the most important function of government, on which the vitality of a

---

[1] Enough has been said of these matters in preceding chapters. But it may be well to refer again to the inscription on the monument of Turia, *CIL*. VI 1527, where the widower records her virtue and their long happy union as rare examples.

state primarily depends, is to secure the well-being of the poor. To us national states, based on community of effort and inherited tradition, and looking to common ends and common hopes, may seem the normal organization of mankind. We may easily forget that it is a system of very recent growth, and that a number of national problems remain unsolved, indeed are causing much anxiety at the present time. But in reviewing the distant past we can at least see the main points without prejudice. We can see that the new machinery of the Roman Empire neither formed a national state nor improved the condition of the poor. It was too vast and too mechanical to do the first ; society was too deeply rooted in slavery for it to undertake the second. So the improvement of the organization effected only thus much, that unlicensed oppression of subject peoples was checked, and by the end of the first century A.D. good government was normal. So far it was well, and the Empire had justified itself. But the apparent prosperity and peace was a mere assertion of the superiority of an organized civilized power to unorganized uncivilized barbarians. That is, it did not essentially differ from the same power when its organization was less perfect in the time of the Republic. In its resources there was far less waste than there had been under the old system, but no vital strengthening, no true national or industrial growth. The framework was changed, but the basis of society remained the same. Ranks, from the noble to the slave, were still there, and the inevitable tendency was for official status to become rank, and for the ingenious machine of Augustus to become an absolute monarchy, putting on the forms of oriental despotism. The check on waste enabled its resources to suffice for a time, but the steady drain of specie to the East in due course exposed the financial weakness of the empire. It was not producing goods to exchange with the products of the East, so the precious metals were drained away. Then came the age of defensive wars, creating a boundless demand for ready money, and the Imperial government, which had put down the extortion practised by individuals under the Republic, was driven to turn extortioner itself. Civil officials, made liable for taxes that they could not raise, were face to face with ruin. To avoid municipal office was as much an object as it had once been to attain it, and laws compelling men of means to serve in honourable posts were one of the many forms of taxation. The empire could not even pay the blood-tax for its own defence. More and more it became the practice to bring barbarians into Roman territory, and to leave to them the defence of the frontiers. Whether the countries included in the empire suffered to any serious extent from malaria, is a subject worthy of detailed inquiry. There is little doubt that Italy did. But there were plenty of other causes at work to promote decay not only in Italy but in the empire at large. None of these can compare in importance with the cessation of active personal interest in public affairs. Great indeed had been the evils of the Republic in its latter days, so great that its fall was inevitable. But its one strong point was that there was still an opening for personal initiative, for independent participation in government, for an ambition not limited to success in pleasing a single master. The murder of Cicero confirmed what the suicide of Cato had assumed, that this opening was now finally closed. The classes from which officials were necessarily drawn had to choose between a politic acquiescence in present facts, or a theatrical and futile opposition, or retirement. The first alternative led to promotion, hardly to satisfaction. The higher a man rose, the more closely he was watched; he either was, or was suspected of being, uneasy under a restraint of which his elevation had made him more conscious. The second led direct to ruin. And retirement was but a temporary evasion, not a lasting remedy. Few could find a life-long occupation in literary pursuits, nor could literature retain its vigour when the free expression of opinion on contemporary topics was exposed to the penalties of treason. In the vast majority of cases, to withdraw from public life meant a wearisome round of debauchery. From gluttonous and profligate nobles even the worst of emperors had little to fear. And so, alike under the law of treason and the family decay hastened by meaningless luxury, the remains of the old nobility disappeared, and a new upper class, largely of freedman origin, gradually arose. The smouldering discontents, and occasional conspiracies, that marked the earlier period of the Principate, led to a last vain revival of republican sentiment in the time of Nero. The generation that could remember the civil wars had passed away. In those who had known the gloomy days of Tiberius, the insane tyranny of Gaius, the domination of women and freedmen under Claudius, the cruel disappointment of hopes by Nero, it was still possible to find men willing to risk their lives in a belated imitation of Brutus and Cassius. Such was still the power of the vague dream of 'freedom' generated by idealizing the past. But the conspiracy failed, and in a few years the deposition of Nero and the civil war that ended by giving the Empire to Vespasian revealed the truth that even the choice of a master no longer rested with Rome or Italy, but with the great frontier armies. Henceforth the man accepted by the army was accepted by Senate and People as a matter of course. The truth dissembled by Augustus now stood confessed before the world. The lesson of Pharsalus was learnt at last.

INDEX

Law-courts closed for lack of magistrates with *imperium* 1175.
Law-courts suspended in a crisis (*iustitium*) 840, 859.
Law-reform, designed by Caesar 1280.
Law, Roman, spread of 215, 217, 223, 936.
Lawyers, growth of professional 232, 673, 827, (1026, 1027, 1032), 1280, (1330), 1373-1377.
(See *Jurists*.)
League, Latin, closed 136.
League, Latin, suppressed 182, 220, 223.
League recognized, see *Lycia*.
Leagues, dissolved by Rome 511, 577.
Leagues in ancient Italy 58-60, 192.
lecticae, litters, palanquins 660, 738, 1323, 1385.
Legal phraseology in literature 406.
legati, see Army.
legationes liberae 1024, 1076, 1302, 1406.
Legends, early, specimens of 106.
Legends, historical value of 105, 107, 131, 229.
leges—alphabetical list of laws directly referred to in text.
Acilia 733, 735, 761, 924.
Aelia et Fufia 652, 819, 988.
Aemiliae 156, 1218.
agraria of 111 B.C. (mover unknown) 750.
Antoniae 1297, 1301, 1305.
Appuleiae 809, 813-815, 818, 823.
Atia 1025.
Aufidia (?) 1050.
Aureliae 944, 958.
Baebia, see *Cornelia*.
Caecilia 1186.
Caecilia Didia 819.
Caelia (647), 791.
Calpurniae 639, 640, 644, (686), 853, (855), 988, 989, 1019, 1027.
Canuleia 110, 120, 121.
Cassiae 647, 791.
Cincia 397.
Claudiae 259, 397, (404), (549), 628-631, (634), 661, (708).
Clodiae 1080-1082, 1084-1086, 1186.
Cornelia Baebia 647.
Cornelia Fulvia 647.
Corneliae 863, 908, 909, 911, 912, 917 -928, 944, 1012, 1018, (1054), 1174.
Didia 648, see *Caecilia*.
Domitia 792, 912.
Fabia 662.
Fannia 648, 672.
Flaminiae 266, 403.
Flavia 1055.
Fufia 1063, see *Aelia*.
Furia 634, 649.
Gabiniae 647, 978, 985, 987, 1194.
Gellia Cornelia 961.
Horatiae, see *Valeriae*.
Hortensia 153, 169, 171, 172, 175.

leges (continued).
Iulia of 90 B.C. 843, 849, 850, (853), (855).
Iuliae 1059, 1060, 1068-1071, 1077, (1081), 1116, 1174, 1220, 1249, 1263-1266, (1283).
Iuniae 715, 889.
Licinia Mucia 821, 822, 836.
Liciniae Sextiae 112, 123-128, 229, 694.
Liciniae 910, 1164, 1183, see *Pompeiae*.
Licinia et Aebutia 652, 736, (833).
Liviae 732, 740, 827-834.
Maenia 173.
Mamilia 770.
Manilia 995.
Maria 753.
Minucia 397.
Mucia, see *Licinia*.
Octavia 751.
Ogulnia 164, 171.
Oppia 325, 397, 648.
Orchia 648.
Papia 1010, 1047, 1123.
Papiria (?) 889, see *Plautia*.
Papiria 857.
Pedia 1324, 1325, (1331), (1333).
Peducaea 761.
Plautia Papiria 843, 853.
Plautiae 857, 858, 873, 910, 911, 926, 929, (1047), (1182), 1183.
Pompeia of 89 B.C. 853.
Pompeiae (1117), 1164, 1182-1185, 1188, 1190, 1208, (1220), (1246).
Porciae 637, (723), (732), (1037), (1188).
Publiliae 81, 155, 172, 173.
Pupia 1190.
Remmia 831.
Roscia 992, (1024).
Rubria 733, (750).
Saufeia 833.
Semproniae 694-699, 711, 723-727, 729 -731, (733), 734, (751), 752, 859, 1038, 1067, 1121, (1178).
Serviliae 761, 786, 809, 825, 911, 924, 1020-1023.
Sextiae, see *Liciniae*.
Sulpiciae 859, 860, 863, 1173.
Terentia Cassia 948.
Thoria 750.
Titia 1328.
Tulliae 1024, 1027.
Valeriae 70, 106, 149, 171, 293, 873, 905, 919.
Valeriae Horatiae 64, 172.
Varia 840, (846), (857-859).
Vatiniae 1063, 1067, 1187.
Villia 615, 616, 619, 620.
Voconia 634, 651.

*leges agrariae 64, 126, (679), 750, (797).
Flaminia 266.
Sempronia Tib. Gracchi 694-699, 711.
Sempronia C. Gracchi 725.

---

 * The following attempt at classification defies an alphabetical arrangement, and is in many respects unsatisfactory. But I think some sort of grouping is necessary, and I have therefore decided to let it stand.

Pergamene—Police 547

Pergamene kingdom made a Province, see *Asia.*
Pergamum and the Attalid kings 348, 361, 377, 402, 417, (420), 421, 428, 430, 476, 482, 580–582, (877), (879), (882), 885, 969.
 Attalus I 421, 430, 433, 436, 437, (482).
 Eumenes II 444, 457, 460, 472, 476, 478, 480, 481, 482, 484, 486, 493–495, 504–506, 509, 512, 522, 529, 540, 549, 551, 581.
 Attalus II (Philadelphus) 476, 484, 506, 526, 529, 540, 551, 581, 583.
 Attalus III (Philometor) 581, 699, 707, 708.
Peripatetic School 426, 878, 885, 1349.
permutationes, see *Money, remittance of.*
Perpernae (or Perpennae).
 M. Perperna (cos. 130) 707, 708.
 (? C.) Perpenna 848.
 M. Perperna (cos. 92, cens. 86) 874, 903.
 M. Perperna 941, 943, 951, 960, 961.
Perrhaebia 471, 494, 504, 513.
Perseus of Macedon 498 and chapter XXXI *passim.*
Persia and the Great King 457.
Persons, status of, important in Roman law 1375.
Perusia (Perugia) 310, 1340.
Pessinus in Galatia 377.
Pet animals 1352, 1369.
Petreius, M. 1041, 1167, 1217, 1252, 1256.
Phalanx.
 early Roman 52, 100, 144.
 Epirote 202, 203, 212.
 Macedonian 438, 439, 440, 513, 514, 533.
 Syrian 479.
Phanagoria 807.
Pharnaces, see *Pontus.*
Pharos and its lighthouse 1238.
Pharsalus and the great battle 1231.
Pherae 468.
Philip II of Macedon 177, 201, 418.
Philip V of Macedon 273, 297, 307, 318, 332, 348, 355, 357, 361, 369, 375, 390, 393.
Philip V, quarrel with Rome, wars etc. 394, 411, 415, 418, 419, 422, 428, 448, 455, (459), 466–472, 474, 481, 482, 486, 487, 493–495, 498–500 (see chapter XXVIII *passim*).
Philip, the sham (Pseudophilippus) 573.
Philippi, campaign and battles of 1334–1336.
Philippus, see *Marcii.*
Philo, see *Publilius, Veturius.*
Philopoemen 369, 413, 432, 435, 462, 463, 465, 472, 488, 496, (576).
Philosophers in Rome 657.
Philus, see *Furii.*
Phocaea (445), (472), 475, (710).

Phocis 434, 441, 444, 470.
Phoenicia 584, 586.
Phoenicians 29, 98, 130, 211, 230, 236–238, (457), 475, 764, (1172).
Phrygia, the greater 709, 716, 727, 804, 807, 875, (930).
Picentes 193, 208.
Picenum 193, 208, 210, 333, 842, 850, 865, 890, 892, 952, 1031, 1114, 1211, 1214.
Pictor, see *Fabii.*
Pictures 1389.
pilum 144, 212, 268, (438), 788, 796.
Pindenissus 1195.
Pinna (841), 845.
Piracy.
 Italian and Ligurian 25, 99, 130, 181, 183, 553, 559.
 western Greek 143.
 Illyrian 267, 273, 415, 565, (804).
 Balearic 710.
 in eastern Mediterranean (Cilicia etc.) (416), 662, 789, 804, 879, 885, 939, 942, 945–949, 965, 966, 1084, 1174.
Piraeus 879, 880.
Pirates ranging Mediterranean 945, 949, 959, 960, 964, 984.
 suppressed by Pompey 988, 993.
Pisae (Pisa) 268, 559, 759.
Pisaurum (Pésaro) 1211.
Pisidia 460, 804.
Piso, see *Calpurnii, Pupius.*
Pistoria (Pistoja) 1041.
Pitane 882.
Pius, see *Caecilii Metelli.*
Placentia (Piacenza) 1200, 1220, 1392.
 (See *Colonies.*)
Plagues, see *Epidemics.*
Plancius, Cn. 1086, 1172.
Plancus, see *Munatii.*
Plautii.
 C. Plautius (censor) 155.
 L. Plautius Hypsaeus (praet. 134) 684.
 M. Plautius Silvanus (trib. 89) 853, 857.
 P. Plautius Hypsaeus (trib. 56) 1178.
Plautus, T. Maccius 406, 424, 658.
Plebeian offices, rules and restrictions of 399, 614, 620, (1246, 1276).
Plebeians and the consulship 621.
 and religious offices 164, 171, 408, 653.
 rich and poor 112, 118, 119, 122, 123, 124–128, 152, 153, 399.
plebiscita 84, 89, 122, 147.
Plebs, origin of 46, 47, 49, 120.
Pleminius, Q. 376.
Plutarch as an authority 525, 720, 732, 776, 777, 808, 820, 841, 858, 896, 972, 1030, 1171, 1282, 1294.
Po, region of 9, 16, 17, 269, 273, 280, 287, 370, 452, (chapter XXXII *passim*), 610, 663, 921.
Poisoning suspected 232, 435, 494, 506, 650, 946, (997), 1067, 1113, 1120, 1366.
Police of Italy neglected 947, 1028, 1350, 1355, 1394.